Sexual Problems in Medical Practice

Harold I. Lief, M.D., Editor-in-Chief

American Medical Association

First Edition — November 1981
    Second Printing — August 1984

Additional copies may be purchased from:
Order Department OP-120
American Medical Association
P.O. Box 10946
Chicago, IL 60610

Sexual Problems in Medical Practice

    Bibliography: p.
    1. Sexual disorders.   2. Sex therapy.   3. Therapist
and patient.   I. Lief, Harold   I. II. American Medical
Association.   DNLM: 1. Sex.   2. Sex behavior.   3. Sex
disorders. WM611 8513
RC566.S492   616.6'9   81-7947

ISBN 0-89970-098-5   AACR2

NEA:84-417-120:10M:8/84

FOREWORD

In 1968, the AMA Committee on Human Reproduction submitted a report to the Board of Trustees recommending that the American Medical Association provide written source material for the physician to improve his understanding and knowledge of human sexuality. In response to this recommendation, the Board of Trustees in 1969 authorized the publication of a book entitled *Human Sexuality*.

The favorable response to this volume demonstrated the need for information to guide the practicing physician in the subtle and complex area of counseling patients with sexual problems. It soon became apparent that a more comprehensive approach would serve the needs of physicians and their patients more fully. This new volume represents the extensive and concerted efforts of contributors, who are proficient in the many aspects of sexual problems for which individuals seek help from physicians.

Whether physicians decide to refer patients who require the most expert assistance to other physicians or to act as counselors or therapists themselves, this book is designed to assist in that choice. This volume should aid physicians in providing optimal personal attention required by patients for their most sensitive and intimate problems.

Special appreciation is expressed to Harold I. Lief, M.D., members of the Editorial Board, and the other contributors to this book, as well as to members of the AMA staff. All of them have most generously given their time to the preparation of *Sexual Problems in Medical Practice* because of their conviction that this volume will be of value to practicing physicians and their patients.

James H. Sammons, M.D.
Executive Vice President

PREFACE

Nearly 10 years have elapsed since the appearance of AMA's first publication dealing with the subject of sex, *Human Sexuality*. In its way, that text was a milestone in alerting physicians to the pervasiveness of sexual problems in modern society and the health implications of these problems for their patients.

In one sense, this new publication is a direct descendant of the first, because it renews and brings up to date discussion of those issues that are so basic to adequate understanding and appreciation of the sexual anxieties, fears and disorders that patients bring to physicians' offices. In a larger sense, however, this is an entirely new publication—clinically oriented, with effective management of patient problems its primary focus.

Two of the three major sections of the book discuss the detection, diagnosis and treatment of sexual disorders. The other major section—the initial one—presents background information that places these later considerations in proper perspective. It draws a picture of modern sexual practices, alerts the physician to cultural differences and other societal influences, and delineates the levels of preparedness, commitment and expertise that physicians need to become successfully involved in the process of counseling and therapy.

The diligent reader may come across certain redundancies if he proceeds through the chapters sequentially. This may be an inevitable consequence of multiple authorship, but in a few instances repetition was intentionally countenanced as being desirable for emphasis or for offering differing views of the same subject. In any event, it was decided that to err on this side was far less heinous than to omit salient material by inadvertence. Information on taking a sexual history, for example, appears in several of the chapters, and appropriately so, to underscore its significance in various contexts and settings.

Some readers may find distressing the lack of a bibliography or suggested reading list. It is hoped that they will utilize the extensive references that accompany most of the chapters to pursue their interest in specific areas. The quantity and quality of these references make a separate bibliography unnecessary.

Our principal objective in this publication has been to be of concrete assistance to physicians as they deal with the day-to-day concerns of their patients in sexual matters. We welcome your comments, criticisms and recommendations on the practical value of this book so that we can strive to come even closer to realization of that objective in succeeding editions.

Harold I. Lief, M.D.

ACKNOWLEDGMENTS

The contributions of all those associated with the production of this book are gratefully acknowledged. Especially do I wish to commend members of the Editorial Board and the AMA staff, whose diligence and dedication to quality have brought this volume to its fullest fruition. Harold I. Lief, MD

Editorial Board

Additional Contributors

Mildred "Mickey" Apter, A.C.S. (Ph.D. Candidate)
The Institute for Advances Study of Human Sexuality,
San Francisco, California.

Ellen M. Berman, M.D.
Associate Professor, Department of Psychiatry, University of Pennsylvania,
Philadelphia, Pennsylvania

Oliver Bjorksten, M.D.
Associate Professor of Psychiatry, Medical University of South Carolina,
Charleston, South Carolina.

John Paul Brady, M.D.
Kenneth E. Appel Professor and Chairman, Department of Psychiatry,
University of Pennsylvania, Philadelphia, Pennsylvania.

John C. Buffum, Pharm.D.
Clinical Pharmacist, Veterans Administration Medical Center, Assistant Clinical
Professor of Pharmacy, University of California, San Francisco, California.

R. Clay Burchell, M.D.
Chairman, Department of Obstetrics & Gynecology, Lovelace Medical Center,
Albuquerque, New Mexico.

Millicent E. Buxton
Information Coordinator, Haight Ashbury Free Medical Clinic,
San Francisco, California.

Sandra C. Cole, AASECT, CSE, CSC
Instructor, Department of Physical Medicine and Rehabilitation/Department of
Psychiatry, The University of Michigan, School of Medicine, Ann Arbor, Michigan.

Theodore M. Cole, M.D.
Professor and Chairman, Department of Physical Medicine,
The University of Michigan, School of Medicine, Ann Arbor, Michigan.

Jackie V. Davison, Ph.D., A.C.S.
Research Associate, Psychohormonal Research Unit,
Johns Hopkins Hospital, Baltimore, Maryland.

Diane S. Fordney, M.D.
Associate Professor, Obstetrics & Gynecology, Psychiatry,
Arizona Health Sciences Center, Tucson, Arizona.

Laurence Hof, M.Div.
Clinical Associate in Family Study in Psychiatry, Division of Family Study,
Department of Psychiatry, University of Pennsylvania, School of Medicine,
Pniladelphia, Pennsylvania.

Arlene B. Kagle, Ph.D.
Private Practice, New York, New York.

Arno Karlen
Karlen Productions, Inc., New York, New York

Robert C. Long, M.D.
Clinical Associate Professor, Department of Obstetrics & Gynecology,
University of Louisville, Louisville, Kentucky.

Terrance R. Malloy, M.D.
Clinical Associate Professor of Urology, University of Pennsylvania,
Philadelphia, Pennsylvania.

William R. Miller, Ph.D.
Director of Clinical Services and Research, Assistant Professor of
Psychology in Psychiatry, Marriage Council of Philadelphia,
Philadelphia, Pennsylvania.

Charles Moser, Ph.D., A.C.S.
Research Coordinator of the Substance Abuse and Sexual Concerns Research Group,
Assistant Professor of Clinical Sexology, Institute for Advanced Study of
Human Sexuality, San Francisco, California.

Lawrence Sharpe, M.D.
Assistant Professor of Psychiatry, Columbia University,
College of Physicians and Surgeons, New York State Psychiatric Institute,
New York, New York.

Stanley H. Shrom, M.D.
Clinical Assistant Professor of Urology, University of Pennsylvania,
Philadelphia, Pennsylvania.

Ralph Slovenko
Professor of Law and Psychiatry, Wayne State University, School of Law,
Detroit, Michigan.

David E. Smith, M.D.
Founder and Medical Director, Haight Ashbury Free Medical Clinic and
Associate Clinical Professor of Toxicology, University of California,
San Francisco, California

Alan J. Wabrek, M.D.
Director Medical Sexology, Hartford Hospital, Hartford, Connecticut and
Associate Professor, Department of Obstetrics & Gynecology,
University of Connecticut, School of Medicine, Farmington, Connecticut.

Alan J. Wein, M.D.
Chairman, Division of Urology, University of Pennsylvania, School of Medicine,
Philadelphia, Pennsylvania.

Josef H. Weissberg, M.D.
Assistant Clinical Professor of Psychiatry, Columbia University,
College of Physicians & Surgeons, New York, New York.

Editorial Advisor

Arno Karlen
Karlen Productions, Inc.

AMA Staff

Project Director
Marilyn A. Krause
Staff Associate, Division of Drugs

Editorial Coordinator
Emanuel M. Steindler, M.S.
Director, Department of Mental Health

Editorial Assistants
Sandra McVeigh
Marsha Meyer
Beverly Rodgers

Research Assistant
Priscilla Murray

Technical Assistants
Patti Stone
Wanda Wade

Foreword

Preface

Acknowledgments

CONTENTS

Part II—Clinical Aspects

Part III—Management Consideration

Appendices

Part I
Basic Information

Chapter 1

Sex and the Physician

Harold I. Lief, M.D.

Dealing with sexual problems of patients is an important part of medical practice and should be a significant concern of almost all physicians. When physicians are comfortable about inquiring into the sexual lives of their patients and when they take the initiative by asking appropriate questions, sexual problems are discovered in 15 to 50 per cent of patients, depending upon the type of practice.[1] Although sexual problems are rarely if ever fatal, many thousands of people are deeply troubled, anxious and depressed because of them. Marital disruption, even divorce, commonly results from untreated sexual problems.

Not all sexual problems confronting the physician are the usual sexual dysfunctions, such as premature ejaculation and impotence in men or orgasmic dysfunction in women. Conflicts over sexual behavior, such as frequency, oral sex and coital positions, are even more common and sometimes more troublesome.[2] Sexual concerns resulting from illness and from medical procedures, such as hysterectomy, mastectomy and colostomy, also require counseling. Physical disorders may bring about sexual dysfunction; diabetes is the most common of these, but there are many others that may adversely affect sexual function. Medications, such as those used to treat hypertension, often cause sexual dysfunction.[3]

Unlike most other subjects in medical practice, sexuality often creates intense feelings in physicians. Because sex is a private and intimate subject, physicians are likely to be uncomfortable when taking a sexual history until they become experienced in treating patients with sexual problems. Uncertain of the patient's response, unaccustomed to talking about sex professionally, and unsure of his own competence in this kind of practice, the physician may be awkward in his early approach to the subject. If he increases his store of information about sex, it will help him considerably in overcoming his almost ubiquitous feelings of anxiety. This volume is designed to help the physician to do that and to prepare him to become more effective in treating patients with sexual concerns and problems.

Tendencies to regard sexual behavior as good or bad, important or unimportant—in short, *values*—are significant considerations. Probably more than in any other dimension of practice, values and ethics have to be taken into account—the physician's as well as the patient's. The physician must recognize that he has sexual values or preferences and that these may differ from those of the patient. The influences—intended and unintended—of these values will be discussed elsewhere in this volume.

In dealing with sexual problems, the physician has a splendid opportunity to practice preventive as well as therapeutic medicine. By assisting a young patient to overcome sexual anxieties and inhibitions, he helps prepare that person for satisfactory relationships throughout life, perhaps eventually for marriage. By counseling a married couple, enabling them to obtain greater mutuality and sexual pleasure, the physician reduces marital discord and may even prevent divorce and its emotional and physical sequelae for the couple and their children.

Marital unhappiness, separation and divorce have been implicated as causative factors in a variety of illnesses, especially depression, which, in turn, often contributes to many diseases. Somers quotes a report of the National Institute of Mental Health: "The single most powerful predictor of stress-related physical as well as emotional illness is marital disruption."[4] Helping patients with sexual problems is more than enriching, important as that is: It is good medical care because, by reducing one of the most common sources of human suffering, it helps prevent illness, the uprooting of families and the resultant social disorganization.

Most sexual problems brought to the attention of physicians, especially to family physicians, are those of couples. Some of these problems are primary causes of marital dysfunction. Most are consequences of other kinds of marital discord and, in turn, perpetuate and increase marital unhappiness. It seems reasonable, then, to make sex counseling and marriage counseling a "package" in the training of physicians and the delivery of medical care. Training in sex and marriage counseling is a logical requisite for primary care physicians—those practicing internal medicine, family medicine and obstetrics/gynecology. It is logical even in pediatrics, for it helps the practitioner to recognize the connections between the parents' relationship and a child's sexual problems. An example of such a connection is the covertly seductive father of a teenage daughter, abetted by a sexually repressed wife, who interferes with the separation that is necessary for a girl in her early adolescence to transfer attachment from her father to male peers.

Sex counseling and couple counseling are not the only ways the physician can practice preventive medicine. Early intervention can occur in many other sexually related clinical situations, such as unwanted teenage pregnancies, premarital counseling, family-planning services during pregnancy, postpartum care and family-life education for teenagers and young adults. The pediatrician and obstetrician, dealing with children and adolescents or with young parents, have excellent opportunities to practice effective preventive medicine.

PHYSICIAN'S ATTITUDES

There is general agreement that the physician's capacity to help his patient is a result of three primary factors: attitudes, skills and knowledge (sometimes called the *ASK* formula). Attitudes can inhibit or enhance the acquisition of skills and even of knowledge; moreover, they can inhibit the transmission of knowledge from physician to patient. In few other aspects of medical practice are attitudes more important than in caring for patients with sexual problems.

4

Physicians have been socialized as boys and men or as girls and women before they become medical students. Sexual feelings, beliefs and values stemming from a particular religious, ethnic and social-class background are often intense and firmly held; therefore, physicians cannot learn about sex in the same relatively dispassionate way that they can study the Krebs cycle. In all of us, an interplay between our beliefs or ideas about sexual functions and dysfunctions on the one hand, and our values or preferences on the other, determines what our attitudes will be.

If a future physician grows up believing that masturbation is sinful, for example, he will retain the value judgment in practice that it is bad; thus he might react strongly and negatively to a patient's discussion of masturbation. If the physician believes that masturbation is normal for unmarried males and females but abnormal and bad in marriage, that judgment would influence the discussion of masturbation with a married partner.

Society impresses on its members many sexual values, some of them so gradually and covertly that they are absorbed and accepted without awareness. In addition, every person has life experiences that subtly leave marks largely outside his conscious recognition. The physician who is unaware of his own moral values may unwittingly try to impose them on the patient. On the other hand, some physicians who are fully aware of their values also try to impose them on patients.

A physician who cannot countenance premarital intercourse under any circumstances is clearly a poor choice for a single girl seeking contraceptive help. The physician who, because of strong religious beliefs, unconsciously regards out-of-wedlock pregnancy as justified punishment for premarital coitus may find it impossible to prescribe a contraceptive even for a girl who has already had an out-of-wedlock pregnancy. It is thus that physicians may project their own values onto the clinical situation.

Similarly, personal attitudes may be held toward such sexual behaviors as oral-genital and anal-genital intercourse, extramarital sex, homosexual practices, sexual expression among the elderly and group sex. Even the idea that women may enjoy and actively pursue sex was strange to many gynecologists until the 1960's.[5] If a physician believes that women are essentially passive and submissive and should be paced by the husband's sexual interests, his attitude toward a woman who reports that she took the initiative sexually and that she actively enjoys it probably affects the way he deals with her.

Every physician who wishes to be a competent sex counselor must try to discern his patients' values and to become more aware of his own. It doesn't matter whether the physician's values are more conservative or liberal than the patient's. The patient may become threatened and respond with shame or anger if the physician attempts to change the patient's values abruptly. A good physician-patient relationship depends on the clarification of values and of possible conflicts between those of the patient and the physician.

ETHICAL ISSUES AND CONCERNS IN SEX COUNSELING

Ethical issues in sex counseling in many ways are like those in other aspects of medical care—professional competence, responsible care, informed consent and confidentiality. However, the intimate nature of sexual function, the self-esteem affected by it and the strong emotions associated with it intensify the significance of such issues. There are also unique aspects of sex counseling (e.g., the enhanced possibility of erotic feelings arising in the patient or the physician, the way in which the patient's and/or physician's erotic feelings are managed) that make accompanying ethical issues an even more important consideration for the physician than they are in medical care in general. (See Chapter 27.)

Imposing Standards (Values). Although the general rule is not to impose sexual standards on patients, the patient's values may be the most significant factors in sexual inhibitions or symptoms. An inhibited couple's puritanical ideas may have kept their sexual pleasure minimal; their values and those of the physician are the keys to successful therapy. Some attitude change toward greater tolerance and permissiveness often occurs, as the physician tries to modify an archaic conscience and rigid standards of behavior. When it happens, it happens slowly, often as a by-product of treatment, rather than by value confrontation and imposition. Occasionally, however, explicit reference to the differences in values of patient and physician is necessary.

In many sex counseling situations, the physician often must take a permission-giving role; e.g., permission to a couple to experiment with new behaviors so that they can expand and enrich their sexual experiences. However, the physician must be sensitive to his patients' values and extremely careful not to jeopardize their trust in him by demanding that they behave in ways that are inimical to their values. The correct timing of interventions is most important; decisions about how and when to offer recommendations should be made on the basis of sensitivity and experience.

Value conflicts between sexual partners are common. The physician's neutrality by no means precludes his making these conflicts as explicit as possible in an attempt to reach a satisfactory resolution.

Competence. The physician must judge whether he has the competence to undertake therapy in a given situation. Certainly, it is unethical for him to promise to deliver more than is possible; even the most skillful practitioners have their share of failures. A physician's competence increases with experience in an ongoing process; yet he has to be reasonably certain that he is not only willing to help, but that his skills are equal to the clinical task. The levels of competence—diagnostician, educator, counselor and skilled therapist—are discussed in Chapter 8 and guidelines are given for judging one's own level.[6]

Exploitation. Exploitation may be financial or sexual. Financial exploitation occurs when the physician continues to treat beyond his level of competence or uses inappropriate therapy merely to retain the patient. Financial exploitation is possible in any clinical situation. Sexual exploitation is more of a possibility in sex counseling than in other forms of counseling or psychotherapy. Patients with sex problems are particularly vulnerable to seduction, and sometimes they themselves use seduction as a magical means of reassurance about being worthwhile, of gaining power over a person perceived as more dominating, or of overcoming inhibitions of sexual desire, excitement or orgasm. The physician who actively or passively engages in erotic contacts with his patient is violating the patient's trust, and there is a very strong likelihood that the patient will be psychically damaged, if not by the contact then by the termination of an illusory love relationship with the therapist. The few authors who claim that sex between patient and therapist is helpful to the patient are unconvincing.[7, 8]

There is a "gray area" in which affectionate touching, hugging even kissing —the "laying-on of hands" in a parental way —may be misinterpreted by the patient as erotic. Malpractice suits have been based on such misconceptions. Without unduly restraining his warmth and affection, the physician must be cautious about the degree and the manner in which he displays affection for a patient. (See Chapter 27.)

Special Therapeutic Techniques. Special techniques, such as the sexological examination and the use of surrogate partners (see Chapter 25), raise ethical issues. Both techniques are controversial. The physician without special training should not carry out these procedures, but he should know about them and the pitfalls that are involved. Very few sex therapists actually watch their patients during sexual encounters; that procedure, too, is highly questionable, and the physician is advised not to refer patients to therapists who use it. It is not only ethically controversial, but it involves invasion of privacy and has potential legal complications.

Recommending sexually explicit books or films is ethical, provided the physician has first determined what his patient's attitudes toward such material are, and provided he does not impose his values in an authoritarian way.

Confidentiality and Informed Consent. Confidentiality and informed consent raise ethical issues as they do in other aspects of medicine, but feelings about violation may be more intense. Many patients would not want others to know about their reasons for seeking help or that they are even undergoing sex therapy. The charged feelings that most people have make it mandatory that the physician explain in detail the procedures and methods he intends to use (see also Chapter 27).

There is a full discussion of the ethical issues in sex therapy and research in the publications on sex ethics by Masters, et al.[9, 10]

Sexual health care is requested by many patients and needed by many more who are too embarrassed to ask for it. A sensitive, thoughtful, caring physician can be of enormous help to such patients. Sexual problems cannot be ignored. Even the physician who is disinterested or uncomfortable with this part of medical care must be willing to listen, to inquire and to refer tactfully and competently. The interested physician who gradually acquires greater competence as a sex counselor will derive a great deal of satisfaction from his efforts—usually short term and often effective. Helping patients with sexual problems can, in fact, be one of the most gratifying aspects of practice.

References

1. Burnap DW, Golden JS: Sexual problems in medical practice. *J Med Educ* 1967; 42:673-680.
2. Frank E, et al: Frequency of sexual dysfunction in 'normal' couples. *N Engl J Med* 1978; 299:111-115.
3. Reichgott MJ: Problems of sexual function in patients with hypertension. *Cardiovasc Med* 1979; 3:149-156.
4. Somers AR: Marital status, health, and use of health services. *JAMA* 1979; 241:1818-1822.
5. Scully D, Bart P: A funny thing happened on the way to the orifice: Women in gynecology text books. *Am J Sociol* 1973; 78:1045-1050.
6. Lief H: Sex education in medicine: Retrospect and prospect, in Rosenweig N, Pearsall FP (eds): *Sex Education for the Health Professional*. New York, Grune & Stratton, 1978.
7. McCartney J: Overt transference. *J Sex Res* 1966; 2:227-237.
8. Shepard M: *The Love Treatment: Sexual Intimacy Between Patients and Psychotherapist*. New York, PH Wyden, 1971.
9. Masters WH, et al: *Ethical Issues in Sex Therapy and Research*, Vol 1. Boston, Little, Brown and Company, 1977.
10. Masters WH, et al: *Ethical Issues in Sex Therapy and Research*, Vol 2. Boston, Little, Brown and Company. (in press)

Chapter 2

Sexuality and Sexual Health

Harold I. Lief, M.D.

Physical sex is only part of a person's sexuality. In a fuller sense, sexuality is the integration of several dimensions—somatic, emotional, intellectual, social and ethical—and constitutes a significant portion of an individual's personality. These dimensions are rooted in each person's genetic inheritance and predispositions, family and cultural influences, other life experiences and the knowledge, behavior and attitudes stemming from psychosexual and psychosocial development. Sexuality, like personality, is an abstract concept greater than the sum of its parts; compared to sex in the narrow sense, it is a useful concept because of its multidimensional nature—it has many facets other than sexual excitement and orgasm.

Healthy sexuality is even more difficult to define, for health also is an abstract and often elusive concept. Although normative (statistical) data contribute to the definition of healthy sexuality, they are too restrictive. As guidelines for behavior, such data leave little room for change and evolution in society and for individual experimentation. The notion of normality as health in the medical sense is also inadequate. Too often it is subject to the vagaries of medical fashion and erroneous medical "fact." (For example, for at least two centuries physicians believed that masturbation caused a host of illnesses, from pimples to blindness, paralysis and fatal fevers.)

The idea of health as an ideal state of physical and mental well-being, fostered by the World Health Organization as a goal that health professionals should strive for, is also unsatisfactory; "perfection" is perhaps even less possible to conceptualize and attain in sexuality than in other aspects of life.

Perhaps "sexual health" has to borrow something from each of these three ideas—normative in the statistical sense, normal in the medical sense and ideal in the philosophical sense. It is best defined in terms of a process of growth and development and its hoped-for consequences: the enhancement of personality, relationships and the capacities for pleasure, intimacy and love.

The capacity to find pleasure in bodily sensations and eventually to exchange this pleasure with another person brings fulfillment; it also heightens self-esteem and concurrently decreases the loneliness and alienation that are inevitable existential experiences in everyone's life. The self-confidence and ability to relate to another person, despite vulnerabilities that flow from these pleasurable experiences, are significant to enhancement of personality.

The close relationships we call *intimacy* are based on sharing both pleasure and pain. The word comes from the Latin verb, *intimare*, meaning *to know*. The free expression of sexual love with another is one of the most important ways to come to "know" someone else. The Bible expresses this by using the word "know" to denote sexual union. (While in a more mundane sense, *knowing* may bring disillusionment, distrust and a decrease in intimacy, *knowing* in the sense of *understanding* and *acceptance* heightens sexual love and intimacy.)

Sexuality is but one of several dimensions of intimacy. Others are affection, expressiveness or the capacity to share thoughts and feelings, commitment to the relationship, compatibility of interest and values, trust, capacity for conflict resolutions, autonomy or independence, and identity. Thus it is possible to be intimate with another person in the absence of a sexual relationship, just as it is possible to have sexual encounters without genuine intimacy. It is the conjunction of sexual expression with the other dimensions of intimacy that allow for the greatest degree of individual and mutual pleasure and growth.

Before we discuss the several factors that may influence sexual health, a fuller description of the components of sexuality is in order.

THE SEXUAL SYSTEM

Sexuality can be described as a system somewhat analogous to the circulatory or respiratory system. Its components are identified as follows:

1. *Biological Sex*: Chromosomes, hormones, primary and secondary sex characteristics.
2. *Core Gender Identity*: Sense of maleness or femaleness.
3. *Gender Identity*: Sense of masculinity or femininity.
4. *Gender-Role Behavior*:
   a. nonsexual gender-role behavior: behavior often associated with masculinity and femininity.
   b. sexual behavior: behavior motivated by desire for sexual pleasure (ultimately for orgasm).

The chromosomal pattern passed on by parents is the most important determinant of one's biological sex, but the chromosomal inheritance may be modified by such factors as immunologic processes (e.g., the H-Y antigen), the effect of or resistance to fetal androgens, and steroids taken by the mother during pregnancy. The presence or absence of fetal androgens or of androgen-sensitive cells programs the central nervous system, especially the hypothalamus, during a critical period of fetal life (between the 6th and 12th weeks) for the development of primary sex characteristics and, later, sexual behavior. An XY fetus will develop into a normal male unless there are androgen-insensitive tissues or a deficiency of fetal androgens, in which case feminizing characteristics will occur. Similarly, excessive androgens in an XX fetus will bring about masculine characteristics. Chromosomal or hormonal abnormalities can create problems of intersexuality (sex errors of the body). If these errors are not corrected early in life, they may lead to conflicts in gender identity or even in core gender identity. However, the sex assigned to the child by parents is, with rare exceptions, more important in determining gender identity than is biological sex.[1] (See Chapter 3.)

10

If there are no problems of intersexuality and if sex assignment and rearing are clear-cut, a secure sense of maleness or femaleness is generally complete by the age of 3. However, some intersex patients and some without an evident biological defect have grave difficulties in developing a secure or appropriate core gender identity. These are transsexuals, of whom a fuller description is given in Chapter 19.

In our culture, doubts and conflicts about masculinity and femininity are ubiquitous, even among those with normal primary and secondary sex characteristics. Perceptions that a child or adolescent has of his secondary sex characteristics contribute significantly to his developing gender identity.

Serious disturbances in gender identity may be important in the creation of paraphilias, such as transvestism, fetishism, voyeurism and exhibitionism. However, much more common are subtler conflicts about gender identity that lead to disturbed relationships—the Don Juan who has to prove his masculinity by sexual conquests, the promiscuous housewife who tries to prove her femininity by finding the elusive orgasm or by demonstrating her attractiveness, the woman who cannot respond sexually because she fears it means being completely dominated or possessed by a male, the husband who objects to coitus with his wife on top because it seems "unmanly."

The "battle of the sexes" is carried out not only in bed but in every area of marital interaction, generally by those who are uncertain of their masculinity or femininity or who fight to gain self-respect by derogating the spouse or restraining the spouse's freedom of choice. A generation ago, masculine and feminine roles were "assigned" by tradition; today roles are much more negotiable, and there are serious problems when negotiation is impossible because of faulty communication or when it breaks down because of disturbed perceptions or fear of compromise.

Partners do not always have the same perceptions of appropriate behavior for a man or a woman. The culture defines, sometimes clearly and sometimes not so clearly, its expectations of males and females, and in this way it shapes the expectations of males and females in each institution in society. For instance, a culture indicates with varying clarity which sex should place primary emphasis on a career or on a family, how much and in what ways each sex should develop aggressiveness and nurturance, and which sex should be leaders of political parties or religious groups or should teach in primary schools or in universities. Furthermore, there is a reciprocal relationship between gender-role behavior and gender identity. How one feels about oneself as masculine or feminine affects behavior in a great variety of settings; conversely, one's behavior in these settings influences feelings about one's sex.

SEXUAL BEHAVIOR

The fact that patterns of sexual behavior in the human are much more varied than in any other animal can be attributed to the considerable influence of learning. At the same time, biological processes limit the possibilities, and they fashion the similarities in sexual behavior that are found in societies with enormously different cultural patterns and institutional forms; e.g., of families, child-rearing, means of production and distribution, religion, education and art.

Similarities include: (1) the patterned sequence of activities involved in self- or mutual-stimulation designed to elicit a reflex orgasm, (2) the physiologic changes in human sexual response termed by Masters and Johnson[2] as excitement, plateau, orgasm and resolution, (3) the primacy of pleasure as a motivation for sexual activity, and (4) the tendency for humans to join together in twosomes for sexual pleasure. (This relationship is sometimes called "pair-bonding.")

What evolves in diverse societies is a standard pattern which, for most people who have reached sexual maturity, includes coitus. In this standard pattern, the male desires to penetrate, the female to be penetrated. Orgastic motivation is independent of reproductive intent. The standard pattern includes several elements in a definite sequence, the schematic organization of which is shown in Figure 1.

The sexual motive state, a mental set that prepares the individual for sexual activity, represents a readiness for sexual initiation and reception. Presumably there are neurohumoral processes in the brain that must be psychologically "received" in order for the sexual motive state to develop. For example, very low levels of testosterone prevent the development of desire in the male and probably in the female as well.

The strength of stimulation varies in different individuals and in the same individual from time to time. The attention the individual pays to inner stimuli also may vary. He may concentrate on them or ignore them. If the inner stimuli are received and attention is focused on them, arousal is built up by the memory of past pleasurable experiences and wishful thought. These, in turn, determine preferred or even exclusive modes of stimulation. Extragenital parts of the body then contribute a supplementary stream of pleasurable excitation to the main flow of genital response, creating genital vasocongestion.

The penetration phase of the sexual pattern varies much less than does the foreplay phase, because pelvic thrusting is based on an innate neural pattern that is part of man's mammalian heritage. Orgasm itself, although a reflex response, is not the same in each individual nor in the same person at different times. The degree of satisfaction generated by the sexual experience also varies. By no means is there always a direct relationship between the intensity of orgasm and the degree of satisfaction; satisfaction depends largely on the context of the sex act and its significance. The latter is based on the nature of the sexual relationship and the participants' past and current life experiences, as well as on the anticipations of the consequences of sexual activity. Unless guilt or anxiety rises to disturbing levels, however, the response is pride, rising self-esteem, general muscular relaxation and, perhaps, sleep.

The standard pattern may be inhibited at any of its levels—the level of desire, of excitement or of orgasm. (Indeed, inhibition may interfere with an

Figure 1. Standard Coital Pattern.

> Submanifest excitation from internal stimulation establishes receptivity to psychologic stimulation.

⬇

> Sensory and intellectual stimulation by automatic mechanisms of arousal.

⬇

> This sets up sexual motive state which mobilizes and organizes the resources of the organism towards attainment of orgastic pleasure.

⬇

> This state elicits automatic responses of preparedness:
> sensory: selective mechanism of attention
> intellectual: selective mechanisms of memory and wishful thought
> motor: engorgement of erectile structures
> glandular: release of sperm; secretion of vehicular and lubricative fluids.

⬇

> Activities of wooing secure consent of mate.

⬇

> Foreplay: collateral stimulation of responsive extra-genital regions sends tributary streams of pleasure into orgastic main stream.

⬇

> Rise of impetus to penetrate—rise of desire to be penetrated.

⬇

> Inplay: intramural stimulation by pelvic thrust.

⬇

> This reflexly evokes pleasurable orgastic peristalsis of genital structures.

⬇

> Sleep.

⬇

> Pride.

From Rado S: Adaptational view of sexual behavior, in *Psychosexual Development in Health and Disease.* New York, Grune & Stratton, Inc, 1949.

earlier phase, namely, courtship or the search for and the finding of a suitable partner, thereby preventing the establishment of a "sexual pair.") Inhibition of the standard pattern is created by anxiety. The sources of anxiety and the various substitute patterns that anxiety and the defenses against anxiety create are discussed elsewhere in this book.

Love. In Rado's words: "Love is a sustained emotional response to the source of pleasure received and expected. It finds motor expression in the trend to keep that source close, in readiness to supply the expected pleasure whenever desired. And, love inspires thought that will idealize its source of pleasure by making it appear as desired, full of perfections and stripped of imperfections."[3]

Often sexual desire is intensified by love. The state of being "in love" combines orgastic desire with two of four currents of love. One is *sensual* and the other *magical*. A couple in love will share these emotions. Sensual love is derived from the sex act itself. Magical love is a revival of the infantile dependence on parents. It signifies that a person is cared for, cherished and made secure as if by magic (instantaneously and effortlessly). The lovers find substitutes in one another for their parents, achieving the illusion of perpetual security. While sensual love, through constant repetition, tends to decrease, magical love waxes and wanes, depending on its modification by reality. The illusion of security is dispelled and then returns temporarily. It is then that magical love increases sensual love and creates moments of intense pleasure, the memory of which sustains the relationship.

Two other currents, *responsible* love and *procreative* love, characterize a mature relationship. A state of responsible love is reached when there is complete trust and selflessness, when each partner values the other as much as oneself. Responsible love maintains the security of the mates. It is a rational as well as an emotional force directing the well-being of the couple by providing for economic security, status and the development of each partner's potential.

Procreative love ensures the survival of the species and promotes a firm basis for the care of offspring. It is the love that mates share with one another and with their children.

The four currents of love—sensual, magical, responsible and procreative— may blend together or they may conflict and create marital disruption or difficulty in choosing a mate. Resulting anxiety may then not only interfere with sexual functioning per se (sensual love), but it may inhibit the full development of other forms of love or may so accentuate one of them that an inappropriate balance results.

Sexual health implies the full development of sexual pleasure (sensual love) and the capacity for good pair-bonding, which in turn depends on a proper combination of, and balance among, magical, responsible and procreative love.

FACTORS INFLUENCING SEXUAL HEALTH

Physiological Factors. Sex assignment at birth should be correct for future gender identity and for satisfying erotic functioning; it should be congruent with chromosomal, gonadal, hormonal and anatomical configurations. In cases of intersexuality, the incongruence should be interpreted to the family so that corrective surgical and/or hormonal intervention can be carried out to achieve and maintain as much congruence as possible. This intervention should take place at the earliest moment favorable for the child to avoid the complications of sex reassignment later in life.

Sometimes there are untoward physiological changes at puberty that influence sexual health, particularly by affecting gender identity. In females, absent or irregular menstruation and delayed or precocious maturation can be influential; in males, gynecomastia (present in 75 per cent of boys at puberty) and undescended testes can have untoward psychological effects. Pride in body development, maturation and physiological processes (e.g., menstruation) enhances sexual health. Anxiety and shame about these processes have deleterious effects. A common example is the girl who unconsciously walks in a stooped manner in order to hide her developing breasts. Such shame about budding sexual development may create lifelong problems with posture.

Handicaps such as physical disability, blindness and deafness do not desexualize an individual. At any age, the sexual needs of the handicapped may be very much like those of the nonhandicapped, although their gender identity and sense of sexual adequacy are often threatened. (See Chapter 15.)

Behavioral Factors. Sex of rearing should be consistent with assigned sex. Any ambiguous attitudes of parents or parent-figures should be identified and corrected. If parents make a clear sexual identification of the child, the child by age 3 will be able to say with conviction, "I am a boy" or "I am a girl."

The child's masturbation and sex-rehearsal play—play that is preparatory for later adult activity—with other children should be accepted and treated with respect by parents, although subject to the socialization of privacy. A child's private and noncoercive sexual exploration should be encouraged; this will permit responsible expression and learning of those pleasurable experiences that prepare the way for more mature ones. If the body and its sensations are a legitimate source of pleasure, it follows that masturbation is not an abnormal way of obtaining pleasure and of learning the processes creating pleasure.

With the upsurge of hormones at puberty, the adolescent's increasingly intense need for erotic expression should be recognized; within appropriate limits, satisfying and nonexploitative ways of meeting these needs should be encouraged. Peer discussion of sexual behavior and attitudes should be recognized as a significant part of sexual learning. Appropriate information and discussion will help the adolescent integrate his sexual behavior and values and will lead to responsible and nonexploitative sex. Adults must understand that sexual development is a life-long process,[4] and that getting a healthy start in childhood and adolescence is the best assurance that sexual expression will continue to be rewarding and fulfilling throughout life.

Educational Factors. Healthy sexual behavior should be taught as a natural function. Parents and parent-figures should give children phase-appropriate information about sexuality. At receptive times in the child's development, the variety of values should be communicated, and the advantages and disadvantages of different lifestyles explored. In such discussions, parents and teachers should encourage responsible sexual decision-making.

Sex education geared to the age of the child should be included in school curricula from the earliest years through graduation from high school.

Sociocultural Factors. Prohibitions of private sexual behavior and some social taboos may contribute to poor sexual health. Because authoritarian attitudes of teachers or therapists may interfere with freedom to inquire, learn and change, such attitudes should be avoided. The culture also tends to promote gender-role stereotyping, which inhibits the flexible use of the self and may adversely affect one's relationships; such stereotyping by society needs to be actively discouraged. Physicians, nurses and other health professionals should be aware of their own gender-role stereotyped attitudes (e.g., the doctor as man and the nurse as woman) and be careful that these attitudes do not interfere with their relations with their colleagues or their *management* of patients.

Negative emotions such as anxiety, shame, guilt and anger inhibit sexual health. Conversely, the positive emotions of joy, pleasure, hope, realistic pride and love facilitate sexual health and personality development in general. In a beneficial circle, positive feelings about oneself as a sexual being become reinforced.

References

1. Money J, Ehrhardt AA: *Men and Women, Boy and Girl. Differentiation & Dimorphism of Gender Identity from Conception to Maturity*. Baltimore, Johns Hopkins Press, 1972.
2. Masters WH, Johnson VE: *Human Sexual Response*. Boston, Little, Brown and Company, 1977.
3. Rado S: An adaptational view of sexual behavior, in Hoch PH, Zubin J (eds): *Psychosexual Development in Health and Disease*. New York, Grune & Stratton Inc, 1949.
4. Gadpaille WJ: *The Cycles of Sex*. New York, Charles Scribner's Sons, 1975.

Chapter 3

Psychosexual Development Through the Life Cycle

Warren J. Gadpaille, M.D.

Psychosexual development is the continuing process by which each person becomes the sexual being he or she is. At any point in life, it represents the cumulative effects of many forces, and it is one facet of psychological and maturational development that is constantly being directed and shaped by three forces simultaneously. One force is biological, including hormonal, physiological and anatomical influences, innate maturational timetables, and cognitive maturation. A second is cultural, including social learning in the family and influences outside the family. A third force is intrapsychic, including normal developmental conflicts; unconscious fantasies, conflicts and attitudes; and the influences of all earlier experiences and emotions that help determine how one approaches and copes with each new biological, cultural and intrapsychic event.

This chapter deals with normal psychosexual development in the Western middle class. Disturbances in sexual development will be mentioned only to illustrate undisturbed development. What will be described is that which is attainable under realistic emotional and environmental influences that encourage the unfolding of sexual potential.

PRENATAL INFLUENCES

The presence of normal sex chromosomes (XY or XX) determines whether the undifferentiated gonadal anlage develops, respectively, into testes or ovaries. In the XY embryo, testes begin to develop and to produce androgens at a fetal age of about six weeks. In the XX embryo, ovaries begin to develop somewhat later.

Sexual development, in contrast with simple sexual differentiation, begins at about six weeks and depends upon the presence or absence of fetal testicular androgens. The external genitalia of both sexes form from the same embryological tissue. In the presence of fetal androgens, the genital tubercle enlarges and becomes a penis. The urogenital folds fuse, enclosing the urethra along the underside of the penis. The labioscrotal swellings fuse at the midline to form the scrotum. At the same time, the Wolffian ducts will begin to form the vas deferens, seminal vesicles and ejaculatory ducts. A separate fetal testicular substance reduces the Müllerian ducts to vestigial remnants. External male genital morphology is complete and irreversible by the end of the 14th week.

In the absence of androgen, the genital tubercle becomes a clitoris. The urogenital groove remains open as the vaginal introitus. The urogenital folds remain in place as the labia minora; labioscrotal swellings remain unfused and enlarge to form the labia majora. The Müllerian ducts form the fallopian tubes, the uterus and the major part of the vagina. The cause of the Wolffian duct to become vestigial is not known. Female genital morphology, like male morphology, is complete and irreversible by the 14th week.

Also beginning at six weeks, but probably extending for a longer period, fetal androgens start organizing parts of the developing brain, especially in the hypothalamus and limbic system, which may mediate behavior and temperament more characteristic of males than of females. At puberty, the hypothalamus will mediate the release of hypophyseal gonadotropins in the acyclic male pattern.

In the absence of fetal androgens, comparable central nervous systems are organized so that at puberty gonadotropins will be released in the typical cyclic female pattern (which accounts for the menstrual cycle), and characteristically female behavior and feminine temperament may be mediated.[1,2]

Another result of normal fetal CNS organization is that, after gonadal maturation, sexual arousal is more easily elicited by a member of the opposite sex than of the same sex.[3] This constitutes an innate heterosexual bias, demonstrable in nonhuman mammals and probably present in humans. In humans, however, this bias can be overridden by a variety of postnatal emotional and learning experiences.

It seems that, in mammals, nature is predisposed to differentiate a female, except for chromosomally determined gonads, unless effective fetal androgens cause male dimorphism. If there are no fetal gonads of either sex, as in Turner's syndrome (chromosomes 45, XO), female morphological and feminine temperamental differentiation occur. They also occur if fetal testes are present and functioning but the androgen is not effectively used by the tissues, as in animal experiments with antiandrogens and in the human androgen insensitivity syndrome. If there are excessive levels of virilizing androgens in a chromosomal and gonadal female, as in congenital hyperadrenocorticism, male morphological and masculine temperamental differentiation occur.*

In considering sexual development, one must distinguish maleness and femaleness from masculinity and feminity. Maleness and femaleness are physical and physiological; for instance, childbearing is a female characteristic. Masculinity and femininity are sex-linked psychological characteristics and social behaviors not directly related to copulation and reproduction. Behavioral scientists disagree over the nature and extent of innate masculine and

---

*For overviews of the vast literature on this principle of embryological differentiation, see Gadpaille,[1] Money and Ehrhardt,[2] and Reinisch.[4] For detailed consideration of the anomalous and pathological conditions that can distort human sexual differentiation and development, see Chapter 18. For a detailed medical discussion, see Jones and Scott.[5]

feminine traits. There is a consensus that any such traits are fragile in humans and can be modified vastly or even destroyed by learning, but the innate characteristics probably set limits within which normal variations occur. The preponderance of cross-species, cross-cultural, observational and experimental evidence is that sex-specific traits do not arise from postnatal learning alone, and that the newborn is not a *tabula rasa* in respect to these variations, however great his or her plasticity.

The evidence is that masculinity and femininity are not polar extremes; brain structures and functions that mediate masculine and feminine characteristics probably exist normally in both sexes.[6,7] Therefore, it is normal for qualities typically associated with either sex to exist in any individual. However, the potential for all sex-related traits and behaviors is not thought to be normally equal in both sexes; certain brain systems and the capacities for some sex-specific responses are not normally as fully developed or capable of function in males, nor are others in females.[6] The modal behaviors and temperaments of the sexes are statistically distinguishable, although normal individuals show varying kinds and degrees of cross-sex traits, and some display more heterologous than homologous traits.

CHILDHOOD

Most physicians are at least superficially familiar with the standard divisions of early childhood psychosexual development into oral, anal and phallic stages. These concepts represent essentially intrapsychic events, and even detailed understanding of them seldom links stage-specific maturation and development with present and future sexuality. In this section, as in those sections about subsequent periods of life, questions that bear directly on patient care will be addressed briefly.* What experiences in any developmental period are essentially sexual? How are they reflected in later sexuality? Which aspects of psychosexual development and sexual identity seem to have critical or optimal periods of development?

The concept of critical periods is familiar in embryology and organogenesis; for example, the 6th to 14th weeks of fetal life are critical for the differentiation of the external genitals. The concept is also relevant to cognitive and psychological development, as has been shown for language readiness and the fixing of the core-gender identity. The principle is that a biologically determined maturational timetable determines the *only* or the *optimal* time for a biological or psychological system to be organized. Before the critical period, the organism is not ready for the system to be organized; after development, whether normal or abnormal, that system is relatively or absolutely fixed. The normal development of systems of a higher organizational level depends on the successful development of early related systems. Therefore, disruption of an early critical-period phenomenon impairs the successful acquisition of certain later systems.[8-10] For components of learning or

---

*For a detailed discussion of normal psychosexual development throughout life, see Gadpaille.[11]

psychological development, the term "optimal period" is preferable to "critical period," because some capacity usually remains for further learning or for modifying what was learned.

Infancy (Birth to 18 Months). Several aspects of infancy are directly sexual. One is learning to accept one's own and others' bodies as good, pleasureful, and trustworthy or as bad, unpleasant, and dangerous. This learning results largely from the manner of mothering—the quality and quantity of touching, holding, and fondling and of physical warmth or its lack. Spitz[12] has shown how soon the quality of mothering is reflected in sex behavior: infants who receive good mothering masturbate by 1 year of age, but those who are poorly mothered do not. A sense of one's body as good or bad also arises from parental responses to genital behavior. The capacity to form bonds with others is strongly influenced in early infancy as well,[13] because of the interactions that produce trust of physical closeness.

Learning core-gender identity—the *sense* of being male or female—is also directly sexual. There are sex differences in newborns, such as boys' greater muscular strength and irritability and girls' more frequent vocalizations and spontaneous smiling (even during sleep) and greater tactile sensitivity.[14] There are reciprocal reactions in parents; they respond differently to boys and girls from the child's birth. They not only handle male and female newborns differently, they tolerate and elicit different behaviors from them. From the time an infant is named, a constant stream of cues teaches it that it is male or female.

Other sexual experiences of infancy are derived from having a male or female body. The mostly invisible and internal female sex organs with their more vague and diffuse sensations on the one hand, and, in contrast, the more external, visible male organs and their more localizable sensations on the other, lay early bases for the different sexual self-concepts, body images, sexual attitudes and qualities, and vulnerabilities felt by females and males.[15]

Infancy is probably the optimal period for achieving trust and enjoyment of physical closeness, as well as the capacity to form healthy and loving bonds, and for acquiring one's core-gender identity. This latter development may continue into early toddlerhood, but core-gender identity is usually irreversible by age 1 1/2 to 2 years.[16]

Toddlerhood (18 Months to 3 1/2 Years). The chief developmental events of this period are the emergence of body autonomy and learning to balance control of oneself with acceptance of social controls. Much of this experience is specifically sexual. During this time, most children become aware of anatomical sex differences. Normally this awareness is not traumatic, but it does stimulate enormous curiosity. Circumstances expose many toddlers to the events of pregnancy and birth, to which they also respond with great curiosity.

Body autonomy involves sexual matters. Along with increased muscular mastery and the drive to explore one's body and the physical environment, there is increased genital exploration, purposeful masturbation, and sex play with others. Toilet training, the paradigm of conflict at this stage, has sexual implications because of the proximity of sexual sensations to eliminatory

20

functions. There is always the danger of learning an inappropriate association between "dirty" bowel functions and sexual sensations; this is a greater emotional hazard for girls than for boys. And as the toddler struggles with the inner conflict between wanting control of his own bowel action and the requirement that he relinquish at least part of it, he may generalize this conflict to feeling that he also does not have an autonomous right to sexual sensations.

Socialization in sex roles increases now, because of the child's greater ability to process information and instruction, and because of his great mobility and social interaction that expose him to role models, chiefly within the family. Which sex he or she belongs to is already fixed; what it means to be that sex is the new horizon. Toddlers begin to identify with and imitate the same-sex parent; some temporary periods of cross-sex identification are normal, but persistent cross-sex identification is not.

In most middle-class families, boy toddlers are more likely to identify with mother than are girls with father. Most fathers work away from home and are not present to serve as role models for children of either sex during most children's waking hours. It is mother's position of power, control, nurturance and creativity to which children of both sexes are more exposed, and her ability to create life is especially obvious if a sibling is born. It is the mother with whom both boy and girl infants first identify during their earliest months. Boys must disidentify with her to achieve a male identity, an intrapsychic task not necessary for girls.[17, 18] All these factors contribute to males having more difficulty establishing a sex-appropriate identity and to that identity being more vulnerable to disruption.[1, 11]

A toddler is encouraged and rewarded for behavior that his parents consider sex-appropriate and ridiculed or punished for deviations. Destructively rigid sex-role stereotyping, when present, begins its damaging constriction by toddlerhood, but the child probably has no awareness of it. Toddlers are affected by evidence within the family of how one or the other sex is valued, as reflected in parents' attitudes toward one another, and by any differential treatment of siblings and other relatives according to sex. A toddler can begin to develop a deep-seated repudiation of his own or the opposite sex if he senses consistent overt or covert disparagement of males or females.

Toddlerhood is the optimal period of language readiness; during these years, children must learn effective verbal communication or carry a major handicap through life. The relationship of such learning to sexuality is not much appreciated, but toddlers' sexual curiosity is not only physical and visual but verbal and cognitive. Accurate words are necessary to normal ego development. Without clear verbal concepts, one cannot bring order to one's world or categorize one's experiences realistically. In no other area of necessary learning does our middle-class culture so cripple a child by failing to answer questions, giving false answers, not providing correct words, or mislabeling sexual anatomy, sensations and functions.[19]

Because these aspects of psychosexual development take place in the optimal period for achieving a sense of physical autonomy, much of this development can be expressed in terms of sexual "rights" that children can best acquire at this time. The principal right is a sense of ownership of one's body. Despite the child having to accept social controls and recognize the rights of others, the outcome of an emotionally healthy toddlerhood is a sense of owning one's body and body products and contents. There are also the rights to one's sex organs and sexual sensations and to value and enjoy them. These rights are inseparable from language skills because of the need for sexual communication; one must feel a right to sexual curiosity and questioning and to correct answers and words with which to form realistic concepts.

The carry-over of this developmental phase into later sexuality is obvious. If it is successfully negotiated, an individual can comfortably accept his or her sexual anatomy, sensations and functions. While there are no functional sexual body contents or products in early childhood, appropriate and relaxed bowel and urinary training translate later into unconflicted attitudes toward semen and ejaculation, menstruation, vaginal secretions and pregnancy.

This period, then, starts the child toward taking pleasure in being male or female, which includes the beginning awareness and acceptance of sociosexual differences. It also provides the foundation for openness to learning about sex and for comfort with sexual knowledge and language. This foundation later leads to ability to communicate with others, especially with partners, about sexual matters.

Preschool Period (3 1/2 to 6 Years). Some subtle but important maturational changes in sexual physiology mark this period. The sensory nerves to the penis and clitoris become fully myelinated by about 3 to 3 1/2 years of age, allowing for more discrete and intense erotic sensation. There is also probably a slight increase in androgen production in both sexes. Because androgen is largely responsible for erotic desire in both sexes and for sensitizing the clitoris and penis to respond sexually to tactile stimulation, this rise enhances the child's sexual drive. Finally, a small amount of clinical evidence suggests that neurophysiological maturation may occur around the beginning of this period which permits sensitizing of the olfactory part of the brain to human sexual pheromones. If this is true, it is analogous to the central nervous system maturation that occurs when male puppies, previously pheromonally insensitive, become responsive to the odor of an estrous bitch; it would mark the onset of comparable heterosexual responsiveness. The same evidence suggests unique sensitivity and different emotional responses to the odors of one's biological parents.[20,21]

Some or all of these factors cause increasing genital eroticism, with an even greater increase in masturbatory activity than in toddlerhood. The most important change is that masturbation is now goal-directed with heterosexual fantasies. It is inevitable for the child to wish to gratify his desires with the opposite-sex person he loves most—usually the parent. This is a manifestation of the Oedipus complex, and it occurs largely outside awareness or in dreams and disguised masturbatory fantasies. But there is no substantial doubt that it occurs, and most parents can recall such seemingly naive comments as, "When Daddy dies and I grow up, I'm going to marry Mommy," or,

"I have a vagina! Why can't I have a baby with Daddy, too?"

These wishes produce fear and conflict. If the child wants to displace or destroy the parent, he fears that the bigger, stronger parental rival will be angry and destroy him. In a child's logic, the punishment would fit the crime; the result is fearful fantasies that his or her sexuality will be destroyed. At the same time, the child loves the rival parent deeply and feels guilty over Oedipal impulses.

Most children of this age know or sense the role of the genitals in coitus; for many reasons, their fantasies of it are often more fearful than pleasant. If they have witnessed intercourse, it is more likely to have seemed violent than joyous to them—at least in a culture where such observations are too rare for repeated exposure to reality to correct that impression. Adults' reactions to being seen are likely to reinforce the child's perception that they were doing something bad and shameful, and parents seldom counteract fearful fantasy with clear information.

A child's sexual anatomy affects the kinds of fears and dangers he imagines. A boy's penis is external and vulnerable; this invites fear of it being cut off, and he may regard female anatomy as proof of that possibility. A girl may believe that in the past her mother deprived her of a penis as punishment for her sexuality. In her wishes for sexual gratification with father, her genital anatomy renders her vulnerable to fantasies of violent penetration and mutilation. Parents are often puzzled about why their otherwise happy preschoolers have nightmares filled with devouring ogres and attacking monsters equipped with penetrating, explosive, or slashing weapons. It is no coincidence that gory fairy tales full of wicked stepmothers and cruel kings appeal especially to this age group.

In a normal family, reality triumphs. The child's fantasies cannot be sustained in the face of the fact that the "rival" parent remains loving and accepting and does not reinforce the fears. And the parents' continued preference for one another in intimacy and the physical impossibility of replacing the parent cannot forever be denied. So reality as well as fear divests the fantasy of much of its unconscious power and forces renunciation of the wish. The Oedipal phase ends with the child beginning to accept and to strive for a definitive identification with the parent of the same sex.

Healthy parental response is crucial to successful resolution of Oedipal conflict, and parents can unwittingly fall short. It may be difficult for a father to be both patient and firm with a persistently intrusive and provocative son, especially when he does not know what the behavior means unconsciously. If he is unreasonably angry or punitive in return, the boy may attribute it to rivalrous retaliation, and this reinforces his fearful fantasies. If there is dissension between the parents, either one may turn to the child out of spite and value the child's love more than the spouse's, making the fantasied rivalry real. Oedipal feelings exist in parents, too; many a parent is shocked and horrified to discover erotic stirrings in response to childish imitations of coquetry or wooing. Frequently such a parent, more often the father, withdraws out of guilt and ends all physical affection and warmth, nonverbally teaching the child that heterosexual feelings are bad.

What is needed—and healthy families can do it without knowing anything about the Oedipus complex—is an openly welcoming attitude toward the child's budding heterosexual interests. In such families, there is no reason to be jealous of the child or to fear one's own responses. The child also should be shown gently but firmly that the parents' physical intimacies are reserved for one another and that, while the child's sexuality is accepted, it must be deferred and eventually directed toward a different partner.

The successful resolution of complex Oedipal processes is essential for psychosexual development. This is the stage when the child first feels, and experiments in fantasy with, heterosexual urges; it is probably the optimal period for the acceptance and fixing of heterosexual preference. Although the child must defer and redirect his urges, he must achieve and retain a firm sense of their basic goodness and acceptability, his right to them, and his right to their ultimate gratification. He also must remain convinced of his right to compete for an appropriate heterosexual partner. Otherwise the stage is set for self-defeating sexual object choices, or for deflected, substitute gratifications.

Early School Years (6 Years to Puberty). This period has often been referred to as sexual latency, because of Freud's belief that there is then an organic diminution of sexual energy. Cross-cultural studies and investigation of children in Western society have not supported this view. In fact, in our society there is a steady increase in the incidence of sexual activity among children during these years.[22, 23] In cultures permissive of childhood sex play, every form of individual, dyadic and group sex play, both homosexual and heterosexual, occurs during these years.

There are two reasons why children in this culture seem to be less sexual. One is that their sexual activity becomes secret because they have learned of adults' disapproval. The persistence of overt public sexual behavior usually indicates some ego pathology, even though the urge to such behavior may be the species norm in permissive situations. A second reason is that an enormous range of new ego-development tasks, most of them not specifically sexual, are ready to be mastered; this makes sexuality less preoccupying.

One ego-development task that is sexual is consolidating sex-appropriate sex-role preference. This started in infancy with the beginning of core-gender identity, continued during toddlerhood as the child experimented with same-sex and cross-sex identifications, and finally settled on identification with the same-sex parent at the resolution of Oedipal conflicts. Now the child, by attending school, is thrust into the larger society. It is probably in these early school years that socialization is most intense and most strongly determines role preference. Sex-roles in the family may have been idiosyncratic; now the child learns more of how the sexes are treated and what is expected of them in the world outside home. Pathogenic family attitudes can be ameliorated, although early learning can be very refractory; family expectations can be so powerful that a child has difficulty learning or accepting different or broader sex-role definitions. On the other hand, a warm and loving family can often insulate a child from the effects of a larger social milieu that adheres rigidly to overly restrictive sex-role stereotypes and is less tolerant of normal but divergent interests and attitudes.

Boys usually have a more difficult sexual identity task in these years than girls. Just when they are struggling to disidentify with mother and identify with father, they enter a school environment where most of the authorities are women. Most teachers prefer orderliness, and women teachers have never been little boys. There are, of course, fine exceptions but at this crucial time the majority of boys are required to act like normal girls in order to be considered "good" and are chastised for behaving like normally rambunctious boys. A very unfortunate consequence of the largely female teaching system is that learning, art, gentleness and considerate manners tend to become associated with femininity. Men could, of course, teach these qualities as primary school teachers and boys could identify with them easily. But boys, in their sometimes desperate internal efforts to disidentify with femaleness, may repudiate these qualities as "sissy" to the detriment of their future school performance and their intellectual, social and emotional potential.

There are later periods when sex-role preference is strongly affected by life experience, but it may well be that basic acceptance of satisfaction with one's sex role—the social expression and consequences of being male or female—are most influenced during this period.

Sex play, if not harshly suppressed, begins in early toddlerhood, and it continues in the school years. But solitary or mutual masturbation, visual or tactile curiosity about others' bodies, and imitations of adult sexual activities are almost universally disapproved of or punished in this society. There are other societies (not all of them preliterate) that have a permissive attitude. There are significant differences in adult sexuality in the two types of cultures. In permissive cultures, adult obligatory homosexuality and paraphilias are virtually nonexistent. In restrictive ones, paraphilias, sexual conflicts, sexual misuse of others, and sexual dysfunctions are endemic. [2, 24-26]

The issues are complex and controversial, but it appears that the consistent prohibition of childhood sex play and curiosity is based more on the moral values of some cultures than on objectively demonstrable benefit to children, either early in life or in adulthood.

PREADOLESCENCE AND ADOLESCENCE

The words "puberty" and "adolescence" are not used uniformly in scientific literature. Puberty is the biological surge of maturation that results in reproductive capacity and adult appearance. Its midpoint is somewhat arbitrarily defined as menarche in girls and the capacity for seminal emission in boys. Adolescence is the variable period of psychological and social response to puberty. Normal pubertal changes are similar throughout the human species, whereas adolescent phenomena vary widely cross-culturally and among individuals.

Prepuberty is a somewhat vaguely delimited but biologically real state when pituitary and gonadal hormones increase much more sharply than during childhood, but the bodily manifestations are not striking. Preadolescence is the corresponding period of diffuse and labile emotional response to these internal changes.

Puberty occurs about two years earlier in girls than boys, and all the body changes may take from one and one-half to four years. Usually at about 9 to 11 years of age, the ovaries produce the sex hormone, estrogen, in increasing amounts; this increase initiates breast and uterine development and the fat distribution that results in typical female body contours. Females also produce male hormones (androgens) which are responsible for the development of pubic and axillary hair and increased growth of the clitoris and labia majora. Androgen is also responsible for erotic desire and the intensity of genital sensation in both sexes. At about the middle of puberty (average, 12 to 12 1/2 years), the hypothalamus has begun its cyclic regulation of sex hormones, and menarche occurs.

Testicles begin to enlarge at about age 12 and start producing increasing amounts of testosterone about a year later. This initiates growth of the penis, pubic hair, and prostate; deepens the voice; and causes characteristic male musculature and bone growth. The ability to ejaculate semen with viable sperm, the equivalent of first menstruation in females, usually is achieved shortly before age 14.

Preadolescence is marked by increasing emotional lability, irritability, and unpredictable shifts from striking maturity to regressive behavior. This turbulence is probably caused by the rising production of sex hormones, which influences behavior before any major physical signs appear; therefore, the youngster has nothing concrete to which to attribute these puzzling feelings. Even when external changes have begun, the youngster still feels more like a child than an adult, has not yet moved into the adolescent social world, and often conveys a sense of being at odds with himself and the world.

Masturbation increases, primarily among boys, and, at least in the American middle class, homoerotic play becomes the most frequent form of sexual exploration with others. Kinsey et al[22,23] found that, among girls, the active incidence of homoerotic play reached its peak at ages 9 to 11 and remained more common than heterosexual play through age 13; among boys, it peaked at 12 and remained more common through age 15. The intrapsychic and cultural forces that make this pattern a developmental norm in our culture are complex and perhaps pathogenic;[25] still, for the vast majority of youngsters, such homoerotic activity is a developmental way station to heterosexuality. The rising tides of sex hormones press for gratification at a time when most youngsters' egos are not yet ready to cope with the emotional risk of heterosexual interaction; they often find it easier to explore their changing bodies and stronger sex drives with their more familiar same-sex peers.

Normal puberty can occur as much as two and one-half years earlier or later than the average. However, markedly early or late puberty can cause serious emotional distress, even lasting problems of sexual self-confidence or even identity for the youngster so physically out of step with his peers (see Chapter 18).

Early adolescence is often, if not normally, a period of considerable emotional stress for many nonsexual reasons, but sexual conflict looms large. There is a recrudescence of Oedipal feelings; often they are stronger and more consciously disturbing than in childhood. It is not uncommon for early adolescents to have conscious fantasies and undisguised dreams of sexual activity with a parent. Parents are more likely to have conscious sexual feelings toward their now handsome young sons or nubile daughters than when their children were 4 or 5 years old. And now the issue of rivalry is no longer academic; a son may be stronger or better looking than his father, a daughter more attractive than her mother.

Both the intensity and potential reality of these feelings help precipitate one of the major tasks of adolescence. This task entails a shift from the parent as primary love object to a nonfamilial heterosexual peer. The early adolescent's first expression of this is often a crude distancing from the parents, especially the opposite-sex parent, by turning away and by derogation; this is a way of denying attraction and the associated conflict.

This is a difficult time for parents who usually have done little to provoke this reaction, do not understand it, and may be struggling with their own guilt-producing conflicts about their newly sexual children.

In cultures that restrict childhood sexuality and provide little sex education, young people are ill-prepared for the intense sex drive and reproductive potential of puberty. Girls are often more ready for heterosocial interaction than are their male peers, who may still be trying to achieve a secure masculine identity. Adult levels of sex hormones tend to accentuate masculine/feminine differences, and even most former tomboys become more traditionally feminine as boys begin to reinforce such qualities socially. Adult society, sharply aware of adolescents' procreative capacity and work potential, increases its pressure toward sex-role conformity. This can cause social and emotional hardships for those who fall outside the culture's norms or who wish to extend beyond them.

Having lacked natural opportunities in childhood to become familiar and comfortable with their own and others' sexual anatomy, sensations, and functions, many early adolescents enter a period of intense, self-preoccupied exploration. Although such heterosexual exploration is officially tabooed, imperative drives usually overcome at least some of the inhibitions. Group parties give way to occasional pairing and most adolescents find some chances for experimentation.

This is essentially a period of self-centered sex even when it involves a partner, although youngsters may think themselves as devoted as Romeo and Juliet. The partner is largely a vehicle for self-discovery. "What will happen to *me* if I kiss him?" "How will *I* feel if I touch her breast?" "What will it do to *me* if she rubs my penis?" Countless bits of self-knowledge must be gained before there is the emotional maturity to concern oneself with another.

By the end of early adolescence, Western middle-class youngsters should have accomplished the resolution of their dependency and reawakened Oedipal conflicts with parents enough to move into the mainstream of adolescent socialization and to begin heterosexual pairing. And they should have gained enough familiarity with, and security about, their own and others' bodies to begin turning their attention more to the partnerships.

No sharp age line marks the beginning of late adolescence; it usually arrives in high school, perhaps around 16 for girls and 17 to 18 for boys. Pair dating is the heterosexual norm, although the pairs may spend much of their time with groups. Sex becomes less self-centered; more attention is given to being part of a relationship. Adolescents who date explore the implications of caring, what one gives and risks in emotional involvement. Many commit themselves to marriage, but the majority of these marriages end in divorce, suggesting that readiness for mature commitment is not to be expected in adolescence.

The recent Western trend has been toward earlier sexual activity, including coitus, but masturbation remains the most common sexual outlet throughout adolescence, even for many of those with coital experiences. This is more true for boys, probably because our society is more accepting of sexual activity in males than in females. The ages at which adolescents begin various sexual activities vary widely according to geographical areas, social classes, and ethnic and other subcultural mores. This variance probably accounts for the disagreement among many studies of adolescent sexual behavior. Those that suggest that coital experience in late adolescence is still the exception[27] probably are not correct for the general population.[28]

A few adolescents begin coitus by 12 or 13. Once a boy or girl starts "heavy petting," there is a tendency to proceed to coitus within months, although some do not do so until adulthood or marriage.[29] By the end of high school in most areas, almost half, or even more than half, of the adolescents have had coitus, and—a significant shift from the past—the proportion is sometimes higher among girls.[11] By the end of the teens, a majority of adolescents of both sexes have experienced coitus at least once. (For an overview of statistical studies and trends, see Chilman.[30])

It must be emphasized that this brief and simplified summary is not meant to suggest ideal standards or healthy norms of adolescent sexual behavior. Emotional readiness is an individual matter, and sexuality is sensibly postponed by many adolescents. The younger or less mature that adolescents are, the less likely are they to think of such consequences as pregnancy and sexually transmitted disease. However, adolescent sexual experience is natural and, regardless of much that has been written about the dangers of coitus to adolescent ego development, there is no evidence that heterosexual coitus *per se* is damaging;[31] experience is important for proper learning. It is an individual's family experience and ego development that determine the impact of sexual experience.

The later the developmental phase, the more difficult it is to define optimal periods, but clinical experience allows some generalizations. Adolescents who fail to shift from primary relationships with their parents to primary relationships with their peers usually find the transition more difficult later in life. Those adolescents who have not established a heterosexual dating pattern with some comfortable sexual activity, whether coital or not, probably reflect enough immaturity or inhibition to have problems in adult sexuality. Also, those whose sexual interactions remain self-centered reveal a delay of both emotional and cognitive maturation. Abstract thought is not normally fully possible until about age 14; until this level of "formal operations"[32] is reached, one cannot understand involvement and commitment, anticipate unexperienced consequences, or plan for the future. However, the fact that such cognitive maturation is possible at that age does not mean that all adolescents achieve it. There is evidence that not more than about half the people in the U.S. ever develop beyond the cognitive level of "concrete operations" characteristic of normal primary school children (aged 7 to 11), and that the percentage of those capable of abstract thought does not increase much after adolescence.[33] The persistence of sexual activity limited to concrete, self-oriented interactions in which the immediate experience remains the most important factor indicates a deficit in sexual development.

ADULTHOOD AND PARENTHOOD

Adult and Marital Sexuality. Procreative adulthood, unlike any previous period, has several optimal paths of psychosexual development. There are no biological or ego-maturation changes that force all normal adults beyond previous levels of sexual development. All but a small minority are sexually active, but many of those who are not lead rich and rewarding lives. The majority marry, but many who do not marry have gratifying sex lives that include emotional involvement, tenderness, and concern. Most people have children. Active parenthood does precipitate new psychosexual developmental issues, but childless couples are not necessarily less sexually mature than those with children. However, because of space limits, this chapter is confined to the typical progression to marriage and parenthood. (For a discussion of alternate adult sexual and marital life styles and decisions about parenthood, see Gadpaille.[11])

To separate young adult or even early marital sexuality from late adolescent sexuality is a somewhat false distinction. Since many persons marry during adolescence, the phases often overlap. However, adulthood is a different psychological stage than adolescence. Many young adults are now postponing marriage and children, and further psychosexual development can occur even when their marital and parental status is no different from when they were adolescents.

Freedom from parental restraint comes with independent living quarters, although the constraints of personal values, conflicts, or developmental deficits do not automatically lessen. Adolescence is thought of as a time of exploration, but, because of the greater opportunities afforded most young adults, many of them engage in even more sexual experimentation. On the other hand, because the intrapsychic progress from adolescence to adulthood entails the crystallization of identity, values, and interests, other young adults will have experimented sufficiently during adolescence and found what they like sexually, and their current experimentation therefore is diminished.

"Permissiveness with affection"[34,35] is becoming the predominant sexual value among young adults; many accept permissiveness even without affection. There is greater incidence of premarital coitus now among women, so that there is now much less difference between the sexes than in the past. A 1972 questionnaire study of white women ages 18 through 24 revealed that 70 per cent of the unmarried and 81 per cent of the married had experienced premarital coitus.*[36] Surveys generally show a higher rate of premarital coitus among young black females compared with young white females, although young black females had fewer partners.[28]

Women's greater acceptance of nonmarital coitus can cause a type of anxiety related to psychosexual development that was once a predominantly male concern—performance anxiety. As women recognize their right to sexual fulfillment, those whose development has interfered with orgasmic response are likely to have doubts about their adequacy as women and as sexual partners.

A characteristic of healthy adult sexuality is the capacity to focus both tender and sexual love on the same person (not necessarily only one person in an individual's lifetime). Both the successful resolution of adolescent development and the early adult experience in sexual relationships are important for the achievement of such fusion, a capacity that is necessary before genuine, lasting commitment to a partner is possible.

Marriage and parenthood are only two of various ways that individuals of the 20 to 40 age period deal with the sexual issues. There is no implication that marriage is either the only appropriate or the most healthy way to manage adult sexuality. Married persons and parents are not by definition healthier than unmarried childless people. Some of the continued development possible within marriage is also possible in unmarried partnerships, but marriage and parenthood are qualitatively different from nonmarriage and childlessness. Marrying and having children each precipitates psychosexual developmental tasks—tasks that may result in further growth, conflict, or disorder— that are not necessarily thrust on persons who are unmarried or childless.

Marriage legally commits couples to try to develop their sexuality cooperatively rather than as individuals; although divorce is more easily obtained than in past generations, persons who are married find it more difficult to separate than those who simply live together. Of course, many married partners never openly discuss their sexual feelings, preferences, or displeasure with one another, but, if such communication did not develop before marriage, marriage does provide both impetus and further opportunity.

Marriage also provides an opportunity for resolving remnants of unconscious sexual guilt related to parental disapproval. Girl friends and boy friends are just that, but a husband or wife has a role earlier held by a parent. A spouse's enjoyment of, even eagerness for, sex play, coitus and variety of sexual expression can promote guilt-free sexual pleasure. The intimacy possible in marriage, the daily experiencing of one another's fluctuating moods and physiological changes, such as those associated with the menstrual cycle, can

---

*These figures cannot be accurately compared with the earlier Kinsey statistics, because the population sample and method are not similar, but other studies[30] show the same trend.

dispel the anxiety-producing mystery of the opposite sex. It also can foster identification with the attitudes and sensations that each sex shares with the other; absence of this cross-sex identification promotes misunderstandings, while its presence diminishes inappropriate aspects of masculine and feminine stereotypes.

Parenthood is a potent force in resolving remaining unconscious sexual conflicts and in further development; it also can precipitate regression and disturbance. Pregnancy awakens new levels of a woman's identification with her own mother. For her husband, it evokes similar identifications with both father *and* mother, since in his primary identification with mother he internalized some of her nurturing qualities. Pregnancy begins to trigger a woman's maternalism and enormously expands her awareness and acceptance of her previously vague internal sexuality; now there are contents and sensations to define it in a new way.

Childbirth turns husbands and wives into parents and even more powerfully precipitates identification with their own parents. The woman gains functional equality with her mother, the man sexual parity with his father. These identifications carry the seeds both of growth and regression or disorder. As in marriage, but far more intensely, the spouse who is now a parent can emotionally facilitate guilt reduction and sexual enjoyment. Becoming a parent also may awaken unresolved Oedipal conflicts in a destructive way; sexual activity may be inhibited if the spouse is unconsciously identified with the sexually tabooed parent.

Parents also identify with their child and continue to do so as the child grows. In each developmental stage, the child reawakens in the parents the emotions, the developmental tasks, and any residual conflicts from that stage in their own lives. Of course, the parent meets each recrudescence not as a child coping with a stage for the first time but with an adult's ego development, able to repair maladaptations and achieve greater health.[11]

To give some simple illustrations, a toddler's sexual curiosity and frank questions may make young parents think about their own use or avoidance of sexual words, and communicate more realistically about sex. A child's increased sexual activity during the Oedipal stage forces many parents to re-evaluate attitudes toward their children's and their own rights to sexual expression, such as the right to masturbation. A man whose father was physically undemonstrative and avoided him, perhaps fearing homosexual taint in such behavior with a son, may discover how natural such father-son affection is and lose some of his own anxiety about affection among men.

Although adolescence is often especially trying for parents, the growth potential is commensurate. Parents who have enough ego flexibility to hear their adolescent children's questions and challenges, and to consider them with respect and intellectual honesty, will benefit as much as their fortunate youngsters. They need not forsake their own sexual values, but, in some cases, they will find that their previously unquestioned values have been opened to the possibility of alternatives, and their own sexual identities may be richer for it.

Replacement by the young is inevitable for all people and painful for many.

It is not true that all parents of adolescents have begun to lose their vigor and sexual attractiveness and capacity; many are in their sexual prime. But it is true that they have fewer remaining years of peak sexuality and reproductive potential than their adolescent children. True replacement does not take place during these years, but the issue starts to become conscious. This can cause severe distress in psychosexually immature parents and in those whose adult sexuality has been less than fulfilling. However, the growing sexual independence of one's children can permit greater sexual freedom and enjoyment. Many parents gain more free time and privacy than they have had since their first child was born. If they have made good use of their relationship, they know so much more about sex and about each other's sexuality that feverishly active adolescents seem like fumbling novices. The reassessments of attitudes and the changes in life-style that accompany one's children's adolescence can bring major achievements in psychosexual development.

MIDDLE AND LATE YEARS

If the extremes are averaged, these periods entail biological changes that make it improbable for most persons to maintain the level of sexual functioning and to have the same emotional responses as in young adulthood. In some ways, then, the developmental changes of middle and later life are not as optimal as those of young adulthood. The middle years are considered to begin for most women when they lose their procreative potential and when most of a couple's children have begun to move away to set up their own homes.

Our culture has been, and largely continues to be, as antisexual toward older people as toward the young. Both implicit and explicit traditional mores make active sexuality acceptable only in married people of reproductive age. The result is that relatively little normal psychosexual development has been acknowledged or studied in the older population.

Diminished fertility and menopause force a woman to think about her sexuality differently. This can be a very difficult time, often of severe depression or even psychosis, especially for women who had emotional conflicts about childbearing or child rearing, whose childbearing potential or desire was unfulfilled, or whose self-esteem was exaggeratedly linked to maternal capacity. Hormonal changes can lead to unpleasant physical symptoms, and then to gradual vaginal changes that may impair sexual responsiveness and pleasure. However, only about 15 per cent of women suffer clinically significant symptoms during menopause;[37] estrogen replacement therapy also can prevent vaginal changes.

Some recent reports suggest a somewhat higher incidence of endometrial carcinoma (which is rather rare under any circumstances) in women taking estrogen postmenopausally, but these reports have been questioned by other investigators. The true risk remains unknown. Whether continued gratifying coitus or the risk involved is more important is best left to each woman and her physician; a simple hysterectomy is usually safe and may be an alternative solution for some women.

There are no male biological changes comparable to menopause. Neither a man's sexual function nor his fertility is lost or even declines sharply because of age alone. Paternity has been documented into the 80's and 90's, and, while almost all authorities report a gradual decline of circulating testosterone in later life, there is not an inevitable correlation with a diminished capacity for paternity. However, some men become depressed or panicky in middle life over their imagined loss of sexual vigor and hurl themselves into illconsidered sexual adventures or new marriages as a means of reassurance.

The (primarily female) biological changes of middle life must be understood as a major impulse toward further psychosexual development, not merely or even mainly as causes of problems, which occur in only a minority of cases. For women whose values have precluded the use of contraception, menopause offers the first opportunity for sex without fear of pregnancy and may bring a great increase in enjoyment. Since these changes typically coincide with the end of preoccupation with active parenting, they allow new leisure for partners to enjoy one another and, for the woman, the possibility of a new or resumed career. The enhanced self-esteem that accompanies a continued sense of personal and social contribution is an antidote to depression and therefore to sexual decline.

In the absence of specific disease, male erectile capacity is never lost as a consequence of age alone. Sexual arousal and achievement of orgasm may, however, take longer; there are longer refractory periods after orgasm; and ejaculation is less forceful and may not occur on every coital occasion. Unless a man misinterprets these changes as decreased virility, they can carry more advantages than disadvantages. They impair sexual impetuosity, but that may have less importance for older couples and be compensated for by longer love play and coitus and the opportunity for more loving attention to the partner as a complete erotic being. Many women express appreciation for older partners for just these reasons.

The advent of grandparenthood is a major life event, but it does not necessarily cause major psychosexual development. Its impact on a person's sexuality is usually peripheral, arising from a sense of still having value and usefulness to one's children and grandchildren. It mitigates concerns over replacement and provides a realistic sense of generational continuity that softens the reality of ultimate death.

One of the most dramatic examples of psychosexual development that sometimes occurs in middle life is that which follows the dissolution of a marriage that has been sexually unsatisfactory. Many couples maintain a sexually and interpersonally unhappy marriage out of the conviction that their children will benefit from an unbroken home. Often these are mismatched people who have tried unsuccessfully to make their relationship gratifying and are capable of previously unattained levels of sexuality with other partners. When their children are no longer dependent, they may wisely separate or divorce and make developmental gains with new partners that transform their many remaining years. Not all middle-age divorces, therefore, should be stigmatized as inappropriate climacteric responses.

As people age, chronic diseases and partners' deaths affect their sexual potential. By age 65, approximately 20 per cent of married men and 50 per cent of married women have lost their spouses through death.[38] There are far more whose spouses, although living, are sexually impaired by chronic illness (this happens to more men than women). Still, the majority of elderly people with willing partners are capable of sexual function and enjoyment. More important still is their right to their sexuality. Many studies have laid to rest the myth of asexuality among the aged.[39-43] While most studies that include women reveal somewhat less sexual activity than among aged men, this is probably caused by unavailability of partners, since many conditions and surgical procedures that severely or totally impair males impair females less or not at all.[44-46]

Even physical conditions that cause some sexual impairment may expand sexual expression—in effect, further sexual development. An impotent man may, with helpful reinforcement, learn new ways to express physical affection for his wife, maintaining both her sexual pleasure and his own masculine self-esteem. Sympathetic, authoritative understanding and encouragement may help those without partners to accept masturbation for the first time as a guiltless source of pleasure. In any event, age and illness cannot completely rob a previously full life of its integrity and dignity.

Physicians involved in direct patient care are in a unique position to influence psychosexual development in healthy directions. Increasingly, the medical profession sees its role as fostering health, not only treating illness. A knowledge of early developmental needs can be of immense benefit to parents and to their children and adolescents. An understanding of how each person returns to the same emotionally charged sexual issues time and again during the life cycle can help the physician make sense out of some of the problems of living that underlie many of the vague, nonspecific complaints that bring people to his office. And the realization that psychosexual development never need end places him in a position to help many older people discover, or retain, a sexually vital life.

References

1. Gadpaille W: Research into the physiology of maleness and femaleness: Its contributions to the etiology and psychodynamics of homosexuality. *Arch Gen Psychiatry* 1972; 26:193-206.
2. Money J, Ehrhardt AA: *Man and Woman, Boy and Girl. Differentiation & Dimorphism of Gender Identity from Conception to Maturity*. Baltimore, Johns Hopkins University Press, 1972.
3. Harris GW: Sex hormones, brain development and brain function. *Endocrinology* 1964; 75:627-648.
4. Reinisch JM: Fetal hormones, the brain, and human sex differences: A heuristic, integrative review of the recent literature. *Arch Sex Behav* 1974; 3:51-90.

5. Jones HW Jr, Scott WW: *Hermaphroditism, Genital Anomalies and Related Endocrine Disorders*, ed 2. Baltimore, Williams & Wilkins Company, 1971.
6. Beach FA: Cross-species comparisons and the human heritage. *Arch Sex Behav* 1976; 5:469-485.
7. Diamond M: Human sexual development: Biological foundations for social development, in Beach FA (ed): *Human Sexuality in Four Perspectives*. Baltimore, Johns Hopkins University Press, 1976.
8. Scott JP, et al: Critical periods in the organization of systems. *Dev Psychobiol* 1974; 7:489-513.
9. Scott JP, et al: Critical periods in behavioral development. *Science* 1962; 138:949-958.
10. Scott JP: Critical periods in organizational processes, in Faulkner F, Tanner JM (eds): *Human Growth: A Comprehensive Treatise*. New York, Plenum Press. (In press)
11. Gadpaille W: *The Cycles of Sex*. New York, Charles Scribner's Sons, 1975.
12. Spitz RA, Wolf C: Autoerotism: Some empirical findings and hypotheses on three of its manifestations in the first year of life. *Psychoanal Study Child* 1949; 3/4:85-120.
13. Bowlby J: Maternal care and mental health. Geneva, Switzerland, (monograph). *World Health Organization*, 1951.
14. Korner AF: Methodological considerations in studying sex differences in the behavioral functioning of newborns, in Friedman RC, et al (eds): *Sex Differences in Behavior*. New York, John Wiley & Sons, 1974.
15. Kestenberg JS: Outside and inside, male and female. *J Am Psychoanal Assoc* 1968; 16:457-520.
16. Hampson JL, Hampson JG: The ontogenesis of sexual behavior in man, in Young WC, Corner GW (eds): *Sex and Internal Secretions*, ed 3. Baltimore, Williams & Wilkins Company, 1961.
17. Greenson RR: Dis-identifying from mother: Its special importance for the boy. *Int J Psychoanal* 1968; 49:370-374.
18. Stoller RJ: Symbiosis anxiety and the development of masculinity. *Arch Gen Psychiatry* 1974; 30:164-172.
19. Gagnon JH: Sexuality and sexual learning in the child. *Psychiatry* 1965; 28:212-228.
20. Bieber I: Olfaction in sexual development and adult sexual organization. *Am J Psychother* 1959; 13:851-859.
21. Kalogerakis MG: The role of olfaction in sexual development. *Psychosom Med* 1963; 25:420-432.
22. Kinsey AC, et al: *Sexual Behavior in the Human Male*. Philadelphia, W.B. Saunders Co, 1948.
23. Kinsey AC, et al: *Sexual Behavior in the Human Female*. Philadelphia, W.B. Saunders Co, 1953.
24. Ford C, Beach FA: *Patterns of Sexual Behavior*. New York, Harper and Row Publishers, Inc, 1951.
25. Gadpaille WJ: A consideration of two concepts of normality as it applies to adolescent sexuality. *J Am Acad Child Psychiatry* 1976; 15:679-692.

26. Gadpaille WJ: Psychosexual developmental tasks imposed by pathologically delayed childhood: A cultural dilemma, in Feinstein SC, Giovacchini PL (eds): *Adolescent Psychiatry*. Chicago, University of Chicago Press, 1978.

27. Offer D: *The Psychological World of the Teenager*. New York, Basic Books Inc, 1969.

28. Kantner JF, Zelnik M: Sexual experience of young unmarried women in the United States. *Fam Plann Perspect* 1972; 4(4):9-18.

29. Sorensen RC: *Adolescent Sexuality in Contemporary America*. New York, World Publishing Company, 1973.

30. Chilman CS: Adolescent sexuality in a changing American society. Washington, DC, U.S. Dept of Health, Education, and Welfare, DHEW Publication No (NIH) 79-1426,1978.

31. Gadpaille WJ: Adolescent sexuality: A challenge to psychiatrists. *J Am Acad Psychoanal* 1975; 3:163-177.

32. Inhelder B, Fiaget J: *The Growth of Logical Thinking from Childhood to Adolescence*. New York, Basic Books Inc, 1958.

33. Kohlberg L, Gilligan C: The adolescent as a philosopher: The discovery of the self in a postconventional world. *Daedalus* 1971; 100:1051-1086.

34. Reiss IL: *Premarital Sexual Standards in America*. New York, Free Press, 1960.

35. Reiss IL: *Family Systems in America*, ed 2. Ainsdale, Ill, Dryden Press, 1976.

36. Hunt M: *Sexual Behavior in the 1970's*. Chicago, Playboy Press, 1974.

37. Weiss E, English OS: *Psychosomatic Medicine*, ed 3. Philadelphia, W.B. Saunders Co, 1957. Group for the Advancement of Psychiatry: *Psychiatry and the Aged: An Introductory Approach*. (GAP Report No. 88). New York, Group for the the the Advancement of Psychiatry, 1965.

39. Finkle AL, et al: Sexual potency in aging males. *JAMA* 1959; 170:1391-1393.

40. Newman G, et al: Sexual activities and attitudes in older persons. *JAMA* 1960; 173:33-35.

41. Freedman JT: Sexual capacities in the aging male. *Geriatrics* 1961; 16:37-43.

42. Rubin I: Sex over 65, in Beigel HG (ed): *Advances in Sex Research*. New York, Harper and Row Publishers, Inc, 1963.

43. Pfeiffer E, et al: Sexual behavior in aged men and women: I. Observations on 254 community volunteers. *Arch Gen Psychiatry* 1968; 19:753-758.

44. Ellenberg M: Sex and the female diabetic. *Med Aspects Hum Sex* 1977 (Dec); 11:30-38.

45. Lord JW: Peripheral vascular disorders and sexual function. *Med Aspects Hum Sex* 1973 (Sept); 7:34-43.

46. Twombly GH: Sex after radical gynecological surgery. *J Sex Res* 1968; 4:275-281.

Chapter 4

The Sexual Response Cycle

Milton Diamond, Ph.D. and Arno Karlen

Questions and problems involving sexual response, including orgasm, underlie many visits to physicians, but only in recent decades has detailed knowledge emerged about sexual response and orgasm. Few aspects of sexuality have been so clouded by misinformation and myth, and in few things are there so much individual variation and misunderstanding between men and women.

People tend to take sexual response for granted unless it changes or is dysfunctional. In such instances it can then cause severe conflict in individuals and between partners. Patients commonly ask, "Why can't I have an erection?" "How does a woman know whether she's had an orgasm?" "Can all women become multiorgasmic?" "Are women less excitable than men?" "Do they become excited more slowly?" "How much sexual desire is normal at my age?" Many patients suffer distress and lasting difficulties because of ignorance or problems about such matters. Many can be helped by a physician who understands the processes and problems involved.

BASIC CONCEPTS[1, 2]

Full consideration of the sexual response must first take into account what has been termed sexual aspects, sexual phases and sexual mechanisms. *Sexual aspects* refers to both the psychological (mental) and physical (somatic) components of a sexual situation.

Sexual phases refers to the various "states" in which an individual might become aroused (excitement) or orgasmic.[2] *Sexual mechanisms* refers to those psychological or physical processes that create these phases. If the phases are the "what" of the sexual response cycle (SRC), the mechanisms are the "how."

Returning to "sexual aspects", a *physical* aspect of sex is external and obvious—erection of the penis or nipples, vaginal transudation ("lubrication") and orgasm. The *psychological* aspects of sex—thoughts, feelings and fantasies—are not always obvious (e.g., someone thinking about sex play may look no different from someone who isn't), arousal may not occur and there is variation among individuals and within individuals from time to time.[2] The psychological aspects of an act or response can be *cognitive* (intentional) or *instinctive* (reflexive). Deliberately touching another person's genitals is a cognitive act. Penile erection and vaginal wetting are reflexive and can happen without apparent reason or conscious wish.

When the mental and somatic aspects of sex do not work together smoothly, the result can be very disturbing. Commonly, disparities between an individual's psychological and physical aspects cause concern: A man may want coitus but not have an erection; a woman may want coitus but not lubricate adequately; a person may want orgasm but be unable to reach it. Also, many people aren't sure whether their partners have reached arousal or climax; some aren't sure whether they themselves have. Therefore, they want to know the signs of arousal and orgasm. Understanding the factors involved in sexual response can help patients solve such difficulties.

OVERVIEW

Masters and Johnson,[3] carrying on the pioneering work of Kinsey et al,[4, 5] gave the first detailed description of the physical changes involved in sexual response. In this discussion, we draw largely on their findings. They separated the full response cycle into four phases: excitement (arousal), plateau, orgasm and resolution. For a more comprehensive view, a resting phase also should be considered,[1, 2] since many individuals often vacillate between resting and excitement and any cycle is best conceived as having a common start and conclusion. Moreover, many clinicians now believe that a desire phase occurs before demonstrable excitement. Although there is a great deal of individual variation in the details of each phase, the overall physical aspects of the cycle are similar for the majority of people. Much remains to be learned about the psychological aspects of the cycle.

Most of the time, a person is sexually at rest (Figure 2). When physical or psychological stimuli give rise to sexual thoughts or desire, the response is the excitement (arousal) phase. In both sexes, excitement is marked by increasing vasocongestion in the genitals and rising myotonia, particularly in the genital area but in other regions as well. This causes penile erection and vaginal wetting, the chief signals of arousal. That is why any condition, disease or drug that affects vasocongestion or myotonia can influence sexual response.

Rising excitement brings a person to the plateau phase. Vasocongestion and muscle tension level off, although sexual interest remains high. This phase may be long or short, depending on the individual's constitution, desire, social learning, experiences and other factors. Some people strive to reach orgasm quickly; others can greatly extend the plateau phase and enjoy doing so; and still others have little control over how quickly they go on toward orgasm.

From the plateau phase, one proceeds to the relatively brief orgasmic phase. Psychological and muscular tension rise rapidly, as do heart rate, breathing and body activity. Then there is a sudden peak and a release of tension. Orgasm, or climax, may be triggered psychologically or physically. Stimulation, resulting in orgasm, may be applied to any part of the body, but the genitalia usually are the primary sites involved. In men, orgasm usually but not always includes ejaculation. Psychological stimulation involves fantasy or the awareness of one's own and a partner's reactions.

The resolution (postorgasmic) phase brings mental and physical relaxation and, unless there are feelings of guilt or conflict, a feeling of well-being. Some

Figure 2

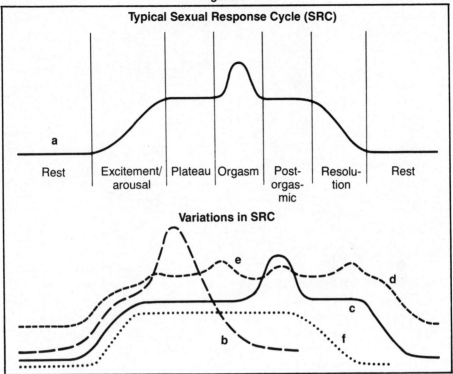

Typical Sexual Response Cycle (SRC)

a

| Rest | Excitement/arousal | Plateau | Orgasm | Post-orgasmic | Resolution | Rest |

Variations in SRC

e

d

c

b

f

people report psychological satisfaction or relaxation without apparent orgasm; to others, not reaching orgasm is intensely frustrating. The former response is more common in women, the latter in men. This phase tends to be different for men and women in other ways as well. Men often become relaxed, passive and physically unresponsive (refractory) to sexual stimulation. Usually the penis soon detumesces and the man again reaches the resting state, perhaps with a period of rest or sleep. Some women also resolve quickly toward rest or sleep, but many remain sexually responsive and show no refractory period; instead they return to the plateau phase, seek further stimulation and reach orgasm again. After two or more orgasms (multiple orgasm), they pass through resolution to rest. Multiple orgasm has been reported in males[6] but occurs only in a very small number, almost all of whom are young.

Many parts of the SRC resemble autonomic stress ("fight or flight") reactions. As excitement builds, the autonomic nervous system brings into play such reactions as increased heart rate and blood pressure, muscle tension, pupillary dilatation, perspiring and finally orgasm. In addition, the involuntary muscles of the blood vessels and genitals relax or contract so that increased blood flow causes swelling of the tissues.

MECHANISMS[1,2]

The entire SRC can be thought of as involving three kinds of mechanisms: arousal, copulatory and orgasmic (see Table 1). The arousal mechanisms depend heavily on sensory input and fantasy; sexual cues are sent to the brain, which interprets and responds to them, and a person is thereby "turned on" or "turned off." Odor, sight, touch, taste, memory and fantasy all may interact to produce arousal. Arousal may occur while the individual is active or passive, and involves both psychological and physical aspects. It is with these arousal mechanisms that erotism is measured (sample measures of arousal are latency to penile erection and vaginal transudation). As arousal builds, copulatory mechanisms come into play to increase the vasocongestion and myotonia that began with excitement. Among the copulatory mechanisms are penile and nipple erection, vaginal sweating and pelvic thrusting. As excitement and copulatory mechanisms become more intense, orgasmic mechanisms, such as ejaculation in men and contraction of the pelvic floor in women, are set in action.

Table 1. Elements of Sexual Response

I. Phases

Resting
Excitement (includes desire)
Plateau
Orgasm
Resolution (includes postorgasmic)

II. Mechanisms

Arousal		Sensory stimuli
Copulatory	*involves*	Erection, sweating
Orgasmic		Ejaculation, muscle contractions

Adapted from Milton Diamond and Arno Karlen, *Sexual Decisions*. Copyright © 1980 by Milton Diamond and Arno Karlen. Reprinted by permission of the publisher, Little Brown and Company.

The sensitivities, or thresholds, of these mechanisms depend on the interaction of biological, social and personal factors. From his culture, a male may learn to give more or less erotic attention to the breasts, or to prefer breasts of a certain size or shape. His personal development may make him respond more or less to such influences. The differences between men and women in certain patterns of response are influenced by innate factors as well. For instance, men may be more responsive to visual stimuli, women to auditory stimuli (words).

Many things can influence arousal, copulation and orgasm. Rest, relaxation, a general sense of well-being and androgenic hormones all lower the thresholds for these mechanisms; hunger, fatigue, depression, progestogenic hormones and many drugs usually raise these thresholds. Anxiety, shame, intrapsychic conflict and preoccupation with other matters also can interfere. Fear and depression reduce desire as well as arousal and excitement. A person who feels rejected in a social, occupational or intimate relationship may not respond to stimuli that would be arousing at other times. Long-range social and individual learning also have effects; for instance, a sexually restrictive background may make sexual responsiveness difficult, while a permissive background may facilitate response.

MALE AND FEMALE CYCLES

The Male SRC.[3] Penile erection, or tumescence, is the first major outward sign of excitement. It results from a cortically mediated or spinal reflex that triggers vasocongestion. Psychological stimuli, touch, warmth, vibration, combined wetness and pressure, and visual and auditory cues all can stimulate erection. The stimuli themselves probably have no specific powers but depend on psychological readiness.

Early in the SRC, vasocongestion makes the scrotum tighten and thicken, and increases the size of the testes by 50 to 100 per cent. Myotonia causes muscles in the spermatic cords and scrotum to draw the testes close to the body; this elevation continues through the plateau and orgasm phase. During resolution, with the reversal of vasocongestion and myotonia, the scrotum and testes return to their normal size and position. The speed of return varies among individuals but seems to be related to the intensity and duration of the excitement and plateau phases. Prolonged testicular vasocongestion ("blue balls") may cause pain and can occur whether or not orgasm has taken place.

Full erection may develop within ten seconds after stimulation begins; this varies according to age, the amount and kind of stimulation and erotic interest. The erect penis is most likely to stay fully firm during the plateau phase, when copulatory mechanisms are operating. Later in the plateau stage, further vasocongestion of the penile corona and glans makes these areas more prominent and red-purple. Erection then remains nearly complete until after orgasm.

It is virtually impossible for the penis to become locked in the vagina. A survey of scientific literature revealed only one confirmed account[7] associated with prolonged vaginismus (tonic contraction of the vagina). Such a lock occurs normally in dogs, wolves and some related species because of vasocongestion at the base of the carnivore penis; this may well be the source of lore about humans locked together.

During orgasm, contractions of the prostate, seminal vesicles and vas deferens are followed by throbbing of the penis as semen is ejaculated. The first contractions are fairly regular and occur at intervals of about 0.8 seconds; subsequent contractions are weaker, irregular and less frequent.

Ejaculation, like erection, is largely reflexive and has its own neurological trigger. There are two phases: emission and ejaculation proper. During emission, the accessory glands and vas deferens empty into the dilated prostatic urethra. Young men are usually aware that this has happened and that ejaculation is inevitable. With age, these phases lose their distinctive character. Recognizing this point of ejaculatory inevitability is important in the treatment of premature ejaculation (see Chapter 12).

The Female SRC.[3] Just as erection signals arousal in males, three vaginal changes signal sexual excitement in females—vaginal sweating (lubrication), expansion of the inner two-thirds of the vaginal barrel and color changes in the labia. All three depend on vasocongestion and myotonia.

Within 10 to 30 seconds after excitement starts, the vaginal walls begin a sweating-like process (transudation). The transudate is clear, slightly slippery, nonoily and has a distinctive odor and taste. This fluid seems to have at least three functions: It lubricates penile movement in the vagina, it neutralizes the usually acidic vaginal environment and its moisture aids sperm survival. (Although typically called "lubricating fluid," the authors consider the term too limiting and prefer the original "vaginal transudate" unless lubrication in coitus is being referred to specifically.) In some women, especially after menopause, there is too little lubrication for comfortable coitus (any water-soluble lubricant can lessen discomfort). This reduced wetting does not necessarily reflect lack of erotic interest or poor sexual technique, any more than copious fluids always indicate intense interest and pleasure. Estrogen levels, vaginal infections and certain drugs also affect vaginal transudation.

As excitement increases, the inner portion of the vaginal barrel begins to balloon; a space greater than is necessary for the penis is thereby created and perhaps provides a receptacle where semen can collect. Increasing vasocongestion turns the vagina from its normal pink color to red. The inner portion of the vagina continues to balloon, a process called tenting. Meanwhile, the outer third narrows and tightens; it is now called the orgasmic platform.

During orgasm, tenting continues and the orgasmic platform contracts, first strongly and rhythmically, then more weakly and at longer intervals. Orgasmic contractions may continue far longer than in men. The woman's awareness of orgasm usually, although not always, corresponds with these contractions; longer more intense contractions are felt as a longer, more intense orgasm. For many reasons—e.g., prolonged excitement without orgasm—vasocongestion may remain after sexual activity; this chronic pelvic congestion, the female equivalent of "blue balls," can cause severe pelvic discomfort and emotional frustration.

Although the clitoris is highly sensitive, its response may be visually slow and undramatic during excitement. It may throb and become more sensitive to touch and pressure, and there is vasocongestion but only rarely erection.[3] It is difficult to see clitoral changes during the plateau phases, for the clitoral prepuce swells, as the clitoris disappears under its hood. This retraction may, in part, be a protective mechanism. Many women enjoy direct clitoral stimulation, but many others find it unpleasant and even painful, especially when the tip rather than the shaft is rubbed. The clitoris may keep disappearing and reappearing as excitement waxes and wanes. During resolution, clitoral swelling diminishes in a way similar to penile detumescence.

Changes in the labia majora and minora during the SRC are affected by parity. In nulliparous women, myotonia makes the labia majora become flatter and thinner during arousal, and they remain so throughout plateau and orgasm. In women who have had children, the labia have developed an extensive vascular network, which becomes congested during sexual response; the labia swell two to three times in size. In all women, the labia minora normally double or triple in size and become reddish purple.

During the plateau, the labia may become deep red or even deep purple. Their prominence and color change signal that orgasm is inevitable if stimulation continues; without these signs, orgasm will not occur. During resolution, a return to normal occurs in two stages, first rapidly and then more slowly.

Changes in movements of the uterus play a dramatic part in the SRC of some women and in their awareness of their response. During arousal, the uterus becomes engorged and lifts upward; the elevation continues through the plateau phase. During orgasm, the uterus contracts rhythmically. Whether a pumping or sucking action occurs, as if to aid sperm transport, is debated.[3,8] Some women are able to distinquish between an orgasm in which there are intense uterine contractions from one in which these contractions are minimal. In five to ten minutes after orgasm, the uterus returns to normal size and position.

Male-Female Differences in the SRC. In some men, the SRC differs from that described above,[3] but men are more consistent than women, both as a group and as individuals from one time to another. Except in old age or when ill, most men usually experience the pattern shown in Figure 2 (*a* or *b*); some experience the pattern in *c*. Having reached the plateau phase, only rarely do they voluntarily stop short of orgasm. Typically, a young man in the resting phase can be aroused quickly, strives for rapid increase in pleasure and wants intensely to move quickly through plateau to orgasm. His sexual focus is sharp and strong and he approaches orgasm with rapid heavy breathing and pelvic thrusting. Orgasm is usually explosive and brief, often with vocal noises, an end of thrusting, retraction of the pelvis and brief loss of awareness. Then he rapidly loses sexual interest and returns to the resting state.

In some women, the SRC is like that typical of males in that resolution occurs quickly. Some may return to the plateau and then to additional orgasms (*d*). For other women, perhaps a majority in our society, excitement builds more slowly, the plateau is prolonged and orgasm is less dramatic (*e*). For still other women, orgasm seems not to be a climax but a passing over to a more relaxed state, with little movement or noise, followed by slow resolution. What they describe as orgasm is not subjectively or objectively much different from a plateau experience, but afterward they feel release of tension, a sense of completion and a desire to talk, rest, cuddle or sleep, all of which suggests that orgasm has occurred. For a number of women, perhaps 10 to 30 per cent, orgasm never or rarely occurs (*f*). For many others, it is intermittently absent.[5, 9, 10]

Responses Common to Males and Females. Except for reactions of the breasts and skin, where females are more responsive, nongenital sexual responses are more alike than dissimilar in males and females.

Erection of the nipples is an early sign of arousal in females and occurs in about half of all males. Vasocongestion enlarges the female breasts and areolae during the excitement and plateau phases, especially in nulliparas and women who have not nursed. The breasts and areolae quickly return to normal size during resolution.

During sexual response, 70 to 75 per cent of women and about 25 per cent of men show the sex flush, a blush or rash-like vasocongestion across the chest, breasts, back and neck. It develops during the transition from excitement to plateau, is most evident at orgasm and disappears quickly during resolution. This striking and common event went largely unnoticed until it was described by Masters and Johnson.[3]

Myotonia and physical activity increase in both sexes during arousal. Much of the movement during genital activity is reflexive, but some is learned. During the plateau phase, myotonia continues to increase and may be especially evident around the mouth and in the strap muscles of the neck. Muscles tense in the thighs, buttocks and toes. When orgasm is imminent, the muscles of the limbs contract and there is carpopedal spasm.

Orgasm brings a peak of muscle tension and activity. There may be dramatic movements of the entire body, especially of the pelvis, or rigor-like tension and tremors. These movements vary a great deal among individuals according to age, health, sexual experience and upbringing. Sometimes the most important factor is how free a person feels to "let go" during the approach to orgasm.

Other organ systems and functions also change during sexual response. As noted earlier, pulse, heart rate and blood pressure almost double. The rate and depth of breathing increase greatly. Saliva may flow freely, whether or not kissing occurs. The anus tightens during excitement; during orgasm it may show typical 0.8-second pulsations. Urination is almost impossible in a nullipara during genital activity; however, the release of urethral sphincters after coitus is often accompanied by an urgent need to urinate. Some women, especially multiparas, release some urine during orgasm because of spasmodic relaxation of the bladder-urethra sphincters.

THE SRC IN AGING

Almost every mechanism and phase of the SRC is affected by aging. The changes, although slow and subtle from year to year, are unmistakable over long periods. In middle age, men reach erection, begin coitus and attain orgasm more slowly. Erection, orgasm and ejaculation all occur with less force and intensity. Erection may take two to three times longer to occur in the 50's than in the 40's, and after 60 a lost erection becomes more difficult to regain. Ejaculation may become more a seepage than a "shot," there is progressive decline in penile sensitivity and the refractory period may last for days.

Aging affects the SRC somewhat differently in women. Aging men still produce androgens, although in decreasing amounts. In women, changes begin in reproductive tissues as estrogen production declines during menopause. About five years after menopause, vaginal transudation is greatly reduced in most women, although it remains adequate for coitus in some. After age 60, transudation may take several to many minutes to occur. The vagina becomes narrower, shorter and less able to expand; the vaginal walls become thin, even tissue-paper thin, so that coitus may be painful. The sex flush is rare or absent after 50. In the minority of aging women who have severe problems in physical response, estrogen replacement therapy may give relief.[7]

For many people, middle age is a time of peak nonsexual pressures—job, career, the "empty nest," financial obligations, midlife readjustments. The resulting depression and anxiety can easily interfere with sexual arousal and activity, just when the physical vigor of response is declining. Midlife sexual problems also can arise in both sexes because of boredom with partners, entrenched marital conflict or a feeling that sex is now inappropriate or shameful. Another common cause of problems is fear of being found unattractive with a resultant withdrawal from sex. People who draw much of their feeling of pride and worth from being erotically attractive may find aging devastating. Seeing themselves age and their responses diminish, some blame themselves or their partners.

Men and women who adjust to age changes may find sexual play and coitus as satisfying in later life as ever before. In aging men, sexual response is more easily influenced by emotions, situations and relationships. For many men, urgency and speed of sexual response becomes uncontrollable less often, and women often become less inhibited, more playful, more sexually self-accepting. Men may become less impetuous and less vulnerable to feelings of intolerable frustrations; women may more gladly accept their own and others' erotism. Life experience may bring to both sexes a more accepting and self-accepting frame of mind. In effect, the responses of men and women become more alike, and this can be a source of increased sexual harmony. Orgasm does become less important to some people, but the body contact and the physical expression of intimacy can make sex an undiminished pleasure.

The frequency of coital activity of most people decreases with aging, but usually in proportion to their levels earlier in life. Those who are vigorous when young are more likely to remain active later; the inactive tend to become less active still. Kinsey et al[4] found that, on the average, men wanted coitus about half as often at 50 as they had in their teens. At age 70 the most common orgasmic frequency was about three times per month. Masters and Johnson[3] found women who, in their 60's and 70's, still produced adequate vaginal transudation and showed little vaginal shrinkage. These women had engaged in coitus or masturbated at least once or twice a week most of their adult lives. Those who did so once a month or less during the decade after menopause had difficulty accommodating the penis when they did try. Sexual mechanisms also last longer and remain stronger in people with regular partners; in fact, the regularity of sexual activity seems to be more important than the frequency. Masters and Johnson concluded that a woman or man with good general health and an interested, interesting partner can have a gratifying sex life even into the 80's. In a minority of older people, perhaps 15 per cent, sexual activity increases with age.[11, 12] Actually, while it is known that activity and healthy functioning are correlated, it is not known which is cause and which is effect.

Situational and social factors, as well as physiological ones, can be detrimental to free sexual expression. For many older people, especially women, the lack of a regular sexual partner or of privacy correlates with a decreased interest in coitus. Moreover, our society has traditionally seen erotism in later life as "undignified." In evaluating sexuality in older persons, the physician should keep such factors in mind and gauge each patient's physiology accordingly.

ORGASM

Overview. No aspect of sexual response has created so much debate as orgasm. Ignorance of what orgasm actually is gave rise to considerable doctrinaire argument in the past among scientists and laymen alike. The acquisition of some knowledge in recent years has, in turn, produced new questions and arguments.

For example, some persons wonder why orgasm is so much more obvious in men than in women. Although some women have dramatic, unmistakable orgasms, the majority do not. Since virtually all men and most women clearly recognize their own orgasms, they often have difficulty understanding that there are women who don't have orgasms or who fail to recognize them if they occur. The picture is complicated by the varieties of orgasmic response reported, from anorgasmia to multiple orgasms in women and the relative absence of either of these extremes in men.

The reasons for inability to reach orgasm are many and, in some cases, remain unknown. Many anorgasmic people report having had strict religious upbringing, feelings of sin and guilt about pleasure, ignorance of their sexual potential and general sexual inhibitions.[13] Nevertheless, many people with comparable backgrounds have no orgasmic difficulties. Sometimes education, training or therapy can make orgasm possible for, and desirable to, anorgasmic individuals.[13, 14]

Orgasm in women may be described as having three subjective stages that occur in rapid succession.[3, 15] The first signals the end of increase in sexual tension; although violent movement may continue, there is a sensation of stopping or floating. This feeling is accompanied or soon followed by intense concentration on pelvic sensations. In the second stage, a feeling of body warmth seems to radiate from the pelvis throughout the body. In the third stage, there is awareness of involuntary genital contractions and throbbing.

Orgasms vary in intensity and quality among individuals and within individuals from one time to another. One question about orgasm that keeps recurring is, "Is there a difference between vaginal and clitoral orgasms?" This question arises from Freud's now discounted theory that sexual maturity in females involves a shift in erotic focus from the clitoris (commonly stimulated in masturbation) to the vagina (stimulated in coitus). But neither this "vaginal transfer" theory nor any other accounts for all the varied research and other reports on orgasm. In fact, several theoretical models have been proposed to describe sexual climax.

Single Model. Kinsey et al[5] were among the first to seriously question that a distinction existed between clitoral and vaginal orgasm. The subsequent research of Masters and Johnson[3] showed that the physiological response is the same whether orgasm is triggered primarily by stimulation of the clitoris, vagina, breasts or even by stroking of the thighs or earlobes. This theoretical model, which has been relied on primarily in this chapter thus far, has received the most attention from physiological and psychological research.

Double Model. It has been argued that not all orgasms fit the single model. According to Fisher, many women say they can distinguish two kinds of orgasm, different both in how they are brought about and in how they are experienced.[15] For example, they describe orgasms caused by clitoral stimulation as warm, ticklish, electrical and sharp and those triggered by vaginal stimulation as deep, throbbing, soothing and comfortable. Fisher also reports that some women prefer one type of orgasm, and some experience the other as unpleasant or even painful. He says that, in attaining orgasm, "the majority (about two-thirds) of women ascribed relatively more importance to direct clitoral stimulation as compared to vaginal stimulation." Although Fisher holds to a theory of two types of orgasm, he does not rate either kind over the other as a sign of psychosexual maturity.

Fox and Fox[16] also describe responses that fit the double model. They see a link between the degree of satisfaction in female orgasm and convulsive vaginal contractions, which vary according to whether there is intromission. The penis, they say, seems to form a tight-fitting plug and thus creates a response different from that in an empty vagina. While this description is based on the laboratory observation of only one couple, some clinical reports of our own echo this finding.

Triple Model. Singer[17] suggests a three-orgasm model. One type is vulval orgasm, similar to that described by Masters and Johnson. It does not vary with the kinds of stimuli that cause it. Another type, uterine orgasm, is said to involve stimulation of abdominal nerves and repeated movements of the uterus; only deep penile thrusting or similar stimulation can set off this response (this type of orgasm was clearly described by Kinsey et al[5]). A third type, blended orgasm, is a combination of the vulval and uterine types. Singer considers no one type of orgasm superior or more mature than another.[17]

It is quite possible, then, that psychological and physical factors combine to produce different kinds of orgasm—if not now measurably different, still different in subjective but real ways. If the multiple-model theories are true, it would seem that usually only clitoral (vulval, single-model) orgasm results from masturbation or oral stimulation and uterine (mixed) orgasm from penile penetration. It is significant that many men, like many women, report somewhat different response and satisfaction from orgasms caused by masturbation or oral stimulation than from those caused by coitus.

Masters and Johnson[3] observed that the female orgasm, as measured by the strength of muscle contractions, is often physiologically more intense when caused by masturbation than by coitus. However, as in other phases of the SRC, intensity is not necessarily a measure of satisfaction. Women sometimes show physical signs of arousal without feeling aroused,[18] and sometimes men have pleasureless erections. Most people apparently prefer the total body involvement and psychological experience of coitus, even though it may be measurably less intense. Some women who never or rarely reach orgasm nevertheless enjoy coitus and their sexual relationship.[19] For some people, orgasm is possible but not desired because it seems to be an unwished-for loss of control.

Comparison of Male and Female Orgasm. There are some basic orgasmic similarities between the sexes. Many of the physiological processes are the same. When masturbating, both sexes take about the same time to reach orgasm: one to two minutes in young men, three to four in women (in coitus this orgasmic time differential may take on great significance). The majority of adult men and women seem to be satisfied by one orgasm most of the time. Women who have multiple orgasms do not usually reach a large number of climaxes, but rather feel satisfied after a few; only a small minority desire five or more. The experience may be found quite exhausting.

Several differences between the sexes also exist. We have noted that a significant minority of women never reach orgasm, and one in seven is multiorgasmic; in healthy men, either extreme is rare. Many women, although they prefer to reach orgasm, can enjoy sexual activity without orgasm. Males are more likely to persist in sexual activity until orgasm occurs, and they reach coital orgasm with comparative ease and regularity. In fact, if a postpubertal male cannot usually reach coital orgasm, physical or psychological dysfunction should be suspected. Another difference is that males reach their highest orgasmic frequencies from about age 15 to 25, followed by a gradual decline throughout life; women experience a peak in orgasmic frequencies in their 30's.[4, 5]

It has been argued that such differences have cultural origins. It is true that females have been sheltered from erotic experience more than males and have had fewer other-sex contacts; thus females' erotism has been more controlled and limited than males. Kinsey et al[5] did find that, in females, a devoutly religious background, a sexually restrictive upbringing and a lack of higher education all correlate with difficulty in reaching orgasm and with reaching it less frequently. In males, such backgrounds correlate with restricted sexual activity but not with impaired orgasmic function.[4] Also, the prevalence of female orgasm varies widely from society to society, and it has probably increased steadily in our society throughout this century.

Other evidence, however, indicates that the differences are not entirely cultural. The capacity for multiple orgasm in many women can hardly be created by cultural forces when the same capacity can be seen in almost no men. The best explanation for orgasmic differences between the sexes seems to be a combination of physiological, cultural and individual forces. One biological reason, we speculate, is that female orgasm is a relatively recent evolutionary development, as are face-to-face copulation and year-round sexual readiness throughout most of life. These factors may be adaptive in helping to create a mutually pleasurable bond in the species that must raise children through the longest childhood in nature. Yet female orgasm, being less deeply rooted physiologically, may be more vulnerable to social and intrapsychic interference.

Attitudes Toward Orgasm and Anorgasmia. About a half century ago, as Western society began to emphasize equality of the sexes and the desirability (or even alleged necessity) of female orgasm, many people rejected the previous claim that proper women were sexually unresponsive. With equally poor reasoning, however, they began to view anorgasmia as a deficit in emotional maturity and a flaw in a relationship. This concept slowly changed, so that anorgasmia became related not to the females' immaturity but to the males' lack of technique. Whereas, theretofore, women were to serve mens' needs, men were now supposed to "give" women orgasms in the service of their own needs. Now, in the past few years some people have tried to further female erotism independent of men;[20] as a result, women are increasingly considered sexual in their own right and responsible for their own orgasms. As Masters and Johnson have stated, sex has shifted from something men do *to* women, through something men do *for* women, to the present where sex is something men do *with* women.[21]

These shifts have not been welcomed by all. If a woman is responsible for her own orgasm, she can no longer easily blame her partner for its absence nor can he feel proud of its presence. The goals of human sexuality and orgasm are repeatedly questioned.[2,17] It is suggested that, if orgasm is desired, one must work at it. A willing partner, however, is a definite if not indispensable asset.

Masters and Johnson have echoed Kinsey's belief that male responsibility for female orgasm is, to some extent, a Western middle/class attitude. Men from lower social levels are likely to think a man should reach orgasm whenever it seems natural to him. Despite middle-class attitudes promulgated in many texts, several researchers believe female anorgasmia probably depends more on a woman's background, development and degree of desire than on her partner's coital techniques or on the extent of foreplay.[5,22] Varied and prolonged love-making and foreplay do facilitate or enhance the orgasmic response of many women, but it has become a perhaps unjustified cliche in the literature on human sexuality that these are always essential for female orgasm and for both partners' satisfaction.[23]

It is also too rarely noted that individuals vary greatly in their liking for and timing of various phases of the SRC. One partner may enjoy a long excitement phase; another may like prolonging the plateau level; another may desire rapid orgasm; still another may enjoy a rather long resolution phase.

Simultaneous orgasm—both partners reaching climax at the same time—has been recommended often during the past half century; couples strive to attain it and even consider its absence to be a sign of sexual incompatibility.

However, some authorities and many couples do not find simultaneity important. They prefer that each partner find pleasure in his or her own time and way. Some feel this way because of differences between the behavior of males and females during orgasm. Most women desire deep vaginal penetration, and/or sustained clitoral stimulation (direct or indirect) and thrusting during climax: however, the majority of men usually stop thrusting during orgasm and retract the pelvis.[3] These desires seem to conflict. Therefore, many people may reach greater satisfaction by nonsimultaneous orgasm, each partner in turn offering the other the most possible pleasure during climax. No one way is best for everyone. And it should be borne in mind that many achieve greater satisfaction in their partners' orgasm than in their own.

The descriptions, comments and speculations in this chapter are meant not as prescriptions but as guidelines for understanding basic sexual responses in an individual and a couple. Much remains to be learned about both the somatic and psychological aspects of response. Meanwhile, in counseling patients, physicians should keep in mind that the range of normal variation is great and that the goal is satisfaction, not adherence to any paradigm of sexual function and feeling.

References

1. Diamond M: Sexual anatomy and physiology: Clinical aspects, in Green R (ed): *Human Sexuality, A Health Practitioner's Text*. Baltimore, Williams & Wilkins Company, 1975.
2. Diamond M, Karlen A: *Sexual Decisions*. Boston, Little, Brown and Company, 1980.
3. Masters WH, Johnson VE: *Human Sexual Response*. Boston, Little, Brown and Company, 1966.
4. Kinsey A, et al: *Sexual Behavior in the Human Male*. Philadelphia, WB Saunders Co, 1948.
5. Kinsey A, et al: *Sexual Behavior in the Human Female*. Philadelphia, WB Saunders Co, 1953.
6. Robbins MB, Jensen GD: Multiple orgasms in males. *J Sex Res* 1978; 14:21-36.
7. Oliven J: *Clinical Sexuality: A Manual for the Physician and the Professions*. Philadelphia, JB Lippincott Company, 1974.
8. Fox C, et al: Measurement of intra-vaginal and intra-uterine pressures during human coitus by radio-telemetry. *J Reprod Fertil* 1970; 22:243-251.
9. Gebhard PH: Female sexuality, in Giese H (ed): *The Sexuality of Women*. New York, Stein and Day, 1970.
10. Raboch J: Studies in the sexuality of women, in Giese H (ed): *The Sexuality of Women*. New York, Stein and Day, 1970.
11. Pfeiffer E, et al: Sexual behavior in aged men and women. *Arch Gen Psychiatry* 1968; 19:753-758.

12. Verwoerdt A, et al: Sexual behavior in senescence. *Geriatrics* 1969; 24:137-154.
13. Masters WH, Johnson VE: *Human Sexual Inadequacy*. Boston, Little, Brown and Company, 1970.
14. Kaplan H: *The New Sex Therapy*. New York, Brunner/Mazel Inc, 1974.
15. Fisher S: *The Female Orgasm: Psychology, Physiology, Fantasy*. New York, Basic Books Inc, 1973.
16. Fox CA, Fox B: A comparative study of coital physiology with special reference to the sexual climax. *J Reprod Fertil* 1971; 24:319-336.
17. Singer I: *The Goals of Human Sexuality*. New York, WW Norton & Company Inc, 1973.
18. Heiman JR: A psychophysiological exploration of sexual arousal patterns in females and males. *Psychophysiology* 1977; 14:266-274.
19. Wallin P, Clark A: A study of orgasm as a condition of women's enjoyment of coitus in the middle years of marriage. *Hum Biol* 1963; 35:131-139.
20. Hite S: *The Hite Report*. New York, Macmillan Publishing Co, Inc, 1976.
21. Masters WH, Johnson VE: *The Pleasure Bond*. Boston, Little, Brown and Company, 1975.
22. Adams C: Sexual responsiveness in college wives, in Demartino M (ed): *Sexual Behavior and Personality Characteristics*. New York, Grove Press, 1966.
23. Karlen A: The soiled pinafore: A sexual theme in psychiatric history, in Karasu TB, Socarides C (eds): *On Sexuality: Psychoanalytic Observations*. New York, International Universities Press Inc, 1979.

Chapter 5

Sociology and Human Sexuality

L. Reiss, Ph.D., and Frank F. Furstenberg, Jr., Ph.D.

Greater toleration of premarital and extramarital coitus and the increased emphasis on sexual gratification in marriage are not novel trends in American society, but the pace of change today probably is unprecedented. There is intense public discussion of what were once exclusively personal matters. Practices that a generation ago were considered socially deviant, such as cohabitation or homosexuality, are tolerated, if not accepted.

The very changes that invite choices also create new responsibilities. The coexistence of "old" and "new" moralities bewilders many people, including the young. Some parents are no longer sure of their own standards, much less what to teach their children. Young people, in turn, are no longer sure of what to do or from whom to get advice.

Amid this confusion, physicians are called upon to provide special knowledge. They often may find themselves in the uncomfortable position of being social arbiters to interpret changing sexual standards. In doing so, they have to venture outside the familiar confines of the traditional medical role and seek information on values and behavior in various segments of society, some far removed from their own. Most cannot be experts in the social, as well as the biological and physical sciences, but they can find in the sociological view of sex much that bears on patient care.

Until rather recently, most sociologists have avoided systematically studying sexual behavior. Since Alfred Kinsey's pioneering studies of sexual behavior appeared some 30 years ago, there has been less reluctance to study sexual behavior, and in the past decade many nationwide studies[1-3] and polls[4-6] have appeared. Although some of these do not bear the weight sometimes placed on them, they have spurred public discussion of such formerly taboo topics as marital and nonmarital sexual relationships, sexual function and dysfunction, orgasm, contraception, abortion, sexually transmitted disease and cohabitation. In fact, the sheer amount of information, some of it based on questionable data sources, presents a challenge to the physician who is called upon to respond to a variety of questions about sexual matters.

PREMARITAL SEXUAL BEHAVIOR

Historical and Cross-Cultural Evidence. Studying a society's sexual behavior and attitudes at one point in time is as limited as looking at a patient's medical condition on one specific day. Accordingly, it makes sense to collect data over an extended period but, in doing so, one must avoid historical cliches. Societies, like people, embellish the past and develop mythologies about it. For instance, some observers talk of a time when premarital virginity prevailed for both sexes, but parish registers as far back as the 16th century reveal that illegitimacy was common in England and many parts of Europe. Even where people disapproved of premarital coitus, babies were born out of wedlock or couples married in haste.[7,8] The records of one Massachusetts church show that 200 years ago one-third of all women married there had confessed fornication to their minister. (Without the confessions, their babies would not have been baptized.) There were doubtless other nonvirgins who, not being pregnant, did not confess. We are not saying that premarital coitus was always as prevalent as it is today, but even 200 years ago we were not essentially a nation of virgins at marriage.[9]

Although premarital coitus was officially condemned strongly in most parts of this country, it was informally condoned by many people as long as a resulting pregnancy led to marriage. Community pressure was sufficient to keep the majority of premarital pregnancies from leading to out-of-wedlock childbirths.[10]

Anthropological evidence shows that American society, seen in a cross-cultural perspective, has been rather restrictive about premarital coitus.[11] Many societies, especially nonliterate ones, give young people more latitude for sexual experimentation after or even before puberty.[12] Nevertheless, few if any cultures have approved of socially "unlicensed" childbearing. Virtually all cultures have some form of marriage rules, at least in part to assign parental rights and responsibilities.[13] It might be said that society tries to regulate sexuality partly in order to regulate parenthood. Modern contraception, allowing a greater separation of sexuality from reproduction, has probably lessened the importance placed on premarital chastity.

Current Behavior. In our society, as in virtually all others,[14] different values have been placed on virginity for men and for women. Men have been tacitly encouraged to violate public standards, women to maintain them. Some early sociological studies of sexual behavior chronicle the struggle between males and females over sexual "license" or "virtue."[15-19]

Recent estimates show that the trend toward greater acceptance of premarital coitus, noted by Kinsey et al in the 1940's, has accelerated since then.[3,20,21] Kinsey found that a rise in the incidence of premarital coitus had begun during the 1920's and had continued at a slow rate in subsequent decades. There is now little doubt that another relatively great shift toward earlier coital experience occurred in the late 1960's and early 1970's. As in the previous era, the changes were more evident among females than males.[1,22]

Some of the most carefully collected data on the sexual behavior of teenage females[20,21] reveal that in 1979 nearly two-thirds of all white women were nonvirgins by age 19. Blacks had a higher incidence of premarital coitus than whites, began coitus earlier and hence were far more vulnerable to pregnancy. Men tended, as in the past, to start coitus earlier than women and to have more frequent and varied experiences. The great majority of men are nonvirgins by their late teens.[3,23,24]

Nonmarital coitus during adolescence is not considered as socially deviant as it was a decade or so ago. Adolescents, however, are not invariably prepared for the concommitants of coitus, as the high rates of teenage pregnancy and sexually transmitted disease show. Critics of the liberalization of sexual standards have sometimes argued that the diminished importance placed on premarital chastity can be traced to the availability of modern methods of birth control, in particular oral contraceptives. In 1976, however, 16 years after the pill became available, most sexually active teenagers had never used oral contraceptives regularly, if at all. It seems unlikely that the advent of the pill or other modern methods of birth control produced the "sexual revolution." As yet, there is no evidence to show that availability of family planning services alters the incidence of premarital coitus in any predictable way,[21,22] although it does seem to aid in containing the risk of pregnancy.[21,25]

Before Kinsey's studies, there was some interest in, but little data about, the sexual practices of people from different social strata or with varying lifestyles. Kinsey et al found that sexual behavior varies by education, occupational level and income—for instance, that the middle and upper classes begin coitus later than the lower classes and are more likely during adolescence to engage in masturbation and petting as alternatives to coitus. More recent surveys[1,21] have found a narrowing of class differences in both sexual behavior and attitudes about sexual practices.

Today the incidence of coitus among adolescent females does not vary much by social class, but there are some differences in the use of contraception and abortion.[21] Lower-class women are more likely to bear children out of wedlock, at least in part because contraception and abortion are less accessible to them and perhaps also less acceptable.[26]

Age also has a powerful influence on sexual values and behavior. Virtually all recent studies show that the young have a more permissive view of premarital coitus than their elders.[27] There are two possible sets of reasons that adults appear to be more conservative. One is that young people are more responsive to changing mores and/or that the risks of pregnancy and STDs do not seem as great to them. Furthermore, the youth culture and its courtship systems promote more permissive standards. The second reason is that parents' social responsibility for their children's behavior makes them less sexually permissive. They often feel they must take the blame if their teenager becomes pregnant or contracts a STD.

To learn which of these two factors was more important,[1] permissiveness was compared among different age groups: among people the same age in differing family situations and, within the adult group, among those who did and did not have teenage children.[1] There were consistent differences by age; however, among the adults, there was considerably more variation between parents and nonparents of the same age. Being in the parental role appears to lower the permissiveness even of adults who accept a great deal of experimentation in their own marital or extramarital lives.

The differences between the values of parent and child often limit communication between them. Adolescents, perceiving parental disapproval, seek information and advice from their peers, thus displacing the parents in sexual socialization. Expecting to have little influence, the parents often abdicate responsibility for providing sexual education in the first place.

In a study of pregnant adolescents and their parents, it was reported that parents were genuinely shocked to discover that their daughters were pregnant, even when they knew that most adolescents in their neighborhood were sexually active.[28] Interviews with the daughters confirmed that they had usually kept their sexual activity secret from their parents. The daughters were inclined to view sex as "something that just happens," leaving to chance whether they became pregnant.[29] The girls who had made their sexual activity known to their parents were far more likely to use contraception and less likely to become pregnant in early adolescence.

With or without parental awareness, the most autonomous youth are more successful at contraception.[30] It seems that if adolescents are well informed and are taught to act independently, they will take steps to avoid unwanted pregnancy—if, of course, they have access to contraceptives, which many do not. Thus, it would seem that the family physician may have a role to play in imparting sexual information to both adolescents and their parents. When indicated, the physician may also assume responsibility for referring the adolescent to a family planning clinic for counseling or contraceptive instruction.

As an aside, it is also worth pointing out that the trend toward nonmarital sexuality, although most visible among the young, has apparently increased in all age groups. A sizable proportion of adults in their middle years live outside marriage, at least for a while, after divorce or a spouse's death.[31] They participate in nonmarital sexuality as do their children, and fewer conceal behavior that years ago they might well have carried out surreptitiously. Many people over 65 also cohabit, some to avoid losing Social Security and other pension benefits, but others simply because they can accept sexuality outside marriage. Physicians should no longer expect older persons who are not married to be sexually inactive.

Consequences. Young people are exposed to complex messages about sex, ranging from explicit encouragement to active discouragement. Although values and guilt may affect the likelihood of sexual behavior, once coitus occurs, guilt does not usually terminate that conduct. Rather, those who feel guilty typically repeat the behavior despite that feeling.[1] Guilt about violating social codes may be less common and acute today with the erosion of commitment to premarital chastity in society at large. However, more than one-third of female nonvirgins felt guilty about their first act of coitus.[23]

Some subcultures still prize virginity highly; young people in these subcultures who want to remain virgins may feel intense conflict over maintaining a standard no longer adhered to by those outside their subculture. On the other hand, as permissive attitudes become more widespread, shame or anxiety over *not* losing one's virginity may increase. Young people may feel ashamed or abnormal if they have not experienced coitus by late adolescence.

Because of the recent relaxation of laws that once virtually denied contraceptives to minors, contraceptive use by adolescents is increasing but is still very irregular.[21] Even college students frequently do not practice birth control at all or regularly.[32] It has been found that over one-quarter of nonvirginal teenage women never used contraception; only 30 per cent always did so.[21]

Ignorance is still a major reason for the young not using contraception.[33,34] Only about 40 per cent of teenage women know when during the menstrual cycle the risk of pregnancy is highest.[21] Many adolescents do not know how or where to obtain contraceptives, which methods to use, or which social agencies offer contraceptive assistance. Moreover, contraception is used less regularly and effectively by those whose sexual behavior is episodic, and this is the case for most adolescents.

Many young women do not receive adequate contraceptive instruction until after they have become pregnant for the first time. Even then, professionals dealing with unwed mothers often try to persuade them that they really had not wanted coitus and that it was not going to occur again.[35] This makes contraceptive planning less likely and a second pregnancy more likely.

Were it not for the legalization of abortion, the number of births to unmarried teenagers would be going up (from the current 30 per cent pregnancy rate among unmarried sexually active teenagers) rather than remaining relatively steady. About one pregnancy in three is terminated by a voluntary abortion. The decision to terminate a pregnancy reflects both the values of the teenager and her family and the cost of obtaining an abortion.[21] Abortion rates vary greatly, of course, from state to state.

Social class, ethnic background and religious factors affect rates of both pregnancy and abortion. Adolescents whose parents finished high school or college are more likely to use contraception regularly than those from less educated families.[21] Young women from low educational backgrounds are more likely to give moral or medical objections to contraception and to perceive their risk of becoming pregnant as less. Regardless of their families' educational background, blacks are somewhat more likely to risk conception and somewhat less likely to use contraception regularly. In general, young women from college-educated families are more willing to seek abortion; they may feel that they have more to lose by an early birth, and certainly they receive more pressure from their families to end the pregnancy.[36] As might be expected, religious values figure importantly in both the likelihood of engaging in premarital sexuality and the willingness to terminate a pregnancy should conception occur. Clearly, a physician is well advised to be sensitive to the different attitudes toward sexuality, pregnancy and parenthood held by various classes, and religious and ethnic groups.

There is evidence that giving birth in adolescence, especially in the early teens, often brings a host of adverse social and economic sequelae. In the U.S., about 250,000 unmarried teenage women give birth each year.[37] Some eventually marry the fathers, but premarital conception greatly increases the chance of separation and divorce. In a study of 400 adolescent mothers, over half of the marriages that occurred after pregnancy ended within five years.[38] Other studies have revealed similar rates.[39,40]

Early childbearing greatly reduces a woman's chances for continued education and economic independence; a majority of teenage parents may go back to school, but the demands of marriage and childbearing often force them to drop out again. Therefore, many lack qualifications for stable employment and must seek help from their families or public welfare. More teenage mothers end up on relief than do teenagers who defer childbearing.

About 780,000 teenage premarital pregnancies occurred in 1976. Roughly 530,000 of them ended in abortion or miscarriage, and the remaining 250,000 resulted in illegitimate children. An additional 320,000 pregnancies involved teenagers who were married before or after the birth occurred.[37]

It has been estimated[25] that over 300,000 fewer premarital pregnancies would occur if teenagers who did not want babies used contraception consistently. It also has been estimated that about 700,000 more premarital pregnancies would occur if no contraception were used.

Editor's Note: *For an update of statistics relating to teenage pregnancy, the reader is referred to a recent report of the Guttmacher Institute[41] which appeared after this chapter was prepared for publication.*

MARITAL SEXUALITY

If we thought that the sociological literature accurately reflected sexual experiences, we might conclude that people's interest in sexuality suddenly declines after marriage. Because sociologists have shown little interest in marital sexual patterns, this discussion is necessarily limited by the paucity of such research.

Historical and Cross-Cultural Patterns. Some scholars believe that the institution of marriage was developed in part to regulate sexual activity in order to control reproduction. Spouses in all cultures are expected to have sexual relations, but there are enormous variations in frequency. In certain cultures, men are ridiculed if they cannot perform coitus nightly; other cultures condone marital coitus only for procreation.

Because sex has been regarded as a strictly private matter in Western society, it is difficult to infer from historical sources whether marital sexual behavior has changed much over time. Nineteenth century books on marriage and medicine reveal a double standard. Men were expected to initiate, and actively seek pleasure in, sexual play; women were encouraged to accept and endure. One medical text written in 1869 said that "there can be no doubt that sexual feeling in the female is, in a majority of cases, in abeyance, and that it requires positive and considerable excitement to be roused at all; and, even if roused (which in many instances it never can be), is very moderate, compared with that of the male."[42] Similar if sometimes less extreme pronouncements can be found in more recent marriage manuals. However, there is good reason to suspect that, as the expressive and companionable features of marriage have become more central, marital sexuality has become more highly valued and women's potential for sexual enjoyment is more clearly recognized. There is even recent evidence that the Victorian era was not as lacking in accepting female sexuality as we once believed.[43]

Contemporary Behavior. The view of gender differences in sexual capacity did not change abruptly. The data from the Kinsey surveys show that marital coitus did not increase among married women born after the turn of the century. On the other hand, coital orgasm did. According to Hunt, the frequency of marital coital activity and orgasm rose somewhat in the late 1960's.[3] While the study contains some of the same limitations as Kinsey's in sampling, reliability, validity and other aspects, the evidence assembled seems convincing that several factors—greater openness about sexuality, the encouragement of mutual enjoyment and of emotional exchange, better knowledge of physical sexual functioning—have contributed to more satisfying sexual relations within marriage. In a study of a representative national sample of women aged 15 to 45, there was an increase in marital coital frequency between 1965 and 1970.[44] About 50 per cent of Kinsey's female sample had tried oral sex; in a survey of 100,000 female readers of *Redbook* magazine,[4] 90 per cent had done so. Anal intercourse had been tried by over 40 per cent of the *Redbook* sample. Masturbation after marriage was reported by 40 per cent of Kinsey's sample of women and almost 70 per cent of *Redbook's*.[4,45] Although the *Redbook* study is not comparable to Kinsey's and its sample is not representative of the nation, the sample probably is representative of a large segment of white middle-class females and does indicate some change in the norm. Some conjugal sexual patterns may have changed because today more couples with unsatisfying sexual relations dissolve their union than such couples did in the past. Certainly, people now place greater value on sexual enjoyment in marriage and are more willing to seek information and help when their expectations are not met.

As old problems are solved, new ones are created. To the extent that sexuality becomes an arena for achievement, it may seem like work rather than play,[46] and expected mutual gratification may place a greater burden on the partners and thus may adversely affect their sexual adjustment and satisfaction. The physician should be equipped to respond to expressions of sexual discontent as couples become more aware of "what they are missing" and more willing to seek advice and aid.

There is some evidence that within long, stable marriages sexual satisfaction fluctuates cyclically rather than declines steadily. More than one study has shown that marital satisfaction drops during the early years of parenthood, reaches a low point when children are teenagers and rises again when they leave home. Being a parent may be rewarding, but it can divert emotion from the conjugal relationship or become a source of conflict affecting the spouses' sexual relations.[47,48] Despite regrets about the "empty nest," couples have time to reinvest in their marriages, and often the result is increased sexual satisfaction.[22]

Sexuality in Middle and Later Life. Coitus becomes less frequent with age for physical and, in many cases, psychosocial reasons. The decrease, however, varies—often in proportion to early-life sexual behavior, especially in men.[45,49] A study of several hundred older people in North Carolina showed that enjoyment of sexuality when younger was the best predictor of sexual performance in old age.[50] In addition, those who began sexual activity early and engaged in sexuality often were more likely to stay sexually active in later life. Since our culture is more encouraging of sexuality for younger people today and since our society is beginning to accept the position that older people can and should be sexually active, more people may be sexually active in later life in the future.

Social Class. It has been believed that the lower social classes have fewer inhibitions and enjoy sexual relations more than the middle class, but empirical data do not agree. Both coital frequency and reported sexual and marital satisfaction are higher in those in the middle-class. This was first reported by Kinsey et al,[45,49] and then explored in depth with smaller samples by [48,51]

All of these studies reveal that education and income correlate positively with coital frequency in marriage. College-educated, middle-class couples also vary their sexual activities more; e.g., they engage in extensive foreplay more often, use more coital positions and engage more often in genital manipulation and oral-genital contact.[45,49] A greater proportion of middle-class women than lower-class women experience orgasm.

In a recent intensive interview study of 50 blue collar-class couples and a comparison group of 25 middle-class couples,[52] vast disparities in the meanings attributed to sexual behavior in the two class groups were detailed. Blue collar-class wives, far more often than middle-class wives, said that they engaged in coitus merely to comply with their husbands' wishes, felt more constrained about initiating sexual activity and more often felt guilty about performing anything other than traditional sexual practices. Many blue collar-class men resented their wives' traditional approach to sexuality; they complained, for example, that their wives always wanted to do it "the same way." Yet, if the wives expressed too open an interest in sexuality, the husbands tended to see this as a threat to their masculinity. In short, in the blue collar-class there was a war between the sexes in the marriage bed, based in part on very different expectations of appropriate gender role behavior.

There are several possible explanations for these class differences. One is the general influences of education and occupational level on interpersonal behavior.[53] It has been argued that people who know more about sexual function may be more skilled in attaining sexual satisfaction. They may be more effective in practicing contraception, thus reducing anxiety about unwanted pregnancy, which often inhibits sexual pleasure. Another possible reason is that insufficient income directly and indirectly strains a marriage. Couples who must divide scarce resources feel resentment over the restrictions imposed on their lives and blame each other for low earnings.[52] Such strains often make sexual relations an arena for marital struggle.

The degree to which couples share activities may have an effect on sexual enjoyment.[53] Lower-class couples with a high degree of communication, task-sharing and mutual interests have more stable and satisfying marriages and sexual interaction.[18] One must hesitate to advance causal arguments, but the same qualities in a marriage that promote communication may also promote sexual adjustment. Lower-class couples who have less interaction generally tend to see sexual relations as a necessary release; those who have more

60

mutuality are more often inclined to view sexuality as an opportunity to express solidarity. For instance, within the lower class group, rates of orgasm and sexual satisfaction are higher for both sexes in couples who shared household work.[18]

Such social class differences complicate the task of a physician who is confronted with patients with sexual and marital dysfunctions. Many lower-class men and women are unaccustomed to discussing their sexual problems with anyone and are not likely to seek a physician's help unless the situation is acute. When they do seek aid, signs of tension relief may be noted merely as a result of open-ended interviews.[52]

Consequences. Sex is increasingly valued as a form of recreation and intimacy. In contrast to the unmarried, many of whom have unintended and unwanted conceptions, married couples are far more successful than ever before in controlling fertility through contraception, sterilization and abortion. In a national sample of married women,[44] it was revealed that sterilization was the most common form of contraception (50 per cent) among married couples aged 35 to 44. A disproportionate number of abortions still occur among low-income women, who are less likely to use contraception effectively.[55] If present educational trends continue, however, we may see greater contraceptive sophistication at all levels of society, thus reducing reliance on abortion. Moreover, recent restrictions on the use of Medicaid funds to pay for abortions can be expected to have an impact on prevalence. Therefore, sexuality may be seen increasingly as separate from reproduction, especially in marriage, a development that will probably influence the nature and quality of sexual relationships.

EXTRAMARITAL SEXUAL RELATIONSHIPS

Historical and Cross-Cultural Background. The double standard pervades sexual relationships, especially extramarital ones, in all societies. The power advantage of males is evident in this phenomenon. Most societies restrict extramarital coitus more than premarital and marital coitus. A cross-cultural survey[11] revealed that, although 70 per cent of the cultures studied considered premarital coitus acceptable, only 20 per cent felt that way about extramarital relations. Many cultures that do accept extramarital coitus do not stress lifelong love relationships in marriage. In Western culture, with our emphasis on love and intimacy between husband and wife, sexuality is a part of a relationship that many couples feel is too intimate to share with others. Thus, extramarital coitus is likely to arouse jealousy.

Almost all cultures do prefer that mates get along congenially, but only some feel that the relationship should or must be monogamous or one of deep love and affection. Traditional Eskimo society, for example, allowed for the addition of new partners as situations demanded. If a man's sister-in-law became widowed, he would probably take her as a second wife, giving her a better chance of survival. These practices were compatible with a de-emphasis on exclusive marital ties and with the stress on sharing that aided survival in that culture.[56]

Men often covertly approve of extramarital adventures for themselves and keep such affairs secret from their wives. Of course, some of their partners are other men's wives, but such a contradiction is not usually acknowledged.[14,22] Today a small number of married people are trying to work out more open arrangements that allow both spouses opportunities for extramarital coitus.

Most societies feel that extramarital coitus is a greater threat to marriage and the family than is premarital coitus. Although a growing proportion of our adult population accepts premarital coitus (20 per cent in 1963; 50 per cent in 1970; 70 per cent in 1975),[22] such radical change has not occurred in attitudes toward extramarital coitus. Less than 30 per cent accept such relationships regardless of the circumstances.

Patterns of extramarital sexual behavior also have been slower to change. Kinsey et al reported that about half of all married men and one-quarter of married women had experienced extramarital coitus at least once by age 40. More recent data from different samples show no increase among men but suggest a rise among women. For example, of women in the *Redbook* study who were born in the 1930's, about 40 per cent had had extramarital coitus.[4] In another study[3] a rise was reported only for wives younger than 25. Changes in premarital sexual behavior do not automatically bring changes in extramarital behavior. For example, in Sweden, which now generally accepts premarital coitus, attitudes and behaviors about extramarital coitus have not changed as dramatically.[57]

Contemporary Patterns. Extramarital coitus has been the subject of relatively little research since that of Kinsey, although some work has appeared in recent years.[4,58,59] Extramarital relationships that involve coitus may predominantly express love or pleasure and also may or may not be accepted by the married couple (i.e., consensual or nonconsensual). (We shall not discuss extramarital relationships that have emotional importance but that do not involve sexual activity.)

There are, then, four types of extramarital sexual affairs: (1) love-focused and consensual; (2) pleasure-focused and consensual; (3) love-focused and nonconsensual; (4) pleasure-focused and nonconsensual. The fourth type— pleasure-focused and nonconsensual—is by far most common for men and probably also for women, although not to the same extent. To some degree, our society has a tradition of tolerating covert extramarital coitus by husbands more so than that by wives.

Pleasure-centered and consensual extramarital coitus may be becoming more common. However, acceptance commonly carries the restriction that extramarital love (as opposed to coitus) should be avoided.[60] Even those with such agreements spare each other details of their affairs. There is a strong desire to keep the extramarital relationship separate from the marriage so as not to upset the marriage relationship.

Such activity sometimes involves "swinging," the exchange of partners. This pattern has recently attracted a great deal of attention.[61-63] In "open" swinging, both spouses act with full awareness of details or in view of one another. Usually, men initiate swinging by talking their wives into it. However, some husbands find that they cannot perform as often as they would like and that their partners are not as attractive as they would like. Also, they may be threatened by wives who discover that they are multiply orgasmic or that they can enjoy sexual relations with women as well as men. Some husbands who talk their wives into swinging later try to talk them out of it.

Love-focused consensual affairs are quite rare. Some occur when the marital relationship, although significant, is far from fully satisfactory. However, some authorities argue that such affairs also occur in very fulfilling marriages and that the affair adds a new dimension rather than compensates for a weakness.[64]

The love-focused and nonconsensual affair is the kind our society has traditionally considered most likely to destroy a marriage. Jealousy can indeed disrupt the marriage if the relationship is discovered. In fact, whenever the extramarital partner becomes the more important one, the marital relationship may be significantly altered. This can happen despite the intention to limit emotional involvement.

Consequences. The mutual effects of marriages and affairs depend in large part on the partners' capacity and desire for intimacy. The traditional romantic view of intimacy is close association, sharing and personal contact in both a physical and an emotional sense whereby one person fills another's needs entirely; obviously some people manage to achieve this, although we do not know how many or how easily. A minority view of intimacy, but a growing one, is the diffuse and partial one. According to this view, one person cannot satisfy all of another's needs for intimacy, and there is room in one's life for several (perhaps almost equally important) sources of support, friendship and sharing on an emotional if not also on a physical level. The diffuse view is held by many people living in communes and by those who espouse group marriage and love-oriented, consensual extramarital affairs.[64] Some marriage counselors agree that the diffuse view of intimacy is more realistic and that the total view expects too much from a mate, thereby inviting resentment and disillusionment.

Another important factor in the effects of extramarital coitus is one's view of sexuality. In our culture (and many others), women have traditionally associated sex with affection and love; men have associated it primarily with pleasure. These differences, although clearly diminishing, are still significant in determining the consequences of extramarital coitus.

The length of the marriage affected by extramarital coitus is also a determining factor.[65] It has been reported that extramarital coitus during the first 12 years of marriage is associated with marital unhappiness, but that this is less true after 12 years.[65] There may be a greater sense of security and a greater tolerance of a mate's private activities in a long-term, stable marriage than in the early years of marriage.

Obviously, there are no simple answers about the outcome of extramarital coitus. The type of extramarital relationship, the type of marriage, the people's views of intimacy and of sexuality and the length of the marriage are only some of the variables. If a patient has problems about extramarital sexuality, the physician should not assume that his own attitude is the same as the patient's; instead, he should try to clarify the situation in order to determine whether or not marital counseling is desired or indicated.

RELEVANCE OF THE SOCIOLOGICAL PERSPECTIVE FOR PHYSICIANS

Physicians are often called upon to give advice or to play the role of social arbiter in matters concerning sexual behavior and values. Thus, it is important for them to be aware of general trends in the society and of their variations in different ethnic and class groups. By gaining such information, physicians may be able to give a more helpful medical opinion, whatever their private moral position may be.

Some physicians will be tempted to label behavior they deem undesirable as "unhealthy" or "sick." If a sexual practice is likely to disturb physiological function, there is a medical basis for calling it unhealthy. However, whether a sexual practice is seen as unhealthy often depends on one's cultural training. For example, a man raised in Latin America who ejaculates in 20 seconds may not consider himself a premature ejaculator nor may his partner; his culture doesn't teach him to expect his wife to reach orgasm as often as he does. In our society, a middle-class man who reaches orgasm in 20 seconds is more likely to label himself a premature ejaculator; a blue-collar man is somewhat less likely to do so. Clearly, the culture helps define "dysfunction."

The fact that sexual values vary between segments of one society, over historical time and during the course of one person's life does not mean that all standards are equally advantageous for an individual or society. Furthermore, changes that are desirable from one point of view may be undesirable from another. For instance, premarital coitus is usually viewed with more disfavor by parents than by their offspring. Reducing hostility to homosexual behavior may threaten certain social interests but it also promotes the interests of others. Abortion is seen by some as life-saving and by others as life-destroying.

Physicians cannot hope to resolve these moral dilemmas for their patients, but they can at least serve as educators. There is much ignorance and misinformation about sexuality that they can help to dispel. Physicians may feel unqualified to fill this void alone; perhaps some feel that it is the responsibility of the family, church, school or family planning clinic. Nevertheless, the task often does fall to them and, when it does, it gives them a responsibility to be well-informed.

In this chapter, some sociological studies of sex that bear on the physician's clinical decision-making and consulting responsibilities are reviewed. Subject matter is confined to premarital, marital and extramarital heterosexual behavior, which has received most study and which requires most of the physician's clinical attention.

Clinical Aspects

Harold I. Lief, M.D.

The sociological data presented in this chapter may appear to the neophyte physician to be interesting and informative, but the information is perceived to be relevant to clinical practice only when the physician starts to experience firsthand the influences of class, religion and ethnicity on the physician-patient relationship and on the management of sexual problems in practice. In addition, the norms of society, which frequently differ in different classes, religions and ethnic groups, affect perhaps even unconsciously the attitudes of physicians as well as of patients. To "bring home" the significance of sociological perspectives to the practicing physician, the following short case illustrations are offered.

Many blacks are sensitive about the widespread myth that blacks are promiscuous:

Case 1: A 32-year-old, attractive, black married woman with two children refused to be interviewed by a white psychiatrist, a member of the research team.[66] She was reluctant to disclose that she had had premarital intercourse, so convinced was she that this would confirm the white psychiatrist's misperception of blacks and that she would have been labeled and stigmatized as "promiscuous." She had no hesitancy, however, in talking with a black psychiatrist who easily obtained her sexual history.

White women married to blue collar workers can resent the often obligatory nature of sex even if they attain orgasm easily:

Case 2: As one woman married to a member of a construction gang expressed it, "My husband always gives me the feeling that he needs my orgasm for his ego even more than I need it for myself, and I resent it bitterly."

The following case illustrates the effects of religious orthodoxy, but in a paradoxical fashion:

Case 3: A 28-year-old woman, married for two years, asked for help because of an inhibition of sexual desire secondary to an inhibition of excitement. She had a very passionate premarital relationship with her fiance, but her excitement and desire ceased on the night of her marriage and had been absent since. When asked for an explanation, she replied, "You see, we were brought up to think of sex as dirty, bad and very sinful, particularly by my mother. She would never in a million years believe I would have sex before marriage. Knowing this, I felt free to have it. Now that I am married, she knows that sex is expected. I feel that she is in the bedroom with me watching every move, and I am paralyzed."

The management of sexual problems is often made more difficult by the values of the physician. Here are a few illustrations:

Case 4: A gynecologist referred to another physician a 17-year-old unmarried woman who had recently given birth to a normal infant. The referring physician had delivered the child but, when a few weeks later he was asked for contraceptive assistance by the young woman, he had turned her down saying "I'll be damned if I will assist you in any way in sustaining your promiscuous behavior." At least the physician was caring enough to refer her to another physician who, in his hierarchy of values, felt that a greater level of immorality than premarital coitus was bringing another unwanted child into the world or having an abortion.

Case 5: A middle-aged married woman with three college-age children suffered from moderately severe hypertension for which she had been treated for some years by an eminent internist. The patient was married to a sadistic, paranoid man who, in fits of rage, would strike her, sometimes inflicting painful bruises and black eyes. She had endured this treatment through many years of marriage, but now that the children were away at school, she began an affair with a kind and affectionate long-time friend. She was, however, troubled by guilt, for this extramarital relationship was counter to her religious upbringing and her own norms of conduct. Despite her guilt, she was having, for the first time in her life, intense sexual feelings and a sense of fulfillment that was altogether missing from her marriage. Her conflict and guilt caused her to confess the affair to her internist from whom she expected sympathy and understanding.

Instead, no doubt because of his own moral strictures, he upbraided her severely and concluded by stating that if she did not cease the affair from that moment on, he could no longer continue as her physician. Fortunately she was able to bring her problems to a psychiatrist who gave her the necessary empathy and arranged for a support network of her friends and relatives that sustained her until she could obtain a divorce and marry her friend and lover. Interestingly, her hypertension, which had existed for many years and had required daily medication, dropped to normotensive levels when her daily marital stress was removed.

It is not uncommon for a physician to recommend sexual behavior that is unacceptable to the patient:

Case 6: A gynecologist, without inquiring about his patient's attitude toward masturbation, suggested to a preorgasmic woman that she masturbate at least two to three times a week. Outraged by the suggestion but too embarrassed to voice her objections, she never returned to the gynecologist but instead consulted another to whom she confided that she had been taught that masturbation was a dreadful sin and that its perpetrator was certain to go to hell.

Conflicts in moral outlook between two generations can be seen in this case, which also illustrates how two parents of the same generation may differ:

Case 7: A couple married for 28 years had a history of growing hostility and increasingly frequent arguments over the past five years, behavior that had led them eventually to sleep in separate bedrooms. The major recent cause of their marital conflict was their divergent attitudes toward the lifestyles adopted by their two daughters, aged 23 and

26. Both were living with male friends in short committed relationships, and both had chosen not to marry—at least for the time being. The father did not particularly like this arrangement, but he accepted it. His wife bitterly opposed her daughters' lifestyles to the point where she had broken off any relationship with them. This had been very painful to her husband, who was intensely angry over his wife's intransigence.

Socioeconomic factors also have significant impact. In the world of financial and emotional impoverishment, some young unmarried women who have opted to carry their pregnancies to term refuse to give up their newborn children. With a tremendous yearning for love, but suspicious of men and distrustful of intimacy, they believe that their love for the child will somehow magically make up for all of the deprivations they have suffered. Although by no means restricted to black women, this attitude is more commonly seen among black women than white women. The differences in frequency probably are due to several causes, one of which is the greater chance of emotional deprivation among blacks. Another possible cause is that the history of black women as the center of the household—the *uterine* unit—in a world of male unemployment, even desertion, may predispose to this choice. Differences in expectations regarding education and employment between blacks and whites may also play a role. The unmarried young woman who has to care for an infant is in a precarious position with regard to her future.

There seems to be a significant difference between lower-class and middle-class people in their attitudes towards seeking help for sexual problems. Blue collar workers, white and black, seem reluctant to label themselves as needing help for this aspect of their lives. They hesitate to discuss problems of sexual disinterest or sexual performance. To them it is stigmatizing. The same attitude seems to exist, although to a lesser extent, with regard to seeking help for marital problems. However, a way out for the professional is possible. If the physician senses this reluctance, but suspects a sexual and/or a marital problem, he can ask if there are any significant "family" problems or concerns. Labeled in this way, the blue collar worker or spouse is more likely to accept help. When referring a patient from this social class to a sex therapist, the physician should keep in mind this possible sensitivity.

We have been discussing some of the ways in which sociological perspectives may assist the physician in helping patients with sexual problems. Many additional dimensions might have been included. There are two final ones: (1) A sociological perspective allows a physician to be on firm ground when he responds to a patient's query on whether certain behavior is usual; and (2) awareness of the great range and variation in sexual behavior demonstrated by sociological data increases the physician's acceptance of practices he might otherwise have found to be immoral or aesthetically displeasing.

References

1. Reiss IL: *The Social Context of Premarital Sexual Permissiveness*. New York, Holt, Rinehart and Winston, Inc, 1967.

2. Simon W, et al: Beyond anxiety and fantasy: The coital experience of college youth. *J Youth Adoles* 1972; 1:203-222.
3. Hunt M: *Sexual Behavior in the 1970's*. Chicago, Playboy Press, 1974.
4. Tavris C, Sadd S: *The Redbook Report on Female Sexuality*. New York, Delacorte Press, 1977.
5. Athanasiou R, Sarkin R: Premarital sexual behavior and postmarital adjustment. *Arch Sex Behav* 1974; 3:207-225.
6. Hite S: *The Hite Report*. New York, Macmillan Publishing Company, 1976.
7. Shorter E: *The Making of the Modern Family*. New York, Basic Books Inc, 1975.
8. Laslett P: *Family Life and Illicit Love in Earlier Generations*. London, Cambridge University Press, 1977.
9. Smith DS: The dating of the American sexual revolution: Evidence and interpretation, in Gordon M (ed): *The American Family in Social-Historical Perspective*. New York, St Martins Press, 1973.
10. Vincent CE: *Unmarried Mothers*. New York, The Free Press, 1961.
11. Murdock GP: *Social Structures*. New York, Macmillan Publishing Company, 1949.
12. Beach FA: *Human Sexuality in Four Perspectives*. Baltimore, Johns Hopkins University Press, 1977.
13. Coser RL: *The Family: Its Structures and Functions, ed 2*. New York, St Martins Press, 1974.
14. Reiss IL: *Premarital Sexual Standards in America*. New York, The Free Press, 1960.
15. Waller W: *The Family: A Dynamic Interpretation*. New York, Cordon, 1938.
16. Green A: The cult of personality and sexual relations. *Psychiatry* 1941; 4:343-348.
17. Whyte WF: A slum sex code. *Am J Sociol* 1949; 49:24-31.
18. Rainwater L: Some aspects of lower class sexual behavior. *J Soc Issues* 1966 (April); 22:96-109.
19. Staples R: *The Black Family: Essays and Studies*. Belmont, California, Wadsworth Publishing Company Inc, 1971.
20. Zelnik M, Kanter JF: Sexuality, contraception and pregnancy among young unwed females in the United States. *Demographic and Social Aspects of Population Growth*. Washington, DC, Government Printing Office, 1972.
21. Zelnik M, Kanter JF: Sexual and contraceptive experience of young unmarried women in the U.S., 1976 and 1971. *Fam Plann Perspect* 1977 (March/April); 9:55-71.
22. Reiss IL: *Family Systems in America, ed 3*. New York, Holt, Rinehart & Winston, 1980.
23. Sorensen R: *Adolescent Sexuality in Contemporary America*. New York, World Publishing Company, 1973.
24. Zelnik M, Kanter JF: Sexual activity, contraceptive use and pregnancy among metropolitan-area teenagers. *Fam Plan Perspect* 1980 (Sept/Oct); 12:230-237.

25. Zelnik M, Kanter JF: Contraceptive patterns and premarital pregnancy among women aged 15-19 in 1976. *Fam Plann Perspect* 1978 (May/June); 10:135-142.

26. Blake J: The teenage birth control dilemma and public opinion. *Science* 1973; 180:708-712.

27. Reiss IL: *Heterosexual Relationships: Inside and Outside of Marriage*, (pamphlet). Morristown, New Jersey, General Learning Press, 1973 (Oct); 1-29.

28. Furstenberg FF Jr: Birth control experience among pregnant adolescents: The process of unplanned parenthood. *Social Problems* 1971; 19:192-203.

29. Luker K: *Taking Chances*. Los Angeles, University of California Press, 1975.

30. Cvetovich G, et al: Sex role development and teenage contraceptive use. *Adolescence* (in press).

31. Glick TC, Spanier GB: Married and unmarried cohabitation in the United States. *J Marriage Fam* 1980; 42:19-30.

32. Reiss IL, et al: Premarital contraceptive usage: A study and some theoretical explanations. *J Marriage Fam* 1975 (August); 37:619-630.

33. Finkel ML, Finkel DJ: Sexual and contraceptive knowledge, attitudes and behavior of male adolescents. *Fam Plann Perspect* 1975 (Nov/Dec); 7:256-260.

34. Presser HB: Guessing and misinformation about pregnancy risk among urban mothers. *Fam Plann Perspect* 1977 (May/June); 9:111-115.

35. Rains PM: *Becoming an Unwed Mother*. Chicago, Aldine, 1971.

36. Shah F, et al: Unprotected intercourse among unwed teenagers. *Fam Plann Perspect* 1975 (Jan/Feb); 7:39-44.

37. Tietze C: Teenage pregnancies: Looking ahead to 1984. *Fam Plann Perspect* 1978 (July/Aug); 10:205-207.

38. Furstenberg FF Jr: *Unplanned Parenthood: The Social Consequences of Teenage Childbearing*. New York, The Free Press, 1976.

39. Presser HB: Early motherhood: Ignorance or bliss? *Fam Plann Perspect* 1974 (Winter); 6:8-14.

40. Furstenburg FF Jr, et al: *Teenage Sexuality, Pregnancy and Childbearing*. Philadelphia, University of Pennsylvania Press, 1981.

41. *Teenage Pregnancy: The Problem That Hasn't Gone Away*. New York, The Alan Guttmacher Institute, 1981.

42. Gordon M: From an unfortunate necessity to a cult of mutual orgasm: Sex in American marital education literature, 1830-1940, in Henslin JM (ed): *Studies in the Sociology of Sex*. New York, Appleton-Century Crofts, 1971.

43. Degler CN: What ought to be and what was women's sexuality in the nineteenth century. *Am Hist Rev* 1974 (Dec); 79:1467-1490.

44. Westoff CF: Coital frequency and contraception. *Fam Plann Perspect* 1974 (Summer); 6:136-141.

45. Kinsey AC, et al: *Sexual Behavior in the Human Female*. Philadelphia, WB Saunders Co, 1953.

46. Lewis S, Brissett D: Sex as work: A study of advocational counseling. *Soc Prob* 1967; 15:8-18.
47. Rollins BC, Cannon KL: Marital satisfaction over the family life cycle: A re-evaluation. *J Marriage Fam* 1974; 36:271-284.
48. Komarovsky M: *Blue-Collar Marriage*. New York, Random House, 1964.
49. Kinsey AC, et al: *Sexual Behavior in the Human Male*. Philadelphia, WB Saunders Co, 1948.
50. Pfeiffer E, et al: Sexual behavior in middle life. *Am J Psychiatry* 1972; 128:1262-1267.
51. Scanzoni JH: *The Black Family in Modern Society*. Boston, Allyn & Bacon Inc, 1971.
52. Rubin L: *Worlds of Pain: Life in the Working Class Family*. New York, Basic Books Inc, 1977.
53. Kohn M: *Class and Conformity*. Chicago, Dorsey Press Inc, 1978.
54. Bott E: *Family and Social Network*. London, Tavistock, 1957.
55. Vaughan B, et al: Contraceptive failure among married women in the U.S. 1970-73. *Fam Plann Perspect* 1977 (Nov/Dec); 9:251-258.
56. Sanders IT: *Societies Around the World*. New York, Dryden Press, 1956.
57. Reiss IL: Sexual customs and gender roles in Sweden and America: An analysis and interpretation, in Lopata H (ed): *Research on the Interweave of Social Roles*. Greenwich, CT, JAI Press, 1980.
58. Reiss IL, et al: A multivariate model of the determinants of extramarital sexual permissiveness. *J Marriage Fam* 1980 (May); 42:395-411.
59. Sponaugle GC: A study of extramarital sexuality in Minnesota, 1978 (unpublished).
60. Ziskin J, Ziskin M: *The Extramarital Sex Contract*. Los Angeles, Nash Publishers, 1973.
61. Gilmartin B: That swinging couple down the block. *Psychol Today* 1975; 8:54-58.
62. Gilmartin B: *The Gilmartin Report*. Seacaucus, New Jersey, Citadel Press, 1978.
63. Bartell G: Group sex among the mid-Americans. *J Sex Res* 1970; 6:113-130.
64. Ramey J: *Intimate Friendship*. New York, Prentice Hall, 1976.
65. Glass SP, Wright TL: The relationship of extramarital sex and length of marriage. *J Marriage Fam* 1977; 39:691-704.
66. Rohrer JH, Edmonson MS (eds): *The Eighth Generation*. New York, Harper and Row Publishing Inc, 1960.

Chapter 6

Understanding the Varieties of Homosexual Behavior

Warren J. Gadpaille, M.D.

A major purpose of this chapter, in addition to providing a background for the physician treating a patient of homosexual orientation, is to counteract overgeneralized preconceptions about homosexual behavior. Probably 1 to 3 per cent of female, and 3 to 6 per cent of male, adults are predominately or exclusively homosexual, and perhaps as many as 33 per cent of all people will have had some kind of homosexual activity during their lives. Few generalizations are scientifically justified about even exclusive homosexuals, much less about a third of the population.

In Chapter 3, it is stated that available evidence indicates that the biologically normal newborn infant probably has an innate neuropsychological and neuroendocrinological bias toward an eventual heterosexual orientation. If this point of view is accurate, it means that, in the absence of biological abnormality, various kinds of unnatural influences are necessary to disrupt heterosexual orientation permanently. However, it implies very little else that is generally applicable to adult preferential homosexuals and nothing at all about the vast number of people with other kinds of homosexual experience.

With respect to adult preferential or exclusive homosexuals, no simple or single cause or source of interference with this apparent innate heterosexual bias is known. It is probable that adult homosexuality can result from many different influences—some known, some speculated, some still unknown.

One possibility is that there is an alteration or aberration in the fetal hormonal (and other) influences that organize the embryonic central nervous system for ultimate heterosexual arousal and responsivity. The altered developmental biology could reverse that bias or diminish or neutralize its strength. Although there is no direct empirical evidence for this as a basis of homosexuality in man, experimental evidence on primates and other mammals, and clinical evidence from studies on human endocrinopathies and genetic disorders suggest that some such altered biology during fetal development may play a significant predisposing role in some or all gender role and orientation deviations.[1,2]

A known cause of homosexuality in some adults is unconscious conflict arising from postnatal rearing influences that make heterosexuality unappeal ing or unattainable. The causes and psychodynamics of such conflicts are varied,[3,6] although some may be more typical than others. There is no doubt that such conflicts are etiologic in homosexual psychiatric patients who are unhappy with their homosexuality; it is not known whether or to what extent they are etiologic in the much larger nonpatient homosexual population, although several researchers[7-9] report typical conflicts in nonpatient research populations also. If aberrant fetal biology plays no role, fairly powerful and chronic (albeit perhaps subtle) influences are probably necessary to deflect the innate heterosexual bias. If (or when) fetal biology is aberrant, a child may have less resistance to relatively minor pathogenic experiences of the sort that might also be found in the histories of many heterosexuals. Homosexuality that arises from interpersonal and intrapsychic conflict may be considered an adaptive response to the psychological repudiation or avoidance of heterosexuality.

There are many social learning theories that explain preferential adult homosexuality on the basis of various postnatal learning and socializing influences and that minimize the importance of unconscious conflict.[10] This approach helps to explain many aspects of the social and psychological lives of homosexuals that are not adequately understandable on the basis of intrapsychic conflict alone. Such theories are clearly necessary to explain such phenomena in other cultures as accepted homosexual activity among preferentially heterosexual adult males, as well as exclusive and enforced, but not adult-prognostic, homosexuality among adolescent males.[11] The theories also explain many developmental phase and nonexclusive manifestations of homosexuality in American culture and *perhaps* some instances of preferential adult homosexuality. But as general explanation, these theories lack credibility because of the one-sided position they take in the nature/nurture interaction, neither extreme of which is scientifically tenable.

Because there are so many unfortunate misconceptions about homosexuality, it is important to stress, as noted in the following paragraphs, what one can *not* assume simply by knowing that a person is primarily aroused by, or is sexually active with, others of the same sex.

To begin with, without taking a careful history, homosexual activity does not by itself indicate which of the many varieties of homosexual behavior is being reflected. It does not even indicate whether the person considers himself or herself to be homosexual.[12]

There are injunctions in Christianity and some other religions against homosexuality, so that whether it is good or bad, acceptable, or sinful and evil is already decided for some people. But on a human ethical level, homosexual activity among consenting peer partners in no way labels someone as bad or evil. Except where homosexual activity itself is deemed criminal, there appears to be no higher incidence of criminality or antisocial behavior among homosexuals than among heterosexuals.

Homosexuality does not necessarily imply diminished function in other areas of life or even an impoverished sex life. There are more homosexuals who feel satisifed and are productive or creative in all walks of life than homosexuals who cannot function effectively because of emotional conflict over their sex orientation.[13-16] Masters and Johnson[17] found in research comparing committed and highly functional homosexual and heterosexual couples (findings not necessarily generalizable to the general population of either group) that the homosexual couples took more time in whole body sensuality and foreplay, were more sensitive to the partner's responses and wishes, communicated more fully and freely about their sensations and emotions during sexual encounters, and were more egalitarian than the heterosexual couples.

Chiefly, one cannot automatically assume that homosexual behavior is, or is symptomatic of, an illness. Clearly it can be, as in the chaotic and indiscriminate pansexuality of some borderline character disorders, just as some manifestations of heterosexuality are grossly symptomatic. If aberrant fetal biological development is found to be the basis of some homosexuality, such cases could possibly be considered one of the sexual anomalies. Perhaps only that unknown proportion of cases of homosexuality that are traceable to identifiable interpersonal and intrapsychic disturbances of psychosexual development can be assumed to follow the medical psychiatric model of illness. Such a model has a known (or knowable) cause, typical onset and chronic course, pathognomonic symptoms, and implications for prevention and for the nature of therapy. Even in these cases, determining what to do about the problem is the sole right and choice of the individual, except in specific instances of misuse against others. A broad range of homosexual persons and homosexual behaviors, perhaps a majority, probably fall outside such a model of illness and reflect a wide variety of motives, origins, and individual and cultural meanings. An excellent historical overview is provided by Karlen.[18]

VARIETIES OF HOMOSEXUAL EXPRESSION

Preferential or obligatory homosexuality elicits the most interest and is subject to the most bias and misunderstanding, even though only a minority of persons who have ever had any homosexual experience fall into this category. Cross-species and cross-cultural evidence suggests that preferential or obligatory homosexuality is qualitatively, not merely quantitatively, different from other expressions of homosexuality.[19] (This category itself is best broken down into diverse types for better understanding, and will be explicated in the following section.)

These people can respond erotically only to members of the same sex, or they are more readily and pleasurably aroused by members of the same sex even when opposite sex partners are available and willing. Their arousal is primarily and specifically erotic; it is not derived from nonsexual motives and dynamics as in the case of pseudohomosexuals. The term "preferential" does not imply that this kind of homosexuality is an expression of conscious choice any more than heterosexuality is. The origins of erotic sexual orientation, although diverse and sometimes obscure, are typically early and outside awareness or decision. Because the emotional attitudes toward this group can so strongly affect medical treatment, they are discussed more fully in the latter part of this chapter.

Developmental homoerotic activity is homosexual in terms of object choice, but it is usually not prognostic of adult homosexuality. It may occur at any or all immature developmental stages in both boys and girls. Kinsey et al[20,21] found that 33 per cent of women and 50 per cent of men recalled preadolescent or adolescent homoerotic play. This subject is discussed in detail in Chapter 18.

Pseudohomosexuality[22] is homosexuality by default. It has been described primarily in males, but complementary motivation may operate in females. The primary conflicts of pseudohomosexuals concern dependency and power, which they associate respectively with femininity and masculinity. If they perceive themselves as weak or inadequate compared to other men, they unconsciously assume that they are nonmasculine, which equals feminine, which equals homosexual.

The most common symptom of this condition is pseudohomosexual anxiety or panic, often when the man finds himself in an all-male environment or when some life situation, such as rejection by a sex partner or losing out to another man in the competitive job market, is perceived as a blow to masculine self-esteem (see Chapter 20). Sometimes these men may act out these conflicts in occasional homosexual behavior, either to test out their perceptions of themselves or in passive resignation to what they perceive as their fate. These experiences are usually not satisfying and are often severely anxiety-producing. But pseudohomosexuality sometimes develops into a pattern of exclusive behavior through restricted learning and socialization and through the absence of emotional freedom to explore heterosexuality.

The childhoods of these men may have been characterized by passivity and isolation from peers, but few remember wishing to be girls or feeling early erotic attraction to males. Masturbatory fantasies and dreams may have homosexual content, but the affective components are more reflective of power and submission then of eroticism. Of course, primarily erotic homosexuality may coexist with conflicts over power and dependence. Pseudohomosexuality is a risk for people of either sex whose developmental conflicts gave them an inadequate sense of masculinity or femininity.

Situational homosexuality is that which occurs among preferential heterosexuals in enforced single-sex environments, such as some armed forces assignments. Usually these people revert later to their heterosexual patterns and no problem is presented to the physician unless the experience precipitates a pseudohomosexual panic (see Chapter 20) or a more lasting pseudohomosexual maladaptation. However, in some enforced single-sex environments, such as correctional institutions and boarding schools, additional characterological qualities (forceful coercion and fearful submission) often color the homosexual activity.

Exploitative homosexuality is that in which people with physical and social power, as in an inmate subculture, force weaker or more submissive people to be sexual objects, usually through anal intercourse but also through fellatio. While there may be unconscious sexual identity conflicts in the exploiters, these are essentially acts of violence in which the penis is used as a weapon or symbol of dominance, as in heterosexual rape. Sexual exploitation motivated by power, dominance and underlying rage also occurs in women's prisons. Male exploiters typically do not consider themselves homosexual and would rarely seek therapy for a sexual conflict.

Enforced homosexuality is the complement of exploitative homosexuality. The attack on masculine or feminine self-image is violent and severe; therapy is strongly indicated, although the circumstances and facilities often make it difficult or impossible. While there is a general and probably accurate consensus that a primarily erotic homosexual preference cannot be induced in anyone in the absence of pre-existing sexual orientation conflicts, there is one report of preferential homosexuals who claim never to have had homosexual tendencies before being forced in prison to be regular sexual objects.[23]

The masculine or feminine identity implications of the insertor and insertee roles in male homosexuality are now considered irrelevant by some authorities; in most middle-class American homosexuals the roles are often alternated, strong preference is expressed by few, and there is little professed correlation between role and masculine or feminine self-image.[24,25] This ambiguity may be highly ethnocentric, however. There are other Western cultures (e.g., some Latin-American societies) and U.S. subcultures (e.g., some ethnic groups and prison cultures) in which insertor and insertee roles are sharply dichotomized as respectively masculine and feminine. Only the insertee is regarded by himself and his peers as homosexual and feminine and is so stigmatized. The insertor in no way feels or is considered homosexual; he suffers no social stigmatization, and his masculinity is not compromised in anyone's eyes.[26] This can be true whether the insertor's act involves intimidation and violence, as in prisons, or is by mutual consent. Such dichotomy is also reported among some male adolescent groups.[27,28] The implications for the physician are that middle-class American sexual values are largely inapplicable to insertors in these cultural contexts; usually only the insertee suffers intrapsychic or social erosion of his sexual identity.

Bisexuality is poorly understood. In a society that strongly stigmatizes homosexuality, bisexuality is usually found in those whose erotic preference is homosexual but who can engage in, and to some extent enjoy, heterosexual relations.

Ambisexuality is distinguished from bisexuality by the equal capacity for enjoying and functioning in sexual activity with either sex. Masters and Johnson[17] have recently reported what appears to be true ambisexuality. In the small number of people so designated, no differences in physiological response, sexual function, or observed or reported erotic pleasure were detectable, regardless of the sex of the partner.

Variational homosexuality, the voluntary expression of a desire for sexual variety, is a form of homosexual activity claimed by some people. It probably springs from a number of different roots in different people. One root *may* be freedom from social bias and avoidance, but others may include unrecognized homosexual preference, conflict over heterosexuality, and the incapacity for emotional commitment to a particular partner or life-style, given the long-term implications and responsibilities of such commitment.

Finally, there is a type of homosexuality seen today that might best be called *ideological* or *political*. It is most prevalent among women in the feminist movement, and it is often proclaimed to be a denial of any sexual need for, or dependence upon, men. It is also sometimes explained as a negation of any innate psychological sex differences, including sexual orientation; this attitude may be found in men or women. Sexual identity conflicts may well masquerade in this guise, but the ideological positions passionately repudiate the idea of psychopathology as their genesis. However, psychiatrists are being consulted more and more by people who have found such ideological homosexual activity incompatible with their basic sexual identities and who experience doubts and conflicts as a result.[29,30]

PREFERENTIAL OR OBLIGATORY HOMOSEXUALITY

The true incidence of stigmatized behavior cannot be determined. Estimates are as high as 10 per cent of males and 6 per cent of females in this country; the higher estimates generally derive from nonrepresentative samples or from writers who may wish to exaggerate the incidence. Without attempting to evaluate the credibility of the various studies and estimates, it is generally considered reasonable that 1 to 3 per cent of females and 3 to 6 per cent of male adults are preferentially or exclusively homosexual.[10,20,21] This means about 6 to 8 million people in the United States today. There do not appear to be any major differences in incidence among the various ethnic groups.

Contrary to much popular misconception, the majority of those who, at any given time, consider themselves (or are considered by researchers according to specific rating criteria) to be preferentially or exclusively homosexual have at some time experienced coitus, and a significant proportion continue to have some degree of heterosexual activity. According to different studies, one-third to over two-thirds of homosexual males report ever having had coitus, and between 10 per cent to 20 per cent had coitus within the year prior to the study.[16,31-34] Between 62 and 85 per cent of homosexual females report having had coitus ever, and 9 to 38 per cent had coitus within the previous year.[16,32,34-36] Twelve per cent to more than 18 per cent of homosexual men are reported to have been married.[16,32,33,37,38] In a study by Bell and Weinberg,[16] half of the ever married white homosexuals of both sexes and nearly three-fourths of the ever married black homosexuals were reported to have had children.

There are important differences as well as similarities between male and female homosexuals. For example, while in one study, about two-thirds of each sex reported "sissiness" or "tomboyism" as children, and while one-third never had shown such behavior, in a comparison group of heterosexuals, only 3 per cent of males reported "sissiness," whereas 16 per cent of females reported "tomboyism."[32] Therefore, cross-gender behavior is more prognostic of adult homosexuality in boys than in girls. Cross-gender behavior in either male or female homosexuals, however, does not necessarily continue into adult life, and probably the majority of homosexuals are not recognizably distinguishable from their heterosexual counterparts.

76

From the data cited earlier, it is clear that more female than male homosexuals have had and continue to have heterosexual intercourse.

The greatest behavioral difference is in partner frequency and change. In a study by Schäfer,[34] homosexual males averaged 15 times as many partners as did homosexual females; 11 times as many males as females had had sex with more than 50 partners; males averaged 16 partners per year, whereas females averaged two. In the Bell and Weinberg study,[16] nearly one-half of the white and one-third of the black males reported at least 500 different sexual partners; another one-third and one-fourth, respectively, reported between 100 and 500 partners. Seventy-nine per cent of the whites and 51 per cent of the blacks reported that more than half their partners were strangers, and 70 and 38 per cent, respectively, had sex only once with more than half their partners. In contrast, 7 per cent of white and 12 per cent of black female homosexuals had 50 or more different partners, and only 6 per cent of both reported that their partners had been strangers. The Schäfer study[34] shows that homosexuals of both sexes shift partners more often than do heterosexuals, and that the difference is much greater between homosexual and heterosexual males than between the two groups of females; comparison with heterosexuals on this point is omitted from the Bell and Weinberg study.[16] Both studies indicate a greater incidence and duration of close, quasi-marital relationships among females, as well as greater focus upon and demand for sexual fidelity in female couples than in male couples.

The label "homosexuality" implies a unity that does not exist. Bell and Weinberg[16] have proposed one possible typology for 71 per cent of the nearly 1,000 homosexuals in their study. There were those who were "coupled," who lived in a quasi-marriage with a partner (the length of the partnership varied widely). Of their 686 males, the "close-coupled" (9.8 per cent) desired considerable closeness and fidelity; the "open-coupled" (17.5 per cent) considered a regular partner important for sex and affection, but, despite considerable jealousy, agreed that each could have other sexual partners. Those called "functional" (14.9 per cent) had high levels of sexual activity, more sexual partners than those in the other groups, little regret over their homosexuality, and fewer sexual problems. The "dysfunctionals" (12.5 per cent) had more regret over their homosexuality and more sexual problems than the others. The "asexuals" (16.0 per cent) had little interest, had little activity and few partners, and also had many sexual problems. The same percentage of lesbians were classifiable, but there were approximately three times as many "close-coupled" and far fewer "functionals," "dysfunctionals" and "asexuals."

Since the study population was entirely from an urban and relatively liberal location (San Francisco area), a question might arise regarding this typology. Although the typology might be applied anywhere, the relative proportions and even their distinguishing characteristics could vary in unknown ways among other populations. And because about 30 per cent could not be classified in this manner, and no psychological data or homosexual/heterosexual comparisons are provided for them, it is not known how the data and characteristics of this large unclassified proportion might modify or invalidate the conclusions drawn.

Whether preferential homosexuals are psychiatrically disturbed is a controversial issue, and one that is highly politicized. Many homosexuals and psychiatrists alike believe that, unless homosexuality is regarded as a normal variation, discriminatory practices against homosexuals will continue. In 1974, the American Psychiatric Association voted to remove homosexuality from its classification of mental illnesses. Yet, in 1977, a survey of 2,500 psychiatrists by *Medical Aspects of Human Sexuality*[39] found that 69 per cent of the respondents regarded homosexuality to be a pathological adaptation. All psychoanalytic theories interpret homosexuality as a consequence of various pathogenic influences and conflicts, and the great majority of psychoanalysts agree with that interpretation. Psychogenic roots are found in virtually all preferential or exclusive homosexuals who have been in analysis, and, as noted before, some researchers report finding such roots in nonpatient populations.

Results of psychological test surveys of nonpatient homosexuals, however, routinely fail to reveal significant pathology in all, or even the majority, of homosexuals tested. In comparison studies, the results vary from finding more to less pathology in homosexuals vs. heterosexuals. In the Bell and Weinberg report,[16] in which a number of significant studies are summarized, homosexuals as a group showed more social and psychological problems than did heterosexuals in the majority of a wide variety of measures, including job stability, psychosomatic symptoms, tension, depression, suicidal ideation and attempts, and incidence of seeking professional help. Females tended to show fewer and smaller differences than did males. However, when the homosexual/heterosexual comparisons were broken down according to the types described above, there were no significant differences in problems reported by heterosexuals and homosexuals of the "close-coupled," "open-coupled," and "functional" types; the "dysfunctionals" and "asexuals" provided most of the problems. Again, the omission of any comparable data about the 30 per cent of unclassified homosexuals makes unknown the applicability of such specific comparisons and conclusions to homosexuals as a group.

The fact that a predominant number of homosexuals (males, essentially) have numerous, and frequently changing, sexual partners who are strangers may or may not be indicative of pathology. There are no exactly comparable data for heterosexuals, but whatever data do exist indicate that heterosexual partner numbers and frequency of change are typically a fraction of that of many or most homosexuals. It is easy to make value judgments (as distinct from psychiatric judgments) about having so many casual partners, but such judgments may have little basis other than moral prejudice or even envy.

The actual reasons for the difference can only be speculated at present. Perhaps homosexual males are freed from the restraints imposed on heterosexuals by females who have a vested interest in commitment, marriage and family. The fact that homosexuals have not identified in sexual orientation with their same-sex parents usually reflects, in clinical populations at least, conscious or unconscious hostility toward the same sex, and this has been found in nonclinical populations as well;[9] such ambivalence could account for the frequent turning from one partner to another. Although it is politically unpopular to state that many homosexuals show disturbed sexual behavior, it is certainly true that when a heterosexual shows a predominance of sex with many partners who are and remain strangers, it is evidence of shallow, narcissistic, impersonal, often compulsively driven, genital rather than person-oriented sex, and is almost always regarded as pathological.

Whatever the clinical or characterological meanings of impersonal, "promiscuous" sex, they do not apply to those homosexuals who are able to establish an intimate, committed partnership. Not only do they appear to be as well adjusted as most heterosexuals, but, as noted above, may express even more caring in sexual relations than heterosexuals do.

Many observers believe that any disproportionate incidence of social and psychological problems among homosexuals is caused by their social stigmatization and the consequent emotional stress. This is a reasonable and attractive explanation because such conditions do cause stress and morbidity among the victims. On the other hand, the one study of those variables in both permissive and nonpermissive environments failed to find that homosexuals in the former environments had fewer psychosocial problems than did those in the latter.[33]

It is clearly inappropriate to stereotype all homosexuals as emotionally disturbed and socially dysfunctional. The prevalence of impersonal sexuality is very likely pathological in anyone who shows it, whether homosexual or heterosexual. Even if preferential or obligatory homosexuality is an adaptation to disturbed psychological development, there is little reason to presume that this adaptation disrupts overall function any more than other kinds of pathogenic developmental influences cause various degrees of emotional dysfunction in perhaps the majority of heterosexuals; it is only that, in heterosexuals, developmental traumata have affected, constricted, or rigidified aspects of their lives other than sexual orientation. The studies comparing psychosocial problems in heterosexuals and homosexuals show conflicting findings. The majority of homosexuals appear to be both socially and psychiatrically satisfied and functional, although perhaps they often lack interpersonal intimacy with their sex partners.

IMPLICATIONS FOR PHYSICIANS

Physicians are only people with a particular kind of professional training. They are subject to the same stereotypic thinking, prejudices, conflicts, inhibitions, and ignorance as are other people, and nowhere is this more true than when they deal with the subject of sex. Misconceptions and unexamined personal attitudes about homosexuality on the part of physicians can result in grave, even life-threatening, disservice to homosexual patients.

Relatively few homosexuals will initially and spontaneously identify themselves as such to a physician, and even fewer will express a desire to change their orientation. For the majority who do not want to change, it is a serious mistake to try to persuade them to change (at least if they are adults), because the attempt will usually destroy rapport and perhaps drive them from necessary medical care. It is useful, however, once trust is established, to ask with nonjudgmental interest, "Have you ever felt unhappy over being homosexual and wished you could be different?" There are those who do want to change and perhaps could but are afraid to say so because they are convinced that it is never possible; for them, the possibilities and alternatives are discussed in Chapter 19.

Homosexual preference or activity is usually found only if specifically asked about in the history. Very few physicians routinely ask such questions, but it is important to remember that any patient may be homosexual, even a married parent whom the doctor has known for some time. The embarrassed reticence of physicians may be rationalized as fear of invading privacy or as conviction that patients would be offended and that no one would admit to homosexual activity. Both offense and denial may occur under the best of circumstances, but they are greatly minimized by a matter-of-fact, nonjudgmental manner.

In the course of routine sexual history (see Chapters 10,11) and after more neutral and introductory questions, it is easy to ask, "When did you first learn about homosexuality? What are your attitudes about it? What, if any, homosexual activity took place during your teen years? As an adult, what concerns, if any, do you have about homosexuality?"

Questions like these will help the physician get into the subject, but unless he probes into possible homosexual behavior, he will miss cues that can be helpful in diagnosis and treatment. Thus, the physician may also ask: "What is your usual preference in sexual partners?" and, if characteristics other than gender are given, "Do you prefer men or women?" If the patient is married or there is evidence of heterosexual activity, one needs to probe further with questions such as, "Do you have any other sexual interests or activities? Do you ever have sex with persons other than your present partner? Do you ever have sex with other men (women)?"

Often a patient with homosexual activity is willing or even eager to discuss it because the activity is related to his reason for coming to the physician. Once a homosexual activity is expressed, the physician should find out about specific practices, frequency, recency, and number of recent partners.

These questions are neither academic nor prurient. Failure to know a patient's orientation dulls a physician's alertness to atypical manifestations or loci of some illnesses or lesions. For example, this is particularly true of sexually transmitted disease, which has a high incidence among homosexual males (two-thirds in the Bell and Weinberg study[16]). Lack of an index of suspicion can lead to failure to examine for a rectal lesion and failure to culture or do appropriate microscopic examinations of rectal or pharyngeal specimens even in the presence of suspicious symptomatology, with potentially serious to disastrous consequences to the patient and often to others.

It is well for a physician to determine which of the various kinds of homosexual behavior a patient's experiences reflect, and whether there are indications for some form of psychotherapy even when change to heterosexuality is not an issue. Persons subjected to enforced homosexuality, even when it was long past, may have serious emotional problems as a consequence. A patient unable to form attachments may need and benefit from professional help regardless of orientation. Homosexuals can suffer sexual dysfunctions just as heterosexuals can.

Societal attitudes, of course, can play a major role in determining how comfortable a homosexual will be with his orientation, and can greatly influence the nature of his self-image. The empathic physician as a practitioner will try to help his homosexual patient achieve a positive sense of well-being and self-worth in the face of social antagonism, while he strives as a health educator and community leader to eliminate the prejudice and stigma that cause so much personal anguish and suffering.

Basic to all good patient care with homosexuals is an open, accepting, nonjudgmental attitude. This is sometimes difficult or impossible for some physicians to achieve, and when personal emotional attitudes interfere with optimal physician-patient relationship and patient care, the ethical course is to explain one's dilemma openly and refer the patient. Every physician treats many patients who enjoy activities, hold beliefs, and engage in life-styles that the physician would not choose for himself or herself. A sick homosexual patient is simply a sick person, entitled to be treated with dignity and respect and to receive whatever care that the medical or psychiatric condition demands.

References

1. Gadpaille WJ: Biological factors in the development of human sexual identity. *Psychiatr Clin North Am* 1980; 3(1):3-20.
2. Diamond M: Human sexual development: Biological foundations for social development, in Beach FA (ed): *Human Sexuality in Four Perspectives*. Baltimore, Johns Hopkins University Press, 1976.
3. Bergler E: *One Thousand Homosexuals: Conspiracy of Silience or Curing and Deglamorizing Homosexuals?* Patterson, NJ, Pageant Books, 1959.
4. Freud A: Studies in passivity, in *The Writings of Anna Freud*, Vol IV. New York, International Universities Press, 1952.
5. Bieber I, et al: *Homosexuality: A Psychoanalytic Study*. New York, Basic Books Inc, 1962.
6. Socarides CW: *Homosexuality*. New York, Aronson Jason Inc, 1978.
7. Evans RB: Childhood parental relationships of homosexual men. *J Consult Clin Psychol* 1969; 33:129-135.
8. Snortum JR, et al: Family dynamics and homosexuality. *Psychol Rep* 1969; 24:763-770.
9. Hendin H: Homosexuality: The psychosocial dimension. *J Am Acad Psychoanal* 1978; 6:479-496.
10. Gagnon JH, Simon W: *Sexual Conduct: The Social Sources of Human Sexuality*. Chicago, Aldine Publishing Company Inc, 1973.
11. Davenport W: Sexual patterns and their regulation in a society of the southwest Pacific, in Beach FA (ed): *Sex and Behavior*. New York, John Wiley & Sons, 1965.

12. Weinberg TS: On 'doing' and 'being' gay: Sexual behavior and homosexual male self-identity. *J Homosexuality* 1978; 4:143-156.

13. Hooker E: The adjustment of the male overt homosexual. *J Project Tech* 1957; 21:18-31.

14. Churchill W: *Homosexual Behavior among Males: A Cross-cultural and Cross-species Investigation*. New York, Hawthorn Books Inc, 1967.

15. Schafer S: Sexual and social problems among lesbians. *J Sex Res* 1976; 12:50-69.

16. Bell AP, Weinberg MS: *Homosexualities*. New York, Simon and Schuster Inc, 1978.

17. Masters WH, Johnson VE: *Homosexuality in Perspective*. Boston, Little, Brown and Company, 1979.

18. Karlen A: *Sexuality and Homosexuality: A New View*. New York, W.W. Norton & Company, 1979.

19. Gadpaille WJ: Cross-species and cross-cultural contributions to the understanding of homosexual activity. *Arch Gen Psychiatry* 1980; 37:349-356.

20. Kinsey AC, et al: *Sexual Behavior in the Human Male*. Philadelphia, WB Saunders Company, 1948.

21. Kinsey AC, et al: *Sexual Behavior in the Human Female*. Philadelphia, WB Saunders Company, 1953.

22. Ovesey L: *Homosexuality and Pseudohomosexuality*. New York, Science House, 1969.

23. Sagarin E: Prison homosexuality and its effect on post-prison sexual behavior. *Psychiatry* 1976; 39:245-257.

24. Harry J: On the validity of typologies of gay males. *J Homosexuality* 1976-1977; 2:143-152.

25. Haist M, Hewett J: The butch-fem dichotomy in male homosexual behavior. *J Sex Res* 1974; 10:68-75.

26. Carrier JM: Sex-role preference as an explanatory variable in homosexual behavior. *Arch Sex Behav* 1977; 6:53-65.

27. Bartollas C, et al: The booty bandit: A social role in a juvenile institution. *J Homosexuality* 1974; 1:203-212.

28. Reiss AJ Jr: The social integration of queers and peers. *Soc Prob* 1961; 9:102-120.

29. DeFries Z: Pseudohomosexuality in feminist students. *Am J Psychiatry* 1976; 133:400-404.

30. DeFries Z: Political lesbianism and sexual politics. *J Am Acad Psychoanal* 1978; 6:71-78.

31. Schofield MG: *Sociological Aspects of Homosexuality* Boston, Little, Brown and Company, 1965.

32. Saghir MT, Robins E: *Male and Female Homosexuality: A Comprehensive Investigation*. Baltimore, Williams & Wilkins Company, 1973.

33. Weinberg MS, Williams CJ: *Male Homosexuals, Their Problems & Adaptation*. New York, Oxford University Press, 1974.

34. Schafer S: Sociosexual behavior in male and female homosexuals: A study in sex differences. *Arch Sex Behav* 1977; 6:355-364.
35. DOB questionnaire reveals some facts about lesbians. *The Ladder* 1959; 3:24-26.
36. Grundlach RM, Riess BF: Self and sexual identity in the female: A study of female homosexuals, in Riess BF (ed): *New Directions in Mental Health*. New York, Grune & Stratton Inc, 1968.
37. DOB questionnaire reveals some comparisons between male and female homosexuals. *The Ladder* 1960; 4:4-25.
38. Manosevitz M: The development of male homosexuality. *J Sex Res* 1972; 8:31-40.
39. Sexual survey #4: Current thinking on homosexuality. *Med Aspects Hum Sex* 1977 (Nov); 11:110-111.

Chapter 7

Classification of Sexual Disorders

Harold I. Lief, M.D.

This chapter will consider the classifications of sexual disorders, using the *Diagnostic and Statistical Manual-III* (DSM-III) of the American Psychiatric Association[1] as the major source. It will emphasize nomenclature and descriptions, and will include passing reference to the effects of developmental influences, anxiety and partner-conflict. Etiology will be discussed in greater depth in subsequent chapters. This chapter will suggest that so-called minor sexual "difficulties" may be of major importance to people.[2] To orient the reader, reference will be made to the diagram "Dimensions of Sexual Dysfunction." That part of the chapter will focus on the factors the physician should consider in making his appraisal.

In most people the desire for sexual pleasure is relatively strong. Although it is possible to inhibit sexual behavior altogether, relatively few people elect a life of celibacy. There is no device by which the intensity of sexual desire can be measured. No doubt it exists along a continuum (the distribution probably is a bell-shaped curve) from the relatively asexual at one end to the highly sexual at the other. Yet the strength of sexual desire for most of mankind during most of a person's life makes sexual behavior an imperative for all but the very few.

Indicative of the "instinctive" nature of sexual function, infants have an erection and female infants demonstrate vaginal lubrication during the birth process.[3] Despite the strength of this inborn reflex response, the developmental path toward the standard pattern of expression (the "standard" subject to the vicissitudes of a particular culture) can be blocked by one or more of three major factors: (1) a biogenic force in which the machinery of the body is not functioning properly, as in congenital disorders or acquired illness; (2) a deviation from the usual developmental pattern of erotic arousal, as in fetishism; and (3) anxiety of sufficient severity to inhibit or distort any aspect of the complicated sequence of events required for the successful completion of sexual activity. (See Figure 3.) An example of this is lifelong premature ejaculation.

Most commonly, an unusual pattern of erotic arousal is conjoined with anxiety over going ahead with the standard pattern of finding, courting and joining in mutual sex play with a partner. This conjunction provides the groundwork for the groups of sexual disorders labeled either *disorders of gender*

Figure 3. Standard Coital Pattern.

Internal stimulation establishes receptivity to psychodynamic stimulation.

Arousal by sensory and intellectual stimulation of each other.

In both mates, this sets up sexual motive state which mobilizes and organizes the organism's emotional and other resources for orgastic pleasure.

In both mates, this state elicits automatic responses of preparedness:
sensory: selective mechanism of attention
intellectual: selective mechanisms of memory and wishful thought
motor: engorgement of erectile structures
glandular: release of sperm; secretion of vehicular and lubricative fluids.

Male woos and secures consent of the female.

Foreplay: mutual stimulation of responsive extra-genital regions sends tributary streams of pleasure into orgastic main stream in both mates.

Male: rise of impetus to penetrate—Female: rise of desire to be penetrated.

Inplay: intramural stimulation by pelvic thrust.

This reflexly evokes pleasurable orgastic peristalsis of genital structures and brings mounting emotional tensions to a climactic discharge in both male and female.

Sleep.

Pride.

From Rado S: An adaptational view of sexual behavior, in *Psychoanalysis of Behavior*. New York, Grune & Stratton, Inc, 1956.

identity or *paraphilias*. (The term *paraphilia* is preferred to past labels, such as perversion or deviation, because it avoids the pejorative connotation of those words.)

Developmentally, any of the various dimensions of the standard pattern can be disturbed. The dimensions of the standard pattern are: (1) core gender identity; (2) gender identity; (3) forms of erotic arousal; (4) strength of desire; (5) capacity for sexual excitement; (6) capacity for orgasm; and (7) capacity for sexual pleasure.

The schema just presented form the basis for the classification adopted by the *Diagnostic and Statistical Manual - III* (DSM-III).[1] It essentially repeats the analysis presented by Freud[4] in 1936:

" . . . one sees merely that the most varied means are employed to impair (sexual) function as: (1) the mere turning aside of libido, which seems most easily to produce what we call pure inhibition; (2) impairment of the execution of the function; (3) the rendering it difficult through the imposition of special conditions, and its modification through diverting it to other aims; (4) its prevention by means of precautionary measures; (5) its discontinuance by the development of anxiety, when the initiation of the function can no longer be prevented; finally, (6) a subsequent reaction of protest against the act and a desire to undo it if it has actually been carried out."

Using more modern terminology, the DSM-III has set forth the following classification of sexual disorders:

Gender Identity Disorders
1. Transsexualism
2. Gender Identity Disorders of Childhood
3. Other Gender Identity Disorders of Adolescence or Adult Life

Paraphilias
1. Fetishism
2. Transvestism
3. Zoophilia
4. Pedophilia
5. Exhibitionism
6. Voyeurism
7. Sexual Masochism
8. Sexual Sadism
9. Other

Psychosexual Dysfunctions
1. With Inhibited Sexual Desire
2. With Inhibited Sexual Excitement (Frigidity, Impotence)
3. With Inhibited Female Orgasm
4. With Inhibited Male Orgasm
5. With Premature Ejaculation
6. (With Functional) Dyspareunia
7. (With Functional) Vaginismus
8. Atypical Psychosexual Dysfunctions

Other Psychosexual Disorders
1. Ego-dystonic Homosexuality
2. Psychosexual Disorders Not Elsewhere Classified

The DSM-III is limited to mental disorders, hence the terms "psychosexual" and "functional" in the DSM-III classification, excluding physical disorders. We prefer to describe these disorders and dysfunctions from a physical as well as a psychological perspective.

Before discussing the sexual disorders listed in DSM-III, it is important to recognize that there are common sexual difficulties that do not merit one of the diagnostic labels given above and yet may cause distress sufficient to create much unhappiness. These difficulties include couple-conflict about sexual frequency, about the degree of feeling associated with sex, aspects of the sexual repertoire, the timing of sex, the degree of participation of the partner and initiation of sex. These difficulties are taken up in some detail in Chapter 11.

GENDER IDENTITY DISORDERS

Only a brief description of such disorders follows, since these are discussed in considerable detail in Chapters 18 and 19. The gender identity disorders are characterized by the individual's feelings of discomfort and inappropriateness about his or her anatomic sex and by persistent behaviors generally associated with the other sex. Gender identity is a personal awareness of one's sex (male, female, or ambivalent) or of one's feelings of masculinity and femininity; it is the inner sense of masculinity or femininity. *Core* gender identity is a sense of maleness or femaleness. Gender role behavior is the outward expression of this personal awareness. Disturbances in gender identity and role behavior are severe disturbances, to be distinguished from feelings of inadequacy generated by thoughts that one is not living up to the concept of gender role behavior (behaving like a man or like a woman). Some feelings of inadequacy about masculinity and femininity are ubiquitous in childhood and adolescence, and remnants of these doubts are found in almost every adult.

Transsexualism is an overriding feeling "of discomfort with one's anatomic sex and a constant desire to be rid of one's genitals and become a member of the opposite sex. The diagnosis is made only if the disturbance has been continuous (not limited to periods of stress) for at least two years; is not symptomatic of another mental disorder, such as schizophrenia; and is not associated with physical intersex or genetic abnormality."[1] The differential diagnosis must be made among true transsexualism, transvestism, cross-dressing and homosexuality. For a more detailed discussion, see Chapter 19.

Gender identity disorders of childhood and other gender identity disorders of adolescence or adult life are discussed in detail in Chapter 18.

PARAPHILIAS

In the paraphilias there is a pattern of erotic arousal that differs from the standard pattern. There may be associated anxiety of varying degrees when there is an attempt to engage in the standard pattern.

The essential features of this group of conditions are persistent and repetitive sexually arousing fantasies, frequently of an unusual nature. They are associated with either "(1) preference for use of a nonhuman object for sexual arousal; (2) repetitive sexual activity with humans involving real or simulated suffering or humiliation; or (3) repetitive sexual activity with nonconsenting partners."[1] Paraphilias, as defined here, represent gross impairment of the capacity for affectionate sexual activity between adult human partners. These disorders are far more common in males than in females.

Fetishism is the preference for nonliving objects as the exclusive means of attaining sexual excitement. The fetishist prefers the fetish rather than the human being associated with it. Such behavior is "safe" in that it avoids the dangers of a real human experience. Not all fetishists require the fetish for gratification, but without it sexual excitement tends to be much less intense. The most common fetish is an article of clothing. Minor fetishistic behavior should not be considered aberrant; however, when the fetishistic behavior becomes acute, relationship problems occur and normal sexual relations tend to be avoided. There is evidence that in some fetishists a biogenic factor is present, namely, abnormal electrical activity in the temporal lobes indicative of temporal lobe epilepsy.[5]

Transvestism is cross-dressing to achieve sexual stimulation. Many transvestites are able to have a reasonably happy sexual relationship if their partner is cooperative. Cross-dressing may become a prominent theme of sexual interaction. Couple-conflict, however, produces anxiety, depression, guilt and shame. Transvestism may be accompanied by other paraphilias, most frequently fetishism.

Zoophilia is an extremely rare disorder in which sexual excitement is produced by the act or fantasy of engaging in sexual activity with animals. Animals are the preferred form of sexual outlet, even when other forms are available.

Pedophilia is a preference for repetitive sexual activity with prepubertal children. Twice as many pedophiles prefer opposite-sex children. Heterosexually oriented males prefer 8- to 10-year-old girls. Homosexually oriented males prefer a partner 10 to 13 years of age. Adults who have no sexual preference choose children under age 8. According to Mohr and co-workers,[6] incestuous pedophilia is found in only 15 per cent of cases. On the other hand, the victim is a total stranger to the pedophile in only 10 per cent of the cases. While in general the pedophiles are males, it is well known that there are women who have sexual relations with young boys. However, they are almost never charged with the crime of pedophilia. Mothers are occasionally involved in incest with their preadolescent daughters, as well as sons.

Exhibitionism is the repeated exposure of one's genitals to an unsuspecting stranger for the purpose of producing sexual excitement. This excitement may be enhanced by the shock reaction produced in the victim. Sexual excitement does not always occur, even though it is the purpose of the act. The victim is usually a female, and rarely is further sexual contact sought unless the exhibitionism is combined with another paraphilia. Only a few cases of female exhibitionism have been reported.[7] Most exhibitionists are married, although they may have performance problems in heterosexual relations.

Voyeurism is the repetitive act of looking, so as to become sexually aroused, at an unsuspecting person (usually a woman) who is in the process of disrobing, who is naked or who is engaging in sexual activity. Orgasm, usually produced by masturbation, may occur during the voyeuristic activity. Ordinarily, voyeurism involves clandestine "peeping"; however, it occasionally occurs with the consent of the participants. Voyeurism is not to be confused with normal curiosity between two persons who know one another.

Sexual masochism is intentional participation in an activity in which the individual is physically harmed or his life is threatened in order to produce sexual excitement, or when the preferred or exclusive mode of experiencing sexual excitement is to be humiliated, bound, beaten or otherwise made to suffer. Masochistic fantasy without masochistic behavior is an insufficient basis for the diagnosis of sexual masochism.

Sexual sadism is a method of stimulating sexual excitement and orgasm by inflicting physical or psychological suffering on the sexual partner. Generally there are insistent and persistent fantasies in which sexual excitement is produced as a result of suffering inflicted on the partner; however, fantasy alone, without behavior, is an insufficient basis for the diagnosis. Sadism is not to be confused with minor forms of aggression in normal sexual activity. The extreme forms of sadism include lust-murder, rape and torture.

Other Paraphilias. This category includes rare types of nonstandard sexual behavior, such as coprophilia (the love of feces), frotteurism (sexual excitement produced by rubbing against an unsuspecting stranger), klismaphilia (autoeroticism produced by a self-administered enema), mysophilia (sexual excitement created by filthy surroundings), necrophilia (sexual excitement produced by sexual activity with a corpse), telephone scatologia (obscene telephone calls) and urophilia (sexual excitement produced by urinating on a victim). Of these, the most common in contemporary society is the obscene telephone call. In this condition, in the safety of his own home, a person calls a woman whom he generally has seen at a distance or perhaps knows only slightly and, while making lewd remarks, masturbates.

Many of the bizarre paraphilias can be enacted in special houses of prostitution. In this way, these houses of prostitution may be serving a unique social function by preventing the victimization of innocent people.

The treatment for paraphilias is considered in Chapter 19. Although primary care physicians should be able to recognize these sexual disorders, referral to a psychiatrist is indicated in most instances.

PSYCHOSEXUAL DYSFUNCTIONS

The previous sections have dealt primarily with disturbances of core gender identity, gender identity, and patterns of erotic arousal, whereas the strength of desire and the capacity for sexual excitement, for orgasm and for sexual pleasure are the dimensions disturbed in the sexual dysfunctions. Freud[4] put it so well that it bears repeating:

"The execution of the sex act presupposes a very complicated sequence of events, any one of which may be the locus of disturbance. The principal loci of inhibition in men are the following: a turning aside of the libido at the initiation of the act (psychic unpleasure), absence of physical preparedness (nonerectability), abbreviation of the act (ejaculatio praecox), which may equally well be described as a positive symptom, suspension of the act before its natural culmination (absence of ejaculation), the nonoccurrence of the psychic effect (of the pleasure sensation of orgasm)."

Masters and Johnson's pioneering physiological research[8] led to a two-phase approach to sexual dysfunctions, namely, disorders of excitement and of orgasm.[9] To this must be added a third phase—that of desire. In addition, excitement has two components—one psychological (arousal), the other physiological (vasocongestion) —which may become "disconnected," e.g., a man may feel intensely aroused and have a limp penis or he may be only partially aroused even while having an erection. The excitement phase, therefore, must be subdivided. It is also possible for a person to go through the entire sexual response cycle with his or her physiological responses being unimpaired and yet feel little pleasure or satisfaction. For this reason the dysfunctions will be summarized on the basis of the acronym, *DAVOS*. In the acronym, *D* stands for desire, *A* for arousal, *V* for vasocongestion, *O* for orgasm, *S* for satisfaction. Anxiety can lead to an inhibition of desire of arousal, which is the psychic equivalent of the physiological vasocongestive response involved in sexual excitement, of excitement itself, of orgasm or of satisfaction. The three-phase response of desire, excitement and orgasm developed for purposes of therapy by Kaplan[10] thus has been expanded into a five-phase response cycle, suggested by Zilbergeld and Ellison.[11]

Inhibited Sexual Desire. Until recently, sex research has overlooked a stage of readiness which Rado[12] called the "sexual motive state," in which erotic thoughts and feelings create a sexual appetite or drive. This state of readiness, or preparation for sexual activity, is a function of the central nervous system, while excitement and orgasm involve the genital organs as well. Since in general the brain is organized for both facilitation and inhibition, it is likely that the centers subsuming sexual interest also have facilitative and inhibitor mechanisms. Direct evidence for this hypothesis has been found in many species. "In the adult the steroid hormones . . . activate, modulate, or inhibit the function of existing neural circuits."[13]

In man, indirect evidence suggests similar mechanisms. Neurotransmitters are involved in facilitation and inhibition. Psychoactive drugs as well as centrally acting antihypertensives may depress sexual desire. Of the sex hormones, testosterone seems to be the most significant hormone affecting sexual interest or libido.[14]

In the inhibition of sexual desire, the readiness to seek out, or at least to be receptive to, sexual cues is decreased or absent. The DSM-III[1] describes it as follows:

"Persistent and pervasive inhibition of sexual desire. The judgment of inhibition is made by the clinician's taking into account factors that affect sexual desire, such as age, sex, health, intensity and frequency of sexual desire, and the context of the individual's life. In actual practice this diagnosis will rarely be used unless the lack of desire is a source of distress to either the individual or his or her partner. Frequently, this category will be used with one or more of the other dysfunction categories."

Inhibited Sexual Excitement. Referring back to the acronym, *DAVOS*, excitement consists of two aspects: psychological and physiological. As the vasocongestive response to sexual stimuli continues, a person becomes aware of his erotic reactions; presumably, via positive feedback, this awareness augments the physiological response. Normally, awareness and vasocongestion are synergistic.

This conscious awareness is what is labeled *arousal*. In some people (the percentage is not known), excitement is not inhibited, but the conscious awareness of the vasocongestive process is, leading to an inhibition of arousal. According to Heiman,[15] more women than men demonstrate this dysfunction. She speculates that the positive feedback of penile erection is an important cue to men, a cue obviously not available to women, who, because of faulty learning and anxiety, are more likely than men to fail to identify or to mislabel bodily sensations.

Ordinarily, inhibition of the vasocongestive process (physiological excitement) is far more common and may occur despite intense arousal. The diagnosis is based on recurrent and persistent inhibition of sexual excitement during sexual activity manifested either by partial or complete failure to attain or maintain erection until completion of the sexual act, or by partial or complete failure to attain or maintain the lubrication- swelling response of sexual excitement until completion of the sexual act. Of course, the physician must ascertain that the individual has engaged in sexual activity that is adequate in focus, intensity and duration. In other words, the physician cannot make the diagnosis in the absence of sufficient sexual stimulation. Here he must use his judgment because of the varying capacity of people, still within normal limits, to respond to sexual stimulation.

Inhibited Female Orgasm. If the clinician judges that there has been adequate sexual stimulation and the female still has a recurrent and persistent inhibition of orgasm, she meets the criteria for this diagnosis. In many instances there is also inhibition of sexual excitement; the inhibition of orgasm is a natural consequence of the inhibition of excitement. However, there are many women who have no inhibition of excitement but are anorgasmic or, to use a more hopeful word, *preorgasmic*.[16] There are varying degrees of preorgasmia: the woman who is not able to attain an orgasm with self-stimulation; the woman who can masturbate to orgasm but is unable to attain an orgasm with a partner despite adequate clitoral stimulation by the partner; the woman who can have an orgasm with reasonable frequency during foreplay but cannot have one during coitus.

The absence of coital orgasm is not necessarily pathological. In some instances this represents a normal variation. Our best estimate is that the majority of women do not have orgasm with regularity during coitus. To determine whether this is a normal variation or whether it represents a pathological inhibition sometimes requires a very thorough appraisal.

Inhibited Male Orgasm. This is usually called *retarded ejaculation*, and occasionally *ejaculatory incompetence*. In this condition there is a delay or absence of either the emission or ejaculation phases, usually both, following adequate sexual excitement. Most commonly there is an inability to ejaculate during intromission, although sometimes the inhibition occurs with masturbation as well.

Premature Ejaculation. This diagnosis is a relative one because it is difficult for diagnostic purposes to use the dimension of time alone. If the man almost always ejaculates prior to intromission, there is no doubt about the diagnosis. If ejaculation occurs soon after intromission, the diagnosis becomes dependent on whether the partner is able to have enough stimulation to achieve an orgasm. Kinsey[17] demonstrated that the average male takes only one and one-half minutes after intromission to ejaculate. Therefore, the diagnosis depends upon the distress of the patient or the partner, and the clinician's judgment of whether the patient has "reasonable control." This takes into account factors such as age and frequency of coitus that affect duration of sexual excitement or, what Masters and Johnson termed, the "plateau" phase.[9]

Dyspareunia. A recurrent pattern of genital pain during or immediately after coitus is the basis for the diagnosis of dyspareunia. This condition is rarely seen in men. Although the most common cause in women is inadequate lubrication, a detailed history and a pelvic examination are necessary to check for a wide variety of physical disorders frequently responsible for dyspareunia. Some examples of these disorders are pelvic adhesions, endometriosis and atrophic vaginitis. The type and site of vaginal pain may indicate the etiology. If vaginismus is the cause of dyspareunia, the primary diagnosis is *vaginismus*.

Vaginismus. The history of recurrent and persistent involuntary spasm of the perivaginal muscles, especially those of the outer third, leads to the diagnosis of vaginismus. The majority of cases are psychogenic. Even if an initial biogenic factor is no longer present, the memory of painful coital attempts may lead to involuntary perivaginal spasm. If vaginismus has been present from the beginning of the marriage, the marriage is usually "unconsummated."

Atypical Psychosexual Dysfunction. This category is for sexual dysfunctions not classifiable by another diagnosis. Examples are genital anesthesia and the female equivalent of premature ejaculation.

OTHER PSYCHOSEXUAL DISORDERS

Ego-Dystonic Homosexuality. This diagnosis is made when a homosexual patient claims distress over homosexual relationships, or over persistent homosexual fantasies and a sustained pattern of overt homosexual arousal, and wishes to become heterosexually oriented. This condition is described in detail in Chapter 20.

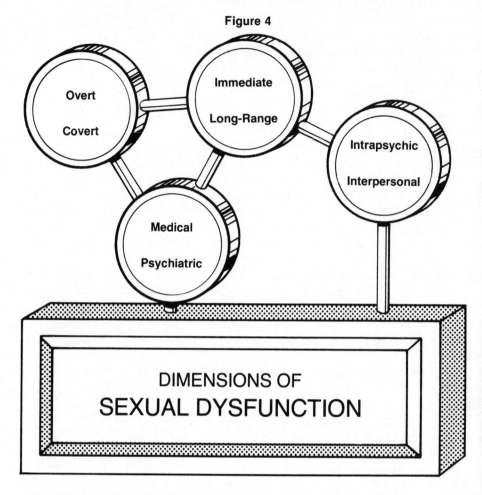

Figure 4

Overt
Covert

Immediate
Long-Range

Intrapsychic
Interpersonal

Medical
Psychiatric

DIMENSIONS OF
SEXUAL DYSFUNCTION

Psychosexual Disorders Not Elsewhere Classified. If an adequate label is not applicable, this category is a convenient catch-all. Examples are the absence of satisfaction despite adequate desire, excitement and orgasm and "Don Juanism," or repeated sexual encounters aimed at inflating a man's pride, wherein the conquest rather than the partner is the dominant theme. Another example is lowered self-esteem and the avoidance of sex because of a negative body image after mastectomy.

Sexual Aversion. This diagnosis is not listed under the Psychosexual Disorders in *DSM-III*, since it is regarded primarily as a phobic disorder. However, it must be included in our classification. Masters and Johnson[3] diagnosed 116 cases of sexual aversion between 1972 and 1977 at the Masters and Johnson Institute. The diagnosis is made only if there is a consistent phobic component, usually manifested by "irrational, overwhelming anxiety at the thought of sexual contact." The anticipatory anxiety is extreme, so much so that some persons with the syndrome find it easier to have sexual intercourse than to undress and touch their sexual partner.

DIMENSIONS OF SEXUAL DYSFUNCTION

Figure 4 demonstrates that sexual dysfunctions may be overt or covert, lifelong or immediate, intrapsychic or interpersonal, and some of them may be traced to significant medical or psychiatric factors. In addition, the dysfunctions may be generalized or situational.

Overt Sexual Disorders. "Overt" may refer to (1) patient's knowledge, (2) presenting complaint, or (3) revelation of the sexual disorder in the course of history-taking in which the presenting complaint was nonsexual. Overt disorders may thus be shared at once ("open") or shared somewhat later ("secret") after the patient feels more at ease with the physician.

The most overt situation occurs when the patient is fully aware of the sexual disorder, viz., impotence, and presents it as his chief complaint. The sexual disorder is less overt when the patient, although fully aware of it, seeks help for another real or imaginary condition. For example, a patient may complain of depression but will reveal his impotence during the course of the interview. On occasion the disorder is fully known to the patient, but he denies its importance. Denial as a defense mechanism may cause the patient to withhold information or to make light of it. A patient with retarded ejaculation, for example, asked, "Why is my wife complaining? She should love it if I can keep going for more than half an hour." He was trying to cover up his own anxiety as well as his wife's justified feeling that her husband was not "giving" to her emotionally as well as sexually.

When the symptom or syndrome is overt, the physician's task is somewhat easier because he does not have to overcome the patient's resistance in order to (a) uncover the connection between the presenting complaint and the underlying sexual disorder, and (b) point out the connections to the patient.

Covert Sexual Disorders. A "covert" sexual disorder is one in which the disorder is not connected in the patient's mind with other symptoms he presents. Symptoms may include fatigue, headache, backache, gastrointestinal disturbances, menstrual irregularities or dysmenorrhea. Osler said of syphilis that it was "the great imitator" of other disease states. Today it may be said more accurately that sexual dissatisfaction plays that role. Identifying and labeling the unconscious connection between symptom and sexual frustration becomes the task of the therapist.

Lifelong and Acquired Sexual Disorders. If the sexual disorder follows a period of normal functioning, it is said to have been *acquired*. The man who develops impotence after he has been able to have satisfactory erections and coitus has "acquired" impotence or, as it is sometimes called, "secondary" impotence. If he has never had an erection sufficient for penetration, he has *lifelong* or "primary" impotence. The differentiation is important in the diagnostic evaluation of the etiology of the disorder.

Generalized and Situational Sexual Disorders. If a disorder, e.g., impotence or anorgasmia, is situational (i.e., occurring only in certain situations or only with certain partners), one can be certain that the problem is psychogenic (unless limited to association with alcohol or drugs). If the disorder occurs in all situations (i.e., is "generalized"), it may be psychogenic, biogenic or a combination of the two. The most typical situation is one in which the sexual dysfunction is restricted to the marriage. In this case the physician has to examine the nature of the marital relationship.

Intrapsychic or Interpersonal Factors. Since anxiety or other negative emotions responsible for sexual disorder or dysfunction are intrapsychic, one might say that all sexual dysfunctions have an intrapsychic component. Differentiation between *intrapsychic* and *interpersonal* in this context means that the dominant etiology can be traced to either intrapsychic or interpersonal factors. If negative associations to sex create anorgasmia in relationships prior to a woman's marriage, clearly the etiology is primarily intrapsychic. On the other hand, if there is a period of good functioning which later deteriorates because of marital conflict, the situation clearly is primarily an interpersonal one, although, as has just been stated, it has to have its intrapsychic components. These dimensions are described in other chapters.

Long-Range or Immediate Causes of Sexual Dysfunction. Causes of sexual dysfunction may be long-range, either interpersonal or intrapsychic, or immediate. *Immediate* factors refer to anxieties about performance, monitoring one's own sexual performance or "spectatoring," exquisite sensitivity to the partner's reaction, avoidance of sex, and avoidance of talking about sex. The immediate and long-range etiologic components are described in detail in subsequent chapters.

Medical and Psychiatric Causes. Some sexual dysfunctions may be attributable to physical illness, e.g., impotence stemming from diabetes. Some may be primarily due to a psychiatric disorder such as inhibition of sexual desire as a consequence of depression. These topics also will be discussed in other chapters.

Sexual disorders may be divided into three major categories: disorders of gender identity, paraphilias and dysfunctions. Because the physican sees many more patients with sexual dysfunctions than with disorders of gender identity or paraphilia, the dysfunctions have been discussed more fully in this chapter. Homosexuality is no longer considered a mental disorder unless it is "ego-dystonic," i.e., distressing to the patient. However, because it still remains of great interest and practical concern to the medical practitioner, two chapters (6 and 20) are devoted to this general subject. In addition to the more organized syndromes, advice and treatment are commonly sought by patients for other sexual concerns and difficulties. Most of them can and should be treated by the primary care physician (see Chapter 11).

References

1. American Psychiatric Association: *Diagnostic & Statistical Manual of Mental Disorders III.* Washington, American Psychiatric Association, 1980.
2. Frank E, et al: Frequency of sexual dysfunction in 'normal' couples. *N Engl J Med* 1978; 299:111-115.

3. Kolodny RC, et al: *Textbook of Sexual Medicine*. Boston, Little, Brown and Company, 1979.

4. Freud S: *Problem of Anxiety*. New York, WW Norton & Company, 1936.

5. Epstein AW: The relationship of altered brain states to sexual psychopathology, in Zubin J, Money J (eds): *Contemporary Sexual Behavior: Critical Issues in the 1970's*. Baltimore, Johns Hopkins University Press, 1973.

6. Mohr JW, et al: *Pedophilia and Exhibitionism*. Toronto, University of Toronto Press, 1964.

7. Hollender MH, et al: Genital exhibitionism in women. *Am J Psychiatry* 1977; 134:436-438.

8. Masters WH, Johnson VE: *Human Sexual Response*. Boston, Little, Brown and Company, 1966.

9. Masters WH, Johnson VE: *Human Sexual Inadequacy*. Boston, Little, Brown and Company, 1970.

10. Kaplan HS: *Disorders of Sexual Desire*. New York, Brunner/Mazel Inc, 1979.

11. Zilbergeld B, Ellison CR: Desire discrepancies and arousal problems in sex therapy, in Leiblum SR, Pervin LA (eds): *Principles and Practice of Sex Therapy*. New York, Guilford Press, 1980.

12. Rado S: An adaptational view of sexual behavior, in Rado S (ed): *Psychoanalysis of Behavior*. New York, Grune & Stratton Inc, 1956.

13. Gorski RA: Sexual differentiation of the brain, in Krieger DT, Hughes JC (eds): *Neuroendocrinology*. Sunderland, Mass, Sinauer Assoc, 1980.

14. Persky H, et al: Plasma testosterone level and sexual behavior of couples. *Arch Sex Behav* 1978; 7:157-173.

15. Heiman JR: A psychophysiological exploration of sexual arousal patterns in females and males. *Psychophysiology* 1977; 14:266-274.

16. Barbach L: *Women Discover Orgasms: A Therapist's Guide to a New Treatment Approach*. New York, Free Press, 1980.

17. Kinsey A, et al: *Sexual Behavior in the Human Male*. Philadelphia, WB Saunders Company, 1948.

Chapter 8

The Physician's Role in Practice and in the Community

Harold I. Lief, M.D.

ROLE IN PRACTICE

Physicians are being consulted more and more for help with sexual problems. The need for help always has been there, but it was often hidden from view. From surveys made in the 1950's to "hotline" data gathered in the 1970's, we have long known that people are troubled in their marital and family relationships more than by other aspects of life, such as work, money, recreation, or even problems with alcohol or drugs.[1] We also know that in three of four instances of significant marital disharmony, there is a sexual problem. Even in "happy" marriages, sexual problems are frequent.[2] With the increased freedom to speak openly about sexual matters and greater public awareness of resources for treatment of sexual problems, the frank demand for treatment increases. In fact, it is fair to say that there is often, if not usually, less embarrassment on the part of the patient than on the part of the physician.

Now that sex is no longer a taboo topic, every imaginable difficulty about sexuality is being brought by patients to the physician's office—questions about sex education, masturbation, homosexuality, sexual functioning, and, most often, problems of sexual inadequacy and sexual incompatibility. More and more persons now take for granted that their physicians and other health professionals will be willing and able to help them with such problems. The success in treating sexual dysfunctions reported by Masters and Johnson[3] and others[4] has become general knowledge, and it has swelled the call for services. Patients used to be ashamed and anxious (and many still are) because it was a blow to their pride to acknowledge a sexual problem or anything that might be construed as sexual ignorance or inadequacy. The physician was ashamed and anxious because the sexual feelings and behaviors were so highly charged emotionally that they touched unexplored, sensitive aspects of the physician's own life; sexual inquiry also might have seemed to be an intrusion into forbidden territory in the patient's life.

Many physicians also frankly admit that their hesitancy has been compounded by their feelings of unfamiliarity. They are not sure how to inquire about sexual matters, nor what to do with the responses. This doubt creates a sense of incompetence and it increases their discomfort in approaching the subject. Much remains to be done both in medical schools and in training programs for physicians in primary care specialties (general practice, family practice, general pediatrics, internal medicine, and obstetrics/ gynecology).[5]

Scully[6] interviewed residents in obstetrics/gynecology and concluded that most of them were unqualified to give sexual counseling and that their lack of knowledge (and the nontherapeutic attitudes of many) affected their diagnostic ability. Moreover, because, as is finally being recognized, the chronically ill, the physically disabled, and occasionally even the terminal patient may require sexual counseling, such patients often arouse strong emotions in the physician; adding the emotionally charged subject of sex makes the situation doubly difficult.

Usually a person who has questions or problems about sex consults the physician he sees and trusts most, *provided the patient believes that the physician is comfortable in talking about sexual matters*. Because these sexual issues are complex and involve many disciplines, the physician needs direction in finding the therapeutic level at which he can best function to evaluate and meet his patients' needs. The following section of this chapter is designed to provide direction of this kind.

Physicians differ in their interests in sexuality and their ability to deal with it in patients. All physicians cannot become sex therapists, but they can gain minimum competence for discovering and identifying sexual problems and referring patients effectively. The interests, knowledge, skills and experience of each physician should determine how much more than that he may or may not be able and willing to do.

Establishing Therapeutic Roles and Tasks

Six levels at which the physician carries out therapeutic roles and tasks with a patient who has sexual concerns can be identified (see Table 2).[3] At the first level, the physician is an evaluator and inquirer. To these roles are successively added those of sex educator, counselor, marital therapist, psychotherapist, and sex therapist.

Evaluator and Inquirer. Whatever their level of competence, all physicians must learn how to inquire and evaluate. In this role, the physician must be comfortable with sexual topics and should put the patient at ease, listen well, show active interest and concern for the patient's feelings, and do nothing to increase shame and embarrassment; the physician also must know how to take a sexual history. The first step is almost always, by asking a few open-ended questions (see Chapter 10), to learn whether the patient has sexual concerns and, if there are any, to give reassurance that these concerns are being listened to, taken seriously, and are not reacted to with discomfort.

For many physicians, routinely asking a few questions about sexual matters is the most unfamiliar and difficult step. Usually a few open-ended questions about specific sexual functions and satisfaction will elicit uncertainties and other problems that exist. A physician can ask how often, or under what circumstances, the patient experiences erectile problems, arousal, orgasm, or sexual or marital conflict. The questions should allow for more than a yes or no answer. It is often useful to ask what the patient likes most or least about sex. The physician's willingness to speak directly about sex gives the patient permission to do so as well.

Table 2
Management of Sexual Problems

Evaluation of Sex Problem Level	Patient (Client) Need	Therapeutic Tasks	Therapeutic Roles
1. Unknown	To be understood	Active (creative) listening (i.e., understand and evaluate).	Evaluator-inquirer
2. Sexual ignorance	Sexual knowledge	Provide accurate information and suggest specific sexual behavior. Follow-up.	Sex educator
3. Sex discomfort/ dysfunction	Comfortable sexual functioning	If physician treats organic factors, reduce or remove discomfort/ dysfunction; make time-limited contract; suggest specific sexual behavior. Follow-up.	Sex counselor; refer to helpful professional if own intervention is insufficient.
4. Interpersonal conflict and sex problem	Assistance with conflict leading to sexual dysfunction	Review, direct, and restore bonding; make contract; suggest specific sexual behavior. Follow-up.	Marital therapist; refer if indicated.
5. Sex problem and intrapsychic conflict	Explore internal conflicts and related interpersonal conflicts	Correlate internal conflicts with sex problem for perspective and resolution.	Psychotherapist
6. All of above	Comfortable use of newly learned sex knowledge, attitudes, and skills	Recognize *hierarchy* of patient needs in rational brief treatment.	Sex therapist

After asking questions, the physician must judge whether any sexual problems uncovered in history taking are within his or her competence. If they are, a plan of treatment should be set up with the patient's full knowledge and consent. If these problems are not within the physician's competence, he should acknowledge this and make a referral to a professional who does have the specialized knowledge and skills required, e.g., a sex therapist, psychiatrist, or marriage counselor, depending on the nature of the problem. Referral itself can hinder as well as help therapy; therefore, it should be made with tact and skill.

After having perceived a sexual concern, the physician should take a detailed marital and sexual (or relationship) history and perform a physical examination, including any needed laboratory tests, to determine whether there are organic or other physiologic conditions affecting sexual function (see Chapters 9 and 10). A help to the physician may be a semistructured sexual interview. (See "Evaluation of Sexual Behavior and Gratification" [Appendix I].)

Sex Educator. Because few physicians have specialized training in psychotherapy, marriage counseling, or sex therapy, the great majority of them and other health practitioners will act as educators and counselors. Some of the most common concerns expressed by patients are those having to do with contraceptives; sexually transmitted disease; their own or their children's sex education and experience; marital discord; sexual dysfunction; sexual conflicts with partners over frequency, preferences and feelings; and simply lack of information. If the problem seems to be largely sexual ignorance, the physician should provide information, make specific suggestions if necessary, and arrange for a follow-up visit. Many sexual myths (e.g., effects of aging, penis size, simultaneous orgasm) abound in our culture.[4] Ideally, every physician should be able to act as an educator as well as evaluator.

A 58-year-old woman complained to her physician that her 65-year-old husband was oversexed because he had shown no decline in his sexual interest after the age of 60. She was certain that such interest would decrease to once a month after that age. Her information was obtained from her bridge-playing friends.

A 28-year-old woman, a college graduate, was seen with the chief complaint of "I am not sure I have a clitoris." Her lawyer-husband was equally uncertain. Needless to say, the woman suffered from an inhibition of sexual excitement and had never been orgastic. Physical examination revealed a completely normal clitoris. In addition to the reassurance of anatomic normality, the examination was helpful in another way. With the aid of a hand-mirror, the patient could identify her clitoris, and her husband, who was observing the examination, was for the first time certain of its location.

Sex Counselor. Counseling requires familiarity with important facets of psychotherapy, and sex therapy, but not the extensive knowledge and experience that ensure competence to deal with almost all kinds of sexual problems. Counseling includes (1) increasing the communication between partners, (2) decreasing the anxiety over sexual performance, (3) decreasing the self-monitoring ("spectatoring") of the dysfunctional partner, (4) a step-wise approach to the restructuring of the sexual experience, the sensate focus pleasuring exercises pioneered by Masters and Johnson,[5] and (5) the treatment of premature ejaculation with the "stop-start" method of behavior therapy.

A couple was referred by the Fertility Clinic because the husband, a 34-year-old business man, had retarded ejaculation. History revealed that the symptom had started seven years earlier at a time when the husband had left a salaried position and had started a business of his own. He was dependent on his wife's earnings as a school teacher and was afraid that if she became pregnant he would not be able to maintain his newly begun business. The retarded ejaculation was his unconscious way of assuring himself that his wife would not become pregnant. Behavior therapy removed the symptom, and his wife became pregnant and delivered uneventfully.

In using such techniques, the counselor must be alert to the defenses and to the sabotage of treatment some couples use to maintain the destructive homeostatic patterns that they have developed over the years, even though they pay a price in loss of love, self-love and pleasure. In fact, some sex problems themselves are such defenses. Despite this warning, it must be recognized that some couples have relatively compartmentalized problems that yield to counseling without any need for the physician to deal with the nuances of intrapsychic or interpersonal forces.

Usually considerable skill is required to judge whether a particular situation will be helped by counseling or whether it requires the psychotherapeutic skills associated with sex therapy. A good rule of thumb is for the counselor to develop a limited "contract" or agreement with the patient or couple. If counseling does not progress in the ways hoped for at the beginning of treatment—for example, after about six sessions—the counselor should seriously consider referral.

A 56-year-old man, impotent after a prostatectomy, was asked by the physician to bring his wife for the initial consultation. The patient stated that in the hospital he had heard that a man becomes impotent after such an operation. He was vague about the source of this misinformation; in any case, his sexual concerns and accompanying anxiety had never been discussed by any of his attending physicians or, if they had, he couldn't remember it. His anxiety was reinforced by his retrograde ejaculation, which he had never understood. He had the usual performance anxiety and self-monitoring or "spectatoring" and a marked concern about his wife's sexual satisfaction. The patient, however, reported that he had good morning erections, but attributed these to a full bladder rather than to a normal sexual reflex-response. His wife confirmed the presence of morning erections and also reassured him about her satisfaction, because she was easily orgastic with clitoral stimulation. For this man, however, the only normal or "natural" form of sex was intercourse. A combination of sensate-focus exercises and education, explaining the mechanism of retrograde ejaculation, the reflex nature of erections, and techniques to reduce spectatoring, all in conjoint sessions with a very supportive wife, was successful in overcoming his sexual problem in only five sessions.

As a counselor, the physician must deal with a host of medical situations with sexual connotations. Obvious examples are the diabetic patient with impotence, the postcoronary patient, the woman concerned about her sexual capacity and functioning after hysterectomy, the patient worried about attractiveness after mastectomy or colostomy, and the physically disabled patient (see Chapters 14 and 15).

Marital Therapist. When sexual problems are a consequence of disorders that are primarily marital, patients can be referred to marital therapists. The physician who is not trained specifically in such skills should make referrals, although physicians who are interested in augmenting their skills should see the couple together for at least several sessions.

A 48-year-old man was impotent with his wife, although he performed satisfactorily on the rare occasions when he had intercourse with other women. His wife was sharply critical of his sexual techniques and demeaned him at almost every opportunity. In a separate session with the wife, the physician learned that she had a long-standing extramarital liaison with a "marvelous lover." It became clear that she had to keep her husband sexually inadequate in order to justify her affair. The physician referred the couple to a marital therapist.

Psychotherapist. The psychotherapist deals with the intrapsychic aspects of marital and sexual problems, although there is always an interaction between intrapsychic and interpersonal dimensions. Most psychotherapists are either psychiatrists or clinical psychologists. Intrapsychic problems are often recognized because they are lifelong (existed before marriage), generalized (exist with all partners or a certain class of partners), can be traced to events or relationships in early life, and often involve symptoms other than marital conflict (e.g., phobias, overanxiety, rituals). Early life events may be traumatic, as in the case of incest (real or fantasied) or rape. But very often symptoms are a consequence of guilt inculcated by religious orthodoxy or the failure to live up to the rigid expectations of parents or parent surrogates. Guilt over the excessive attachment to the parent of the opposite sex (the "Oedipus complex") is a frequent finding.

Sex Therapist. A sex therapist is defined as one who has had specialized training beyond basic professional education, at least 200 hours of supervision in sex therapy, and at least 500 hours of clinical work in an approved training program. Sex therapy is a form of psychotherapy that encompasses skills in both individual and marital therapy. There are few formal sex therapy training programs, and the number of trainees is much smaller than the need for therapists. Most competent therapists have learned their skills in apprentice fashion, taking care to gain as much as possible from skilled supervisors. They have had a major commitment to sex therapy as a specialty. The physician who wants to make the commitment to learn sex therapy and to give it a substantial part of his professional time can contribute a great deal to the health needs of his community (see Chapter 26). The zealous dilettante, on the other hand, will do little but use time and money inefficiently to the patient's detriment and his own dissatisfaction.

Physician-Patient Interaction

Each physician should find his optimal level of involvement in sexual health by honestly analyzing his own personal comfort, professional interest, knowledge of sexual matters, therapeutic skills, and priorities in using professional time. The physician who finds it difficult to avoid a morally judgmental attitude about certain sexual behaviors should know that this attitude is never appropriate at any therapeutic level; too often patients sense such attitudes, despite attempts by the physician to conceal them. If a physician finds that his attitude is counterproductive, he should inform patients who have sexual concerns that, although such concerns are valid, they are not matters about which he can be helpful, and he should then make a referral. This procedure prevents conflict within the physician, resistance and disappointment on the part of the patient, and disruption of rapport between the physician and patient.

A gynecologist realized that he did not condone premarital intercourse, and because of his attitude could not provide contraceptive counseling to teenagers, even for those with a history of pregnancy. He also recognized that contraceptives were hardly likely to promote sexual activity in already sexually active young women. Despite this knowl-

104

edge, his moral stance made it necessary for him to refer sexually active teenagers to colleagues who did not have his moral strictures. Thus he provided much better care than he would have if he had felt impelled to deliver a sermon to his young patients.

The physician-patient interaction needs constant re-evaluation. Some physicians can counsel adults very well but are not effective with teenagers or the elderly. The gender of the physician and the patient is not usually important, but in some cases it may be (see Chapter 10). Social class and educational differences can impair therapeutic effectiveness through differences in language, attitudes, life experiences, and practical options. Indigent patients may be unable to obtain child care, or cannot come for visits during regular office hours for fear of losing their jobs, or may be unable to buy books and therapy aids. One must be aware of, and find ways of working with, such limitations. Ethnic and racial differences may present problems. Patients who speak little English usually do not do well in therapy unless it is carried on in their native tongue by someone who shares their background. Their sexual mores, roles and expectations may differ greatly from those of the physician.

In sex evaluation, counseling and therapy, the risk of irrational reactions by both the physician and patient is greater than in most areas of medical care. Elements of transference and countertransference may appear and may be different for each patient. (These are irrational reactions to another person based on partial identification of that person with someone else, often a parent, who has had an important influence in shaping one's life. Transference is the irrational reaction of the patient to the physician; countertransference is the irrational reaction of the physician to the patient.)

Personality conflicts and nontherapeutic attachments sometimes occur. It is not unusual for a physician to be attracted to a patient and even have some degree of erotic arousal. Medical students are frequently flustered when experiencing such feelings and sensations, especially for the first time. It would be of great help to them if they could realize that their reactions are not at all unique. Although a physician may not have control over his feelings, he does have control over his behavior. There is no valid professional reason for amatory contact between the therapist and the patient; however, surveys indicate that approximately 10 per cent of physicians report such sexual contact.[7] There is a gray area, of course, where an affectionate touch or even an embrace may be misinterpreted by the patient. Malpractice suits based on such misinterpretations have occurred. The physician must guard against these forms of behavior, especially with emotionally disturbed patients, while at the same time recognizing that a cold and detached demeanor that serves as a protective device against emotional involvement with patients may seriously impair therapy.

If the physician believes that a sexual involvement is possible, or if he does not know how to manage a particularly seductive patient, referral is in order. It is the physician's responsibility to make referrals in a scrupulously ethical and professional way. Where no acceptable facilities exist, the physician may have a stronger obligation, morally at least, to try to help the patient by his own efforts.

Referrals. Referring patients requires knowledge of the resources in one's community. It is difficult to evaluate the skill and experience of other professionals, and it must be remembered that some of the best counselors and therapists are not physicians. However, not all sex therapists are competent. The referring physician must evaluate their ethics, treatment formats and professional credentials. A person qualified as a professional may not truly be qualified as a sex therapist, despite claims that he is. It helps to know something of the history of previous referrals to the sex therapist, to obtain the opinion of colleagues, and to know of papers published or presented by the specialist.

The physician also should have full knowledge of the facility to which he is referring his patient (i.e., the kind of services it offers, if it does follow-ups, the treatment costs, whether it is affiliated with a reputable medical facility, whether its location is convenient for the patient, the degree of communication possible between the clinic and the referring physician). Directories[8] listing centers that offer marital, family and sex therapy, as well as training resources, may provide some information for referrals, but these lists require continuous updating. The responsibilities of the physician in relation to sex therapy clinics have been helpfully delineated in a report by the AMA House of Delegates in December, 1977 (see Appendix II).

Continuing Education

Physicians also can learn about the latest developments in both sex education and sex therapy through publications of the Sex Information and Education Council of the United States (SIECUS) and through conferences, symposia and courses sponsored by various organizations and institutions. The "SIECUS Report," published six times a year, lists workshops in sex education held throughout the country, and is a valuable resource for learning about recent publications in the field and about studies of sex education.

The American Association of Sex Educators, Counselors, and Therapists (AASECT) sponsors sex education workshops of its own and through its journal, the *Journal of Sex Education and Therapy*. This publication also helps to keep the sex educator up to date. A physician who wishes to develop expertise in sex education should contact both organizations.

There are opportunities for the physician to acquire additional training in sex therapy; e.g., the *Journal of the American Medical Association* annually publishes a special issue on continuing education courses. Courses on sex therapy are listed under the subject heading "Psychiatry". Workshops are often part of a medical specialty's annual meeting agenda. A new video clinic has been developed on sexual dysfunction for instructive viewing in the hospital or in the physician's office or home. It is available from the American Medical Association.

University-affiliated courses include the following: The Human Sexuality Program of the University of California-San Francisco offers several continuing education courses for the practicing professional. The University of Pennsylvania program at the Marriage Council of Philadelphia conducts a full-time 11-month training program on marital and sex education, therapy and research; two positions are available for nonpsychiatric physicians each year. The University of Minnesota Medical School offers a comprehensive 12-week program on sexual health care for practicing physicians and residents. A two-week program is available each summer at Indiana University's Institute of Sex Research.[8]

The aforementioned are only some of the sources and programs available to the physician; however, it should be noted that legitimate and comprehensive educational programs in sex therapy are not prevalent. Some medical schools have developed excellent curriculum courses for the student and resident, but these courses, unfortunately, are the exception rather than the norm.

The vast number of problems involving sexual function increase the demand for services, and patients' higher expectations of the health practitioner's ability to handle sexual problems create a situation for which the physician should determine and use his highest possible level of competence in managing sexual problems. The practitioner must learn the basic skills of evaluation, education and counseling or else neglect an increasingly important aspect of practice. Recognizing the etiology and complexity of a patient's problem can help the physician to decide whether or how to treat a problem or refer the patient to a specialist. In this process, the evaluation of sexual problems and the determination of therapeutic roles and tasks are inseparable.

ROLE IN THE COMMUNITY

In addition to the roles of educator and counselor for his patients and with parents of younger children and adolescents, the interested physician can play a role in community sex education. If it is true that much sexual dysfunction and unhappiness can be *prevented* as well as cured or ameliorated, the key to prevention is in sex education in the home, school, church and college. Yet it is difficult to prove that sex education prevents sexual disorders, including dysfunctions, for two reasons: (1) the complexity of psychosexual development and behavior, and (2) the failure to agree on standards for adequate sex education, especially in schools.

The complexity is exemplified by the description of five components of psychosexual dysfunction: (1) disturbances of the physiologic response cycle; (2) disturbances of the perceptual component, e.g., through anesthesia; (3) disturbances of subjective satisfaction; (4) distress associated with sexual myths and ignorance; and (5) sociosexual relationship distress.[9] It is possible, for example, for a person to have no physiological disturbance and yet be dissatisfied with sex, even to the point of anhedonia (absence of pleasure). Because the natural history (precursors, onset and development without intervention) of the sexual dysfunctions is not well known,[10] the best time for preventive intervention is unclear.

Agreement on the standards for adequate sex education is a goal still to be reached. Evaluation research needs to take into account such matters as "whether the class was interesting or boring; whether the teacher was adequately trained; whether the class was a comprehensive, semester-long treatment or a single hurried lecture; whether students were stimulated to think about how they communicate with their partners about sex; or whether only the 'facts' were presented."[11] Evaluation research should lead to a clearer understanding of the relevant factors. Increased understanding should lead to a greater consensus about standards.

It is ironic that sex education in schools has been attacked because it does not accomplish much or, on the other hand, that it does too much, namely, that it allegedly promotes irresponsible sex behavior, even promiscuity. The critics in the first group usually point out that sex education fails to decrease the incidence of teen-age pregnancy or venereal disease. This goal for sex education is unrealistic because these health problems are affected by a wide variety of social factors, such as community mores, family background, peer relations, social environment and social policies.[12] Clearly, sex education is only one of the influences on sexual behavior. (For a review of research evaluating school sex education, see Scales and Gordon.[13])

Some of the salient findings in recent evaluation research are that sex education programs increase the reporting rate for sexually transmitted diseases, that these programs may be effective in reducing pregnancy rates among teenagers, and that the rate of repeated nonmarital pregnancies is markedly decreased by special programs aimed at pregnant teenagers.[14]

An Institute of Sex Research study[14] using control and experimental groups revealed that sex education made students "more permissive about kissing and hugging, but more conservative about sexual intercourse . . . more tolerant about sexual relationships . . . and less tolerant of exploitative relationships . . . more aware of ethical considerations and of the feelings of others." It also found that "sex education substantially increased knowledge of sexual anatomy and reproductive functions." The study concludes that "sex education can presumably only promote rather than assure healthy sexual attitudes and can be only one factor in a preventative approach to sexual disorders and problems."[12]

Physician as Consultant in the Community. The evidence seems to point to the usefulness of sex education. What, then, are the potential roles for an interested physician? He can be (1) a teacher of teachers; (2) a consultant to individual schools, to school systems, and to churches; (3) a guest lecturer, workshop organizer, or participant in PTAs and other lay groups; (4) a participant in radio and TV commentaries or talk shows; (5) a writer for the popular press or participant in developing audiovisual materials; and (6) a citizen-parent active in developing community organizations that promote sex education, research and treatment.

As teacher of teachers, the physician can have a greater effect in a school or school system than if he enters a classroom himself as a teacher.[15] (It is the rare physician who has the skills to be an effective teacher for school children.) Informal contact between physicians and interested teachers or school administrators is the usual process. The physician should be aware that parents may become suspicious of such efforts as a possible intrusion into an area of privacy. It is wise, then, either to have the seminars for teachers approved by the parent organization or to include some parents in the seminars with the teachers.

When the physician is acting as a consultant, he should explore the expectations and fears of the school (or church) administrators, the parents and the teachers. Based on their beliefs and the attitudes expressed, he also should respect the wishes of these segments of the community. If he is consultant to a senior high school, some interviews with student leaders also are appropriate. He should be cognizant of any anticipated community opposition and advise the administrators of ways to reassure anxious parents. He may be consulted about curriculum, format, teaching aids and teacher competence. If he himself is not competent to deal with some of these aspects, he should inform the appropriate people. Nothing is worse for a consultant than to create expectations that cannot be fulfilled.

When appearing as a participant in public discussions, the physician should make certain that he knows the audience, their level of information, and, in general, what attitudes he may expect. If he is helping to plan a program, he should determine the concerns of the audience; e.g., does the audience want to hear about sexually transmitted diseases, teenage pregnancy, or the role of sex in teenage relationships?

Some physicians have been active in promoting local groups concerned with starting or augmenting community sex education. (Examples are SIECIND and SIECONN—the Sex Information and Education Councils of Indiana and of Connecticut.) In this way, they can join groups who have similar interests and become much more influential. Opportunities of this kind are available in those states that mandate sex education, such as Hawaii, Kentucky, Maryland, Michigan, Missouri, New Jersey and North Dakota, as well as Washington, D.C. (California, incidentally, mandates sex education for all health professions.)

Additional useful information for the physician can be found in a symposium, "The Physician and Sex Education."[16] This monograph contains useful information on the techniques of effective sex education in schools, as well as on preparing the schools and parents in the community.

Sex education should promote healthy sexuality, including knowledge and information, interpersonal communication about sexuality, and discussions of sexual attitudes and values. It should not attempt to influence behavior directly, nor should the primary goal of sex education be "disaster insurance," namely, the elimination of sexually transmitted diseases or teenage pregnancy.

References

1. Gurin G, et al: *Americans View Their Mental Health*. New York, Basic Books Inc, 1960.
2. Frank E, et al: Frequency of sexual dysfunction in 'normal' couples. *N Engl J Med* 1978; 299:111-115.

3. Masters WH, Johnson VE: *Human Sexual Inadequacy*. Boston, Little, Brown and Company, 1970.
4. Kaplan HS: *The New Sex Therapy*. New York, Brunner/Mazel Inc, 1974.
5. Lief HI: Sex education in medicine: Retrospect and prospect, in Rosenzweig N, Pearsall FP (eds): *Sex Education for the Health Professional*. New York, Grune & Stratton Inc, 1978.
6. Scully D: Skill acquisition in obstetrics and gynecology: A surgical speciality, and implications for patient care. University of Illinois, Chicago Circle, 1976. (Dissertation)
7. Kardener SH, et al: A survey of physicians' attitudes and practices regarding erotic and nonerotic contact with patients. *Am J Psychiatry* 1973; 130:1077-1081.
8. Directories of the American Association of Marital and Family Therapists (AAMFT) Upland, Calif, and of the American Association of Sex Educators, Counselors, and Therapists (AASECT), Chicago.
9. Sharpe L, et al: A preliminary classification of human functional sexual disorders. *J Sex Marital Ther* 1976; 2:106-114.
10. Qualls CB: The prevention of sexual disorders: An overview, in Qualls CB, et al (eds): *The Prevention of Sexual Disorders: Issues and Approaches*. New York, Plenum Press, 1978.
11. Scales P: How we guarantee the ineffectiveness of sex education. *SIECUS Report* 1978 (March); 6:1-3.
12. Calderone MS: Is sex education preventative?, in Qualls CB, et al (eds): *The Prevention of Sexual Disorders: Issues and Approaches*. New York, Plenum Press, 1978.
13. Scales P, Gordon S: The effects of sex education: A review and critique of the literature, in Gordon S, et al (eds): *The Sexual Adolescent*. North Scituate, Mass, Duxbury Press, 1979.
14. Sarrel PM: The university hospital and the teenage unwed mother. *Am J Public Health* 1967; 57:308-313.
15. Gadpaille WJ: Sex in the schools: Your stake in the battle over sex education. *Med Economics* 1970 (January); 1-13.
16. Homel SR: The physician and sex education. *Pediatr Clin North Am* 1969 (May); 16(2):327-525.

Part II
Clinical Aspects

Disturbances in the Physician-Patient Relationship: Effects on Sexual Functioning

Daniel H. Labby, M.D.

With the exception of the minority that are based on organic disease, sexual dysfunctions may be considered to be psychologically induced maladaptive behaviors. They can, therefore, be greatly influenced by suggestion, especially from an influential authority figure in a therapeutic role. If the physician-therapist is at ease with problems of sexual health, he will have an extraordinary opportunity to be helpful, but if he is insecure with his own sexual identity, is graceless or clumsy, and particularly if he is insensitive, the dysfunction can be intensified.

The therapist's manner and his general skill with language, as well as his capacity to produce a comfortable alliance with his patient, are critical in making his efforts either therapeutic in the best sense or destructive and harmful. Moreover, what is left unsaid, undone or avoided may be as important as what is said. For example, the simple omission of the sexual history can suggest to the patient that sex is unimportant or is a part of his life that doesn't matter to the physician. The patient also may feel that the physician is unwilling to address the issue and is personally vulnerable because he is uninformed and untrained to manage such problems.

The physician not only may omit doing what is proper, but he may do what is improper and, to cover his confusion, offer misconceptions and misinformation. Or he may use unclear language, jargon, vulgarity and inappropriate humor, all of which are unprofessional and detract from the dignity of the patient's concerns. The careless use of language can easily lead the physician into many traps, such as perpetuating old myths ("You know and I know that your impotence is more likely due to your age than anything else.") or premature and empty reassurances, ("Lots of happily married women rarely or never have orgasms.")

The practitioner who seeks comfort in the use of jargon and flippant language ("How's you sex life?" "Can you do your 'homework'?" "Are you okay in the bedroom?") may get exactly what he deserves from his patient, which is an uninformative "okay." Each party thereby avoids dealing with the subject and no help is provided. Contrast this approach with a more feeling one, such as: "I would like to know everything I must understand about you to be of the most help. For example, can you help me understand something about your sex life?" or, "Are you sexually active?" and, "Are you satisfied with your sex life?" In general, it is best to avoid euphemisms such as "your intimate life," and to call sexual health exactly what it is. The physician's approach should be such as to make certain that sexual dysfunction will be neither overlooked nor exacerbated.

The physician's basic attitudes will influence his case-finding ability. A GAP report, *Assessment of Sexual Functioning*,[1] convincingly states: "The frequency with which sexual problems are identified in medical practice reflects the physician's initiative in seeking sexual information and his ease in discussing sexual material. Reports have shown that very little sexual disclosure is made by unselected patients when the physician conveys distaste for such discussion; frequency of disclosure rises when he asks questions about sex that are specifically indicated by the patient's situation; it rises significantly higher when sexual questions are routinely included in the interview by a physician who is himself undisturbed by their inclusion."

THE SEXUAL HISTORY

Taking a sexual history obviously can have a very powerful therapeutic effect in and of itself, especially if it is done skillfully. Often, this is the first opportunity for the patient to find words for his problems and share his concerns with another human being. Although the value of such ventilation is highly significant, much of the advantage understandably can be cancelled out by ineptness on the physician's part. Awkward questioning, statements that reflect the physician's moral standards, insistence on inappropriate explicit detail, and misplaced sexual curiosity on the part of the physician (whose interest may be more prurient than professional) are easily sensed by the patient and are counterproductive.

The physician also can terrorize a patient by simplistic and unrealistic instructions, such as, "Can't you go right ahead with a second erection and satisfy your partner if you ejaculate too fast?" or by demands and imperatives: "You should voluntarily be able to relax the spasm in your vagina enough to allow your husband to enter with a full erection." "If you don't take care of your impotence now, it's obvious what you can expect as you get older." Such clumsiness can perpetuate and intensify sexual distress.

Three interrelated areas have been identified as causing difficulty in the course of learning how to take a sexual history: problems arising from the physician's personal attitude, those related to lack of clinical experience and those derived from an ineffective coping strategy.

Problems Arising from a Physician's Personal Attitudes. By taking a sexual history, the physician emphasizes its legitimacy; the degree of his comfort and ease can be a powerful influence on producing comfort and ease in the patient. Good rapport is best achieved by using language in such a way that it is not sermonizing, moralizing, judgmental or biased. If there is also acceptance and understanding of sexual values that are dependent on social class attitudes, open trust and confidence can develop.

As Comfort[2] has said, "As a minimum [the physician] should be able to deal with reassurance and first-aid or first-trial experiences, and should present the face of an unembarrassed, nonjudgmental and sexually positive listener."

Very often the patient will silently appraise the doctor as a fellow human being with a sex life of his own. Each is a sexual person and either or both may become sexually aroused. In fact, there is risk at this point of seductive behavior, which can produce inappropriate professional behavior and even overt sexual expression. It is the physician's responsibility to provide and maintain a realistic and workable professional atmosphere. There is an undeniable intimate quality to sexual history-taking that is not present when questioning is focused on other organ and behavior systems.

Problems Related to Lack of Clinical Experience. The shift to taking a sexual history can occur during the course of the medical inventory. Strategies differ with the individual style of the physician. The questioning can be managed gracefully following the obstetrical, gynecological and menstrual history in women or the genitourinary history in men, and it may be introduced by an expression of concern for the patient's sexual health, as noted above.

If the patient demurs, it is best to delay taking the sexual history until a comfortable, trusting alliance has been developed. Inexperienced therapists may not appreciate the importance of allowing sufficient time for this type of relationship to develop. The delay also provides an interval of thought and recollection for filling in details, long since forgotten but retrievable, so that they can be shared with the physician when trust is established.

Problems Derived from Premature Reassurance and the Need to Deal with Anxiety. As already indicated, the physician risks powerful adverse effects if he offers premature and empty reassurances or flip explanations. These may save the physician time and embarrassment, but it can do the patient a grave disservice. A dubious alternative is to offer advice based on solutions the physician already has worked out in his own sex life; these are usually inappropriate to the patient's. If the physician uses such techniques to "get it over with" or to cover anxiety and avoid losing control, the patient's confidence will be destroyed. Patients are sensitive to such tactics. The physician who, in addition, loses his professional objectivity and probes the patient's experience in the hope of getting treatment for his own sexual dysfunction will only reveal his discomfort and sacrifice his professional stance.

THE PELVIC EXAMINATION

Most patients like to be told that their genitalia, internally and externally, are quite normal. Thus, a woman may be anxious to know if she has an intact hymen, if her clitoris is in "the right place and big enough," or if there are malodorous discharges and other odors that may be bothersome to her partner.

It is better for the physician to wait until the examination is completed rather than respond with quick, empty reassurances. For example, to be told that "your clitoris is not very big but it is probably going to be okay," will inevitably be destructive to a woman's sexual self- confidence and future adjustment.

Tunnadine[3] has stated it well: "We find the vaginal examination includes several aspects of the patient's sexual attitudes, through ideas of the physical nature of her genitals, to her emotional attitudes toward her own femininity, and also something of her physical behavior and psychological attitudes during intercourse. All of these may help us to detect sexual difficulty without her need to confess it in words and to understand something of its nature."

The pelvic examination, therefore, provides an opportunity for good or for mischief, and the physician is strongly advised to avoid ambiguity, bias, guesswork and uncertain information. Patronizing attitudes, the "pat on the head," will never allow an anxious, tense patient to relax sufficiently for a satisfactory examination. When a workable relationship is established, even the most frightened and irrational fantasies of the patient can be shared.

There is an important experiential difference between examining male genitalia and examining the female pelvis. As Tunnadine[3] again points out, "The structure, purpose and the pleasure potential of the penis are obvious from an early age. The vagina, in contrast, is, of course, hidden, mysterious and, for the woman until recently, not to be touched or explored. The range and strangeness of individual fantasies are such that one can question and speculate for a lifetime without guessing right; the communication has to come from the patient."

The physician who suggests that a woman's genitalia are somehow different or deviant will only perpetuate her myths and confirm her unexpressed fears.

MALE GENITAL EXAMINATION

Males also come to examination with suspicions and anxieties, particularly about their genital normality; the adequacy of their testicular and genital size; the possible long-term effects of testicular atrophy following mumps, injury or genital herpes; or the effects of the circumcised or uncircumcised state. Almost always the concern over a real or imagined physical defect will be an ego-saving device that enables the patient to avoid any psychological introspection about root causes.

IATROGENIC MISHAPS

The zealous use of manipulation procedures, such as urethral dilatation, prostatic massage or seminal vesicle stripping, may produce impotence, ejaculatory incompetence or other sexual handicaps. These possible consequences should be explained in advance to avoid damage to the patient's sexual self-confidence and self-concept. Some problems also may arise during the course of sexual dysfunction therapy. All the negative influences may come to focus here: inadequate evaluation of the patient's history, personal prejudice, insensitivity, ambivalence, over-certainty, the perpetuation of myth and superficial unsound advice.

The following clinical illustrations will make these points more vivid:

A 48-year-old male had normal sexual function in his marriage but was found, on routine examination, to have mild, maturity-onset diabetes mellitus. Being an informed person, he read that diabetes occasionally may be associated with impotence and, with some anxiety, attempted to have intercourse that very night. Quite predictably and to his horror, he found that he was impotent. On reporting this to his physician the next day, he was abruptly told: "You must have vascular damage," and was given a brief but pointed lecture. His anxiety and panic were thereby perpetuated and the impotence proved completely unresponsive to injections of vitamin B12 or androgen. (These medications are frequently prescribed; except in special situations, they are useless other than as placebos.)

The critical historical fact that was overlooked was that the impotence had occurred after the patient read the book on diabetes. It was discovered on referral that he did indeed have erections in the morning, during sleep, during daytime fantasy and during masturbation. With reassurance, re-education and operant conditioning therapy, he responded well, his sexual confidence was restored and he has remained potent for more than four years.

A 32-year-old housewife, unable to have orgasms, reported this to her physician, who simply duplicated what he deemed to be the relevant pages from Masters and Johnson's *Human Sexual Inadequacy* and instructed her to "go home and practice in a warm tub." When this proved frustrating and futile, he instructed her husband to rub her clitoris the way he himself might want to masturbate.

A 42-year-old woman was instructed to simulate orgasm in order to restore her husband's erectile capacity.

A 58-year-old posthysterectomy patient was the victim of "permission-granting" when her physician instructed her to go home and "resume your regular sexual relationship" without inquiring as to its previous quality. He also never acquainted her with the fact that the capacity to function sexually is not dependent on having a uterus.

An example of how "doctor-power" combined with insensitive language can prove devastating is provided in the following case:

A 68-year-old male was found to have a hard prostatic nodule and was advised that a perineal prostatectomy was necessary. The resident urologist, in the interest of "informed consent," stated, "We can save your life from cancer but it will cost you your manhood." The patient was shocked but agreed to the procedure, was operated upon and pursued a smooth convalescence, but he became depressed and soon reported having no erections at any time.

Each visit to his surgeon reinforced the notion that this was expected and predictable. Because of the depression, he was seen in consultation, at which time the above story was disclosed with the additional information that his wife had cooperated by not permitting the patient to occupy their double bed; she had insisted that he move to another room. The wife later explained this was done so that he would not attempt intercourse even though he had seemed interested. It would only have ended in failure, she said, and she did not want to perpetuate his depression. Moreover, she believed that his cancer might be contagious. The husband revealed that he had been using all kinds of fantasies to induce an erection, but his failure to obtain an erection only proved that "the doctors were right all along." It was pointed out to him that he was not only fulfilling their prophecy but that, indeed, they may have influenced him and even "ordered" him to be nonerectile. His wife was then reassured about her cancer phobia.

Their sexual rehabilitation eventually was accomplished, based on no-demand for sexual intercourse and suggestions for genital pleasuring and contact that would ensure modest but usable penile erection. This procedure eventually became possible, and orgasm for both was achieved with a partially erect penis through penile-clitoral direct stimulation and some intravaginal containment. It was unfortunate that the resident's explanations included a word so richly suggestive and emotionally charged as "manhood." He could have simply indicated that the patient might expect some effect on his erectile capacity postoperatively and then answered any further questions.

Sexual interviewing and examination can be an emotionally charged and frightening experience for both patient and physician. The opportunity for being helpful as well as the chance of damaging the patient confront the physician. Increasing one's knowledge about the pitfalls possible in this aspect of medical practice is the surest way to avoid them.

References

1. Group for the Advancement of Psychiatry: Assessment of Sexual Function: A Guide to Interviewing. (*GAP Report No. 88*). New York, Group for the Advancement of Psychiatry, 1973.
2. Comfort A: Primary care for six basic sexual problems. *Mod Med* (Dec) 1974; 42:25-34.
3. Tunnadine P: Psychological aspects of the vaginal examination. *Med Aspects Hum Sex* (April) 1973; 7:116-138.

Chapter 10

Sexual Interviewing Throughout the Patient's Cycle*

Harold I. Lief, M.D., and Ellen M. Berman, M.D.

Sexual interviewing is the most important skill needed to become a competent sex counselor. Once the clinician's knowledge and experience are adequate, he has little difficulty asking about a patient's cardiovascular or gastrointestinal system; this is not usually true of making inquiries about a patient's sexual system.

As Green[1] states, "Memorizing a series of questions pertaining to masturbation does not guarantee that the clinician considers the area worthy of time expenditure and hardly eliminates embarrassment when reciting the questions of a middle-aged patient of the opposite sex. The patient may never have discussed masturbation; may harbor considerable conflict, embarrassment and guilt over the subject; and does not see where it is especially relevant to his or her medical history."

When the interviewer experiences strong feelings, such as sexual arousal, shame, anger, anxiety, or disgust, the interviewing situation changes; all too often, the physician's values, beliefs and attitudes differ from those of his patients. Managing one's own feelings while being sensitive to those of the patient requires a reasonable degree of comfort with the subject matter.

In this chapter, we discuss sexual interviewing throughout the patient's life cycle. A complete and thorough review would require a booklet, and indeed the Group for the Advancement of Psychiatry (GAP) has already prepared a monograph on this subject.[2] Numerous films, videotapes and audiotapes about interviewing patients with sexual problems also are available (see Chapter 25).

Most sexual problems occur in the context of an on-going relationship; nine of 10 adults marry and long-term relationships are also common in the unmarried. Although it is possible to have a viable marriage with unsatisfactory sex, or an "unhappy" marriage with satisfactory sex, sexual difficulties frequently cause marital problems and vice-versa. At the Marriage Council of Philadel-

---

*Reprinted by permission from "Sexual Interviewing of the Individual Patient Through the Life Cycle" in Oaks WW, et al (eds): *Sex and the Life Cycle*. New York, Grune & Stratton, Inc, 1976, 1-11.

phia, for example, about 80 per cent of couples who request help for marital difficulties have sexual problems. In about half of these couples, the sexual problems are of sufficient severity to warrant a combination of marital and sexual therapy. Even when the sexual problem is the presenting complaint, in about 20 per cent marital conflict is the primary cause of the sexual dysfunction. Therefore, some knowledge of the techniques of assessment in the interviewing of couples is particularly helpful to the physician.

INTERVIEWING COUPLES

The first interviews with couples are likely to be disconcerting to the medical student or physician. Since interviewing skills are learned almost entirely through interviewing individual patients, the novice feels inadequate when interviewing couples. Yet with practice, he can quickly learn a few basic skills:

1. Have the partners talk with one another as much as possible in order to assess and support their communications; usually simply asking the couple to turn and speak to one another will get them started.

2. Check the perceptions of one partner with the other partner. ("What do you think of what your wife just said?" "Hearing your husband just now, what were your feelings?" "Would you like to add or subtract from what your spouse has said?")

3. Determine their expectations of, and disappointments with, their relationship.

4. Ask what each can do to help the situation. ("Now that we have heard your concerns about your spouse's behavior, what would you like him to do about it?" "And what can *you* do to improve your relationship?")

A few such basic questions generally maintain the interview, allow the physician to keep control, and direct the interview in helpful ways. If one partner becomes agitated, the physician should step in and assume control. It is a rare person who refuses to quiet down when the physician indicates that this form of behavior is sabotaging the purpose of the interview, which is to understand the couple's relationship.

The goals of the interview should be to collect historical material, understand current levels of adaptation, identify problems and begin to seek agreement about a course of action. Even without special training in marital therapy, the physician can help many couples. Furthermore, when he is beyond his depth, he knows that he can refer a couple to someone with the necessary specialized training and experience.

INTERVIEWING INDIVIDUAL PATIENTS

The need remains for interviewing the individual patient, however, especially because one-to-one interviewing is the method learned by medical students and physicians and is the starting point for learning interviewing skills.

The variables, aside from the unique and idiosyncratic aspects of the patient's problems, that affect an interview include the following:

Gender of the Patient and the Therapist. For women, female role training and, for some, the impact of the menstrual cycle can significantly influence interest in and attitudes toward sex. A man is subject to different biologic vicissitudes; an aging man's decreased interest in sex, perhaps as a consequence of decreased sexual tension (and ejaculatory content and force), may be highly significant.

A woman therapist may elicit different attitudes, and hence different communications, from her patient than would a man. For instance, some women insist on going to a female gynecologist; others insist on a male. Attitudes towards one's own sex and the different patterns of identification and complementation between the patient and the physician will influence the content and process of an interview.

Women physicians are often perceived to be more accessible, although some women still feel that a woman cannot be a good physician. Among urban educated women there has been recently a very strong demand for female physicians. In recent years, male patients have become more accepting of female physicians. A male physician with a female patient are more likely to develop parent/child-type interactions, unless both work against it. This type of relationship goes against the need of the patient to be involved intelligently in her care. A male physician with a male patient may develop interactions which ignore feelings. Male physicians may be particularly uncomfortable with homosexual male patients.

The Patient's Age. This is an obvious variable and we will not belabor it. Clearly, the techniques of communicating with a 4-year-old, a prepubertal child, an adolescent, a mature adult and an elderly patient are different. Toys are usually necessary to discern a young child's thoughts and feelings, but such an approach would be regarded as absurd by an adolescent. Often the major obstacle in interviewing an adolescent is his distrust of the therapist. Many physicians caught in their own value structure find this age-group particularly difficult to work with. The adult in midlife, with 20 or more years of sexual function or dysfunction behind him, has needs and problems different from those of the young adult, whose experience is still somewhat limited. Aging patients may cause the younger physician to become frustrated with chronic disease and to fear his own aging. Many physicians are still not comfortable with the idea that old people are sexual, and they avoid the subject with them entirely. (See the section in this chapter on Interviews at Different Life Stages.)

Communication Problems. When talking about their sexual problems, almost all patients show a discomfort that varies with the patient's age. The child's great difficulty in articulating feelings is paralleled by the adolescent's unwillingness to reveal his sex life for fear that the information may be used against him or be shared with his parents. Because of the widespread myth that older people should have a declining interest in sex, many of them are deeply ashamed of talking to physicians about sexual concerns.

Normative Crises. At each stage of the life cycle, one faces new circumstances and tasks—starting school, puberty, dating, choosing between college or going to work, selecting an occupation, getting married, pregnancy, the first child, being a parent, settling down, changing job or marital partner, living together without children, retirement, illness and death in the family. Each new task may be a turning point. These times of decision present both a threat and a challenge; they create opportunities for growth, as well as possibilities of regressive behavior and symptom formation. Because these normative crises influence overall behavior, sexual function may be affected minimally or profoundly. As the interviewer gathers information, he must keep these stages of the life cycle in mind and try to determine the impact that they may have on sexual function.

Types of Problems. The nature of a sexual disturbance affects the interview. Interviewing a patient whose chief complaint is an overt sexual problem, such as impotence, is different from interviewing a patient who does not recognize that sexual frustration or conflict lies behind the headache, gastrointestinal symptoms, or low back pain that he describes as his major concern. The patient who has preferred homosexual behavior and who wishes to become heterosexually oriented and the preferential homosexual who has no such wish but seeks help for impotence, present diverse challenges to the interviewer. Homosexual patients with impotence or orgasmic dysfunction are not unusual in sex dysfunction clinics, but can be startling to the family physician, who may assume "conversion" to heterosexuality is indicated for such cases at all times. This is usually not so. These cases should generally be referred for evaluation to a sex therapist.

Social Class and Ethnic Background. Patients with an ethnic or social-class background dissimilar to that of the interviewer often use unfamiliar words or phrases to denote a variety of sex organs and sexual behaviors (e.g., "man in the boat" for clitoris). In like manner, the physician's professional language may be obscure or completely unknown to the patient.[3] If the therapist uses the terms "fellatio" and "cunnilingus," a few patients may be familiar with them, but many more will understand "oral-genital sex" or "going down."

Moreover, people from different ethnic or social backgrounds frequently do not trust each other. The patient's distrust of the therapist may cause the patient to conceal his sexual fantasies and behavior, and the therapist's biases may be manifested as tactlessness, brusqueness, contempt, sarcasm or astonishment, which, with rare exceptions, have no place in the interview.

The values of the patient may affect the interview. For example, patients from a lower social class may feel that discussing sex is a stigma and a threat to self-esteem, especially to one's femininity or masculinity. The authors have found that people from lower-class black communities may refuse to see a *marriage* or *sex* therapist because to do so would imply that something was wrong with their marital or sex lives; on the other hand, they often come willingly for counseling from a *family* therapist.

People from different social classes may also perceive their stages in life differently from the interviewer. For example, the lower and middle classes seem to have differing attitudes toward the effects of aging on sex and marriage. In addition, one must take into account the divergent ideas about women's roles during young adulthood and middle life in various social classes and ethnic groups (see also Chapter 5).

The women's movement has been primarily a middle-class phenomenon, but changing cultural roles affect women everywhere. For example, a working mother with small children may still feel bound to do all of the housework and cooking (traditional roles), while working in a job that has become available to her only because of recent cultural changes, e.g., telephone lineperson. This kind of role duality may be puzzling for the middle-class physician.

Normative behavior also has to be judged in the context of social class. In some cultural settings, even so-called latency-age and prepubertal children may engage in coitus. In this country, early coitus tends to occur in cultural settings of excessive crowding, poverty and open or indiscriminate sexuality.[4]

The Nature of Relationships. A patient's relationships help to determine the direction as well as the content of an interview. If the patient is married or has a semipermanent relationship, the interview must deal with sexual aspects of that relationship. If the patient is homosexual, the content of the interview will differ from that of the heterosexual interview. For example, the homosexual's attitude toward society's view of homosexuality is a key element absent from an interview of a heterosexual. If the patient is involved in group sex or other nontraditional sexual behaviors, the interviewer must consider behavior patterns and the values or meanings attached to the behaviors. These sexual behaviors may occur as carefully thought out life-plans or as self-destructive patterns. Representing another special situation is a patient who complains of impotence in extramarital liaisons but remains potent with his wife, who in turn is having successful encounters with her lovers.

The Patient's Expectations. The interview is shaped by the patient's "agenda." His expectations must be made explicit in the course of the interview. He may expect his sexual problem to be cured magically by a pill or injection, or by getting his spouse to change, perhaps to become multiorgasmic. He may wish to have simultaneous orgasms with his partner, to become a "stud," or, as one patient put it, to become "someone who can screw any dame I meet anywhere in the world, even after a casual acquaintance." Such unrealistic expectations affect the interview; they can easily sabotage the therapist's efforts unless the magical, grandiose or self-defeating nature of the "script" can be made overt and eventually modified or eliminated.

The Physician's Professional Identity. Patients' expectations and attitudes differ according to their perceptions of the professional's occupational role. A man may have completely different attitudes toward being interviewed by a urologist than by a psychiatrist. A woman may feel differently about being interviewed by a gynecologist rather than her family physician. The patient coming to a marriage counselor for sex therapy brings a different perspective from the one in which he consults his general practitioner.

Unless he has previously talked to his family physician about sexual concerns, the patient may hesitate to raise such concerns because he does not know how the physician will respond. The patient may fear that he will be brushed off or will not be taken seriously, or, even worse, that he will be humiliated. He may expect his physician to be concerned about physical causes of his problem and unconcerned about his marriage or other psychological factors. On the other hand, he may expect a marriage counselor to inquire about his marriage and perhaps his feelings, but to miss some important physical aspects.

BASIC PRINCIPLES OF TAKING A SEXUAL HISTORY

Before we discuss interviewing at different stages of life, some general principles should be mentioned:

1. *The physician should be comfortable and at ease.* Despite the intimate nature of the inquiry, the physician has society's sanction to ask his patient questions about matters usually kept private. If the patient does not raise concerns about sexual functioning, the physician should initiate the discussion.

Many physicians are concerned, if only unconsciously, about the possibility of a seductive approach by a patient. If it occurs, the interviewer must judge whether it is conscious and deliberate. If it is, it should be dealt with directly but tactfully; for instance:

"Many patients with sexual problems develop the notion that someone other than their spouses would be a better lover, and the physician to whom these intimate details are confided becomes a source of attraction. I think we need to talk about it, understand it, and realize that making such a fantasy a reality would be injurious to you and to me, so it is out of the question."

If the fantasy is outside of the patient's awareness, the physician must watch carefully for its influence on interviewing and therapy and broach the subject only if it becomes a source of resistance to treatment.

2. *The physician should establish empathy with the patient*, and do so before launching into the details of the sex history. Trust and confidence are built up slowly, but the basis of a therapeutic alliance can be created in the first few minutes of the interview by the therapist's warmth, compassion and understanding. Quickly identifying and labeling the patient's feelings is one of the best ways to start building empathy.

3. *The physician's values must not have a negative effect on the interview.* He cannot escape into fake neutrality or avoid having sexual values, but his awareness of his preferences and biases should enable him to prevent their unwarranted intrusion in the interview.

4. *The greater the physician's knowledge, the more skillful the interview*, unless discomfort or prejudice interferes.

5. *Questions should be as precise as possible within the limits imposed by tact.* Questions that are too general, such as "How is your sex life?" should be avoided, because a positive reply may be a false positive.

6. *Emotionally charged areas should be approached gradually.* The physician should use bridging questions, going from the less emotionally charged matters to those with more impact; e.g., from menarche to dating to petting to coitus, from body concerns and nudity to masturbation, from adolescent homosexual encounters to adult homosexuality.

7. *Questions should progress from "learning" to "attitudes" to "behavior."* The physician should proceed from asking how the patient learned about certain

sexual behaviors, such as homosexuality, to attitudes toward that issue, and then to the actual behavior; e.g., "At what age did you first learn that some people are attracted physically to members of the same sex?" "What were your early attitudes about that?" "What are your attitudes now?" "What kind of homosexual experiences have you had?"

8. *If it seems necessary, the physician should state—before asking about it—that a certain sexual behavior is common.* This is reassuring to the patient and reduces potential embarrassment. For example, "There has been a lot of talk these days about oral-genital sex. What are your feelings about that? Your experiences with it?" Or, "Premarital intercourse is fairly common. What are your attitudes toward it? Your actual experience with it?"

INTERVIEWS AT DIFFERENT LIFE STAGES

Before Puberty. Most sexual interviewing of young children takes place through the parents, and the physician's attitude is often a model for the parents. If the physician talks about sexual matters openly, honestly, simply and consistently, they may do so as well. Most of the physician's efforts are in education; i.e., correcting the parents' misconceptions and myths. Many parents tend to react in one of two polarized ways: either they exaggerate the child's sexual behavior and see it as abnormal, or they deny what is obvious to a skilled observer. Pediatricians report that many mothers do not "see" the child's masturbation even when the child is fondling his genitalia in the examining room.

Direct observation of the mother and child may provide additional clues. Their faces often reveal anxieties and inhibitions about sex; e.g., the blushing and stammering of a mother talking about her child's sex play with the child next door.

Communication with young children is best done through toys. If, for example, the situation to be explored is one of child molestation, the pediatrician or family practitioner can set up a structured play situation and ask the child to respond. A free, unstructured play situation also may be used. It is entirely appropriate to talk with the child seriously about a doll's experiences, feelings, interests and concerns.

With older children, it is often better to speak directly. The interviewer can use the technique of "generalizability" saying, "Other kids have found it worthwhile to tell me what happened and how they felt."

He must always be careful about the difference in meanings attached to the words he uses. To him, the word "feel" is an abstraction about emotions, but it may mean "touch" to the child. Similarly, the child may associate the word "why" with a punitive attitude, since some parents often use "why" when disapproval is forthcoming.

Adolescence (Puberty Through 19). Inteviewing an adolescent is strongly affected by the turbulence of this stage of life. A GAP report[2] has stated: "It is naive to expect the adolescent patient to be reasonable, open and cooperative during the period when he is undergoing rapid and apparently unpredictable mental and physical changes. These changes require the adolescent to distance himself from the parents and all the other adults he associates with them. Moreover, he must justify or rationalize behavior, prompted by his search for identity, his fear of his own drive toward independence, his fear of sexual impulses toward his parents, and the threat of engulfment he senses in being close to a strong adult. A view of the adult (physician) as untrustworthy allows him to justify his discomfort on the grounds that he is being victimized by someone hostile and treacherous."

The interviewer is in a dilemma. He faces the adolescent's distrust but cannot deal with it by indirection or a gradual approach. He has to face the sexual problem head on. Any vacillation invites greater hostility and increases the initial barrier between patient and physician.

The adolescent's distrust makes the issue of confidentiality more important than at other times in life. A blanket reassurance about confidentiality may be unwise, for there are times when the physician must discuss with the parents issues about which they are already concerned. The adolescent recognizes this fact and is prepared to accept it, provided the interviewer shows him enough respect to state from the beginning the limits of confidentiality, and promises to discuss beforehand any possible talk with the parents.

Precise stipulations about what is and is not confidential are necessary. The physician can suggest that the young patient tell him what he wishes to remain secret, and then give the patient assurance of obtaining his permission before discussing those matters with the parents. The physician must make clear, however, that if the two of them disagree about disclosure, the physician's judgment must prevail.

When there is no overt sexual problem, but guilt (e.g., about masturbation) is reflected by the adolescent's symptoms, sexual fantasies, or behavior, a long exchange is usually advisable before specific questions about sexuality are asked. When adolescent sexual problems are covert, rapport is even more necessary than with the adult patient.

Because adolescents often have to put on an air of bravado about sexuality, the interviewer must not be fooled by the patient's dress and manner. Under the bravado may lie much anxiety and embarrassment.

The interview is also shaped by the young person's sexual concerns. These may be fear of intimacy, anxieties about sexual performance, guilty fears about sex, and fear of bodily damage ("castration" anxiety). Concerns about pregnancy, sexually transmitted disease, homosexuality and marriage are also common. For example, if the adolescent expresses some concern about homosexual inclinations, the interviewer must ascertain if the adolescent is really "turned on" by members of his sex, or is putting in sexual terms a nonsexual dysfunction involving feelings of inadequacy in sports or other competitive situations. If homosexual arousal is present, does the adolescent see this as a problem and, if so, is the problem related to the attitudes of family and friends and society at large, or is it because he wishes to change his sexual orientation?

Each sexual concern has its own special content, and the interviewer's skill depends partially upon the extent of his knowledge of the subject.

Early Adulthood (Ages 20 to 29). As a person enters young adulthood, he must pull up his roots and develop independence and autonomy. These needs are in sharp conflict with the pull back to the security offered by his family. Anxieties about developing new relationships, especially intimate ones of long duration that may or may not lead to marriage, are almost ubiquitous. The fear of intimacy, of course, may extend throughout this entire decade of life. It may be the nature of the patient's relationships, not sexual performance itself, which is the primary problem.

Concerns about performance are extremely common. Premature ejaculation is especially frequent; young men with a great deal of sexual tension may take some time to learn control over ejaculation. The problem of impotence begins to occur more frequently in the later half of the decade and becomes still more common in the 30's and 40's. Orgasmic dysfunction in women also is common, especially coital anorgasmia after years of having been orgastic in intercourse. This may be secondary to inhibition of desire and/or excitement.

If the patient is married, interactions between marriage and sex must be carefully explored. Obviously sexual dysfunction may lead to critical problems in marriage, and resentment, guilt and fear created by the marriage can interfere with sexual behavior.

Marital stress usually appears or increases with the wife's pregnancy and birth of the first child. A sudden upsurge of patterns that evolve from the patient's own triangular relationships with his parents assert themselves and may affect sexual adjustment. As relationships become more complex, the interview must cover more territory.

Early Midlife (Ages 30 to 40). Many people experience a crisis in their early 30's. They try to assess where they are, where they have come from, and where they will be going. They take stock of their work and family life and decide whether they want to commit themselves to it or set off in other directions. For this reason, extramarital relationships become common at this stage. Many people act out their uncertainties or test them out in new relationships.

By this time, more than 90 per cent of people are married,[5] and the marriage is a major focus of interest in sexual interviewing; in fact, the two are inseparable. If the decision is made to stay in the relationship, there follows a time of settling down, in which commitments are made to marriage and work. Chronic incompatibility about dependence, power and intimacy, and intrusions of family, friends, work and recreation often affect sex. Preoccupation with work and boredom are also common sources of sexual disharmony. If a couple's sexual communication was inadequate to begin with, there may be secrecy concerning their real feelings about their sexual adjustment. To deal with sexual problems, one must deal with the marital problems.

Later Midlife (Ages 40 to 60). In the first part of this stage (usually 40 to 45), there is a need to redefine one's life and perhaps to change it before it is too late. Often this need is expressed as a wish or demand to change the marital relationship. If this is impossible, extramarital relations may be a substitute. While more couples than not have greater satisfaction after their teenage children leave home, for some people this period brings a new burden. Thrown back on their own resources, the couple may have a flare-up of sexual difficulties.

In addition to proofs of aging, such as menopause in women and changes in physical condition in men, there is a marked increase in anxiety about diminishing masculinity and femininity and a reactive wish to prove one's gender capacity. Many men divorce their wives and marry younger women; most older women, however, do not have a similar option.

With physiological changes, sexual desire and activity often decrease (although not as much as many physicians assume) and there is a consequent falling-off of sexual gratification. However, with the man's increased capacity for control of ejaculation, there may be a compensatory increase in the quality of sexual encounters. Most men seeking therapy at this age do so because of impotence, and most women because of complaints of infidelity. Complaints about orgasmic dysfunction, which peak between 30 and 35, decline in frequency.

Late Life (After Age 60). Anxieties about diminishing sexual function are the most important single reason for seeking sex and marriage counseling at this stage. These anxieties threaten intimacy and security, which are necessary to deal with the threats of desertion, loneliness and chronic illness. Depression is often a prominent symptom at this stage of life and can decrease sexual drive markedly in both women and men.

There tends to be an abrupt discontinuity around age 75, when a person becomes "old-old" rather than "young-old." Illness and physical dysfunction increase sharply. There also can be a marked drop-off in sexual functioning, although this is not true for men in good health. For them, there is no drop-off between the ages of 69 and 79; instead sexual activity remains at the same level.[6] In other words, for "biologically advantaged" men, sexual interest is maintained during the 60's and 70's.[7] Women beyond the age of 60 are less active sexually, primarily because partners are less available.[8]

When interviewing elderly patients, the physician must be aware of the impact of myths about aging. If patients accept society's notions about decreased sexual function, they may be too embarrassed to talk about and certainly to initiate discussion of sexual concerns. Many physicians share these myths about the effects of aging and fail to show interest in what may be an important aspect of the older person's life.

For an older person, as for a young child or adolescent, trust in the physician is essential if the patient is to reveal thoughts or feelings that may be shameful and embarrassing. Building trust slowly by allowing ventilation of feelings, by scheduling relatively short interviews that do not tire the patient, and by permitting him to project onto the physician his magical expectations may be the best way to gain the patient's confidence.

With continued practice in sexual interviewing, a physician's skills will increase proportionately. The growing sense of competence enhances one's comfort, the most important ingredient in eliciting information about the patient's sexual concerns. The physician should take whatever opportunities are available to observe skillful marital and sex therapists conduct interviews, either through live demonstrations or through a growing library of films and videotapes.

References

1. Green R: *Human Sexuality: A Health Practitioner's Text*, ed 2. Baltimore, Williams & Wilkins Company, 1975.
2. Group for the Advancement of Psychiatry: Assessment of Sexual Function: A Guide to Interviewing *(GAP Report No. 88)*. New York, Group for the Advancement of Psychiatry, 1973.
3. Vincent CE (ed): *Sexual and Marital Health: The Physician As a Consultant*. New York, McGraw-Hill Book Company, 1973.
4. Hammond B, Ladner J: Sexual socialization in Negro ghetto, in Broderick C, Bernard V (eds): *The Individual, Sex and Society*. Baltimore, Johns Hopkins University Press, 1969.
5. Glick PC, Norton AJ: Marrying, divorcing and living together in the U.S. today. *Popul Bull* 1977; 32(5).
6. Martin CE: Sexual activity in the aging male, in Money J, Musaph H (eds): *Handbook of Sexology*. New York, Elsevier- North Holland Publishing Co, 1977.
7. Pfeiffer E, et al: The natural history of sexual behavior in a biologically advantaged group of aged individuals. *J Gerontol* 1969; 24:193-198.
8. Pfeiffer E, Davis GC: Determinants of sexual behavior in middle and old age. *J Am Geriatr Soc* 1972; 20:151-158.

Chapter 11

Sexual Concerns and Difficulties and Their Treatment

Harold I. Lief, M.D.

Sexual dysfunction, such as inhibition of excitement or orgasm, is not the only source of sexual and marital dissatisfaction. Other kinds of problems can be grouped into sexual *concerns* and sexual *difficulties*. Sexual concerns involve questions about such things as normalcy, body image, fears of rejection and fears of aging. Sexual difficulties involve issues causing conflicts between partners, such as differing attitudes toward oral sex, timing of sex, amount of foreplay and frequency of sex.

Sexual difficulties create more sexual and marital dissatisfactions than do dysfunctions. According to Frank and her associates,[1] this is particularly true of the wives: "For both the man and the woman, the strongest predictor of sexual dissatisfaction was the number of sexual difficulties reported by the wife, suggesting that among all the kinds of sexual problems, it was the wives' difficulties that were the least well tolerated." Although these re-searchers did not differentiate between concerns and difficulties, labeling them all "difficulties," the differentiation presented here should help clarify this heretofore amorphous category of sexual problems.

SEXUAL CONCERNS

Concerns may not become problems unless they lead to inhibition of per-formance or sexual dissatisfaction. If they create conflict with the spouse or other partner, they turn into difficulties. Following are some of the more common sexual concerns:

Normalcy. One of the most frequently encountered concerns is "Am I nor-mal?" This question may be asked about any facet of sex: viz., "Is it normal to have orgasm only with clitoral stimulation but not with intercourse?" "Is it normal for me (or for my spouse) to desire oral sex?" "Is it normal for me to feel disgusted by oral sex?" "Is it normal to desire sex three or four times a week?" or "only once a month?" "Is it normal to go to sleep right after sex?" "What about my husband's masturbation—is that normal?" "I have fantasies about another person—am I kinky?" The list of concerns about "normalcy" is almost endless. For example, a woman complained about being "frigid." On inquiry, she replied that she no longer had multiple orgasms—merely one per encounter. Ridiculous as this may seem to the physician, the patient was dissatisfied with sex because her expectations were not being realized. Her definition of normalcy included being able to have multiple orgasms.

Relaxation. Some people are unable to relax prior to sexual intercourse. Frank[1] found that 47 per cent of "happily married" women had this complaint. One of the basic ingredients of "good sex" is the ability to relax. The physician should attempt to discover if the tension occurs because sex is considered bad, sinful, dirty or disgusting, or if it is a consequence of fear of performing poorly, fear of the partner's criticism or a subtle manifestation of hidden anger. (Of course, if such fear or anxiety persists and is chronic rather than transitory, it constitutes a dysfunction rather than a concern.) Also causing tension are guilt feelings because of infidelity.

Identifying and labeling the correct reasons for sexual tension may be therapeutic in themselves. The underlying anxieties are often based on misinformation and sexual myths that can be corrected by appropriate information. Often, muscle-relaxation techniques practiced 20 to 30 minutes prior to a sexual encounter are very helpful in reducing tension.

Secrets. Some of the underlying causes of sexual tension may not be unconscious; instead they may be secret, not shared with the spouse or partner. Some of these are secret fantasies and wishes; for example, many people have fantasies about other partners. They are often reassured when they find that this is the most frequent of all fantasies and is perfectly normal in happily married people. On the other hand, such a fantasy may reflect marital dissatisfaction, in which case treatment of the couple may be required. Other fantasies and wishes include sado-masochism, desire for oral sex or other types of erotic "turn-ons" that the individual is afraid to share with his or her partner.

It is not only the teenager who may be guilty and fearful because of secret masturbation. A married person also may be ashamed of masturbation and too embarrassed to discuss it with the partner. Secret masturbation is a good example of how a concern may turn into a difficulty if the partner discovers the masturbation and is angered by it. Other secrets that create concern include clandestine extramarital sex or homosexual activity. Secret performance anxieties also are often a concern.

Case 1: A young man of 18, a college freshman, reported that he had had a steady girlfriend all through high school, but had a great deal of tension in sexual activity because of retarded ejaculation and a particular need to involve feet and shoes in his pattern of erotic arousal. Fearful of confiding this to his girlfriend, sexual relations became more and more troublesome until he gradually developed impotence. When he eventually confided in his girlfriend, the concern became a difficulty because she was not as sympathetic and understanding as he had hoped.

Case 2: A physician kept his cross-dressing hidden from his wife for five years. When his secret became too burdensome, he arranged "accidentally on purpose" to have his cross-dressing discovered by his wife. His cross-dressing then became a major difficulty in their relationship. Fortunately, the wife insisted that her husband receive treatment; her participation in the treatment was an essential ingredient of therapy.

Case 3: A 34-year-old man, married for 12 years, had managed to keep his homosexual activities secret from his wife. Fearful of being arrested by the police after one of his homosexual encounters, he confessed to his wife. This is another example of how a concern became a major difficulty.

The treatment of secret concerns follows the same general guidelines as employed for the unconscious sources of tension. Catharsis is an important dimension of treatment. The reduction of shame and guilt in some instances may be curative in itself. Sharing the secret with the partner does not inevitably lead to conflict and marital difficulty. Sometimes the partner is most sympathetic, understanding and supportive.

Case 4: A 45-year-old minister told his physician about his concerns over secret homosexual fantasies. The physician, knowing the wife, suggested that he share these fantasies with the wife. The wife was so supportive and understanding that the husband's impotence quickly disappeared. Their entire sexual relationship was enhanced by the sharing of these fantasies. On some occasions the partner is relieved to learn about the secret because he or she had ascribed their sexual tension to some other more troublesome cause; e.g., "He/she does not love me anymore." Sometimes the patient is greatly relieved to find that the partner has had similar fantasies, which they now can share.

It is not always easy for the physician to know whether the sharing of a secret will help or damage the relationship. When he is uncertain, the exploration should be with the patient, and the secret should not be shared until the physician is reasonably sure that this will be helpful. The intrusion of the physician's values may cause difficulty.

Case 5: A physician, who was more tolerant of other partner fantasies than was the patient, pushed the patient to share her fantasies with her husband. The husband could not accept the fact that his wife had fantasies of another man, and the physician's unfortunate recommendation led to serious marital conflict.

Body Image. Concerns about body image and their reflections on masculinity and femininity are ubiquitous among teenagers and common among adults of all ages. It is a rare male who, in his teenage years, does not have some concern about the size of his penis. Many male adolescents are concerned about their total body configuration, perhaps worrying that it may not sufficiently reflect an image of masculinity. It is for this reason that male adolescents flock to body-building centers. Transmitting the information to the patient that disparity in penis size during the flaccid state is rarely reflected in similar discrepancies during erection, and that the average depth of the vagina is 4 1/2 inches, is often reassuring. Similarly, female adolescents are concerned about their total body configuration. Many of them place unusual emphasis on their breasts. If there is shame about sexual development, a young girl may attempt to hide her breast development by walking bent over. Others may seek to augment their breast contours by padded bras. These concerns are not limited to adolescents.

Case 6: A 35-year-old physician discovered that his wife was having an extramarital relationship. In a bitter argument, she told her husband that her lover had a much larger penis than he did. The husband went into a profound depression, believing that he had a penis too small to be effective in sexual relations. On two occasions he sought to pressure a urologist into giving him a penile prosthesis and was not at all reassured by the urologist's examination and statement that the penis was of normal size. He was so convinced that he had an unusually small penis that he became suicidal.

Body image concerns appear frequently after ablative surgery leading to external bodily changes. The most important of these are mastectomy and colostomy. These procedures often lead to a profound sense that one is no longer physically attractive and a conviction that the partner will no longer be sexually interested.

Mastectomy. The breast is perhaps the most important symbol of femininity in our culture and in many others as well. Furthermore, the breast is a source of sexual stimulation for the woman and of sexual arousal for the man. Witkin[2] points out that the woman's postmastectomy concern may be not only the fear of her partner's aversion but also of his pity which, too, is perceived as a form of rejection. Pity reinforces her feelings of deficiency, incompleteness and worthlessness.

The physician must inquire about the patient's concepts of femininity, her previous sexual experiences, concerns about the renewal of sexual activity and her perception of her partner's responses. Unfortunately, few physicians take the time or make the effort to help patients deal with these concerns. A study conducted by the Masters and Johnson Institute[3] demonstrated that only 4 of 60 women had discussed sexual concerns with a member of the health-care team prior to discharge from the hospital, although half the group would have welcomed such discussion if a professional had brought it up. Sometimes there is not even a discussion with the patient about the possibilities of breast reconstructive surgery, a procedure of great help to many women.

The same study demonstrated that changes in sexual behavior were significant after surgery. One-third of the women had not resumed intercourse as long as six months after hospitalization. There was a decrease in orgastic capacity, in frequency of intercourse and in female initiation of sexual activity. Breast stimulation as a part of foreplay decreased substantially, a change that lasted for years. Changes in coital position and in nudity indicated an increase in self-consciousness about their bodies.

Although most men make a good adjustment to their partner's mastectomy, a subgroup of men experienced some feelings of aversion. It has been suggested that preventive care should include involvement of the man in the decision-making process regarding surgery and in in-hospital desensitization programs during postoperative recovery in which the man views the operative site and assists in changes of the dressing; these steps should facilitate the husband's development of comfort and sense of involvement.

Ostomy. Fears of partner-rejection are common following surgery that creates artificial openings in the abdomen for the passage of feces or urine. In men, surgery for cancer or inflammatory bowel disease that requires an ileostomy or colostomy often produces impotence, retrograde ejaculation or a loss of the ability to ejaculate. Some women report dyspareunia or loss of erotic sensations and, hence, of arousal. In addition to these biogenic consequences, the concerns about the partner's reactions may cause or augment existing sexual dysfunctions. Physicians and nurses usually neglect to discuss the impact of the ostomy on the patient's sexuality, and this omission may increase a patient's apprehension. Decreased feelings of attractiveness and concern about the partner's reactions should be a matter for inquiry and discussion by the health-care team. A patient's concern about the impact of bodily changes upon sexual functioning should always be explored.

Prostatectomy, in addition to its physical consequences (see Chapter 14), may create sexual concerns. Transurethral prostatectomy causes impotence in only 5 per cent of men, yet many men mistakenly believe that impotence is inevitable. If this belief is not corrected by the physician, psychogenic impotence may occur. On the other hand, retrograde ejaculation is an aftermath in at least 75 per cent of all types of prostatectomy.[4,5] If the patient is not informed about this probability, retrograde ejaculation will cause concern when it occurs.

Case 7: A 55-year-old married man sought help for impotence six months after a prostatectomy. It was clear from his history that this was a case of psychogenic impotence, because he had good erections in the morning. Among other things, he was greatly concerned about the fact that he saw no evidence of ejaculation. He did not understand that his ejaculation was retrograde. He claimed that no physician had ever explained this mechanism to him. It was not clear whether this was true or whether he had so much anxiety about the surgery that he had not absorbed the information. The concern over the apparent absence of ejaculation was the most important factor in the etiology of his impotence.

Surgery on the reproductive organs has direct consequences for gender identity. Less direct, but equally important, may be the consequences of any serious systemic illness that creates a sense of weakness or modifies one's appearance. For example, a few days after being in intensive care for a potential myocardial infarction, a patient was doing push-ups in his room.[6] His fear that he might lose his effectiveness as a lover was of more concern to him than the threat to his life.

Unfortunately, gender identity may be sufficiently precarious so that it is adversely affected by such surgeries as sterilization, hysterectomy or prostatectomy. Vasectomy or tubal ligation also may create concern about sexual functioning, usually because of confusion between fertility and potency or sexual competence. A conscious or unconscious equation of procreative and sexual capacity may, after such surgery, impair sexual functioning. The concern can usually be eliminated or reduced by the physician through inquiry, identification of the underlying concern and education. Occasionally, it is the partner rather than the patient who is apprehensive.

Case 8: A 48-year-old schoolteacher asked for psychiatric consultation because of two persistent symptoms. One consisted of a flow of saliva to the point where, standing in front of the class, she would shower the children in the front row. The other was a severe case of athlete's foot, one so severe that she had traveled from her home on the Gulf Coast to the Mayo Clinic for evaluation. Her medical history revealed that she had a hysterectomy several months before the onset of these symptoms. When asked about her concerns about hysterectomy, she said, "Oh, I have none. I went to the medical library and spent several weeks reading all the available texts. I learned that hysterectomy should have no effect on a person's sexual abilities." In this case, the patient's great apprehension about the effect of hysterectomy was defended by this unusual library research and her denial of the consequences that she mistakenly believed would result from the operation. Rather than in the middle of her body, she had developed symptoms at the upper and lower ends. This was an unusual case of both upward and downward displacement.

Life Cycle. Although the sexual problems that arise in marriage constitute the most frequent and most important need for professional intervention, additional characteristic sexual problems arise during the life cycle.[7] Some of the more frequent problem areas, discussed in detail in other chapters of this volume, are the following:

Assisting children and their parents to deal with issues of sexual development, such as concerns about masturbation, sex play with other children, menstruation, wet dreams, sexual fantasies and coital activity among teenagers. "How do I, as a parent, talk to my children about sex?" is a question often asked of physicians.[8] Concerns of teenagers may include masturbation, penis size, how far to go during petting, how sex relates to love, same sex arousal, contraception, premarital coitus, sexual performance and abortion. Adults young and old have questions concerning sexual performance, compatibility, family planning, genetic counseling, abortion, adoption and stress. Separation, such as occurs with divorce or death in the middle-aged or elderly, creates special sexual problems. The loss of companionship and affection in those cases may be even more important than the decrease in sexual opportunities, although the interest in sex itself among the elderly is characteristically unrecognized or minimized by the physician. Aging brings with it its own set of concerns which include increased need for genital stimulation, increase in the refractory period for men, decrease in the quantity and force of the ejaculate and the drying and thinning of the vaginal mucosa (unless there is steroid replacement therapy).

In most instances, reassurance is all that is needed. The physician is more likely to be "heard" if he discusses the pros and cons of sexual decision-making than if he forcefully expresses his own value position.[9]

SEXUAL DIFFICULTIES

Any of the concerns discussed previously may become *difficulties* if couple-conflict results. Arguments between couples about what is "normal" are common. Generally, the partner who desires a particular sexual behavior, e.g., oral sex, will label it *normal*, whereas the partner who has some aversion to it will label it *abnormal*. The term "abnormal" also can be applied in a pejorative way to issues of frequency as well as sexual behaviors or desires (fantasies).

As discussed earlier, a secret revealed may create serious difficulty; for example, the bisexual husband who confides his homosexual behavior to his wife. Differences in parental attitudes toward children, sexual behavior or even life-styles frequently lead to conflict. Differences in attitudes about such matters as contraception, child-spacing, number of children and sterilization also can create difficulties.

Some of the most common difficulties are:

Frequency of Sex. This is perhaps the most ubiquitous difficulty of all. "If I'm able to drag him away from the football game on TV he seems to like sex, but why should I have to pressure him? You would think sex would be more fun than listening to Howard Cosell." Or, "She never wants sex, she always says she is too tired or has a headache."

Timing of Sex. Conflicts over the time that sex is desired are frequent as well. Some partners are "morning" people; others are "night" persons. People who do not go to bed at the same time or who wake up at different hours often have trouble programming their sexual lives.

Setting for Sex. Some people like to have sex in the same place, the same way, all the time. If such a person is married to someone who likes variety, conflict is inevitable. One person may prefer a romantic setting, whereas the partner may be indifferent. One may wish to schedule sex; the other may prefer it to be "spontaneous." Often people have different desires with regard to nudity, "lights-on" and privacy.

Case 9: A 50-year-old woman, married at age 15 because of an unplanned pregnancy, had negative feelings toward sex all her life. She had never been orgasmic. It was her habit to have sex with her bedroom door open so she could listen to her children during the night. This habit, which augmented her inability to relax during any sexual activity with her husband, persisted even after their children were grown. The husband had always resented this but had given into his wife's demands for fear that she would reject his sexual advances altogether.

Foreplay. The second most frequent difficulty among women (found by Frank and associates) was the feeling that there was too little foreplay (38 per cent). This was the most frequent complaint among men (21 per cent). Some subjects also complained about the incompetence of their partners, even if the duration was sufficient. "He doesn't know how to turn me on."[1]

Repertoire. Conflicts about which behavior can be included are common. Most frequent of all are differing desires about oral sex. Other aspects of foreplay, such as penile stimulation, clitoral or breast stimulation and anal stimulation, also can lead to couple conflict. Occasionally one partner wishes a variant, such as troilism (three partners) or group sex, and is opposed by the partner. Conflicts are also encountered about the use of drugs or alcohol prior to or accompanying sex.

Coital Positions. Physicians often hear about conflicts over coital positions. "Why does he insist on doing it doggy-fashion; I feel humiliated." "He wants me on top; I feel it's not feminine." Or, "Why does she only want me to use the 'missionary' position?"

Timing of Penetration. "He always thinks he knows when I'm ready. If I ask him to wait, he gets angry."

Type and Timing of Orgasm. "Shouldn't we be having our orgasms at the same time?" "What's wrong with her, that she cannot have an orgasm with intercourse?" Often, it is the husband who is disturbed by his wife's lack of coital orgasm, believing it to be a reflection on his competence as a lover. He needs to be informed that this is a usual variant, that perhaps 50 per cent of women do not have coital orgasms regularly.

Afterplay. A frequent complaint is that the partner does not show enough regard or concern. "He goes right to sleep after sex; he doesn't even kiss me goodnight."

Passion. Women especially complain that their mates make love mechanically without much passion. There may be insufficient tenderness as well as intensity. Likewise, many men wish their partners were more erotic or imaginative.

Affection. One partner (usually the woman) believes that an expression of affection inevitably will be interpreted as an invitation to sex, and that if sex is not desired at that time, it will lead to an inhibition of the expression of affection. Affection and sex need to be fused during the sex act and separated at other times.

Many concerns can be eliminated by education. Certainly questions about normalcy fall into this group. When the concern is related to strongly held beliefs and feelings, e.g., "oral sex is repugnant," education may not suffice. The physician must evaluate the patient's degree of flexibility. If there is considerable inflexibility and resistance to the educational statements of the physician and the belief is causing marital conflict, the physician must seek some way to circumvent the conflict. If negotiation and compromise do not work and the conflict is serious, referral to a marital therapist is called for, although the therapist may not be able to do much more.

It is often possible to get marital partners to accept a "contract" in which each agrees to a set of expectations and obligations. In resolving conflicts over sexual frequency, coital positions, and amount and time of foreplay, this approach is helpful. Many times one person does not realize the concerns of the other partner or how important they are to the other. When better communication is effected, couples often resolve their difficulties without much outside assistance.

In summary, you, as a physician, should undertake the following:

1. Identify and categorize the problem.

2. If the issue is an educational one, inform the patient about anatomy, physiology and "norms."

3. Point out that sexual expression is varied and that what one person "feels" may be normal for him or her. It is useless to try to conform to some

"ideal" form of sexual expression. A good example is the issue of "normalcy" during intercourse. If only a small percentage of women experience orgasm during coitus, the woman who does not attain orgasm is not, per se, abnormal.

4. If the problem is creating a marital conflict, decide whether conjoint couple-counseling is to be recommended and then decide further whether you want to treat the couple yourself or refer the couple to a marital therapist.

5. If you do the counseling yourself, make sure that the concerns or difficulties are effectively communicated to the partner.

6. If the couple cannot reach some method of conflict-resolution, aid them in reaching a contract—a set of agreements concerning each one's expectations of the other and obligations to the other.

7. If they cannot agree on a "contract," refer them to a marital therapist.

8. In any case, schedule re-interviews six weeks, three months, six months and one year later. This on-going contact will permit you to see to what extent the conflict has been settled and if additional treatment is necesary.

References

1. Frank E, et al: Frequency of sexual dysfunctions in 'normal' couples. *N Engl J Med* 1978; 299:111-115.
2. Witkin MH: Sex therapy and mastectomy. *J Sex Marital Ther* 1975; 1:290-304.
3. Frank D, et al: Mastectomy and sexual behavior: A pilot study. *Sexuality & Disability* 1978; 1:16-26.
4. Badorsky M, et al: Effect of benign prostatic hypertrophy on sexual behavior. *Med Aspects Hum Sex* 1976 (Feb); 10:8-22.
5. Finkle AL, Prian DV: Sexual potency in elderly men before and after prostatectomy. *JAMA* 1966; 196:125-126.
6. Halberstam M, Lesher S: *A Coronary Event*. Philadelphia, JB Lippincott Company, 1976.
7. Lief HI: Medical aspects of sexuality, in Beeson PB, et al (eds): *Textbook of Medicine*, ed 16 (in press). New York, WB Saunders Co, 1981.
8. Calderone MS, Johnson EW: *The Family Book About Sexuality*. New York, Harper & Row Publishers Inc, 1981.
9. Diamond M, Karlen A: *Sexual Decisions*. Boston, Little, Brown and Company, 1981.

Chapter 12

Sexual Dysfunction: Diagnosis and Treatment

Alexander N. Levay, M.D., and Lawrence Sharpe, M.D.

Sex is a natural function. Almost everyone is born with a potential for normal sexual function; early experiences, especially cultural and family influences, shape psychosexual development, subsequent sexual behavior and sexual response. When not physical in origin (see Chapter 14), sexual dysfunctions are caused by conflicts or faulty learning leading to disruptive emotional states, such as anxiety, fear or anger, which inhibit what would otherwise be pleasurable sexual activity.[1,2]

There is a natural sequence of sexual development in childhood that is analogous to alimentary, motor, cognitive and other kinds of development (see Chapter 3). Not only genital but many nongenital experiences of early childhood, such as closeness with parents and competitive and aggressive play with siblings, can affect sexuality. All behaviors are subject to inhibition and reinforcement throughout childhood. Cultural and family factors can determine which behaviors are reinforced, modified or suppressed. The association of sexual behavior with anxiety, rage, pain and guilt lays the groundwork for dysfunctional adolescent and adult sexuality.

In sexual dysfunction, distressing emotions such as anxiety prevent desired sexual activity with a desired partner. Such distress often also affects a partner's responsiveness or satisfaction. The aim of therapy is to overcome distress by removing inhibitions laid down early in life, by reducing intrapsychic conflict (see Chapter 13) or by manipulating the environment to eliminate or minimize the emotions that produce distress.

Of all the distressful emotions, anxiety is the most common. Even in the absence of anxiety, temporary disruption of any stage of the sexual response cycle can occur. Too much food or alcohol, the sudden crying of a child, or preoccupation with work or family problems may produce a sudden loss or diminution of desire, arousal or orgasm. A sexually secure person sees such an occurrence as temporary, like a bout of sleeplessness or loss of appetite. However, a person subject to sexual anxiety may interpret such an event as the onset of severe and perhaps permanent dysfunction. Subsequent sexual activity is begun with apprehension over repeating the earlier failure. If not overcome by successful subsequent experiences, the apprehension becomes sustained anxiety and leads to an entrenched self-fulfilling prophecy of sexual dysfunction.

There are many factors that precipitate anxiety. A common one in male teenagers is the fear of not performing adequately, and the possibility of pregnancy is a fear that is common in teenagers of both sexes. In more experienced persons, these factors are more idiosyncratically determined. Performance anxiety can develop later in life or can be reawakened by any stressful event, such as a new method of contraception, a new sexual partner, divorce, bereavement, or the sudden appearance of sexual maturity in one's teenage child.

The fear of failing again augments any underlying intrapsychic conflict. Even in the absence of an underlying conflict, performance anxiety is usually sufficient to inhibit performance—a vicious circle—a fear of failure leading to another failure which, in turn, leads to increased performance anxiety and still another failure.

Other immediate causes of sexual dysfunction are "spectatoring" (the monitoring of one's own performance to the detriment of the perceptual and proprioceptive cues necessary for arousal), exquisite sensitivity to anticipated negative reactions from the sexual partner, anger and guilt.

Etiologic factors may be divided into three groups: the *immediate* causes discussed above, *interpersonal* factors, and *long-range psychological* factors (the major emphasis of Chapter 13).

Masters and Johnson[3] emphasized the concept of the sexually functioning couple. Reciprocal marital and sexual relationships establish a couple *system;* ignoring this fact limits a physician's understanding and therapeutic skills. For example, there may be an unspoken collusion to avoid facing the discomfort of mutual sexual frustrations. Some sexual dysfunctions are masked in the relationship and become apparent only with another partner. Conversely, either member of a dysfunctional couple may be able to function satisfactorily with other partners.

There is a wide diversity in types of sexual behavior (e.g., coital, manual, oral, anal), in frequency of sexual contact, in time spent in each phase of the response cycle and in the entire cycle, and in the kinds and levels of emotion expressed. Couples should not be made to feel that their mutually pleasurable activity is dysfunctional because it does not meet an arbitrary standard of normality. Some physicians mistakenly consider high sexual frequencies after middle age to be abnormal, but they take low frequencies for granted. Couples beyond middle age should be informed that any mutually comfortable sexual frequency is normal, as it is at any other time of life.

Because there is no consensual standard of sexual functioning for individuals or couples, dyadic sexual "difficulties" develop when partners' preferences differ and cause dissatisfaction. A dysfunction arises when one or both partners have trouble functioning sexually. The end result of the dysfunction may become the acceptance of a sexless relationship. In such cases, the physician must be careful to classify the relationship (but not the individuals) as conflicted or dysfunctional. Needless to say, treatment of the couple cannot proceed unless both members acknowledge that their relationship is dysfunctional and they are motivated to work on their problems. Occasionally, it is possible to treat only one member of the couple who may, depending on the nature of the problem, find help.

INHIBITED SEXUAL DESIRE IN EITHER SEX

Inhibited sexual desire (ISD) is persistent indifference to sexual activity. It can be lifelong (primary) or it may follow a period of normal sexual desire (acquired or secondary). It may occur in all situations and with all partners (generalized) or only in certain circumstances or with certain partners (situational).

An attractive, 45-year-old, highly successful lawyer in her second marriage sought treatment for depression and sexual inactivity. Her husband had not approached her sexually for five years. During this time she had occasionally masturbated with extreme guilt and with anger at her husband for making her feel compelled to do so. She had fantasies about sexual involvements outside the marriage, which also produced anger and guilt. While she was unsure why the problem began, she dated it from the time she had had a tubal ligation. For a while she had tolerated her husband's lack of sexual interest. The recent information explosion in the media had prompted her to seek help.

The marriage had been happy during the first 10 years. Her husband had typically initiated their sexual activity and it was satisfactory, although she had always desired more frequent contact than he. Furthermore, although he felt constrained by no religious restrictions, he insisted that no contraceptive of any kind be used. Over the first 10 years of marriage, three children were born; then she decided to have a tubal ligation. He consented with great reluctance. After the operation, he sought sexual contact less often, and over the past five years had never initiated it. On the rare occasions when she initiated contact, she felt humiliated that he was unwilling. She was convinced that he had a sexual dysfunction and felt that he was rejecting her as a wife, a woman and a lover. She wanted help for him, for herself and for the marriage.

After many failed attempts to convince him to attend a session with a sex therapist, the husband finally did so, but in a defensive, hostile mood. He insisted that he loved his wife and appreciated all her qualities as a woman, wife and lover but said that he had had no sexual feelings for several years and had not even masturbated. Although he was close to 50, he did not give the common rationalizations of excessive work or age. He simply stated that he lacked desire and resented his wife's pressures.

Couple therapy was unexpectedly successful in a short time through the clarification of two issues. First, the husband still loved his wife and sexual inactivity did not indicate rejection of her. Second, he remained angry at her overriding his wish that she not undergo sterilization. These problems were fully explored during therapy and sexual activity was resumed. Sexual activity was satisfactory, although still less frequent than the wife would have wished.

Primary lack of desire is rare. Clinically, it seems to be more common in women than in men, although that may be changing. Few people with inhibited desire express it as a complaint unless their partners insist; occasionally someone does complain because he or she has become increasingly aware of the dysfunctional nature of the condition. Some people without desire can engage in sexual activity with a partner (as a "duty" or to meet a partner's expectations) and go through all the physiological stages of arousal and orgasm without ever feeling desire or satisfaction. Even if they do experience satisfaction, as some do, the inhibition of desire may remain undiminished. Again, it is usually the partner who is distressed because of the person's lack of involvement.

The complexity of this disorder requires early referral to experts in psychodynamic and sexual therapy. The treatment of long-term sexual inhibition is difficult. Motivation is generally low, and the pathological intrapsychic factors are so strong and associated with so much anxiety that they are hard to unravel except in long-term therapy. If such patients can overcome their anxiety and engage in masturbation or sexual activity with a partner, behavior modification techniques can be tried. Treatment may then begin with the therapist initially side-stepping the pathological intrapsychic factors.

A very attractive 24-year-old woman who had been married for four years complained that she had never experienced any sexual desire, had never been orgasmic, and, although she did not find sexual activity repugnant, had never had any satisfaction from it. She was the only child of overprotective and rather puritanical parents, but no developmental events could be found to account for these symptoms.

Her dating experiences had not been unusual, but she had never enjoyed teenage petting. One of the things that attracted her to her husband was that he was an expert wooer and had a reputation as a ladies' man. She hoped that, with his experience, he would be able to introduce her to the mysteries of sexual pleasure. During courtship he honored her wishes to avoid coitus before marriage, although he continued his ardorous pursuit. The marriage was progressively disastrous; her lack of sexual desire and response increasingly frustrated both of them and made the husband feel justified in seeking extramarital encounters. The emotional bond between the couple was still strong, however, and they desired to save the marriage.

They were treated as a couple. At first the wife remained passively accepting and resisted her husband's advances to become involved in sexual activity. Therapy was aimed at making her aware of her sensations and making the husband a therapeutic partner, encouraging her in self-exploration. The therapist acted as an objective teacher and permission giver. The wife gradually responded to this form of therapy.

It should be kept in mind that biogenic causes of lifelong inhibited sexual desire (ISD), even if rare, do exist. In men it is almost always associated with low testosterone levels, usually below 250 mg per cent. Sometimes this occurs in conjunction with hyperprolactinemic states. If lifelong ISD is biogenic, endocrine therapy instead of, or in addition to, psychotherapy usually is indicated.[4]

Secondary lack of desire is far more commonly felt as distressing, and it is more often presented as a problem to a physician. Libido may disappear suddenly or slowly and there is a clear change in frequency of functioning. This may be the first sign of a nonsexual physical illness or mental disorder. The most common disorder affecting desire is a major depressive illness, although adrenalectomy, Addison's disease and Symmond's disease can have similar effects. Loss of desire also can result from an acute physical illness or an extended debilitating or disabling physical disorder. The chief complaint is usually related to the major physical or mental condition; successful treatment of the underlying condition often restores libido.

The etiology of psychogenic inhibited desire may be difficult to identify. It may have a variety of complex and idiosyncratic mechanisms and sources: low self-esteem, feelings of hopelessness and helplessness, depression and general anhedonia are common. The most frequently identified factor is inhibition with dysfunction in other areas of the sexual response cycle: repeated experiences of premature ejaculation, erectile dysfunction or dyspareunia frequently induce loss of sexual desire. Some people retain a desire to masturbate, but loss of desire may be complete.

Those who lose desire because they have sexually dysfunctional partners have actually suppressed their desire rather than sought other outlets. They also have commonly suppressed anger and resentment toward their mates and feel some degree of aversion.

Bereavement, separation and divorce can also lead to temporary loss of desire. After a period of mourning, normal sexual desire usually returns, but when it does not, therapy is required. Loss of desire also sometimes occurs after extended sexual inactivity associated with separation from a desired partner.

Many people expect or accept loss of sexual desire in both sexes because of aging and, in women, after menopause. Although there is a decline in sexual frequency and of arousal mechanisms (tumescence and vaginal wetting), aging need not (and usually does not) lead to loss of desire; many patients in whom loss of desire is a self-fulfilling prophecy can regain desire through education and psychosocial support.

Many idiosyncratic sources of diminished sexual desire lie in religious, social and family taboos and in early-life sexual experiences. Fetishism, other paraphilias and homosexual orientation also may be sources of lack of desire for one's partner.

It has been postulated that there is a normal distribution curve for sexual desire and responsiveness; it is not known, however, what percentage of people with hypoactive sexual desire are at the lower end of this distribution. There also may be natural changes in desire that are not reactions to the psychological stresses of everyday life but that may cause a person to seek treatment. These areas still have not been explored in depth and remain fertile fields for research.

Usually loss of desire can be understood and treated only if the therapist understands the relationship between the patient and the sexual partner. In fact, this relationship is sometimes the chief cause of the disorder. Most commonly, the partners have unequal sexual desire; one sees the other as "undersexed" or "oversexed," and the one with greater desire misinterprets the other's lesser desire as loss of interest or affection, and suffers a blow to self-esteem. If communication between the partners is poor, serious difficulties can develop in the entire relationship, as can a lack of sexual desire. Treatment can be much more effective if a deep bond still exists. Establishing communication about sexual feelings and needs, and learning cooperation for mutual and individual satisfaction, can rapidly reverse the problem. In some couples, there are psychodynamic factors, such as power struggles, "sibling rivalry" and fear of being overwhelmed or exploited by the partner's needs, all of which indicate interpersonal conflict. Such couples need extensive psychodynamic treatment by a marital specialist.

In some couples, other bonds are still intact, but the erotic bond has atrophied or has been suppressed. Desire and arousability may still exist, expressed in coitus with other partners or masturbation. Many such couples maintain close and mutual interests in their children, in business and in social activities. Many never express lack of sexual desire as a problem, for they resort to masturbation or affairs. When such couples do seek therapy, it may be for marital therapy even though sexual difficulties exist.

If the partners have no emotional commitment, sexual desire is usually absent. Treatment is almost always unsuccessful in such cases because of lack of motivation.

A 34-year-old businessman saw a physician at his wife's insistence; their coital frequency had fallen to once a month, and he seemed to her to be mechanical about it. She was demanding a return to the more romantic and passionate love-making of the earlier years of their marriage. They had wed when she was 18 and he 22, and they had three children. He told the therapist and his wife that the diminished frequency and intensity of love-making was caused by the stress and fatigue of his job. However, in an individual session with the therapist, he confided that his wife no longer met his fantasy ideal of a pubescent girl and that he was finding it more difficult to feel excited by her. Sexual activity with pubescent girls was the center of his fantasies; he found satisfaction in using pornography and occasionally with prostitutes. He said it was true that sexual activity with his wife now seemed routine and a duty.

This case of secondary, situational inhibition of desire was difficult to treat, for neither partner could fulfill the other's desires. Furthermore, the husband's unwillingness to share his reasons with his wife made her increasingly angry at him. Finally she sought and obtained a divorce.

A businessman in his mid-30's had an inhibition of sexual desire ever since his marriage six years earlier. He had no such inhibition prior to marriage, and had a very active sexual life then with many partners. His history revealed, however, that he had been engaged to marry, and had been deeply in love with, a young woman about 10 years earlier. She had died in a tragic accident. Further investigation revealed his marked fear of making a commitment to his wife because of his underlying fear of loss and abandonment. When sensate focus exercises for the couple proved unrewarding, individual psychotherapy was instituted and led to a gradual resolution of the inhibition of sexual desire. In his case he had masturbated almost daily; thus, there was no loss of libido per se but a fear of intimacy.

A 32-year-old woman consulted a therapist because of an inhibition of desire, at times approaching an aversion to sex. When she did have sex, however, she thoroughly enjoyed it and was invariably orgastic. She had two disastrous marriages that included physical abuse and infidelity. She had felt free and uninhibited and highly responsive during the first marriage, but subsequent relationships gradually became more and more difficult as her inhibition of desire increased. It was only when she initiated sex that she felt she had the situation under sufficient control and could enjoy it. Even though she was living with a man who, in almost all respects, would have been an excellent marital partner, she was afraid to give any control to the man and would invariably reject his sexual advances. Her previous experiences had led her to believe that women were exploited and abused and, although there was no evidence of this in her current partner, it was difficult for her to change her belief that had developed as a consequence of her previous marriages.

A couple in their 50's sought help because the woman was distressed that her husband seemed disinterested in sex and was rejecting her requests for it. She had been a sexually responsive and orgastic woman throughout more than 30 years of marriage. The current dysfunction started three years previously when the woman, then 50, had a marked increase in irritability, postmenopausally. Although estrogen replacement therapy had helped somewhat, breakthrough bleeding and fear of cancer caused her to stop taking estrogens. As for the husband, one argument three years before in which his wife had said some hurtful things so rankled him that he had not been able to forgive her. His anger toward her for her irritability and excessive demands had led to an almost total absence of sexual desire. Marital therapy was successful in removing his anger and restoring their previous excellent sexual relationship.

DYSFUNCTIONS OF PERFORMANCE IN MALES

Inhibited Sexual Excitement (Erectile Dysfunction)

This disorder is defined in the DSM-III as "partial or complete failure to attain and/or maintain penile erection until the completion of the sexual act in the male."[5] This definition assumes that sexual desire is present, that the environment is suitable, and that "sexual activity is adequate in focus, intensity, and duration." This definition includes the rare cases of male erectile difficulty during masturbation.

Most patients with impotence find kissing, touching and even genital contact pleasurable, but the arousal component of these behaviors is blocked either continuously or intermittently. If this blocking occurs frequently, it can lead to diminished desire, in which case inhibited sexual desire is a secondary diagnosis.

Erectile dysfunction is always obvious and causes concern, even though its occasional occurrence is a natural part of most men's experience. The outcome depends on how a man interprets it. Most men accept it enough to be able to go on to further sexual experiences unimpeded. Their partners are usually even less concerned. However, some men, after even one episode of impotence, approach sexual activity with dread and monitor their performance. This fear may well be borne out: The man's attention shifts from his pleasure to the degree of his penis' tumescence or flaccidity. Treatment must focus on eliminating spectatoring and the underlying anxiety.

Total, lifelong impotence is extremely rare; most men have masturbated to erection (97 per cent) and have experienced erection during sleep or upon awakening.[6] Far more women report lifelong inhibited arousal, although a careful history may reveal that lubrication occurs during dreams or at other times but is not identified as sexual arousal. The disparity in the frequency of complaints about lack of arousal between males and females is not surprising, because arousal is more obvious in males. Different social and parental expectations of boys and girls about self-exploration and pleasuring also may play a part. There is also strong peer-group support among males for sexual activity, including masturbation, and much less among females. Boys have added opportunity for experimentation and stimulation, since urination in the male usually involves touching the genitals. It is perhaps not surprising that many more females (30 per cent[7] in one study and 22 per cent in another study[8]) than males (3 per cent in both studies) report never having stimulated their genitals.

Secondary inhibition of sexual arousal is the sexual dysfunction men most often present for treatment. It may be situational, i.e., limited to certain environments or certain partners. It usually occurs with a man's wife, and one of the most common causes is a couple believing the myth that sexual activity declines with aging and ceases at some time in midlife. The condition is also associated with such stresses as midlife crises, concerns about health, business pressures, childrearing, and marital discord.

A 54-year-old executive who had been married happily for more than 25 years complained of erectile dysfunction. Over the past four years he had increasing difficulty in reaching erection or in maintaining it long enough to penetrate. Before this period, he and his wife had coitus regularly and with mutual satisfaction.

The problem had begun during an ocean voyage; the wife was apprehensive that people in the adjoining cabins would realize they were having coitus. One night the husband became rather drunk and tried to force himself on his reluctant wife but could not achieve erection. On their return home, he again attempted coitus but was disturbed by the screams of their youngest child who was having an argument with an older sibling. Since those occasions, coitus had become less frequent and increasingly difficult for him. He felt growing anxiety, and he constantly checked the extent of his erection. At first he ascribed the erectile problem to aging or ill health, but when a thorough medical examination revealed no physical problem, he realized that, despite his age, he should not be having erectile dysfunction.

This was a typical case of erectile dysfunction caused by misinterpretation of normal events, and it responded well to an explanation of the origin of the problem.

A 38-year-old attractive and sexually responsive woman had gradually lost her capacity for arousal as a consequence of her husband's impotence during the past three years. Not wishing to undergo the frustration of his inability to complete vaginal penetration and feeling awkward about suggesting more intense foreplay, she gradually resigned herself to being "turned off" rather than to re-experience sexual frustration. When her husband regained his potency after treatment, her capacity for sexual excitement was quickly restored. In the process she learned to be a more effective communicator and less dependent on his erectile competence.

A 46-year-old man and his wife sought marital therapy. He was impotent in about 75 per cent of their sexual encounters. Ridicule and scorn were heaped upon him by his wife. In fact, her belittling attitude was expressed almost constantly. After a few sessions, the therapist learned that the wife was carrying on an extramarital relationship and was very much in love with the other man. In order to justify to herself her extramarital relationship, she had to maintain her husband's impotence. His sexual failure provided the excuse she needed to continue her liaison with her lover. This marriage ended in divorce.

Some people do not function well sexually with their spouses, but do so with other partners. Some function well only on vacation and not in their own homes. Others find that condoms or other contraceptives inhibit their excitement. Treatment in these cases should be focused on the underlying anxieties.

One of the most common causes of inhibited sexual excitement is using alcohol to the extent that it dulls the senses and inhibits erection, ejaculation and orgasm. Many prescribed and unprescribed drugs, as well as some organic conditions (e.g., diabetes) also can inhibit excitement. Thus, the physician should consider these as possible sources of dysfunction (see Chapter 17 and Chapter 14, respectively).

Dysfunctions at other stages of the sexual response cycle, such as premature and retarded ejaculation, often lead to inhibited sexual excitement; the repeated disappointment and stress of sexual failure at these stages raise anticipatory anxiety at earlier stages. Dysfunctions involving sexual excitement are usually accompanied by spectatoring, performance anxiety and goal orientation (see Chapter 13).

Inhibited Male Orgasm

Inhibited male orgasm is "the recurrent and persistent inhibition of the male orgasm as manifested by a delay or the absence of either the emission or ejaculation phases or, more usually, both following an adequate phase of sexual excitement."[5] This may not cause a man distress, so clinicians rarely see a patient with this disorder. Masters and Johnson[9] reported 17 cases in 10 years. In fact, some men with this condition are proud of maintaining erection for a long time and repeatedly satisfying partners. However, a man's partner may believe that he is withholding his ejaculation as a way of withholding himself from her, and she takes it as a personal rejection. Consequently, such men sometimes appear for therapy because of problems in relationships. Some seek help because they feel they are not experiencing the sexual excitement and pleasure they know through masturbation. Occasionally the couple seeks treatment because the retarded ejaculation creates frustration over the consequent infertility.

The diagnosis of retarded or absent ejaculation is not based on how long it takes to reach orgasm. The duration of all phases of the sexual response cycle varies among individuals and from one occasion to another. Many people vary the amount of time at any stage of the sexual response for their own satisfaction or their partners'. Retarded or inhibited ejaculation exists when a man wishes to pass from the plateau stage to ejaculation but cannot. With increased striving for ejaculation, his distress increases, ejaculation becomes more difficult, and pleasure diminishes. If ejaculation does occur, it is relatively unsatisfying. Men with this condition usually do not have the same problem with masturbation but do have it with manual-genital and oral-genital contact with partners.

The etiology of retarded or inhibited ejaculation remains controversial, but it often involves internal conflicts over powerful aggressive impulses and fantasies about coitus and ejaculation that the man finds unacceptable. Often the problem is lifelong, but it sometimes develops after a traumatic incident (such as discovering a partner's infidelity), after the onset of repressed or suppressed anger toward the wife following a period of good sexual functioning, or because of conflicting wishes to impregnate the partner and fear of the consequences of her pregnancy. Some cases arise from conditioning by masturbatory practices; for instance, unusually rough stimulation of the penis by hand or by thrusting against bed sheets or other dry, rough surfaces. Such patients often complain of inadequate stimulation by their partners and seek other means of increasing stimulation, without success.

Treating retarded ejaculation is usually very difficult, and success may be followed by relapse. Sometimes the emotional dynamics of the couple are involved with the relapse, so treatment requires cooperation and motivation by both partners. Progressive behavioral therapy is used over a period of weeks; vigorous manual stimulation to orgasm by the partner is followed by vigorous manual stimulation and insertion just as ejaculation is about to occur, followed by male superior insertion while the woman continues manual stimulation at the base of the penis until ejaculation. These exercises are continued until ejaculation can be controlled consistently.

A 34-year-old clerical worker was unable to ejaculate coitally, although he had no problem maintaining his erection and ejaculating by masturbation. He sought therapy because he had recently met a woman he wished to marry.

He gave a history of lifelong inability to ejaculate except during masturbation by lying prone and rubbing against rough linen sheets. His problem had made him increasingly avoid coitus for fear that not ejaculating would provoke derision. He had not had coitus for five years.

The patient's fiancee was eager to help him with his problem, and joint sex therapy was undertaken. He was soon able to ejaculate through masturbation by the partner approximating the earlier solitary masturbation against a rough surface. Then he became able to ejaculate through oral and manual stimulation. Marriage plans went ahead, and the couple continued therapy until regular intravaginal ejaculation was achieved, although the couple came to prefer oral sex.

A couple in their mid-30's were referred by the Infertility Clinic. The wife, a schoolteacher, desperately wanted to have a child. However, the husband had retarded ejaculation for the past six years, after a six year period of good sexual functioning. At that point in their marriage he was in the process of starting a new business. In financial difficulty, he was dependent on his wife's income in order to be assured of financial success. Although his wife wanted to become pregnant, a pregnancy would mean that she would have to give up her job and her income. Faced with this conflict, he developed retarded ejaculation. The husband was dependent on his wife emotionally as well as financially but had enormous difficulty in expressing the tender, affectionate feelings he felt for her. These were concealed by constant bantering and teasing, with an edge of sadism. His life experiences had led to the belief that women were somewhat parasitic. His need to get was stronger than his desire to give, particularly since he feared that giving would promote additional demands.

Therapy consisted of behavioral therapy described above and individual psychodynamic psychotherapy for the husband. Over a four month period it was successful, and the wife became pregnant and had an uneventful delivery.

Premature Ejaculation

Premature ejaculation, like inhibited ejaculation, is a problem of lack of ejaculatory control: "Ejaculation occurs before the individual wishes it, because of recurrent and persistent absence of reasonable voluntary control of ejaculation and orgasm during sexual activity."[5]

Defining this condition has always been a source of controversy. In the past, authorities diagnosed the ejaculation as premature if it occurred within 30 to 60 seconds after penetration or even by the number of penile thrusts. Some have mislabeled the condition as impotence. Masters and Johnson[9] define it in terms of partner satisfaction—when a man cannot control his ejaculation after vaginal penetration so that a fully orgasmic partner fails to reach orgasm at least half the time.

The DSM-III definition quoted above depends on a person's subjective sense of regulation, not on arbitrary limits of time, thrusts or even personal satisfaction. This seems more practical, since some men and their partners are not distressed by rapid ejaculation. Men who ask for help feel distress and sexual dissatisfaction, and so do their partners.

Men with premature ejaculation seem to pass rapidly from the excitement phase to ejaculation without experiencing the plateau phase with its pleasure and build-up of tension. Such response, with or without distress, is normal in adolescence; this is not premature ejaculation, as control has not yet been learned—something that will come with experience. However, for some individuals this is the beginning of a long-lasting behavior pattern. By the time they ask for help, their fear of premature ejaculation is so strong that the prospect of sexual activity provokes anxiety.

Most cases of premature ejaculation are primary, in that the condition has always existed. In the rare cases in which it is secondary, it is usually associated with a specific psychosexual stress. Long, enforced sexual abstinence may produce rapid ejaculation when sexual activity is resumed; most men rapidly regain voluntary control, but, in some, premature ejaculation apparently becomes established with increasing anxiety. All men with premature ejaculation (as opposed to normal rapid ejaculation), experience anxiety, which is central to the dysfunction. The initiation of sexual activity is viewed by both partners with apprehension, and completion of sexual activity is associated with a decreasing level of satisfaction. As a secondary phenomenon, sexual desire becomes inhibited and, in some men, erectile capacity is also impaired.

Unconscious intrapsychic conflict seems to appear less often in premature ejaculation than in most sexual dysfunctions. The anxiety is conscious, and treatment must be aimed at reducing it. Behavioral techniques can help many patients experience greater pleasure and satisfaction and increase their control over the duration of any phase of the sexual response cycle.

An 18-year-old male complained of rapid ejaculation. He had been very active sexually for four years with many partners and usually was so sexually excited by thinking about forthcoming contact that after only seconds of physical contact, while still fully dressed, he would ejaculate. This was highly embarrassing, and he felt the ejaculation was obvious to his partner, although none ever mentioned it. After ejaculation, he would continue sexual play, reach erection again, maintain it for a reasonable length of time, and ejaculate again coitally, leaving himself and his partner more satisfied. Sometimes, anticipating sexual activity later in the day, he would masturbate, but this did not always prevent ejaculation on initial contact.

Although the young man considered himself a premature ejaculator, his behavior was far from abnormal for an adolescent. His anxiety over what he perceived as a dysfunction was laying groundwork for real sexual dysfunction. Treatment was aimed at teaching him to regulate the timing of his arousal and ejaculation by masturbating alone and then having sexual activity with a partner.

The clinical observation that some cases of premature ejaculation are situational, with improvement being noted with other partners, indicates that interpersonal conflict leading to anger and anxiety serves to maintain the dysfunction. The sexual partner's cooperation and her willingness to delay her own satisfaction are essential to treatment. She must be helped to accept noncoital means of sexual satisfaction while learning to help her partner. If couples show such cooperation, treatment is often rapidly successful and the relapse rate is low. An uncooperative partner makes successful treatment difficult and may even prevent success indefinitely.

Patients with premature ejaculation who also have serious personality or interpersonal problems that create marital discord are the most difficult to treat. Individual therapy, couple therapy, or both are required before the sexual problem can be solved. The physician should refer such patients for specialized care.

A 37-year-old engineer had experienced rapid ejaculation throughout his marriage, but his wife, who also reached orgasm quickly, had learned to accommodate him and often their orgasms were simultaneous. During the two years before he sought treatment, the husband had become more involved in his work, which he found increasingly frustrating. He often let out this frustration on his wife and children, thereby creating serious strains in the marriage. He ejaculated even more rapidly, so that his wife could no longer time her orgasm to his. This increased his sense of failure—now not only as a worker and father but as a lover and husband.

Although the couple presented a sexual problem, treatment had to concentrate first on their marital strains and the husband's misdirected anger. With renewed feelings of intimacy in the marriage, the couple was able to proceed to the sexual problem, and they responded rapidly to the standard sequences of exercises for learning new sexual techniques.

DYSFUNCTIONS OF PERFORMANCE IN FEMALES

Inhibited Sexual Excitement

The DSM-III definition, as it pertains to females, characterizes this disorder as "the partial or complete failure to attain and/or maintain the lubrication-swelling response—until the completion of the sexual act."[5]

Usually a woman can tolerate lack of full excitement and still engage in coitus. However, passive participation by women is becoming less common today, as sexual pleasure has become more positively identified for women as well as for men.

It is common for a man to see a woman's arousal as a reflection of his own sexual prowess and attractiveness; her lack of excitement causes apprehension or resentment and therefore creates tribulation for both partners. Another man may recognize a real inhibition in a partner's enjoyment and want her to learn to experience her sexuality fully. Such a man may encourage his partner to seek treatment.

Inhibited excitement may be the consequence of fear of pregnancy, menopause, hysterectomy, marital discord or the "empty nest" syndrome. Of these etiologic factors, marital discord is by far the most common.

Inhibited Female Orgasm

Anorgasmia (or, as some prefer, preorgasmia) is defined in DSM-III as "the recurrent and persistent inhibition of the female orgasm as manifested by a delay or absence of orgasm following a normal sexual excitement phase during sexual activity which is judged by the clinician to be adequate in focus, intensity and duration."[5]

This definition includes women who have experienced desire and excitement but never orgasm, those who can achieve orgasm through masturbation or clitoral stimulation by her partner but not through coitus, and those with situational anorgasmia who reach climax only in certain circumstances or with certain partners and not with other desired partners. The inability to experience orgasm through coitus alone may be a normal variation of female sexual response, although in some people it reflects pathological inhibition.

Distress over anorgasmia varies among women and over time for some women. Often more distress is felt by the spouse, who infers some deficiency on his part. This is especially likely if a man misperceives female orgasm as a man's responsibility, something a man "gives" to a woman.

Although Masters and Johnson have reported that there is no physiological difference between "vaginal" and "clitoral" orgasm,[3] patients' reports and data from sex-therapy clinics show that about 50 per cent do not regularly experience orgasm during coitus, even after extensive treatment. (In a reasonably representative survey, Hunt found that 53 per cent of women experienced coital orgasm nearly always, and that 40 per cent experienced it between one-quarter and three-quarters of the time.)[10]

Primary anorgasmia—never having experienced orgasm by any means—is not uncommon, affecting perhaps 10 per cent of adult women in the United States.[7] Secondary anorgasmia—the onset of anorgasmia in a woman who has been orgasmic in masturbation and coitus—is not uncommon, but the diagnosis is usually secondary to inhibition of desire, even though the inhibition of orgasm may have occurred first.

A woman who does not masturbate and finds no orgasmic fulfillment in coital activity may well develop an aversion to all sexual activity. She may experience physical discomfort caused by prolonged vasocongestion, involuntary muscle irritability and an extended resolution phase. Some women develop dyspareunia or even vaginismus.

Two common causes of primary anorgasmia are the unrealistic fear of the loss of control that occurs at climax and fear of closeness or fusion with the partner. Inability or unwillingness to communicate with the partner, poor techniques by the partner or premature ejaculation are commonly associated with secondary anorgasmia. Attitudes learned during childhood and adolescence play a significant role for many women in our society. They learn when young to think of sexual activity, especially orgasm, as animalistic, too aggressive and unfeminine. Other psychological factors may also be important (see Chapter 13).

A 38-year-old married woman requested treatment for anorgasmia. She had masturbated to orgasm as an adolescent but stopped when she married. Her husband had been her only sexual partner, and, although the marriage was happy and satisfying and she responded to his sexual advances with excitement, she had never experienced orgasm through several kinds of sexual activity with him.

Recently she had rediscovered masturbation and was usually orgasmic, but it caused her some feelings of guilt and low self-esteem. She now wished to reach orgasm in love-making with her spouse and was increasingly anxious because she could not. The husband was unaware of her lack of satisfaction, because she had never dared to confide in him and had often pretended to have an orgasm.

The couple were treated to reduce the wife's goal orientation and spectatoring. Through concentration on her sensations, contraction exercises of the pubococcygeus muscle, and the husband's continuing support, treatment was slow but eventually successful.

Treatment must be aimed at correcting fears and misconceptions. It must also help a woman increase her assertiveness and sexual initiative, and support her in realizing that her sexual activity is for her own enjoyment as much as her partner's. Progressive exercises in masturbation and in sex play with her partner may help her to become more familiar with her desires and sexual responses and to achieve satisfaction.

Typically, as a woman falls out of love with her husband, inhibition of desire, excitement and orgasm takes place. A careful history, however, reveals that orgasm is the first response to disappear, then excitement, and finally desire. It is as if the bodily responses are inhibited before complete awareness of the sexual turn-off develops into a full-scale inhibition of desire.

A 35-year-old woman, married for 12 years to a man several years older, had gradually become disillusioned over her husband's extreme passivity. Not only did she have to take the lead in parenting their four young children, but she had to stand up to her dominating and controlling in-laws. Disgusted with her husband's low income (as a professional person he was earning only about $13,000/year), she became a highly placed executive earning over $40,000 a year. Her disrespect for her husband developed until she had lost her capacity to attain orgasm. Gradually her decrease in sexual excitement led to complete disinterest in having any sexual activity with her husband. An extramarital affair in which she was highly responsive and orgastic accentuated her marital inhibition of desire.

Dyspareunia

Dyspareunia may be considered as either an organic or psychogenic condition, or as a mixture of both. Dyspareunia is "functional," as the DSM-III puts it, "when the presence of recurrent and persistent genital pain in either the male or female is associated with coitus, is not caused exclusively by organic factors and is not a symptom of lack of lubrication or vaginismus in the female."

Since biogenic factors are frequent in both male and female patients with complaints of dyspareunia, a careful and full physical examination for localized genital pathology is essential before a diagnosis of functional dyspareunia can be considered. In males, in whom the disorder is infrequent, conditions such as phimosis, Peyronie's disease, nonspecific urethritis or prostatitis are the most common organic disorders leading to pain during coitus. In females, many cases of dyspareunia have an organic basis, most of which are associated with localized genital conditions, such as episiotomy scars, pelvic disorders and most commonly endometriosis.

In women, functional dyspareunia frequently co-exists with vaginismus, sometimes in conjunction with other minor physical disorders of the genital area. Vaginismus may be the primary cause of dyspareunia. At times the dyspareunia occurs first and evolves into vaginismus. Other sexual dysfunctions often appear after the experience of dyspareunia, including lack of desire, lack of lubrication and inhibition of orgasm. The male partners frequently experience problems with sexual desire and occasionally erection. In the male with *functional* dyspareunia, there is usually a severe underlying psychopathological condition requiring expert psychiatric assistance. In the female, the etiologic conditions for the disorder include a lack of understanding about techniques of sexual stimulation and the types of personality that are prone to overreact to minor pain, to develop phobic reactions, to suppress hostility toward the partner, and to respond to stress with symptoms of conversion hysteria.

Although there may be clinical evidence to suggest the presence of one of these mechanisms in the individual patient, it has become a widely accepted fact that many patients can be treated with great success without a lengthy psychotherapeutic undertaking or the need to know whether any of these mechanisms may be operating.

Occasionally the physician will be consulted by a patient who complains of pain during or immediately after orgasm. In such cases, penetration and pelvic thrusting often proceed without any discomfort and the pain is restricted to the experience of orgasm. Most frequently there is some pelvic pathology, and intense uterine contractions in these patients contribute to the pain. In other patients, pain seems to be in the perivaginal muscles. In these women, Kegel exercises, consisting of alternating contraction and relaxation of the perivaginal muscles, primarily the pubococcygeus (the same contractions that a woman would use if she must stop the stream abruptly in the middle of urination), helps to alleviate the discomfort.

The physician should bear in mind that the DSM-III[5] definition of "functional dyspareunia" excludes difficulty with vaginal lubrication. Although several biogenic factors contribute to lack of lubrication, the usual cause is a psychogenic inhibition of sexual excitement. Attempted coitus when there is relatively little vaginal lubrication is probably the most frequent precursor of dyspareunia. Concern over repetitive experiences of pain during intercourse heightens the woman's anxiety and decreases her vaginal lubrication, and a vicious circle begins.

The type of pain is often of help diagnostically. For example, endometriosis is often associated with pain that occurs with deep penile thrusting and that often increases premenstrually.

Treatment is based on the techniques of relaxation, desensitization and re-education, with specific attention paid to the role of the pelvic musculature in the coital act and recognition of pelvic, genital and muscular sensations, which are used to aid the patient in the control of the pelvic musculature. Such treatment also has proved successful in those cases of dyspareunia that were initiated by localized genital or pelvic pathology, but in which the painful symptom persisted after the underlying condition had been successfully treated. The spouse is an added therapeutic element in this disorder by helping his wife to identify her responses and helping to organize their love-making to allow the relaxation-desensitization re-education process to operate.

Vaginismus

Vaginismus is defined as a condition in which there is recurrent and persistent spasm of the musculature of the outer one-third of the vagina that interferes with coitus. It is "functional" when not caused exclusively by organic factors, and tends to be the least common of the female sexual dysfunctions.

The primary form of this disorder, in which the female has never experienced sexual activity without vaginismus, is *more* common than the secondary form, in which the symptom develops after a period of functioning without the spasm. Minor spasms and potential pain in the vagina are not uncommon when the young, menarchal female makes the first attempt to insert a tampon, but the majority of females with this experience do not proceed to develop functional vaginismus. In the minority of cases, the spasm is present on the initial attempt to insert a tampon or one's fingers in masturbation, and the condition becomes established. The symptom is generally associated with discomfort, pain and a psychic fear bordering on panic, which is often ill-defined and centers around thoughts of injury, harm or irreparable destruction of the internal organs. In such cases, pelvic examination is difficult and is resisted, and the insertion of a speculum or more than one finger on vaginal examination is impossible. Attempts at penile insertion, even when the patient has lubricated sufficiently, are invariably met with severe spasm and resistance.

156

The presence of vaginismus in the marriage invariably leads to severe relationship problems, and frequently other functional sexual symptoms, including loss of sexual desire, appear in both partners. Persons with vaginismus are not necessarily frigid or lacking in sexual feelings, although the persistence of the symptom after several attempts at intercourse may make them appear to be so to their spouse and to themselves.

The *most frequent* presentation of vaginismus in the primary care physician's office is the type associated with a localized physical condition, such as vaginitis, in which the fear is directly associated with the local disorder. With successful treatment of the underlying condition, this type of vaginismus disappears, although in some women, because of anticipatory anxiety, it persists as a secondary functional vaginismus.

Therapy is straightforward once the condition is diagnosed and treatment of any underlying organic pathology is successful. By the use of the sexological examination (see Chapter 25) and vaginal dilators of increasing size, the patient slowly becomes tolerant of the insertion of objects into the vagina. Some therapists prefer the use of fingers, first using the patient's own fingers and then the partner's, and conducting the desensitization in an atmosphere free of sexual demand. At a suitable point in this form of treatment, the spouse's penis is substituted for fingers. This behavioral form of treatment is almost always successful and only rarely does a couple require referral for individual psychotherapy or marital therapy.

Sexual Aversion

Some patients develop a general conscious state of aversion toward all or some form of sexual activity, based on phobic mechanisms. These patients often show phobic symptoms in other areas of their daily life. Such patients' sexual problems are intimately involved with, and are an integral part of, a phobic disorder, which requires expert psychiatric diagnosis and treatment. In some instances, women respond readily to nongenital stimulation but cannot bear to be touched or caressed genitally. In others, only intromission is phobically avoided.

A couple in their late 20's sought help because of an unconsummated marriage of five years duration. They had never been able to achieve intromission. The wife would not even allow her husband to touch her genitalia. Despite that, she was frequently orgastic with breast stimulation. As often happens in cases of unconsummated marriage, the husband was markedly inhibited sexually, and he passively accepted his wife's control of the situation. In this way he could avoid facing his own anxieties about sexual performance. The wife required intensive individual psychotherapy before the dysfunction was alleviated.

A 22-year-old woman sought help because of inability to permit vaginal penetration. In sexual activities with her fiance she was responsive and even orgastic with genital stimulation, but she froze when penetration was attempted. The engagement was cancelled.

Behavioral therapy of about three months duration was successful. Within six months she was able to have intercourse with a different young man, whom she eventually married.

The rapid reversal of sexual dysfunction is rewarding for both the patients and therapist. However, maintaining improved function may require continued attention to intrapsychic and interpersonal factors. To maintain their gains in therapy, both partners must adjust their sexual activity to their other daily needs and its place within the marriage and the family.

References

1. Freud S: *The Problem of Anxiety*. New York, Norton, 1936.
2. Lief HI: Anxiety, sexual dysfunctions, and therapy, in Fann WE, et al (eds): *Phenomenology & Treatment of Anxiety*. New York, Spectrum Publishing, 1979.
3. Masters WH, Johnson VE: *Human Sexual Response*. Boston, Little, Brown and Company, 1966.
4. Kaplan H: *Disorders of Sexual Desire*. New York, Brunner/Mazel Inc, 1979.
5. American Psychiatric Association: *Diagnostic & Statistical Manual of Mental Disorders - III*. Washington, DC, American Psychiatric Association, 1977.
6. Kinsey AC, et al: *Sexual Behavior in the Human Male*. Philadelphia, WB Saunders Co, 1948.
7. Kinsey AC, et al: *Sexual Behavior in the Human Female*. Philadelphia, WB Saunders Co, 1953.
8. Miller WR, Lief HI: Masturbatory attitudes, knowledge and experience: Data from the sex knowledge and attitude test (SKAT). *Arch Sex Behav* 1976; 5:447-466.
9. Masters WH, Johnson VE: *Human Sexual Inadequacy*. Boston, Little, Brown and Company, 1970.
10. Hunt M: *Sexual Behavior in the Seventies*. Chicago, Playboy Press, 1974.

Chapter 13

Intrapsychic Factors in Sexual Dysfunction

Alexander N. Levay, M.D., Josef H. Weissberg, M.D., and Sherwyn M. Woods, M.D.

Most cases of sexual dysfunctions have psychogenic roots. A minority of cases also have organic causes. Sexual dysfunction of purely organic origin is rare; even in many sexually dysfunctional diabetics, there is an interplay of organic and psychological forces (see Chapter 14).

It would be convenient if one psychological conflict or diagnostic category was uniformly associated with a given sexual dysfunction, but this is not the case (see Chapter 12). Any psychiatric syndrome can exist along with any sexual problem. Clinically, many individuals with severe psychopathology, even psychosis, function quite well sexually. Conversely, many people without demonstrable psychopathology have sexual dysfunctions. Nevertheless, intrapsychic factors help create and perpetuate most dysfunctions.

Occasionally, uncomplicated cases of sexual dysfunction are simply the result of lack of knowledge, insufficient experience, or faulty learning. However, in many instances, faulty learning leads to ignorance, because an individual's intrapsychic conflicts block the assimilation of correct information.

Intrapsychic factors consist of (1) emergency or "negative" emotions such as anxiety, guilt, shame and anger, (2) beliefs that, coupled with feelings, create inhibiting attitudes, and (3) conflicts between opposing attitudes, thoughts, or wishes. Much of this chapter will be devoted to a discussion of these intrapsychic or internal conflicts.

An intrapsychic conflict is illustrated by the woman who is raised in a stern, moralistic family and who may not be free to enjoy sex because her sexual impulses are in conflict with childhood-derived attitudes that sexual pleasure is dirty, sinful and shameful. Indeed, sexual pleasure increases a sense of guilt. Anorgasmia and even vaginismus may be consequences of the conflict between the drive for sexual expression and the repressive attitudes absorbed during childhood. These repressive attitudes may persist unconsciously despite intellectually more liberal views (e.g., that sex is normal, healthy and pleasurable) derived from adult exposure to more flexible social and cultural viewpoints and by the liberalization of religious and educational institutions.

Although a patient with such deep-seated problems should be referred to a skilled psychotherapist or sex therapist, many dysfunctions caused by intrapsychic conflict can be modified without extensive psychotherapy. Often, re-education and encouragement by an authority, such as a physician sex counselor, are enough to reduce dramatically the inhibition and thus the conflict.

Sometimes the immediate causes of sexual dysfunction are the primary ideologic factors. Of these immediate causes, performance anxiety is almost always present.

PERFORMANCE ANXIETY AND GOAL ORIENTATION

Case 1: A 45-year-old professional man had always experienced premature ejaculation shortly after insertion. He satisfied his wife manually and often timed insertion so that she would reach climax when he ejaculated after a few pelvic thrusts. Still, he approached coitus dreading failure. Above all, he feared her silent accusations that he had deprived and disappointed her and her strongly implied belittlement of him as a man. He was extremely successful and a hard worker, and their sex life was further diminished by his fatigue. He could take no solace in his wife's orgasms, because both he and she believed they were not produced the "right" way.

Many people view coitus not as natural and enjoyable, but as a performance that tests their worth as men or women. They tend to think of sex as being for their partners, not themselves; therefore, their partner's satisfaction becomes the measure of their own prowess. This attitude is reinforced by society's emphasis on competition and achievement, especially for men. When a man with conflicts about competition pairs with an inhibiting or overdemanding woman, his performance anxiety may become severe enough to cause dysfunction. And by focusing so much on their partners' orgasms, men can induce performance anxiety in their partners, which leads to further deterioration of their sexual experience.

Performance anxiety is particularly amenable to brief counseling by the primary care physician who must redirect the patient's emphasis from performance to involvement in the pleasure of love-making for oneself. Accomplishing this switch from performance to involvement almost invariably increases the partner's satisfaction as well.

Case 2: A 35-year-old mother of three who had married her childhood sweetheart believed that she had never been orgasmic in 17 years of marriage, despite her almost frantic attempts to achieve this state. She felt completely inadequate and guilty, believing she had deprived her husband of a response that she overvalued as the only proof of love. In fact, her husband had a lifelong history of premature ejaculation that played an important role in perpetuating their sexual difficulties, but it was concealed by the wife's self-deception. She had recently begun masturbating and complained that even then she was unresponsive. Close questioning revealed that she had experienced perivaginal muscle contractions, and when it was explained to her that these were orgasms, she was amazed to learn that she had indeed been orgastic.

The couple responded easily to counseling. The wife was encouraged to appreciate her husband as a cooperative and caring lover; he was urged to concentrate on and enjoy his own experience. They used the stop-start technique described by Kaplan.[1] (The woman intermittently stimulates the penis to help the man learn to prolong arousal without ejaculating.) The husband mastered his performance anxiety and learned ejaculatory control. She relaxed with her husband, and there was dramatic improvement in their sexual function and enjoyment.

160

This rather sophisticated woman had managed to maintain an island of ignorance about orgasm. Her defective self-esteem, her husband's defensive pressuring, her inability to experience conscious anger at him, and her mistaken belief that orgasms are always explosive all made it impossible for her to permit her own orgasms to reach consciousness. This is an example of the blocking sensations from awareness referred to in Chapter 12.

Goal orientation, like performance anxiety, diverts attention from pleasurable experience to striving for orgasm. This preoccupation with success rather than with pleasure, although often presented as a complaint, is frequently a defense against unconscious conflict. Such conflict often involves fear of loss of control, with which orgasm is commonly equated. Often permission-giving, education, and use of specific methods of sexual behavior therapy, (e.g., sensate focus, stop-start) reverse the sexual dysfunction, but sometimes more extensive exploration and therapy are necessary.

SPECTATORING

Case 3: A 55-year-old diabetic male developed erectile difficulty. In a sexual situation, he became deeply preoccupied with the state of his penis and as a result remained impotent. He approached his wife with dread of failure and often avoided sexual activity. As his spectatoring diminished in intensity during treatment, he was able to manage only partial erections. On returning home after a three-week hospitalization for an acute illness, he and his wife were enjoying their relief and sex was far from their minds. When he was surprised by a sexual impulse, he was able to experience a full erection and to have unimpeded and highly pleasurable coitus.

In spectatoring, a person becomes an anxious and driven observer of his own experience. It is common to all sexual dysfunctions involving performance anxiety and goal orientation. Some amount of spectatoring is probably universal, but usually it occupies only a small part of one's mind. When it takes much of a person's attention during sexual activity, adequate functioning is impossible. Often if spectatoring is limited to natural awareness, sexual functioning improves dramatically.

Patients with medical and surgical illnesses are often prone to spectatoring as they become preoccupied with how or if their illness will affect sexual performance. The physician who is sensitive to such concerns, and intervenes early with appropriate information, support, and reassurance, performs a service of enormous importance to his patients.

Early conditioning or faulty learning can make people equate sex with love, violence, power, domination, sin, the forbidden, the dirty, or the revolting. Sex may be thought of as something reserved for those older or younger than oneself, as a weakening activity, or as a performance on command. And sometimes a seeming obsessive preoccupation with performance may conceal a fear of loss of control. Sexual functioning may well become impaired.

FEAR OF LOSS OF CONTROL

Case 4: A 30-year-old single man was distraught about being able to reach orgasm only if he entered his partner's vagina from the rear. Brief psychotherapy and behaviorally oriented sex therapy, aimed at reducing his obsession with performance by increasing awareness of his own sensations, had been only temporarily successful.

Only with long-term psychoanalysis did this man resolve his sexual problem. The central issue was his unconscious terror that losing control in orgasm would make him aware of repressed memories of early sexual experiences with his mother and sister, over which he felt terrible guilt. During rear entry he could not see his partner's face, so there was less risk that during the ecstasy of orgasm he might fantasize the face of the mother or sister he still desired. During treatment he became aware of other problems related to these conflicts; the most important of these was his need to select women who were married or involved with someone else and therefore with whom he was not likely to have a sustained relationship.

SEX EQUATED WITH VIOLENCE

Case 5: A 56-year-old man had a lifelong history of erectile difficulty accompanied by strong fears of failure and of being rejected and condemned by his partner. In his second marriage he had experienced partial relief of his inhibition and rather good sexual function. However, a year before he entered treatment, his wife became ill and six months later she died of cancer. At his first visit, he reported performance anxiety and expressed shame and self-loathing at desecrating his wife's memory by wanting sex with other women. He had not resumed dating; his anxieties were caused by anticipatory fantasies.

Early in treatment, he had a dream that clearly illuminated his unconscious fear of aggression. In the dream he was naked in bed with his older sister and had a full erection. His sister asked if he thought his penis would fit inside her the right way. He expressed concern that he would hurt her. The scene shifted to coitus with his recently deceased wife; while he was actively thrusting, her appearance rapidly deteriorated until she looked as she had when dying. The patient awoke, still aroused but feeling anxious and guilty.

This patient's dream was a clear expression of a long-standing equating of sex with aggression. His problem was severely worsened by the death of his wife because of an unconscious conviction that her illness and death were evidence of his murderous impulses toward her. His penis was a weapon that could damage and destroy women. His impotence had long been an attempt to protect women he loved from the violence and destruction that he associated with the sexual act.

Our culture seems to predispose many people to equate sex with violence. Boys typically are taught early that assertion, competition and aggression are part of masculinity, and this almost inevitably applies to sex in terms of equating sex with aggression.[2] Many do not perceive the difference between appropriate sexual assertion and inappropriate aggression (injurious behavior). Yet they also learn that women should be treated with respect and gentle deference. In early adolescence, boys commonly regard sex as exploitative and are incredulous when they discover that women find sex noninjurious and even pleasurable. Many girls are raised to be nonaggressive and to express sexual interest more through enticement than through assertiveness. In the past two decades, cultural attitudes have been changing; now one often encounters men who fear being overwhelmed and depleted by sexually desirous and insistent women, and women who fear injuring or alienating men with sexual demands.

162

SEX EQUATED WITH POWER

Case 6: A woman in her mid 30's brought her much younger lover to her appointment with her physician. She appeared to be in great distress as she recounted that her current lover had developed premature ejaculation. She felt that the one thing she had perfected to an art was her sexuality and his dysfunction was a slap in the face. It also threatened her deeply as a reflection on her sexual prowess. She expressed a firm intention to end the relationship unless he could become his former self immediately.

The symptom had developed suddenly and dramatically. She was undergoing therapy for vaginal candidiasis and casually mentioned that she felt pain during coitus. The physician's questions revealed that her partner's premature ejaculation was caused by his wish to avoid coitus, so as not to cause her pain, but she remained unreassured and distraught. Her sexual history included many gratifying affairs, the majority with married men, which she initiated by being actively seductive until the man fell in love with her. She would then suddenly lose interest and look for a new conquest. Never before had a man "failed" her sexually, and she interpreted it as a loss of her feminine power. Her frequent terminations of relationships expressed her fear of intimacy and involvement. Her treatment proved unsuccessful, because she was not motivated to change and denied having any problems. She continued to insist that her only problem was an inadequate man.

People who are power-driven tend to dominate their partners as a defense against intimacy. Many of these people are fearful of being exploited and overwhelmed by their partners, and are reassured by their ability to seduce and thus to control them. This way of making threatening figures innocuous may succeed in preventing intimacy; if there is an additional threat from the partner, then a further defense, such as impotence or sexual unresponsiveness, may be created. Also, a dominating person's partner may react with resentful passive resistance, i.e., "withholding" sexual functioning. The partner seems to go along with the other's need to dominate, but unconsciously resists by becoming "unable" to respond.

SEX AS DIRTY OR SINFUL

Case 7: A 50-year-old social worker refused to touch her husband's genitals or permit him to touch hers out of fear that by either act she would somehow contaminate him. For many years this did not interfere with coitus; intercourse would take place without any previous genital stimulation. The couple requested therapy when he became impotent, since she would not stimulate him manually or orally. His first episode of impotence was unrelated to her problem, but then was maintained by her attitudes. As a child, the woman had received frequent warnings that sex and the genitals were unclean. She was required to wash not only her hands but her genitals as well after each visit to the bathroom. The physician instructed the couple to use disposable surgical gloves when stimulating one another; this resulted in sufficient stimulation for both, and the husband's impotence was cured.

Early experiences condition many people to consider sex dirty or sinful. Explicit parental instruction may be responsible, but almost subliminal perceptions of unacknowledged attitudes may be just as influential. Some children seem to absorb cultural attitudes that sex is bad or dirty despite an apparent absence of inhibitory attitudes at home. Many people with such attitudes do not have difficulty with coitus, but are repelled by certain kinds of sex play, such as oral-genital contact or even kissing. This becomes a problem if the partner has difficulty becoming aroused. Obviously, conflict is inevitable if a functional partner insists on activity that is inhibited in the spouse.

Many young people avoid sex because they consider it reserved for adults; they believe that to be sexual is to be grown-up and independent. Their sexual inhibition reflects reluctance to give up dependence on parents or parent substitutes. Some of these people avoid sex completely; others permit sexual play but avoid "grown-up" intimacy such as emotional commitment, coitus, or orgasm. Still others have several partners and avoid contraception; they are rejecting adult responsibility for their sexuality. The evaluating physician, however, should distinguish irresponsible behavior from the childish playfulness that often characterizes the healthy sex activity of the young.

It is unusual for a person to shift rapidly from feeling that sex is for older people to feeling that sex is reserved for the young. But this shift may occur with or without a change in physiological capacity. Men in cultures that value a high frequency of orgasm may experience an "over-the-hill" syndrome in their middle 30's when the capacity for repeated ejaculation begins to wane. It is not unusual for such men to seek younger, more vigorous, and stimulating partners in an effort to resolve their concern with their own waning sexuality and attractiveness. Unfortunately, physicians can unwittingly contribute to men's distress over aging by reinforcing their concerns about fading prowess with such comments as, "What do you expect at your age?"

INTIMACY, COMMITMENT AND LOVE

Experience during each phase of life contributes to the ultimate nature of one's sexual and emotional relationships. The foundations of intimacy and commitment to another person, including the sexual, begin in infancy and childhood. Trust, autonomy, and sexual and personal identity are but a few elements of this foundation. A child uses play to master anxiety, and an adolescent's curiosity and experimentation bring comfort with his own body and then with others'. If the foundation has been laid and a stable personal and sexual identity has solidified, late adolescence and young adulthood are likely to cause a shift from dependent ties with family to new ties of love and commitment outside the family.

This is obviously an enormously complex developmental task subject to a wide variety of traumas and distortions. Each distortion has a potential for interfering not only with the present but with future development. If a boy's relationship with the first woman in his life, his mother, is one of mistrust and emotional distance, he will continue to be influenced profoundly by this. For example, trust is important for the play and peer relationships that are necessary for adolescent exploration of relationships. These, in turn, are necessary for the adolescent to achieve a sense of gender-role adequacy. It is no wonder that children who do not trust one or both parents tend to be suspicious adults; they often are masochistically drawn to untrustworthy people and, therefore, have experiences that confirm their distrust. Sexually, distrust is often expressed as inability to relax and experience orgasm or even arousal. Many such people have an intense fear of vulnerability, which they defend against by avoiding situations that would leave them emotionally exposed.

It is testimony to the basic strength of the human emotional constitution that so many people reach adulthood with their basic sexual functioning intact. For most of them, developmental experiences shape their erotic preferences, their style of sexual expression, and their preferences in behavior and partners. Sometimes the misperceptions of reality distortions are so severe that psychotherapy is needed to undo the developmental damage.

Case 8: A 35-year-old professional man began psychotherapy when he became despondent over his inability to sustain a love relationship. He had numerous affairs, but none lasted more than a few months. Early in each affair, he was strongly attracted and sexually potent, but later he lost sexual and emotional interest and had difficulty sustaining erection. The patient was an only child; when he was 4, his father died and the boy was raised by his mother in a highly intimate relationship of mutual dependence. The chief intrapsychic factor in this patient's sexual problem was castration anxiety arising from his unconscious equating of loved women with his mother. As soon as he cared for a woman, he had to withdraw and desexualize the relationship to avoid conflict over his incestuous feelings. Only when a relationship was casual could he allow himself full potency.

This is a form of the "madonna-prostitute complex";[3] in severe cases, a man may be potent only with prostitutes.

Case 9: A couple in their middle 30's sought help because the husband felt extreme anxiety and depression over his wife's rejection of his advances. He was deeply distressed by not being allowed to fondle his wife's breasts or genitalia; he believed this denial proved that she did not love him. After unsuccessful attempts, he would become very angry and then lapse into deep sadness and prolonged crying. The wife did care about him deeply, and the marriage was otherwise quite successful. However, because of early childhood experiences of molestation and body invasion (frequent enemas), she could not tolerate being touched sexually. Nevertheless, she had no difficulty initiating sexual activity. Putting her in charge and repeatedly reassuring him enabled the couple to work out their dysfunction. In this case, a referral for individual therapy was necessary for the wife, to allow her to work out the conflicts that perpetuated her phobia.

Some people find that they cannot behave sexually without being in love. Others see sexual refusal or inhibition as a denial of love. Some very loving couples who share negative feelings or values about sex can have a very stable relationship in which sex has little or no part. Problems arise, of course, when such values are held by only one partner. Some disorders of desire reflect problems of this type.

Case 10: A 25-year-old man sought counseling at the insistence of his wife. Both were medical students who shared deep religious convictions, and they planned lives as medical missionaries. Their marriage was happy and full except that he did not satisfy her strong sexual drive. His sexual drive had been virtually nonexistent since adolescence, a reflection of his asceticism and obsessive-compulsive renunciation of all "base instincts." He was not amenable to therapy, but his wife was helped to understand that her husband's lack of sexual interest did not show lack of love. She ultimately decided that masturbation was better than marital discord or separation.

When couples experience sexual problems, a physician may well find difficulties in one or both partners that antedate the marriage. When people pair, their individual problems interact and then can be solved most often by treating the couple as a unit. This is also true of homosexual couples, who are subject to some of the same sexual dysfunctions and conflicts. If the long-range intrapsychic conflicts in either heterosexual or homosexual persons are severe, individual psychotherapy is indicated.

SEX SEEN AS NURTURANCE OR DEPLETION

Case 11: A young couple complained of the husband's inability to sustain erection after penetration. The wife repeatedly awakened him every night, asking him to insert his penis while he hugged and kissed her as if she were a little girl. If he failed to comply, she flew into a rage and beat him. She was readily orgasmic when her clitoris was stimulated, but she did not accept this as a substitute for coitus. She was reluctant to stimulate his penis and did so grudgingly; if he did not develop an erection soon after stimulation began, she became angry again.

The wife had a severely deprived childhood. She had a childhood history of inserting objects into her vagina. She described fantasies of being "filled-up" by her husband, and she equated coitus with childhood experiences of nurturance and feeding. The couple's treatment proved more difficult than anticipated. Despite the history of inserting objects into her vagina during childhood, as an adult, the wife had developed difficulty in inserting things into her vagina— such as fingers, tampons and a diaphragm—an excellent example of the behavioral consequences of the conflict between infantile and adult sexuality. She also had trouble accommodating her husband's penis when treatment helped to maintain his erection. She complained of pain and often moved as if to dislodge his penis.

As treatment progressed, her anger subsided and she became subdued and depressed. Her infantile, unconscious wish to be fed sexually was in conflict with her wishes for adult sexual function and gratification. Her husband experienced her as depleting and insatiable and protected himself from her impossible demands by becoming sexually dysfunctional.

Some people experience sex primarily as a way of servicing and feeding their partners. When "giving" is combined with difficulty in permitting oneself to "get," resentment develops. This resentment often takes the form of perceiving sex as depleting and unhealthful. In men, this may cause retarded ejaculation. Women with this inner conflict may use somatic complaints to avoid sex.

LIFE-CYCLE STRESSES

Sexual functioning can be strongly influenced by physical illness, stress, anxiety, or depression. Some people respond to their anxiety and tension with increased desire, using sex as a tranquilizer. Others respond with decreased libido or impaired sexual functioning, which often causes additional anxiety that compounds the problem.

Each period of life has characteristic conflicts, and physicians often encounter them in practice. Adolescents, for example, often equate sex with independence, adulthood, and separation from family. It is often clinically difficult to distinguish healthy sexual playfulness and experimentation from driven behavior or sexual activity that may signal an impending identity crisis. Parenthood also often brings sexual problems (e.g., as a consequence of rivalry with a child, itself a repetition of earlier sibling rivalry).

Case 12: A 28-year-old man developed retarded ejaculation and became a compulsive womanizer after the birth of his son. He deeply loved his son and sought treatment not for the sexual problem but because he began having dreams of harming the child. His rivalry with a younger brother for his mother's attention had been dormant during his marriage; now it was recalled by his unconscious resentment and jealousy over his wife's attentiveness to their infant. This is an example of a sexual problem that cleared up with very little direct discussion or intervention as the patient became aware of his jealousy and rivalry and of their consequences.

Lately, clinicians have begun to pay much more attention to the midlife crises of patients in their 40's and early 50's. These crises often occur in women whose lives have centered on raising children who have now left home; in men who have achieved lifelong goals and now question the validity of those goals; and in men who are forced to recognize that they have not achieved their goals and probably never will do so. The existential questions, "Who am I, where have I been, and where am I going?" may affect their sexual lives; decreased libido and sexual function, real or imagined, may follow. Intrapsychic factors that have been dormant or only marginally disruptive may flare up into serious problems, or previously resolved problems or dysfunction may reappear.

Health and the fear of loneliness are increasingly significant factors as a person ages. If partners are available and health is good, most people in their 60's and 70's continue to lead active sex lives. Appropriate education and counseling can often be of enormous value in helping them adjust to aging. Unfortunately, sometimes an intrapsychic conflict in the physician impedes such adjustment. One physician, asked by a 68-year-old patient why his erections were no longer as firm, responded jokingly, "What do you care about that for at your age?" Many people, including professionals, have a need to deny that the elderly are sexually interested and active—perhaps a carryover of the child's need to deny that his parents are sexual, coupled with a denial of their own ultimate aging.

A great variety of intrapsychic factors can affect disorders of desire and of functioning and the way sex is used interpersonally. Distortions of intrapsychic development lead to conflicts that exert a direct effect on sexual behavior through defensive operations necessary to reduce anxiety, guilt, or shame. Such conflicts also exert indirect effects by interfering with sexual learning and with capacity for intimate relationships. Even when intrapsychic factors are complex, many patients respond dramatically to support, permissiveness, specific suggestions, and exercises designed to promote new learning. When these fail, or if the problems appear to be severe and complex, psychotherapy is indicated. In those instances, consultation with a specialist is helpful in order to determine the most appropriate form of treatment. That may be short-term or long-term psychotherapy dealing with patients' general psychological problems, rather than therapy specifically directed toward the removal or alleviation of their sexual problems. If their sexual problems persist, however, more specific sex therapy should be instituted.

References

1. Kaplan H: *The New Sex Therapy*. New York, Brunner/Mazel Inc, 1974.
2. Woods SM: Violence: Psychotherapy of pseudohomosexual panic. *Arch Gen Psychiatry* 1972; 27:255-258.
3. Freud S: On the universal tendency to debasement in the sphere of love (Contributions to the psychology of love), in Strachey J (ed): *The Complete Psychological Works: Standard Edition*, 24 Vols. London, Hogarth Press, 1953-1974.

Chapter 14

Effects of Physical Illness on Sexual Functioning

Alexander N. Levay, M.D., Lawrence Sharpe, M.D., and Arlene Kagle, Ph.D.

The need to treat an illness, unfortunately, too often overshadows all other considerations for both physician and patient. A mistaken belief that asking about sex is untimely or unseemly keeps the patient from seeking information and reassurance or the physician from offering them. Some patients, on their own or with their partners, can cope with even devastating effects of illness on their sexual functioning. But many others need their physician's knowledge, care and support.

BACKGROUND FACTORS

Physical illness can interfere with sexual desire or ability because of organic, psychological and interpersonal factors. A physician must understand all three types to deal with any patient's sexual difficulties.

Sexual function may diminish or cease because of such organic factors as pain, immobility, changes in body function, disfigurement or the demands of dealing with a temporary or permanent disability. In most cases, total or partial sexual activity can be resumed when these factors are ameliorated by treatment, education, permission and reassurance.

More often sexual function is influenced by psychological factors, such as fears, moods and defensive behavior, that alter or inhibit sexual interest. Probably the most common fears are about death, disability, preoccupation with body integrity and dependence. Denial of the illness or its severity is common. Shock, anxiety, detachment or suppression of feeling, as well as depression and regression also occur frequently. In addition, many patients are angry, demanding, needy, manipulative, resigned or withdrawn. The emotions that emerge usually reflect the patient's characteristic ways of coping with stress.

The patient's emotional response almost always affects sexual functioning, but there are no simple correlations. Anxiety arising from the physical illness often leads to concern about current or future sexual functioning. There may be loss or increase of desire, or a shift to more aggressive or passive sexual behavior. For example, increased anger may result in more aggressive sexual behavior or, conversely, more passive behavior. Being more demanding may be expressed in increased sexual contact as a way of becoming close, or in decreased sexual contact with the wish to be taken care of in nonsexual ways by the spouse.

Illness may also affect the motivation to have sex. Sex may be used to secure reassurance and nurturing, or as a symbolic test of potency, power and attractiveness. Thus, a postcoronary patient may wish to engage in sex to become close to his partner or to reassure himself of his physical intactness; a mastectomy patient may wish to engage in sex to demonstrate that she is still desirable although disfigured.

A patient's reaction affects the partner, who in turn affects the patient. Illness may elicit the partner's nurturing, parental behavior; anger and intolerance; or feelings of loneliness or abandonment. Patients who react to illness with withdrawal or anger make many partners feel excluded, helpless or confused. In some cases, both parties are so fearful that sex will be difficult or harmful that, in a misguided attempt to protect one another, they abandon physical intimacy; this can then undermine emotional intimacy. In other couples, illness brings closeness, cooperation and sharing. In still others, illness creates or extends distance and discord. Because of these varied possibilities, dealing with the couple is an important part of treating the patient's emotional and sexual relationship.

Virtually any illness can affect sexual interest and activity. Fortunately, in most cases, adverse effects are minimal and as transitory as the illness itself. Most couples return to their preferred level of sexual involvement after a cold, a broken leg or an appendectomy. But some conditions can have more serious and long-lasting effects. These include certain major illnesses; many surgical procedures; conditions that cause chronic discomfort, limit mobility or are disfiguring; and any illness affecting the urogenital and reproductive systems.

Illnesses can affect sexual functioning in three ways. Some produce direct physical sexual dysfunction (organic). Others cause no organic sexual impairment but can trigger psychological reactions that lead to sexual dysfunction (psychogenic). Still others produce organic impairment leading to partial dysfunction, which in turn may trigger psychological reactions causing full sexual dysfunction (organo-psychogenic). In every case, the physician must deal with both the physical illness and the psychological reactions to it.

Some organic sources of sexual dysfunction are paraplegia and postsurgical conditions (e.g., radical prostatectomy) that affect the nerves responsible for sexual response. The psychological reactions can be devastating.

Psychogenic sexual dysfunction can arise from conditions as different from each other as coronary heart disease and disorders requiring pelvic surgery. A man may become impotent after routine hernia repair or suprapubic prostatectomy if he mistakenly believes that the procedure harms sexual function. For the same reason, a woman may become sexually unresponsive after hysterectomy or mastectomy.

Among the causes of organo-psychogenic sexual dysfunction are end-stage renal disease and some antihypertensive medications. These can create partial or temporary organic dysfunction which, if aggravated by psychological factors, can result in complete and permanent dysfunction. Reversing the organic problem by kidney transplant or changing the medication does not always relieve the sexual dysfunction; when severely debilitating psychological factors are present, they also must be resolved before sexual function can return.

People with some illnesses may have any of the above three kinds of problems. Men with diabetes mellitus who complain of erectile difficulties may show total, partial or no organic impairment when tested in a sleep laboratory.

Clearly a physician should not label any sexual dysfunction as solely functional, but should approach it along both organic and psychological lines. (Some screening questions and treatment techniques to use with patients experiencing sexual difficulties that are related to illnesses are given later in this chapter.)

Unfortunately, research on physical illness and its effects on sexual function is sparse. There are few studies on the physiology of organic impairment so that in many cases the mechanisms that cause loss of function remain undetermined. There also are very few surveys of sexual behavior following specific illness, and findings are usually limited to questions concerning frequency of intercourse and do not include a full range of sexual behaviors. Most of these reports are based on small samples, and few findings have been replicated. The reactions and observations of patients' partners have rarely been included. Physicians with extensive clinical experience in this area who have developed treatment plans for sexual problems related to physical illnesses can help colleagues and patients by publishing their findings or otherwise making them known.

ILLNESS WITHOUT ORGANIC SEXUAL IMPAIRMENT

Coronary Heart Disease. Cardiovascular disease, particularly myocardial infarction, is known to affect sexual functioning. Recent major monographs, textbooks and symposia on cardiology are beginning to address this aspect of the disease and recovery from it.[1,2]

Although no organic component has been implicated, between one-third and one-half of all men who have suffered myocardial infarction report having diminished desire and coitus even several years later.[3,4] Some men, however, report increased sexual activity.[2,5] Similar increases and decreases also have been noted in women.[6] The changes in both sexes are thought to be related to emotional changes and to altered interaction with partners.

These seemingly contradictory findings are more understandable when one explores patients and their partners psychologically. Some patients push themselves to be sexually active to prove that they are intact, strong or attractive.[7] This may reflect a need to deny that the condition is life-threatening. Despite more frequent sexual activity, there may be problems; a patient striving to prove intact function may become a spectator to his own sexual behavior and feel "performance anxiety." The final result is often erectile, lubricatory or orgasmic problems.

Some postcoronary patients and their partners become unduly cautious, fearful of aggravating the condition and of causing further coronary thrombosis, even death.[8,9] Such fears may reflect general depression, anxiety and preoccupation with the illness. The final result can be loss of desire or disruption of arousal or other phases of the sexual response cycle. Angina, dysrhythmia and congestive heart failure can have similar effects.

Unfortunately, a patient's sexual concerns, fears and even dysfunctions often remain unexplored. In many cases, when factual information alone is needed, it is not given by the physician or, if given, it is not heard by the patient.[10] Any discussion of sex should include the partner and be timed so that the patient can absorb the information with minimal anxiety. Ideally, such a discussion should not be merely part of discharge instructions but should be initiated by the physician as soon as the patient's concern shifts from immediate survival to future functioning.

In a recent study of 100 wives of patients who had myocardial infarctions,[11] "nearly all (the wives) stated that they would prefer to receive sex instructions together with their husbands and have the opportunity to explore their concerns and fears."

It stands to reason that the partner of a cardiovascular patient would have a major influence on the success or failure of rehabilitation, and that the sexual needs of the partner, as well as of the patient, should therefore be given adequate consideration. The study found that, although the wives were not relieved of their fears by the information they received, that fact was not important enough to deter them from returning to sexual activity. Fear, however, may have affected both the quality and frequency of their activity, the authors observed. Any recommendations or suggestions should be reinforced several times during convalescence so that questions or concerns can be dealt with before difficulties develop.

It is important for a patient to know how much energy is actually expended in sexual activity. Hellerstein and Friedman's classic study of cardiac and normal patients showed that the mean maximal heart rate (a measure of oxygen consumption) during sexual activity with a familiar partner is 97.5; it rises to a peak of 117 for the period of orgasm.[1,3] The mean maximal heart rate during normal office work, including walking, climbing stairs and doing paper work, is 120. Obviously many daily activities demand as much or more "work" than coitus.

The "met" is a convenient measure of energy use. It is the energy expenditure per kilogram of body weight per minute of a subject sitting quietly in a chair. (In a 70 kg man, one met is approximately 1.4 calories per minute or 3.5 ml oxygen per kg per minute.) A champion athlete can perform at 20 mets; the average person strolling at a level of 1 mph performs at 1.5 mets; running 5 mph at 8 mets; and an average, fully recovered, postinfarct patient has a performance capacity of 8 mets. It is now generally agreed that if a postmyocardial infarction patient can exercise at a level of at least 3 mets, sexual activity with a familiar partner may be resumed.

A recent and as yet unreplicated finding reported by Fletcher and Johnston[12] strikes a cautionary and potentially alarming note. A small sample of postmyocardial infarction patients fitted with a halter monitor and meeting the above criteria for exercise tolerance were instructed to engage in sexual activity during the following 24 to 48 hour period. Much to the surprise of the investigators, a sizeable proportion of study subjects showed serious electrical instability manifested by frequent and often multifocal ventricular beats, sometimes appearing as bigeminy or coupling. In one instance, there were even brief runs of ventricular tachycardia. These serious phenomena occurred most frequently during sexual activity with an unfamiliar partner or with masturbation, but they occurred with familiar partners as well. Since there were no such irregularities with activities that produced a comparable or greater work load on the heart, it seems clear that, if these findings are confirmed, sexual excitement and activity may prove to be singularly stressful and therefore more hazardous to postcoronary patients than previously thought.

It is not as yet clear what mechanisms are involved or how much of this response is due to the psychophysiological stress response of the sexual experience, and how much to the psychophysiology of sexual arousal itself. There also was an iatrogenic stress factor complicating this study in that patients were told to have sex, and this meant, in effect, that their physicians were "watching."

From these findings, patients who experience ventricular arrythmia only during sexual activity should undergo halter monitoring.

The cardiac stress test is readily available and adequate, and the results and their significance should be fully shared and discussed with the patient and partner.

Many patients, especially those who were not physically fit before the myocardial infarction, tend to become debilitated by bedrest afterward. Such patients have decreased exercise tolerance and often mistakenly believe that their limitations are the result of permanent damage caused by muscle loss. They must be told that this is not true, and a supervised general fitness program should be started so that normal activities, including sex, can be resumed.

Most patients and their partners have an emotional need to be physically close during the stressful period of convalescence, but many fear that any physical intimacy may lead to sexual arousal, which they consider dangerous. They should be reassured about the low risk of sudden cardiac disorder during coitus once adequate screening procedures have been passed. While more research is needed, most studies to date show that less than 1 per cent of all sudden deaths can be attributed to coital activity. The vast majority of these deaths involve partners other than spouses, unfamiliar settings and the previous consumption of a great deal of food or alcohol.[13]

In light of these findings, it seems reasonable to allow a couple to resume sexual activity gradually as exercise tolerance increases. This often occurs before the 8- to 12-week period of abstinence that most cardiologists prescribe. Because resuming even partial sexual activity, such as manual or oral sex, is important to most patients and partners in order to maintain emotional closeness and to avoid sexual dysfunction or phobia, few restrictions need be offered. Only if the patient is in poor physical condition or has other disabilities, such as continued angina on exertion or cardiac arrhythmia, should sex be limited; in these cases, the physician can suggest the prophylactic use of coronary vasodilators or antiarrhythmic medication. The physician can also teach and encourage active sexual behavior by the partner, such as partner-superior (patient-prone) or lateral coital positions and manual and oral stimulation. If the patient is totally incapacitated, the partner can be advised to masturbate when aroused. Holding, fondling and kissing in tender but nonarousing ways should always be suggested as a way for the couple to maintain closeness and a sense of being cared for and loved.

Cerebral Vascular Accident. Stroke, like coronary heart disease, is life-threatening. If severe, it can leave a person with major disabilities, including inability to communicate. Even less severe strokes may cause loss of mobility, cognitive impairment and changes in affect, including rage and depression. The patient can seem very much "not himself." Dependence becomes a real problem as well as an emotional issue, and the patient's family is often disoriented by these changes, especially if the patient was active, verbal and independent before the stroke. While the patient and the family attempt to cope with these changes, sex may have a low priority, but as recovery proceeds it can gain great importance.

Several aspects of impairment affect sexual function. The patient may not be able to move some parts of the body easily or at all. There may be sensory impairment affecting parts of the sexual apparatus directly or other components of the sexual system. No matter how mild the stroke or impairment, the patient's body image and sense of attractiveness may be badly damaged. As in cardiac cases, the patient and partner may fear that sex will be harmful or cause another stroke. All of these factors can lead to sexual dysfunction even if the neuromuscular components of the sexual system are sufficiently intact.

In a study of 105 stroke patients under age 60, 43 per cent reported decreased frequency of coitus, but only 29 per cent reported decreased libido.[14] It is not clear what caused them to limit coitus—perhaps debility and pain, fear related to the disease, the partner's feelings or the couple's shift to noncoital acts which they were reluctant to discuss. Whatever its origin, this decrease in coitus could probably be reversed in many couples by a physician's approval and instruction.

Perhaps because stroke more often attacks older people, who until recently were widely thought of as being uninterested in sex, there is almost no literature on how strokes affect sexual response and behavior. More specific help awaits the publication of research and clinical reports.

Hypertension. This is one of the most common conditions treated in general practice, yet the sexual effects of the illness and of its treatment are not very well known. Untreated hypertension rarely seems to affect sexual activity, even though in persistent cases there is decreased cardiac output and, during coitus, a rise of blood pressure as high as 260/150 mm Hg.[15]

The lack of knowledge about the effects of sexual activity on hypertensive patients suggests that physicians make conservative recommendations—that physically and emotionally stressful intercourse should not occur until the condition is under reasonable control.

When hypertension is adequately managed, the patient's sexual behavior should still be monitored. Asking patients about their sexual activity can provide the information necessary for counseling, both to prevent sexual difficulties and to maximize compliance with medical instructions.

If sexual difficulties do occur, the resulting anxiety can lead to sexual dysfunction. Such dysfunction may complicate treatment of the hypertension, because there is evidence that a significant number of patients will discontinue medication rather than suffer sexual side effects. As with diabetes and other conditions where any given patient may or may not have organic components to his sexual dysfunction, believing that the sexual problem results from the illness or the medication can maintain the sexual problem. The physician may elect to refer the patient for intensive sexual therapy in such cases.

While sexual functioning is generally not impaired in undiagnosed cases of hypertension, difficulties often occur when the patient learns of the illness and treatment for it begins. Organic sexual dysfunction caused by certain antihypertensive drugs is fairly common. Alpha antiadrenergic drugs block ganglionic receptor sites in the sympathetic nervous system; the decrease in sympathetic stimulation can produce inhibited or retrograde ejaculation. Impotence also commonly occurs; in some cases, this is probably at least in part a psychological reaction to the changes in ejaculation.

Oral diuretics and hydralazine hydrochloride, which do not affect the ganglionic system, and beta antiadrenergic drugs, such as propranolol hydrochloride, are very effective in treating certain cases of hypertension and fortunately do not usually cause sexual complications. Most patients treated for hypertension can be advised that sexual side effects occur in a small percentage of cases, but that controlling the dosage or changing the medication can eliminate these effects. To minimize the risk of creating a negative placebo effect, the physician will have to use his judgment as to when to introduce this information to highly anxious and suggestible patients.

Hypertensive patients may need support and information for psychological reasons. Some believe that their condition can be made worse by excitement, even though it is under medical control, and family and friends routinely instruct them to relax and not become upset or excited. Many patients and their spouses abstain from sexual activity, assuming that sexual excitement is dangerous, even though abstinence can create discord and distress. Other patients deny the symptoms or diagnosis of hypertension and continue all normal activities, including sexual ones. Many will also discontinue prescribed medication if they think it interferes with sexual function. A number do not tell their physicians they have done so, and even stop seeing them altogether.

Bronchopulmonary Conditions. Bronchopulmonary conditions, including allergies, chronic obstructive pulmonary disease (COPD), asthma and emphysema, can affect sexual function. Many patients are cautious or fearful about sexual activity because its respiratory demands create dyspnea and hypoxia, which they associate with life-threatening situations. Recent studies of COPD[16,17] and asthma reveal a high incidence of erectile difficulties, which were psychogenic rather than organic. Labby[18] wrote: "Emotional factors are most often of prime importance and any sexual difficulties are probably best seen as an integral part of the patient's emotional history." Dependency needs and fear of separation seem to be the major etiological elements. The effects on sexuality of conflicts about such feelings have already been described.

When sexual difficulties develop during these illnesses, referral may be necessary for treating the intrapsychic elements of both the disease and the sexual dysfunction. At the same time, a primary care physician can help many patients by making pragmatic suggestions, such as how to reduce respiratory requirements during sex.

Allergic and asthmatic reactions may be induced or worsened when vaso-congestion of nasal membranes occurs simultaneously with sexual arousal. These reactions can be minimized by scheduling medication so that it is most effective when the patient usually has coitus. A simple but very helpful suggestion is to keep inhalers and other medications at the bedside.

A couple's sexual patterns may require more oxygen consumption than is possible for someone with COPD and emphysema, particularly when he is in the prone position. The couple should be advised to have coitus in a sitting posture so that the partner does most of the thrusting. They should also be encouraged to enjoy sex play to orgasm as an alternative to coitus, or to extend sex play so that coitus is briefer.

ILLNESSES INVOLVING ORGANIC AND PSYCHOGENIC IMPAIRMENT

Diabetes Mellitus. This is most often used as an example of a disease that organically impairs sexual function. Some patients with erectile problems have undetected diabetes mellitus,[19] and some with treated diabetes also have erectile problems.

Yet in any specific case it is difficult to determine to what extent the diabetic pathological process is responsible for the sexual problem, and to what extent the psychological mechanisms of performance anxiety and spectatoring are playing a part. Some patients with erectile problems also lose sexual desire (although this is not a symptom that they present). Their plasma testosterone levels are normal, so loss of desire is secondary to erectile dysfunction and not a primary effect of diabetes on endocrine function.[20,21]

About one-half of diabetic men experience erectile difficulties. Research shows that this problem is unrelated to the patient's age or to the severity or duration of the diabetes.[21-23] Abel reports erectile dysfunction in 84 per cent of the male diabetics he examined, with 30 per cent clearly "organic," 44 per cent partially organic and 26 per cent psychogenic.[24] The neuropathy underlying sexual dysfunction may be primarily metabolic (through changes in the sorbital pathway) or primarily vascular, leading to small arteriole sclerosis and thus to direct neural damage. Direct arteriole damage in the corpora cavernosa and corpus spongiosum leads to further erectile problems. One study has shown lesions of the autonomic nerves in the corpora cavernosa, but the small sample and lack of a control group make these findings inconclusive.[20]

There is also evidence that the arteries supplying the penis develop occlu-

176

sive lesions similar to those occurring in the extremities that cause claudication.[25] Thirty patients between the ages of 30 and 56 (12 of whom were diabetic) with a history of erectile dysfunction of more than one year, demonstrated these lesions on arteriography of the penile arterial bed, which correlated with an absence of pulsation in the dorsal penile artery. In four clearly psychogenic impotent patients these findings were not present.

In diabetes of recent onset, good control of the illness and counseling for psychological concerns often completely eliminate erectile difficulties. Apparently these patients were experiencing reversible neuropathy caused by a primary metabolic disorder. One would expect the patients with more serious vascular neuropathy to respond less well to treatment. However, performance anxiety and spectatoring usually come into play whatever the underlying organic mechanism and as such require counseling or therapy. If sleep studies show total (organic) erectile dysfunction, penile implants can be recommended if the couple insists on regaining coital activity (see Chapter 25).

A very small number of men report retrograde ejaculation or impaired orgasm. Men usually retain the ability to ejaculate despite loss of sustained arousal, although recent evidence indicates that a significant proportion of diabetic males do experience various ejaculatory difficulties. These seem to be correlated with the presence of signs and symptoms of a neurogenic bladder, suggesting sympathetic neuropathy as causation.[26]

Similar findings have not been reported consistently among females. Kolodny[21] found an absence of orgasm in 35 per cent of previously orgasmic female diabetics, but other studies report no such incidence.[22,23] Ellenberg[27] wrote: "There are not demonstrable differences between diabetic females with or without neuropathy regarding sexual interest and orgasm. Even more startling is the lack of any effect of diabetes on female sexual performance." Women seem to be unaffected or have difficulties only with orgasm, which involves the sympathetic nerves; they do not have problems with arousal, which involves parasympathetic responses.

So far, no neurological or other physiological factors have been found to account for differences between diabetic men and women. These differences may result from inexact measurement, as decreased arousal is less obvious in women. If scientific measurement rather than patients' reports are used to determine arousal, more similarity may be found between the sexes.

It is obviously difficult, then, to confidently label a diabetic patient with sexual dysfunction as "organically impaired." A diabetic man's impotence may result from minimal organic changes that are magnified by psychological factors. Comparable changes may occur but go unnoticed in diabetic women. Medical control of diabetes alone may not relieve sexual fears.[28] Therefore, a diabetic man may need considerable support and possibly therapy to avoid or overcome secondary impotence. A diabetic woman may not have this problem, but she needs extra gynecological information and supervision, since hyperglycemia and glycosuria make her highly susceptible to vaginal infections, especially monilial vulvovaginitis.

Renal Failure. Sexual dysfunction appears, or worsens if present, in one-half of all men and one-quarter to one-half of all women who suffer renal failure.[18,29] The reduction in libido, coital frequency and orgasm varies with differences in treatment.

Uremia causes sexual dysfunctions, especially loss of libido and impotence, which often are not alleviated by dialysis. In fact, one-third of men and one-quarter of women report increased dysfunction after uremia is brought under control.

Dialysis at home is associated with better sexual function than hospital outpatient treatment, but it does not prevent considerable loss of desire and potency in many patients.[29] In a report by De-Nour,[30] several psychological factors were implicated in loss of libido and potency in dialysis patients. Depression, loss of dominance in the marriage and negative attitudes of the spouse toward illness and the provision of chronic care were all found to be negatively correlated with sexual functioning. Evaluation of the couple prior to beginning dialysis therapy is recommended to identify the possible presence of these factors. When marked depression occurs, a course of antidepressants may be tried. Therapy for the couple or for the healthy partner also may be necessary to deal with negative feelings and behaviors toward the patient.

Reports on sexual function are mixed for patients given renal transplants. Many return to sexual function, but 20 to 30 per cent of men do not.[31,32] Such patients need support and sometimes sex therapy to restore sexual function. Some studies suggest that improvement is limited to women.[18] When renal transplants do restore sexual function, it happens spontaneously without therapeutic intervention.

A comparison between male patients with chronic renal disease undergoing hemodialysis with a group treated by renal transplants indicates that long-term dialysis does not reverse the fall of testosterone levels, the high levels of luteinizing hormone (LH) or follicle stimulating hormone (FSH), or the severe spermatogenic damage.[33]

The etiology of sexual dysfunction in renal failure is not clear. Several factors may be responsible. Uremic neuropathy often affects the autonomic nervous system and may reduce erectile capacity via impairment of the parasympathetic system. Early treatment is important in preventing such neuropathy; it can be reversed by renal transplant.[32] There is some evidence that uremia affects Leydig cells, reducing testosterone production.[34] Some uremic patients who do not undergo dialysis show increased libido when treated with testosterone.[35,36]

Additional factors have recently been reported, which may account for the presence of impaired sexual functioning.[37,38] A decreased level of zinc appears to affect the production of testosterone; replacement therapy in a small group of patients seemed to reverse this effect, with a concomitant improvement in sexual responsiveness. Most recent evidence indicates that a consistent elevation of prolactin occurs in patients with chronic uremia that is not corrected by hemodialysis. Prolactin has been found to be associated with diminished sexual arousal and desire, possibly by interference with the production or peripheral utilization of testosterone or by a central effect.

Finally, other medical conditions underlying or complicating the uremia, such as vascular disease and diabetes, or the treatment of these conditions, such as drug therapy for hypertension and depression, may produce or perpetuate sexual dysfunction.

Clearly an interplay of organic and psychological factors contributes to sexual problems in end-stage renal failure. The physician must not be lulled into assuming that sexual difficulties can be forgotten after a renal graft; psychogenic problems continue in many patients after the organic problem has been resolved. Such patients need support and sometimes therapy to restore sexual function. Those who remain on dialysis may require even more help.

Decreased libido may call for couple counseling. One can encourage the patient to engage in sexual play even if the illness diminishes desire and arousal; it may help to urge the spouse to be encouraging, since love and support always aid sexual interest. And sex can be encouraged as soon after dialysis as possible, when the effects of uremia are lowest. Psychotherapy for the couple may help if changes in roles and dependence interfere with marital adjustment.

Cancer. Despite increasing cure rates, cancer remains one of the most dreaded diseases; it is associated with disfigurement after surgery, long and painful illness and a high probability of death. It is not surprising that physicians often give the patient's sexual life low priority. Yet cancer may involve areas of the body associated with sexual functioning, and treatment often involves massive changes in body image and integrity. It can activate all the psychological problems previously discussed. In the final phase, disability, hospitalization and the imminence of death can disrupt sexual function completely.

Patients with cancer must first deal with the possibility of their own death. This is awesome, frightening and emotionally overwhelming. Even if treatment has been successful, many patients continue to fear recurrence. If initial treatment has only ameliorated the condition or slowed its spread, the patient may live with considerable pain, with the side effects of continuing treatment (especially chemotherapy and radiation), with loss of function and with increased dependence on others. All of these circumstances may undermine libido or sexual function. Also, the spouse often has new responsibilities and anxieties and may experience sexual difficulties, especially if the spouse feels guilty about "imposing" sex on the patient or is physically and emotionally turned off by the effects of the illness.

Radical surgery, especially colostomy, ileostomy, prostatectomy and radical cystectomy, often injures the nerve plexi responsible for erection and orgasm. Even when no direct harm is done to areas involved in sexual function, problems may occur because of damage to the patient's self-image and sense of attractiveness.

Many ostomy patients and their spouses adapt over time, but the stoma is visually unpleasant and malodorous, and there may be such sexual problems as erectile difficulty and, in women, a decrease in the ability to have multiple orgasms.[39] About one-third of the men and women questioned in a long-term follow-up study reported diminished libido.[40] Over one-half of the men were not having sexual relations, and 21 per cent of the women experienced pain or lack of sensation during coitus.

Many such couples need support and counseling to resume their sexual relationships. One can suggest bedtime attire that covers the stoma and appliance but allows easy access to the rest of the body; robes and nightgowns are better in this respect than pajamas. Societies of ostomy patients can be of practical help with these and other problems.

Surgery in the pelvic area, more than any other surgery, disrupts sexual function. In the past, radical procedures were too often used with little concern for the quality of the patient's life if he or she survived. Many patients lost sexual function because nerve plexi were severed. Today, cure rates are higher and surgeons have developed techniques that avoid these problems.[41] However, radical retroperitoneal prostatectomy and abdominal-perineal resection must transsect either the sympathetic hypogastric plexus or the pudendal nerve, interfering with the nerves mediating erection of the penis.[42] In most cases, the resulting organic impotence is total. Such sexual expression as kissing and caressing can be encouraged, since libido and the need for closeness and love remain despite loss of erection or orgasm.

Surgery that directly affects the genitalia is usually threatening to sexual function and to confidence in one's capacity for such functioning. Many patients and their partners wrongly assume that cancer in these sites, even if removed, precludes sexual activity. In some cases, this assumption stems from fear of contagion or of exacerbating or reactivating the disease. Some women mistakenly believe that the uterus is essential to sexual function and that hysterectomy will make them asexual. In a study of 89 patients who underwent hysterectomy and oophorectomy for noncancerous conditions, 37 per cent reported a deterioration in sexual relationships, which they associated with the operation. Most who showed such effects had expected the operation to diminish their sexual feelings and activities.[43] Hysterectomy is also psychologically very threatening to some husbands, who feel it has made them infertile by proxy; it is therefore a blow to their masculinity.

It is essential that the physician give preoperative counseling and dispel any misconceptions of the patient and partner. As Labby[18] has said: "Preoperative prophylaxis is of the essence in avoiding demoralizing postoperative emotional states. Preoperative knowledge of the patient's emotional life is fundamental: a positive statement that sexual expression can follow the same pattern after surgery that it did before, should help dispel the myth that gynecologic surgery destroys sexual response."

Treatment and surgery should, whenever possible, maintain sexual function. The vast majority of patients with cervical carcinoma (stages I and II) who are treated by radiotherapy undergo narrowing and obliteration of the vagina, pelvic fibrosis and coital discomfort or pain. These effects rarely occur in patients treated by surgery alone; sexual dysfunction, therefore, is proportionately less common.[44] Most radiologists say that regular examinations during therapy and the use of dilators when necessary prevent the occurrence of such strictures.

Radiation therapy does not disrupt sexual function in men treated for testicular tumors. Patients with seminoma treated with radiation alone show little change in sexual function; in one-third of the cases, there is lower semen volume. Of patients with nonseminomatous tumors treated surgically, more than 80 per cent reported decreased semen volume and 20 per cent reported sexual difficulties.[45] Obviously, such findings should be carefully considered when treatment decisions are made. Since many men and women associate semen with sexual as well as reproductive potency, any possible change in semen volume should be explained before surgery. This will lessen the chance that such change will erode a person's sexual self-image and lead to dysfunction.

The surgery most traumatic to women seems to be mastectomy, because it so vastly changes feminine appearance and body image.[46] Ervine[47] says that the patient's initial reaction is to feel "mutilated, repulsed, desexed, frightened and depressed," although most women and their spouses do, with support, adjust and return to full sexual function.

Several measures can be used routinely to help mastectomy patients. Byrd[48] recommends (1) early mobilization of the involved shoulder and upper extremity, so that there is a full range of motion by the time of hospital discharge; (2) immediate use of a temporary prosthesis (as early as two or three days after surgery); and (3) a permanent prosthesis as soon as the wound has healed adequately. Resuming interest in make-up, bed time attire, hairdo and other aspects of appearance also should be encouraged to help the patient and partner reduce the sense of trauma to the woman's body and body image and to maintain sexual attractiveness and interest.

The patient and partner also should be reassured that the surgery in no way decreases sexual function and that coitus may be resumed without hazard. With such active support from the physician, most women and partners can make an excellent psychological as well as physical recovery.

In recommending a return to sexual activity after this or any other surgery, the physician should be specific. Saying something indefinite, such as "You can have intercourse soon," may be variously interpreted as meaning three days or three months. If patients or spouses seem reluctant to resume a sexual relationship, the physician should take time and care to understand their underlying concerns or fears and to help work them out.

Urological Illnesses. Any condition that affects the genitals directly or indirectly can precipitate sexual dysfunction. Dysfunctions may arise partly from organic factors, inasmuch as many urological illnesses cause pain during coitus. However, one should keep in mind that these conditions can be dramatized and used as excuses for abstinence by patients who want to withdraw from sexual activity for other reasons.

Cystitis, urethritis and prostatitis can cause sexual discomfort and dysfunction. Lower urinary tract infections occur most commonly in women 24 to 48 hours after genital activity, especially if it was vigorous and prolonged; this suggests that minor local trauma predisposes to infection. Postmenopausal women are particularly vulnerable to such mechanical trauma, probably because of the effects of lack of estrogens. To help eradicate recurrent urethritis and cystitis, a physician should remind patients to empty their bladders before and after sexual activity and to drink liberal amounts of fluids. In chronic cases, long-term antibiotic therapy and washing the area around the urethra before sex have been suggested.[49]

Many women with recurrent bladder and urethral infections come to associate sexual activity with pain and develop secondary anorgasmia, dyspareunia and even vaginismus. They and their partners need support if they are to return to comfortable sexual activity. Specific medical recommendations and information help not only to end the infection but to reassure the couple that the condition is not permanent. Women who develop vaginismus should receive dilation (see Chapter 12). Those who develop more serious psychosexual conflicts may need referral for intensive psychotherapy.

Men experience sexual difficulty associated with prostatitis and some unusual conditions of the genitalia, such as undescended testicles, a tight foreskin, chordee and Peyronie's disease. These conditions can cause considerable pain or worry about malformation and malfunction. Prompt medical attention and sympathetic reassurance are essential to minimize medical and psychological effects and to avert serious dysfunction.

Any illness or congenital defect causing sterility also can lead to sexual difficulty. Dysfunction in such instances is strictly psychogenic; loss of reproductive capacity is often inaccurately associated with loss of sexual function. Some couples need patient, extended counseling.

Other Medical Conditions. A number of illnesses and procedures in addition to those discussed above are associated with high rates of sexual dysfunction. In many situations, the physician will have to rely on his own clinical experience, observations and judgment, because little or no data may be available.

Liver diseases, such as cirrhosis and hepatitis, can cause failure to metabolize estrogens properly, so these hormones accumulate in the blood stream. In men, the results are gynecomastia and diminished libido and arousal. It is not clear to what extent these problems are psychogenic, as well as somatogenic, although both factors may well be at work.

Endocrine disorders can increase or decrease androgen levels. Men or women with hypothyroidism, women with Addison's disease and men with feminizing testicular tumors causing depressed androgen production often experience reduced desire or arousal. Women with masculinizing tumors of the adrenal glands and Cushing's syndrome, both of which can elevate androgen production, may experience increased libido and such masculinizing effects as hirsutism and deepening of the voice.

Hormonal abnormalities have recently been identified as a significant source of impotence. While most cases of impotence undoubtedly are psychogenic (see Chapter 25), Spark et al[50] reported that 37 of 105 impotent patients had disorders of the hypothalamic-pituitary-gonadal axis that were not suspected prior to screening for serum testosterone levels. After correction of the primary problem, appropriate hormonal therapy restored potency in 33 of these patients.

Hematological illnesses, including sickle cell disease and leukemia, have been known to cause priapism. This can result in permanent sexual impairment and patients with these conditions may be afraid to participate in any sexual activity if they are aware of this possibility. Should such permanent impairment occur, some patients can be helped with penile implants if their basic condition permits such a procedure and the patients and their spouses desire it.

Neurologic disorders, such as multiple sclerosis and syringomyelia, can disrupt central nervous system pathways and reflex arcs essential to sexual function. Any aspect of sexual response, from arousal to orgasm, may be affected. However, because many patients with these conditions retain sexual function, it may be difficult to differentiate between psychogenic and organic components.

MANAGEMENT OF SEXUAL PROBLEMS

The first step in the medical management of sexual problems is taking a sexual history. Knowing a patient's past sexual function is essential; it enables the physician to educate, reassure and orient a patient faced with illness. Telling a patient who has always had sexual problems that a treatment or surgical procedure will not change sexual function hardly gives relief. Similarly, taking a sensitive and careful sexual history can keep a physician from mistakenly assuming that an elderly or unmarried patient will not mind losing sexual function.

Seven questions are usually sufficient to gain a basic understanding of the patient's sexual function. Exactly how one phrases them depends to some extent on one's own style and on the patient. Most important is that the patient know that the physician is as comfortable, natural and professionally interested in this aspect of health as in others—no more and no less.

1. A good opening question, after general queries about marriage and social life, is: "How is the sexual part of your life?" Putting the question this way tells the patient that sex is a natural function, and that knowing about it is important to the physician's ability to provide the best possible care. Since the question is open-ended, it helps the physician gain a sense of how the patient views those areas of his life. Responses range from a spontaneous outpouring of concerns, fears and disappointments through perfunctory replies to aversive disclaimers. All provide useful information about basic attitudes and possible areas of further exploration.

It is almost always important to proceed to more structured questions in order to obtain factual details. Occasionally one finds a patient who is unduly anxious or unwilling to consider the topic or answer the question; the physician can protect the patient's right to privacy without sacrificing good medical care by dropping the subject but reserving the option of asking again if it is necessary for complete management.

2. A good follow-up question is: "How often are you having sex?" This requires only a numerical answer, not a description, which is difficult for many patients to give.

3. Whatever the answer, one can go on to more specific questions about sexual activity: "What type of sexual activity are you having—manual, oral or coital?" By naming several types of sexual behavior, the physician gives the patient acceptable terms and promotes the idea that all of these behaviors can be discussed.

4. "How often do you masturbate?" should be asked of all patients, whether or not they have available partners. The question indirectly helps to teach patients that in many situations masturbation is natural and healthy. It is particularly important to know the patient's premorbid attitude toward masturbation, because recommending masturbation may be helpful during rehabilitation. For example, a woman who has had a hysterectomy and oophorectomy, who is not on hormone replacement therapy and who does not have a sexual partner may be advised that masturbation will help maintain vaginal lubrication and avoid atrophic vaginitis. How this suggestion is made, if at all, depends on the patient's attitude and history.

5. This question is meant to probe for difficulties that the patient has not described: "Many people experience sexual problems at some time in their life. What problems have you experienced? Desire? Erection? Lubrication? Orgasm? Enjoyment? Pain?" By making this question open-ended, the physician encourages the patient to view a problem as something that happens to many people, and that can be discussed with the physician and solved. The information also may be useful in medical management. For example, a man with a premorbid history of erectile dysfunction will probably need special support and counseling both before and after a routine prostatectomy.

6. If the partner has not been interviewed, it is important to learn something of his or her sexual response: "How is it for your partner?" Often difficulties are ascribed to partners: a patient may talk about his partner's anorgasmia rather than his own difficulty in becoming aroused. This open-ended question can provide rich material about how the spouse is viewed as a mate and sexual partner. Ideally, the partner also should be interviewed, because evaluating sexual function very often requires considering the patient as part of a couple.

7. The last question is: "What physical concerns or medical problems have you or your partner had that affected your sexual functioning?" This allows patients to discuss concerns about the size or function of their genitalia and to raise sexual concerns about past or present illnesses, medications and surgical procedures. Among these factors may be previous pelvic infections, sexually transmitted disease, complications of pregnancy or medical conditions discussed earlier in this chapter.

These seven questions are sufficient to elicit the presence of functional as well as organic sexual problems if they exist. Further exploration is needed if problems emerge, but often the physician does not have to deal with them beyond offering a referral.

The timing of these questions is important: To obtain maximum information and help the patient as much as possible, the physician should not ask them during an emergency examination for the primary condition. The history should be taken, preferably from both spouses, when the acute phase of illness is past and convalescence begins. Convalescence is also a good time to ask about any concerns that the patient's illness may have caused about future sexual functioning.

With new patients who receive a complete work-up, it is important to include sexual history routinely. Physicians who have not asked such questions may find doing so difficult or uncomfortable. Usually they can be asked naturally after questions about marital and social adjustment, or they can be included in the system review. To avoid negative implications, the physician should not sandwich these questions between bowel and urinary problems nor pose them after asking about venereal disease.

To learn how much, if any, sexual impairment has organic sources, one should routinely ask the following questions of patients who acknowledge sexual difficulties or who have experienced illnesses or treatments associated with sexual dysfunction:

For Men:
1. How often do you have morning erections? Are they as firm as ever?
2. During masturbation, is the erection full or partial? Do you have an orgasm? Is there any ejaculate (semen)?
3. When was the last time you experienced a full erection with your partner?
4. When was the last time you had an orgasm with your partner?
5. How often do you feel an urge to have sex? Is this different from before?

For Women:
1. When was the last time you felt lubricated (wet) with your partner? Is this different from before?
2. When was the last time you had an orgasm with your partner? Do you have orgasms more or less often? Have your orgasms changed in any way? Has the way you reach orgasm changed?
3. During masturbation, do you lubricate? Do you have an orgasm? Has this changed in any way?
4. How often do you feel an urge to have sex? Is this different from before?

In evaluating the answers, the physician will find that several factors stand out in problems that are primarily psychogenic. Libido may be diminished or absent, but morning erections and ability to masturbate are intact. Some good sexual function may still occur under special circumstances, such as on vacation or when the children are away. Any such positive experiences greatly improve the prognosis, for they suggest that full sexual function is physically possible.

If a patient has not tried to masturbate, the physician can prescribe it as a step in diagnosis. Patients who have a negative attitude toward masturbation may offer resistance or only token compliance; such an attitude must be taken into account in evaluating self-reports. If the patient can masturbate with full erection to orgasm, organic impairment can be ruled out. Sometimes, however, emotional inhibition is so severe that masturbation is also impaired. In such cases, the presence of morning erections suggests organic intactness, but long-standing dysfunction can affect even morning erections, either directly or by the patient's inattention to them. In some such cases, referral to a sleep laboratory is very useful to record the natural tumescence which occurs during REM sleep. The patient can be awakened and shown his erectile capacity.

If the answers to the questions above suggest no organic problems, the situations must be handled circumspectly. Many patients hope for a "medical" problem, since the inability to function is deeply threatening, especially to some men's sense of masculinity. Also, many patients are deeply distressed by the idea that the problem may be "mental." Therefore a patient should be told of findings in a way that is not unduly discouraging or alarming and that helps to motivate his acceptance of treatment.

Some answers that patients give to screening questions suggest that there is an organic basis for their problems. Continuing libido with some sexual sensation or function suggests organic impairment—for example, a man who continues to desire sex and have orgasms and who experiences no performance anxiety despite lack of erection. However, such a man need not give up having a sexual relationship. The enjoyment of sex can always be maintained, if only through alternatives to coitus. This has been shown by the creative responses of many paraplegics and their partners who have learned to compensate for the handicap (see Chapter 15).

A special point should be made about the sexual needs of patients when they are hospitalized, especially for long periods. Hospital personnel usually consider patients to be asexual and allow them little privacy; there is little or no opportunity for patients to be sexual with a partner or even to masturbate. Sexual involvement beyond inconspicuous kissing and touching is usually considered inappropriate or even objectionable. This contradicts the matter-of-fact way that physicians and nurses are taught to deal with other private body functions, such as elimination and bathing. These outdated attitudes disregard a patient's right and need to maintain sexual function. A patient's sexuality should be accepted along with other aspects of personality and behavior.

Monitoring. In interim or update histories, the same questions should be asked as in the original history. Monitoring is needed as sexual dysfunction fluctuates, stabilizes, worsens or improves. For instance, it is useful to inquire of a postcoronary patient if his sexual activity has returned to a satisfactory level. An arthritic patient with ankylosis of the hip joint should be asked whether relatively pain-free movement of the thigh is still possible during intercourse. Especially in chronic conditions, an interim history also allows the physician to address new problems before they create excessive distress.

If disability makes coitus impossible or the disease interferes with the patient's wish or need to be sexual, sexual play with the unafflicted partner should be encouraged, as should masturbation. Intensive counseling or therapy can be suggested to deal with the patient's sense of loss in not being fully functional, or if the partner cannot adjust to alternate forms of sexual pleasure.

No matter how serious or trivial their ills, people come to a physician with feelings, fears, concerns and ideas that are highly individualized. Each patient needs to be considered as a person rather than a case. The effects of physical illness on sexual function also vary among individuals. People who have been comfortable with and enjoyed their sexuality have a strong but not necessarily spoken wish to maintain it; those who have found sexual activity difficult or unpleasurable may find in physical illness an excuse to withdraw from sex. In either case, the physician's role is the same: to help the person live as full a life as possible, sexually and otherwise.

References

1. Hellerstein HK, Friedman EH: Sexual activity and the post-coronary patient. *Med Aspects Hum Sex* 1969 (March); 3:70-96.
2. Kavanagh T, Shepard RJ: Sexual activity after myocardial infarction. *Can Med Assoc J* 1977; 116:1250-1253.
3. Hellerstein HK, Friedman EH: Sexual activity and the post-coronary patient. *Arch Intern Med* 1970; 125:987-999.
4. Block A, et al: Sexual problems after myocardial infarction. *Am Heart J* 1975; 90:536-537.
5. Dengrove E: Sexual responses to disease processes. *J Sex Res* 1968; 4:257-264.
6. Abramov LA: Sexual life and sexual frigidity among women developing acute myocardial infarction. *Psychosom Med* 1976; 38:418-425.
7. Rosen JL, Bibring GL: Psychological reactions of hospitalized male patients to a heart attack. *Psychosom Med* 1966; 28:808-821.
8. Adsett CA, Bruhn JG: Short-term group psychotherapy for post-myocardial infarction patients and their wives. *Can Med Assoc J* 1968; 99:577-584.
9. Bilodeau CJ, Hackett TP: Issues raised in a group setting by patients recovering from initial myocardial infarction. *Am J Psychiatry* 1971; 128:73-78.
10. Tuttle WB, et al: Sexual behavior in post-myocardial infarction patients, (letter). *Am J Cardiol* 1964; 13:140.
11. Papadopoulos C, et al: Sexual concerns and needs of the postcoronary patient's wife. *Arch Intern Med* 1980; 140:38-41.
12. Johnston BL, et al: Sexual activity in excercising patients after myocardial infarction and revascularization. *Heart Lung* 1978; 7:1026-1031.
13. Ueno M: The so-called coition death. *Jap J Leg Med* 1963; 17:333-340.
14. Kalliomaki JL, et al: Sexual behavior after cerebral vascular accident. *Fertil Steril* 1961; 12:156-158.

15. Howard EJ: Sexual expenditure in patients with hypertensive disease. *Med Aspects Hum Sex* 1973 (Oct); 7:82-92.

16. Kass I, et al: Sex in chronic obstructive pulmonary disease. *Med Aspects Hum Sex* 1972 (Feb); 6:33-42.

17. Luparello TJ: Asthma and sex. *Med Aspects Hum Sex* 1970 (March); 4:97-107.

18. Labby DH: Sexual concomitants of disease and illness. *Postgrad Med* 1975; 58:103-111.

19. Deutsch S, Sherman L: Previously unrecognized diabetes mellitus in sexually impotent men. *JAMA* 1980; 244:2430-2432.

20. Faerman I, et al: Impotence and diabetes: Studies of androgenic function in diabetic impotent males. *Diabetes* 1972; 21:23-30.

21. Kolodny RC, et al: Sexual dysfunction in diabetic men. *Diabetes* 1974; 23:306-309.

22. Rubin A: Sexual behavior in diabetes mellitus. *Med Aspects Hum Sex* 1967 (Dec); 1:23-25.

23. Barnett DM: Diabetic impotence unrelated to treatment. *Hosp Trib* 1973 (Oct 8); p2.

24. Abel G, et al: Paper presented at the Sixth Annual Conference of the International Academy of Sex Research. Tuscon, AZ, Nov 1980.

25. Michal V, Paspichal J: Phalloarteriography in the diagnosis of erectile impotence. *World J Surg* 1978; 2:239-247.

26. Abel G: Personal communications, 1981.

27. Ellenberg M: Sex and the female diabetic. *Med Aspects Hum Sex* 1977 (Dec); 11:30-38.

28. Masters WH, Johnson VE: *Human Sexual Inadequacy*. Boston, Little, Brown and Company, 1970.

29. Thurm J: Sexual potency of patients on chronic hemodialysis. *Urology* 1975; 5:60-62.

30. De-Nour AK, Shanan J: Quality of life of dialysis and transplanted patients. *Nephron* 1980; 25:117-120.

31. Phadke AG, et al: Male fertility in uremia: Restoration by renal allografts. *Can Med Assoc J* 1970; 102:607-608.

32. Salvatierra O, et al: Sexual function in males before and after renal transplantation. *Urology* 1975; 5:64-66.

33. Holdsworth SR, et al: A comparison of hemodialysis and transplantation in reversing the uremic disturbances of male reproductive function. *Clin Nephrol* 1978; 10:146-150.

34. Guevara A, et al: Serum gonadotrophin and testosterone levels in uremic males undergoing intermittent dialysis. *Metabolism* 1969; 18:1062-1066.

35. Wilkey JL, et al: The effect of testosterone on the azotemic patient. *J Urol* 1960; 83:25-29.

36. Finkle AL, Thompson R: Alternatives to androgenic hormones in treating male impotency. *Geriatrics* 1972; 27:74-76.

37. Levy NB: Sexual maladjustment to maintenance hemodialysis and renal transplantation, in Levy NB (ed): *Living or Dying: Adaptation to Hemodialysis*. Springfield, IL, Charles C Thomas, 1972.

38. Gomez F, et al: Endocrine abnormalities in patients undergoing long-term hemodialysis. *Am J Med* 1980; 68:522-530.
39. Dlin BM, et al: Psychosexual response to ileostomy and colostomy. *Am J Psychiatry* 1969; 126:374-381.
40. Druss RG, et al: Psychologic response to colostomy. *Arch Gen Psychiatry* 1969; 20:419-427.
41. Weinstein M, Roberts M: Sexual potency following surgery for rectal carcinoma. *Ann Surg* 1977; 185:295-300.
42. Bernstein WC: Sexual dysfunction following radical surgery for cancer of the rectum and sigmoid colon. *Med Aspects Hum Sex* 1972 (March); 6:156-163.
43. Dennerstein L, et al: Sexual response following hysterectomy and oophorectomy. *Obstet Gynecol* 1977; 49:92-96.
44. Abithol MM, Davenport JH: Sexual dysfunction after therapy for cervical carcinoma. *Am J Obstet Gynecol* 1974; 119:181-189.
45. Brachen RB, Johnson DE: Sexual function and fecundity after treatment for testicular tumors. *Urology* 1976; 7:35-38.
46. Huffman JW: Sexual reactions after gynecologic surgery. *Med Aspects Hum Sex* 1969 (Nov); 3:48-57.
47. Ervine CV Jr: Psychologic adjustment to mastectomy. *Med Aspects Hum Sex* 1973 (Feb); 7:42-65.
48. Byrd BF Jr: Sex after mastectomy. *Med Aspects Hum Sex* 1975 (April); 9:53-54.
49. Adatta K, et al: Behavioral factors and urinary tract infection. *JAMA* 1979; 241:2525-2526.
50. Spark RF, et al: Impotence is not always psychogenic: Newer insights into hypothalamic-pituitary-gonadal dysfunction. *JAMA* 1980; 243:750-755.

Chapter 15

Sexual Health and Physical Disability

Theodore M. Cole, M.D., and Sandra S. Cole

SEXUALITY

Each time a physician sees a new patient many human issues emerge. Sexuality is one of them. Before the decade of the 70's, most medical publications about sexuality addressed disease and reproductive aspects of sexual function. Now sexual health has become an acceptable area for physician-patient interaction.

Publications, conferences and seminars have changed the role of sexuality in the overall rehabilitation process and have established it as a legitimate health concern for men and women with physical disabilities.[1-3] However, even now not everyone agrees that sexuality is important to the adult with a physical disability. Some health professionals believe that the immediate post-trauma hospitalization period is too early for the disabled person to be concerned with sexual issues. Hospitalized disabled patients who participated in two studies are reported to have considered sexual function least important when compared to such other physical functions as ambulation, moving from bed to wheelchair, and bowel and bladder function.[4,5]

If sexuality is treated as sex organ function or if conclusions are drawn on the basis of surveys of hospitalized persons who are still in the early stages of disability adjustment, the broader and deeper meaning of sexuality may be overlooked. Sexuality is more than genitality or sex acts. It should be broadly thought of as an avenue toward intimacy and reflected in all that a person is and does.

Intimacy is of great importance to people and nearly everyone is capable of experiencing it: The prospect of isolation from intimacy is fearful. Problems may arise when physicians and/or patients equate intimacy with sex acts. If physicians avoid discussing sexuality with disabled patients, they may lose a natural avenue to understanding and talking about intimacy. The result may be to isolate the disabled person even further, producing more fear and more disability. Physicians should understand that adherence to a limited genital concept of sexuality may exclude those whose physical disabilities have caused their genitals to be lost, damaged or denervated. Similarly, if sexuality is restricted to interaction between partners, the widowed and the unmarried may be overlooked. Or, if sexuality is confined to heterosexual intercourse, other aspects of sexual expression, for example solitary masturbation or homosexuality, may be restricted.

When feelings of intimacy occur between two people, a very special relationship develops that includes mutual comfort, acceptance and trust. As a result, couples are able to be unguarded and to expose their "bad" as well as "good" points with a feeling of safety.

The ways in which two people express their intimacy are legion. Intimacy is the eye contact that says, when others are talking, "I know how you are feeling about what we are hearing." It is the comment made in public with special meaning for only the two. It is a touch, a hand hold, a hug, or a kiss for no special reason other than contact. It is sitting and lying together, holding, cuddling, talking, or saying nothing with comfort and ease for the warmth and closeness it provides. It is expressed in private jokes, pet names, carefree laughs and gentle caresses. Intimacy like this is always sexual but not necessarily genital or even erotic. Intimacy also may include intense expressions of body and genital contact, however comfortably achieved, in an atmosphere of open communication. The object of intimacy, however, is much more than the orgasm of sexual intercourse.

Comfort or discomfort with sexuality may influence how one person interacts with another, how a physician relates to a patient, or how a person interacts with his or her sexual partner. In order to have a full capacity for intimacy, one must have a healthy self-concept. Sexual health, in turn, is part of a healthy self-concept.

There is strong evidence for a distinct relationship between self-esteem and sexuality in people with physicial disabilities as well as in those who are able-bodied.[6] Positive self-esteem may enhance a patient's ability to develop compensatory mechanisms for re-entering society following disability.

Rehabilitationists know that successful work leads to increased self-esteem, causing the patient to continue in a work activity that has produced the increased self-esteem.[7] Such activities will benefit the patient by making him less willing to accept a dependent role. In the case of a physically disabled person, this may result in fewer complaints and reduce the need for outside medical support.

Similarly, the achievement of intimacy with a partner may lead to increased self-esteem and may further encourage the individual to continue other activities, such as employment. These activities may not only satisfy the disabled patient but may also decrease feelings of uselessness and castration, resulting in less social withdrawal and, therefore, less need for outside social support. This reduces social and economic costs to the community. Activities deliberately designed to increase the patient's self-esteem thus may help conserve health care resources and reduce the cost for society in general.

Medical articles and periodicals written for people who have physical disabilities are now emphasizing that sexual rehabilitation should be expected from rehabilitation professionals.[8,9] Institutional prohibitions which, until recently, have discouraged expressions of intimacy between patients and their partners are giving way. In some institutions, privacy rooms are now available, and residents can use them with their partners for intimate exchange that may or may not include sexual activity.

SEXUAL DYSFUNCTIONS ASSOCIATED WITH PHYSICAL DISABILITIES

As shown in other chapters in this book, the more common sexual dysfunctions are often rooted in dysfunctional sexual attitudes, behavioral problems, problems of interpersonal relationships, or early traumatic sexual experiences. Any of the common sexual dysfunctions may occur in an adult with a physical disability, whether they are induced by the disability or not. The physician should be acquainted not only with the usual sexual dysfunctions, however, but also with the ways in which sexual function may be changed by physical disability. He also must be aware of the fact that it may take years to adjust sexually after a severe disability.

As in the able-bodied population, the physician should not overlook the fact that bisexual and homosexual orientations exist among disabled people. Value judgments in this area are no more appropriate for the physician than they would be in other areas of patient care. It would be inappropriate to refer a patient on the basis of sexual preference alone. However, referral for sexual counseling may be made if the patient identifies problem areas and service needs that go beyond the physician's interest or training.

Classification of Disabilities

Physical disabilities can be grouped into four categories with respect to sexual function. Placement in a category depends on the person's age at the time of onset and the progressive or stable nature of the disability.

Type I disabilities are those that begin at birth or before puberty and are nonprogressive, such as congenital brain injury, limb amputation in early life, congenital loss of sight or hearing, and mental retardation.[10] Persons with these disabilities experience a lifetime of being different from their peers. The overly protective or guilt-laden attitudes of society or parents may have had an inhibiting effect upon their psychosocial maturation. Experiences that are important to adolescents may be either unavailable or consciously kept from them. As a result, some disabled persons may emerge from adolescence with maturational deficits and lack certain social skills. They may find themselves in an adult world wishing to be sexually sophisticated but lacking the requisite preparation.

Type II disabilities also begin before puberty and therefore may have essentially the same effect on adult sexuality as Type I disabilities. However, they are progressive and the child can never be sure that his or her body will not become even more dysfunctional with time. Examples of these disabilities include juvenile rheumatoid arthritis, childhood-onset diabetes mellitus, muscular dystrophy and cystic fibrosis. Because of the progressive nature of these disabilities, the children may be regularly involved in medical treatment programs that require much of their energy. They may have a poor body image, a feeling of being sickly, an unwillingness to regard their bodies as being able to provide sensual pleasure, and a belief that they are incapable of achieving intimate relationships.

Type III disabilities are those that occur in adult life and are stable. Examples include traumatic spinal cord injury, amputation[11] and disfiguring burns. Persons so disabled can recall when they were normal. This reference point may be helpful in the effort to re-establish their psychosexual identity. Further, they may already have learned the interpersonal skills necessary to develop satisfying adult sexual relationships. These skills may be modified and continue to serve them after they are disabled.

Type IV disabilities are the degenerative diseases that will affect most adults who live to be old. They include, for example, degenerative heart disease, stroke, cancer, arthritis and chronic renal disease. Their onsets are often gradual and their course progressive, thus allowing for slow adjustment to the disabling process. However, like Type II disabilities, Type IV disabilities produce an unstable base from which patients can plan their lives. Patients with these disabilities may find it necessary to invest considerable energy in maintaining their health, and they may have great difficulty looking upon themselves as "well even though disabled."

Evaluation of Disabilities

All four types of disabilities can be manifested in sexuality as solitary or partnership problems, fertility concerns, or body image issues. Therefore, depending upon the nature of the disablement, sexuality may be affected in the areas of masturbation, coitus, positioning techniques, sex-role stereotypes, procreational ability, or self-acceptance.

The duration of the disability often plays an important role in the patient's awareness of a sexual concern or dysfunction. In a sample of recently hospitalized patients with spinal cord injuries, almost 50 per cent believed that their sexual adjustment was good and only 9 per cent rated it as poor at the time of discharge from the hospital.[12] However, a year or two later, 38 per cent stated that their sexual adjustment was now poor. This suggests an early lack of awareness of the influence of physical disability upon sexual activity.

For many disabilities, the work tolerance of the patient can be predicted by knowing the severity of the disability, age, and the health status before disability. Sexual activity is no different. Under comfortable circumstances, cardiovascular stress during sexual intercourse does not exceed that caused by climbing two flights of stairs. However, if less stress must be recommended, the patient can be assured that there remains, to the extent of one's imagination, a wide variety of sexual expressions and techniques to enjoy. Or, if neuromuscular disorders limit mobility or postures, the patient can be asked to explore the partner's willingness to assume responsibility for body positioning. Loss of finger dexterity may be compensated for by use of the mouth if both partners agree. Virtually no disability prohibits recumbency and closeness in bed. The overall benefits of seeing oneself as capable of giving and receiving sexual pleasure may far outweigh the risks to the body. The risks of foreclosing on the human need for intimacy may greatly overshadow the risks of physical harm resulting from intimate acts between two people who care for one another.

It must always be kept in mind that intimacy and sexual contact do not require sexual intercourse or orgasm.

194

It is beyond the scope of this chapter to enumerate all of the sexual concomitants of the many disabilities that may affect men and women. However, the physician should be aware of some of the psychological, physiological and interpersonal alterations that may be imposed by the physical disability.

Medical. There are several resources to whom the patient may turn when medical evaluation is needed to assess sexual function. A physician skilled in family practice, physical medicine and rehabilitation, internal medicine, urology, gynecology, or neurology may obtain a proper medical history, perform an appropriate physical examination, and interpret the necessary laboratory reports. The physician has basically two tasks: (1) to include or exclude treatable medical disease or impairment that may have an influence upon sexual function, and (2) to diagnose medical causes for sexual problems that, even though not remediable by medical treatment, must be understood in order to facilitate adjustment and proceed with rehabilitation planning.

A variety of genital and reproductive impairments may occur in the various physical disabilities. At one end of the spectrum is loss of the genitals themselves due to trauma or disease (usually cancer). The male can lose part or all of the penis and testicles. In the female, vaginal closure or loss of the vulva, uterus, ovaries and breasts can result in sexual dysfunction. In these more obvious situations, initiation of discussion of the meaning of these losses and the sexual adjustment problems they may be causing is important, since there may be a need for the patient to explore the potential for an expanded view of sexual activities and gratifications. Some people who have lost their external genitalia continue to describe their sex lives as active and satisfactory. This suggests that if other aspects of adjustment to disability are adequate, sexual performance and gratification can be achieved.

Less vivid but still devastating dysfunctions can occur in persons who lose sensation in their genitals due to metabolic diseases, such as diabetes mellitus, or nervous system disorders, such as multiple sclerosis and spinal cord injury. Not only may the individual receive less sensation but physical orgasm may not occur, and potency and fertility may be lost in the male. Sometimes, a patient may erroneously conclude that the loss of fertility and sensation is synonymous with the loss of emotional feelings and capacity for intimacy in general. The patient may withdraw behind a barrier of seeming indifference to sexual stimulation, forgetting that the largest part of one's sexuality is in the psyche, not in the genitals.

The medical and surgical conditions that lead to loss of accustomed function of the genitals may produce sexual dysfunctions. Examples include developmental or degenerative anomalies of the sex organs themselves or of the circulation supplying them. Some orthopedic or neurological disorders may limit a person's sexual repertoire. Loss of mobility, as may occur in arthritis, multiple sclerosis, stroke and cerebral palsy, can make traditional positioning for intercourse painful or impossible. Persons so affected may conclude that they can no longer engage in coitus. Some persons whose medical conditions necessitate drainage from urethral catheters or ileostomies to collection bags may be emotionally unable to accept the appliances. Even their partners may become convinced that the sex organs can no longer be used for pleasure. Endorsement of continued sexual desires and feelings combined with counseling may expand the patient's concept of sexuality beyond genital function alone. With patience and support, patients and/or partners may be able to begin their adjustment as sexual persons. Then, with specific help or referral to a sex therapist or a counselor who understands sexuality and physical disability, the patient and/or partner may begin to deal productively with this aspect of physical disability, which when untreated has the potential for creating severe conflict and often personality disorders.

Psychosocial. Sexual dysfunction following a physical disability may not be organically related to the disability. Some patients may attribute their sexual dysfunction directly to the physical disability and thus overlook dealing with its psychological components. However, the psychological aspects of sexual dysfunction may be as disabling as the medical aspects.

A case in point is vaginismus. A woman with multiple sclerosis and skeletal muscle spasticity may experience painful intercourse caused by involuntary contraction of the muscles of the pelvic floor which she believes to be the result of spasticity. However, anxiety can greatly increase spasticity caused by central nervous system disease. In this case, relief of sex-related anxiety will help reduce spasticity during intercourse and, thus, vaginismus. The separation of medical from psychological influences will be necessary before useful therapy can commence.

In the male, sexual dysfunction, such as premature ejaculation, impotence, or retarded ejaculation, may result from a medical illness, a psychological reaction, or both. Multiple sclerosis would seem to explain impotence in a man with the disease, yet counseling and removal of sexual anxieties often improve his genital function.

These examples suggest that sexual dysfunction may be a result of organic or psychological disorders or, as is probably true in the majority of instances, a combination of both. However, the physician will find that some persons are unwilling to accept their own adjustment problems as an explanation for sexual dysfunction. They would rather invoke as explanation a medical problem over which they have no control. Referring such patients to a sex therapist may prove rewarding after the physical losses caused by the disability have been assessed and discussed. Information on these physical losses should be given to the therapist to whom the patient is referred if that therapist is unfamiliar with physical disability.

Interpersonal. In addition to medical and psychological issues within the patient, the sexuality of the spouse or partner also must be considered. For example, an able-bodied spouse's sexual frame of reference to the partner may be dramatically altered by the disfiguring burn on the partner's face. Or a spouse whose partner has survived a life-threatening heart attack may consciously or unconsciously withhold sexual advances for fear that sexual activity may expose the partner to further risk. These conflicts can best be resolved by treating the couple as a sexual unit.

Other Evaluation Techniques. Openness and frankness are important techniques used to evaluate sexual dysfunction in adults. Openness and frankness about one's own feelings of sexuality, however, do not imply disclosure of personal sexual preferences or activities. The physician may find that he can facilitate the patient's thinking and discussion by saying, for example, that it is perfectly natural for anyone to have "turn-ons" and "turn-offs" and that sexual arousal may follow a variety of stimuli. Yet, it is important that the physician not impose his own values upon the patient by advocating or opposing certain activities or points of view. It is also important for him to validate reasonable concerns that the patient might have and continue to work with the patient and/or partner to enhance sexual well-being. The physician should also let the patient know that he does not regard certain sexual activities as unusual or abnormal. For example, in talking to a man who is recovering from a crush fracture of the pelvis which also caused injury to intrapelvic nerves and organs, the physician may wish to learn whether the patient's genitals can function sexually by asking "How often do you masturbate now?" By asking "how often" rather than "do you masturbate" the physician is telling the patient that masturbation is a natural activity for many people. It then may be easier for the patient to talk about his attempts rather than to hide them in the belief that masturbation is abnormal. This method of questioning avoids unnecessary confrontation of the patient or partner and facilitates truthful responses in a comfortable atmosphere.

The physician can also help a patient by supplying him with texts and pamphlets that address sexual health and sexual concerns. They illustrate the various approaches that can be taken and the devices available to enhance sexual function and expression in persons with physical disability.[13] This assistance is much the same as might be provided for those persons with other problems. In addition, when appropriate, the physician can help the patient find referral resources for in-depth counseling in personal adjustment, just as he would provid help to locate resources to facilitate physical mobility or self-care.

While it is necessary for the physician to encourage physically disabled patients to realize their own potential for achieving satisfactory sexual function, he must do so carefully to avoid false hopes, undue optimism and unrealistic expectations.

It is hoped that this chapter will encourage physicians to consider sexual adjustment as a significant goal of rehabilitation. Not to do so may mean a rehabilitation failure. The medical, psychological, social and vocational rehabilitation of a patient is not likely to be complete or successful without satisfactory sexual rehabilitation as well.[14]

References

1. Cole TM, Glass DD: Sexuality and physical disabilities. *Arch Phys Med Rehabil* 1977; 58:585-586.
2. Comfort A: *Sexual Consequences of Disability*. Philadelphia, GF Stickley & Company, 1978.

3. Robinault I: *Sex, Society, and the Disabled*. New York, Harper & Row Publishers, Inc, 1978.
4. Hanson RW, Franklin MR: Sexual loss in relation to other functional losses for spinal injured males. *Arch Phys Med Rehabil* 1976; 57:291-293.
5. Spergel P, et al: Sex—a rehabilitation issue: What priority and when. *Arch Phys Med Rehabil* 1976; 57:562.
6. Weiss AJ, Diamond MD: Sexual adjustment, identification, and attitudes of patients with myelopathy. *Arch Phys Med Rehabil* 1966; 47:245-250.
7. Cole TM: Sexuality and physical disabilities. *Arch Sex Behav* 1975; 4:389-403.
8. Labby DH: Sexual concomitants of disease and illness. *Postgrad Med* 1975; 58:103-111.
9. Scheingold LD, Wagner NN: *Sound Sex and the Aging Heart*. New York, Human Sciences Press, 1974.
10. de la Cruz FF, LaVeck GD: *Human Sexuality and the Mentally Retarded*. New York, Brunner/Mazel Inc, 1973.
11. Kent S: Coping with sexual identity crises after mastectomy. *Geriatrics* 1975; 30:145-146.
12. Regional Spinal Cord Injury System of Minnesota, Theodore M. Cole, M.D., Director. (Unpublished report)
13. Mooney TO, et al: *Sexual Options for Paraplegics and Quadriplegics*. Boston, Little, Brown and Company, 1975.
14. Cole TM, Cole SS: The handicapped and sexual health. *SIECUS Report* 1976; 4:1-10.

Chapter 16

Sexuality and Mental Disorders

Sherwyn M. Woods, M.D., Ph.D.

Sexual behavior, like all human behavior, represents complex interplay among intrapsychic, interpersonal, biological and social factors. In both the emotionally healthy and ill, it is part of, and affected by, an individual's general behavioral patterns. Furthermore, sexuality often is expressed in a wide variety of nonerotic emotions, such as love and hate, and feelings of dependence, power and hostility. An individual's personality and emotional conflicts, whether or not there is a diagnosable psychiatric disorder, may be expressed as a sexual dysfunction or disorder; more commonly, however, they help determine sexual fantasy and behavior. Psychic factors also help determine which acts are considered erotic and which partners are selected. The adage is true: One man's perversion is another man's boredom.

PSYCHIATRIC ILLNESS AND SEXUAL DYSFUNCTION

Psychiatric disorders are not usually associated with specific sexual dysfunctions or symptoms. Rather, pre-existing sexual patterns are modified by the advent of psychiatric illness. The disorder may accentuate some behavior or cause acting out of impulses and fantasies that were previously unconscious or restricted to fantasy, or it may result in inhibition of sexual expression, or a turning away from other persons, so that sexuality becomes much more self-centered or autoerotic.

The same factors that produce psychiatric illness may produce a sexual disorder. The simplest and most obvious example is an organic lesion in an area of the brain that directly influences sexual behavior; such a condition is likely to produce both an organic brain syndrome and a disorder of sexual behavior simultaneously. More often, however, the anxiety, guilt or shame that results in neurotic symptoms or a psychotic decompensation also may affect sexual impulses, fantasies or behavior. Such conflicts may emerge in adult life but they are usually rooted in early development. A person whose life experience and inner conflicts have led to general inhibition of assertiveness is likely to have generalized this inhibition to sexual learning and behavior.

Sexuality also may be influenced by the effect of a psychiatric disorder on general mental functioning. For example, the organic brain syndromes are associated with impaired cognition (intelligence, language, learning, memory), and such defects obviously impair a person's capacity to relate to others sexually. Both the functional and organic psychoses are characterized by impairment of the ability to distinguish what is real from what is unreal. The resulting delusions, hallucinations or disordered perceptions may result in bizarre behaviors and relationships, including sexual ones. The autism and impaired thinking of a schizophrenic often severely interfere with, or distort, communications and relationships with others.

Any mood, from depression to elation, can affect sexual interest. Not surprisingly, changes in sexual behavior occur in psychiatric disorders characterized by mood alterations. Similarly, the severe anxiety or panic state that may accompany an acute neurosis is likely to interfere with sexual functioning. These effects on sexuality, which are not inevitable, are more likely in acute than in chronic states.

Psychiatric illness is often associated with disturbed physical or physiological functioning. The disturbance may be caused by the debilitating effect of severe or chronic stress, anxiety or depression. Increased energy states, such as those that accompany mania and amphetamine psychosis, make more energy available for sexuality. Physiologic (and thus sexual) function also can be greatly altered by drugs. These include drugs that can cause psychiatric illness as well as the neuroleptic and antidepressant agents used to treat such disorders (see Chapter 17).

Sexuality also can be affected if psychiatric illness changes one's ability to seek out and form comfortable relationships. This ability requires self-esteem, confidence, assertion and skills in communication. All of these may be severely undermined in a person with a psychiatric disorder and can have direct or indirect effects on sexual expression. Sexual function with a partner also requires a sense of adequacy and security about one's masculinity or femininity. In our culture, gender-role adequacy is extremely vulnerable to any sense of failure, not merely sexual failure. People with psychiatric disorders may have many social, vocational or interpersonal failures.

Sexual attitudes, behavior and skills are continually influenced by learning. When psychiatric illness alters the way one views oneself or others, relationships and experiences that are necessary for sexual development will not take place. This is especially true during important developmental periods, such as puberty and adolescence, and childhood as well. For example, if parents are ill or emotionally unavailable, particularly at the earlier stages of a child's development, there is the possibility of inadequate parenting that may have effects on the child's subsequent sexuality.

The fact that there is no consistent relationship between any specific psychiatric illness and disordered sexuality has been demonstrated in many studies. Winokur et al[1] compared 50 normal, 50 psychotic and 100 nonpsychiatric medical patients and found that the three groups did not differ significantly in frequency of coitus or orgasm. Woodruff et al[2] found no correlation between altered sexual behavior and the diagnosis of neurosis; also, divorce was not more likely in neurotic patients. Schaefer[3] found no relationship between "mental health" and sexual responsiveness in psychologically "maladjusted but non-neurotic" women, and Raboch and Bartak[4,5] found no differences between orgasmic and nonorgasmic women in the occurrence of neurotic symptoms. Coppen,[6] however, found that normal individuals attain orgasm more consistently than neurotics, schizophrenics or depressed patients. McCulloch and Steward[7] found no differences in sexual satisfaction between normal females and psychiatric outpatients or between neurotics and schizophrenics.

Fisher's exhaustive study of women[8] revealed no relationship between degree of maladjustment and sexual responsiveness. His data clearly show that a woman can be seriously maladjusted and still be normally responsive. The only significant correlations with women's sexual responsiveness are education, social class, practice effects and perhaps being an only child. Fisher believes it to be a myth that consistency of orgasm is related to mental health, femininity, attitudes toward mother, aggressiveness, guilt or religiosity. However, Pinderhughes et al[9] found that most psychiatrists and 39 per cent of psychiatric patients they studied believed that problems in sexual function might contribute to psychiatric disorders. Eighty per cent of the psychiatrists and almost 50 per cent of the patients believed that psychiatric disorders might interfere with sexual function. Graham[10] studied married men and women about to begin analytic psychotherapy and compared them to a group who had already been in such therapy; he found that therapy does result in more frequent and satisfactory coitus.

It is not surprising that many studies fail to find a direct correlation between psychiatric illness and the presence or absence of orgasm, specific sexual symptoms or sexual dysfunction. Emotional conflict and psychiatric disturbances may or may not be expressed in sexual symptoms; more commonly, they affect the nature, style and degree of satisfaction. At least three elements in sexual experience may be affected: desire, pleasure and performance. For example, a chronically depressed woman with low self-esteem and feelings of unworthiness may have no problem reaching orgasm, but she may feel little pleasure. Alternatively, these feelings may determine her selection of sexual partners and her way of relating to them; she may, for example, select only men she sees as depreciated or who match her own devalued self-image, or she may be compulsively promiscuous in an attempt to prove her worth.

The sexual dissatisfaction associated with psychiatric illness is often reflected more in the patient's partner than in the patient. For example, an obsessional man may be quite undisturbed about his distant, cold and mechanical sexuality; however, it may greatly upset his partner. A hate-filled patient may use sex to express aggression but seem quite normal to superficial observation or in simple terms of potency or consistency of orgasm.

DIAGNOSIS AND EVALUATION

When the clinician attempts to assess the relationship between psychiatric illness and sexual functioning, the evaluation proceeds as it would for any patient. A sexual history and physical examination are essential. Psychiatric patients are as vulnerable to physical illness as anyone else, and their sexual complaints may be based on physical disorders unrelated to their psychiatric problems. A schizophrenic patient also may be diabetic or have a neurologic lesion that is causing sexual symptoms unrelated to the psychosis. In fact, severely disturbed patients may be so preoccupied or disorganized by their psychiatric disturbances that they fail to offer information about medical symptoms.

Sometimes a psychiatric history suggests that a sexual complaint may be related to the psychiatric disorder, as when the symptoms of both are simultaneous in onset, exacerbation and remission. This never, however, precludes the necessity for a careful physical examination. Also, it must be remembered that sexual symptoms may precede or follow the development of psychiatric symptoms, sometimes by several months. In trying to learn whether sexual complaints are secondary to psychiatric illness, the clinician should watch for organic, psychological or behavioral factors that may have a common etiology. For instance, secondary impotence is not surprising in an obsessional man who feels guilty about sexual impulses and plagued by doubts about his masculinity; neither is loss of sexual interests. The clinician might suspect an unrelated etiology if the depression lifts without previous sexual interest returning. A great many psychiatric patients are given antianxiety, antipsychotic or antidepressant drugs early in their illnesses. The physician must be particularly alert to possible side effects of such drugs, such as loss of libido and interference with erection or ejaculation (see Chapter 17).

ORGANIC MENTAL DISORDERS

Organic mental disorders may be secondary to drugs, tumors, infections or other factors that alter brain function. Such disorders usually cause disturbances in intellectual functions and memory, and often the psychiatric history reveals a change in personality—and sometimes (but not always) in sexual expression as well. Sexuality may be altered by reduced intellectual function or by the release of social inhibitions, which in turn results in impulsiveness, loss of judgment or asocial behavior. Some patients perform sexual acts in inappropriate ways, times or places. No specific sexual disorders are associated with organic mental disorders, except when a brain lesion is located in an area that regulates sexual functioning. This happens in the Kluver-Bucy syndrome[11] in which destructive organic damage of the temporal lobes, such as may result from head injury, are associated with hypersexuality as a release phenomenon (in the Jacksonian sense). Psychomotor seizures can involve sexual behavior, such as coital or masturbatory movements, as can ictal or preictal behavior. However, psychomotor epilepsy is commonly associated with reduced sexual drive.[12] Small and Small list several organic conditions that may have sexual symptoms.[13]

AFFECTIVE DISORDERS

Depression or its precursors can occur in infancy, childhood or adolescence and can have a profound influence on sexuality.[14] The sexual symptoms accompanying depression—reduced or greater than usual sexual expression—are similar in the young and old. Constant masturbation may be a child's frantic attempt to relieve anxiety or depression and achieve neuromuscular relaxation. Depression in puberty may lead to social withdrawal and a decrease in developmental sex play, which interfere with the development of heterosexual maturation, skills and comfort. Depression in later adolescence or early adulthood may produce impulsive attempts to counteract decreasing libido or potency through drugs or promiscuity.

Most clinicians agree that depression usually reduces sexual desire. The results of one survey by Lief show that 80 per cent of psychiatrists believe that depressed patients have decreased libido and sex activity; however, only 29 per cent believe that a majority of depressed patients become impotent.[15] Lief points out that there is absolutely no evidence to support the popular clinical belief that impotence and anorgasmia are common results of depression.

Ayd found that 60 per cent of his depressed patients experienced lower libido.[16] Renshaw believes that depression is associated with a reduction of all drives and appetites, including sexual ones, and that impotence is often secondary to performance anxiety.[17] Spencer and Raft found decreased sexual desire was the most common and most severe symptom in their depressed patients.[18] They say that this may be a part of the patients' general withdrawal from their surroundings and from interpersonal relationships.

Depressed patients often lose their capacity for enjoying sexual fantasies, an important element in the preliminary phase of sexual arousal. Many patients are often filled with guilt and self-recrimination. They may be obsessed with past sexual transgressions or fantasies and become very self-punitive about their sexuality. The underlying hostility present in many depressives may be expressed by sexual withdrawal from the partner or spouse, or the patient may become so fearful of the anger that appears or threatens to appear during sexual contact that there is defensive withdrawal.

Spencer and Raft suggest the possibility that catecholamine derangements in depression may be a direct or indirect factor in such patients' decreased sexual responsiveness.[18] Renshaw[19] reported the successful use of doxepin in treating sexual dysfunctions in depression, but it is not known how much alleviation of dysfunction is caused by neurophysiologic effects and how much by the psychological effect of reduced depression. There is still insufficient evidence about the general effectiveness of psychotropic agents in sexual dysfunction associated with depression. It must be remembered that tricyclic antidepressants, which are often used to treat depression, sometimes inhibit ejaculation in men and delay orgasm in women.

Sometimes sex activity may be increased early in depression. This often occurs in an attempt to raise self-esteem, to confirm sexual identity or to boost lagging sexual interest.[18] Sometimes there is compulsive nocturnal masturbation in order to attain sleep, or promiscuity or frantic sexual activity in an attempt to reverse the depression in manic-depressive psychoses.[14]

Impotence or diminished sexual appetite in middle-aged males has been found to threaten their sense of masculinity and causes impulsive sexual acting out. A parallel phenomenon occurs in women (or men) as an attempt to relieve loneliness and sadness or as a frantic attempt to prove that sexual attractiveness and capabilities are not lost. Such behavior may ultimately make the depression worse by producing guilt, shame and self-recrimination. A marked change in an individual's usual sexual pattern, such as promiscuity, homosexual experimentation or compulsive masturbation, may be a sign of an underlying depression, especially in adolescents.

In manic-depressive psychosis, many observers believe that the hypomanic phase often is evidenced by an increase in sexual interest and activity.[20,21] The general acceleration of thought, speech and motor activity may be associated with increased sexual thoughts and desires. Hypersexuality may be the presenting or first symptom of a manic episode. This usually takes the form of a sharply increased frequency of heterosexual intercourse, a frantic search for many partners or constant seductive behavior. Renshaw counsels that intense agitation and activity, with seemingly driven and excessive sexual activity, should alert a clinician to the possibility of a first manic-depressive episode.[14]

Tsuang found that of 100 manic patients, 30 per cent had increased sexual drive and 15 per cent had decreased sexual drive.[21] The pre-illness sexual lives of those who became hypersexual were not particularly unusual. Winokur et al analyzed sexual behavior during 100 manic episodes of 61 hospitalized patients.[22] They found decreased interest in sex in 13 per cent of the episodes, no change in 22 per cent, and some sort of hypersexuality in 65 per cent. No differences were found between men and women.

SCHIZOPHRENIA

The effects of schizophrenia on sexuality are quite variable. They depend on whether the illness is acute or chronic, on whether it develops early or late in life and on the extent of the disruption in overall social functioning. Sexual disturbance in schizophrenia may come from distorted interpersonal relationships or as a direct consequence of acute psychosis, with its confusion, impulsiveness, hostility, autism and distorted sense of reality.[23] However, schizophrenia does not necessarily preclude adequate sexual functioning.[24] Barker, for example, found high orgasmic capacity in schizophrenic females.[25] Rado[26] believes that a basic characteristic of schizophrenia is anhedonia (pleasure deficiency) combined with distorted body awareness, which consequently affects sexual behavior.

Schizophrenia often causes deterioration in relationships, including sexual ones.[27] Weiner[28] believes that the patient's sexual life is almost always disturbed. The person either shuns virtually all sexual relationships or suddenly engages frantically in many relationships with no sense of satisfaction. Sexual activity, if it occurs, is often detached from the partner and sometimes involves hostility or sadism.[29]

Some clinicians report that there is increased sexual desire and frequency, especially of masturbation, among their patients in the early stages of the illness.[30] Others[31] have found decreased sexual drive to be the most common early sexual dysfunction in schizophrenic reactions, although 24 per cent of their sample noted increased sexual interest. Skopec et al[32] report that schizophrenic patients often show great intellectual preoccupation with sex but not necessarily a great deal of sexual activity.

Another basic characteristic of schizophrenia is a strong but confused preoccupation with one's own body and self, along with great difficulties in interpersonal relationships. Satisfactory heterosexual behavior, therefore, becomes difficult or impossible. This situation may leave masturbation as the only sexual outlet; its frequency also may increase in the person's attempt to relieve the general anxiety and tension associated with stress. How the patient views coitus depends on pre-existing values and attitudes, colored by the conflicts and impulses involved in the psychosis. Fantasy life often expresses the range of the patient's sexual conflicts and anxieties, is sometimes quite bizarre and is associated with delusions or hallucinations.[23]

During periods of active psychosis, sexual behavior may be quite erratic and include displays of hostility, impulsiveness or bizarre attempts at seduction. Chronic sexual offenders are not usually found among schizophrenic patients, and perversions are no more common than in other patients.[23]

There is little literature on the effects of other functional psychoses on sexual function. One interesting syndrome is erotomania (the Clerambault syndrome), in which a female patient has a delusional belief that a man, usually considerably older and often a prominent figure, is much in love with her. The belief arises from a grandiose fantasy aimed at relieving feelings of being unlovable. Such patients are usually diagnosed as paranoid or paranoid schizophrenic.[33]

NEUROSIS AND NEUROTIC PERSONALITIES

Some schools of psychiatric theory, particularly psychoanalysis, have long held that sexuality is a central issue in human development. In this view, how sexuality is managed, especially in infancy and childhood, has a profound effect on the development of neurotic symptoms or neurotic personality patterns later in life. In contrast, studies have indicated that neurotic individuals do not differ from normal individuals in sexual dysfunction, frequency of intercourse or orgasmic capability.[1,2,4,5,8,34] Besides having serious methodological flaws, some of these studies raise arguments that are specious, because psychoanalytic theory does not hold that developmental conflicts over sexuality necessarily result in sexual dysfunction or even specific sexual symptoms.

Developmental conflicts involving sexual and aggressive drives help create values, attitudes about the self and others and interpersonal styles that influence sexual learning. Psychodynamic theories hold only that emotional conflicts related to the management of sexual and aggressive drives, especially during childhood and adolescence, influence how these drives are expressed later in life.

One's sexuality at any moment in time represents a complex interaction among historically derived and conflict-shaped drive management, social values and previous learning and conditioning. Sexual dysfunctions are only one possible outcome of conflict. More common outcomes are reduced personal satisfaction, painful emotions about sexuality (anxiety, guilt, shame), distorted interpersonal behaviors, neurotic influences on choice of partners and the use of sex to express nonsexual emotions, such as hostility, dominance, aggression or dependence. Sex behavior can be either an avoidance of intimacy or a way to achieve it.[35]

Neurotic persons do not have the personality disorganization or loss of contact with reality that characterizes the psychotic. They may be quite functional in most aspects of their lives yet suffer painful emotions, such as anxiety or depression, or unpleasant symptoms, such as phobias, obsessive thoughts, compulsive rituals, fugue states or conversion reactions. Often these symptoms are caused by conflicts over sexual impulses or behaviors that are unacceptable or frightening. For instance, a phobia, conversion hysteria or panic reaction may be a defensive attempt to ward off unacceptable sexual impulses.

Sexuality also may be influenced indirectly by a neurotic process. The neurosis may distort feelings about self-worth, attractiveness, communication skills or the ability to engage in the social interchanges that precede sexual relationships. It can affect one's capacity for intimacy, or the degree of ambivalence about one's partner, or influence the selection of that partner. These influences not only produce immediate emotional distress but interfere with developmental learning. A neurotically depressed adolescent may suffer extreme anxiety or guilt about masturbation or sexual experimentation; equally important is the effect of that depression on the adolescent's socialization and peer relationships. Adult sexual behavior will be profoundly affected by the self-esteem, social skills and sense of gender adequacy that do or do not solidify during adolescence.

Most neurotic persons, if studied in sufficient depth, show conflict or unhappiness about their sexuality or their ability to relate sexually to others. Such conflict must be inferred if the individual is too anxious or ashamed to acknowledge the problem, or if repression or denial excludes the problem from conscious awareness. As noted earlier, the influence on sexuality sometimes is disturbing not to the patient but to the patient's partner. Looking for the influence of current or developmental conflict solely in narrow sexual terms, such as orgasmic capability or erectile potency, is like looking for microbes with binoculars!

The neurosis most often associated with sex-related symptoms is hysteria. Purtell et al[36] reported that 86 per cent of their patients with conversion hysteria had sexual problems, compared to 29 per cent of a control group. In conversion hysteria, the symptom is often a defense against unacceptable sexual or aggressive impulses. For instance, hysterical blindness may be a reaction to unacceptable voyeuristic impulses, or hysterical fits a response to unacceptable sexual excitement. A similar mechanism may occur in certain phobic reactions and other neurotic symptoms.

The person with a hysterical personality, sometimes associated with hysterical neurosis, is typically histrionic, emotional and seductive.[37,38] The seductiveness is usually used to manipulate others in order to satisfy the patient's narcissistic and child-like dependency needs. Such patients are often sexually unresponsive, despite their superficial seductiveness.

The obsessive-compulsive neurotic is plagued by obsessive thoughts and/or compulsive rituals; these are recognized by him as absurd, but acute anxiety ensues if they are not carried out. The personality is typically perfectionistic, intellectualizing, rigid and overcontrolled. These persons experience considerable anxiety, shame and guilt about sexual and aggressive impulses, are afraid of spontaneity and are highly performance oriented. In its severe form, this neurosis can be as incapacitating as a psychotic illness; in its milder and more common form, it may occur in quite functional and otherwise successful people. Sexual difficulties include mechanization of sex, impotence, premature ejaculation, retarded orgasm, compulsive genital acts and upsetting fantasies of carrying out some "unacceptable" sexual behavior.[39]

Obsessional neurotics confuse sexuality, hostility and aggression in themselves and others; this confusion contributes to their strong need to be always in control of themselves and others. They greatly fear loss of control; of course, giving oneself up to sensation and allowing oneself to relinquish control are an important part of sexual pleasuring and orgasm.

Salzman[40] describes how even a severely obsessional man may achieve a satisfactory adjustment and perform the sexual act perfectionistically according to the latest sex manual and with proper consideration for the partner. The act, however, is stilted, unspontaneous, routinized and often boring to the partner. Obsessional neurotics with difficulties of potency or orgasm sometimes have less of a problem with prostitutes or in fleeting affairs, in which the partner is seen as a depreciated person. Such an attitude reduces the need for perfect performance and makes control less crucial.

OTHER PERSONALITY DISORDERS

In personality disorders, the patient's personality is maladaptive and usually is disturbing to others but not necessarily to the patient. The obsessive-compulsive and histrionic personalities have been mentioned above; others are the schizoid personality, with its social seclusiveness and avoidance of intimate relationships, and the antisocial personality. Specific sexual symptoms may or may not be present in those with personality disorders. Usually the patient's sexuality simply parallels and is consistent with his nonsexual behavior and relationships.

Someone with an antisocial personality is likely to engage in sex without regard for the feelings of others or for cultural norms and have little guilt in doing so. Often such a person uses sex primarily to manipulate others. A schizoid individual, being turned inward, is likely to be more comfortable with autoeroticism and sexual fantasies than with intercourse. When sexual relationships do occur, they are likely to reflect the same emotional detachment as other relationships.

Jacobs[41] has suggested that certain sexual problems and dysfunctions in marital relationships are typical of couples who have different specific personality types; e.g., an obsessive-compulsive man married to an hysterical woman. The specificity of these patterns has not yet been confirmed by others.

Since sexuality represents biological, psychological and social factors, psychiatric illness affects sexual function by directly or indirectly influencing one or several of these factors. Sexual knowledge, attitudes, values and behavior may be shaped by the influence of such illness on development and learning. The result may be specific sexual symptoms or changes in attitudes toward oneself and others that shape sexual expression. When disturbed sexuality causes further stress and anxiety for the psychiatrically disturbed patient, therapeutic intervention is needed.

References

1. Winokur G, et al: Developmental and sexual factors in women: A comparison between control, neurotic and psychotic groups. *Am J Psychiatry* 1959; 115:1097-1100.
2. Woodruff RA, et al: Divorce among psychiatric out-patients. *Br J Psychiatry* 1972; 121:289-292.
3. Schaefer LC: Sexual experiences and reactions of a group of 30 women as told to a female psychotherapist. Columbia University, 1964. (unpublished doctoral dissertation)
4. Raboch J, Bartak V: A contribution to the study of the anesthetic-frigid syndrome in women. *Cesk Psychol* 1968; 64:230-235.
5. Raboch J, Bartak V: The sexual life of frigid women. *Psychiatr Neurol Med Psychol* 1968; 20:368-373.
6. Coppen A: The prevalence of menstrual disorders in psychiatric patients. *Br J Psychiatry* 1965; 111:155-167.
7. McCulloch DJ, Stewart JC: Sexual norms in a psychiatric population. *J Nerv Ment Dis* 1960; 131:70-73.
8. Fisher S: *The Female Orgasm: Psychology, Physiology, Fantasy*. New York, Basic Books Inc, 1973.
9. Pinderhughes CA, et al: Psychiatric disorders and sexual functioning. *Am J Psychiatry* 1972; 128:1276-1283.
10. Graham SR: The effects of psychoanalytically oriented psychotherapy on levels of frequency and satisfaction in sexual activity. *J Clin Psychol* 1960; 16:94-95.
11. Oppenheimer H: *Clinical Psychiatry: Issues and Challenges*. New York, Harper & Row Publishers, Inc, 1971.
12. Pincus JH, Tucker GJ: *Behavioral Neurology*, ed 2. New York, Oxford University Press, 1978.
13. Small IF, Small JG: Sexual behavior and mental illness, in Freedman AM, et al (eds): *Comprehensive Textbook of Psychiatry*, ed 2. Baltimore, Williams & Wilkins Company, 1975.
14. Renshaw DC: Sexuality and depression in infancy, childhood and adolescence. *Med Aspects Hum Sex* 1975 (June); 9:24-25.
15. Lief HI: Commentary: Current thinking on sex and depression. *Med Aspects Hum Sex* 1977 (Dec); 11:22-23.
16. Ayd FW Jr: *Recognizing the Depressed Patient*. New York, Grune & Stratton Inc, 1961.
17. Renshaw DC: Sexuality and depression in adults and the elderly. *Med Aspects Hum Sex* 1975 (Sept); 9:40-62.
18. Spencer RF, Raft D: Depression and diminished sexual desire. *Med Aspects Hum Sex* 1977 (Aug); 11:51-61.

19. Renshaw DC: Doxepin treatment of sexual dysfunctions associated with depression, in Medels J (ed): *Sinequan (Doxepin Hydrochloride): A Monograph of Recent Clinical Studies*. Amsterdam, Excerpta Medica, 1975.
20. Arieti S: Sexual conflict in psychotic disorders, in Wahl CW (ed): *Sexual Problems Diagnosis and Treatment in Medical Practice*. New York, Free Press, 1967.
21. Tsuang MT: Hypersexuality in manic patients. *Med Aspects Hum Sex* 1975 (Nov); 9:82-89.
22. Winokur G, et al: *Manic Depressive Illness*. St Louis, CV Mosby Co, 1969.
23. Shulman BH: Schizophrenia and sexual behavior. *Med Aspects Hum Sex* 1971 (Jan); 5:144-153.
24. Landis C, et al: Psychological and physical concomitants of adjustment in marriage. *Human Biol* 1940; 12:559-565.
25. Barker WJ: Female sexuality. *J Am Psychoanal Assoc* 1968; 16:123-245.
26. Rado S: *Psychoanalysis of Behavior*, Vol II. New York, Grune & Stratton Inc, 1962.
27. Johnston R, Planansky K: Schizophrenia in men: The impact on their wives. *Psychiatry Q* 1968; 42:146-155.
28. Weiner H: Diagnosis and symptomatology, in Bellak L (ed): *Schizophrenia: A Review of the Syndrome*. New York, Logos Press, 1958.
29. Frank L: Humanizing and dehumanizing aspects of human sexuality. *Dis Nerv Syst* 1969; 30:781-783.
30. Lukianowicz N: Sexual drive and its gratification in schizophrenia. *Int J Soc Psychiatry* 1963; 9:250-258.
31. Varsamis J, Adamson JD: Early schizophrenia. *Can Psychiatry Assoc J* 1971; 16:487-497.
32. Skopec HM, et al: Sexual behavior in schizophrenia. *Med Aspects Hum Sex* 1976 (April); 10:32-47.
33. Hollender MH, Callahan AS III: Erotomania or de Clerambault syndrome. *Arch Gen Psychiatry* 1975; 32:1574-1576.
34. Winokur G, Holemon E: Chronic anxiety neurosis: Clinical and sexual aspects. *Acta Psychiatrica Scandinav* 1963; 39:384-412.
35. Chrzanowski G: Sex behavior as clue to mental disease. *Med Aspects Hum Sex* 1971 (March); 5:200-209.
36. Purtell JJ, et al: Observations on clinical aspects of hysteria: Quantitative study of 50 hysteria patients and 156 control subjects. *JAMA* 1951; 146:902-909.
37. Chodoff P: The diagnosis of hysteria: An overview. *Am J Psychiatry* 1974; 131:1073-1078.
38. Nemiah J: Hysterical neurosis, conversion type, in Freedman A, et al (eds): *Comprehensive Textbook of Psychiatry*, ed 2. Baltimore, Williams & Wilkins Company, 1975.
39. Barnett J: Sex and the obsessive-compulsive person. *Med Aspects Hum Sex* 1971 (Feb); 5:34-97.
40. Salzman L: *The Obsessive Personality*. New York, Science House, 1968.
41. Jacobs LI: Sexual problems and personalities in four types of marriage. *Med Aspects Hum Sex* 1974 (March); 8:160-178.

Chapter 17

Drugs and Sexual Function

John Buffum, Pharm.D., David E. Smith, M.D.,
Charles Moser, Ph.D., Mickey Apter, Ph.D. (Candidate), Millicent Buxton,
Jackie Davison, Ph.D.

Drugs have always played a part in human sexuality. One has only to look at some of the old herbals or recipes for aphrodisiacs to get an idea of the large number of compounds that were brewed and ingested to enhance the performance of the man or woman who had no interest or of the man who was unable to sustain an erection. Many of these early concoctions contained substances that looked like the sexual organs. The oyster may have been used because of its resemblance to the vulva; ginseng may have been used because of its resemblance to the penis.[1,2]

EVALUATION OF THE LITERATURE

When we read the literature, we would like to see well-designed studies with solid conclusions upon which clinical judgments can be made regarding drug selection. For some reason, studies concerning drug-induced effects on sexual function are rare in the literature. Most available data are generated by studies addressing other questions, although there are some data from isolated case reports. The problem is further compounded by review articles that do not critically analyze the data that they cite.

In order to provide useful information, studies and reports should meet certain criteria:

1. The gender of subjects should be made explicit. Frequently studies do not mention how many males and females completed the study. This makes incidence data difficult to interpret, especially if the study involves gender-specific dysfunctions, such as erectile or ejaculatory failure.

2. There should be a control group. Certain population groups (e.g., hypertensive patients) have a higher incidence of sexual dysfunction, even when not taking medication.[3]

3. The age and marital status of the population should be specified. For example, a decrease in frequency of sexual activity is sometimes associated with increasing age.[4-7] Also, persons who were once married and do not remarry tend to have intercourse more frequently than those who remain in first marriages for long periods of time.[8]

4. Other drugs taken should be investigated. It is difficult to draw conclusions if one is not sure which drug is causing a problem.

5. Reports should indicate how the investigators obtained their data. There can be a big difference in the significance of results, depending upon whether

a patient is interviewed, is given a questionnaire or has simply volunteered information.[7,9,10]

6. It is important to know at what dosage the dysfunction occurs. It is also important to know whether that dose is adequate to treat the disease.

7. It is useful to know if there was any history of sexual problems before the patient began taking the drug. Some patients have been known to use drugs as an excuse for not having sex.

8. The term "impotence" should be defined. It has been used for everything from decreased desire to failure of ejaculation. It most commonly is used synonymously with erectile failure.

9. Studies should determine how long the patient was taking the drug before the sexual dysfunction began. Was tolerance noted? How long did the dysfunction last before the drug was discontinued?

10. It is important to know if the patient had any other disease state(s) or postsurgical condition that might have predisposed him to sexual dysfunction.

11. It helps to know if there was patient compliance—if the drug actually was taken as it was prescribed.

12. The duration of the study should be indicated so that the recorder can know whether it was long enough for adverse effects to occur. Some studies are not of sufficient duration.

13. Not all studies can employ a double-blind design, but it helps to eliminate any placebo effect or bias if neither the patient nor the researcher knows what is being ingested.

14. Randomization of patients helps to prevent any bias in patient selection. Again, not all studies can be set up in this way, but the data would be more reliable if they were.

15. Crossover design allows comparison of the patient response with the drug and without. Differences in patient response become apparent with this design.

DRUG EFFECTS PRODUCING SEXUAL DYSFUNCTION IN MALES

Decreased desire—The action of certain drugs that block dopamine receptors has been associated with decreased sexual behavior in animals.[11] Antiandrogens block the action of testosterone and act specifically on central sexual behavior mechanisms. Other drugs that can decrease desire include those that lower serum testosterone (e.g., narcotics), those that have dysphoric effects (e.g., antineoplastic agents) and centrally acting antihypertensives.

Decreased erection due excessive sympathetic stimulation—Sympathomimetic drugs may decrease erection by mechanisms that have not yet been elicited. They increase muscle blood flow and decrease cutaneous blood flow, possibly creating a type of steal syndrome by diverting blood away from the penis.

Decreased emission due to alpha-sympathetic blockade—Alpha-adrenergic blocking agents, as well as drugs that block both alpha- and beta-adrenergic transmission, inhibit innervation of the vas and epididymus, causing de-

212

creased emission. As a result, there is less or no movement of semen into the posterior urethra and therefore less stimulation for ejaculation.

Retrograde ejaculation due to alpha-sympathetic blockade of the internal urethral sphincter—Alpha-adrenergic blocking agents block the innervation responsible for internal sphincter closure.

Decreased erection and ejaculation due to decreased spinal reflexes—Certain centrally active drugs cause a progressive, nonselective decrease in central nervous system function that interferes with these particular reflexes. This affects both the sympathetic and parasympathetic systems.

Inhibition of erection and ejaculation due to ganglionic blockade—Both parasympathetic and sympathetic systems have ganglia that are blocked by ganglionic blocking agents. These agents are seldom used outside of intensive care units, where sexual functioning is rarely a consideration.

DRUG EFFECTS PRODUCING SEXUAL DYSFUNCTION IN FEMALES

Decreased desire—Same mechanism as for males.

Decreased lubrication—Drugs which decrease vaginal congestion decrease the sweating effect responsible for lubrication. This might occur as a result of either decreased spinal reflexes or ganglionic blockade, as in males.

Delayed orgasm—Some drugs have caused difficulty in achieving orgasm, possibly by a mechanism similar to that in males, i.e., rerouting blood and decreasing pelvic congestion.

DRUGS THAT AFFECT SEXUALITY

In the following sections, drugs with known effects on human sexuality are evaluated. When known, sexual dysfunction incidence data, dosages, duration of effects and mode of action are discussed.

Hormones

Androgens are used for several purposes, ranging from replacement therapy to marrow stimulation and cancer chemotherapy.[12] When their use in serious illness is necessary, consideration of their effect on sexual function becomes less important. For less critical indications, such as the treatment of certain types of "impotence," the physician should weigh all possible side effects, including adverse sexual effects.

When there is clearly a deficiency in testosterone production, replacement therapy with androgens is indicated and results can be dramatic. When there is no such deficiency, the efficacy of such therapy is questionable. Testosterone by itself has been used in sexually dysfunctional elderly men, occasionally with good results, although the placebo response is probably responsible in most cases. However, there is no reliable evidence that androgen replacement is beneficial in aging men.[12] In fact, it may be quite harmful. Prostatic cancer has been reported following androgen therapy.[13,14] This is most likely due to stimulation of a pre-existing but slow growing neoplasm in tissue responsive to androgens. Other undesirable effects include edema, jaundice, hepatic cancer, steroid fever, impotence, gynecomastia and azoospermia. Exogenous androgen also may inhibit gonadotropin secretion, leading to a decline in spermatogenesis.[12]

When anabolic steroids are used to enhance athletic performance, a practice that is not recommended, endogenous testosterone production may be suppressed and erectile dysfunction may result.[12] In one study, norethandrolone, an anabolic steroid, was administered to seven men for 8 to 25 weeks; all showed decreased libido, potency and testicular size, and azoospermia.[15] Some recovery occurred 24 to 26 weeks after treatment was discontinued, but permanent testicular damage was noted. In a 10-subject study, one of five men taking methandrostenolone in a dose of 25 mg/day complained of marked diminution of libido. There was no complaint from any of the five who received 10 mg/day.[16]

Until about 1974, prescription products containing testosterone, yohimbine and nux vomica (strychnine) were available for use in impotence. It is significant that, despite "double-blind crossover studies" purporting to show efficacy, marketing of these products was discontinued.[17-19]

Antiandrogens are of experimental interest as possible therapy for sex offenders. The goal is to reduce the sexual desire of criminal sex offenders in order to prevent the recurrence of sex crimes. Cyproterone acetate, currently not marketed in the United States, is one of the most potent antiandrogens known.[12] It acts through competitive inhibition of all androgens at the androgen-sensitive target organs. Its "selective action at the hypothalamic mating centers" accounts for its ability to inhibit libido.[20] This drug has progestational, androgenic and antiestrogenic activities as well.[12] Doses of 50 to 200 mg/day orally plus 300 to 600 mg every week or two have resulted in partial to complete inhibition of sexual activity.[20] Sexual desire decreases in 10 to 14 days and returns to normal within two weeks after the drug is discontinued.[12] Medroxyprogesterone acetate, chemically a progestin, is seeing experimental use in the United States as an antiandrogen for the treatment of sex offenders.[21] In one study only three of 20 patients showed recurrences of sexually deviant behavior while on a medication regimen of from 200 to 600 mg/week of medroxyprogesterone acetate.[21] One of the relapses was clearly related to alcohol abuse. Of 11 patients who discontinued medication against medical advice, 10 relapsed. The injectable aqueous suspension is the preferred dosage form because of its long duration of action (once or twice a week dosing) and certainty of administration.

Progestins are indicated mainly in the treatment of female reproductive disorders, for contraception in women and in the treatment of outflow obstruction secondary to benign prostatic hyperplasia in men.[22-24] Progestins have been reported to cause decreased desire and impotence in males.[23-26] Of 19 patients taking medrogestone, six taking 15 to 30 mg/day showed a decrease in sexual activity.[23] (The study did not clearly differentiate between decreased desire and impotence.) In one patient, there was a rebound increase in sexuality when medrogestone was withdrawn. In another study, gestonorone caproate, in doses of 200 mg intramuscularly every week for two to three months, caused impotence in 21 of 30 patients being treated for benign prostatic hyperplasia.[25] When hydroxyprogesterone caproate was used in 45 patients being treated for outlet obstruction, impotence occurred in 11.[24] The mechanism for the sexual dysfunction may be related to the antiandrogenic effects of the progestins.

Estrogens are administered to women for replacement therapy or for contraception, but they also have been used in males for the treatment of breast and prostatic carcinoma.[22] Because of their ability to decrease sexual desire in males, estrogens have been employed to control deviant sexual behavior, but other adverse effects, such as nausea, vomiting and feminization, limit their usefulness.[21,27] Although there have been many reports in the literature regarding changes in sexual desire and excitement after oral contraceptive use, when the studies are well controlled the results usually show no statistically significant change.[28,29] It appears that there are about as many women who experience an increase in sexual interest and responsiveness as experience a decrease or no change.

Corticosteroids are used in many illnesses, ranging from shock to dermatitis. Although they are capable of suppressing the hypothalamic-pituitary-adrenal axis and causing a variety of undesired effects, no cases of sexual dysfunction have been directly attributable to them.[30]

Antihypertensive Agents

By their very nature, drugs used to lower blood pressure might be expected to have some effect on sexual function. These agents act by decreasing sympathetic stimulus to the arteriolar and venous vasculature by various mechanisms.[31]

Spironolactone, a competitive aldosterone antagonist diuretic, acts by binding to the kidney cytosol mineralocorticoid receptor[32] and has caused decreased libido, impotence and gynecomastia.[33-35]

In one study, the incidence of impotence with large doses (400 mg/day) was reported to be about 30 per cent;[35] this dysfunction also has been reported with lower doses (50 to 100 mg/day).[33,34] A decrease in sexual desire is common, but there are no incidence data.[34,35] The mechanism for these sexual side effects is thought to be the drug's antiandrogenic action that inhibits the binding of dihydrotestosterone to its cytosol protein receptor.[32,36]

Although other diuretics have been implicated as causing sexual dysfunction, the evidence is sparse. In one comparative study,[37] 32 per cent of the patients reported difficulty with erection and 14 per cent reported difficulty with ejaculation while using an unspecified diuretic, but there were no controls. In another study of patients taking hydrochlorothiazide (50 mg/day), the incidence of sexual dysfunction was 9 per cent compared with 4 per cent in a normotensive control population, but again there was no hypertensive control population.[38] In one study of 67 patients (sex unspecified) who were taking hydrochlorothiazide 100 mg daily, there were three cases of decreased libido.[39] There were no controls. In another study, chlorthalidone was associated with impotence in four of ten patients.[40] Again, there was no control group, so it is difficult to draw conclusions. One report cites five cases in which chlorthalidone was associated with impotence and decreased libido when taken either alone or in combination with other drugs.[41] In all cases sexual function improved when chlorthalidone was stopped. In most diuretic studies, sexual dysfunction is not reported as a side effect.

Methyldopa, a centrally acting hypotensive which may have some peripheral action,[31] has been reported to cause decreased sexual desire, failure of erection and failure of ejaculation in doses of 1 to 3 gm/day.[8,9,40,42-49] Studies reporting decreased libido—probably due to a central effect—indicate that the incidence is 7 to 14 per cent.[40,45,47] Failure to ejaculate occurs in 7 to 19 per cent of patients and probably is secondary to the sympathetic blocking effect.[9,43,46,50,51] The most common sexual dysfunction is failure of erection, which, depending on the study, has an incidence of 2 to 80 per cent.[9,10,42-45,50-53] This effect may be due to a steal syndrome or shunting of blood away from the penis because of the drug's vasodilating action.

Propranolol, a beta-adrenergic blocking agent, is active against both $beta_1$ and $beta_2$ receptors.[54] It has been reported to cause decreased libido and decreased erection.[38,43,54-62] Reports of decreased libido show that the incidence is only about 1 to 4 per cent in both males and females.[55-57,63] Decrease in erection is more common and has a reported incidence of up to 28 per cent.[43,58-63] One study indicated an incidence of unspecified sexual dysfunction in 23 per cent with a combination of propranolol, hydralazine and hydrochlorothiazide.[38] The mechanism of action for decreased erection may be the increased alpha sympathetic tone as the beta effects are blocked, an action that tends to decrease blood flow to the penis.[54] Sexual dysfunction caused by propranolol seems to be dose-related, with the incidence being greater when doses exceed 320 mg.[55]

Metoprolol, a $beta_1$ selective blocking agent, has not been associated with sexual dysfunction in a study of 10,088 hypertensive patients.[64] A possible reason for the lack of sexual side effects is that metoprolol is relatively cardiospecific and has no effect on skin or resting muscle blood flow, as opposed to propranolol, which reduces both.[65] Beta blockers, including both propranolol and metoprolol, have been associated with isolated cases of Peyronie's disease.[66] The etiology is unknown.

Nadolol is a nonspecific beta blocker similar to propranolol. In a study of 9,837 hypertensive patients there were 30 reports of "sexual dysfunction" (not specified).[67] This would appear to be an incidence of 0.3 per cent. However, because the number of males and females completing the study was not specified it is difficult to determine incidence data. The dosages used were 40 to 240 mg/day, with the majority taking 80 or 160 mg/day. There should be little difference in side effects between propranolol and nadolol, and because propranolol's sexual side effects are seen at higher doses (see above under *Propranolol*) it would be reasonable to assume that this would also be true for nadolol. At the doses used, however, "no correlation was found between side effects and dosage."[67]

Clonidine, a centrally acting $alpha_2$-adrenergic agent, has been reported to cause failure of erection and decreased libido.[48,49,68-71] Other studies, however, indicate that the drug has no sexual effects.[72-75] One small study mentioned that decreased libido and impotence occurred in seven of 10 patients.[48] These results are probably due to the drug's central depressant effects. Failure of erection is more commonly reported, and an incidence of 4 to 70 per cent has been noted.[48,49,68-70] This effect may be due to the same mechanism that may be operative with methyldopa: the shunting of blood away from the penis caused by generalized vasodilation. These effects have been reported over a wide dosage range (from 0.2 to 4.8 mg).[73]

Guanethidine acts peripherally to block postganglionic adrenergic neurons. It has been reported to cause a decrease in erections, failure of ejaculation (probably failure of emission) and decreased libido.[9,43,75-81] In one study, mildly decreased libido was observed in 29 per cent of the patients,[76] probably due primarily to a central effect, for guanethidine has been reported to cause depressive reactions.[8,43,75,76,78,81] A wide-ranging incidence of 4 to 100 per cent for impaired erection[9,43,50,75-77,81,82] and 2 to 100 per cent for ejaculation has been reported in the literature. With respect to the latter, most patients complained of "dry sex" (i.e., normal orgasm with no ejaculation). When retrograde ejaculation was specifically tested for, it did not occur.[83] The impaired erection is probably due to a shunting of blood away from the penis, while the ejaculation failure is due to the blockade of sympathetic innervation for emission. Guanethidine has a much greater effect on the short adrenergic neurons innervating the genital organs than on the long neurons. It can produce functional and histologic damage that may persist for several months.[84] These side effects have been seen with doses exceeding 25 mg/day.[9,43,75-80]

Hydralazine is a peripherally acting vasodilator that directly relaxes the vascular smooth muscle.[43] No sexual dysfunction has been reported with hydralazine alone. One case of erection failure was noted when the drug was used with hydrochlorothiazide.[85] Impotence and undefined sexual dysfunction were reported in 19 to 23 per cent of patients receiving propranolol, hydrochlorothiazide and hydralazine.[38,59] Considering the possible effect of propranolol on sexual function, one could surmise from these studies that hydralazine has an additive effect. Any effect hydralazine might have may be due to the shunting of blood away from the penis. In one case, erectile failure occurred following the addition of hydralazine to a propranolol and furosemide regimen.[86] The author noted that the patient still had morning erections, so it would appear that something else may have been the cause.

Prazosin acts peripherally and has some sexual side effects, also possibly caused by shunting of blood away from the genitals. In doses of 3 to 20 mg/day, failure of erection has been reported in 0.6 to 4 per cent of patients,[87,88] and "sexual dysfunction" in 9 per cent.[42] Because of its alpha$_1$-adrenergic blocking action, prazosin might be expected to adversely affect ejaculation, but this action has not been reported.[71]

Phenoxybenzamine is an alpha$_1$-adrenergic blocking agent that can suppress the emission phase of ejaculation and also cause retrograde ejaculation[71,89-91] with doses of 40 to 60 mg/day. Partial inhibition of ejaculation develops in 32 to 50 per cent of patients.[58,91] The adverse effects on ejaculation are probably due to the blocking of the alpha-adrenergic receptors that innervate the internal genitalia.

Reserpine has been associated with decreased libido, failure of erection and failure of ejaculation.[48,49] There are no incidence data on decreased libido alone, but one study indicated that the incidence of decreased libido or erection was 46 per cent.[48] Other studies indicate that the incidence of impotence was 11 to 33 per cent.[43,59] In one small study, failure of ejaculation occurred in 14 per cent of the patients.[43] Decreased libido is most likely due to reserpine's central nervous system catecholamine-depleting effects. Impotence is probably a peripheral effect secondary to a shunting of blood away from the penis. Sexual dysfunction is seen with doses ranging from 0.1 mg[59] to 0.5 mg.[43,48] In these studies, a thiazide diuretic was used with reserpine.[43,48,59]

Psychotherapeutic Agents
Antipsychotic Drugs

These drugs have three main pharmacological actions that can affect sexual response. They all block dopamine in the central nervous system,[10] and this may have adverse effects on sexual desire through the mechanism of hypothalamic-pituitary-gonadal axis supression.[92-94] Most also have an alpha-adrenergic blocking action[95] that can interfere with innervation of the internal genital organs, and some have a vasodilating action that might interfere with erectile response by shunting blood away from the genitals.[95]

With the notable exception of thioridazine, there have been few studies on the sexual side effects produced by the *phenothiazines*. Thioridazine is notorious for its interference with ejaculation; the incidence ranges from 30 to 57 per cent.[75,92,96-111] It is not clear whether retrograde ejaculation or inhibition of emission is involved in the ejaculatory dysfunction. Inhibition of erection occurs about 54 per cent of the time.[99,106,107] Decreased libido has been seen in isolated cases,[97,106,107] and there have been three reports of total lack of orgasm.[102,103,107] Mesoridazine,[112] chlorpromazine,[113] fluphenazine,[114] perphenazine,[108] trifluoperazine,[108] butaperazine,[108] haloperidol and chlorprothixene[115] also can interfere with emission and/or ejaculation, but the reported incidence has been very low.

Antidepressants

Sexual side effects are rather rare with tricyclic antidepressants. There have only been 14 cases of impotence reported to the FDA in the past eight years.[116]

Amitriptyline, the most wide used and most anticholinergic tricyclic, showed no greater frequency of impotence than the others. In addition to their anticholinergic action, tricyclics block the "amine pump" preventing reuptake of norepinephrine and/or serotonin.[117] It is this mechanism which is most likely responsible for any sexual side effects.

In addition to amitriptyline, administration of protriptyline, imipramine and desipramine has been associated with decreased libido and inhibition of erection and ejaculation,[118-124] but incidence data are scarce. Because decreased

218

libido is frequently seen as a symptom of depression, it is difficult to distinguish drug effects from those of the disease process.[125,126]

Monoamine oxidase inhibitors also affect sexual function. In one small study, tranylcypromine, which chemically and pharmacologically resembles amphetamine,[125] was reported to cause increased libido as well as both impotence and spontaneous erections in doses of 20 mg/day.[118] It is difficult to draw conclusions about the sexual side effects from these data.

Phenelzine and isocarboxazid[124,127-130] have been reported to cause inhibition of erection and difficulty in achieving orgasm in men. (Difficulty in achieving orgasm in women was reported with phenelzine only.) These effects disappear rapidly on withdrawal of the drug. The etiology of these side effects is unknown, but the changes in levels and synthesis of norepinephrine peripherally may be a possible mechanism.

Lithium, which is used in the treatment of bipolar depressive disorders, was reported in one study to cause "impaired sexual function" and "decreased sexual appetence."[131] The sexual effects were described in only two patients, and then only as impotence. It was not stated whether the patients were male or female, so incidence data cannot be determined from this study. Sexual function returned to normal when lithium was discontinued.

Sedative-Hypnotic and Antianxiety Drugs

There are no published cases of sexual dysfunction associated with administration of *meprobamate*, a sedative-hypnotic used in the treatment of anxiety,[132] and the manufacturer does not list any. However, like other sedative-hypnotics, meprobamate depresses spinal reflexes. It could cause decreased sexual response, especially if used in conjunction with other central nervous system depressants, such as alcohol.

The only published reports of sexual dysfunction occurring with a *benzodiazepine* have been with chlordiazepoxide. There was one case of impotence[133] and one case of failure of ejaculation.[134] The manufacturer of diazepam indicates only that "changes in libido" have occurred infrequently. The manufacturer of oxazepam states that "rare instances" of "altered libido" have occurred. There are no such warnings concerning flurazepam. Because of the general depressant effects of benzodiazepines, inhibition of spinal reflexes that affect sexual function might be expected to occur with large doses, accumulation or concomitant administration of another depressant.

There are no specific studies on the sexual side effects of *barbiturates*, but reports indicate that the pattern is similar to that with the other depressants. The barbiturates show a tendency to produce a biphasic response; there is an initial beneficial effect on sexual desire, usually followed by a decrease in ability to maintain erection.[135,136] The dose levels were not given.

Although there are no well-controlled studies on the effects of *methaqualone* on sexual function, this drug has acquired a street reputation for sexual enhancement.[137-140] It has been documented that methaqualone increases sexual arousal[135,139,140] and produced a total body tingling sensation.[138-140] Any increased libido, however, is most likely due to decreasing inhibitions. One report indicated that it seemed to work better in women; if used in excess by men, it actually had a deleterious effect on sexual performance and drive.[137] (It has been noted that persons taking methaqualone tend to be ataxic, with a weakness of the extremities, and have been known to fall down stairs as a result.[139-142] Methaqualone also has been shown to have an inhibitory action on polysynaptic pathways and to produce hind limb weakness in animals.[142] Such action could be the cause of impotence when larger doses are used.)

Ethanol (ethyl alcohol) is a general central nervous system depressant that has both long- and short-term adverse effects on sexual functioning. The failure of erection and increased libido described by Shakespeare in Macbeth,[143] for example, is short-term and is well known to most men who have attempted to function sexually following excessive alcohol ingestion. People have different thresholds for sexual dysfunction that are related to their blood alcohol level. Central nervous system effects tend to be more pronounced when levels are rising than when falling.[144] Erectile dysfunction may have more than one cause. Ethanol impairs spinal reflexes, which causes both decreased sensation and decreased innervation for erection, but it also has been shown to decrease serum testosterone levels.[144]

One study in which serum testosterone and luteinizing hormone (LH) levels were measured in males before, during and after acute alcohol ingestion showed that, as blood alcohol levels increased, plasma testosterone levels decreased and LH levels increased.[145] The speculation was that the increase in LH levels may have been associated with the increased libido that accompanies acute alcohol ingestion. Decreased serum testosterone, on the other hand, may lead to decreased erection. These effects usually are transient and diminish as the blood alcohol level falls. A similar study was done in women with different results.[146] In this study there was no reduction of serum testosterone or increase in serum LH. There were no consistent effects on progesterone, estradiol, FSH or prolactin.

There are, however, permanent effects related to decreased testosterone levels. A study of normal males given alcohol over a four-week period showed that decreased testosterone production was coupled with an increased metabolic clearance.[144] Long-term alcoholics also have been noted to have hyperestrogenemia secondary to alcohol-induced liver damage, in which the liver converts a higher proportion of androgens to estrogens.[147,148] A combination of decreased testosterone and hyperestrogenemia is probably the cause of the feminization, gynecomastia, sterility, impotence and decreased libido seen in some alcoholic males.

In one study of 17,000 alcoholic males, 8 per cent complained of impotence.[149] In half of these cases, the impotence was irreversible; in the other half, sexual function returned following several months of abstinence from alcohol. Decreased libido was not mentioned in this study.

Results of a study of 16 nonalcoholic women, who were shown erotic films and given alcohol while being measured with a vaginal photoplethysmograph, indicated that alcohol caused decreased objective signs and increased subjective perception of sexual arousal.[150] This would indicate that vaginal vasocongestion decreases with increasing intoxication, just as does penile erection, its counterpart.

In one study of 44 female chronic alcoholics, 20 per cent said they never experienced orgasm and 36 per cent said they had orgasms less than 5 per cent of the time.[151] It is not clear whether this anorgasmia was related to the adverse physiological effects of alcohol, to the social consequences of alcoholism or to some aspect of the alcoholism-prone personality.

Stimulants

Amphetamine and related compounds are central nervous system stimulants or sympathomimetics[152] and have been reported to cause increased libido, impotence and delayed ejaculation in males[136,153-155] and increased libido and delayed orgasm in females.[153-155] Changes in sexual function due to amphetamine use are usually quite variable within any given study. Mazindol, a non-amphetamine anorexiant, has been anecdotally reported to cause an "aphrodisiac effect" in about 5 per cent of female patients.[156]

Newer data indicate that the dosage, route of administration, habituation and social setting play a great part in determining a user's sexual response to the amphetamine.[155] Smaller oral doses tend to be associated with enhanced sexual desire in both men and women. Small doses also seem to help sustain erections and produce some delay in ejaculation in males, but the results are less clearcut than in females. Some women report that amphetamine enhanced their ability to achieve an orgasm, possibly because of the increased libido and longer duration of the sexual act. Larger doses of amphetamine (up to 1 gm/day) tend to be associated with sexual dysfunction, with males reporting impotence and both males and females reporting anorgasmia.[155]

Another interesting effect of amphetamine is that some users will engage in sexual acts that they would avoid under non-using circumstances.[153-155]

The mechanisms by which amphetamine alters sexual function have not been determined, although they are probably related to the drug's central nervous system effects on monoamine oxidase, catecholamines, serotonin and dopamine and to its peripheral effects on catecholamines.[152,157]

Cocaine also has been reported to have both positive and negative effects on sexual function that are similar to those of amphetamine. Cocaine has a wide reputation as an aphrodisiac among users.[135,158,159] In large doses, erection may be decreased.[158]

There have been reports of spontaneous erections occurring following intravenous injection of both cocaine and amphetamine.[159] Multiple orgasms have been reported to be facilitated with both drugs.[158] Cocaine has been used as a douche with resultant local anesthetic effects, systemic stimulant effects, and purported effects of contracting vaginal musculature.[159]

There are no controlled studies on the effects of cocaine on human sexual activity, and doses have not generally been reported.

Opiate Analgesics

Heroin (diacetyl-morphine), a synthetic morphine derivative with a high abuse and addiction potential, causes decreased libido, retarded ejaculation and impotence.[136,160-163] In one study, 61 per cent of heroin addicts reported impaired libido, which returned to normal after detoxification;[162] in contrast, libido was not affected in any of the control subjects. In the same study, impotence was reported by 39 per cent of the addicts compared to 7 per cent of the controls, and delayed ejaculation by 70 per cent of the addicts but by none of the controls. Premature ejaculation has been reported in a larger number of heroin users.[160,161] It seems to be more prevalent in addicts when they are undergoing detoxification than when they are drug-free or taking heroin.[160] It has been suggested that this dysfunction may be a symptom of withdrawal, because it subsided as the other symptoms did.[164] One study suggests that premature ejaculation may reflect pre-drug functioning rather than being a withdrawal symptom.[160] The implication is that those taking heroin may use the drug for self-medication to prevent premature ejaculation.

The mechanism of action for these changes in sexual function is thought to be due to heroin's acute suppression of luteinizing hormone (LH) release followed by secondary drop in plasma testosterone levels.[165] The decrease in LH levels may be associated with decreased libido, and decreased testosterone may lead to impotence. Mirin et al felt that reduction of sexual drive may act as reinforcement for continuing opiate use.[165]

In one study of 40 heroin-using women, 24 noted decreased libido, one had increased libido, and one complained of delayed orgasms since the onset of her addiction.[166]

There are no current reports in the literature linking *morphine* and *codeine* with sexual dysfunction. However, it may be assumed that morphine acts in much the same way as heroin, since heroin is rapidly hydrolyzed to morphine by the body and many of its pharmacological effects occur as a result of this process.[167] With larger doses, codeine also might affect sexual function.

Methadone, a synthetic narcotic analgesic with properties pharmacologically similar to those of morphine,[167] has been implicated in causing decreased libido, failure of ejaculation and failure of orgasm.[160-162,168-171] The incidence of decreased libido ranged from 6 to 38 per cent, of erection failure from 6 to 50 per cent, of retarded ejaculation from 5 to 22 per cent, and of orgasm failure from 5 to 88 per cent.

Whether heroin or methadone causes more sexual dysfunction is controversial. In all the studies, the incidence of sexual dysfunction was reported to be significantly higher in users of both heroin and methadone than in drug-free controls.[160-162,171] Much of the ambiguity could probably be resolved if dosages of the methadone and heroin were known. In most studies, the dose levels were not indicated. A study comparing high and low doses of methadone in maintenance programs suggests that dosage significantly influences the incidence of sexual side effects.[160,172]

Because methadone is cleared from the body slowly, there is always a fairly high concentration of the drug in the body throughout the day[161] when it is used in a treatment regimen, whereas heroin levels tend to rise and fall depending upon availability. In one study, it was found that testosterone levels were lower in methadone patients than in heroin users or control subjects, possibly due to the constant presence of methadone in the body.[161] The significance of this observation is not known. The function of the secondary sex organs was found to be markedly impaired in the methadone patients in contrast to heroin users or controls, but this finding did not correlate well with the serum testosterone levels.

Miscellaneous Drugs and Chemicals

Marijuana has been reported to have both positive and negative effects on sexuality, but no definitive study in humans has yet been conducted. In extremely large doses, as taken by chronic hashish users in India, it has caused both decreased libido and inability to perform.[173,174] In more moderate doses, it has enhanced sexual function.[135,175]

The mechanism of action of the sexual adverse effects of marijuana is not understood. One study concluded that plasma testosterone was decreased in chronic intensive marijuana smokers,[176] but this observation was not confirmed by a later study.[177] Enhancement of sexual function appears to be due to heightened sensory experience and to anticipation.[135,175,178] This greater sensory awareness is the basis for the suggestion that marijuana be used to augment sensate focus exercises for those who are unable to respond to nongenital caresses.[158]

Lysergic acid diethylamide (LSD-25), once used experimentally as an adjunct to psychotherapy,[179] has no acceptable medical use currently. Results of reports on the sexual side effects of LSD are conflicting and the studies are poorly designed. Some users have said they had no sexual feeling whatsoever, whereas others had deeply moving sexual emotional experiences.[135,136,157] Doses were not mentioned in any of these studies.

3,4-Methylone dioxyamphetamine (MDA), an amphetamine derivative, is not used in medicine, although it has been tested as a possible adjunct to psychotherapy.[180] MDA reportedly enhances communication and emotional feelings, thus potentially facilitating sexual performance.[158,182] There have been no reports of sexual dysfunction occurring with use of MDA, but because of its similarity to amphetamine, it can be assumed that with increasing doses erections would be impaired. In addition, possible central nervous system effects could interfere with sexual desire.

The sexual effects of other lesser used psychedelics, including psilocybin, mescaline and ibogane, have not been carefully studied. In an excellent review article, Gawan discusses what is currently known about their historical use and possible effects on sexual function.[158]

Phencyclidine (PCP), an animal tranquilizer now banned from veterinary practice under federal law, is widely abused by youth. Chronic abuse with large doses has been observed to be associated with adverse effects on erection and ejaculation.[182] PCP's use for sexual stimulation, however, apparently is confined largely to a small minority of homosexual males; the diverse effects reported are dose related.[182]

Cimetidine is a histamine H2 receptor antagonist used to suppress gastric acid secretion.[183] There are 30 cases of male patients who developed a progressive decrease in libido and failure of erection within 1 to 28 weeks after being given 1 to 1.2 gm of cimetidine per day.[183-185] Normal sexual function returned within two weeks in two of the four patients in whom follow-up was reported. Breast pain or gynecomastia also has been reported in males during cimetidine therapy,[186,187] and one young woman developed galactorrhea.[187] Another woman complained of "sex inhibition."[185]

The mode of action for the sexual dysfunction is thought to be the drug's possible antiandrogenic activity, although the possibility of a direct effect on the seminiferous tubules cannot be ruled out.[188,189]

The fibrinolytic inhibitor, *aminocaproic acid*, is used to treat excessive bleeding due to systemic hyperfibrinolysis. There is one report of six instances of "dry ejaculation" with no impotence or decrease in libido occurring in a group of 25 patients.[190]

Disopyramide is used in the treatment of ventricular arrhythmia. One patient with renal failure being maintained following atrial fibrillation developed impotence after he had been taking disopyramide for six months.[191] The impotence was attributed to the drug's anticholinergic effects that emerged when the blood levels became excessive. Sexual function returned when the dose was reduced. Another 35-year-old male with normal renal function, taking 300 mg daily, developed erectile failure after three weeks of disopyramide therapy.[192] Sexual function returned six days after withdrawal of the drug.

Thiabendazole is an anthelmintic used in the treatment of parasitic infections. There were two cases of impotence occurring among 23 males and females being treated for trichinosis with thiabendazole.[193] No data were provided on the patients, the specific dose employed, or the onset or duration of sexual dysfunction.

Digoxin is used in treating congestive heart failure and certain cardiac arrythmias. In one study, 5 of 14 males (36 per cent) showed decreased sexual desire following long-term administration of digoxin.[194] Decreased erection was reported by 5 of 14 and decreased frequency of sexual relations by 6 of 14 (43 per cent). These effects were thought to be due to estrogen-like activity of the digoxin.[194,195] Digitalis glycosides have also caused gynecomastia in males.[196]

Clofibrate is a hypolipidemic agent used primarily in the treatment of types III, IV, and V hyperlipoproteinemia.[197] One large survey indicated an incidence of sexual dysfunction of 14 per cent in patients taking clofibrate, although in the same survey there was a 10 per cent incidence with placebo alone.[198] In another report, impotence occurred in 3 of 100 patients.[199] Sexual function returned to normal in two of the patients following withdrawal of the drug; the third required continuation of clofibrate therapy, and his impotence never resolved.

The anticholinergic agent, *methantheline bromide*, usually is used as an antispasmodic.[200] In one study, patients being treated with unspecified doses of methantheline were surveyed for sexual side effects.[201] Impotence developed in almost all patients soon after therapy was initiated and disappeared soon after the drug was discontinued. Methantheline has a particularly high ratio of ganglionic blocking to antimuscarinic activity, and this is the most likely cause of erectile failure.[200]

224

Ketamine hydrochloride is a dissociative anesthetic most commonly used in surgery in children.[202] There is one report of ketamine being administered to prevent erections in patients undergoing cystoscopy.[203] Twenty-five patients were given a dose of 1 mg/lb body weight during induction. Erection did not occur in any of the patients. In two other cases, ketamine was given to patients who developed erections during cystoscopy and detumescence resulted.

Tobacco smoking was associated with erectile dysfunction in two young men.[204] Blood flow studies showed increased flow, and erectile capacity was restored following discontinuation of smoking.

Insecticides and herbicides have been implicated as causing impotence in four of five workers.[205] The exact chemical was unknown, however, because the workers had been exposed to 18 toxic compounds. All four complained of difficulty in achieving and maintaining an erection; one worker experienced delayed ejaculation. After contact with the chemicals had been stopped and methyltestosterone therapy started, the impotence resolved in 2 to 12 months. It was not clear if the methyltestosterone aided in the recovery or was super-fluous. It was suggested that a possible etiology for the dysfunctions involved potentiation of testosterone metabolism by dieldrin, a chlorinated hydro-carbon.[206]

Impotence has been reported following prolonged exposure to *nitrous oxide*.[207] This was a delayed symptom in seven of 15 patients who developed myeloneuropathy, which was slowly reversible when there was no further exposure to the gas.

Antibiotics have caused secondary yeast infections by suppressing normal vaginal flora. Such infections can produce inflammation and result in dy-spareunia until they are effectively treated. Women taking broad spectrum antibiotics, such as tetracycline, should be apprised of this potential side effect. Live yogurt douches have been used successfully to maintain normal vaginal flora.[208]

There have been reports of impotence secondary to use of *disulfiram*, an aldehyde dehydrogenase inhibitor given to treat alcoholism,[209] but it has not been established whether the sexual dysfunction was caused by the drug or the alcohol.[210] When disulfiram was first introduced, the incidence of impo-tence was reported to be 10 to 12 per cent, but this high incidence was be-lieved to have been due to the high dosages employed at the time (2 gm/day).[211] In a recent study, it was found that doses of 500 mg/day are capable of altering the hypothalamic-pituitary-gonadal function of normal men.[210] In this study, no sexual dysfunction was reported, even though some hormone levels and responses were affected.

Cancer chemotherapy agents, particularly alkylating agents (such as *chlorambucil, cyclophosphamide*) and *procarbazine* have been associated with gonadal dysfunction in men and women and gynecomastia and impotence in men.[212,213] In adult males there is a marked decrease of testicular volume, severe oligospermia or azoospermia and infertility, which seems to be related more to the total dose administered.[212] Combination chemotherapy is asso-ciated with longer lasting effects than are single agents. Reversibility is related to total dose, type of drug and duration of time off therapy.[212] The effects in women include vaginal epithelial atrophy, endometrial hypoplasia, amenorrhea and menopausal symptoms, such as "hot flashes," vaginal dryness and dyspareunia.[212] These agents can accelerate onset of menopause, especially in women over 40. These effects are secondary to direct toxic effects on the ovaries resulting in ovarian fibrosis and follicle destruction with resultant decrease in serum estradiol.[212] Data suggest that 50 per cent of women treated with combination chemotherapy will become amenorrheic.

DRUGS TO ENHANCE SEXUALITY

Aphrodisiacs have been traditionally thought of as substances capable of stimulating sexual interest in the absence of other sex stimuli. Many substances do tend to enhance certain aspects of sexual interest and response in humans when sexual inclination already exists. Some examples already have been mentioned. This section will review studies on other drugs which have been tested for aphrodisiac properties.

Volatile nitrites (amyl nitrite, isobutyl nitrite, isoamyl nitrite) are vasodilators that are currently used by some individuals to enhance sexual pleasure. They are reputed to prolong orgasm, or the perception of orgasm, following inhalation just prior to orgasm.[214,215] They also are thought to relax the anal sphincter to facilitate anal intercourse.[216] To date, there are no studies that substantiate or disprove these effects. The nitrites' mode of action is unknown. One author thought the prolongation might be due to cerebral ischemia,[217] although that would be doubtful, considering the mode of action and circumstances of use (inhalation while lying down). The vasodilation with reflex sympathetic compensation could have an effect on the perception of orgasm.[218] Some males also discovered that if inhaled at the wrong time, volatile nitrites can cause immediate detumescence. This effect is used clinically during cystoscopy and following adult circumcisions to prevent erection.[219]

Bromocriptine mesylate is a dopamine agonist derived from ergot and is used in hyperprolactinemic states to inhibit the secretion of prolactin by the pituitary. Because of the association of dopaminergic stimulation with increased sexual activity in animals, it was thought that a dopamine agonist such as this might be useful in the treatment of impotence.[220-222] In one study on hyperprolactinemic patients with pituitary tumors, potency was restored in some cases.[222] In a study on chronic hemodialysis patients, bromocriptine in doses of 5 mg/day improved sexual function in six of seven patients.[223] In three other studies, however, impotent patients who had no endocrine disturbances showed no improvement with bromocriptine in doses of 5 to 7.5 mg/day.[220,221] Bromocriptine may have a role in treating impotence caused by hyperprolactinemia and appears to be most effective when testosterone levels are normal.

Levodopa, a dopamine precursor used in the treatment of parkinsonism,[224] was reported to cause hypersexual behavior in 8 of 908 parkinsonian patients.[225] This is an incidence of only 0.9 per cent, and the authors believed that the enhanced sexual behavior was probably due to a more general hypomanic syndrome, because it was almost always associated with other symptoms suggestive of hypomania.

In other smaller studies, the conclusions were more enthusiastic.[226-228] In one study, psychotic symptoms were reactivated in 10 schizophrenic patients after administration of levodopa.[153] Much of the acting out took on a sexual form. In the same study, increased sexual interest developed in three of six nonschizophrenic psychiatric patients receiving levodopa. The authors noted that the extent of the effects seemed to correlate with the amount of hypersexual behavior occurring before the drug was taken. In their words, "We suspect that amphetamine and levodopa might prove to have aphrodisiac effects in those who 'need' them least and not prove helpful to those who could most benefit from such effects."[153]

In another study, it was noted that increased sexuality seems to occur while the parkinsonian symptoms can still be seen.[229] When the symptoms disappear because of the levodopa treatment, the hypersexuality tends to decrease.

There is one report of two patients who developed ejaculation difficulties with levodopa.[230] Erection and orgasm occurred normally in conjunction with either failure of emission or retrograde ejaculation. It was not clear from the report which occurred. The doses used were 2.5 to 3 gm/day.

Any increased libido in man associated with administration of levodopa probably would be produced by the same mechanism reported in animals. Why this effect should occur in relatively few humans but in most animals has not been determined. Why levodopa caused two isolated cases of ejaculatory problems is not clear either.

Parachlorophenylalanine (PCPA) is an inhibitor of serotonin synthesis that has been used in the treatment of migraine headaches.[231] In one uncontrolled study, administration of PCPA was shown to be associated with increased levels of sexual excitation in migraine patients.[232] In a later study on male migraine patients, oral PCPA plus a placebo given intramuscularly was compared with intramuscular placebo plus oral placebo and oral PCPA plus intramuscular testosterone.[231] PCPA and testosterone significantly increased the total number of daily erections. PCPA alone was no better than a placebo. An earlier study showed that testosterone alone also was no better than a placebo.[232] Apparently such stimulation with use of PCPA has been reported only in those patients with migraine.[231] It also has been noted that there is a decrease in libido in migraine patients.[231] Because migraine headaches have been associated with increased serotonin levels and PCPA decreases serotonin levels, it is reasonable to assume that PCPA might enhance sexual arousal in those with this condition.

L-tryptophan, a serotonin precursor, has been used experimentally in the treatment of multiple sclerosis and schizophrenia.[233] The hypothesis that loading doses of L-tryptophan may increase levels of serotonin and result in decreased libido has been tested,[11] but significant changes in sexual motivation did not occur. In another uncontrolled study of 56 patients with migraine headache, the author felt that he could "express the impression of a reduction of sensuality."[232] The sexual effects of L-tryptophan, however, do not appear to be significant.

Yohimbine is an alkaloid obtained from various sources, most notably the corynanthe yohimbe. It has been used to treat impotence and as an aphrodisiac[158] and has been incorporated into products containing methyltestoste-rone and nux vomica as a treatment for the "male climacteric."[17-19] As noted earlier, these products were taken off the market. Yohimbine is classified as an alpha$_2$-adrenergic blocking agent and has been noted to be a model anxiety-producing agent in doses of 0.1 mg/kg intravenously.[71,234] The dose used for aphrodisiac purposes was 5 mg orally.[235]

Several studies have noted that patients with uremia have low plasma zinc levels,[236] and it is well known that sexual function decreases in uremic men and women.[236-239] One study suggested "strikingly improved potency in all patients" when *zinc* was administered in dialysate fluid to four uremic patients undergoing hemodialysis.[236] A placebo did not improve sexual function in any patient. Results of the study suggest that zinc deficiency may be a major cause of abnormalities in testosterone synthesis or metabolism in those with uremia, but that oral zinc does not increase plasma zinc levels in uremic pa-tients. It has also been reported that older patients have low preoperative serum zinc levels.[240] Oysters have a particularly high zinc content (about 50 to 100 times that found in most foods),[241] which may be responsible for their almost legendary aphrodisiac properties in "tired old men."

Clomiphene citrate is an antiestrogen usually used in the treatment of ovula-tory failure in women desiring pregnancy.[22] Use of the drug in a male alcoholic resulted in increased testicular size, resolution of impotence and improvement of libido. Clomiphene was given to this patient to treat Laennec's cirrhosis complicated by gynecomastia, testicular atrophy, impotence and loss of libido.[242] Although the dose was increased from 50 to 200 mg/day over a four-month period, the authors felt that maximum response can be obtained from a total dose of 50 mg/day. It was believed that clomiphene corrected the androgen-estrogen imbalance by blocking the estrogen excess and/or stimulat-ing the hypothalamic-pituitary axis. The improvements in sexual function lasted eight months after cessation of treatment, at which time the patient reverted to his pretreatment status.

Pheromones are substances secreted by animals to attract members of the opposite sex through the olfactory sense.[243] Work on human pheromones is in its infancy, but it is known that when these substances are secreted by females of lower species, they have very powerful sexual attraction effects on the males. In one study, some short-chain fatty acids that were thought to be crucial pheromonal components were isolated from the vaginal secretion of human females.[244] Alpha androstenol, a pheromone isolated from human male sweat, has been tested by the perfume industry.[245] It was found to be so attractive to human females that it may be incorporated into a new after-shave.[246] Pheromones may well prove to be the only true aphrodisiacs.

Many substances can alter the sexual response cycle in man, either positively or negatively. Many of the drugs used therapeutically have been reported to have adverse effects on sexuality. The possibility of such effects should be taken into account when these drugs are used clinically. Many substances that are used and abused recreationally also have profound effects on sexual response. Some are used in such a manner that they mitigate underlying sexual problems. Treatment of a drug abuser's habit, therefore, may prove unsuccessful without treatment of his pre-existing sexual problems and concerns.

Certain substances have been used since the beginning of mankind to enhance sexuality. Some of the preparations have been used fairly successfully and their reputation has been passed down through the millennia. However, thus far, no aphrodisiac has survived the rigors of scientific scrutiny. As long as humans place value on optimal sexual functioning, there will be a demand for drugs that enhance that function. For the scientific community to meet this challenge, more effective and relevant study designs will have to be utilized to separate fact from fancy.

Authors' Note: *As this book goes to press, important new data concerning the neuropharmacology of erection have become available. The widely accepted view that erection and lubrication are mediated primarily by the parasympathetic nervous systems with a sympathetic component is now being questioned.*[247,248] *Studies in animals and humans have shown that atropine, which blocks the parasympathetic system, does not block erection in males or lubrication in females.*[248,249] *In addition, studies in animals have also shown that acetylcholine, a parasympathetic neurotransmitter, does not produce erection.*[250-252] *When human penile erectile tissue was measured for choline acetyltransferase, which is necessary for parasympathetic activity, none was found, although norepinephrine was present.*[253]

Neuromorphologic studies of human penile tissue have shown scant distribution of parasympathetic fibers and numerous catecholaminergic (sympathetic) fibers.[254] *In addition, one study showed that when acetylcholine was added to a penile tissue bath preparation there was minimal contraction in only two of 24 strips*[254]—*clinical observations that seemed to bear out the lack of effect of anticholinergic drugs on erection. In reviewing the literature for this chapter it was apparent that the drugs which tended to cause erectile failure did not have anticholinergic action, whereas most had some effect on the sympathetic system or were hormonal in nature.*

Nonproprietary Names and Representative Tradenames of Drugs

Aminocaproic acid—*Amicar*
Amitriptyline hydrochloride—*Amitid, Amitril, Elavil, Endep, SK-Amitriptyline*
Bromocriptine mesylate—*Parlodel*
Butaperazine maleate—*Repoise*
Chlordiazepoxide hydrochloride—*Librium*
Chlorpromazine hydrochloride—*Thorazine*
Chlorprothixene—*Taractan*
Chlorthalidone—*Hygroton*
Cimetidine—*Tagamet*
Clofibrate—*Atromid-S*
Clomiphene citrate—*Clomid*
Clonidine hydrochloride—*Catapres*
Cyproterone acetate—*Androcur* (Investigational)

229

Desipramine hydrochloride—*Norpramin, Pertofrane*
Diazepam—*Valium*
Disopyramide phosphate—*Norpace*
Disulfiram—*Antabuse*
Ethinyl estradiol—*Estinyl,Feminone*
Fluphenazine—*Prolixin*
Flurazepam hydrochloride—*Dalmane*
Guanethidine sulfate—*Ismelin*
Haloperidol—*Haldol*
Hydralazine hydrochloride—*Apresoline*
Hydrochlorothiazide—*Esidrix, HydroDiuril, Oretic*
Hydroxyprogesterone caproate—*Delalutin*
Imipramine hydrochloride—*Imavate, SK-Pramine, Tofranil*
Isocarboxazid—*Marplan*
Ketamine hydrochloride—*Ketaject, Ketalar*
Lithium carbonate—*Eskalith, Lithane, Lithonate, Lithotabs*
Levodopa—*Dopar, Larodopa*
Mazindol—*Sanorex*
Medrogestone—*Colprone* (Investigational)
Medroxyprogesterone acetate—*Depo-Provera*
Meprobamate—*Equanil, Meprospan, Miltown*
Mesoridazine besylate—*Serentil*
Methadone hydrochloride—*Dolophine*
Methandrostenolone—*Dianabol*
Methantheline bromide—*Banthine*
Methaqualone—*Quaalude, Sopor*
Methyldopa—*Aldomet*
Oxazepam—*Serax*
Perphenazine—*Trilafon*
Phenelzine sulfate—*Nardil*
Phenoxybenzamine hydrochloride—*Dibenzyline*
Prazosin hydrochloride—*Minipress*
Propranolol hydrochloride—*Inderal*
Protriptyline hydrochloride—*Vivactil*
Reserpine—*Reserpoid, Sandril, Serpasil*
Spironolactone—*Aldactone*
Thiabendazole—*Mintezol*
Thioridazine hydrochloride—*Mellaril*
Tranylcypromine sulfate—*Parnate*
Trifluoperazine hydrochloride—*Stelazine*

References

1. Kaplan H: *The New Sex Therapy*. New York, Brunner/Mazel Inc, 1974.
2. Siegel RK: Ginseng abuse syndrome: Problems with the panacea. *JAMA* 1979; 241:1614-1615.
3. Bulpitt CJ, et al: Change in symptoms of hypertensive patients after referral to hospital clinic. *Br Heart J* 1976; 38:121-128.
4. Karacan I, et al: Sleep-related penile tumescence as a function of age. *Am J Psychiatry* 1975; 132:932-987.

5. Levine SB: Marital sexual dysfunction: Erectile dysfunction. *Ann Intern Med* 1976; 85:342-350.
6. Reckless J, Geiger N: Impotence as a practical problem. *DM*, 1975 (May).
7. Bulpitt CJ, et al: A symptom questionnaire for hypertensive patients. *J Chronic Dis* 1974; 27:309-323.
8. Lief HI, Persky H: Personal communication, 1980.
9. Prichard BN, et al: Bethanidine, guanethidine and methyldopa in treatment of hypertension: A within-patient comparison. *Br Med J* 1968; 1:135-144.
10. Alexander WD, Evans JI: Side effects of methyldopa, (letter). *Br Med J* 1975; 2:501.
11. Hyyppä M, et al: Neuroendocrine regulation of gonadotropin secretion and sexual motivation after L-tryptophan administration in man, in Sandler M, Gessa GL (eds): *Sexual Behavior: Pharmacology and Biochemistry*. New York, Raven Press, 1975.
12. Murad F, Gilman AG: Androgens and anabolic steroids, in Goodman L, Gilman A (eds): *The Pharmacological Basis of Therapeutics*. New York, Macmillan Publishing Co, Inc, 1975.
13. Guinan PD, et al: Impotence therapy and cancer of the prostate. *Am J Surg* 1976; 131:599-600.
14. Sarfaty G: The use of androgens in the male climacteric. *Med J Aust* 1972; 2:571.
15. Frasier SD: Androgens and athletes. *Am J Dis Child* 1973; 125:479-480.
16. Freed D, et al: Anabolic steroids in athletics. *Br Med J* 1972; 3:761.
17. Bruhl DE, Leslie CH: Afrodex: Double-blind test in impotence. *S Tex Med Rec Ann* 1963; 56:22-23.
18. Miller WW Jr: Afrodex in the treatment of male impotence. A double-blind cross-over study. *Curr Ther Res* 1968; 10:354-359.
19. Sobotka JJ: An evaluation of afrodex in the management of male impotency: A double-blind crossover study. *Curr Ther Res* 1969; 11:87-94.
20. Laschet J, Laschet L: Anti-androgens in the treatment of sexual deviations of men. *J Steroid Biochem* 1975; 6:821-826.
21. Berlin F, Meinecke C: Treatment of sex offenders with antiandrogenic medication: Conceptualization, review of treatment modalities and preliminary findings. *Am J Psychiatry* 1981; 138:601-607.
22. Murad F, Gilman AG: Estrogens and progestins, in Goodman L, Gilman A (eds): *The Pharmacological Basis of Therapeutics*. New York, Macmillan Publishing Co, Inc, 1975.
23. Paulson DF, Kane RD: Medrogestone: A prospective study in the pharmaceutical management of benign prostatic hyperplasia. *J Urol* 1975; 113:811-815.
24. Meiraz D, et al: Treatment of benign prostatic hyperplasia with hydroxy progesterone-caproate: Placebo-controlled study. *Urology* 1977; 9:144-148.
25. Palanca E, Juco W: Conservative treatment of benign prostatic hyperplasia. *Curr Med Res Opin* 1977; 4:513-520.

26. Heller CG, et al: Effects of progesterone and synthetic progestins on the reproductive physiology of normal men. *Fed Proc* 1959; 18:1057-1065.
27. Golla FL, Hodge R: Hormone treatment of the sexual offender. *Lancet* 1949; 256:1006-1007.
28. Gambrell RD, et al: Changes in sexual drives in patients on oral contraceptives. *J Reprod Med* 1976; 17:165-171.
29. Bragonier JR: Influence of oral contraception on sexual response. *Med Aspects Hum Sex* 1976 (Oct); 10:130-143.
30. de Lange WE, Doorenbos H: Corticotrophins and corticosteroids, in Dukes MNG (ed): *Meyler's Side Effects of Drugs*. New York, American Elsevier Pub Co, 1975.
31. Nickerson M, Ruedy J: Antihypertensive agents and the drug therapy of hypertension, in Goodman L, Gilman A (eds): *The Pharmacological Basis of Therapeutics*. New York, Macmillan Publishing Co, Inc, 1975.
32. Rose LI, et al: Pathophysiology of spironolactone-induced gynecomastia. *Ann Intern Med* 1977; 87:398-403.
33. Greenblatt DJ, Koch-Weser J: Gynecomastia and impotence: Complications of spironolactone therapy, (letter). *JAMA* 1973; 223:82.
34. Zarren HS, Black PL: Unilateral gynecomastia and impotence during low-dose spironolactone administration in men. *Milit Med* 1975; 140:417-419.
35. Spark RF, Melby JC: Aldosteronism in hypertension: The spironolactone response test. *Ann Intern Med* 1968; 69:685-691.
36. Loriaux L, et al: Spironolactone and endocrine dysfunction. *Ann Intern Med* 1976; 85:630-636.
37. Dollery CT, Bulpitt CJ: Alpha-methyldopa in the treatment of hypertension: Long-term experience, in Onesti G, et al (eds): *Hypertension, Mechanisms & Management*. New York, Grune & Stratton Inc, 1973.
38. Hogan MJ, et al: Antihypertensive therapy and male sexual dysfunction. *Psychosomatics* 1980; 21:234-237.
39. Yendt E, et al: The use of thiazides in the prevention of renal calculi. *Can Med Assoc J* 1970; 102:614-620.
40. Pillay VKG: Some side-effects of alpha-methyldopa. *S Afr Med J* 1976; 50:625-626.
41. Stessman J, Ben-Ishay D: Chlorthalidone-induced impotence. *Br Med J* 1980; 281:714.
42. Kochar M, et al: Prazosin in hypertension with and without methyldopa. *Clin Pharmacol Ther* 1979; 25:143-148.
43. Bulpitt CJ, Dollery CT: Side effects of hypotensive agent evaluated by a self-administered questionnaire. *Br Med J* 1973; 3:485-490.
44. Johnson P, et al: Treatment of hypertension with methyldopa. *Br Med J* 1966; 1:133-137.
45. Horowitz D, et al: Effects of methyldopa in 50 hypertensive patients. *Clin Pharmacol Ther* 1967; 8:224-234.

46. Lauwers P, et al: Methyldopa in the treatment of hypertension. *Br Med J* 1963; 1:295-300.
47. Newman RJ, Salerno HR: Sexual dysfunction due to methyldopa, (letter). *Br Med J* 1974; 4:106.
48. Laver MC: Sexual behaviour patterns in male hypertensives. *Aust NZ J Med* 1974; 4:29-31.
49. Mroczek WJ, et al: Comparison of clonidine and methyldopa in hypertensive patients receiving a diuretic: A double blind crossover study. *Am J Cardiol* 1972; 29:712-717.
50. Vejlsgaard V, et al: Double-blind trial of four hypotensive drugs (methyldopa and three sympatholytic agents). *Br Med J* 1967; 2:598-600.
51. Seedat YK, et al: A comparison of alpha-methyldopa (Aldomet) and ST155 (Catapres) in the treatment of hypertension. *S Afr Med J* 1970; 44:300-301.
52. Kedia K, Markland C: The effect of sympathectomy and drugs on ejaculation, in Sciarra DJ, et al (eds): *Control of Male Fertility*. New York, Harper & Row Publishers, Inc, 1975.
53. Dollery CT, Harington M: Methyldopa in hypertension, clinical and pharmacological studies. *Lancet* 1962; 1:759-763.
54. Nickerson M, Collier B: Drugs inhibiting adrenergic nerves and structures innervated by them, in Goodman L, Gilman A (eds): *The Pharmacological Basis of Therapeutics*. New York, Macmillan Publishing Co, Inc, 1975.
55. Hollifield JW, et al: Proposed mechanisms of propranolol's antihypertensive effect in essential hypertension. *N Engl J Med* 1976; 295:68-73.
56. Knarr JW: Impotence from propranolol? (letter). *Ann Intern Med* 1976; 85:259.
57. Prichard BN, Gillam PM: Treatment of hypertension with propranolol. *Br Med J* 1969; 1:7-16.
58. Warren S, et al: Long-term propranolol therapy for angina pectoris. *Am J Cardiol* 1976; 37:420-426.
59. Veterans Administration Cooperative Study Group on Anti-hypertensive Agents: Propranolol in the treatment of essential hypertension. *JAMA* 1977; 237:2303-2310.
60. Warren SC, Warren SG: Propranolol and sexual impotence, (letter). *Ann Intern Med* 1977; 86:112.
61. Zacharias FJ: Patient acceptability of propranolol and the occurrence of side effects. *Postgrad Med J* 1976; 52(suppl 4):87-89.
62. Bathen J: Propranolol erectile dysfunction relieved. *Ann Intern Med* 1978; 88:716-717.
63. Burnett W, Chahine R: Sexual dysfunction as a complication of propranolol therapy in men. *Cardiovascular Med* 1979; 4:811-815.
64. Klinnert U: Studies on the antihypertensive activity of metoprolol in practice. *Munch Med Wochenschr* 1978; 120:1091-1094.

65. McSorley P, Warren D: Effects of propranolol and metoprolol on the peripheral circulation. *Br Med J* 1978; 2:1598-1600.
66. Pryor J, Kahn O: Beta blockers and Peyronie's disease, (letter). *Lancet* 1979; 1:331.
67. Jackson BA: Nadolol: A once daily treatment for hypertension multi-centre clinical evaluation. *Br J Clin Pract* 1980; 34:211-221.
68. Ebringer A, et al: The use of clonidine (Catapres) in the treatment of hypertension. *Med J Aust* 1970; 1:524-526.
69. Khan A, et al: Clonidine (Catapres): A new antihypertensive agent. *Curr Ther Res* 1970; 12:10-18.
70. Onesti G, et al: Clonidine: A new antihypertensive agent. *Am J Cardiol* 1971; 28:74-83.
71. Hoffman B, Lefkowitz R: Alpha-adrenergic receptor subtypes. *N Engl J Med* 1980; 302:1390-1396.
72. Raftos J, et al: Clonidine in the treatment of severe hypertension. *Med J Aust* 1973; 1:786-793.
73. Clonidine appears useful against hypertension. *JAMA* 1971; 215:2048-2050.
74. Amery A, et al: Hypotensive action and side effects of clonidine-chlorthalidone and methyldopa-chlorthalidone in treatment of hypertension. *Br Med J* 1970; 4:392-395.
75. Money J, Yankowitz R: The sympathetic-inhibiting effects of the drug Ismelin on human male eroticism, with a note on Mellaril. *J Sex Res* 1967; 3:69-82.
76. Bauer GE, et al: The reversibility of side effects of guanethidine therapy. *Med J Aust* 1973; 1:930-933.
77. Seedat YK, Pillay VKG: Further experiences with guanethidine—A clinical assessment of 103 patients. *S Afr Med J* 1966; 40:140-142.
78. Bauer GE, et al: Guanethidine in the treatment of hypertension. *Br Med J* 1961; 2:410-415.
79. Lowther CP, Turner RG: Guanethidine in the treatment of hypertension. *Br Med J* 1963; 2:776-781.
80. Veterans Administration Multi Clinic Cooperative Study Group on Antihypertensive Agents: Controlled trial of bethanidine and guanethidine in severe hypertension. *Circulation* 1977; 55:519-525.
81. Schirger A, Gifford RW: Guanethidine, a new antihypertensive agent: Experience in the treatment of 36 patients with severe hypertension. *Proc Staff Meetings Mayo Clin* 1962; 37:100-108.
82. Rosenbloom SE, et al: Technic of control drug assay, III. Comparison of guanethidine, mecamylamine and a placebo in the hypertensive patient. *N Engl J Med* 1963; 268:797-803.
83. Kedia K, Markland C: Effect of pharmacological agents on ejaculation. *J Urol* 1975; 114:569-573.
84. Jandhyala BS, et al: Effects of prolonged administration of certain antihypertensive agents. *J Pharm Sci* 1974; 63:1497-1513.

85. Keidan H: Impotence during antihypertensive treatment, (letter). *Can Med Assoc* 1976; 114:874.
86. Ahmad S: Hydralazine and male impotence, (letter). *Chest* 1980; 78:358.
87. Pitts NE: A clinical evaluation of prazosin, a new anti-hypertensive agent. *Postgrad Med* 1975; 58:117-127.
88. Amery A, et al: Double blind cross-over study with a new vasodilator—prazosin—in the treatment of mild hypertension. *Excerpta Medica Int Cong Series* 1974; 331:100-110.
89. Green M, Berman S: Failure of ejaculation produced by dibenzyline. *Conn State Med J* 1954; 18:30-33.
90. Moser M, et al: Clinical experience with sympathetic blocking agents in peripheral vascular disease. *Ann Intern Med* 1953; 38:1245-1264.
91. Vlachakis N, Mendlowitz M: Alpha- and beta-adrenergic receptor blocking agents combined with a diuretic in the treatment of essential hypertension. *J Clin Pharm* 1976; 16:352-360.
92. Laughren TP, et al: Effects of thioridazine on serum testosterone. *Am J Psychiatry* 1978; 135:982-984.
93. Siris SG, et al: Effect of dopamine blockade on gonadotropins and testosterone in men. *Am J Psychiatry* 1980; 137:211-214.
94. Arato M, et al: Endocrinological changes in patients with sexual dysfunction under long-term neuroleptic treatment. *Pharmakopsychiatr Neuropsychopharmakol* 1979; 12:426-431.
95. Byck R: Drugs and the treatment of psychiatric disorders, in Goodman L, Gilman A (eds): *The Pharmacological Basis of Therapeutics*. New York, Macmillan Publishing Co, Inc, 1975.
96. Shader R: Sexual dysfunction associated with thioridazine hydrochloride. *JAMA* 1964; 188:1007-1009.
97. Freyhan F: Loss of ejaculation during Mellaril treatment. *Am J Psychiatry* 1961; 118:171-172.
98. Singh H: A case of inhibition of ejaculation as a side effect of Mellaril. *Am J Psychiatry* 1961; 117:1041-1042.
99. Kotin J, et al: Thioridazine and sexual dysfunction. *Am J Psychiatry* 1976; 133:82-85.
100. Amdur M: Confirming a side effect. *Am J Psychiatry* 1976; 133:864-865.
101. Clein L: Thioridazine and ejaculation. *Br Med J* 1962; 2:548-549.
102. Taubel D: Mellaril: Ejaculation disorders. *Am J Psychiatry* 1961; 119:87.
103. Datshkovsky J: Mellaril: Ejaculation disorders. *Am J Psychiatry* 1961; 118:564.
104. Heller J: Another case of inhibition of ejaculation as a side effect of Mellaril. *Am J Psychiatry* 1961; 118:173.
105. Greenberg HR, Carrillo C: Thioridazine-induced inhibition of masturbatory ejaculation in an adolescent. *Am J Psychiatry* 1968; 124:991-993.
106. Witton K: Sexual dysfunction secondary to Mellaril. *Dis Nerv Syst* 1962; 23:175.

107. Haider I: Thioridazine and sexual dysfunctions. *Int J Neuropsychiatry* 1966; 2:255-257.
108. Blair J, Simpson G: Effect of antipsychotic drugs on reproductive functions. *Dis Nerv Syst* 1966; 27:645-647.
109. Shader R, Grinspoon L: Schizophrenia, oligospermia and the phenothiazines. *Dis Nerv Syst* 1967; 28:240-244.
110. Girgis S, et al: Aspermia: A survey of 49 cases. *Fertil Steril* 1968; 19:580-588.
111. Green M: Inhibition of ejaculation as a side-effect of Mellaril. *Am J Psychiatry* 1961; 118:172-173.
112. Shader R: Sexual dysfunction associated with mesoridazine besylate (Serentil). *Psychopharmacologia* 1972; 27:293-294.
113. Greenberg HR: Inhibition of ejaculation by chlorpromazine. *J Nerv Ment Dis* 1971; 152:364-366.
114. Bartholomew AA: A long-acting phenothiazine as a possible agent to control deviant sexual behavior. *Am J Psychiatry* 1968; 124:917-923.
115. Ditman KS: Inhibition of ejaculation by chlorprothixene. *Am J Psychiatry* 1964; 120:1004-1005.
116. Petrie WM: Sexual effects of antidepressants in psychomotor stimulant drugs. *Mod Probl Pharmacopsychiatry* 1980; 15:77-90.
117. Hollister LE: Tricyclic antidepressants. *N Engl J Med* 1978; 299:1106-1109.
118. Simpson GM, et al: Effects of antidepressants on genito-urinary function. *Dis Nerv Syst* 1965; 26:787-789.
119. Ruskin DB, Goldner RD: Treatment of depressions in private practice with imipramine. *Dis Nerv Syst* 1959; 20:391-399.
120. Greenberg HR: Erectile impotence during the course of Tofranil therapy. *Am J Psychiatry* 1965; 121:1021.
121. Everett HC: The use of bethanechol chloride with tricyclic antidepressants. *Am J Psychiatry* 1975; 132:1202-1204.
122. Couper-Smartt JD, Rohman R: A technique for surveying side effects of tricyclic drugs with reference to reported sexual effects. *J Int Med Res* 1973; 1:473-476.
123. Nininger JE: Inhibition of ejaculation by amitriptyline. *Am J Psychiatry* 1978; 135:750-751.
124. Comfort A: Effects of psychoactive drugs on ejaculation. *Am J Psychiatry* 1979; 136:124-125.
125. Hollister LE: Treatment of depression with drugs. *Ann Intern Med* 1978; 89:78-84.
126. Beaumont G: Sexual side-effects of clomipramine (Anafranil). *J Int Med Res* 1977; 5(suppl):37-44.
127. Wyatt RJ, et al: Treatment of intractable narcolepsy with a monoamine oxidase inhibitor. *N Engl J Med* 1971; 285:987-991.
128. Friedman S, et al: A follow-up study on the chemotherapy of neurodermatitis with a monoamine oxidase inhibitor. *J Nerv Ment Dis* 1978; 166:349-357.
129. Bennet D: Treatment of ejaculatio praecox with monoamine oxidase inhibitors. *Lancet* 1961; 2:1309.

130. Rapp M: Two cases of ejaculatory impairment related to phenelzine. *Am J Psychiatry* 1979; 136:1200-1201.

131. Vinarova E, et al: Side effects of lithium administration. *Activ Nerv Sup* 1972; 14:105-107.

132. Mindham R: Hypnotics and sedatives, in Dukes MNG (ed): *Meyler's Side Effects of Drugs*. New York, American Elsevier Pub Co, 1975.

133. Usdin GL: Preliminary report on librium, a new psychopharmacologic agent. *J La Med Soc* 1960; 112:142-147.

134. Hughes JM: Failure to ejaculate with chlordiazepoxide. *Am J Psychiatry* 1964; 121:610-611.

135. Gay GR, et al: Drug-sex practices in Haight Ashbury, or "the sensous hippie", in Sandler M, Gessa DL (eds): *Sexual Behavior: Pharmacology and Biochemistry*. New York, Raven Press, 1975.

136. Parr D: Sexual aspects of drug abuse in narcotic addicts. *Br J Addict* 1976; 71:261-268.

137. Weissberg K: Sopers are a bummer. *Berkeley Barb* 1972 (Sept 1-7); p13.

138. Inaba DS, et al: Methaqualone abuse: "Luding out." *JAMA* 1973; 224:1505-1509.

139. Kochansky GE, et al: Methaqualone abusers: A preliminary survey of college students. *Dis Nerv Syst* 1975; 36:348-351.

140. Gerald MC, Schwirian PM: Nonmedical use of methaqualone. *Arch Gen Psychiatry* 1973; 28:627-631.

141. Ager SA: Luding out. *N Engl J Med* 1972; 287:51.

142. Bhargava KP, et al: The muscle relaxant activity of methaqualone and its methyl congener. *Br J Pharm* 1972; 44:805-806.

143. Shakespeare W: *Macbeth*. Act II, Scene 3.

144. Gordon GG, et al: Effect of alcohol (ethanol) administration on sex-hormone metabolism in normal men. *N Engl J Med* 1976; 295:793-797.

145. Mendelson J, et al: Effects of acute alcohol intake on pituitary-gonadal hormones in normal human males. *J Pharmacol Exp Ther* 1977; 202:676-682.

146. McNamee B, et al: Lack of effect of alcohol on pituitary-gonadal hormones in women. *Br J Addict* 1979; 74:316-317.

147. Van Thiel DH, Lester R: Sex and alcohol: A second peek. *N Engl J Med* 1976; 295:835-836.

148. Gordon GG, et al: Hypogonadism and feminization in the male: A triple effect of alcohol. *Alcoholism: Clin Exper Res* 1979; 3:210-211.

149. Lemere F, Smith JW: Alcohol-induced sexual impotence. *Am J Psychiatry* 1973; 130:212-213.

150. Wilson GT, Lawson D: Effects of alcohol on sexual arousal in women. *J Abnorm Psychol* 1976; 85:489-497.

151. Sex and female alcoholics. *Human Behavior*. 1979 (April), 56-57.

152. Innes IR, Nickerson M: Norepinephrine, epinephrine in the sympathomimetic amines, in Goodman L, Gilman A (eds): *The Pharmacological Basis of Therapeutics*. New York, Macmillan Publishing Co, Inc, 1975.

153. Angrist B, Gershon S: Clinical effects of amphetamine and L-dopa on sexuality and aggression. *Compr Psychiatry* 1976; 17:715-722.

154. Bell DS, Trethowan WH: Amphetamine addiction and disturbed sexuality. *Arch Gen Psychiatry* 1961; 4:74-78.

155. Smith DE, et al: Amphetamine abuse and sexual dysfunctions: Clinical and research considerations, in Smith DE (ed): *Amphetamine Use, Misuse and Abuse*. Cambridge, GK Hall, 1979.

156. Friesen LVC: Aphrodisia with mazindol, (letter). *Lancet* 1976; 2:974.

157. Patrick RL: Amphetamine and cocaine: Biological mechanisms, in Barchas JD, et al (eds): *Psychopharmacology: From Theory to Practice*. New York, Oxford University Press, 1977.

158. Gawin FH: Drugs and Eros: Reflections on aphrodisiacs. *J Psychedel Drugs* 1978; 10:227-236.

159. Ellinwood EH, Rockwell K: The effect of drug use on sexual behavior. *Med Aspects Hum Sex* 1975 (March); 9:10-12.

160. Mintz J, et al: Sexual problems of heroin addicts. *Arch Gen Psychiatry* 1974; 31:700-703.

161. Cicero TJ, et al: Function of the male sex organs in heroin and methadone users. *N Engl J Med* 1975; 292:882-887.

162. Cushman P Jr: Sexual behavior in heroin addiction and methadone maintenance. *NY State J Med* 1972; 72:1261-1265.

163. De Leon G, Wexler HK: Heroin addiction: Its relation to sexual behavior and sexual experience. *J Abnorm Psychol* 1973; 81:36-38.

164. Cushman P, Dole VP: Detoxification of rehabilitated methadone-maintained patients. *JAMA* 1973; 226:747-752.

165. Mirin SM, et al: Opiate use and sexual function. *Am J Psychiatry* 1980; 137;909-915.

166. Bai J, et al: Drug-related menstrual aberrations. *Obstet Gynecol* 1974; 44:713-719.

167. Jaffe JH, Martin WR: Narcotic analgesics and antagonists, in Goodman L, Gilman A (eds): *The Pharmacological Basis of Therapeutics*. New York, Macmillan Publishing Co, Inc, 1975.

168. Kreek MJ: Medical safety and side effects of methadone in tolerant individuals. *JAMA* 1973; 223:665-668.

169. Cassidy WJ: Maintenance methadone treatment of drug dependency. *Can Psychiatr Assoc J* 1972; 17:107-115.

170. Espejo R, et al: Sexual performance of men on methadone maintenance. *Proceedings - National Conference on Methadone Treatment* 1973; 1:490-493.

171. Handbury R, et al: Adequacy of sexual performance in men maintained on methadone. *Am J Drug Alcohol Abuse* 1977; 4:13-20.

172. Crowley TJ, Simpson R: Methadone dose and human sexual behavior. *Int J Addict* 1978; 13:285-295.

173. Hollister LE: The mystique of social drugs and sex, in Sandler M, Gessa DL (eds): *Sexual Behavior: Pharmacology and Biochemistry*. New York, Raven Press, 1975.

174. Chopra G: Man and marijuana. *Int J Addict* 1969; 4:215-247.

175. Nowlis V: Categories of interest in the scientific search for relationships (i.e., interactions, associations, comparisons), in Sandler M, Gessa DL (eds): *Sexual Behavior: Pharmacology and Biochemistry*. New York, Raven Press, 1975.

176. Kolodny RC, et al: Depression of plasma testosterone levels after chronic intensive marijuana smoking. *N Engl J Med* 1974; 290:872-874.

177. Mendelson JH, et al: Plasma testosterone levels before, during and after chronic marijuana smoking. *N Engl J Med* 1974; 291:309-310.

178. Zinberg NE: Marijuana and sex, (letter). *N Engl J Med* 1974; 291:309-310.

179. Groff S: The use of LSD in psychotherapy. *J Psychedel Drugs* 1970; 3:52-62.

180. Naranjo C: *The Healing Journey*. New York, Pantheon Books Inc, 1974.

181. Weil A: The love drug. *J Psychedel Drugs* 1975; 8:335-337.

182. Smith DE, et al: PCP and sexual dysfunction. *J Psychedel Drugs*. (to be published)

183. Wolfe MM: Impotence on cimetidine treatment, (letter). *N Engl J Med* 1979; 300:94.

184. Peden NR, et al: Male sexual dysfunction during treatment with cimetidine. *Br Med J* 1979; 1:659.

185. Gifford LM, et al: Cimetidine postmarket outpatient surveillance program—Interim report on phase I. *JAMA* 1980; 243:1532-1535.

186. Hall WH: Breast changes in males on cimetidine, (letter). *N Engl J Med* 1976; 295:841.

187. Fave GP, et al: Gynaecomastia with cimetidine, (letter). *Lancet* 1977; 1:1319.

188. Van Thiel DH, et al: Hypothalamic-pituitary-gonadal dysfunction in men using cimetidine. *N Engl J Med* 1979; 300:1012-1015.

189. Winters SJ, et al: Cimetidine is an antiandrogen in the rat. *Gastroenterology* 1979; 76:504-508.

190. Evans BE, Aledort LM: Inhibition of ejaculation due to epsilon aminocaproic acid. *N Engl J Med* 1978; 298:166-167.

191. McHaffie DJ, et al: Impotence in patient on disopyramide, (letter). *Lancet* 1977; 1:859.

192. Ahmad S: Disopyramide and impotence, (letter). *South Med J* 1980; 73:958.

193. Hennekeuser HH, et al: Thiabendazole for the treatment of trichinosis in humans. *Tex Rep Biol Med* 1969; 27:581-596.

194. Neri A, et al: Subjective assessment of sexual dysfunction of patients on long-term administration of digoxin. *Arch Sex Behav* 1980; 9:343-347.

195. Navab A, et al: Estrogen-like activity of digitalis. *JAMA* 1965; 194:30-32.

196. Le Winn E: Gynecomastia during digitalis therapy. *N Engl J Med* 1953; 248:316-320.

197. Eder H: Drugs used in the prevention and treatment of atherosclerosis, in Goodman L, Gilman A (eds): *The Pharmacological Basis of Therapeutics*. New York, Macmillan Publishing Co, Inc, 1975.

198. Coronary Drug Project Report: Clofibrate and niacin in coronary heart disease. *JAMA* 1975; 21:455-457.

199. Schneider J, Kaffarnik H: Impotence in patients treated with clofibrate. *Atherosclerosis* 1975; 21:455-457.

200. Innes IR, Nickerson M: Atropine, scopolamine and related antimuscarinic drugs, in Goodman L, Gilman A (eds): *The Pharmacological Basis of Therapeutics*. New York, MacMillan Publishing Co, Inc, 1975.

201. Schwartz NH, Robinson BD: Impotence due to methantheline bromide. *NY State J Med* 1952; 52:1530.

202. Price HL: General anesthetics (intravenous anesthetics), in Goodman L, Gilman A (eds): *The Pharmacological Basis of Therapeutics*. New York Macmillan Publishing Co, Inc, 1975.

203. Gale AS: Ketamine prevention of penile turgescence. *JAMA* 1972; 219:1629.

204. Forsberg L, et al: Impotence, smoking, and beta-blocking drugs. *Fertil Steril* 1979; 31:589-591.

205. Espir ML, et al: Impotence in farm workers using toxic chemicals. *Br Med J* 1970; 1:423-425.

206. Peck AW: Impotence in farm workers. *Br Med J* 1970; 1:690.

207. Layzer RB: Myeloneuropathy after prolonged exposure to nitrous oxide. *Lancet* 1978; 2:1127-1139.

208. Smith DE: Personal communication, 1979.

209. Ritchie JM: The aliphatic alcohols, in Goodman L, Gilman A (eds): *The Pharmacological Basis of Therapeutics*. New York, Macmillan Publishing Co, Inc, 1975.

210. Van Thiel DH, et al: Disulfiram-induced disturbances in hypothalamic-pituitary function. *Alcoholism: Clin Exper Res* 1979; 3:230-234.

211. Ewing JA, et al: Roundtable: Alcohol, drugs and sex. *Med Aspects Hum Sex* 1970 (Feb); 4:18-34.

212. Schilsky RL, et al: Gonadal dysfunction in patients receiving chemotherapy for cancer. *Ann Intern Med* 1980; 93:109-114.

213. Greenberg MS, et al: Gynecomastia after chemotherapy. *Clin Res* 1979; 27:386A.

214. Sigell LT, et al: Popping and snorting volatile nitrites: A current fad for getting high. *Am J Psychiatry* 1978; 135:1216-1218.

215. Perlman JT, Adams GI: Amyl nitrite inhalation fad, (letter). *JAMA* 1970; 212:160.

216. Labataille LM: Amyl nitrite employed in homosexual relations, (letter). *Med Aspects Hum Sex* 1975 (April); 9:122.

217. Louria DB: Sexual use of amyl nitrite, (letter). *Med Aspects Hum Sex* 1970 (Jan); 4:89.

218. Kramer ND: Availability of volatile nitrites, (letter). *JAMA* 1977; 237:1693.

219. Welti RS, Brodsky JB: Treatment of intraoperative penile tumescence. *J Urol* 1980; 124:925-926.

220. Ambrosi B, et al: Study of the effects of bromocriptine on sexual impotence. *Clin Endocrinol* 1977; 7:417-421.

221. Cooper AJ: Bromocriptine in impotence, (letter). *Lancet* 1977; 2:567.
222. Thorner MO, et al: Long-term treatment of galactorrhoea and hypogonadism with bromocriptine. *Br Med J* 1974; 2:419-422.
223. Bommer J, et al: Improved sexual function in male haemodialysis patients on bromocriptine. *Lancet* 1979; 2:496-497.
224. Franz DN: Drugs for Parkinson's disease: Centrally acting muscle relaxants, in Goodman L, Gilman A (eds): *The Pharmacological Basis of Therapeutics*. New York, Macmillan Publishing Co, Inc, 1975.
225. Goodwin FK: Behavioral effects of L-dopa in man. *Semin Psychiatry* 1971; 3:477-492.
226. Benkert O, et al: Effects of L-dopa on sexually impotent patients. *Psychopharmacologia* 1972; 23:91-95.
227. Brown E, et al: Sexual function and affect in parkinsonian men treated with L-dopa. *Am J Psychiatry* 1978; 135:1552-1555.
228. O'Brien CP, et al: Mental effects of high-dosage levodopa. *Arch Gen Psychiatry* 1971; 24:61-64.
229. Hyyppä MT, et al: Is L-dopa an aphrodisiac in patients with Parkinson's disease? in Sandler M, Gessa GL (eds): *Sexual Behavior: Pharmacology and Biochemistry*. New York, Raven Press, 1975.
230. Hällström T, Persson T: L-dopa and non-emission of semen, (letter). *Lancet* 1970; 1:1231-1232.
231. Sicuteri F, et al: Aphrodisiac effect of testosterone in parachlorophenylalanine- treated sexually deficient men, in Sandler M, Gessa DL (eds): *Sexual Behavior: Pharmacology and Biochemistry*. New York, Raven Press, 1975.
232. Sicuteri F: Serotonin and sex in man. *Pharmacol Res Commun* 1974; 6:403-411.
233. Broadhurst AD, Rao B: L-tryptophan and sex behavior. *Br Med J* 1977; 1:51-52.
234. Ingram CD: Some pharmacologic actions of yohimbine and chlorpromazine in man. *Clin Pharmacol Ther* 1962; 3:345-352
235. Aviado D: *Kranz and Carr's Pharmacologic Principles of Medical Practice*. Baltimore, Williams & Wilkins Company, 1972.
236. Antoniou L, et al: Reversal of uraemic impotence by zinc. *Lancet* 1977; 2:895-898.
237. Abram H, et al: Sexual functioning in patients with chronic renal failure. *J Nerv Ment Dis* 1975; 160:220-226.
238. Levy N: Uremic sex. *N Engl J Med* 1977; 297:725-726.
239. Holdsworth S, et al: The pituitary-testicular axis in men with chronic renal failure. *N Engl J Med* 1977; 296:1245-1249.
240. Hallböök T, Hedelin H: Zinc metabolism and surgical trauma. *Br J Surg* 1977; 64:271-273.
241. Murphy EW, et al: Provisional tables on the zinc content of foods. *J Am Diet Assoc* 1975; 66:345-355.
242. Bjork JT, et al: Clomiphene citrate therapy in a patient with Laennec's cirrhosis. *Gastroenterology* 1977; 72:1308-1311.

243. Keverne E: Pheromones and sexual behavior, in Money J, Musaph H (eds): *Handbook of Sexology*. New York, Elsevier Publishing, 1977.

244. Sokolov J, et al: Isolation of substances from human vaginal secretions previously shown to be sex attractant pheromones in high primates. *Arch Sex Behav* 1976; 5:269-274.

245. Browne M: Sweat may be marketable. *New York Times*, reprinted in *San Francisco Chronicle*, Jan 2, 1980.

246. Durden-Smith J: How to win the dating game: By a nose. *Next* 1980; 1:85-89.

247. Newman HM, Northup JD: Mechanism of human penile erection: An overview. *Urology* 1981; 17:399-408.

248. deGroat WC, Booth AM: The physiology of male sexual function. *Ann Intern Med* 1980; 92:329-331.

249. Wagner G, Levin RJ: Effect of atropine and methylatropine on human vaginal blood flow, sexual arousal and climax. *Acta Pharmacol Toxicol* 1980; 46:321-325.

250. Dorr LB, Brody MJ: Chemodynamic mechanisms of erection in the canine penis. *Am J Physiol* 1967; 213:1526-1531.

251. Siroky MB, Krane RJ: Mechanisms of penile erection: A neuro-pharmacologic study. *Surg Forum* 1979; 30:535-546.

252. Domer FR, et al: Involvement of the sympathetic nervous system in the urinary bladder internal sphincter and in penile erections in the anesthetized cat. *Invest Urol* 1978; 15:404-407.

253. Melman A, et al: Alterations in the penile corpora in patients with erectile impotence. *Invest Urol* 1980; 17:474-477.

254. Benson GS, et al: Neuromorphology and neuropharmacology of the human penis: An in vitro study. *Clin Invest* 1980; 65:506-513.

Chapter 18

Sexual Identity Problems in Children and Adolescents

Warren J. Gadpaille, M.D.

Among the several components of sexual identity are core gender identity (an inner conviction of being male or female), sexual preference (preferences for emotional and social qualities and for roles perceived as masculine or feminine), and sexual orientation (preferential or obligatory sexual arousal by heterosexual, homosexual or other objects). Sexual identity also includes cultural beliefs, stereotypes of masculine or feminine behavior and each individual's perception of how he or she conforms to them and to his or her own expectations. There may be difficulties in one or more aspects of sexual identity, and the various aspects do not develop or become relatively firm at the same time.

The subject of *conflicts* in sexual identity raises the issue of distinctions between normal and abnormal sexuality. This is a sensitive matter because ethnocentric concepts of normal and abnormal have too often been assumed to have universal validity and, unfortunately, have been equated with "good" and "right" or "bad" and "evil," causing discrimination against those whose sexual behavior falls outside their culture's norms.

Some expressions of sexual identity, however, are clearly abnormal, e.g., transsexualism, in which an individual of one chromosomal, gonadal, anatomical and physiological gender maintains that he or she is "really" the opposite sex and is simply in the "wrong" body. However, no attempts will be made here to define sexual normality in any species-valid sense.[1]

This chapter discusses sexual identity problems in terms of age-related developmental stages, because this approach seems to be of most practical value to physicians. At each stage beyond infancy, problems representing normal developmental conflicts are differentiated from those considered pathological. Problems of pathology are elucidated as having primarily either organic or psychological etiology.

CHILDHOOD

Infancy (Birth to 18 Months). Limited behavior and communication make objective signs of sexual identity problems in infants rare. Many of the learning experiences that affect sexual identity have not yet taken place, although core gender identity is already being learned, perhaps definitively. In rare instances, evidence of the most severe sexual identity dysfunction, transsexualism, is already manifest.[2] This early onset has led to speculation that a disorder of fetal sex hormone is etiologically significant in transsexualism, but the data thus far do not support that explanation.[3] In any event, physicians should not expect to be consulted about transsexualism at this early stage.

Some organic and intersex conditions that often cause sexual identity problems later in life are evident at birth, but only those that produce ambiguous or anomalous external genitalia usually are recognized. An increasing awareness of the possibility of sexual anomalies should alert physicians to test for vaginal patency at birth by insertion of a catheter, even when the newborn's genitalia seem normally female. Internal sexual morphology, however, is seldom examined for, unless atypical external morphology is observed.

The external conditions most likely to be noted are ambiguous genitalia (enlarged clitoris with or without some degree of labial fusion) in girls with hyperadrenocorticism or whose mothers were exposed to androgenic substances in the first trimester, ambiguous genitalia in male pseudohermaphrodites, microphallus and hypospadias or epispadias. Extremely rare is the condition of true hermaphroditism. Definitive medical or surgical intervention can be undertaken and completed immediately for some of these problems, such as progestin-induced female pseudohermaphroditism. In the majority of cases, medical management can only begin at the time of diagnosis. However, crucial decisions affecting sexual identity must be made immediately after birth to prevent sexual identity problems. This process often involves complex determinations of chromosomal, gonadal, hormonal and anatomical sex, and sometimes delicate decisions about the appropriate sex of assignment and rearing.

There are three basic principles in intersex management and planning in infancy:

1. Although there have been some exceptions noted,[4] almost all children develop the healthy and unconflicted sexual identity to which they are assigned and by which they are reared, provided that this identity is unambiguously adhered to by parents and others who knew the initial dilemma, and even if the assignment contradicts all the biological determinants of sex.[5]

2. Sex of assignment and rearing is usually best decided on the basis of the predicted anatomical capacity for optimal adult sexual function.

3. Even in a genetic male, if a functional penis cannot be expected to develop naturally, it is preferable to rear the child as a girl, because the surgical and hormonal methods for creating a satisfactory female sexual appearance and sexual function are much more successful than those for creating a functional artificial penis.

An exception is a recently discovered condition, steroid 5α-reductase deficiency,[4] an inherited condition in which a 46, XY gonadally and hormonally normal male is born with what appear to be normal female genitalia. These patients lack the enzyme necessary to convert testosterone to dihydrotestosterone, on the presence of which fetal development of the penis, penile urethra and scrotum depend. Even though some of these children have been reared unambiguously as girls, the pubertal growth of these same tissues becomes testosterone dependent. A bifid scrotum and functional-sized (though hypospadic) penis develops, a normal male physical and psychosexual pubescence ensues, sexual desire is toward females, sexual performance is usually heterosexual and the individuals are fertile. Even though apparently rare, these cases appear to be exceptions to both the principle of the prepotency of sex of assignment and rearing and to the generalization that a functional penis cannot develop from what looks like a normal infantile clitoris. There are laboratory tests that detect the presence of steroid 5α-reductase, and the rarity of the condition should not mitigate against appropriate testing at birth in any ambiguous or suspected case, because these children would better be reared as boys.

Children and their parents need a great deal of support to cope with an intersex condition. The disorder and any medical or surgical procedures used for treatment must be described in a manner that eliminates or minimizes uncertainty about the child's assigned sex and prevents ambiguity in the rearing of the child. Explanations should provide the family with answers to questions asked by curious relatives and friends about surgery or hospitalizations.

The physician should avoid terms like "hermaphrodite," "mixed sex," or "organs like the opposite sex." Except when parents need to know technical details, it is almost always possible to describe the condition as a not uncommon one in which nature did not entirely "finish" forming the genitals, and to indicate that any continuing medical measures are a way to complete the job so that the child can be as normal as possible.

When the child is old enough to want and need some explanation, the same one is often most appropriate, at least until the patient is old enough (adolescent or adult) to have to take over medical management or cope with any reproductive impairment resulting from the condition or the surgery. If true hermaphroditism is discovered, it is both psychologically and medically important to remove all organs and signs of the sex opposite to that of assignment and rearing, because the clinician must be able to reassure an adolescent truthfully that no contradictory organs exist in his or her body.

The above merely introduces the complexities of intersex conditions. The reader should refer to Jones and Scott[6] for a comprehensive discussion of the biological, medical and surgical aspects and to Money and Ehrhardt[4] for discussion of the psychological aspects.

Toddlerhood and Preschool Period (1 1/2 Years Through 5 Years). During this period, many aspects of normal development can become the basis of sexual identity problems. The first object of identification for both boys and girls is a mothering female; it is entirely normal for children of this age to show both same-sex and cross-sex identification. As they explore their identities, they magically assume that they can be whichever sex they wish. The early feminine identification of boys adds to the frequency with which they imitate or express the wish to be like mother or other females. Intermittent (but not predominant or preferred) cross-sex identification or behavior in boys and girls usually does not indicate sexual identity problems.

If parents or other important adults misinterpret such manifestations, however, problems may ensue. For example, a father who sees his son playing with dolls or wanting to wear an apron and help mother cook may think he is effeminate or a potential homosexual. The father may withdraw and reject, ridicule and disturb the boy's masculine development by becoming unavailable as a role model and by convincing the child that he must, indeed, be unmasculine. Such conflicts can be induced by either parent in children of either sex, although in this culture, at least, cross-gender behavior is usually more censured in boys than in girls by parents of both sexes, and fathers tend to be more concerned with clear sex differentiation than mothers.

Both envy and fear of the opposite sex occur normally in preschool children. Girls may envy male genitals as something they do not have and may fear them as potentially damaging. Boys may fear female genitals as seeming to confirm the possibility of castration and may envy females' capacity for creativity and their dominance in the world of the toddler. These normal internal struggles can become pathological, with the child rejecting his or her own sex, when parents and other adults fail to value the sexes equally.

In proportion to how narrow or how broad cultural definitions of masculinity and femininity are, a greater or lesser number of normal children fall outside those limits. Pathology does not necessarily exist in the girl who is more active and competitive than her society considers to be normal, or in the boy who is more quiet and emotionally responsive. There is a wide overlap of virtually all characteristics considered to be sex-specific, and efforts to force a given child to conform to social stereotypes may fail. The child can be only what he or she is. Rejecting the child's individual qualities can cripple sexual identity; a little girl, for example, can begin to develop the conviction that she has no right to think of herself as feminine if she differs from the norm.

A physician is often consulted by parents who are afraid there is a dire sexual disorder when they misperceive their toddler's behavior as abnormal. Reassurance is often enough. In some cases, damage may already be in process and special efforts, such as family therapy, may be necessary to change the parents' attitudes and expectations.

During this period, Oedipal conflicts are most intense (see Chapter 3). The conflict caused by fear of the fantasied retaliation by the "rival" same-sex parent may cause the unconscious wish to submit to that rival as a love object to retain his love and appease him. Also, some parents render heterosexuality genuinely unattractive or fearsome through their relationship with one another or with the child. Obligatory or preferential homosexuality may sometimes have such a background.

Organic conditions, such as genital malformations, begin to produce subjectively perceived sex identity problems in this period. In some cases, complete correction must be deferred until this or later maturational phases; in other cases, nothing will have been done even though it has been possible to take corrective measures. During these years, most children become clearly aware of anatomic sex differences; body image formation, especially with respect to the genitals, is a major component of sexual identity. Toddlers begin to compare themselves with others, although the impact of such comparisons will be greater in the school years. More important, those whose genitals remain ambiguous may continue to suffer from ambiguous gender identity messages in their rearing by parents, older siblings and others. Since core gender identity is essentially fixed early in this period, such ambiguity can leave permanent scars.

Any delay in correcting remediable conditions should be discouraged. The child and especially the parents need counseling to dispel uncertainty about sex of assignment and rearing, and to try to repair any emotional consequences that have already occurred. However, correction carries risks of its own. Surgery causes emotional trauma, sometimes severe, to sexual body image and consequent sexual identity, just when the child is struggling with concern over body-part loss and physical integrity, especially as expressed in castration anxiety and penis envy. Whether surgery is performed mainly to prevent further emotional damage due to genital ambiguity, or whether it is medically unavoidable, as in some cases of second- or later-stage repair of hypospadias, careful psychological counseling and follow-up for the child are imperative.

Precocious puberty, whether idiopathic or organic, can occur even before age 5. Cases with specific pathology demand immediate treatment.[7] When treated early enough, these conditions need not cause a child serious sexual identity problems unless the reactions of others make the child believe he is sexually abnormal. Even conditions that virilize as well as cause precocious puberty in girls, such as hyperadrenocorticism, need not disturb normal core gender identity if the girls are treated early and raised unambiguously. Girls with hyperadrenocorticism show some cross-sex social and play behavior and preferences,[8,9] and there is an above-average incidence of psychosexual pathology and homosexual activity in cases treated both early and late.[10,11] A possible parallel has been noted in boys exposed to excessive levels of female hormones *in utero*. They are less aggressive, less assertive and less athletic than controls.[12]

Whatever the cause of precocious puberty, its physical consequences are irreversible. These children and their parents need support through the developmental years to help protect them against stigmatization and to prevent their atypical physical maturation from causing conflicts about sexual identity.

Disturbances in core gender identity become set and behaviorally obvious during this period. If one follows the most rigorous criteria for diagnosing primary transsexualism,[3] transsexuals already are firmly set in their cross-sex behavior and preferences. These children cross-dress whenever possible, they hate and avoid all activities and interests of their own biological sex and they are interested only in those of the opposite sex. Boys are extremely feminine in apppearance and behavior; girls are very masculine. These children are already aware of intense gender dysphoria. Their parents either foster their cross-gender identity or make no effective efforts to interfere with it.

Disturbances in sexual orientation often, if not usually, begin before school age, although overt expressions of same-sex erotic attraction are not yet common. Many preferential or obligatory homosexuals recall conscious, erotically tinged attractions to persons of the same sex before starting school. By the end of early childhood, many prehomosexual boys avoid rough-and-tumble and action-oriented play with other boys; they prefer to play with girls and to engage in feminine activities, and some already have cross-dressing tendencies. A complementary pattern is often seen in prehomosexual girls. These children often express a preference to be of the opposite sex; peer disapproval may begin this early, but they feel less distress than transsexuals. These patterns often do not yet draw the attention or concern that they will during the early school years.

Disturbances in sex-appropriate behavior are a separate entity, both clinically and conceptually. The younger the child, the more difficult it is to distinguish such disturbances from those of core gender identity or of sexual orientation, and to differentiate disturbances from normal variations. Cross-sex role preference may reflect not problems of core gender identity or sexual orientation, but a child's observation of, or belief that there is, preferential treatment of the opposite sex or denigration of his own sex within the family. Sometimes the same-sex parent or, less frequently, an older sibling or other important relative displays behavior or a personality that makes him or her unacceptable to the child as someone with whom to identify. Parents, siblings or other relatives may systematically negate and demean the child's sex-appropriate behavior.

Cross-sex interests and behavior—effeminacy in boys and tomboyism in girls—is common in psychogenic sexual identity problems observed during this period. These are temporary or intermittent in normal children. When persistent (especially effeminacy in boys), they herald significant conflict. By age 5, a boy who consistently prefers to play with dolls and girls and is indifferent to trucks, fire engines and strenuous noisy play with other boys is probably expressing a sexual identity problem.

Psychogenic problems in children of this age are seldom brought to a physician for evaluation and treatment. Because one or both parents usually play the major role in producing those problems, they are likely to be selectively inattentive to the signs of their influence, and often have an unconscious vested interest in the child's skewed development. Furthermore, until a child goes to school full time, he is not often subject to extended observation by many objective adult outsiders. Therefore, even blatant signs of sexual identity disorder are usually ignored, rationalized as "a passing phase" or even encouraged.

Most very young children who are brought to a physician because of incipient sexual identity problems, however, are children whose normal behavior has been misperceived by poorly informed but basically normal parents. When severe problems are presented for consultation, the therapeutic considerations are essentially the same as those discussed in the following section.

Early School Years (6 Years to Puberty). This period has been called latency; the early psychoanalytic theory of an organically determined diminished sex drive during these years[13] has made many people overlook the active sexuality that does occur at this stage. While sexual behavior *per se* is not the focus of this chapter, the importance of the child's sexuality in these years gives this period considerable prominence in sexual identity development. (For a detailed review of normal sexual behavior and development during latency, see *The Cycles of Sex*.[1])

There is increased interaction with the environment during this time, when the child is moving out of the parental cocoon into the wider world of peers and teachers. This process heightens the possibility that masculine and feminine stereotypes may distort atypical but normal interests and attitudes into conflicted or pathological sexual identity. School children can be very cruel, and they may place a normal but studious boy who is not interested in sports in the same category as effeminate boys who have serious sexual identity conflicts. Some athletic coaches even exceed children in shattering the sense of masculinity in normal boys if they are not as competitive as the coaches expect them to be. Tomboyism is not as stigmatized as effeminacy, but girls too can be made to doubt their femininity if they deviate from the stereotypes of the community.

Toward the latter part of this period, homoerotic play begins to increase. For the vast majority of youngsters, this is not prognostic of homosexuality and they are seldom disturbed about it. However, their parents may be horrified and, by their actions and attitude, may convince the child he is abnormal. They often seek medical advice, although they may find it difficult to accept even the most knowledgeable reassurance that such play is usually just part of growing up. (Differentiating homoerotic play from prehomosexual behavior is discussed more fully in the following section on Preadolescence, when such behavior is at its peak.)

No new forms of organic sexual pathology having implications for sexual identity necessarily become manifest at this stage. Some, however, may appear adventitiously at this time. Idiopathic precocious puberty may now occur; it requires family and child counseling and a careful medical work-up to rule out acute and/or treatable pathology. The virilizing effects of hyperadrenocorticism in girls may reach medical attention for the first time. Unexpected evidence of true hermaphroditism may turn up, such as a uterus, tube and ovary in the hernial sac of a phenotypic male. Vaginal examination prompted by abdominal pathology may reveal vaginal agenesis. A pediatrician may become suspicious of a girl's unusually short stature, especially if it is accompanied by other stigmata sometimes associated with Turner's syndrome; even then, definitive investigation, such as chromosomal study, may be postponed to await the test of puberty. But these are chance occurrences in latency and are not precipitated by its biological characteristics as a maturational stage.

When visible body or genital abnormalities have not been repaired or may not be fully correctable, they become particularly troublesome to a child because of the emotional and ego development characteristic of latency. Body and genital comparison is ubiquitous in the showers and toilets of schools— perhaps less so among girls than boys, but this difference is diminishing.

Children with uncorrected conditions respond intensely to their own perceptions of their pathology, as well as to the real or imagined reactions of others.

By this stage, when Oedipal conflicts are resolved or resolving and same-sex identity is becoming firm, there is intense emotional investment in the genitalia and sexual body image. There has also been time for doubts and conflicts to develop. Children with anomalous genitalia are now more likely to feel deep shame and alienation and to try to hide their differences, yet at school they are even more exposed to thoughtless and cruel teasing by peers and even by adults. Some of these children also have been exposed to parental rejection, ambivalence or ambiguous sexual rearing. All of this behavior obviously has serious consequences for sexual identity problems and increases the child's sense of sexual inadequacy.

Girls whose mothers were exposed to androgenic substances during the sixth to twelfth week of pregnancy and who developed progestin-induced hermaphroditism constitute one group of children who have no *active* organic pathology, but who, in this period, show behavioral sequelae of fetal androgenization (some of these sequelae may have been evident earlier). Even if this condition is recognized at birth, the anomalous genitalia immediately repaired and the girls assigned and reared unambiguously as females, they show more tomboyism than average. However, there is no disturbance of core gender identity or, so far as is known, of later sexual orientation. They expend more energy than average and show a preference for boys' toys, games and interests.[14,15] The possibility of analogous behavioral shifts in fetally estrogenized boys has already been mentioned.

Primary transsexualism is evident in this age period to anyone who pays attention to the child. Typically, the child's cross-gender identity has been fostered at home, and questions raised by relatives or neighbors have been brushed aside; now the child confronts the full community and for the first time feels the weight of social disapproval and rejection. This makes the child miserable without modifying his inappropriate identity in the least. It is usually in this period that primary transsexuals first come to medical attention because the parents also cannot ignore the pressure from others. The diagnosis of primary transsexualism in females at this age is often less clear than that in males because of society's greater tolerance of cross-sex preferences in girls. The recognition of this condition depends partly on how adamantly the girl refuses to be socialized as a boy and partly on parents' and other adults' sensitivity to her behavior.

Because of the causative influence of both parents, the treatment of childhood transsexualism is very difficult or impossible; at best, it is complex and lengthy,[3] requiring prolonged intensive individual or group therapy with a therapist of the same sex as a role model. Intensive therapy for both parents is very important, but it has been virtually unachievable. Some mothers of male transsexuals have been seriously engaged in treatment, but no fathers have thus far consented. The mother usually tries to undermine the child's shifts toward sex-appropriate identity. No treatment of any male childhood transsexual has yet been followed long enough to assess adult outcome, but there are some optimistic signs in those who began treatment by age 6 or 7. Treatment of female childhood transsexuals is even less well studied and understood.

The classic prehomosexual signs are seen during the latency years in about two-thirds of boys and girls who later become preferential or obligatory homosexuals.[16] Among boys, these signs are persistent preference for girls' toys and activities, girl playmates and the company of female adults; relative lack of interest in body-contact sports and other rough play with boys; fear of physical injury; occasional or frequent cross-dressing; the expressed wish to be a girl; and feminine identification in family-role play.[16-18] Among girls, signs include preference for boys' toys, activities and clothes; lack of interest in dolls or domestic activities; preference for male playmates; preference for aggressively active play and sports; and cross-gender wishes.[16,18]

The physician must be cautious in making a prognosis. In one study,[16] about one-third of preferential homosexual men and women did not report a childhood history of cross-sex behavior and preference, and 16 per cent of women who were heterosexual reported childhood tomboyism. A follow-up of 16 men who were considered to be effeminate boys[19] revealed that 10 became heterosexual. In the discussion of effeminacy and tomboyism later in this chapter, it will be seen that it is not yet possible to be sure what kind of adult sexual identity disorder will follow from persistent childhood effeminacy or tomboyism.

Some, but not all, prehomosexual boys are aware of same-sex erotic preference quite early in childhood; such youngsters are most likely to become homosexual adults. Also, more homosexuals than heterosexuals report very early sex activity with a partner, sometimes while still in so-called latency. Suggestions for differentiating this behavior from nonprognostic homoerotic play are discussed in the section on Preadolescence.

Disorders of sex-appropriate social behavior and erotic preference during this period have the same possible experiential and intrapsychic backgrounds as in the preschool years. However, school-age children begin having much broader exposure to different sex roles. They become more aware of the relative value that society accords to males or females and to their respective roles. When conflicts over sex role preference exist in the absence of deep confusions of core gender identity or sexual orientation, they are usually caused by family or social discrimination.

Persistent effeminacy and tomboyism are common in sexual identity problems that appear in childhood. As already noted, much less is known about tomboyism than about effeminacy. In a comparative study of markedly effeminate boys and their families and of a control group of noneffeminate boys and families, Green[18] found that the early life experiences of the effeminates included:

1. Parental fostering of, or unconcern about, effeminate behavior during the earliest years, e.g., cross-dressing, which usually begins very early; two-thirds of Green's sample showed it by age 4, the remainder by age 6.

2. Lack of psychological separation from the mother, caused in part by excessive holding of the baby.
3. Maternal overprotection and inhibition of rough-and-tumble play with other boys.
4. Greater availability of female than male companions and playmates in the early years.
5. Actual or emotional unavailability of a consistent adult male role model.
6. Strong paternal rejection of the young boy.
7. Unusual physical beauty, which may influence adults to treat the boy as a girl.

Green[20,21] cautions against assuming that pathological effeminacy necessarily derives solely from interpersonal influences, and also observes that effeminacy is not necessarily prognostic of adult gender-identity disturbance of any kind. However, there is expert consensus that markedly effeminate boys are at higher risk of developing one of three forms of atypical sexual identity—transsexualism, transvestism or homosexuality.

It is not yet known how therapy of effeminate boys affects their adult adaptations. In addition, in a civil-libertarian climate, ethical questions are sometimes raised about intervening in the sexual orientation even of children. However, there are two reasons for immediate and vigorous therapeutic efforts. First, our society shows no signs of rapid and definitive liberalization; the effeminate boy is already stigmatized, and he is made miserable by the teasing of peers and most adults. Second, more emotional distress than happiness can be predicted for an adult who has the sexual identity problems for which an effeminate boy is at risk. Even if, after years of deep distress and conflict, the transsexual obtains sex-reassignment surgery and medication, he can be only an incomplete, imitation woman at most. For the adult transvestite, emotional conflict and the deleterious effects of the cross-dressing compulsion on his life and marital relations are well documented. The preferential or exclusive homosexual is, and probably will continue to be, stigmatized even if he feels no distress over his orientation. If only a few of these sources of unhappiness can be forestalled, early therapy seems justified.

Another sexual identity problem—transvestism—may become manifest during these years. Transvestism is defined as fetishistic cross-dressing, to distinguish it from transsexualism and from homosexual cross-dressing, which caricatures females. It is almost exclusively a male disorder, characterized by erotic arousal accompanying the wearing of female clothes and masquerading privately or publicly as a female. As early as 4 to 6 years of age, some people who later become transvestites were aware of genital excitement while cross-dressing.[3] Transvestism does not involve disturbed core gender identity; transvestites are characteristically preferentially heterosexual. When a child's cross-dressing is accompanied by erotic arousal, it is not a phase that will be outgrown; immediate therapy is indicated.

PREADOLESCENCE AND ADOLESCENCE
Normal developmental behavior in this period that most likely gives rise to sexual identity problems is homoerotic play. In the American middle-class, this becomes most common in preadolescence. In the great majority of chil-

dren (see Chapter 3), it is not prognostic of adult preferential or obligatory homosexuality. But by this age, most children are aware of the stigma attached to homosexuality; they also may sense that it is not the most natural way to express their sexual drives, may feel great shame and may worry intensely about whether it means that they are homosexual. Most parents who become aware of such activity feel horrified disapproval. A physician, usually the first person they turn to for counsel, then must differentiate phase-appropriate homoerotic play from that which reflects a significant underlying problem in sexual orientation. The distinction usually is not possible on the basis of behavior.

Mutual masturbation is the most common homoerotic act of both sexes, but any homosexual behavior (e.g., fellatio, cunnilingus, anal intercourse) may occur normally at this phase. It is sometimes of prognostic significance when a youngster seems compulsively preoccupied with one of the less common phase-appropriate acts, such as anal intercourse by a boy, but this is not really a reliable criterion. However, other criteria can aid in differentiation.

The early cross-gender behavior of younger children who are at risk of developing sexual identity problems has been described. When such behavior forms the background of preadolescent homoeroticism, it is quite likely more than a passing phase. Since phase-appropriate homoeroticism typically occurs among age peers, if a boy or girl is willingly involved with an adult, the probability of a sexual orientation problem is strong; the same conclusion is warranted if the youngster is aware of feeling "in love" with someone of the same sex.[22] Predominantly homosexual masturbatory fantasies have prime diagnostic value; they are not found in children without sexual orientation disorder. If preadolescents are already aware of preferential or exclusive homoerotic arousal and express it openly, no further signs need be sought.

Preadolescents are not much more capable than younger children of assessing the social and emotional consequences of a homosexual life style. For the same reasons discussed earlier, it is preferable to try to get these youngsters into therapy that maximizes the possibility of a shift to heterosexuality.

Early, but not premature, pubescence can cause conflict. Most early-maturing boys enjoy greater prestige among their peers, and their sexual identity is enhanced. But some feel freakish, odd, are fearful that they cannot live up to the more mature sexual image they project and may develop lasting doubts about their masculine adequacy. Early-maturing girls generally do not enjoy higher peer prestige. Since girls usually experience puberty two years before boys, the girl in whom menarche occurs at 10 feels doubly isolated from peers of both sexes and may feel more self-conscious than proud about her fulsome body.

Organic or intersex conditions that come to light, as in latency, usually do so by accident rather than because maturation forces recognition. In a few instances, early sexual experimentation reveals vaginal agenesis, which dictates immediate search for the underlying pathology. Girls with the pure form of Turner's syndrome (characterized only by short stature and streak ovaries) are usually thought of only as small and slow to reach puberty. As time passes, intersex individuals who have suffered ambiguous gender identity rearing show increasing symptoms of gender identity confusion.

No new psychogenic sexual identity problems are pushed into overt expression by prepubertal maturation. Those that come to light in this period arise from greater age, longer experience of conflict and more extensive social interaction. Atypical and cross-gender role preferences cannot as easily be ignored by the child or the community. Some fetishistic cross-dressers begin to show signs now, and more future preferential homosexuals begin to recognize their sexual orientation, although many will long continue to deny it to themselves or believe that they will get over it.

Early Adolescence. Normal developmental conflicts are usually continuations of those that began in preadolescence. Homoerotic activity remains a significant part of early adolescent behavior, and the same criteria for differential diagnosis apply as in preadolescence.

By definition, adolescence cannot begin until pubescence occurs, but from a practical medical viewpoint, problems caused by early or late puberty usually show up during the early and middle teens. The mean age of menarche in girls in the United States is about 12.5 years, the normal range 10 to 16.5; the mean age of first seminal emission in boys is 14, with a normal range of 11 to 16.[23] A widely accepted rule of thumb is that pathology need not be assumed unless puberty is more than 2 to 2 1/2 years earlier or later than the mean. That is, there can be a normal spread of pubertal changes of at least four years among each sex and of six years across the sexes. These figures are valuable to physicians, but they offer little consolation to worried adolescents near either end of the range. The 15-year-old boy with the body of a child may be desperately self-conscious, perhaps to the point of being phobic about sports participation and public showers. He is generally ignored by girls while many friends are involved in dating and heterosexual experimentation. He will almost inevitably be insecure in his masculine self-image. The doubts about masculine adequacy engendered during these years of most intense preoccupation with sexual body image may become permanent, even though within a year or two the boy may catch up with or even surpass most of his age mates. If he is subjected to ridicule or has interests outside the cultural stereotype of masculinity, if his insecurities make him postpone sociosexual learning, if the gap between his own and his peers' sexual development continues to widen—any such influences can magnify his doubts about sexual adequacy into convictions of sexual inadequacy, and sometimes an asexual or even homosexual adaptation.

Significantly early or late puberty, then, can cause serious sexual identity problems for both boys and girls. Such youngsters need help, but they may not express their worries openly to a physician because of their embarrassment. The physician should be alert to distress about pubertal timing and pursue it gently but directly whenever it is suspected. Of course, any signs of endocrinopathy must also be pursued, but even in their absence, reassurance is more effective if it follows a physical examination that gives the adolescent confidence that the doctor has a real basis for his reassurance. Photographs of nude adolescents the same age as the patient at every stage of pubescence are especially comforting; they can be found for boys in Tanner[23] and for both sexes in Conger.[24]

Puberty and early adolescence bring to light several organic and intersex conditions that usually are not evident in childhood. Turner's syndrome is finally diagnosed because of the complete absence of puberty. (For details on tests, pathognomonic findings and treatment, see Jones and Scott.[6]) Exogenous estrogen will produce the external physical changes of puberty and feminine appearance. These girls deserve and, unless retarded, can understand a complete explanation of their condition. They need serious, repeated reassurance that their sexual function can be entirely normal and that they can be mothers by adoption. They can receive further valuable support based on research showing that such women are extremely feminine, are excellent mothers and have an unusual degree of emotional stability.[25-27] I have treated an adolescent who attempted suicide because she was convinced that she was not a "real woman" and would never be attractive to men or have a normal sex and family life. She responded dramatically to a straightforward explanation and to reassurance that could be shown to have a factual basis.

Failure to menstruate, even though other pubertal changes have taken place, can have many causes; one is vaginal agenesis. In some girls, this is a relatively simple consequence of incomplete Müllerian duct development, and the girl has normal ovaries, tubes and uterus; in others, there is faulty development of the other internal sex organs as well. Whether reproductive capacity can be established depends on many factors, but vaginal agenesis is relatively simple in terms of healthy sexual identity. These patients have been reared as girls and, in the absence of sexually pathogenic influences, have a normal female core gender identity, heterosexual orientation and feminine sex role preferences. Vaginoplasty is usually safe and successful and permits full sexual function, including orgasm. The best time for this procedure must be determined for each individual. Unless the young woman's sexual identity is fragile for reasons other than the physical anomaly, careful support and reassurance, including follow-up to ensure the continued patency and adequacy of the artificial vagina, should obviate serious disturbances in sexual identity.

A more striking intersex condition that is sometimes revealed when menarcheal failure and vaginal agenesis are investigated is the androgen insensitivity (testicular feminizing) syndrome. In the fully developed form of this familial disorder, the body cells of a genotypic male are completely insensitive to androgen. The conceptus is an XY male and develops normal testes, but because of cellular insensitivity to androgen, the external genitalia differentiate as female, the normal result of a lack of (effective) fetal androgens during the sixth to fourteenth weeks. The infant is born with normal looking female external genitalia and is assigned and reared as a girl. It is postulated that the fetal hypothalamus is insensitive to the organizing influence of androgen, so there is no innate masculine behavioral or sexual orientation bias to interfere with development as a girl with normal appearance, feelings and behavior. There are no ovaries or other female reproductive organs, and the abdominal testes produce normal amounts of androgens. At puberty the estrogen normally produced by the testes and the adrenal glands cause breast growth and other female body characteristics—a phenotypically normal looking pubescent girl.

Only laparotomy prompted by lack of a vagina reveals the absence of other female structures and the presence of testes (which must be removed because of the heightened risk of malignancy). Although medically dramatic, this condition causes few major problems of sexual identity. The patient will be infertile and will require vaginoplasty with administration of exogenous estrogens after the testes are removed. However, normal female sexual identity has already occurred, and if the patient can be helped to resolve the emotional trauma of discovering her lack of reproductive potential (the true genotypic condition may or may not have to be revealed), sexual identity problems generally do not occur. Emotional tragedies have occurred when the physician and family, discovering the adolescent to be a genotypic, gonadal and hormonal male, have tried to switch the youngster's sexual identity to that of a male. Such attempts invariably fail, causing only emotional turmoil and dysfunction.

In some, but not all cases, the more masculine behavior and preferences of girls exposed to fetal androgens gradually diminish at adolescence. Such hormonal predispositions often give way to the influence of postnatal sex of rearing. It is possible, as Green[20] postulates about tomboyism, that as culturally approved feminine characteristics begin to be strongly reinforced by adolescent male peers, there is great additional pressure to develop more typical femininity.

Because body preoccupation is painfully intense in early adolescence, anomalous genitalia or atypical secondary sex characteristics can cause not only sexual identity problems but even psychotic depression and suicide. That is why in cases of true hermaphroditism, all organs of the sex opposite to the sex of rearing should be surgically extirpated, so that the physician can honestly assure the adolescent that no contradictory sex organs exist.

The gender dysphoria of primary transsexualism reaches a peak of painful intensity in early adolescence. Adult body configuration and genitalia intensify the rejection of what the individual considers to be the "wrong" anatomy. Adult sex drive coupled with the impossibility of functioning as members of the sex to which they feel they "really" belong are deeply frustrating realities that transsexuals cannot deny. Some early-adolescent boys surreptitiously obtain and use estrogens to effect body changes. Some already begin to press for sex-reassignment surgery, but their youth weighs against irreversible procedures being performed, even though there are only three reports of a successful shift of core gender identity in an adolescent or older transsexual.[28-30]

Distinguishing preferential homosexuality has already been discussed, as have the ethical considerations of treatment. The practicalities of treatment are another matter. After adolescents identify as homosexual and accept that identity, not many voluntarily enter therapy to shift their orientation even when the rationale for doing so is fully explained. While the ethics of accepting subadult judgment are debatable, it is probably as unethical to enforce treatment as it is impossible to force treatment success. Even for those who reject their homosexuality and want to change, there may be difficulties. While it is often thought that it is easier for psychotherapy to bring about a shift in sexual orientation in adolescence than it is in adulthood, the dynamics of adolescent development may negate successful therapy.[31] Nonetheless, physicians should know that there is a significant proportion of success in the therapy of those who want to change their homosexual orientation. Adolescents deserve reassurance that they do stand a reasonable chance of being able to shift with proper therapy if they want to (see Chapter 6).

Problems of atypical sex role preference have increasingly different meanings for boys and girls as they reach adolescence. Among boys, those problems that persist into adolescence are most often concomitants of core gender or sexual orientation problems, because there are fewer social rewards of feminine roles and more ostracism of feminine men than of masculine men. Unless such behavior is unconsciously motivated and beyond the person's control, there are strong pressures to relinquish such behavior.

In girls, there may be the same association of cross-sex role preference with deeper confusions of sexual identity, but somewhat different social forces affect girls than boys. Despite advances in female opportunity and reward outside family roles, some inequities in sex-role valuation remain. Furthermore, woman's maternal and nurturing role *within* the family is often undervalued. Girls' repudiation of certain feminine roles can reflect social reality or subjective misperceptions or both. This may lead to internal conflicts; when a girl has developed a sex-appropriate core gender identity and sexual orientation but feels she cannot accept the feminine role, she may come to doubt her femininity and her sexual identity as a woman.

The symptoms of transvestism increase with age. Some adult transvestites became so when they were very young children; more developed the overt syndrome as they approached adulthood. Physicians who work with adolescents are not uncommonly consulted when an adolescent boy has been caught stealing the underclothes of his mother, sister or a neighbor. Inquiry usually reveals that these garments enhance erotic arousal and are used in masturbation. Persistent behavior of this sort in adolescence almost always represents some degree of disturbance in normal psychosexual development and requires psychiatric evaluation.

Late Adolescence. Normal developmental conflicts play little part in sexual identity problems during this stage of development. By this time, both the incidence and frequency of nonprognostic homoerotic play is very low or zero.

Sometimes attendance at single-sex boarding schools has sexual consequences. Such schools are fewer in number today, but some adolescents are given little or no choice about attending them. For the vast majority of children, they reduce the opportunity and sometimes seriously impair the capacity to learn normal heterosocial and heterosexual interactions. Homosexual activity is widespread in such schools long after it is phase-appropriate, and homosexual victimization of the younger and weaker often occurs, much as in prisons. The best therapy is preventive, by avoiding such unnatural environments.

The only intersex condition not usually diagnosed before late adolescence is Klinefelter's syndrome. Those afflicted with it are phenotypic but infertile males with a 47, XXY genotype. Testes are small, adult penis size tends to be below normal and persistent gynecomastia may occur at puberty (only that symptom may come to medical attention in early adolescence). There may be enough testosterone produced for average virilization,[6] but it is often below normal; sex drive may be normal as well.[4] Those with atypical body changes at puberty are subject to disturbed sexual body image and identity.

There is disagreement about whether men with Klinefelter's syndrome are or are not at high risk of developing sexual identity disorders.[4,6,32,33] Many are heterosexual but homosexuality, bisexuality, transvestism and serious gender dysphoria seem to occur more often than in the general population. The infertility is irreversible, but the gynecomastia is amenable to plastic surgery. Some patients may achieve normal sex drive with exogenous use of testosterone, but others are unresponsive. Supportive therapy may be very helpful to adolescents with this disease, especially if it is begun before severe sexual identity problems become fixed.

Delayed or absent puberty caused by organic pathology, especially in boys, is commonly not discovered until the late teens. The etiology varies, it is often untreatable and it sometimes is life compromising. As in other conditions not evident in childhood, normal rearing can protect the child from major disorders of sexual identity, but not from the trauma to his sense of male adequacy caused by failure to achieve puberty or to look like or function sexually as a man. Of course any treatable condition should be treated immediately, but diagnosis and treatment of delayed sexual maturation is highly complex and still experimental.[34]

Many transsexuals of both sexes are trying to live as members of the opposite sex by late adolescence, and quite a number do so successfully. Many such males use estrogens to appear more feminine. Requests for sex reassignment surgery increase in this age group and are sometimes desperate. Unfortunately, many people are diagnosed as transsexuals on the sole criterion of request for sex-change surgery, and irreversible procedures may be undertaken without adequate medical preparation or psychiatric justification. It is advisable to refer these patients to well-established multidisciplinary gender-identity clinics associated with universities.

Homosexual orientation is often clearly recognized by late adolescence, although the behavior may remain suppressed and the individual may still hope that it is a passing phase. It is now important for the physician to differentiate preferential or exclusive adult homosexuality from other sexual orientation problems in which the motivation for homosexual behavior is not primarily erotic attraction.

The different types of homosexuality are described in Chapter 6; recommendations and therapy (where appropriate) vary considerably according to the nature and emotional meaning of the activity.

By late adolescence, most problems of sex-role preference that do not involve core gender or sexual orientation conflicts are consciously perceived as ideological. Such cross-gender preferences are more common in females, possibly because of both the real and the perceived social disadvantages of their roles.

THERAPY

This discussion can offer only a summary of the basic principles of recognizing and treating (or referring) sexual identity problems in children and adolescents. As with other emotional problems, most can be prevented, for they result from pathogenic interactions and misperceptions. Physicians cannot cure the ills of the human condition or produce a sexually healthy society, but they can often inform and educate parents and others before predictable problems develop. The physician can understand normal psychosexual development, the behavior to be expected during its stages and the normal developmental conflicts that are likely to occur and that can be rendered harmless through knowledge. One can discuss these matters with parents, teachers and significant others ahead of time.

Even when problems are not prevented and begin to develop, education and explanation often remain the physician's most helpful tools. Helping the child or adolescent and the meaningful adults in his life to understand what is happening, and why, often makes therapy unnecessary if the problem has not yet become internalized or fixed.

The younger the child, the more necessary it is to involve the entire family in therapy for a sexual identity problem. An adolescent may have enough ego development and live sufficiently outside the family milieu to make intrapsychic changes through psychotherapy despite family attitudes. But a young child lives entirely within the environment that, in most cases, causes, contributes to, or fails to prevent the problem. The therapist and the child are usually helpless unless the family also can change.

The principle of earliest intervention is axiomatic in medicine and nowhere more so than in intersex conditions. Because many components of sexual identity are fixed or most strongly influenced early in life, the sooner that ambiguities can be resolved, especially in the parents' minds, and decisions made about sexual assignment and rearing, the more trouble-free will be the development of the child's sexual identity. The principle of earliest intervention is also true for surgical correction of anomalous sexual organs, although surgery must often be delayed by the facts of developmental anatomy until long after first diagnosis. However, surgical correction and medical intervention are almost never enough; repeated, long-term follow-up with emotional support is usually necessary. Some psychological consequences of organic conditions are probably inevitable, although with optimal treatment the person may cope with them very effectively.

Intersex conditions require the services of one or more specialists, and this raises issues about the continuing role of the referring primary care physician. The patient or the family may be confused about whose patient one is. While

259

the primary care physician may not be involved in the actual medical or surgical treatment of some conditions, he would be the logical and least expensive person to manage many of the conditions in which maintenance treatment or medication is required and, in most instances, he will get the patient back for the medical care of unrelated illnesses.

It is in the patient's best interests that the specialists and primary care physician confer or at least communicate as fully as possible; the family physician must understand the condition and the goals of treatment in order to be in a position to answer the patient's and family's questions in a way that is consistent with the goals set and the answers given by the specialists. This consultation requires initiative on the part of both primary physician and specialist. Sometimes the specialists may not furnish full information, especially if the referring doctor is not easily available or lives in a distant community. At the same time, the family physician may not know what to ask to provide noncontradictory answers to questions such as, "Can I have a baby?" and then "Why not?" It is the specialists' duty to see that the family physician is prepared for his patient to return and ask many of the same things that were explained by the specialists, as well as questions not thought of previously. It is unfortunately true that specialists sometimes neglect to prepare and inform the patient carefully, leading to misinformation and fears about the condition and its consequences. The real burden of this aspect of treatment sometimes falls upon the family practitioner. For this reason, it is also in the patient's best interests for the specialists to make a point of reinforcing the patient's therapeutic alliance with his or her primary physician. Many intersex conditions require a continuing team approach between patient, family physician and specialists.

The same issues sometimes arise over psychogenic gender identity problems. When specific psychotherapy is indicated, the family physician probably will not be actively involved but, with the patient's consent, it is often useful that he be informed about the problem and its management, because many times his reinforcement and support are crucial to success. In instances where the problem arises from parents' or patients' misunderstanding of normal developmental behavior, the psychiatrist may wish to bring the referring physician more fully into the therapeutic plan since he may have both a better established rapport and more frequent opportunities to offer corrective education.

For early cross-sex behavior—effeminacy and tomboyism—group therapy with other such conflicted youngsters using behavior modification techniques, has been investigated most and seems to offer some advantages.[20] It provides a social group in which the children are not teased and rejected and can learn sex-appropriate behavior from same-sex models. They can monitor each other's inappropriate mannerisms in mutually acceptable, less scornful ways. Even in childhood, cross-sex behavior sometimes represents such firmly internalized sexual identity problems that intensive psychotherapy is necessary along with or instead of group therapy. The parents also must be involved in therapy if possible. Internal conflict and social mislearning may contribute in

260

different proportions to gender identity problems. Knowing which plays a larger role may help guide the choice of therapy; that assessment is usually best made by a specialist in such problems. In general, relearning therapies, such as behavior modification and conditioning, often suffice for problems in which mislearning was preponderant; depth therapies (psychoanalysis and related therapies) are more often called for if confused sexual identity reflects unconscious conflict. Unfortunately, even when unconscious conflict is clearly present in adolescence, youngsters may not be amenable to analysis. Sometimes only superficial intervention is possible, and resolution depends on willingness to pursue the problem further in young adulthood.

There is evidence suggesting that many important aspects of sexual identity, including heterosexual or homosexual orientation, may be strongly influenced or even fixed at a much younger age than has generally been thought. The apparent fluidity of much of sexual identity may be an artifact of the enormous human capacity for learning, which can obscure the healthy limits of variability in childrearing. There are far more unanswered questions than solid facts about this issue, but the possibility that crucial aspects of sexual identity may be acquired very early and the recognition that the misery caused by sexual identity disturbances can be devastating, together urge caution against delay in addressing any indication of a problem.

References

1. Gadpaille WJ: *The Cycles of Sex*. New York, Charles Scribner's Sons, 1975.
2. Stoller RJ: *Sex and Gender: On the Development of Masculinity & Femininity*. New York, Jason Aronson Inc, 1968.
3. Stoller RJ: *Sex and Gender Vol II: The Transsexual Experiment*. New York, Jason Aronson Inc, 1976.
4. Imperato-McGinley J, et al: Androgens and the evolution of male-gender identity among male pseudohermaphrodites with 5α-reductase deficiency. *N Engl J Med* 1979; 300:1233-1237.
5. Money J, Ehrhardt AA: *Man and Woman: Boy and Girl: Differentation and Dimorphism of Gender Identity from Conception to Maturity*. Baltimore, Johns Hopkins University Press, 1972.
6. Jones HW Jr, Scott WW: *Hermaphroditism, Genital Anomalies and Related Endocrine Disorders*, ed 2. Baltimore, Williams & Wilkins Company, 1971.
7. Barnes ND, et al: The central nervous system and precocious puberty, in Grumbach MM, et al (eds): *Control of the Onset of Puberty*. New York, John Wiley & Sons, 1974.
8. Ehrhardt AA, et al: Fetal androgens and female gender identity in the early-treated adrenogenital syndrome. *Johns Hopkins Med J* 1968; 122:160-167.
9. Lewis V, et al: Genital operations in girls with the adrenogenital syndrome: Subsequent psychologic development. *Obstet Gynecol* 1970; 36:11-15.

10. Ehrhardt AA, et al: Influence of androgen and some aspects of sexually dimorphic behavior in women with the late-treated adrenogenital syndrome. *Johns Hopkins Med J* 1968; 123:115-122.
11. Money J, Schwartz M: Dating, romantic and nonromantic friendships, and sexuality in 17 early treated adrenogenital females aged 16-25, in Lee PA, et al (eds): *Congenital Adrenal Hyperplasia.* Baltimore, University Park Press, 1977.
12. Yalom I, et al: Prenatal exposure to female hormones: Effect on psychosexual development in boys. *Arch Gen Psychiatry* 1973; 28:554-561.
13. Freud S: Three essays on the theory of sexuality. *Standard Edition of the Complete Works of Sigmund Freud.* London, Hogarth Press, 1953.
14. Ehrhardt AA, Money J: Progestin-induced hermaphroditism: I.Q. and psychosexual identity in a study of ten girls. *J Sex Res* 1967; 3:83-100.
15. Ehrhardt AA, Baker SW: Fetal androgens, human central nervous system differentiation, and behavior sex differences, in Friedman RC, et al (eds): *Sex Differences in Behavior.* New York, John Wiley & Sons, 1974.
16. Saghir MT, Robins E: *Male and Female Homosexuality.* Baltimore, Williams & Wilkins Company, 1973.
17. Bieber I, et al: *Homosexuality.* New York, Basic Books Inc, 1962.
18. Green R: *Sexual Identity Conflict in Children and Adults.* New York, Basic Books Inc, 1974.
19. Lebovitz P: Feminine behavior in boys: Aspects of its outcome. *Am J Psychiatry* 1972; 128:1283-1289.
20. Green R: Atypical sex role behavior during childhood, in Freedman AM, et al (eds): *Comprehensive Textbook of Psychiatry,* ed 2. Baltimore, Williams & Wilkins Company, 1975.
21. Green R: Childhood cross-gender behavior and subsequent sexual preference. *Am J Psychiatry* 1979; 136:106-108.
22. Fraiberg S: Homosexual conflicts, in Lorand S, Schneer HI (eds): *Adolescents: Psychoanalytic Approach to Problems and Therapy.* New York, Paul B. Hoeber Books, 1961.
23. Tanner JM: *Growth at Adolescence,* ed 2. Oxford, England, Blackwell Scientific Publications, 1962.
24. Conger JJ: *Adolescence and Youth.* New York, Harper and Row Publishers, Inc, 1973.
25. Shaffer JW: Masculinity-femininity and other personality traits in gonadal aplasia (Turner's syndrome), in Beigel HG (ed): *Advances in Sex Research.* New York, Paul B. Hoeber Books, 1963.
26. Ehrhardt AA, et al: Female gender identity and absence of fetal gonadal hormones: Turner's syndrome. *Johns Hopkins Med J* 1970; 126:237-248.
27. Money J, Mittenthal S: Lack of personality pathology in Turner's syndrome: Relation to cytogenetics, hormones and physique. *Behav Genet* 1970; 1:43-56.
28. Barlow DH, et al: Gender identity change in a transsexual. *Arch Gen Psychiatry* 1973; 28:569-576.

29. Barlow DH, et al: Gender identity change in a transsexual: An exorcism. *Arch Sex Behav* 1977; 6:387-395.
30. Davenport CW, Harrison SI: Gender identity change in a female adolescent transsexual. *Arch Sex Behav* 1977; 6:327-340.
31. Gadpaille WJ: Homosexuality in adolescent males. *J Am Acad Psychoanal* 1975; 3:361-371.
32. Money J, Pollitt E: Cytogenetic and psychosexual ambiguity: Klinefelter's syndrome and transvestism compared. *Arch Gen Psychiatry* 1964; 11:589-595.
33. Pauly IB: Adult manifestations of male transsexualism, in Green R, Money J (eds): *Transsexualism and Sex Reassignment*. Baltimore, Johns Hopkins Medical Press, 1969.
34. Kulin HE, Reiter EO: Delayed sexual maturation, with special emphasis on the occurrences of the syndrome in the male, in Grumbach MM, et al (eds): *Control of the Onset of Puberty*. New York, John Wiley & Sons, 1974.

Chapter 19

Treatment of Sexual Disorders

Warren J. Gadpaille, M.D., and Harold I. Lief, M.D.

DISORDERS OF GENDER IDENTITY AND GENDER ROLE IN ADULTS

The major forms of gender identity disorders in adulthood are trans-sexualism and some forms of transvestism. In addition, there are disorders resulting from organic pathology or anomaly and problems caused by atypical sex role preferences not associated with transsexualism.

Transsexualism

There are two major professional positions on adult transsexualism. The first holds that true transsexualism exists from earliest childhood, whereas persons who become convinced of a cross-gender identity later in life, after having accepted, identified with and even functioned in accord with their anatomical sex during part of childhood or adulthood, constitute a different diagnostic entity.[1] The second position is that those who reach a conviction of cross-gender identity should be regarded as transsexual regardless of their gender identity and/or diagnostic categories.[2,3] This author favors the generic diagnosis "gender dysphoria syndrome" for both groups and regards the first as true, or primary, transsexuals and the second as secondary transsexuals. Further diagnostic descriptions should accompany the term secondary trans-sexualism.

Primary transsexualism is discussed in terms of the problems it causes a child or adolescent (see Chapter 18). Its etiology seems to be different for males and females. Male transsexuals seem not to have differentiated fully from their mothers and to have failed to develop a male identity. The mothers' own gender identity conflicts and psychodynamics, according to this theory, foster the sons' female identity, in part through prolonged, nude physical closeness. The sons whom these mothers choose for such excessive closeness are usually especially attractive as infants; the fathers seem to make no significant effort to interfere with their distorted development. In such cases, the early cross-gender identity appears to develop without conflict. Aside from their conviction of being the opposite sex, male transsexuals with this background do not exhibit signs of psychosis on psychological tests.[4,5]

Female primary transsexualism is probably not an equally conflict-free development. Logically, the same prolonged early symbiosis with mother would result in female core-gender identity. Fewer such girls have been studied, but the evidence suggests that often their mothers are depressed and emotionally unavailable. Their fathers, conventionally masculine men, are unable to be supportive of their depressed wives, and future transsexual girls, while still very young, are emotionally pressed into (or assume of their own accord) father's role as mother's caretaking mate. To the degree that they fulfill this role, they are rewarded and encouraged; they are also rewarded if they continue to identify with their fathers' masculine interests and activities. Often the parents recall that these girls seemed to them singularly unattractive as newborns, and many were given names or nicknames that are neither unambiguously feminine nor masculine.[1]

Secondary transsexualism can become manifest at any time in adulthood, even late in life, after any of a variety of sexual life styles that did not include cross-gender identification. At times, the conviction of cross-gender identity may develop after the individual has functioned within his or her anatomical sex for many years, even after fathering or bearing children. It has been noted that transvestism may progress to transsexualism,[3] and this change has been recorded both in younger and aging transvestites.[2] Sex reassignment surgery has been requested by some homosexuals, by those with masochistic perversions, by those with severely schizoid character disorders, as well as by those with other disorders.[2] Some very effeminate, cross-dressing homosexuals decide that they wish to become females.

Professionals may have strong doubts about the firmness of cross-gender convictions in many or even most secondary transsexuals. Results of clinical evaluation and psychological testing indicate that quite a number are clearly disturbed. But one cannot avoid taking them seriously. Most are very importunate in demanding sex reassignment surgery; some have already had preliminary surgical or cross-sex hormone treatment, and they may express serious suicidal tendencies growing out of their gender dysphoria.

Treatment ideally should be psychiatrically managed, preferably at a multidisciplinary, university-affiliated gender identity clinic. Only the broad principles of treatment will be discussed in this chapter, but in sufficient detail so that the primary referring physician can offer initial guidance to both the patient and family and make knowledgeable recommendations.

The physician's first inclination, understandably, is to urge that the condition be cured. Efforts to reverse primary transsexualism in adolescents and adults have almost all failed. There are however at least three documented cases of reversal; two used behavior modification techniques[6,7] and one is reliably reported to have resulted from exorcism.[8] Psychoanalysis and dynamic psychotherapy have thus far been of no avail. In any event, few such individuals are motivated for therapy aimed at change or are even amenable to the suggestion. Reversing cross-gender identity is much more likely to succeed in secondary transsexuals, but they too are highly resistant. Change is most likely to be possible as a byproduct of the preparatory stages of sex reassignment.

When transsexualism is secondary to serious psychiatric illness, or if suicide is deemed imminent, emergency or involuntary hospitalization and treatment may take precedence over attending to the gender dysphoria. However, if a person requests sex-reassignment surgery and is sufficiently functional, there is often no recourse but to begin a complete workup for the procedure. Complete psychiatric and physical examinations are necessary to differentiate primary and secondary transsexualism, to assess areas and degrees of psychiatric illness and ego strengths and to rule out intersex or other organic pathology. The patient must be fully apprised of the many risks and emotional coping tasks confronting anyone seeking sex change even under the most favorable conditions.[2] Sometimes the sober facts of the enormous emotional and social tasks ahead and of the technical limitations of producing functional genitalia of the opposite sex (especially female-to-male) make the less determined reassess their wishes and even to try to reverse them.

Most patients persist in requesting sex change. The consensus today among the most reputable professionals in the field is to require that the patient live, pass and work continually as a member of the desired sex for an extended period, usually from six months to two years. During that time, only heterologous hormone therapy is given. This often has a calming and reassuring effect on a determined transsexual. It produces physical and physiological changes that give the patient some sense of what it would be like to be the opposite sex and also facilitates passing as the opposite sex. The patient must be warned that, while most of the changes caused by hormone therapy are usually completely reversible, some are not (e.g., the deepening of the voice, the male pattern of hair growth in females given androgens). Estrogens given to males can produce irreversible testicular atrophy, infertility and some penile atrophy.[9] Regular psychiatric follow-up during this trial period is important to help the patient deal with the difficult emotional tasks that may be encountered. Occasionally only hormone therapy is requested.

During this trial period, the majority of applicants for sex change drop out of the prolonged program. Some are too impatient to tolerate the delay and seek a less cautious surgeon who will perform the desired surgery on the patient's request alone. Others are secondary transsexuals who discover that their desire for reassignment is not lasting or that passing as the opposite sex does not magically solve their problems. During this time, some become amenable to psychotherapy, and some are forced into it by desperation or as a result of suicide attempts.

With those who successfully complete the trial period and persist in their wish to have surgery, the physician or gender identity clinic still must make difficult medical decisions. Primary transsexuals have the best prognosis, although serious questions arise even about them.[1] For secondary transsexuals, especially those with past or current serious psychiatric illness, the prognosis is poorer. The physician or clinic may face the Hobson's choice of refusing surgical reassignment to a severely disturbed patient because experience dictates that he or she is a very poor risk, while at the same time knowing that the chance of suicide is very high because of the patient's dysphoria, and that therapy to relieve the patient's desperation may not be available, accepted or effective.

Follow-up studies of surgically treated transsexuals indicate high patient satisfaction, but these reports are open to serious question.[1] None of the studies distinguishes primary and secondary transsexuals and an objective outsider may be hard pressed to agree with the self-reported success of some patients—for instance, those who turned to prostitution and had frequent criminal involvements and legal difficulties.

Even most of those patients who are seemingly satisfied require psychotherapy after surgery. Often the emotional stresses of living a biologically false role have just begun. Most surgically reassigned transsexuals want "heterosexual" relationships and marriages, and many achieve them. However, all realize that they can never totally secure the new sex they wish to be and this factor alone can contaminate their relationships. Because surgical reassignment from male to female can be both esthetically and functionally more successful than the reverse, males reassigned as females have the easier task; however, doubts and conflicts about themselves and their partners may become crippling whether they conceal or reveal their original sex. For the female reassigned as a male, the inability of plastic surgery to produce even a remotely normal penis, much less one that is sexually functional, makes it virtually impossible to conceal her original sex in a long, intimate relationship. Her potential for a debilitating sense of inadequacy and for doubts about the true heterosexuality of the female partner seem even greater. Nonetheless, pairings perceived as successful do occur,[10] and, for many transsexuals, the new life seems preferable to the old despite the problems.

Many families of primary transsexuals need as much or more understanding guidance than the transsexuals themselves. This may be true when the patient still has meaningful family relationships even though the family likely had contributed to the transsexualism originally. With such families, nothing is gained by assessing blame and generating guilt, because they are powerless to undo the original emotional damage.

Many secondary transsexuals seek treatment when older; some have wives or husbands and children. For their spouses and children, there is usually disruption of the family and great emotional distress. Some live on in their families as new "aunts" or "uncles"; occasionally some will remarry in their new sex and adopt their own children. Any of these solutions present children with bizarre emotional traumas and tasks with as yet unknown psychopathological consequences. A sympathetic ear, a nonjudgmental presentation of the facts and support through the transition may be all the physician can offer in these cases.

Gender Identity Disorders with Organic Causes

Most gender identity disorders, regardless of etiology, begin and are fixed before adulthood, but those with organic causes may come to medical attention only after adolescence. (Their early manifestations and treatment are discussed in Chapter 18.) Even if severe pathology or trauma in adulthood destroys the genital organs or disrupts or reverses normal sex hormone production, one would not expect alteration of a firmly established gender identity, however much the sense of masculine or feminine adequacy may be affected.

People with intersex problems who are not seen until adulthood may or may not have gender identity problems, depending on whether their rearing as males or females was consistent or ambiguous. Undoing the damage of ambiguous gender rearing is not usually possible. If the patient identifies with, and prefers to be, one sex more than the other, it may be advisable to undertake whatever medical and surgical procedures are feasible to make the patient's anatomy and physiology as consistent as possible with the predominant gender identity. Looking like and functioning as that sex may make the patient amenable to therapeutic help. Behavior modification techniques may enhance social function in that sex role, and dynamically oriented psychotherapy may help resolve conflicts associated with an uncertain sense of gender identity.

Atypical Sex-Role Behavior

A person's sex-role behavior and preferences may be inconsistent with both cultural expectations and his or her own unconflicted gender identity and heterosexuality. It is debatable whether these sex-role behaviors can be considered disorders unless they arise from internal conflict or pathogenic developmental influence. There are effeminate men and masculine women who display no other evidences of gender identity disorder.

It is true not only in this society but cross-culturally that there is little advantage in a man's being thought unmasculine or a woman's being considered unfeminine. Such stigmatization is especially unwarranted when the man's or woman's gender identity, sexual orientation and parental functions are perfectly congruent with biological sex. Many people to whom this happens suffer social derision; some of them genuinely or defiantly ignore the derision or fight back. To those troubled by either the stigmatization or the inconsistencies between their true sexual identities and the way they appear to others, a creative behavioral therapist can devise techniques for teaching them more culturally acceptable mannerisms and behaviors.

PARAPHILIAS

Paraphilia—a word derived from the Greek roots "para," meaning "along side of," and "philia," meaning "love,"—was first used by the pioneer American psychiatrist, Adolf Meyer, who wished to avoid the pejorative term, "perversion." Even "deviance," although an improvement, is not quite neutral. For those reasons, the DSM-III Committee on Psychosexual Disorders of the American Psychiatric Association resurrected the almost forgotten term, "paraphilia."

Even though paraphiliac disorders often involve criminal acts or, at least, acts for which the perpetrators could, if discovered and apprehended, be prosecuted, to achieve an objective and dispassionate concern for the patient, it was necessary for the DSM-III Committee to put greater distance between the social or public perception of the paraphilias and the health professional's perception. To a certain extent, the term "paraphilia" accomplishes the decriminalization and neutralization of deviant sexual behavior and allows the physician to help a distressed patient without the repugnance or even moral outrage that might inevitably accompany more pejorative labels.

Not all persons who exhibit paraphiliac behavior are distressed. Many come to the physician's attention because the behavior distresses the spouse, usually the wife (paraphiliac disorders affect males far more frequently than females), or because the behavior has become a criminal offense and the patient a "sex offender,"[11,12] who is referred by some agency of the criminal justice system.

The physician need not feel that he has to condone behavior, such as pedophilia or exhibitionism. His task is to set aside personal prejudices and try to understand the origins of the paraphiliac behavior under review, in order to make decisions about patient care. Of course, the degree of social offense varies enormously. At one end of the spectrum is the fetishist who is carrying out a victimless act; at the other end is the lust-murderer whose aberrative script requires extreme violence to accomplish sexual arousal. In the first instance the physician may be curious, even puzzled, by the fetishism, whereas he may be outraged by the fetishistic lust-murder. Whatever the severity of the behavior, however, the physician's posture should be "detached concern."

Within the range of paraphiliac behavior, paraphiliacs are a heterogeneous group engaging in diverse sexual activity. Their degree of psychopathology varies from mild to severe and the degree of danger to the public ranges from nonexistent to grave. Moreover, there is no direct correlation between any of the paraphilias and character structure or personality trait. These are also heterogeneous and very diverse.

Fortunately, the primary-care physician has only to retain his equanimity and detached concern long enough to obtain a reasonably accurate history that will enable him to make an appropriate referral to a psychiatrist.

The primary-care physician should emphasize to the patient the inherent dangers of the paraphiliac behavior, both legal and social, and stress the importance of psychiatric care. The physician should be considerate and compassionate while indicating willingness to continue medical care during and after psychiatric treatment.

Principles of Paraphiliac Behavior

Treatment of the paraphilias should not be undertaken by a nonpsychiatric physician. All cases should be referred to a psychiatrist. The primary-care physician, however, should understand the nature of the therapy for these disorders so that he has an adequate basis for evaluating the help that the patient receives from the psychiatrist.

Patients with paraphilias are difficult to treat, and the results of therapy are often disappointing. Seldom do patients seek treatment on their own. As indicated above, more often they are referred by their wives or by the courts. Occasionally they request treatment because of the threat of legal action or of divorce. The prognosis is much more optimistic if the patient's concern about his deviant behavior is sufficient to cause him to seek help on his own. If motivation is inadequate, the patient will skip therapy sessions; avoid "homework" assignments; resist revealing his fantasies or dreams; and use passive-aggressive maneuvers with the therapist, such as arriving late, forgetting sessions and diverting the attention of the therapist to irrelevant issues.

Knowledge of some general principles about the behavior of paraphiliacs will contribute to the physician's understanding and may be helpful as well in educating the patient's spouse:

1. Although there are exceptions, for the most part there is not a progression from minor to major offenses; e.g., from voyeurism to lust-murder.

2. Minor paraphiliac fantasies are common. In many individuals, they remain fantasies and are never carried out in behavior. Some dysfunctions, such as inhibition of desire or impotence, may be defenses against the conscious awareness of unacceptable fantasies. Homosexuality also may be a way of repressing erotic imagery that causes castration anxiety.

3. A paraphilia is characterized by repetitive fantasies and repetitive compulsive behavior patterns.

4. Most, if not all, paraphilias are based on childhood trauma. The traumatized child turns the situation around to emerge in adult life as the triumphant victor. Stoller[13] postulates that there is always an element of aggression in paraphiliac behavior, a defense against real, not fantasized, childhood trauma. In his view, the desire for revenge to erase the past, coupled with the paraphiliac's inability to completely obliterate the danger, creates the need for him to carry out the act over and over again.

Therapeutic Approaches

The principal objectives of any therapy are to increase heterosexual responsiveness and decrease paraphiliac behavior. Within this framework, the therapist attempts to help the patient establish a rewarding sexual relationship (in a few cases of paraphilias this might be a homosexual relationship) and to improve sexual functioning within that relationship. The therapist usually tries to help the patient control his undesirable sexual behavior rather than to reduce his interest in it. If this proves to be impossible, the therapist helps the patient adapt to his deviant role.

Almost all of the psychotherapeutic approaches used in the treatment of sexual dysfunctions have been used as well in the treatment of other sexual disorders. Group therapy has its strong advocates,[14] and most treatment programs for sexual offenders have used this form of treatment primarily or exclusively. Marital therapy proves useful if the spouse's behavior encourages or facilitates the behavior pattern causing distress or if the spouse's support is essential to treatment management. The two approaches used most frequently in the treatment of paraphilias are individual psychodynamic psychotherapy[15] and behavior therapy.[16]

Studies attempting to assess the outcome of therapy for paraphilias usually have been uncontrolled and, with few exceptions, have not compared different techniques. Often, with the exception of homosexuals who are attempting to develop heterosexual interests, the group of patients is heterogeneous and represent a lumping together of "sexual deviants." It would be more useful for evaluating therapies if the groups of patients were more homogeneous (e.g., fetishists only, exhibitionists only). Invariably, because the number of patients with paraphilias is small the significance of the results remains questionable. Of the uncontrolled studies, the best results were shown with 12 transvestites and fetishists, two-thirds of whom improved.[17]

Controlled studies that have compared different treatment methods have failed to demonstrate that one form of therapy is superior to another; e.g., behavior therapy vs psychotherapy. Whatever therapy is used, it seems to have at least as much effect on increasing interpersonal responsiveness as it does on decreasing deviance.[18]

Individual Psychotherapy. In this form of treatment, the therapist attempts to:

1. Discover the patterns of thoughts, feelings and behavior that precede the episode of deviant behavior. It is not uncommon for increased alcohol intake to be a significant aspect of the behavior preceding an "acting out" episode. Curtailing the alcohol intake is an obvious therapeutic approach. However, sometimes conflict with the spouse (playing the mother-role?) is a precipitating factor.

2. Remove the anxiety or depression that is part of a precursor pattern.

3. Increase the capacity of the patient for a better sexual relationship with a committed partner.

Behavior Therapy. Behavior therapy involves conditioning in the therapist's office and assigned tasks at home. It employs aversive techinques[17] (the use of punishment to decrease unwanted behavior), or positive methods such as systematic desensitization ánd operant conditioning.[16,18] In the treatment of paraphilias, aversive therapy is less promising than rewarding the patient for more appropriate and satisfying sexual behavior. If heterosexual approaches create anxiety or anxiety precedes the deviant act, reduction of anxiety through desensitization (see Chapter 25) can be very helpful. A primary technique is the use of controlled fantasy, in which a more adaptive fantasy is substituted for the paraphiliac one immediately before orgasm, either with masturbation or coitus.

A 40-year-old man, impotent in his heterosexual encounters, revealed that his masturbatory fantasies involved sex with another male penetrating him anally. Immediately prior to orgasm he would see himself as a woman. He had never had an adult homosexual experience. Treatment included his looking at a centerfold picture of a nude woman and fantasizing about it just before orgasm, and then gradually doing so earlier and earlier during masturbation. This treatment was combined with therapy to decrease his anxiety during sexual contacts with females. Eventually he became sufficiently comfortable with women to get married.

Multi-Modal Orientation

Lazarus[19] has developed a multiple approach based on the acronym BASIC ID. Seven different modalities are explored: *B*ehavior, *A*ffects, *S*ensations, *I*mages, *C*ognitions, *I*nterpersonal Relationships, and *D*rugs or other Medical Procedures. Therapy does not "attack" each of the dimensions, but each must be explored to understand the patient's problems adequately. "Perhaps the simplest way of expressing the multi-modal rationale is to underscore that comprehensive psychotherapy at the very least requires the correction of irrational beliefs, unpleasant feelings, deviant behaviors, stressful relationships, intrusive images, negative sensations, and possible biochemical imbalances."

In undertaking the treatment of a patient with a sexual disorder, the therapist has to keep in mind the influence of the spouse. The spouse may be helpful or may sabotage the treatment for her own neurotic reasons.

A 35-year-old professional man, married for eight years, came for treatment after his wife discovered him cross-dressing. He had begun to feel so guilty about cross-dressing, which he had done prior to as well as during his marriage, that he had unconsciously manipulated the situation so that his wife was certain to discover his behavior. His episodes of cross-dressing were almost always a consequence of sexual failure with his wife (usually her rejection of his request for sex). On at least one occasion an episode occurred after a competitive failure— failing to win his club's tennis tournament— which he had been expected to do. The patient's wife had been previously married to an aggressive and domineering man who insisted on having sex whenever he wanted it and in whatever way he wanted it. On the rebound, she married a passive, gentle man, although she did not know about his cross-dressing. She insisted on having sex *only* when she initiated it and with her on top during intercourse. The patient's frustration, anger and self-depreciation grew in intensity, and his cross-dressing increased in frequency until he was discovered by his wife. During the first several months of treatment, in which the therapist was seeing the couple conjointly as well as seeing the husband individually, the couple attended a costume party. With great glee the wife revealed that she had dressed her husband in her own female tennis outfit as his costume!

This shows that treatment of the patient alone, without attempting to change the wife's attitudes and behavior, would certainly have been doomed to failure.

Adaptation to a Deviant Role

Sometimes, the therapist can best help the patient by assisting him to adapt to, rather than change, his deviant role. In such a case adaptation often can be facilitated by counseling the patient's partner to accept the paraphilia.

A masochistic male who was involved in a long-term relationship with a divorced female came for treatment of impotence. He disclosed that his partner was dismayed by his mild bondage desires (wanting to be tied to the bed). After the couple was seen conjointly, the woman was able to decrease her negative feelings toward the bondage behavior and learned to participate freely in the bondage game. The patient's impotence disappeared and sexual gratification for both increased.

Transvestism

Because of the fact that it is often confused with transsexualism, transvestism has been selected from among the paraphilias for extended discussion. Although in rare cases transvestism will evolve into transsexualism, the two disorders are distinct diagnostic entities that require different treatment objectives and approaches.

Transvestism basically means dressing in clothes of the opposite sex, but its clinical meaning is more limited. It is a compulsion, apparently peculiar to exclusively or predominantly heterosexual males, to cross-dress under the pressure of unconscious sexual identity conflicts and anxieties. Typically, the cross-dressing is fetishistic; that is, it enhances or is necessary for sexual arousal, although sometimes arousal is absent, denied or fades away even though the compulsion continues. Women may dress as men for a variety of psychopathological motivations, but the fetishistic quality and erotic arousal accompanying cross-dressing is typically missing.

As boys, transvestites are typically masculine but may fantasize about cross-dressing or being female. Cross-dressing usually begins in childhood or adolescence, and only occasionally in adulthood. Some transvestites say that their cross-dressing was initiated by their mother, an older sister or other female relative or in some cases by their father, often ostensibly as a punishment; others claim it was self-initiated. Usually cross-dressing involves sexual arousal from the start or is soon associated with it. At first, cross-dressing is accompanied by masturbation. Later it may be used to increase arousal with a partner or may be necessary in order to have intercourse. Transvestism usually progresses from partial to complete, and from secret to private-within-the-home to publicly trying to pass as a woman. Masochistic and bondage/dominance scenarios are often acted out along with the transvestic behavior.

Except for the few who become secondary transsexuals, transvestites greatly value their male genitals and their heterosexuality, although some report occasional homosexual encounters, usually when cross-dressed. Transvestism is invariably a sign of emotional illness. Transvestites are prone to depression, and suicide attempts are common. Useful reviews have been published concerning the developmental psychodynamics, which are varied and complex.[3,20]

Despite such problems, few transvestites voluntarily seek professional help even if they experience subjective distress over their cross-dressing. They tend to be highly defensive and to deny that their activity is indicative of disorder. Most who seek medical attention are forced to do so by wives or by courts (if their cross-dressing results in arrest), or as a result of suicide attempts or of injury resulting from masochistic behavior. If they can be engaged in therapy at all, it must be with a qualified mental health professional who specializes in such disorders. The results are often disappointing. Few of these patients are motivated to seek psychoanalysis, and few are appropriate candidates for it, even though analysis is probably the only modality that could restructure the unconscious sources of their transvestism. Various forms of behavior modification and group therapy have been reported, but the prognosis for adults is poor.

As might be expected, most transvestites have poor marriages that end in divorce. Some wives are shocked to discover their husbands' transvestism.

Wives who are relatively healthy emotionally disengage themselves from the marriage unless the husband is amenable to therapy. But a surprising number of wives condone or even encourage and cooperate in the cross-dressing. These women have complementary sexual conflicts of their own,[4] and many are discontented even though they deny any major strain on their marriages.[21] They may complain to their physicians, but the physicians often run into a brick wall when they try to help them explore and modify their contributory roles. Wives who had no prior knowledge of the transvestism and play no overt or covert role in the cross-dressing often need, and are deeply grateful for, support during a husband's therapy or the period of painful decision-making if he resists or does not respond to treatment.

Other Forms Of Treatment

Often drugs are used in the treatment of the paraphilias (e.g., anticonvulsants if temporal lobe seizures precede or accompany episodes of fetishism, psychotropic drugs to counteract any depression or anxiety that may be triggering paraphiliac acts). Of special interest are the antiandrogens;[22] cyproterone acetate and methyloestrenolone have been used in Europe and medroxyprogesterone acetate (MPA) has been used experimentally in the United States. Cyproterone acetate reduces sexual desire and impairs erectile and orgastic capacity in men. The drug acts on testosterone binding sites, including those in the brain, to inhibit the hypothalamic-pituitary-testicular axis. Although it has been used with great effectiveness in the treatment of sex offenders in Europe, this drug has not been approved by the FDA for clinical use in the United States. The ban primarily has been due to ethical considerations. MPA acts primarily on the pituitary to cause a decrease in LH and, thus, a decrease in testosterone levels. MPA is presently marketed in the United States for other indications and is undergoing clinical trials in the United States for use in sex offenders.

Measuring Sexual Arousal

Techniques for measuring sexual arousal through the presentation of different types of stimuli (e.g., erotic writing, pictures, films) have been developed for experimental and therapeutic purposes. Abel[23] and others have used the penile transducer to objectively measure the arousal pattern of those persons termed by Abel as "sexual aggressives" (rapists and child molesters, for the most part). The patient is asked to fantasize sexual scenes, to watch videotapes or slides depicting a variety of sexual behaviors or partners, or to listen to audiotaped descriptions of sexual scenes. The patient's erection measured by the penile transducer, can be calibrated as a per cent of his full erection. In this way his response to a variety of stimuli can be measured, ranging from pure aggression, through a mixture of aggression and sex, to intercourse between consenting adults. The patient then is alternately given instructions to become aroused and to suppress arousal through concentration so that his capacity to control sexual excitement can be determined.

Treatment Objectives And Recommendations

Based on their studies of sexual aggressives, Abel and his coworkers[23] offer a list of treatment objectives and recommendations. These are applicable even if the paraphilia does not involve overt aggression. (One hypothesis is that *all* paraphilias are based on unconscious aggression as a defense against specific childhood trauma).

1. Decreasing deviant sexual arousal. Various behavior therapy techniques, as well as medroxyprogesterone, might be used to reduce those fantasies and impulses that precede the sexual aggressives' paraphiliac behavior.

2. Developing adequate heterosexual arousal.[18] If the paraphiliac is unable to have adequate sexual arousal with adult partners, he cannot perform sexually with them unless he uses deviant behavior. Masturbatory conditioning and systematic desensitization are effective in assisting the patient to develop heterosexual arousal with adult partners.

3. Developing heterosocial skills. Many paraphiliacs lack the skills required to establish a relationship with another adult. Various techniques, including modeling, role-playing, social reinforcement and video feedback performance, can help the patient achieve these skills.

4. Training in assertiveness. It is not uncommon to find that a lack of assertiveness leads to inappropriate sexual aggressive behavior in a situation in which the patient thinks he has full control. Assertiveness training can be used to decrease this compensatory aggression.

5. Training in empathy. If the paraphiliac has great difficulty in achieving intimacy, especially with females, or does not understand the effect of his behavior on others, these skill deficiencies can be assessed and treated systematically.

6. Attaining of sexual knowledge. If paraphiliac behavior is partly due to ignorance, this ignorance can be assessed through a variety of sex knowledge inventories and then corrected.

7. Treating sexual dysfunction within the marital unit. As indicated earlier, the treatment of specific sexual dysfunctions (e.g., impotence or premature ejaculation, preorgasmia or significant marital problems) may help significantly to reduce the patient's paraphiliac behavior.

Although all seven components of treatment may not be necessary for each patient, evaluation must be carried out to determine the patient's needs. Follow-up is essential to ensure that the patient has learned not only how to control his deviant behavior, but how to initiate and maintain activities that are more rewarding than his previous deviant ones, thereby enabling him to reinforce his new behavior pattern and form a new nondeviant relationship with society.

EGO-DYSTONIC HOMOSEXUALITY

The phenomenology of homosexual behavior is discussed in Chapter 6. Here are discussed only sexual conflicts for which some homosexuals request treatment.

Discussing the treatment of homosexuals does not imply that all homosexuals should be treated with the aim of a shift to heterosexual orientation. Unless a person forces his homosexuality upon others—a misuse of sexuality that is no more characteristic of homosexuals than of heterosexuals—it is a private matter to be respected in every way. But some homosexuals seek treatment for sexual problems, and some wish to become heterosexual. The primary physician needs sufficient information to provide treatment or referral.

The recent pressure for homosexual rights has fostered positive changes, but it has also created some medical attitudes that can be detrimental to some homosexuals. In the militant belief that all problems related to the homosexual's orientation are caused by society's antihomosexual attitudes, some psychiatrists, both heterosexual and homosexual, refuse to treat a homosexual who requests change; they even refuse, regardless of how desperate the patient's state of mind, to refer the person to another psychiatrist who can and will treat him.[24] Forcing a prohomosexual ideology on a patient is no more medically ethical than forcing treatment designed to produce unwanted change to heterosexuality.

Another detrimental position, held by some homosexuals and groups, is ignoring or denying the scientific literature and insisting publicly that preferential or exclusive homosexuality cannot be changed. This attitude not only discourages some persons who are miserable over their homosexuality and could change, but it also affects the beliefs of some physicians. Most physicians now in practice have had no training in sexual behavior; most medical schools now offer some courses in human sexuality, but the average young physician still has less clinical knowledge about sexuality than about most other areas of medicine. The physician who is not informed may discourage a homosexual who is seeking change rather than make a helpful referral.

The published data on shift in orientation among homosexuals of both sexes after psychoanalysis or psychoanalytically-oriented psychotherapy are remarkably consistent: About one-third or more of those patients who wish to change and who remain in treatment become exclusively heterosexual, and about one-third more become bisexual or preferentially heterosexual.[25-28] A somewhat higher reversal rate has been reported with the use of psychoanalytic group therapy in groups composed entirely of homosexuals.[29]

Behavior modification therapy is more controversial on certain grounds. Statistical follow-up results are poor to questionable.[30-31] Ethical problems arise regarding the use of aversion therapy (the use of electric shock, emetics or other unpleasant stimuli to extinguish arousal by homosexual objects). Furthermore, the loss of homosexual arousal does not mean that a person will become heterosexually arousable. More recent behavioral techniques avoid aversive stimuli and attempt to replace homosexual arousal by heterosexual arousal. These methods hold more promise, but the number of patients is very small and no statistically significant follow-up studies have been published. For a review of treatment modalities, rationales and statistics, see Karlen.[32]

Masters and Johnson[33] have recently reported successful shift to preferential or exclusive heterosexuality in over 70 per cent of homosexual clients who were dissatisfied with their homosexuality. A modification of their therapy techniques for sexual dysfunction was used. Some professionals have questioned whether their patient population is representative, and Masters and Johnson have not published their therapeutic procedures in adequate detail to permit replicative studies; thus, it is not known how generally applicable their results may be. However, this is a potentially effective and practical new modality for homosexuals who wish to shift to heterosexuality.

Some homosexuals who want to change have a far better than average chance of doing so, some far worse. Prognosis for change depends on many variables in family relationships, motivation, sexual history and ego strength.[25,28]

Since a reasonable proportion of homosexuals can become heterosexual with sufficient motivation and appropriate therapy, the physician must know to whom to refer them. All such persons require referral to a mental health professional, but the majority of such professionals are quite pessimistic about these patients; either they were taught that outmoded attitude or they were not trained for such work and their previous attempts were unsuccessful. If the physician does not know of specialists in this field, it is often wise to consult the department of psychiatry at the nearest medical school or the local psychiatric association, or to be sure that the therapist to whom one makes referral is a certified psychoanalyst or other qualified mental health professional with successful experience in working with homosexuals. Should any question exist, it is entirely in order to contact that physician and explore his or her attitudes and experience in working with homosexuals who wish to become heterosexual.

Special dilemmas arise concerning homosexuals whose sexual behavior is of a criminal nature, such as rapists, homosexual pedophiles and those who commit homosexual incest. Some states provide for enforced treatment of homosexual criminals, itself a policy of questionable ethics and legality. The issue is confused by the legal position that prisoners are incapable of giving valid informed consent. There exist very promising forms of therapy for criminals who exhibit sexual dyscontrol, both homosexual and heterosexual—not only aversive techniques, but the use of antiandrogens[34] and androgen-depleting chemicals.[35] These agents cause reversible diminution or elimination of sex drive, and during this time therapy often has succeeded in removing the compulsion toward antisocial behavior. Many heterosexual and homosexual offenders would gladly accept such treatment in preference to long jail sentences and the likelihood of continued and uncontrolled antisocial impulses. However, such therapy is often unavailable because federal and/or state laws invalidate a criminal's right to consent to it. A physician faced with a patient in such a dilemma should refer him to the most authoritative professionals in the area who may have experience in helping the patient obtain judicial consent to treatment.

Some homosexuals who profess no desire to shift their orientation present many of the same sexual dysfunctions as heterosexuals, such as primary and secondary impotence, retarded ejaculation and female anorgasmia (premature ejaculation is rarely a male homosexual complaint). The therapy for these dysfunctions is essentially no different than with heterosexual pairs,[33] except that it requires a therapist or cotherapists sufficiently free of sexual biases to proceed regardless of the patients' orientation.

Different problems are posed by homosexual patients who do not wish to change but whose emotional distresses are in some way directly related to their homosexuality. For instance, some effeminate males and their female counterparts are socially and occupationally stigmatized; others feel shame that impairs their self-confidence and assertiveness. It is often useful to help them find and use the services and emotional support of local homophile organizations. Special assertiveness training groups also may be beneficial.

The main complaint of many homosexuals (more males than females) is difficulty in finding partners for lasting, committed, monogamous relationships. Social disapproval of homosexuality may increase this difficulty, but it is not clear whether this is a major factor. Homosexuals have not identified in sexual orientation with the same-sex parent, an identification that is the natural outcome of a healthy family childhood. It is predictable, therefore, to find ambivalence or even hostility, whether conscious or unconscious, toward someone the same sex as the parent who was unacceptable as a sexual model. Such hostility is ubiquitous among those seen clinically. It is not known to what extent this is true of the nonclinical population; however, to whatever extent it is, difficulty with long-term commitments may be a built-in liability of homosexual orientation.

Every homosexual patient deserves to be treated in accordance with his or her wishes, not the bias of a psychiatrist. Nevertheless, the psychiatrist owes it to a patient to discuss any unrealistic expectations. Sometimes patients with serious symptoms and deep emotional conflicts ask that they be cured without dealing with sexual orientation. Perhaps in some cases this is possible, but in most people the various aspects of mental and emotional function influence each other. A patient who opens himself to change must recognize that he is also opening himself to exploring the dynamic origins of all his development, including sexuality. Not all homosexuals who discover the origins of their orientation do or need to shift it but, in psychoanalytic therapy, previously denied conflicts or dissatisfactions over homosexuality may emerge and reassessment of the possibility or desirability of change may occur.

The treatment of patients with the diagnosis of a gender identity disorder, paraphilia or ego-dystonic homosexuality should be carried out by psychiatrists or other experienced psychotherapists. The primary-care physician must be sufficiently informed and concerned, even in the face of strong inner feelings that may be aroused by the nature of the sexual acts under consideration, so that he can establish and maintain a therapeutic relationship. Taking a careful history and making an appraisal, including the degree of severity of the behavior and of the patient's personality organization, will enable the physician to make a more informed referral. The patient's interview with the primary-care physician may "make or break" the possibility of treatment. The physician, if understanding and concerned, will help the patient accept treatment; if the physician is shocked, angered or disgusted, he may effectively prevent any possibility of treatment.

References

1. Stoller RJ: *Sex and Gender, Vol II: The Transsexual Experiment*. New York, Aronson, 1976.
2. Meyer J: Clinical variants among applicants for sex reassignment. *Arch Sex Behav* 1974; 3:527-558.
3. Person E, Ovesey L: Transvestism: New perspectives. *J Am Acad Psychoanal* 1978; 6:301-323.
4. Stoller RJ: Transvestites' women. *Am J Psychiatry* 1967; 124:333-339.
5. Stoller RJ: *Sex and Gender*. New York, Science House, 1968.
6. Barlow DH, et al: Gender identity change in a transsexual. *Arch Gen Psychiatry* 1973; 28:569-576.
7. Davenport CW, Harrison SI: Gender identity change in a female adolescent transsexual. *Arch Sex Behav* 1977; 6:327-340.
8. Barlow DH, et al: Gender identity change in a transsexual: An exorcism. *Arch Sex Behav* 1977; 6:387-395.
9. Morgan AJ Jr: Psychotherapy for transsexual candidates screened out of surgery. *Arch Sex Behav* 1978; 7:273-283.
10. Green R: *Sexual Identity Conflicts in Children and Adults*. New York, Basic Books Inc, 1974.
11. Gebhard PH, et al: *Sex Offenders*. New York, Harper and Row Publishers Inc, 1965.
12. Resnik H, Wolfgang M: *Treatment of the Sex Offender*. Boston, Little, Brown & Company, 1972.
13. Stoller RJ: *Perversion: The Erotic Form of Hatred*. New York, Pantheon Books, 1975.
14. Peters JJ: Children who are victims of sexual assault and the psychology of offenders. *Am J Psychother* 1976; 30:398-421.
15. Meyer JK: Individual psychotherapy of sexual disorders, in Sadock BJ, et al (eds): *The Sexual Experience*. Baltimore, Williams and Wilkins Inc, 1976.
16. Bancroft J: The behavioral approach to sexual disorders, in Milne H (ed): *Psychosexual Problems*. Baltimore, University Park Press, 1976.
17. Marks IM, et al: Sexual deviants two years after electric aversion. *Br J Psychiatry* 1970; 117:173-185.
18. Barlow DH: Increasing heterosexual responsiveness in the treatment of sexual deviation: A review of the clinical and experimental evidence. *Behav Ther* 1973; 4:655-671.
19. Lazarus AA, Rosen RC: Behavior therapy techniques in the treatment of sexual disorders, in Meyer JK (ed): *Clinical Management of Sexual Disorders*. Baltimore, Williams and Wilkins Inc, 1976.

20. Ovesey L, Person E: Gender identity and sexual psychopathology in men: A psychodynamic analysis of homosexuality, transsexualism, and transvestism. *J Am Acad Psychoanal* 1973; 1:53-72.
21. Beigel HG: A weekend in Alice's wonderland. *J Sex Res* 1969; 5:108-122.
22. Walker PA: The role of antiandrogens in the treatment of sex offenders, in Qualls CB, et al (eds): *The Prevention of Sexual Disorders*. New York, Plenum Press Inc, 1978.
23. Abel GG, et al: Aggressive behavior and sex. *Psychiatr Clin North Am* (Apr) 1980; 3(1):133-151.
24. Davison GC: Homosexuality and the ethics of behavioral intervention: Paper 1. Homosexuality, the ethical challenge. *J Homosexuality* 1977; 2:195-259.
25. Bieber I, et al: *Homosexuality: A Psychoanalytic Study*. New York, Basic Books Inc, 1962.
26. Mayerson P, Lief HT: Psychotherapy of homosexuals: A follow-up study of nineteen cases, in Marmor J (ed): *Sexual Inversion*. New York, Basic Books Inc, 1965.
27. Kaye HE, et al: Homosexuality in women. *Arch Gen Psychiatry* 1967; 17:626-634.
28. Hatterer LJ: *Changing Homosexuality in the Male*. New York, McGraw-Hill Book Company, 1970.
29. Hadden SB: Treatment of male homosexuals in groups. *Int J Group Psychother* 1966; 16:13-22.
30. Freund K: Some problems in the treatment of homosexuality, in Eysenck HJ (ed): *Behaviour Therapy and the Neuroses*. Oxford, Pergamon Press, 1960.
31. Feldman MP, MacCulloch MJ: Aversion therapy in management of 43 homosexuals. *Br Med J* 1967; 2:594-597.
32. Karlen A: *Sexuality and Homosexuality*. New York, WW Norton & Company, 1971.
33. Masters WH, Johnson VE: *Homosexuality in Perspective*. Boston, Little, Brown and Company, 1979.
34. Laschet U: Antiandrogen in the treatment of sex offenders: Mode of action and therapeutic outcome, in Zubin J, Money J (eds): *Contemporary Sexual Behavior: Critical Issues in the 1970s*. Baltimore, Johns Hopkins University Press, 1973.
35. Money J, et al: 47,XXY and 46,XY males with antisocial and/or sex offending behavior: Antiandrogen therapy plus counseling. *Psychoneuroendocrinology* 1975; 1:165-178.

Chapter 20

Anxiety in Men About Homosexuality

Sherwyn M. Woods, M.D., Ph.D.

Homosexual preoccupations and anxieties are by no means rare in heterosexual men. Physicians, particularly those working with adolescents or young adults, frequently encounter heterosexual men who have become anxious because of homosexual thoughts, dreams or "impulses." Although less common, similar anxiety also may occur in homosexual men who have not yet recognized and accepted their homosexuality or are struggling with the conflict of whether or not to act on their homosexual wishes and impulses. The DSM-III[1] labels this syndrome "ego-dystonic homosexuality."

In the more usual situation, a heterosexual man, often at time of stress or crisis, will begin to experience obsessional homosexual thoughts, fleeting or even elaborate homosexual fantasies, homosexual dreams, or severe anxiety or hostility in the presence of homosexual men. Such episodes may be occasional or episodic, or the individual may become preoccupied, even obsessed, with the ideation; the frequency and intensity of the episodes depend on personality and other neurotic conflicts that may exist.

The most common clinical presentation is anxiety, sometimes of panic proportions. Common precipitants include being thrown into intimate proximity with other men, as in a military or dormitory situation; a loss of masculine pride and self-esteem, as after a failure in sexual performance; a social or vocational failure; or use of marijuana or alcohol, which releases inhibitions and allows awareness of such preoccupations. Some patients have neurotic depression; others simply complain of obsessional homosexual thoughts or fantasies. Since men in our culture have difficulty discussing anything that impugns their masculinity, patients are often reluctant to reveal the source of their anxiety or depression. Sometimes the conflict is so threatening that it is driven out of conscious awareness, and the patient fails to connect it to his symptoms. Still others complain only of the somatic equivalents of their anxiety or depression, such as sleeplessness, vague or unusual body sensations, and body preoccupations.

Homosexual anxiety is particularly common in student health centers. Probably a great many male patients are treated symptomatically for anxiety and depression without the physician being aware that concerns about homosexuality are an important etiological factor.

Studies of male medical students have revealed that 37.5 per cent expressed considerable fear of "latent homosexuality," although actual and overt homosexuality were relatively rare.[2,3] Review of a random sample of 200 medical students, interns and residents seeking psychiatric consultation at a student psychiatry service showed similar results.[4] It is doubtful that the findings would be different in any other population of young male professionals. Psychotherapists commonly encounter anxiety about homosexuality, and Bieber et al[5] reported that only 41 per cent of their heterosexual male patients were free of homosexual concerns. Homosexual trends (defined as anxiety, fantasies, dreams, obsessive thoughts, or fears of homosexuality) were found to be moderate or severe in 42 per cent and mild in 17 per cent of the patients. At least half of any group of male patients in psychotherapy are likely at some time to talk about such concerns or express worries about becoming homosexual.[6]

Anxiety about homosexuality also occurs in middle-aged or older men, but less frequently than in young men. In such older males, there is usually a history of transient homosexual anxieties earlier in life. The greater clinical incidence in younger males is no surprise; they are learning to deal with sexual drives and attempting to achieve masculine adequacy and self-esteem. Any failure in masculine self-esteem, no matter what its source, may be expressed in the form of fears about homosexuality.

Women also have anxiety about homosexuality and conflicts about feminine self-esteem,[7-9] but they rarely show the severe anxiety and panic states about homosexuality seen in men. It has been suggested that the reason is society's more positive attitudes toward masculinity.[9] In this view, a woman is not so threatened if she discovers she has masculine aspirations. Women in our culture characteristically respond to a loss of feminine self-esteem with sadness, depression and despair, while men are more likely, at least initially, to respond to loss of masculine self-esteem with severe anxiety. Other theorists explain this discrepancy by developmental differences in the way boys and girls manage castration anxiety.

PSEUDOHOMOSEXUALITY

To understand homosexual preoccupations and fantasies in heterosexual men, one must recognize that these feelings may stem from either sexual or nonsexual conflicts. Ovesey established the basic psychodynamics of this important clinical distinction in a series of classical papers.[7,10-14] He and other clinicians believe that *non-erotic motivations*, such as strivings for dependence and power, also can give rise to homosexual ideation or fantasies in heterosexual patients.[6,8,15-17] Few of these patients are overtly bisexual or suffer from true latent homosexuality, i.e., homosexuality that is not yet in conscious awareness. To presume, as was usually done in the past, that such thoughts or fantasies must stem from unconscious and repressed homosexuality is dangerous. In the majority of such patients, homosexual fantasies and ideation are unaccompanied by erotic feelings, arousal or behavior. Ovesey says: "I found that in every such instance. . .the fantasies were motivated either by dependency needs or by power needs. . .through the symbolic use of genital organs for nonsexual purposes."[14] In other words, the imagery is homosexual in form but the underlying motivation is not erotic in nature.

The patient understandably misinterprets these fantasies as being truly homosexual, but in fact they are only symbolically so. If one studies heterosexual males who experience homosexual thoughts or fantasies, the large majority have no associated erotic arousal or desire for homosexual activity.[6,8,15-17]

Homosexual ideation and fantasy, then, are best understood by examining three possible motivations—sex, dependence and power. The sexual component, aimed at erotic gratification, produces "true homosexual anxiety," and the associated conflicts are "true homosexual conflicts." The dependence and power components use the ideation of genital organs and acts to express nonsexual motives. Dependence and power motivations are more accurately termed "pseudohomosexual," and the associated anxiety, "pseudohomosexual anxiety."[9]

Homosexual males can have both pseudohomosexual and true homosexual (erotic) motivations. In fact, in homosexuals the dependence and power elements play a large role in determining the nature of the actual homosexual act, as well as the types of partners sought.[9]

Since the majority of males who are preoccupied with homosexual fantasies or thoughts are struggling with pseudohomosexual rather than true homosexual conflicts, one should take care not to presume latent homosexuality unless there is evidence of erotic desire or arousal. Arousal may be acknowledged directly by the patient or inferred on the basis of orgastic dreams or erotic fantasies involving homosexual activity. A man's pseudohomosexual anxieties are most often precipitated by a crisis of masculine self-esteem arising from failure to live up to his own criteria of masculinity or adult adequacy.[9,15] Because these criteria are often quite unrealistic, it is no surprise that such persons also frequently experience considerable depression.

Common precipitants of pseudohomosexual anxieties are failure in self-assertion, often in power struggles with other men; competitive defeat by other men, especially in love or work; failure to achieve a sense of activity and dominance in relationships with women, resulting in intense feelings of shame about submission or passivity; threatened or actual exposure of deep, shameful dependency needs; and real or imagined inadequacies in heterosexual performance. When these problems occur, they commonly do so at normal maturational milestones, such as falling in love, marrying and becoming a parent.[15]

Homosexual ideation may arise in response to interference with important defensive adaptations, such as pathological dependency or problems with power figures. Any adaptive failure in life, be it social, sexual, or vocational, may be perceived unconsciously as a failure in fulfilling the masculine role and thereby give rise to fears of homosexuality. The unconscious thought process is: I am a failure → I am castrated → I am not a man → I am like a woman → I am homosexual. These ideas are derived from culturally determined stereotypes and attitudes about the relative value and status of men and women.

In our society, masculinity is equated with strength, dominance and superiority; femininity with weakness, submissiveness and inferiority. Men tend to identify such masculinity with success and such femininity with failure. This equation is a caricature of the social definition of masculinity and of the social judgment that "femininity" and homosexuality are failures for which a man must suffer humiliation. When men suffer inhibitions of assertion or experience adaptive life failure, they experience the pseudohomosexual equation and thereby call into play psychological defenses that use dependence or power to repair damage already done or to ward off future damage. Unfortunately, this tactic only aggravates the situation. For example, an adult who experiences failure and distress in an important sexual, social, or vocational situation may develop powerful unconscious wishes for infantile dependence—to be cared for, protected, and nurtured and to have others take all responsibility for his welfare. Such wishes are humiliating to adult masculine pride.

The situation may be further aggravated by another unconsious symbolic mental process: The individual wishes to recapture masculine strength by absorbing or "transfusing" it from another and stronger male. Since the penis is a strong symbol of masculine power and since sucking, or "taking in," is a strong symbol of infantile dependence, fantasies or dreams ensue that involve clutching at a strong male, sucking on a man's penis, or capturing the penis anally. In this way, the dependent male attempts to repair his sense of masculine inadequacy by appropriating another's masculine strength. However, such efforts are doomed to failure, not only because they are "magical" and symbolic, but because they are interpreted literally by the patient as being homosexual and increase the very anxiety they were meant to alleviate.

A 28-year-old recent law school graduate was about to try his first case and was severely reprimanded by the judge for failure to attend to some technicality. This occurred in open court and the patient felt humiliated in front of both his clients and the other lawyers, with whom he felt very competitive. That evening he tried to find solace with his girlfriend and found for the first time that he could not maintain his erection. During the night he dreamed that he was being cuddled by a large and powerfully built older man and that after a while he began to suck on this man's penis with a sense of contentment and relaxation. The patient awoke in panic. Over the next several weeks he became obsessively preoccupied with looking at men's crotches and wondering about the size of their genitals. At no time did he feel erotic arousal and there was no history of homoerotic arousal or experience. The patient appeared in his physician's office with a severe anxiety panic based upon fear that he was becoming a homosexual.

Such patients have fantasies or dreams of fellatio, anal intercourse, or stroking, fondling, or in some other way experiencing another man's maleness or strength. Men with obsessive-compulsive personalities are particularly prone to organize their obsessional thinking or behaviors around such feelings. They also may become frantic about the possibility of losing control and acting on their "impulses." Such men are almost invariably preoccupied with feelings of masculine inadequacy—that their bodies are feminine, their penises too small, their manliness questioned by others.

The unassertive male may attempt to deny his weakness by acting out its opposite in a compensatory striving for power.[11] Dependence and power strivings can be considered as opposite sides of a coin. The power-driven dependent male is constantly in competition and views relationships with men in terms of dominance and submission; in his view, the weaker male is forced to submit, like a woman, to the stronger male. Such men are so certain of their inadequacy that they usually concede defeat in advance. They chronically anticipate humiliation of their masculine pride. Chronic pseudohomosexual anxiety leads to a paranoid expectation of homosexual assault, frequently symbolized in the form of anal rape.[12] Such individuals are preoccupied with feelings of powerlessness, fantasies of physical assault, and expectations that they will be caught off guard and rendered powerless. This is consistent with the observation that the conflict in paranoid men arises from fear of retaliatory attack, injury and destruction by more powerful males whose power they would like to steal.[18,19]

Anxiety about homosexuality is particularly common in patients who respond to success with anxiety instead of pleasure.[13,15] They present symptoms of anxiety or depression after attaining life goals. Some men try to avoid anxiety by unconsciously sabotaging their potential success in advance. Such a man projects his own envy onto other men, presuming that they will attack, castrate and humiliate him should he have the audacity to be successful or powerful.

A senior medical student with an excellent academic record wanted to drop out of medical school a few months before graduation. Though exclusively heterosexual in behavior and arousal, he was panic stricken that he was "becoming gay." During his senior year he had become increasingly uncertain of his desire to be a physician and had become phobic of strange or dimly lit places because of fantasies that he would be "attacked from the rear." This fear had gradually merged into fantasies and dreams of being forced by the attacker to perform fellatio and submit to anal intercourse. His symptoms had their source not in repressed or latent homosexuality but in dependence and power conflicts rising from Oedipal rivalry with his physician father. His symptoms had been precipitated by anticipation of receiving his medical degree. He unconsciously equated this with a rivalrous attack on his father. His pseudohomosexual fantasies and fears revived his feeling of certainty that only humiliation and defeat could follow such competition and his unconscious wish to magically incorporate his father's power, symbolized by the father's penis.

Fear of homosexual assault in a power struggle leads some patients to violence in an attempt to ward off the humiliation of competitive defeat or of dependent longings.[16] This violence may be directed at the physician. In these cases, violence is a defensive and restorative act to reclaim masculine self-esteem by aggressively dominating and overpowering another. It also denies the passive and dependent longings that the patient symbolically links to femininity. The mental equation is: I dominate, control, annihilate → I am not castrated → I am not a woman → I am not a homosexual.

Unconscious pseudohomosexual conflicts also may be expressed in competitive, compulsive and stereotyped attitudes and behavior in relationships with women. Such chauvinism is neurotic and extends beyond any cultural bias of Western society. Like violence, it can be an attempt to ward off a sense of masculine failure (symbolized as homosexuality) through depreciation of women. Such men are very vulnerable to anxiety about homosexuality when their defenses fail or when their chauvinistic attitudes are challenged, as by an encounter with a capable or "liberated" woman.[17]

We have said that pseudohomosexual conflicts may coexist with true homosexual conflicts. The physician may encounter heterosexual patients who have unconscious erotic homosexual desires combined with pseudohomosexual conflicts.

It is essential that the physician recognize the extent of panic and the sense of personal devastation that can be experienced by patients struggling with either true or pseudohomosexual conflicts. Despair to the point of suicide or suicidal ruminations are not uncommon; neither are hypermasculine behavior, a propensity to violence, or compensatory and frantic heterosexual activity. Don Juanism is much more often a response to pseudohomosexual anxiety than to latent homosexuality.

If it is quite clear that the conflicts are pseudohomosexual rather than homosexual, the physician's firm, unequivocable statement that the patient is not a homosexual but is using homosexual constructs to symbolize other problems will usually bring great relief.[14,16] Such reassurance should not be given until the physician is certain that the anxiety is actually pseudohomosexual; otherwise it may accentuate rather than relieve the patient's fears. Patients with either severe problems or with mixed problems should be referred for psychiatric consultation and treatment. Again, the physician must be sensitive to the possibility that the patient will consider such referral further evidence of his inadequacy and masculine failure. However, even patients with true homosexual anxiety are reassured by the fact that many exclusively homosexual men can become exclusively heterosexual with psychotherapy; it follows that it would be less difficult for a heterosexual male to resolve homosexual conflicts and anxieties.[15]

TRUE HOMOSEXUAL ANXIETY

True homosexual anxiety, as mentioned earlier, arises from erotic motivations that produce homosexual fantasies, impulses, dreams, or behavior. When motivation is erotic, ideation is usually associated with sexual arousal. A man in whom this is true may have a history of episodic homosexual experience, report erotic feelings in the presence of men, and masturbate to fantasies of homosexual activity. Classical psychoanalytic theory ascribed this to repressed homosexual impulses remaining from a normal bisexual developmental phase. Many analysts now question this concept[8,10] as does the author, preferring to view most homoerotic impulses as a defensive retreat from heterosexual anxieties.[8,9,20] Unconscious conflict during the developmental process may create fear and a sense of danger about heterosexual interests; this can lead to a fearful renunciation of heterosexuality and a defensive diversion of sexual impulses to the "safer" homosexual object.

If such dynamics have been a profound part of psychosexual development, a person will reach adolescence or young adulthood with a basically homosexual orientation. There is usually a history of homosexual experiences or arousal, but these experiences may have been so threatening that the person tried to repress or deny them.

Similar conflicts of a lesser degree may leave an individual basically heterosexual but with a residue of true homosexual conflicts and some potential for homoerotic interest. This interest may be expressed as fleeting homosexual arousal or erotic fantasies or it may be blocked from consciousness, to emerge only at times of heightened heterosexual anxiety—on the occasion of first coitus, of emotional intimacy with a valued woman, or of marriage or parenthood. Since there are almost always pseudohomosexual conflicts as well, sexual, vocational, or social failures that threaten masculine self-esteem or arouse intense feelings of powerlessness and dependence may precipitate homosexual ideation or interest. If powerful and unacceptable homosexual awareness or arousal rises toward consciousness, it may lead to a "homosexual panic."

Patients experiencing homosexual panic represent true psychiatric emergencies. They run a high risk of severe psychiatric decompensation or even suicide. Such reactions may be particularly deep and disruptive in adolescents who often feel blocked from seeking professional help because of fearfulness about telling their parents of their problem.

In patients struggling with severe psychoneuroses or incipient psychoses, the failures in repression and general disruption of psychological defenses may cause psychiatric decompensation to be ushered in by way of a homosexual panic. Obsessional and paranoid individuals are especially prone to homosexual and/or pseudohomosexual conflict.[13,16,18,19] Psychotic patients may have considerable homosexual preoccupations, including delusional beliefs; in most cases, the pseudohomosexual issues are of greatest importance.

ANXIETY ABOUT HOMOSEXUALITY IN MEDICAL PRACTICE

Not all individuals with homosexual and pseudohomosexual anxiety are found in the offices of psychiatrists and in psychiatric emergency rooms. Most of these people never reach psychiatrists' offices, and many do not disclose their anxiety and conflict to their personal physician. However, medical illness and medical and surgical procedures can ignite smoldering pseudohomosexual anxieties. Illness brings enforced passivity, dependence on others, invasions of privacy, and a sense of not controlling one's destiny. Medical procedures may involve touching the genitals or insertion of fingers or instruments into the anus, mouth or urethra. Moreover, such procedures are done by a physician, usually male, who is clearly in a dominant, controlling role. Indeed, the physician is often seen as a parent figure and is invested with the same omnipotence a child ascribes to a parent. It is difficult to imagine another circumstance more likely to revive or aggravate a male's anxiety about masculine inadequacy, dependence, powerlessness, enforced submission, or castration.

A patient with severe problems may respond with a major psychiatric illness or crisis. Some patients develop pathological dependence; others forego medical or surgical treatment because it provokes intolerable anxieties. In more common and less severe situations, there is still potential for disruption or alteration of the physician-patient relationship, which interferes with medical treatment. Noncompliance may arise from a wish to secretly triumph over the physician's orders; hostile and hypermasculine behavior may be expressed toward female medical personnel, or pathological dependence on the physician may prolong recovery or result in hypochondriasis. Some malpractice actions may well be motivated by retaliatory wishes as a defense against pseudohomosexual conflicts that have developed in the context of the physician-patient relationship. In patients with latent homosexual problems, illness or the relationship with the physician may precipitate either a homosexual panic or a pseudohomosexual panic arising from conflict over dependence or power.

Pseudohomosexual conflict and anxiety are not uncommon in physicians and may distort professional behavior.[2,3] An obvious example is medical students who report that they often "forgot" or avoided doing genital or rectal examinations because of their own discomfort. It is easy for a physician to rationalize such behavior and even easier to avoid discussing the patient's sexual history or concerns out of discomfort.[2] Some physicians defensively overcompensate with omnipotence or authoritarianism in order to keep patients at a safe distance. It is easy to convey explicitly or implicitly what one does not want to hear of the patient's homosexual anxieties and thus avoid one's own. Such attitudes not only damage the physician-patient relationship but may prevent the patient from using what may be his only avenue toward finding help for what can be devastating anxiety.

Anxiety about homosexuality in either homosexual or heterosexual men should be given the same careful, unbiased consideration by the physician that he would give any other medical complaint. If this indeed is a major cause of concern for the patient, it is definitely a problem that needs to be addressed. If the underlying source of the anxiety cannot be easily determined and the patient's fears relieved, the physician should refer the patient to a specialist in this type of problem.

References

1. American Psychiatric Association: *Diagnostic & Statistical Manual of Mental Disorders III*. Washington, American Psychiatric Association, 1980
2. Woods SM: A course for medical students in the psychology of sex: Training for sociocultural sensitivity. *Am J Psychiatry* 1969; 125:1508-1519.

3. Woods SM, Natterson J: Sexual attitudes of medical students: Some implications for medical education. *Am J Psychiatry* 1967; 124:323-332.

4. Woods SM: Unpublished data

5. Bieber I, et al: *Homosexuality: A Psychoanalytic Study of Male Homosexuality*. New York, Basic Books Inc, 1962.

6. Bieber I, Bieber T: Heterosexuals who are preoccupied with homosexual thoughts. *Med Aspects Hum Sex* 1975 (April); 9:152-168.

7. Ovesey L: Masculine aspirations in women: An adaptational analysis. *Psychiatry* 1956; 19:341-351.

8. Bieber I: The meaning of homosexual trends in therapy; a round table discussion. *Am J Psychoanal* 1964; 24:60-76.

9. Ovesey L, Woods SM: Pseudohomosexuality and homosexuality in men: Psychodynamics as a guide to treatment, in Marmor J (ed): *Homosexual Behavior: A Modern Reappraisal*. New York, Basic Books Inc, 1980.

10. Ovesey L: The homosexual conflict: An adaptational analysis. *Psychiatry* 1954; 17:243-250.

11. Ovesey L: The pseudohomosexual anxiety. *Psychiatry* 1955; 18:17-25.

12. Ovesey L: Pseudohomosexuality, the paranoid mechanism, and paranoia: An adaptational revision of classical Freudian theory. *Psychiatry* 1955; 18:163-173.

13. Ovesey L: Fear of vocational success: A phobic extension of the paranoid reaction. *Arch Gen Psychiatry* 1962; 7:82-92.

14. Ovesey L: *Homosexuality and Pseudohomosexuality*. New York, Science House, 1969.

15. Bieber I: Homosexual dynamics in psychiatric crisis. *Am J Psychiatry* 1972; 128:1268-1272.

16. Woods SM: Violence: Psychotherapy of pseudohomosexual panic. *Arch Gen Psychiatry* 1972; 27:255-258.

17. Woods SM: Some dynamics of male chauvinism. *Arch Gen Psychiatry* 1976; 33:63-65.

18. Wolowitz NH: Attraction and aversion to power: A psychoanalytic conflict theory of homosexuality in male paranoids. *J Abnorm Psychol* 1965; 70:360-370.

19. Higdon JF: Paranoia: Power conflict or homosexual projection? *J Operation Psychiatry* 1976; 7:42-45.

20. Abernethy V: Dominance and sexual behavior: A hypothesis. *Am J Psychiatry* 1974; 131:813-817.

Chapter 21

Sexual Issues in Reproductive Counseling

Alan J. Wabrek, M.D., and R. Clay Burchell, M.D.

The physician who provides reproductive counseling can make the interchange more meaningful and effective by taking into account some well-known aspects of human behavior and discussing the sexual and relationship issues involved. Physicians, because of their education and experience, have a unique opportunity to become "significant others" to patients in this rather personal area of counseling.

THE TEENAGE PERIOD

Pierson[1] has emphasized that physicians should examine their own attitudes and feelings about adolescents in general and adolescent sexual activity specifically. She states, "I have become quite comfortable with the fact that intercourse can and may represent nothing more than a contemporary version of what was once termed 'heavy petting'; most sexually active individuals of any age or sex will readily acknowledge that not every act of intercourse is endowed with profound human value except for that of that moment." Gray and McGinnis[2] found that adolescents with sexual problems often receive the same kind of "fatherly" advice which they had always found less than helpful at home. This can be compounded by the physician who perceives the patient as his or her own daughter. Seaman[3] found that " . . . common is the paternalistic but kindly practitioner who wishes to spare his young patients embarrassment. So delicate is he, that he may fail to render the service he contracted for." Tyrer[4] has considerable experience in this area and has emphasized that, to be effective with teenagers, the physician must always be sincere, honest and sympathetic, and assure them that confidentiality will be maintained.

The teenage years should be a time of transition from child to adult. To make this transition successful, an individual must have the experience of overcoming repeated challenges: One does not grow and develop without the stimulus of challenging problems. On the other hand, growth may be arrested if a problem is so great that the individual is faced with failure.

Sexual involvement is a particularly difficult issue in contemporary society, because it can become overwhelming so quickly. In terms of potential problems and stress there is, for example, a gigantic difference in kissing, sexual caressing and coitus. One leads naturally to another, and the inexperienced individual may move quickly and inadvertently from kissing to intercourse, viz., from sexual involvement with few problems to sexual involvement with the potential for enormous problems. An unplanned and unwanted pregnancy can overwhelm both partners and initiate "instant maturity" which may produce lifetime sequelae.

The earlier that pregnancy occurs in a woman's life, the more vulnerable she is to such sequelae; this is especially true for adolescent pregnancies. Hornik[5] has emphasized that early childbearing can make it very difficult to fulfill the functions of adolescence in our culture, i.e., separation from parents, determination of a sexual role and identity, development of a value system and choice of a vocation. Pregnancy puts considerable stress on the teenager and may force her to bypass important stages of psychosexual maturation, because she is suddenly expected to fulfill the adult role of motherhood and parenting that at times is difficult even for a mature woman.

Teenage mothers often have unrealistic expectations of their children's growth and development, and they will frequently slap or spank an infant or young child long before he can be expected to understand. Many teenage mothers are not particularly nurturing; in a study in Georgia of children who were neglected or abused, 58 per cent had parents who had begun childbearing in their teens.[6] Approximately 80 per cent of teenage marriages that are precipitated by pregnancy end in divorce.

It is important for the physician to impart information on sexual behavior and relationships in the context of reproductive counseling of adolescents. Most physicians would agree that an individual should not begin childbearing in her teens and that permanent harm should be avoided by limiting inadvertent actions taken on the basis of inexperience. There is a conflict here, because learning about sexual relationships has to involve danger. Some risks must be taken to gain experience; postponing all dating until after age 20 also would be a risk. One of the difficulties that sex counselors face is that they may be searching for perfect alternatives when, from a practical point of view, they should be helping the patient find the best option among several less-than-desirable alternatives.

Some of the best reproductive counseling is provided in contraceptive clinics after the patient has sought help. Unfortunately, counseling at this juncture does not usually prevent the first pregnancy or the first fear of pregnancy. If young people would listen, this same applied education could be imparted earlier, but it would be based on an assumption that society may not wish to enunciate or acknowledge: that because some young teenagers will become sexually involved, they need to know how to use contraceptive devices and methods before they engage in intercourse.

Admittedly, several aspects of such education are controversial. Effective contraception does require motivation and planning, which means that sexually involved individuals must be helped to acknowledge and accept what they are doing. It also is true that contraception requires some degree of sexual competence.

These are not, however, insurmountable obstacles. The American Academy of Pediatrics[7] supports this approach and recommends medical consultation and effective contraceptive advice and methods that are consistent with the teenager's physical and emotional needs. Medical consultation should be available to teenagers whose sexual activity exposes them to risk of pregnancy. There has been a marked increase over the years in the proportion of unmarried teenagers who use contraceptive devices (see Figure 5).

From an idealistic point of view, it may seem that our efforts should be turned to helping a person give up sexual involvement when it is clearly detrimental. Practically, such an approach is difficult and rarely effective.

Figure 5

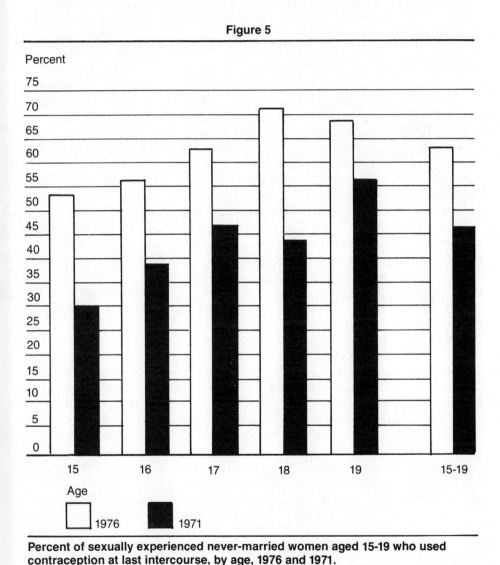

Percent of sexually experienced never-married women aged 15-19 who used contraception at last intercourse, by age, 1976 and 1971.

Reprinted with permission from *Family Planning Perspectives*, Volume 9, Number 2, 1977.

ADULTHOOD

Whereas the problems of the teenage period involve learning about sexuality and relationships, the problems of the middle period involve correlating reproduction with a life pattern. Women are taking more responsibility for themselves, are working to a greater extent and are less willing to be passive about reproduction. Appropriate decisions regarding matters such as contraception, sexual involvement during marriage, relationships during pregnancy and the problems of infertility all require effective knowledge and ability to relate to others. The sexual and relationship issues in reproductive counseling are crucial. The knowledge that another pregnancy will not heal a drifting marriage or bring children closer to a mother may not prevent a woman who needs affiliation from becoming pregnant. Often attention to the issues of vulnerability and intimacy prevents the pregnancy much more effectively.

The middle years are a time for living rather than learning. Although there is sexual, relationship and reproductive involvement, counseling may not be sought or needed unless problems occur. The focus of counseling is mostly on pregnancy and parenting as they affect a woman's sexual responsiveness either directly or indirectly through her partner. Other important questions are: How do different contraceptive methods enhance or inhibit sexuality? How does infertility affect a couple? How does sexual dysfunction cause infertility, and how can the diagnosis and treatment of infertility cause a sexual problem? How do adoption and abortion influence sexuality?

Use of Contraceptives. For many females for whom nonmarital intercourse is prevalent, orgasmic inability or inconsistency reflects psychological inhibitions, but in some instances it may be related to contraceptive measures. The problem may arise through a direct pharmacologic effect or because of the psychological reactions to contraception. Bardwick[8] found a decrease in orgasmic frequency among a sample of collegiate women who were taking oral contraceptives. She attributed this to the guilt and anxiety that the women experienced about being sexually active, although hormonal effects cannot be entirely ruled out. Well-educated, otherwise mature and well-informed women may be abysmally ignorant of sexual and contraceptive information because of prior avoidance of such information when it was needed or desired.

There are important interconnections between relationship dynamics, choice of contraceptive agents and sexual response that should be considered and explored by the prescribing physician. Specific contraceptive methods each may have advantages and disadvantages with respect to sexual functioning.

These methods include the use of diaphragms, creams, foams and jellies inserted into the vagina, or a condom rolled down over the penis. Those persons having short-term sexual relationships usually interrupt the sexual response cycle to put these agents in place. Regular partners are more likely to incorporate the mechanics of insertion or covering into foreplay and, therefore, are likely to be more comfortable with these temporary contraceptives.

The advantages and disadvantages of various temporary contraceptive methods on sexual functioning are summarized in Table 3.

Table 3
Advantages and Disadvantages of Different "Temporary" Contraceptive Methods on Sexual Functioning

Method	Advantages	Disadvantages
1. Oral Contraceptives	Not related to sexual activity Allows for spontaneity No need to touch genitals Fear of pregnancy virtually zero	May interfere with sexual response, with some females experiencing a decrease in desire, arousal or orgasm
2. Intrauterine Device (IUD)	Not related to sexual activity Allows for spontaneity	Need to put finger in vagina to check for string Glans penis may be irritated by end of string
3. Diaphragm	Used only when needed Adds lubrication Facilitates coitus during menses by sequestering menstrual flow	May interfere with spontaneity Woman needs to be comfortable touching genitals Can be forgotten Less cervical stimulation Can be dislodged if female superior during intercourse
4. Creams, Jellies, Foams	Adds lubrication Use only when needed	May interfere with spontaneity May be distasteful with oral/genital sex play
5. Condom	Decreases sensitivity of glans	Male annoyed at using
6. "Morning after Pill"	Allows for spontaneity No need to touch genitals Used only as needed	Used for contraception in past Not recommended today (urogenital abnormalities)

The permanent methods of contraception—vasectomy, tubal ligation and hysterectomy—all have the advantage of removing any fear of pregnancy. Menses also cease after hysterectomy and no longer affect sexual activity. The potential psychological disadvantages of a vasectomy or tubal ligation include such factors as the feeling less of a man or woman or anger because the decision was "forced" by the partner. After hysterectomy, the major sexual effects will be experienced by the woman during orgasm. Normally, contractions of the uterus and outer third of the vagina occur during orgasm; obviously after a hysterectomy, the uterine contractions will no longer be felt. Whether this is perceived as a loss will depend on how much the woman focused on these contractions prior to the hysterectomy. Pomeroy[9] has suggested that such contractions may have occurred without either the woman or her partner being aware of them. Some women become nonorgasmic during intercourse after a hysterectomy. This may be because cervical "jostling" and peritoneal stimulation served as a trigger for the orgasm. Further research is needed to clarify this. Perhaps supracervical hysterectomy could be an acceptable operative procedure for these women.

The potential disadvantage of all three permanent methods of contraception is that desire for sexual activity in both the man and the woman may be decreased if pregnancy is no longer a possibility. Some people connect sex and reproduction so strongly that (usually unconsciously) they lose interest in sex that has no chance of being reproductive. This phenomenon is observed much more often in women than in men.[10]

A 38-year-old woman with four children described her fantasies while engaged in sex with her husband. Over the years her favorite fantasy was that of having repeated intercourse with a wealthy, powerful man and then becoming pregnant and giving birth to his child. After her tubes were tied (about a year before coming for help because of an inhibition of sexual desire for her husband), she felt worthless. She stated, "My regard for myself was wrapped up in my capacity to bear children. When that capacity was gone, I felt worthless." The fantasy she used to replace the one just cited was that of being a prostitute who, while pretending to the male that he was in complete charge of their sexual relationship, would manage through devious ways to retain complete control. This patient's basic feelings were that she was being used by men, that she did not have charge of her own life and that her value in life was to bear children.

The change that has occurred in sexual mores is another problem that confronts people who have been married for more than 10 or 15 years. They can experience a great deal of pressure sexually if they grew up with one set of sexual "rules" and now, because of death or divorce, are forced into an open society where many of the rules are different. The following case illustrates some of these points.[11]

After her 10-year marriage ended in divorce, a woman came for counseling because of her inability to cope with the "dating game." The woman had been a virgin before marriage and, although very responsive in her marriage, did not want to be sexually involved on a casual basis. Virtually every man she wanted to go out with let her know that he did not want to date if coitus was out of the question until they had known one another for some time. During the period of her marriage, the sexual mores in this country had undergone a tremendous shift for which she was not prepared. Any individual may be uncomfortable with changes in societal ethics, but many of the formerly married suddenly bear the full brunt of change.

Couple Relations and Pregnancy. The anticipation of pregnancy may create intrapsychic conflict. The woman whose feminine security hinges on a bride-like figure may become increasingly concerned over "disfigurement" during pregnancy and may need more sexual reassurance. For many women, especially those from educationally and financially deprived backgrounds who have too many children to take care of, sexual relations may be viewed as something to be avoided. Anticipatory dread rather than participatory pleasure may precede sexual acts. The so-called "introversion" of pregnancy[12] may interfere with marital sexuality. The husband may interpret his wife's behavior as desire not to relate to him in an intimate or sexual way, and that can be responsible for interpersonal conflict.

These feelings often result in a complete misunderstanding about sexual activity during pregnancy. The woman may feel "undesirable" because of her enlarging abdomen and unconsciously reject her husband's sexual invitations. Many husbands are concerned about causing injury to their wife and the baby.

In discussion, it is common to find that both desired each other but were restrained by subjective concerns.

Interpersonal conflict also may be precipitated when a couple is confronted with an unwanted pregnancy. It is very easy for individuals in this instance to blame one another rather than accepting their own responsibility. Interpersonal conflict associated with pregnancy can also occur when, for example, after a 25-year marriage, a lonely and dejected wife feels that her unfaithful husband can thereby be erotically recaptured, and the estrangement of her progressively more independent teenage children can be arrested by another baby. An additional child may have served that purpose in the past, but now the problems are just compounded. Interpersonal conflict also occurs when the wife elects to become pregnant again instead of getting a job which her husband feels could help support the family.

Sexual desire and responsiveness during pregnancy has been a relatively neglected area of research.[13] Masters and Johnson[14] reported that there was a decrease in sexual frequency during the first trimester (mostly due to psychological factors), then an increase in frequency and responsiveness during the second trimester (allegedly due to increased pelvic congestion), and then a decrease during the third trimester (due to physical discomfort). Solbert et al[15] retrospectively interviewed 226 women just after childbirth and found that sexual frequency decreased from when pregnancy was discovered until delivery. In order to avoid the retrospective method, Tolor and DiGrazia[16] administered a questionnaire to 161 pregnant women almost equally distributed over the three trimesters of pregnancy. The authors reported a "characteristic decline both in sexual interest and sexual activity as the pregnancy progresses," with the most pronounced trend during the third trimester. Pasini[17] interviewed 100 women after childbirth and with a retrospective technique confirmed the findings of Tolor and DiGrazia. Kenny[18] found that sexual behavior of pregnant women remained "about the same" except for the third trimester when desire, frequency and enjoyment decreased.

One clearcut change during pregnancy is the woman's increased desire for physical closeness. The increased need to be held was first reported by Hollender and McGhee.[19] A common sense hypothesis confirmed by Pasini was that women who had a positive attitude toward pregnancy maintained or improved an already good relationship, while women who had negative feelings toward pregnancy experienced a decrease in sexual satisfaction.

Although coitus during pregnancy is common and generally sanctioned medically, a recently reported large-scale study of amniotic fluid infections points up the desirability of caution. Both the incidence and severity of infection were significantly greater when the mother had coitus at least once a week during the month before delivery. Fatalities among infected infants were nearly five times more frequent in those whose mothers had coitus during pregnancy than in those whose mothers abstained during this time.[20] The reason for these differences is not clear. The use of condoms to prevent infection may be wise.

Understanding some of the woman's emotional and psychological reactions during pregnancy will enable the clinician to be most helpful. As the fetus progresses through phylogeny, pregnancy for the woman may be thought of as a sort of "psychological ontogeny." In other words, as the fetus progresses through the biological past, the woman at the same time relives her psychological past. During pregnancy, through a process of regression, she may return in part to certain aspects of her childhood. The pregnant woman does not have to analyze the nature of, or motivations for, her fears—she may need help to feel secure.

After delivery, most women experience mild depression, often called the "new baby blues."[21] It usually occurs one to three days following delivery, is self-terminating and requires nothing more than support and encouragement. Whether this depression is secondary to hormonal withdrawal or to loss of the fetus is unknown, but it certainly does point up the degree of vulnerability that the postpartum woman commonly experiences. The new mother needs a great deal of "mothering" herself, just at a time when she must learn to do the mothering. She may go through a period of sexual detachment during this time. As LaBarre[22] points out, the young husband who unconsciously looks to his wife as a mother will unconsciously resent his children as rivals, since the mother's distribution of energy and attention is changed with the arrival of the baby. At the same time, the increasing need to be dependent that is experienced by many women during pregnancy and early motherhood may be particularly stressful for the husband, who may not be able to provide her with need fulfillment.

The physician should counsel the couple in order to alleviate their fears, point out the normality of the process and hopefully decrease the incidence of stress for both of them.

Infertility. The sexual and psychological problems of the infertile couple often have been overlooked or knowingly neglected.[23] During the past several years, awareness of factors influencing fertility has grown and it is becoming clearer that sexual dysfunction may be the cause of infertility or a consequence of infertility, its workup or its treatment, or a coincidental finding. Amelar et al[24] have reported that male sexual dysfunction is either the primary factor or a major contributor in 10 per cent of infertile marriages, including (1) difficulty in obtaining or maintaining an erection for penetration, (2) premature ejaculation occurring before penetration, (3) ejaculatory incompetence or retarded ejaculation, or (4) retrograde ejaculation. In women, vaginismus or dyspareunia may preclude intercourse.

Sexual dysfunction also may occur during the course of a protracted medical workup for infertility. Some men become extremely upset by repeated requests for semen samples collected by masturbation.

Scheduled intercourse around the time of ovulation also can present problems. Ginsberg and associates[25] described "the new impotence": The newly found female sexual freedom seems to have caused increased complaints of impotence by younger men. It will be interesting to see, as several authors have suggested,[26-28] whether and by how much impotence will increase as the male member of the infertile couple must change his perspective from "sex on desire" to "sex on demand." Stress may alter spermatogenesis and ovulation significantly. To affect spermatogenesis, stress must be extreme and not what is usually seen under ordinary life pressures. In women, stress frequently leads to amenorrhea.

Artificial insemination is another aspect of infertility that creates problems. A recent nationwide study of artificial insemination by donor (AID) shows that 10 per cent of the physicians queried used the technique occasionally to assist single women wishing to have children.[29] This is a subject that is arousing increased legal, medical and ethical concern. The effect of AID on sexual functioning of the couple during and after pregnancy has not been studied.

Genetic Concerns and Abortion. Fear of pregnancy or of producing an abnormal child may lead to sexual avoidance or dysfunction. In fact, the fear of passing undesirable personal characteristics—a personal congenital anomaly or a family trait—on to progeny may be one dynamic behind ejaculatory incompetence.[30] This possibility should be explored in all males with retarded ejaculation.

There are no known physical consequences that directly preclude a return to normal sexual functioning in women who have undergone an abortion, be it spontaneous, elective or therapeutic. In the 1950's, Kinsey and associates[31] found that 90 per cent of unmarried postabortal women resumed premarital coitus after abortion. The psychological sequelae of abortion only rarely include sexual dysfunction.

Adoption. The literature is replete with observations, but no good data, on young women who have had out-of-wedlock pregnancies, have given their babies up for adoption and have been unable to conceive after marriage.

Orr[32] in 1941 reported on the apparently frequent occurrence of pregnancy after adoption—sometimes in a matter of days. Sandler[33] maintained that the relief of tension and anxiety occasioned by adoption can lead to spontaneous pregnancy. Yet, when Weir and Weir[34] studied 438 couples, of whom 44 per cent adopted children and 56 per cent did not, they determined that the pregnancy rates were essentially the same for both groups during a period of more than five years. Tyler and coworkers[35] analyzed consecutively adopting parents to determine the subsequent pregnancy rates. They concluded that only 4 per cent of adoptive parents conceived within a time interval short enough to make a cause-and-effect relationship between adoption and pregnancy reasonable.

No studies were found relating to the effect of adoption on subsequent sexual functioning of the adoptive parents.

THE MENOPAUSAL PERIOD

Kinsey[31] made the important observation that it is impossible to determine if the decline in frequency of sexual activity with age is due to physiological, psychological or social factors. Kobosa-Munro[36] states that there is a significant increase in the number of older women in this country and their sexuality is often ignored. Newgarten[37] studied 100 women aged 20 to 65 about their attitude toward the menopause. When they were asked the question, "May women have an upsurge in sexual interest during menopause?" the ones who answered in the negative were, for the most part, the youngest in age, i.e., premenopausal. Only 4 of the total of 100 women felt that loss of fertility was the worst thing about the menopause, yet it is widely believed that this is the underlying dynamic responsible for the feeling of diminished femininity in menopausal women. Masters and Johnson[14] found that the human female is fully capable of arousal and orgasmic response well into her 80's if regularly exposed to stimulation and, unlike her male counterpart, the elderly female remains capable of multiple orgasms.

Easley[38] emphasized that the woman had traditionally been valued for her ability to produce large families. Now with the world struggling with overpopulation, as Fathalla[39] puts it, "the female reproductive system is an abnormal phenomenon." The statement may be too strong, but his insightful point should be well taken. As overpopulation has become more and more of a problem and as family size has decreased, there is more emphasis on a woman's sexual responsiveness than on her "reproductive" responsiveness.

During menopause, the ovaries secrete decreasing amounts of estrogen, and vaginal dryness and dyspareunia may result. Dyspareunia is minimized if the woman remains coitally active; sexual abstinence for any reason may lead to development of dyspareunia.

The importance of having a socially sanctioned sexual partner is a major limiting factor for many older menopausal women.[40] Only a small number of elderly widows remarry. Traditionally in our society, women have married men slightly older than themselves. Often the man becomes sexually incapacitated because of illness. The older woman whose husband is ill, impotent or deceased may have very little opportunity for sexuality or even close relationships with other individuals, for that matter. Unfortunately, this isolation can be caused to some extent by the woman's own narrow perspective and her inability to even recognize the many opportunities for meeting her personal needs.[11]

THE PHYSICIAN IN REPRODUCTIVE COUNSELING

Physicians have many advantages as reproductive counselors. They are often in the "right place at the right time" and, like it or not, they will be placed in a counseling role. Even in a team approach, physicians are often crucial in decision-making because they usually are the final authority as to what is medically desirable. Since reproductive counseling is medical as well as personal, it is important for involved physicians to be understanding and to integrate both perspectives.

There are also some problems for physicians as counselors; the most common one is time. To find out how someone feels and thinks, a crucial aspect of the counseling process, takes time. If insufficient time is allotted, the physician simply will not question in a way that promotes understanding; the patient, receiving nonverbal messages of impatience, will then not attempt to reveal all her feelings.

302

Another problem is confrontation. Most physicians see their role as helping to relieve pain and suffering. They have been trained in, and are comfortable with, the concept that treatment may cause pain temporarily. The same is true in counseling. There are times when the physician must explore painful options so that the patient can arrive at the best answer. Confrontation is also a problem for the patient. Patients are usually protective of physicians; if they receive a nonverbal message that the physician is uncomfortable, they will avoid a subject.

A physician friend who became interested in counseling attended a course in which he saw an explicitly sexual film about homosexuality. At the time he was quite upset, but he began to examine his own feelings and said three or four years later that he had become comfortable with the subject as a result of seeing that film. He was surprised to find that, as his attitude unconsciously changed, gynecologic patients who had been in his care for a long time told him that they were homosexuals. When asked why they had said nothing before, they could not really answer but did say that gradually they felt he would be accepting. This is a good example of how change in a physician's attitude can allow patients to feel comfortable enough to tell the truth.

Another aspect of counseling that can cause problems for patients is hidden physician bias. Patients assume that when a physician gives an opinion it is based on medical knowledge rather than on personal experience. Effective counseling, however, is often based on the counselor's feelings, thoughts and suggestions; the foundation or basis of the physician's opinions should be stated so that any bias is in the open. In this way, the counselor allows and even helps protect the patient against bias. It can be harmful when a patient thinks a suggestion is based on scientific truth when, in reality, it is based only on personal feelings.

The line between being an authority (expert) and being authoritarian is often thin. This causes problems for patients in counseling. Virtually all of medicine except psychiatry is based upon examination, laboratory tests, evaluation of data and advising the patient what is best. Thus, the physician spends a great deal of his professional life in making judgments and, because of this, may tend to be judgmental in counseling. For example, after hearing the problem, the response might be: "You should do this." In counseling, it is more helpful to patients to suggest rather than to judge. The difference in one respect is small; in another it is huge! The response would be subtly different: "I think you might consider doing this" or, even better, "It seems to me on the basis of what you have said that doing this might be the better option." The words are not very different, but the difference in behavior is enormous because implied in a suggestion is the *equality* between the physician and patient. Therefore, the physician's opinions can be considered and, if appropriate, easily rejected by the patient. If the physician is authoritarian, however, in his manner or in his words, the patient must either accept or fight, and thereby is not allowed to make a decision.

There are other problems of primary concern to physicians. One is physician anxiety concerning the old common law (or judge-made) rule that the consent of a parent or guardian is required before a doctor may provide any kind of medical treatment for a minor. It is responsible, in part, for some of the difficulty that minors have in getting proper contraceptive care. Twenty-six states and the District of Columbia explicitly affirmed by statute or court decision the right of young people under the age of 18 to consent for contraceptive care. Although a state may require parental *notice* and parent/child *consultation* for prescription contraceptives (for example Michigan), and possibly even nonprescription contraceptives, no state requires parental *consent* for contraception.[41] The fact that there is no specific affirmation statute or decision in any state does not mean that minors in that state cannot consent. As Paul et al[42] concluded, " . . . in many, if not most, of these (other) states, there is reason to believe that teenagers who have the capacity to give informed consent may consent to all sex related medical care." On May 24, 1976, the United States Supreme Court held that, under Titles XII and XX of the Social Security Act, states may not require a minor to have parental consent in order to obtain contraceptive services from federally subsidized programs.[43] Although physicians are concerned about possible civil liability for assault or malpractice, the logic of the Supreme Court holding in *Danforth*[44] appears equally applicable to any rule requiring parental consent with reference to sex-related medical services.

Ethical considerations always seem to pose a problem for counselors. "How can I assist another person in being involved in something I do not believe in?" is a question every counselor has asked. On the other hand, "How can I as a physician not take care of someone in need just because I don't happen to entirely support what they are doing?" With the proviso that the physician should enable the person to do nothing illegal, it seems to us that each counselor must work out a personal code of ethics and decide what care can be provided. Many will differentiate between personal and professional ethics so that in reproductive counseling they would provide contraception for purposes that they might not personally condone for themselves. This is a difficult problem for which there is no easy solution.

The rewards for effective counseling are often as great for physicians as for their patients. If there is one word that describes effective counseling it is *understanding*. A physician can be most helpful if he or she just takes the time to understand the patient. What is not always recognized is how beautiful and joyous it is to have the privilege of being allowed to understand other human beings.

References

1. Pierson EC: Gynecologic approach to counseling the sexually active young woman. *Clin Obstet Gynecol* 1978; 21:235-248.
2. Gray MJ, McGinnis S: Role of the gynecologist and the emerging woman. *Clin Obstet Gynecol* 1978; 21:173-181.
3. Seaman B: *Free and Female*. Greenwich, Conn, Fawcett Crest, 1972.

4. Tyrer LB, et al: Meeting special needs of the pregnant teenagers. *Clin Obstet Gynecol* 1978; 21:1199-1212.
5. Hornik E: How teenagers, their parents, and their doctors can all grow up, in Nash EM, et al (eds): *Marriage Counseling in Medical Practice*. Chapel Hill, University of North Carolina Press, 1964.
6. Klein L: Antecedents of teenage pregnancy. *Clin Obstet Gynecol* 1978; 21:1151-1159.
7. Marinoff SC: Contraception in adolescents. *Pediatr Clin North Am* 1972; 19:811-819.
8. Bardwick JM: A predictive study of psychological and psychosomatic responses to oral contraceptives, in Bardwick JM: *Readings on the Psychology of Women*. New York, Harper and Row Publishers, Inc, 1972.
9. Pomeroy WB: *Girls and Sex*. Harmondsworth, Middlesex, Penguin Books, 1971.
10. Erikson EH: *Dimensions of a New Identity*. (Jefferson Lectures in the Humanities, 1973). New York, WW Norton & Company, 1974.
11. Burchell RC: Counseling the formerly married. *Clin Obstet Gynecol* 1978; 21:259-267.
12. Freedman AM, et al: *Modern Synopsis of Psychiatry II*. Baltimore, Williams & Wilkins Company, 1976.
13. Lief HI: Sexual desire and responsivity during pregnancy. *Med Aspects Hum Sex* 1977 (Dec); 11:51-52.
14. Masters WH, Johnson VE: *Human Sexual Response*. Boston, Little, Brown and Company, 1966.
15. Solbert DA, et al: Sexual behavior in pregnancy. *N Engl J Med* 1973; 288:1098-1103.
16. Tolor A, DiGrazia PV: Sexual attitudes and behavior patterns during and following pregnancy. *Arch Sex Behav* 1976; 5:539-551.
17. Pasini W: Sexuality during pregnancy and postpartum frigidity, in Money J, Mosaph J (eds): *Handbook of Sexology*. Amsterdam, Excerpta Medica, 1977.
18. Kenny JA: Sexuality of pregnant and breastfeeding women. *Arch Sex Behav* 1973; 2:215-229.
19. Hollender MH, McGhee JB: The wish to be held during pregnancy. *J Psychosom Res* 1974; 18:193-197.
20. Naeye RL: Coitus and associated amniotic-fluid infections. *N Engl J Med* 1979; 301:1198-1199.
21. Yalom ID, et al: Postpartum blues syndrome. *Arch Gen Psychiatry* 1968; 18:16-27.
22. LaBarre W: The triple crisis: Adolescence, early marriage, and parenthood, in *The Double Jeopardy: The Triple Crisis*. National Council on Illegitimacy, New York, 1969.
23. Walker HE: Sexual problems and infertility. *Psychosomatics* 1978; 19:477-484.
24. Amelar RD, et al: *Male Infertility*. Philadelphia, WB Saunders Co, 1977.
25. Ginsberg GL, et al: The new impotence. *Arch Gen Psychiatry* 1972; 26:218-220.

26. Bullock JL: Iatrogenic impotence in an infertility clinic: Illustrative case. *Am J Obstet Gynecol* 1974; 120:476-478.
27. Noyes RW, Chapnick EM: Literature on psychology and infertility. *Fertil Steril* 1964; 15:543-558.
28. Kaufman SA: Impact of infertility on the marital and sexual relationship. *Fertil Steril* 1969; 20:380-383.
29. Artificial insemination by donor: Survey reveals surprising facts. *JAMA* 1979; 241:1219-1220.
30. Wabrek AJ, Wabrek CJ: Ejaculatory incompetence. *Conn Med* 1976; 40:450-451.
31. Kinsey AC, et al: *Sexual Behavior in the Human Female*. Philadelphia, WB Saunders Co, 1953.
32. Orr DW: Pregnancy following the decision to adopt. *Psychosom Med* 1941; 3:441-446.
33. Sandler B: Conception after adoption: A comparison of conception rates. *Fertil Steril* 1965; 16:313-333.
34. Weir WC, Weir DR: Adoption and subsequent conceptions. *Fertil Steril* 1966; 17:283-288.
35. Tyler ET, et al: Occurrence of pregnancy following adoption. *Fertil Steril* 1960; 11:581-589.
36. Kobosa-Munro L: Sexuality in the aging woman. *Health and Social Work* 1977; 2:70-88.
37. Newgarten B, et al: Women's attitudes toward the menopause, in Newgarten B (ed): *Middle Age and Aging*. Chicago, University of Chicago Press, 1968.
38. Easley EB: Sex problems after the menopause. *Clin Obstet Gynecol* 1978; 1:269-277.
39. Fathalla MJ: Is gynecological cancer the result of an "obsolete" reproductive system? *Discovery* 1977; 1:1.
40. Pfeiffer E, et al: The natural history of sexual behavior in a biologically advantaged group of aged individuals. *J Gerontol* 1969; 24:193-198.
41. A review of state laws and policies. *Fam Plann Pop Reporter* 1977; 6:4.
42. Paul ER, et al: Pregnancy, teenagers and the law. 1976. *Fam Plann Perspect* 1976; 8:16-21.
43. A review of state laws and policies. *Fam Plann Pop Reporter* 1976; 5:(6)85-86.
44. 428 US 52, Planned Parenthood of Missouri v. Danforth (1975).

Chapter 22

Sexually Transmitted Diseases

Milton Diamond, Ph.D., and Arno Karlen

Several decades ago, the dramatic success of sulfonamides and penicillin in treating the most common general infections and sexually transmitted diseases made many physicians think that these devastating illnesses would, like smallpox, soon be of historical interest only. As any general practitioner can attest, such a millenium has not come to pass. Under the illusion that sexually transmitted diseases have been conquered with antibiotics, many U.S. medical schools have not fully educated physicians in their treatment for at least a decade.[1] Patients and practicing physicians are also to blame. Rosebury[1] asks: "Why is all the elaborate searching out of patients and contacts necessary, the cajolery, the specially trained investigators? The answer... is obvious, venereal disease is shameful... venereal disease control entails mainly a change of attitude." These diseases continue to be among the most pressing and underrated problems in public health and in many physicians' private practices.

For several reasons, the "classic" venereal diseases (VDs) are presently included in a more broadly termed category: sexually transmitted diseases (STDs). (Although the two terms are still used interchangeably, the latter is preferred as a more accurate description.) STDs refer to infections spread by coitus, by oral-genital contact or by anal-genital contact. Only in rare cases is it possible to conclude that "toilet seats and towels" and not people are vectors for these infections. Some nongenital diseases, such as hepatitis, may be spread by sexual activity, and a small number of STDs are sometimes transmitted in ways other than by sexual contact.

Changes in sexual behavior continue to alter traditional disease epidemiology, and the number of diseases that can be transmitted sexually is growing. Oral-genital and anal-genital activities have fostered diverse modes of disease transmission and manifestation. Recently, oral-anal contacts, for example, have resulted in venereal amebiasis, shigellosis and giardiasis.[2]

Over the years, the fight against STDs has been changing direction.[3] Until the first quarter of this century, all effort was directed toward influencing sexual behavior toward abstinence or monogamy: with abstinence or monogamous relationships, people would remain free of STD, and moral and legal restraints were called upon to foster such relationships. With the increase in nonmonogamous relationships during World War I, the focus turned toward influencing other preventive behaviors. Condoms were advertised for "the prevention of disease" and people were warned to be selective in choosing a partner.

The emergence of the "antibiotic era" brought with it an attempt to influence so-called illness and treatment behaviors rather than social behaviors. Since it was found that many patients eschew even preliminary preventive measures against STDs, individuals are now warned to seek diagnosis of all suspicious signs of illness (e.g., genital sores, pain, discharge) and to follow their physician's advice regarding treatment. It is this last emphasis that places most responsibility upon the physician. The primary care physician should increase his efforts to detect signs of various STDs, investigate them all and treat all suspected or proved cases of STD. Whether to moralize is open to debate. Most patients prefer treatment without unwelcome moralizing.

INCIDENCE AND TRANSMISSION

STDs can be spread by both heterosexual and homosexual contact. The incidence seems to be increasing, particularly among teenagers and male homosexuals; in both population groups, active protective measures (e.g., condoms) against STDs are rarely used. Despite popular myths, public health officials think that heterosexual prostitutes are responsible for only a relatively small percentage of cases of syphilis (perhaps 1 to 5 per cent). The figures for prostitute-related gonorrhea are less certain, but they also are probably low in most areas with stable populations.[4] Nonmonogamous behavior in the non-prostitute population has increased significantly.

With the exception of nongonococcal urethritis (NGU), there seems to be a higher rate of STD in lower socioeconomic groups. The 1965 National Health Survey[5] found that the prevalence of syphilis was nine times greater in blacks than in whites. This difference may be due to higher incidence, greater reluctance to seek treatment or decreased availability of adequate treatment. However, the class difference in STD rates at least partly reflects the tendency to report public but not private cases. NGU is reported more often among private patients; it appears to be more prevalent in college students, in the more affluent and in whites.

Reporting by the private physician as required by public health laws is strongly recommended. However, studies conducted by the American Social Health Association in 1963 and 1971 showed that only about 12 per cent of STD cases treated by U.S. physicians were reported to local health authorities.[4] In a recent study in Denver, for example, it was estimated that approximately 60 per cent of cases seen by private physicians were not reported.[6]

The epidemiology of STDs is beginning to receive increased attention from social scientists. Studies indicate that in large cities, despite tourists, conventioneers, servicemen in transit and people traveling for business, residents most often contract STD from other residents. In small and medium-size towns, STDs are only somewhat more likely to be contracted from people outside the locale. Practitioners in locales with large tourist or military populations, however, should remain alert to uncommon types of STD.

The great spread of STDs among male homosexuals comes not only from the difficulties in diagnosis and in making gay males aware of the risks of STD and how to avoid it, but from the tendency of many to have anonymous or near-anonymous sex partners inside or outside their immediate social communities.

STD is most often contracted in nonmarital relations, although, of course, the spouse may then be infected or become a carrier. There often is a ping-pong effect of mutual reinfection among all the partners involved when examination and treatment of all parties are not adequate. All partners must receive treatment if therapy is to be effective. A physician must realize that moralizing may turn a patient away or make him or her be silent about possible venereal infection in self or in partners.

Physicians should be aware that courts have begun to recognize the right of a victim to sue a person who knowingly transmits an STD without informing him or her as sexual partner.[7] Physicians are protected against suit when they reveal a patient's illness or contacts to health authorities.

Specific therapies are indicated below. There are general considerations, however. With widespread and repeated use of antibiotics, there is the possibility that resistant strains of many pathogens may develop (e.g., penicillinase-producing gonococci). Penicillin dosages to treat gonorrhea have risen steadily over the years but now appear to be leveling off.

In most states, minors may be examined and treated for an STD without parental consent; many clinics and practitioners consider confidentiality to be in the minor's best interests if the young patient thinks that revelation would create severe difficulties. There have been no reports of physicians being convicted for treating a minor who has an STD.

Free or inexpensive clinics have been subsidized by state and local governments on the theory that illness and misery probably would be worse without financial aid to help control the infections.

The following sections outline the most common STDs, their identifying features and recommended treatment. For convenience, summaries are given in Table 4. As with other diseases, proper management depends upon individualization of diagnosis and adequate follow-up.

CLASSIC SEXUALLY TRANSMITTED DISEASES[8-10]

Gonorrhea

Now, as it was a half century ago, gonorrhea is one of this country's most prevalent infectious diseases.[3,11] More than 1,000,000 cases of gonorrhea have been *reported* annually in the United States for the past three years, but over 2,000,000 cases are estimated to *occur* annually. The young and economically disadvantaged suffer the most; nearly 90 per cent of reported cases occur in those 15 to 30 years old. Women bear most of the burden, for over 90 per cent of the complications and 85 per cent of the costs from gonorrhea accrue to them or their offspring.[12]

The organism that causes gonorrhea (*Neisseria gonorrhoeae*) exists in the mucous membranes of the urethra, cervix, anus and throat. A man has at least a 20 per cent risk of catching gonorrhea after a single exposure to an infected woman, whereas the risk is 50 to 60 per cent in a woman.

TABLE 4. SEXUALLY TRANSMITTED DISEASES SUMMARY

GONORRHEA

Etiology
Neisseria gonorrhoeae
A non-motile, gram negative diplococcus. 0.6 μ to 1.0 μ in diameter.

Prevalence
1,013,436 (468.3/100,000) cases reported in 1978. Highest reported case rates are in age groups 20-24 and 15-19.

Clinical Presentation
Men have dysuria, frequency, and urethral discharge that is usually purulent and often more severe in the morning. Women experience vaginal discharge and cystitis. About 5-20% of men and 60-85% of women have no symptoms.

Diagnosis
Presumptive identification— Microscopic identification of typical gram negative, intracellular diplococci on smear of urethral exudate from men or endocervical material from women OR positive oxidase reaction of typical colonies from specimen obtained from anterior urethra, endocervix or anal canal, and inoculated on Modified Thayer-Martin Medium.

Therapy
Aqueous procaine penicillin G, 4.8 million units IM at 2 sites with 1 g of probenecid orally OR tetracycline HCl, 0.5 g orally q.i.d. for 5 days, 10 g total OR ampicillin, 3.5 g or amoxicillin, 3 g, either with 1 g of probenecid orally.

Complications
Epididymitis
Pharyngitis
Meningitis
Septicemia
Arthritis
Endocarditis
Conjunctivitis in Newborn
Salpingitis
Pelvic Inflammatory Disease (PID)

SYPHILIS

Etiology
Treponema pallidum
A motile spirochete with 6-14 spirals and ends pointed with finely spiral terminal filaments. 6-15 μ in length.

Prevalence
21,656 (10/100,000) infectious cases reported in 1978. Highest reported case rates are in age groups 20-24 and 25-29.

Clinical Presentation
Primary syphilis: Classical chancre is painless, eroded papule with a raised, indurated border. Atypical lesions are common; multiple lesions may occur. Extragenital chancres may appear on any part of body. Unilateral or bilateral lymphadenopathy may accompany.
Secondary syphilis: Various cutaneous and mucous membrane lesions, alopecia, generalized lymphadenopathy, mild constitutional symptoms.

Diagnosis
Demonstration of *T. pallidum* from exudate of primary or secondary lesions by darkfield microscopy. Typical lesions, reactive reagin test for syphilis (VDRL or RPR), and FTA/ABS will confirm except in early primary cases.

Therapy
Benzathine penicillin G, 2.4 million units IM at 1 visit OR aqueous procaine penicillin G, 4.8 million units total: 600,000 units IM daily for 8 days OR tetracycline HCl, 500 mg orally q.i.d. for 15 days.

Complications
Late syphilis
Congenital syphilis

NONGONOCOCCAL URETHRITIS (NGU)

Etiology
1) *Chlamydia trachomatis*— estimated to cause NGU in about 50% of cases. An obligate intracellular parasite. Diameter 250-500 nm.
2) *Ureaplasma urealyticum*— estimated by some workers to cause NGU in about 30% of cases. A mycoplasma of the T strain, less than 150 nm in diameter.
3) *Other Etiologic Agents*— estimated to cause NGU in 10-20% of cases.
   Trichomonas vaginalis
   Candida albicans
   Herpes simplex
   Coliform bacteria

Prevalence
Age distribution of nongonococcal urethritis parallels that of other sexually transmitted diseases, notably gonorrhea. Recurrences are very common.

Clinical Presentation
Urethral discharge varies from profusely purulent to slightly mucoid. Dysuria may or may not be present. In half of the cases, the incubation period appears to exceed 10 days. Some men may have asymptomatic infection.

Diagnosis
Clinical picture of dysuria and/or urethral discharge; discharge on examination; polymorphonuclear leukocytes on urethral smear negative for *Neisseria gonorrhoeae* and negative culture for gonorrhea on Modified Thayer-Martin Medium.

Therapy
Tetracycline, 500 mg q.i.d. for 7-21 days.
Many clinicians recommend similar therapy for sexual consorts.

Complications
Epididymitis
Prostatitis
Proctitis
Cervicitis
Salpingitis
Reiter's Disease
Ophthalmia neonatorum

TRICHOMONIASIS

Etiology
Trichomonas vaginalis
A motile protozoan with 4 anterior flagella and a short, undulating membrane. 5-15 μm in length.

Prevalence
Prevalence ranges from lower than 5% of private gynecologic patients to as high as 50-75% of prostitutes. Colonization rates are higher among women than men.

Clinical Presentation
From no signs or symptoms to erythema and edema of external genitalia and frothy greenish-gray vaginal discharge. Granular vaginitis may include punctuate hemorrhages and may involve the cervix. Most men are asymptomatic, though some may present with urethritis.

Diagnosis
Microscopic examination of wet mount of vaginal discharge. Papanicolaou smears may show the parasite.
Culture methods are available and are more sensitive.

Therapy
Oral metronidazole 2 g p.o. STAT OR 250 mg t.i.d. for 7 days. Advise patient against consuming alcohol. Treat steady sex partners.

Complications
Rare
Epididymitis
Prostatitis

GENITAL HERPES INFECTION

Etiology
Herpes virus
A spherical DNA virus, enveloped, with cubic symmetry. 150 nm.

Prevalence
Prevalent among adolescents, young adults, and the sexually active.

Clinical Presentation
Vesicular lesions on vulva, perineum, vagina, and cervix in women; lesions on penile shaft, prepuce, glans penis, and (less frequently) scrotum and perineum in men. Recurrent infections. Tender adenopathy, dysuria, and constitutional signs more common with primary infections than those recurring.

Diagnosis
Clinical appearance of herpetic lesions.
Papanicolaou smears from lesions, stained to show multinucleated giant cells with intranuclear inclusion bodies.
Tissue culture.

Therapy
No specific therapy is available. Symptoms may be relieved by warm baths.

Complications
Keratitis
Encephalitis
Neonatal Herpes Infection

VULVOVAGINAL CANDIDIASIS

Etiology
Candida albicans
A dimorphic gram positive fungus that appears as oval, budding yeast cells, has hyphae and pseudohyphae. 3 X 6 μm.

Prevalence
Saprophytic in the oropharyngeal and gastrointestinal tracts in 50% of the population and in the vagina in 20% of nonpregnant women.

Clinical Presentation
Vulva is usually erythematous and edematous. Vaginal discharge, when present, may be thick and white, resembling cottage cheese. Occasionally discharge is thin and watery. Satellite lesions may spread to the groin. Many women have no symptoms. Sexual partners may develop balanitis or cutaneous lesions on penis.

Diagnosis
Microscopic examination of gram-stained smears of introital or vaginal wall scrapings. Microscopic examination of wet mount of vaginal discharge. Culture on Sabouraud's modified agar.

Therapy
Nystatin vaginal suppositories b.i.d. for 7 to 14 days OR niconazole vaginal cream daily for 7 days. Discuss with patient predisposing factors and means of avoiding a recurrence.

Complications
Nil

TABLE 4. SEXUALLY TRANSMITTED DISEASES SUMMARY (Con't.)

CORYNEBACTERIUM VAGINALE VAGINITIS OR HEMOPHILUS VAGINALIS VAGINITIS

Etiology
Corynebacterium vaginale
or
Hemophilus vaginalis
Gram negative pleomorphic coccobacillus, precise taxonomy not decided. Measures 1-3 μm X 0.4-0.7 μm.

Prevalence
Cultured from 23-96% of women with vaginitis. Recovered from 0-52% of asymptomatic women.

Clinical Presentation
Homogenous, relatively thin, occasionally frothy vaginal discharge, usually gray-white. Punctuate hemorrhages and vulvar irritation are occasionally seen. Between 10% and 40% of culture-positive patients have no symptoms.

Diagnosis
Clinical picture, microscopic examination, and culture. Gram stain of vaginal exudate may show tiny, gram negative coccobacilli ("clue cells") adhering to vaginal epithelial cells, though specificity of this finding is low. Wet mount far less sensitive than gram stain.

Therapy
Oral ampicillin 500 mg q.i.d. for 7-10 days (examine patient for syphilis or gonorrhea before prescribing this regimen, as ampicillin may mask symptoms) OR oral metronidazole 250 mg t.i.d. for 7 days.

Complications
Nil

PEDICULOSIS PUBIS

Etiology
Phthirus pubis
Pubic louse, an oval, grayish insect which becomes reddish-brown when engorged with blood. 1-4 mm in length.

Prevalence
Age group of patients affected by pubic lice parallels that of patients with gonorrhea. Transmitted during sexual intercourse, very rarely by bedding or clothing.

Clinical Presentation
Erythematous, itching papules. Nits or adult lice adhering to pubic hair or hair around the anus, abdomen, and thighs.

Diagnosis
Clinical observation of lice OR microscopically, by identification of nits at base of hair.

Therapy
1% Y-benzene hexachloride lotion 25% benzyl benzoate lotion. Combine with appropriate antimicrobials if secondary infection is noted.

Complications
Rare
Impetigo
Furunculosis
Pustular eczema

SCABIES

Etiology
Scarcoptes scabiei
The adult female mite is 300-400 μm long and has 4 pairs of short legs. Posterior legs end in long bristles. Male is 100-200 μm in length.

Prevalence
Transmitted via close bodily contact, often incidental to coitus, infested bedding and clothing.

Clinical Presentation
Linear burrows 1 to 10 mm in length, often with a red papule which contains the mite. Scratching may produce excoriation. Most common sites are finger webs, wrists, elbows, ankles, penis. Nighttime itching is characteristic.

Diagnosis
Identifying the burrows and microscopic identification of the mites.

Therapy
25% benzyl benzoate emulsion.
Y-benzene hexachloride crotomiton.
Combine with appropriate antimicrobials if secondary infection is noted. Trace and treat family, domestic, and sex contacts.

Complications
Impetigo
Pustular eczema

GENITAL WARTS (CONDYLOMA ACUMINATA)

Etiology
Human papillomavirus
A small DNA virus, icosahedral, of the papovarirus group.

Prevalence
Age distribution of venereal papillomatous lesions parallels that of patients with gonorrhea.

Clinical Presentation
Flesh-colored to pinkish papillary or sessile growths which occur around the vulva, introitus, vagina, cervix, perineum, anus, anal canal, urethra, and glans penis.

Diagnosis
Clinical appearance.
Histology.
Electron microscopy.

Therapy
Podophyllin 10-25% in tincture of benzoin, applied weekly.
Electrocautery.
Curretage.
Cryotherapy.

Complications
Rare
Malignant change

LYMPHOGRANULOMA VENEREUM

Etiology
Chlamydia trachomatis
An obligate intracellular parasite. Diameter 250-500 nm.

Prevalence
Occurs frequently in tropical and semi-tropical regions, although 348 cases (0.2 per 100,000) were reported in the U.S. in 1977.

Clinical Presentation
Primary lesion is an evanescent, painless vesicle or superficial non-indurated ulcer on the genitalia. Adenopathy of the regional lymph nodes is common. A frank purulent proctocolitis may signal rectal involvement. Rare.

Diagnosis
Clinical picture. Complement Fixation Test (CFT), significantly positive with a titer of 1:16 or higher in more than 80% of cases. Material for Frei Skin Test is no longer available.

Therapy
Tetracycline 500 mg orally q.i.d. for 2-3 weeks OR gentamicin 40 mg IM b.i.d. for 2 weeks.

Complications
Rare
Elephantiasis
Urethral, vaginal, or rectal stricture from cicatrix following healing. Massed pelvic glands; occasional bony involvement.

GRANULOMA INGUINALE

Etiology
Calymmatobacterium granulomatis
A non-motile coccobacillus that is gram negative. Size 2 μm X 0.8 μm.

Prevalence
Though fairly common in a few underdeveloped nations, frequency has declined from a high of 2611 cases reported in 1949 to 75 in 1977 in the U.S. More common among men and women, and in southern States.

Clinical Presentation
Single or multiple subcutaneous nodules may erode through the skin, producing clean granulomatous, beefy-red lesions (usually painless).

Diagnosis
Clinical picture. Intracytoplasmic rods ("Donovan's bodies") in large mononuclear cell from biopsy material stained with Giemsa or Wright's stain.

Therapy
Tetracycline 500 mg orally q.i.d. for 2-3 weeks OR sulfasxazole 4 g orally, followed by 500 mg q.i.d. for 3 weeks. Fluctuating gland masses indicate a need for aspiration.

Complications
Rare
Elephantiasis
Rectal strictures producing tenesmus, pain, and constipation.
Men: Ulcerative and fistular lesions of urethra, penis, scrotum
Women: Ulcerative genital lesions

HEPATITIS B INFECTION

Etiology
Hepatitis Virus—Type B
A virus of probable DNA nucleic acid content, 26 mμ or less.

Prevalence
Common among homosexuals and prostitutes.

Clinical Presentation
Onset is usually insidious, with vague abdominal discomfort, anorexia, nausea, arthralgia, which often progresses to jaundice. Fever may be absent or mild. Asymptomatic, anicteric hepatitis may occur.

Diagnosis
Detection of hepatitis B surface antigen (HBsAg) in blood by radioimmunoassay, passive hemagglutination, or other techniques.

Therapy
Symptomatic

Complications
Death
Carriers (Uncommon)
Cirrhosis (Late & Rare)

CHANCROID

Etiology
Hemophilus ducreyi
A coccobacillus that is non-motile, non-acid-fast, gram negative. Size 1-1.5 μm X 0.6 μm.

Prevalence
May occur in conjunction with other genital infections, particularly genital herpes and syphilis.

Clinical Presentation
A ragged, tender ulcer that is not indurated ("soft chancre"), its base covered with gray or yellow necrotic exudate. May be multiple ulcers. Tender inguinal adenopathy, usually unilateral. Women contacts are usually asymptomatic.

Diagnosis
Clinical appearance. Exclude possibility of syphilis through absence of indurated lesions and negative darkfield. Gram stained exudate from lesion or aspirates from nodes may reveal short, gram negative rods, OR culture on blood agar or media with blood derivatives.

Therapy
Sulfasoxazole 1 gm orally q.i.d.. OR tetracycline 500 mg q.i.d. for 10-14 days OR kanamycin 500 mg IM t.i.d. for 5-7 days. Fluctuating gland masses will call for aspiration.

Complications
Chronic fistulas of gland masses in groin.

Symptoms and Complications. Within two to six days after intercourse with an infected person, men usually experience dysuria and/or discharge. Although the severity of symptoms and duration of the incubation period may vary, approximately 80 to 95 per cent of these infected men will seek medical care. As many as 5 to 20 per cent of males will have no symptoms (or only mild symptoms), and it is these men who account for up to 50 per cent of male-to-female transmission because of the long duration of infection and ignorance of infectiousness.

Infected women usually are asymptomatic 60 to 85 per cent of the time, or have symptoms that fail to suggest a sexually transmitted infection to them or, unfortunately, to their physician. It is critical that physicians consider gonorrhea as a possible cause in women with dysuria, frequent urination, discharge, menstrual abnormalities and pelvic pain and that they obtain cultures on selective media from these patients.

Nearly all female-to-male transmissions occur because the woman is unaware of her infectiousness. Ten to 20 per cent of women with gonorrhea will develop pelvic inflammatory disease (PID).[13] PID is the most frequently encountered, most incapacitating and most serious complication of gonorrhea. It has been reported to be the most common cause of sterility in women and is a major cause of pelvic surgery and tubal pregnancy. Prompt, adequate therapy and follow-up for PID are mandatory. However, prevention through early treatment of gonorrhea is by far preferable because some patients with PID undergo its sequelae despite adequate therapy for this disorder.

Other complications of gonorrhea include disseminated infection (mostly arthritis and tenosynovitis), epididymitis, bartholinitis and conjunctivitis.

The majority of infections of the rectum and throat are asymptomatic; hence, they do not alert the patient to seek care or avoid sexual contact. Such sites of infection are especially important to consider when counseling homosexuals or their partners.

Diagnosis. In symptomatic males with urethral discharge, a gram-stained specimen that shows typical gram-negative diplococci within leukocytes is highly sensitive and specific for gonorrhea. In males without symptoms or with a negative gram-stained smear, an intraurethral culture on selective media (e.g., modified Thayer-Martin media) should be performed. The gram stain is much less reliable in females. Although gram stains of the cervix may be helpful clinically, their sensitivity seldom exceeds 50 per cent; therefore, cervical cultures are recommended. Cultures from the anal canal will improve the yield in women, and they are recommended in male homosexuals and for test-of-cure in women. Throat cultures should be used when oral-genital contact is suspected or revealed.

When disseminated infection is suspected, blood cultures should be accompanied by appropriate cultures from all other possible sites prior to the initiation of antibiotic therapy.

Treatment. Uncomplicated gonorrhea in men or women may be treated with one of the following regimens:

Aqueous procaine penicillin G (APPG) 4.8 million units injected intramuscularly in divided dosages at two sites, with 1 gm of probenecid orally;
or
tetracycline hydrochloride 0.5 gm orally four times a day for five days;
or
ampicillin 3.5 gm or amoxicillin 3 gm, either drug given with 1 gm of probenecid, orally. The first regimen is slightly more effective than the latter two.

Treatment failures and patients infected with penicillinase-producing strains (see below) should be given a single intramuscular injection of spectinomycin hydrochloride 2 gm.

Follow-up cultures for test-of-cure should be obtained three to seven days *and* 21 days after completion of therapy. Examination, culturing and treatment of all known sexual partners are critical to prevent reinfection and additional transmission.

Complications of gonorrhea require more intensive follow-up, and their management requires more prolonged antibiotic therapy.

Syphilis

This has been one of the most feared and devastating diseases of recent centuries. Although the overall prevalence of syphilis and its complications has declined dramatically in the past few decades, more than 20,000 cases of primary and secondary syphilis were reported in the United States in 1978.[10]

Syphilis is caused by the spirochete, *Treponema pallidum*, which usually enters the body through a break in the mucous membrane or skin. Every organ is susceptible to the disease's effects. Most of the increase in the incidence of early syphilis reported during the past decade has been among homosexual men.

Symptoms and Complications. Syphilis was called "the great imitator" by Osler because its many symptoms (especially in the late stages) mimic a host of ills. The primary stage usually begins 9 to 90 days after exposure, with an average of three weeks until symptoms are observed.[14] A chancre typically appears at the site of infection—usually the penis, vulva, cervix, mouth or anus. When the chancre occurs in the vagina, cervix or anus, it can easily go unnoticed. A chancre is typically a painless, indurated papule that disappears within a few weeks even without treatment. If undetected and untreated, syphilis progresses to its secondary stage after several weeks. Patients with secondary syphilis usually have generalized symmetrical lesions on the skin and/or mucous membranes. These nonpruritic lesions are often accompanied by patchy loss of scalp hair, malaise and low-grade fever. One of the most common findings is generalized lymphadenopathy.[14] As with the primary chancre, such symptoms may resolve without therapy and recur, usually within the first year.

After many years of latency, there follows the tertiary (late) stage. Persons with late syphilis are no longer infectious to sexual partners, but one of three who remains untreated will suffer late manifestations that usually involve the cardiovascular or nervous system.

Congenital syphilis may result in stillbirths or neonatal death. Surviving children often bear such stigmata as notched teeth, deformed bones and visual and hearing problems.

Diagnosis. A definitive diagnosis of syphilis is based on clinical history combined with results of a physical examination and laboratory tests. The spirochete in primary or secondary syphilis may be visualized directly through a dark-field microscope: A moist sample from the skin or mucous membrane lesion is obtained and a standard glass slide with cover slip is prepared. The presence of typical, motile cork-screw shaped spirochetes is usually diagnostic, but other spiral organisms often can be differentiated by the experienced observer. Even when they are present, however, spirochetes may not be detected. Clinical suspicion warrants serologic testing and patient follow-up.

The first and simplest serologic test is a nontreponemal one, such as the Venereal Disease Research Laboratory (VDRL) test. The quantitative VDRL test is the most useful one for follow-up of patients to assess adequacy of treatment. Biologic false-positive VDRL tests may occur in patients with other infections, autoimmune disorders or for no apparent reason. Test repetition and clinical assessment often are helpful in resolving difficult cases. To confirm doubtful cases, use of a more specific (treponemal) test is indicated (e.g., FTA-ABS, MHA-TP). If neurologic involvement is suspected, cerebrospinal fluid examination (including a CSF-VDRL test) is strongly recommended.

Most states require testing for syphilis before marriage and during pregnancy; most physicians test for syphilis when pregnancy is confirmed to safeguard against congenital syphilis (often combined with tests for rubella). Many hospitals require such tests on all admissions.

Treatment. The stage, duration and history of the disease determine treatment. The following regimens serve as a guide. Upon initial detection of primary, secondary or early (less than one year's duration) latent syphilis, benzathine penicillin G, 2.4 million units (1.2 million units in each buttock), is given intramuscularly. This is the drug of choice for early syphilis because effective treatment is provided in a single office visit. When initial detection occurs after one year's duration, benzathine penicillin G is administered in the aforementioned dose for three successive weeks for a total of 7.2 million units; alternatively, aqueous procaine penicillin G is given in 15 consecutive daily doses of 600,000 units each (total of 9.0 million units).

For patients who are allergic to penicillin, either tetracycline hydrochloride or erythromycin 30 gm (0.5 gm four times a day for 15 days) is administered. For tertiary syphilis, the period of treatment is extended to 30 days (total of 60 gm).

Following treatment, the patient should avoid sexual contact until cure is demonstrated. Blood tests should be repeated monthly for three months, then every three months for a year. Frequent routine screening for all STDs is recommended for persons at high risk.

THREE "MINOR" SEXUALLY TRANSMITTED DISEASES

The minor STDs are chancroid, lymphogranuloma venereum (LGV, tropical bubo) and granuloma inguinale (Donovan's disease). All cause genital skin sores and glandular swelling and all may be mistaken for syphilis. These STDs are seen far less often than gonorrhea and syphilis in the United States.

Symptoms and Diagnosis. Chancroid is classically characterized by the occurrence of tender, ragged, nonindurated ulcers on the external genitals of males. Many of the ulcers are associated with tender, often unilateral, inguinal lymphadenopathy. Although the diagnosis is often made on the basis of clinical suspicion after syphilis and genital herpes have been ruled out, the use of selective media for isolation of the causative agent, *Haemophilus ducreyi*, shows promise for the future. Female contacts are usually asymptomatic.[11]

Painless, often evanescent, papules or superficial nonindurated genital ulcers often characterize LGV. Frequently, the patient does not seek treatment until the lesion enlarges and/or inguinal adenopathy is evident. Purulent proctocolitis may accompany rectal involvement. Demonstration of *Chlamydia trachomatis* by specialized tissue culture technique or serologic response to the LGV-complement fixation test may facilitate the clinical diagnosis.

Granuloma inguinale is a rare disorder caused by the bacterium, *Calymmatobacterium granulomatis*. Single or multiple granulating ulcers characterize the disease clinically. Diagnosis is confirmed by microscopic demonstration of the intracellular stage of the organism (Donovan bodies) within stained macrophages.

Treatment. Sulfisoxazole is preferred for chancroid and tetracycline or ampicillin is preferred for granuloma inguinale and LGV. For chancroid, the dosage of sulfisoxazole is 1 gm orally four times daily for at least two to three weeks; for LGV and granuloma inguinale, 500 mg of tetracycline is given orally four times daily for two to three weeks. More prolonged therapy may be necessary in patients with advanced infections.

OTHER SEXUALLY TRANSMITTED DISEASES

In addition to these so-called classic and "minor" sexually transmitted diseases, other STDs constitute major reasons a physician is consulted for genital problems.

Nongonococcal urethritis (NGU). In the male, signs and symptoms resemble gonorrhea, but the incubation period is usually 7 to 14 days, the discharge is usually less purulent and associated dysuria is less common. NGU is at least as prevalent as gonorrhea in men. The Center for Disease Control estimates that over 2.5 million cases occurred in the United States in 1979.[15]

Studies have clearly implicated *Chlamydia trachomatis* as the etiologic agent in up to 50 per cent of cases of NGU and *Ureaplasma urealyticum* may be the cause in 20 to 25 per cent; *Trichomonas vaginalis* and herpes genitalis are uncommon causes. *Chlamydia trachomatis* can be isolated in up to 30 per cent of women who are sexually exposed to NGU. It is implicated as a cause of epididymitis in men and purulent cervicitis and salpingitis in women. *Haemophilus vaginalis* is also a common source of NGU in males as well as vaginitis in females.

Vertical transmission of the agent occurs during parturition; inclusion conjunctivitis in newborns and a distinctive pneumonia syndrome in infants are sequelae.

Gram-stained specimens of urethral discharge fail to demonstrate gonococci, but they contain at least four leukocytes per high-power field. Tetracycline hydrochloride is given orally in a dose of 0.5 gm for at least seven days. Persistent symptoms may indicate reinfection. Partners also may require treatment.

Genital herpes. This has become recognized as one of the most common and serious of the STDs. Genital herpes, caused by herpes simplex virus, has an incubation period of two to seven days. In cases of primary (first episode) infection, vesicles may develop and ulcerate; these highly infectious lesions are often accompanied by fever, lymphadenopathy and malaise. The skin lesions heal spontaneously within 10 to 20 days, but up to two-thirds of patients will suffer frequent and unpredictable recurrences. In typical cases, the clinical diagnosis is evident, but it may be confirmed by demonstration of multinucleated giant cells on stained smears. Diagnosis in asymptomatic persons or in those with atypical lesions must be confirmed by virus culture.

Treatment is symptomatic to relieve discomfort and prevent secondary bacterial infection. Sitz baths, hot wet compresses and anesthetic creams are prescribed. Although several "cures" have been announced, controlled clinical trials have demonstrated that none reduces recurrences or significantly shortens the duration of symptoms.

Several studies have strongly correlated an association between genital herpes in women and cancer of the uterine cervix.[16] Although evidence of a causal relationship with cervical cancer is inconclusive at this time, women with genital herpes should be strongly encouraged to have annual or semiannual Pap smears. Disseminated herpetic infection of the newborn may occur when infants are infected during birth. Over 50 per cent of affected infants die or suffer permanent sequelae. Cesarean section at term (prior to or within four hours of the rupture of membranes) is recommended if the mother has active genital lesions.

Condyloma acuminatum (venereal or genital warts). This papovavirus causes warts in moist genital or anal areas. The moist lesions, which are usually painless and filiform or cauliflower-like, vary in size from millimeters to centimeters. On drier skin, the warts are usually smaller, harder and grayish-pink. Cosmetic concerns motivate most patients to seek treatment, but the warts may be uncomfortable and should be treated.

For small warts, a solution containing 20 per cent podophyllin in a tincture of benzoin is applied topically. The solution should be washed off within two to four hours. Electrosurgery or cryosurgery may be effective for resistant lesions. The warts may recur after therapy. If they are located on or under the foreskin, circumcision is sometimes advised.

318

Trichomoniasis ("trich"). This common vaginal infection is caused by the flagellated protozoan, *Trichomonas vaginalis*. Typical symptoms include itching and a yellow-green, often frothy, discharge. The vulva may be red and painful. An immediate specific diagnosis can be made by wet-mount, microscopic examination of the motile, pear-shaped flagellated organism from vaginal discharge, but selective culture is considerably more sensitive. Men rarely show signs (such as dysuria or itching) of trichomoniasis, but they are often asymptomatic carriers.

Treatment is fairly standard for the patient and the sex partner: 250 mg of metronidazole is given orally three times daily for 7 to 10 days. Alternatively, 2 gm (eight tablets) for each partner may be prescribed. Alcohol is prohibited during the treatment period, because the combined effect of the two drugs can cause moderately severe abdominal symptoms.

Pediculosis pubis (crab lice) and scabies. Pediculosis pubis are minute crab-like parasites similar to common body lice. Patients usually notice the lice or their nits (eggs) near pubic hair roots. Itching varies in severity. They are usually transmitted by intimate contact with an infected person or by contaminated bedding or clothes.

Scabies is caused by the gravid female mite (*Sarcoptes scabiei*) that burrows into the skin and deposits feces and eggs. Itching may be quite severe, especially at night. The characteristic distribution of scabies includes skin creases of the hands, fingers, wrists, toes, genitals, axillae and areolar areas of the breasts. Scabies may be transmitted sexually or nonsexually via contact with people, infested bedding or clothes. Like pediculosis, scabies is usually diagnosed clinically and is confirmed by microscopic viewing of the arthropod or its tracts.

For treatment of both infections, lindane (gamma benzene hexachloride) lotion is applied to the affected areas and allowed to remain for 12 to 24 hours, followed by a soap shampoo. Application may be repeated once in four to seven days. Excessive use of this lotion can cause allergic reactions and care must be exercised when infants are treated. Close household contacts and sexual partners should be treated simultaneously. Contaminated bedding and clothes should be laundered or dry cleaned.

Molluscum contagiosum. This viral disease causes a variable number of smooth lesions with a central depression. Although the virus may be transmitted sexually, it is usually transmitted nonsexually and is commonly seen in school children. The lesions may eventually disappear without therapy, but treatment with excision, desiccation or chemotherapy is recommended.

Hepatitis. It recently has been recognized that hepatitis viruses may be transmitted sexually. Hepatitis A is spread via the fecal-oral route and, therefore, usually is contracted by ingestion of contaminated water or food. Close personal contact or sexual relations also may be responsible for spread of the disease. However, as yet, no positive correlation between sexual behavior and hepatitis A has been demonstrated.

In contrast to hepatitis A, HBsAg antigen associated with hepatitis B has been detected in saliva, semen, urine, serum bile, menstrual blood, vaginal secretions, ascitic fluid and pleural fluid of those individuals infected with hepatitis viruses. Therefore, hepatitis B can be easily contracted by sexual contact. The disease appears to be transmitted commonly by prostitutes and between homosexual males. In one study[17] of homosexual men attending STD clinics, over 60 per cent showed evidence of past or present infection.

There is epidemiologic evidence that non-A, non-B hepatitis also may be acquired sexually. However, because no serologic tests are currently available to diagnose non-A, non-B hepatitis, definitive proof of the venereal spread of this infection must await the development of reliable detection techniques.

Candidiasis (monilia, thrush). These organisms are present in the mouth, vagina or intestines of approximately 50 per cent of healthy individuals. The organisms multiply in the vagina or under the foreskin and can produce symptoms such as severe itching and a thick, white "cottage cheese" discharge. Women often become symptomatic during periods of high progesterone activity, such as during pregnancy or with use of certain oral contraceptives. Symptomatic multiplication of the organisms may accompany debilitating illness, diabetes or antibiotic or immunosuppressive therapy. Diagnosis is by microscopic identification of budding yeasts upon examination of the discharge on a slide containing 10 per cent potassium hydroxide.

For treatment, nystatin vaginal suppositories are inserted morning and night for two weeks or 2 per cent miconazole vaginal cream is applied nightly for two weeks. The cream also can be used to treat balanitis in men or vulvitis in women.

Persistence of symptoms following therapy may require retreatment, but the clinician should be alert to the possibility that diabetes mellitus or other debilitating diseases may be present.

PREVENTION OF SEXUALLY TRANSMITTED DISEASES

A few measures taken by physicians could probably help appreciably to reduce the incidence of STDs.

1. The physician should realize that STDs and their carriers are common in all levels of society. Carriers are a major threat to public health and screening should be done *routinely*. This includes considering the possibility of STDs when taking the history and conducting a careful genital, rectal and oral examination, especially in patients who may be sexually active or who have genital symptoms. No group of patients is immune except those who are sexually abstinent. Those who are monogamous may have partners who are not. In taking a history of any patient, the physician should include inquiry on possible sexual activities that may lead to the condition under investigation. The clinician also should be aware of behavior that suggests the person is at high risk of contracting STDs, although patients may be reluctant to reveal all aspects of their sexual behavior. The physician should not belittle the concern of any patient. Any request for an STD examination should be accorded the same respect as any other patient concern.

2. All patients should, at some appropriate time, be considered candidates for instruction in how to avoid and detect STDs. It cannot be assumed that

this instruction is being given by some other person or agency. Sexually active nonmonogamous patients should learn that any new sexual partner may be a "silent" carrier, that "nice" people from "good" homes do catch and transmit STDs, and that using a condom prevents the transmission of many infections. Washing the genitals with soap and water before sexual activity, douching and/or urinating soon afterward, and using contraceptive foams and jellies during intercourse help prevent STDs. Patients must be advised that oral contraceptives do not protect against STDs.

Most sexually active people know about STDs, but do not take steps to avoid them,[3,18] perhaps because of embarrassment, unwillingness to "ruin the mood," willingness to "take the gamble," or because they deny the risk as it pertains to themselves. Some individuals, for various psychological reasons, deny the possibility of disease or the expiation from guilt that treatment offers. The extent of the risk and the serious consequences should be made known to patients.

3. The physician should make sure that the patient knows that any bump, sore, pain, discharge or discoloration of the genitals, anus or mouth, in oneself or one's sexual partner, should arouse suspicion and be cause for a medical examination.

4. Every patient must be warned against self-diagnosis and self-treatment. Patients should be advised to follow a treatment regimen strictly and to avoid sexual contact until the STD is cured. Partners should be encouraged to have an examination and treatment. The physician must, in the broadest scope, consider the public health aspects of the disease under treatment.

It is perhaps unfortunate that any group of diseases should have become associated with love and sex, two of life's greatest pleasures. But for many people, life is constantly providing a testing ground for their willingness to risk incurring pain in the pursuit of such pleasures. The philosophical and moral issues—let alone the health issues—involved are not always clearly seen nor even considered, and certainly they are not evaluated equally by all. To most physicians, trained in decision making and having lived a life of denial to fulfill future goals, such risk taking might appear to signify frivolous behavior. Nevertheless, many individuals do seek love or sexual satisfaction at the risk of pain, and many commonly rely on feelings and intuition and the desire for immediate rewards despite possible long-term "punishment." The forces of religion, law and public health have yet to prove effective in reversing this trend.

Regretably, despite all individual efforts by personal physicians, the STDs are probably going to persist as important public health problems. The sexual behavior of people and the attitudes of the public toward STD victims are difficult to change. The situation may halt or reverse itself with a massive public media campaign and effective advances in disease detection and treatment, but this will not occur overnight. Thus, it falls to the primary care physician to encourage in each patient an attitude of prevention, detection and treatment—and concern for the welfare of others as well as himself. This might best be done by demonstrating true humanistic and holistic concern for the patient so that the consequences of gambling with one's mental and physical health are recognized and the individual can make the most appropriate sexual decisions.[19]

Acknowledgment

Appreciation is extended to Dr. James W. Curran, Chief Operational Research Branch, Center for Disease Control, Atlanta, and Dr. Richard T. Arnest, of the STD Clinic, Diamond-Head Health Center, Honolulu, for their learned review of this paper.

References

1. Rosebury T: *Microbes and Morals: The Strange Story of Venereal Disease*. New York, Ballantine Books Inc, 1973.
2. Owen RL, et al: Venereal aspects of gastroenterology. *West J Med* 1979 (March); 130:236-246.
3. Darrow WW: Approaches to the problem of sexually transmitted disease prevention. *Prev Med* 1976; 5:165-175.
4. Sagarin E: Swinging through the VD tree. *Physician's World* 1974 (April); 2:70-74.
5. Brooks GF, et al: Repeated gonorrhea: An analysis of importance and risk factors. *J Infect Dis* 1978; 137:161-169.
6. Rothenberg RB, et al: Reporting of gonorrhea by private physicians: A behavioral study. *Am J Pub Health* 1980; 70:983-986.
7. The law: Housen vs Duke. *Time* 1976 (May 31); 45-46.
8. Fiumara NJ: The sexually transmissible diseases. *DM* 1978 (Dec); 25:1-63.
9. Keith L, Brittain J: *Sexually Transmitted Diseases*. Aspen, Colorado, Creative Infomatics Inc, 1978.
10. U.S. Dept of HEW, Public Health Service, Center for Disease Control: Sexually Transmitted Diseases Summary, 1979.
11. McFalls JA: Frustrated fertility: A population paradox. *Popul Bull* 1979 (May); 34:2.
12. Curran JW: Cost-effectiveness analysis: Presentation at National VD Seminar. San Diego, September 1977.
13. Felman YM, Nikitas MA: Pelvic inflammatory disease. *NY State J Med* 1980; 80:635-638.
14. Fiumara NJ: Assessing gonorrhea, nongonococcal urethritis, and syphilis. *Consultant* 1980 (April); 20:246-250.
15. Felman YM, Nikitas MA: Nongonococcal urethritis: The sexually transmitted disease of the 1980s. *Sex Med Today* 1980 (March); 8-13.
16. Platts WM: The changing face of sexually transmitted disease. *NZ Med J* 1979; 90:248-251.
17. Schreeder M, et al: Hepatitis B in the male homosexual, (abstract), in: *Epidemic Intelligence Service Conference* 1979; 24.
18. Hart G: *Sexually Transmitted Diseases*, (pamphlet). Burlington, North Carolina, Carolina Biology Readers, Carolina Biological Supply Company, 1976.
19. Diamond M, Karlen A: *Sexual Decisions*. Boston, Little, Brown and Company, 1980.

Chapter 23

Sexual Exploitation and Aggression

William R. Miller, Ph.D., and Diane S. Fordney, M.D.

Sexual assault refers to nonconsenting sexual behavior, whether physical, visual, or verbal. Rape is the most common and traumatic type, but voyeurism, exhibitionism, frotteurism, obscene telephone calls, and coercive sexual contact between husband and wife also are covered by the term.

There is no accurate estimate of the number of sexual assaults that occur each year, because many victims do not report the sexual assault, because there are differences in the reporting practices of individual police departments, and because the legal definitions of assault among the various states vary. However, government statistics on rape indicate that sexual assault is a major social problem affecting thousands of victims each year. The incidence of rape is 1:2,000 women in suburban and rural areas and 1:1,000 women in urban areas; these statistics suggest that, projected over a woman's lifetime, 4 or 5 of every 100 women will be raped. Rape now accounts for 6 per cent of violent crimes.[1]

Sexual assault frequently has devastating psychological consequences and sometimes results in serious physical injury, disease, or death. Types that cause no physical injury and relatively little psychological insult include obscene telephone calls or letters; frotteurism (rubbing the penis against the victim's body, most commonly in subways or buses); exhibitionism (exposing the genitals to an unwilling witness); and voyeurism (peeping into windows to view nudity or private sexual activity).

Most of these acts have in common the perpetrator's anonymity; his physical distance from the victim; the occurrence of the act in a situation in which harm to the victim is unlikely; the usually random choice of victim; and, with the exception of obscene phone calls or letters, the brief duration of the act. They rarely lead to more serious sexual aggression.[2] Although temporarily upset, most victims experience no adverse effects and are not likely to be subjected to recurrent assaults; support and reassurance are usually all that the victim requires.

Victims of obscene communications may suffer recurrent harrassment which often causes greater stress and fear, particularly if the victim begins to believe that she is known to the writer or caller. Actions aimed at stopping the assaults should be encouraged. Callers can be discouraged by hanging up the phone, blowing a whistle into the mouthpiece, or changing the telephone number. Engaging the caller in conversation only encourages him.

The recipient of obscene letters is usually more fearful, because she knows that the writer has her name and address. Recurrent assaults of this type should be reported to law enforcement officials. Many such harrassers have modes of operation known by the police, and the writer may be identified from police records. Victims of such messages should increase precautions for personal security by locking their doors and should avoid being alone in isolated or potentially dangerous areas.

People who repeatedly commit sexual assaults (e.g., obscene communication, frotteurism, exhibitionism, voyeurism) are almost always men and have been characterized as timid, inhibited, and lacking in social skills. They rarely are guilty of more serious sex offenses, and their behavior is often compulsive and fraught with anxiety, shame and guilt.[3]

Other forms of sexual assault typically produce much greater trauma and more often come to the attention of the physician. Although they have no common term or label, they all have in common the direct performance of sexual acts upon another person without his or her consent.

Rape is the most familiar of these assaults and, in fact, some people refer to all of these assaults as rape. However, most legal jurisdictions define rape as nonconsensual sexual intercourse. Nonconsenting oral-genital and anal-genital sexual assaults are most often referred to as sodomy or involuntary deviate sexual intercourse, not rape. Sexual molestation of children and adults by means of forced genital fondling also may be included in this class of sexual assaults.

Although rape of males by sodomy does occur, the vast majority of rape victims are women age 18 to 45; next most common is rape of adolescent and prepubertal girls. Rape of preadolescent males by males is slightly more common than rape of adult males, except in prison.[3] Only isolated reports of sexual molestation or rape of men by women have appeared.

The effects of rape and sexual molestation and the treatment of victims depend upon the specific nature of the assault, the victim's reactions and age, and the time elapsed since the event.

RESPONSES TO RAPE AND SEXUAL MOLESTATION

Adult Victims. Clinical and research studies have shown a rather consistent picture of the psychological impact of rape and molestation.[3-5] The victim's actions are abnormal for the first several hours or even days after the assault, ranging from hysteria, sobbing muteness, or a trance-like state to stoicism, indifference, flippancy, hostility, rigid self-control, or apology.[4]

Subsequent reactions vary according to the adaptive and coping capacities of the victim. However, there are several fairly predictable responses that have been described as the "rape trauma syndrome."[4] During the acute or disorganization phase, which may last from a few days to weeks, the victim typically has difficulty in sleeping; disturbances in appetite, including anorexia, nausea and vomiting; focused or diffuse fear and anxiety; physical complaints ranging from generalized soreness to localized pain; and repetitive thoughts about the assault. The long-term reorganization phase may last from months to years. The usual response pattern includes a disruption of the routine of living; continued sleep disturbances, particularly nightmares; and a variety of phobias.

Married victims are also confronted with the need to deal with the issue of intimacy and sex with their husbands. It is not possible at this time to characterize the typical response of husbands to the rape or molestation of their wives. Limited research suggests that husbands and boyfriends of victims are angry and resentful toward the victim.[6] Male partners may feel personally wronged if they have the attitude that the woman is the male's exclusive property. Other research, however, indicates that a very different type of response may be characteristic of the husbands of rape victims.[7] They often respond initially with fear, which may be associated with some inappropriate sense of responsibility for the assault; e.g., "I should not have been working that night." The fear and self-blame dissipate rather quickly and are replaced by a dramatic rage response, with the rage being directed at the rapist, not at the victim.

Adolescent and Child Victims. The reactions of adolescent and child victims are similar to those described above for adult victims, but there are also variations due to the personality and developmental differences between young and adult victims.

As with adults, young victims manifest both an acute disorganization phase and a long-term reorganization process following rape or sexual molestation, and their immediate emotional response to the sexual assault may range from very expressive to very controlled.[4] The acute phase of the trauma syndrome is characterized by disturbances in sleeping and eating, excessive fears, repetitive thoughts about the assault, and a variety of physical complaints similar to those of adult victims. In addition, the adolescent or child often experiences additional disruptions as a result of the family's emotional response.

The most common and disruptive response of families to the rape or molestation of a child is the need to blame someone: generally the rapist, the child, or themselves.[4] Although the potential for psychological damage to the child is obviously high if parents blame the victim for the assault, excessive or intense blame directed by the parents at either the assailant or themselves also can be harmful. Murderous rage directed toward the rapist may remind the child of the violence of the assault itself and lead the young victim to believe that her own family is capable of extreme aggression. In addition, when parents blame themselves, they may reinforce the child's initial anxiety about trusting people again, or they may become overprotective and smothering.

The long-term reorganization phase for the adolescent and child victim is similar to that of the adult victim in that there is a disruption of the normal living routine, nightmares and continued sleeping disturbances, and the emergence of phobias. Problems in school frequently develop, including poor academic performance, poor peer relationships, truancy, or school phobia. Sexual fears and concerns are particularly important for the young victim, since she is often not very knowledgeable about sexuality and, in many cases, is a virgin prior to the assault. The sexual aspect of the assault also puts an additional strain on the family because the parents are forced, often for the first time, to deal with their child's sexuality.

MANAGEMENT

Adult Victims. Several important and sometimes conflicting factors must be kept in mind when treating the victims of rape or sexual molestation in the hospital emergency room. First, the victim has suffered a major emotional trauma and requires emotional support, guidance and information. In addition, there may be physical trauma that requires appropriate medical treatment. Finally, the examining physician must assume a medicolegal role; i.e., he is expected to collect information during the examination that eventually may be used as evidence in a legal proceeding. In order to meet these needs and requirements, it is important to establish a procedure for managing victims of rape and to train the hospital staff who might deal with these victims in the special procedures required.

Treatment of the victim is probably most effective and efficient when a team approach is used.[8] The team should include a person who can provide the necessary emotional support, use crisis intervention techniques, and guide the victim through the hospital procedure. A second team member is an emergency room nurse who coordinates the treatment program and explains the procedures to the patient. The third team member, the physician, has a medicolegal role.

It must be noted that the physician's medicolegal responsibilities do *not* require him to determine whether a rape or sexual assault actually did occur. The physician's responsibility is to collect and record information, not to interpret or make judgments. In fact, the physician not only is not responsible for interpreting or judging the data, he is not able to make an accurate determination of the truthfulness of the victim's statements on the basis of the examination in the emergency room. Of course, the physician may find no evidence of semen or physical trauma, but neither of these negative findings precludes the possibility of rape or sexual assault. Also, the physician's opinion of the victim's credibility is a personal one, not a medical or professional opinion.

In addition to the fact that the physician has no legal responsibility for evaluating the truthfulness of the victim's statements, there are two important reasons why the physician should not make such an evaluation. First, the assumption that the victim is lying may consciously or unconsciously bias the way the physician conducts the examination and collects the evidence. Secondly, if the examining physician decides that the victim is lying about the assault, then it is possible that this judgment will be demonstrated to the victim in some way, e.g., in a cold or even hostile manner of interacting. The danger, of course, is that if the patient is not lying, the physician is contributing to additional victimization.

Because the physician needs to be an objective observer and recorder of data and to refrain from making personal judgments, it is important for him to have someone else present to act as an advocate and counselor. In most major cities, this support person is a specially trained worker from a rape crisis center who is on call at the emergency room. This person usually provides both crisis intervention and the option of continued support through telephone hot-lines or counseling groups. The examining physician must be aware of the resources of the rape crisis center, women's groups, and mental health facilities in the community so that appropriate referrals can be made if no support person is available in the emergency room.

Hospital personnel should place a high priority on the rapid examination and treatment of rape victims, because collection of legal evidence should begin with as little delay as possible. Since it can be assumed that most victims are confused and emotionally upset, it is important that the victim be informed of all treatment procedures in writing as well as verbally.

Medical care should entail a history, including a description in the victim's words of the time, place and nature of the assault; physical examination; laboratory testing; treatment; and arrangements for follow-up services.[9] Life-threatening conditions, such as head injuries or bleeding lacerations, must be treated first.

If there are no major injuries, the physician should interview the patient to obtain and record a description of the assault. Next, he should perform the physical examination and note the condition of the victim's clothing and the presence or absence of bruises, cuts, or other signs of violence. He should look carefully for signs of trauma to the genitals or other affected parts of the body, and he should collect specimens for laboratory testing. Finally, he should arrange for medical follow-up to check for pregnancy, genital injury, and sexually transmitted disease and make referrals for crisis counseling and support.

Assembling an office "rape kit" will simplify and expedite the physician's job.[10] A typical kit contains consent forms for treatment and the collection of legal evidence, a history form designed for sexual assault cases, a physical examination form, a list of telephone numbers of law enforcement officials and crisis and counseling centers, and information on reporting to police and on the victims' emotional reactions. The kit also should include items necessary for specimen collection: a bag for clothing; small envelopes for foreign material found on the victim's person, such as grass, gravel, or fingernail samplings; sterile swabs for collecting vaginal, vulvar, oral, or anal secretions and dried semen or blood on the body; glass slides in cardboard cases; small syringes connected to polyethylene tubing to obtain cervical mucus and vaginal pool samples; test tubes for holding syringe or swab samples; a comb to collect any of the assailant's pubic hair that may be on the mons; a medium for *Neisseria gonorrhoeae* culture; and labels.

Examining cervical mucus may be the only way to identify sperm from 6 up to 96 hours after an assault. In addition to a wet mount to be examined immediately for motile sperm, a dry mount is needed for later use by a police technician. Samples of dried or wet blood and of vaginal or other secretions can be used by police laboratories for acid phosphatase determination, blood typing, and A, B and O typing of vaginal secretions or semen. Care must be taken to handle this physical evidence in a way that does not break the chain of evidence. Everyone who handles specimens should sign a sheet stating that he has done so and, if there is no police official present to receive the evidence, it should be labeled and kept in a locked drawer until it can be given to the police.

Samples should be taken from any orifice penetrated by the assailant to obtain cultures for gonorrhea and a baseline serum test for syphilis. Some authorities advocate immediate treatment of all victims for both syphilis and gonorrhea;[9] other authorities advise waiting for the results of the culture and of a second serum test six weeks later in order to avoid unnecessary exposure to penicillin or other medication. This decision depends on the physician's confidence in the victim returning for further treatment.

Pregnancy is possible for any fertile woman not using an oral contraceptive or intrauterine device. Some clinicians recommend administration of 5 mg of estrogen for five days to avert implantation;[9] others believe that the side effects of this treatment are too great to permit its routine use. A follow-up visit after one or two weeks is advisable, and menstrual extraction can be done easily at that time if any question of pregnancy remains. A serologic test for syphilis should be scheduled after six weeks for an untreated victim.

Child and Adolescent Victims. When the victim of rape or sexual assault is a child, the management procedures described above may be modified. The sexual assault of children provokes profound anger in parents and professionals, and the child is often frightened by these reactions and confused about the cause. A stable, comforting parent in the examination area is an asset during the interview and examination; an extremely anxious one should be asked to remain outside.

The physician should question the child in simple language; if this is unproductive, the physician should not persist. Children are often frightened by white coats and a manner of professional distance. Taking off the coat and holding the child while asking questions can do much to allay anxiety. Explaining each step of the examination in a calming way to the child and letting her help you, if she is old enough, can ease and speed up the procedure. Having the parents in constant attendance in the hospital room is comforting for the child.[11]

If a child was raped, examination of external genitals often reveals lacerations, bleeding, or other physical trauma. If the damage is extensive, hospitalization is required and a surgeon competent in repair techniques may be needed. Vaginal and rectal lacerations in children may be associated with dissecting hematomas which are life-threatening and require rapid intervention and hospital observation.

A discussion with the parents that includes explanations may be time-consuming, but it is essential. Prolonged counseling can be referred, but some points must be handled immediately. Parents who are angry, weeping, or hysterical increase the trauma for the child; they must be calmed and cautioned to be supportive, loving, and in control around the child. If they cannot, other adults the child knows and responds to should be called.

Many prepubertal children do not understand the social implications of sexual assault. Even if unhurt physically, they are frightened and often convinced that they have done something bad to make their parents react so strongly. If there is a possibility of additional sexual assaults, parents should be urged to remove the child from the environment. In all other ways, the parents should attempt to allow the child's life to go on as usual. Her questions about the assault should be answered honestly, simply and briefly.

In contrast to young children, teenagers generally are aware of the social implications of sexual assault. They need counseling and loving support from their parents and require more reassurance than do adults of postrape normality and more reassurance than children that they did not cause the rape. Parents in anguish often say, "Why didn't you listen to me?" They must be reminded that the teenager was the victim and that it cannot be assumed that she contributed to the assault.

Finally, some mention should be made of homosexual assaults upon male children. Sexual activities with the boy typically would include caressing and fondling, masturbation and mutual masturbation, fellatio, and/or anal intercourse. Most attention in this area has been given to the molestation of strangers by homosexual pedophiles; i.e., adult males with an exclusive sexual preference for male children as subjects of sexual gratification. There is increasing evidence, however, that many sexual assaults against young boys are perpetrated by members of their own family.[12]

The boy's reaction to a homosexual assault is influenced by several factors, including the identity of the perpetrator, whether there was a single incident or multiple incidents over a period of time, and the degree of force or violence that was involved. In some cases, the boy does not exhibit any overt behavioral reactions, appearing instead to be calm and unconcerned. Negative responses include guilt, psychosomatic complaints, disruption in sleeping and eating patterns, and school phobias.[4]

The general procedures for management of female child and adolescent victims discussed previously also apply to the male child victim. In the medical examination, however, special attention should be paid to the following: any genital or rectal trauma; possible gonorrheal infection of the pharynx, urethra and rectum; and the possible presence of foreign bodies in the urethra or rectum.

Medical management of sexual assault victims consists of immediate evaluation and treatment and two follow-up visits—one after one or two weeks and the other after six weeks—to check for pregnancy and sexually transmitted disease and to evaluate the patient's ability to cope with the psychological trauma. The management of child victims requires some modifications in the procedure, mainly different counseling and support strategies, and methods of dealing with parents.

References

1. Federal Bureau of Investigation: *Uniform Crime Report*. Washington, DC, Federal Bureau of Investigation, 1979.

2. American Psychiatric Association: Psycho-disorders. *Diagnostic & Statistical Manual of Mental Disorders III*. Washington, DC, American Psychiatric Association, 1977.

3. Amir M: *Patterns in Forcible Rape*. Chicago, University of Chicago Press, 1971.

4. Burgess AW, Holmstrom LL: *Rape: Victims of Crisis*. Washington, DC, Robert J Brady & Co, 1974.

5. Russell DEH: *Politics of Rape*. New York, Stein & Day, 1975.

6. Silverman DC: Sharing the crisis of rape: Counseling the mates and families of victims. *Am J Orthopsychiatry* 1978; 48:166-173.

7. Miller WR, et al: *The Effects of Rape on Marital and Sexual Adjustment*. Philadelphia, Marriage Council of Philadelphia, 1979. (unpublished)

8. Hilberman E: *The Rape Victim*. Washington, DC, American Psychiatric Association, 1976.

9. American College of Obstetrics and Gynecology: Alleged sexual assault. *ACOG Tech Bull* (November) 1978.

10. *Report of the District of Columbia Task Force on Rape*. Washington, DC, District of Columbia City Council, 1973.

11. Caprero V: Sexual assault of female children. *Ann NY Acad Sci* 1967; 142:817.

12. Burgess AW, et al: *Sexual Assault of Children and Adolescents*. Lexington, MA, Lexington Books, 1978.

Chapter 24

Incest

Domeena C. Renshaw, M.B., Ch.B., M.D.

The family exists in all societies, and marriage or sexual contact usually is not allowed between any members of the nuclear family other than husband and wife.[1,2] The incest taboo includes intercourse as well as noncoital acts and homosexual contact.

Over the past century, many scientists have believed that there is an instinctive aversion to incest and that "inbreeding" causes mental and physical defects. The matter is still debated today. Some investigators[3,4] claim to have found negative effects of inbreeding, while others have argued that any such effects are probably so small that throughout history they would have passed unnoticed.[5]

One argument for at least a strong cultural factor in the incest taboo is that in virtually all cultures definitions of incest extend beyond the nuclear family, often according to socially defined relationships (designated kin) rather than biological kinship. A society may even encourage first-cousin marriages, while banning coitus with step-siblings and step-parents.[1] In only a handful of societies are aunts and uncles potential sexual or marital partners, and almost all cultures ban sexual relationships with at least one kind of cousin.[6]

Sexual feelings and fantasies are a normal part of everyday life and easily arise between family members. Incest fantasies have not been studied but are prevalent, both in literature and when careful in-depth histories are taken. Powerful and persistent messages, however, are given to every member of society, from early childhood on, that one's closest relatives should be objects of love and loyalty but not of sexual desire. Both conscious and unconscious controls are developed within the family in each new generation, and the children are expected to continue to exercise these sexual controls when they themselves become parents. One generally accepted interpretation is that the deeply rooted taboo protects the family from being destroyed by sexual rivalries and role conflicts. Therefore, sexual impulses toward close relatives are strictly controlled, repressed or denied.[7]

Incest may arouse strong aversive feelings that often preclude an objective assessment. Few persons—including physicians and others—can comfortably discuss incest in depth and detail.

SOCIAL ASPECTS

With the exception of biological mother-son sexual relationships, incest occasionally has been permitted to some people in a handful of societies; e.g., in the royal families of the ancient Incas, Rome, Egypt and Hawaii and among the Azande of Africa.[8,9] Apparently latitude has been given in such cases to perpetuate a ruling family in the interest of political stability. In certain isolated rural subcultures in the United States, in island and mountain cultures, and in parts of Europe, incest is covertly or even semi-overtly accepted by some people, especially with designated kin.[7,10,11]

It has been surmised[12] that the greater the complexity of the cultures, the more the incest taboo seems to be eroded. Some of this incest is with designated kin; stepkinships are excluded from incest prohibition in some penal codes.[13]

Many textbooks state that incest is rare, even statistically negligible, but family physicians and other health-care and social-aid professionals know that this is not so. Incidences of one to a few cases per million[2] in Western populations draw on studies of convicted incest offenders (usually father-daughter incest, including stepfathers). Often incest between siblings and cousins occurs in adolescence and remains undetected.[14,15]

First-cousin incest in one study of sex offenders is reported as probably most frequent, involving perhaps 3 to 4 per cent of the U.S. population; less common, in descending order,[11] is incest with siblings, aunts, siblings-in-law, uncles, fathers and mothers (unfortunately, few studies distinguish fathers and stepfathers). One study of a small, perhaps atypical, group of women revealed incest rates as high as 15 per cent;[16] in another study, the reported incidence was 9 per cent.[17]

In a report on a collection of father-daughter cases,[18] it was estimated by extrapolation that there are 25 million women in the United States who are permanently damaged by father-daughter sexual activity. However, many reviewers question both the data and the conclusions.[19]

Incest is not easily admitted, even to skilled researchers and clinicians. Eliciting details of incestual experiences often takes time, trust and explicit questioning. (Table 5 suggests questions for face-to-face data-gathering. The questions also may be self-administered as a first step toward further discussion.) Incest history may emerge in a crisis, as when a physician is consulted about real or feared pregnancy. Incest is rarely presented as a complaint to psychiatrists (2 per cent in one study in a scan of 6,000 cases seen over a period of three years at a midwest university outpatient clinic), but it may be elicited in a thorough psychiatric history in about 5 to 9 per cent of cases.[17]

In a private practice in Minneapolis, data were analyzed on 32 patients seen over a 15-year period. They experienced incest without revealing a specific clinical profile for either partner.[20]

Unless a horrified neighbor rushes to the police, the first professional to whom the problem is presented may be a clergyman or a family physician; occasionally a child seeks out a teacher for protection, after not having been believed at home that incest occurred. The physician may be the first or only professional sought voluntarily by the family, usually because pregnancy has occurred.

FAMILY AND INTERPERSONAL ASPECTS

The McGill Forensic Clinic in Montreal,[21,22] reporting on the psychodynamics of father-daughter incest, indicates that most of the men involved who have more than one daughter engage in incest with each in turn. The fathers are described as immature and jealous, although most are good providers and faithful to the family. Their wives are more reluctant than they are to accept treatment, and they feel guilty and angry at themselves for not having protected their daughters. The families were helped when all members openly collaborated to keep the father away from the girls.

Incest occurs typically with warnings or injunctions to secrecy or in warm collusion: "It's our secret. No one else in the world should know." The latter may well be the case when the incest results not from coercion but from persuasion, tenderness and promises of rewards. Often, however, threats or force are involved in both the act and the injunction to secrecy: e.g., "If you tell anyone, I'll kill you."

Keeping the secret can cause great anxiety and preoccupation. Daily contact between the incestuous partners may create much tension in both and, in some cases, fear of retaliation. Telling the secret may be a relief, but also may create fear of loss of love of the family member or violence to self.

A child may well become confused about right and wrong, good and bad. In the first place, society consistently teaches its children that when they grow up they will find love and sex partners outside the family. Yet, if a loved father tells his daughter that their pleasurable sexual behavior together is good, why shouldn't mother or others know? On the other hand, if he has threatened to beat her if she tells anyone, how can it be good or right? Sex, love, pleasure and punishment all become blurred.[17,20,23,24]

In very young siblings, normal sex exploration and sex play (without coitus) is not considered incest by law or by most persons.[6] Between adult and child and between teenagers, incest is legally taken to mean regularly occurring full heterosexual intercourse.[13,25] However, heterosexual or homosexual sex play without coitus may lead to orgasm. Though there may be legal debate about the sex play being incest, the emotional responses of pleasure, guilt, conflict, preoccupation and anxiety may be the same as for coitus. Forceful sex play may be upsetting or painful, and threats by siblings, as by adults, to ensure secrecy may cause anxiety. Persistence of pressure or recurrence of forceful sex play between family members may cause physical or emotional trauma.[25] Forceful intercourse is rape incest when family members are involved, with protection an important priority.

BREAKDOWN OF INCEST TABOOS

Fragile incest controls may break down under the influence of alcohol or drug abuse, with uncontrolled strong sexual needs or under emotional distress. Overcrowding and family disintegration also may weaken the incest barrier.[2]

When the incest taboo breaks down, the evaluating physician must try to discover why, although some of the important reasons can be difficult to ascertain. Some of the puzzling issues are:

Why did an adult need to turn to a child relative for sexual expression? Was there a faulty sexual relationship between the parents?[26]

Table 5
INCEST HISTORY: FLOW SHEET

Name: _____

Date: _____

	Never		Sometimes		Frequently	
Fantasy only						
Breast/Genital fondling						
Deep kissing						
Masturbation of you						
Masturbation by you of kin						
Oral—genital						
Anal contact						
Intercourse						
Climax a) you b) kin	a)	b)	a)	b)	a)	b)
Pregnancy						
Fear						
Pain						
Guilt						
Shame						
Thoughts about incest						
Dreams about incest						
Reporting to another						
Police/Hospital						

(Rels. = relationship)	Good	Average	Poor
Rels. between mother and father			
Sex rels. between mother and father			
Rels. mother and self a) past b) now			
Rels. father and self a) past b) now			
Rels. incest partner and self a) past b) now			
Relationship with teacher			
Relationship with minister			
Relationship with spouse now			

Kinship of person who made sex overtures: _____

Was he/she drinking at the time: _____ Threat? _____ Violence: _____

Did he/she have   a) sex with other family? _____ b) Psychiatric problem? _____

Your age at time: _____   Kin's age at time: _____

How did it end? _____

_____

_____

Did you like this person? _____

Do you see each other now? _____ Details: _____

_____

_____

_____

Told to keep secret? _____ Feelings about the secret? _____

_____

_____

Did you tell? _____ Details: _____

_____

_____

_____

Did someone else tell? _____

Details: _____

_____

_____

_____

Pregnancy (if any): _____ Outcome: _____

_____

_____

_____

Pre-occupations with incest (present)? _____

Pre-occupations with incest (past)? _____

Dreams about incest (present)? _____

Dreams about incest (past)? _____

Reading about incest (past) _____ Present: _____

Does your spouse know about this? _____

Reaction: _____

_____

_____

Need for Psychotherapy (past) _____ Present: _____

Sex problems in past: _____

Sex problems now: _____

Details: _____

_____

_____

_____

What helped you most to handle or resolve your feelings about the incest: _____

_____

_____

_____

_____

Domeena C. Renshaw, M. D.
Loyola of Chicago—December 1980

Why did a teenager seek sex from a sibling? Were there excessive restrictions on peer dating?[7]

Did incest controls fail because of excessive use of alcohol or drugs? Psychosis? Senility?[2]

Why, in some cases, were not incest taboos learned—because of mental retardation, psychosis, or other reasons?[2]

What are the covert sexual values in the family's subculture?[6]

Why were parents not protective? Was there subliminal knowledge of the incest by a mother who claimed to disbelieve her child's report but was relieved not to receive her husband's sexual demands?[17,26-28]

Why were stepkinship incest taboos not acquired in a newly formed family? Is a new stepfather younger than his wife and closer in age to his stepdaughter? Was there enough time or awareness of possible peer attraction to avoid sexual expression with new stepkin? Was there enough effort on the part of the mother to protect family members from excess sexual stimulation and tempting intimacy with the stepfather?[26]

DEALING WITH REPORTED INCEST

The physician must first determine whether reported incest is fantasy or fact; this may be extraordinarily difficult to do. If the patient is a child, the determination is critical; local child-abuse laws may require that the incident be reported to a legal authority. Moreover, if incest has occurred, the child needs protection and the family needs counseling if they will accept it. Sometimes checking with the family will confirm the incest, but the child may become upset and change the story. If the report is based on fantasy or is otherwise false, as on occasion it may be, the person accused needs protection from destructive legal entanglement.

Investigating alleged incest can be difficult for many physicians because of their lack of knowledge about, and their discomfort with, this topic or of the law. It may be easier to disbelieve the child or to collude in a coverup than to pursue a history. Knowledge about incest may reduce discomfort enough to permit skillful professional handling of the subject (see Table 5 for questions that may help in evaluation). Details must be elicited by gentle yet specific questioning. Blaming and lack of respect make the questions appear to be an interrogation rather than expressions of concern.

The trauma of incest varies in depth and extent. The presence of force or affection, age, pregnancy and frequency of the act all help to shape the outcome of the experience. It has been stated that incest leaves life-long psychic and sexual disability.[4,18,25] However, it may not always be disabling or traumatic.[7,14,15,17,19,24,28,29]

A potentially significant aspect of the incest episode, whether real or imagined, is internal conflict between enjoying the sex act and experiencing guilt over it. This conflict may result in anxiety. For the partners, the sexual aspect may have been more novel and enjoyable than frightening.[28,29] The panic, blame and fighting among family members upon discovery of the incest,[17] however, might be long and memorable enough to create a lasting generalized feeling that *all* sex is wrong, destructive or evil.[4,9]

Vulnerability to any stress varies with age and coping capacity. Whether incest involves a 6-year-old or a teenager, a retarded child or a precocious one, is obviously relevant in this respect. In addition to the victim and perpetrator of incest, other family members are always involved either directly, indirectly or by default;[26][27][30] thus, the family situation also must be evaluated.

Some individuals express no guilt or conflict about incest that they experienced in early life. They may have understood that the partner had a strong sexual desire, reduced inhibitions (due to excessive drinking or drug use), or a driven need (as in manic-depression). If it is known that the partner also had sexual contact with others in the family, self-blame may be reduced. In addition, guilt may be dispelled and forgiveness extended if the partner (father) was known to have been rejected by his appropriate sexual partner (mother) or if he was known to have other emotional problems.

The physician also can ease residual guilt feelings by helping a patient to realize that, as a young child, he or she had limited understanding of the sex act and was still physically and emotionally dependent on the parent who made sexual contact. Moreover, self-blame can be relieved by reflecting that responsibility also lay with the disbelieving, nonprotective or uninvolved parent who may have ignored the incest even when it was reported.[17,26,30] Such insights may exist at the time or may be attained in retrospect with or without psychotherapy.

Adults. When an *adult* patient reveals that incest took place in her childhood or adolescence, management should follow these lines, provided the physician is not uncomfortable with the process:

1. Evaluate by gathering explicit data on the role and responsibility of patient, partner and other family members.

2. Help the patient to gain perspective with adult hindsight.

3. Ask about injunctions to secrecy at the time of the act and mention that keeping such a secret normally may engender anxiety and be a heavy burden for a child. This may serve to clarify for the patient some of her current emotional tension.

4. Explore childhood efforts to obtain help from other family members, teachers or clergymen and emphasize that this is the most that a child could have done.

5. Mention that incest occurs more often than is realized and is always difficult to discuss. This assurance reduces a sense of uniqueness and helplessness. It gives hope of coping with the stress to know that others have experienced incest and have adjusted well.[5,7,17,28,29]

6. Give credit to patients for the strengths shown in their coping efforts until now.

7. Commend the patient for courage in having shared the secret now and promise to keep the information confidential.

8. Sketch out the family interactions. Point out where relationships (e.g., mother/father) were weak enough for the incest to have occurred. Such recapitulation of the event by an objective authority is integrative and therapeutic. It also can build trust and confidence by showing that the therapist has listened carefully and with concern.

9. Make a contract for dealing with the incest issue: You might say, "This is important, and we will have to discuss it again when I can schedule another half an hour." Then say you will spend a few such visits, if the patient wishes, and "if this is not enough, perhaps we can discuss referral to a psychiatrist." This means the physician accepts the person, is involved and is not overwhelmed by the secret. It also is a declaration that the incest can be discussed nonjudgmentally and that there is hope for healing the incest wound.

Children. If the situation involves recent sexual molestation of a child by an adult, different steps must be taken. First, problems such as pregnancy, physical damage or disease must be addressed. Too often only the "target symptom" of pregnancy is dealt with, as if it existed in a vacuum, because the physician wishes to avoid "entanglements." Nevertheless, pregnancy produces agonizing difficulties; the baby is living evidence of the incest, so the problem cannot be forgotten or concealed if the baby is raised within the family, as sometimes happens.[7,26] Role confusion, arising if the baby's father is also its grandfather, or its mother also its sister, may complicate the infant's adjustment. Adoption may be refused by a close-knit family isolated from the community; it remains the family's right to rear the infant. Supportive long-term professional assistance from a family service agency or the family physician may be helpful and valuable, but it may be refused.

The physician also must determine if child incest included violence. Will it recur? What family strengths are there to work with to prevent recurrence? Is there a healthy sex life between mother and father? Is the incestuous partner alcoholic, pedophilic (fondles other children as well as his own) or mentally-ill? Will he accept treatment? Will the family accept family therapy, which is optimal treatment?[21,26,30,31] Often therapy reveals that the mother-father relationship is weak and requires attention if the couple's sexual needs are to be met without one of them turning to a child again. The adults, however, may consider incest acceptable for their family and refuse intervention.

If the child, under family pressure, fearfully denies the initial report of the incest, the physician should seek help and advice from legal and community resources, such as a hospital child-advocacy team or a local social service agency.

Panic, however, with hasty involvement of legal machinery, can hurt both the physician-patient relationship and the family. Time for an adequate evaluation of the patient and family is essential. They will need preparation for the fact that incest is a criminal act, and they must be told that, by law, the incident must be reported to the police as a preliminary to obtaining a court deposition.

This is not a time for moral outrage on the part of health professionals, who must provide support, understanding and acceptance of the child, incest partner and family. Acceptance does *not* imply condoning incest. But accusation and precipitous arrest of the incestuous adult may fragment or even destroy the family. Severe hardship may follow arrest of the father provider. Legal "treatment" may hurt the child victim further by isolation, institutionalization (sometimes without active treatment) and jailing (therefore, separation and loss) of the father.[32] The broken family may be unable to reconstitute after the father returns if no positive changes have occurred—unless the mother is more aware and protective, the family more integrated or the child removed.[32] Resentment may lead to violent retaliation toward witnesses.

In most states it is a misdemeanor for a physician not to report a case of a sexually abused child, yet the report rate to child protective services by physicians is low.[33] Reasons given for nonreporting included "harmful to the family," "handled more easily privately," and "dissatisfied with state agency management."

It will take time to change the subcultural tolerance of incest that a family might have, but prolonged contact with the larger culture through supportive treatment by a public health nurse, mental health professional or physician may help to emancipate a child socially and emotionally or encourage the family to avoid recurrence of incest.[21,31]

Some believe that treating incest might be more effective if the act were decriminalized to prevent hasty police intervention that often destroys the family. Incest is not always violent nor does it always involve child abuse. Family disorganization and poor role definition usually exist[2,20] and may become foci of individual and family therapy. Alcoholism, drug abuse or mental illness, if a factor, requires treatment. If the family is too chaotic to respond to crisis intervention or long-term family therapy, the child must somehow be protected. It may be necessary to get help into the home in the form of a visiting nurse or case worker. Child therapy facilities often are not available.

A physician's time is well spent if it is directed toward preventing additional family disruption. Any family member may show immediate or delayed anger, denial, anxiety, withdrawal, depression, resistance or manipulation. Incest may be upsetting but not crippling; many resilient persons adjust. The furor must be controlled, as must the physician's own sense of alarm, for the sake of the troubled family.[34]

References

1. Murdock GP: *Social Structure*. New York, Free Press, 1965.
2. Weinberg SK: *Incest Behavior*. New York, Citadel Press, 1976.
3. Schull WJ, Neel JV: *Effects of Inbreeding on Japanese Children*. New York, Harper & Row Publishers, Inc, 1965.
4. Adams MS, Neel JV: Children of incest. *Pediatrics* 1967; 40:55-62.
5. Yorukoglu A, Kemph J: Children not severely damaged by incest with a parent. *J Am Acad Child Psychiatry* 1966; 5:111-124.
6. White LA: The definition and prohibition of incest. *Am Anthropol* 1948; 50:416-435.
7. Wilson PJ: Incest, a case study. *Soc Econ Studies* 1963; 12:200-209.
8. Ford CS, Beach FA: *Patterns of Sexual Behavior*. New York, Harper & Row, Publishers, Inc, 1970.
9. Poznanski E, Blos P: Incest. *Med Aspects Hum Sex* 1975 (Oct); 9:46-76.

10. Parsons T: The incest taboo in relation to social structure and the socialization of the child. *Br J Sociol* 1954; 2:101-117.
11. Gebhard PH, et al: *Sex Offenders: An Analysis of Types*. New York, Harper & Row Publishers, Inc, 1965.
12. Cohen T: The disappearance of the incest taboo. *Human Nature* 1978 (July); 72-78.
13. American Law Institute: Incest. Model Penal Code Proposed, Final Draft Sec 230.2, 1962.
14. Kinsey AC, et al: *Sexual Behavior in the Human Male*. Philadelphia, WB Saunders Company, 1948.
15. Kinsey AC, et al: *Sexual Behavior in the Human Female*. Philadelphia, WB Saunders Company, 1953.
16. Halleck SL: Emotional effects of victimization, in Slovenko R (ed): *Sexual Behavior and the Law*. Springfield, IL, Charles C Thomas, 1965.
17. Renshaw DC: Healing the incest wound. *Sex Med Today* 1977 (Oct); 27-41.
18. Armstrong L: *Kiss Daddy Goodnight*. New York, Hawthorn, 1978.
19. Ramey JW: Dealing with the last taboo. *SIECUS Report* 1979 (May); VII:5.
20. Westermeyer J: Incest in psychiatric practice. *J Clin Psychiatry* 1978; 39:643-648.
21. Cormier BM, et al: Psychodynamics of father-daughter incest. *Can Psychiatr Assoc J* 1962; 7:203-217.
22. Cormier BM, Boulanger P: Life cycle and episodic recidivism. *Can Psychiatr Assoc J* 1973; 18:283-288.
23. Bender L, Blau A: The reaction of children to sexual relations with adults *Am J Orthopsychiatry* 1937; 7:500-518.
24. Bender L, Grugett AE Jr: A follow up report of children who had atypical sexual experience. *Am J Orthopsychiatry* 1952; 22:825.
25. Reiffen D: Protection of children involved in sexual offenses. *J Crim L Criminol Police Sci* 1959; 49:222-228.
26. Machotka P, et al: Incest as a family affair. *Fam Process* 1967; 6:98-116.
27. Renshaw DC, Renshaw RH: Incest. *J Sex Educ Ther* 1978; 3:3-7.
28. Nobile P: Incest the last taboo. *Penthouse* 1977 (Dec); 117-158.
29. Pomeroy W: Incest—A new look. *Penthouse* 1976 (Nov); 8-13.
30. Lukianowicz N: Incest: I. Paternal incest. *Br J Psychiatry* 1972; 120:301-313.
31. Eist HI, Mandel A: Family treatment of ongoing incest behavior. *Fam Process* 1968; 7:216-252.
32. Maisch H: *Incest*. London, Andre Deutsch, 1973.
33. James J, et al: Physician reporting of sexual abuse of children. *JAMA* 1978; 240:1145-1146.
34. Renshaw DC: *Incest—Understanding and Treatment*. Boston, Little, Brown and Company, 1981. (in press)

Chapter 25

Additional Therapies

Editor's Note: This chapter elucidates therapeutic techniques not previously covered in this volume.

The section on sexological examination authored by Domeena C. Renshaw, M.D. and Harold I. Lief, M.D. illustrates a special educative tool that can be used with the patient and partner when pathological causes for a dysfunction have been ruled out. Sexually graphic material (Oliver J. Bjorksten, M.D.), when utilized with discrimination, can be an effective adjunctive aid in therapy.

The benefit of helping patients improve their understanding and knowledge of, and attitudes toward, sexuality is examined in the section on sexual enrichment programs (Laurence Hof, M.D.). However, when there is severe sexual inhibition, with intense anxiety, systematic desensitization (J. P. Brady, M.D.) may be necessary.

The age-old technique of hypnosis has been refined and, today, hypnosis for sexual problems (Domeena C. Renshaw, M.D.) has a respected role in medicine, whereas, the relatively new use of partner surrogates (Domeena C. Renshaw, M.D. and Harold I. Lief, M.D.) as a form of treatment is highly controversial. The surgical treatment of impotence (Alan J. Wein, M.D., Terrence R. Malloy, M.D. and Stanley H. Shrom, M.D.) with a penile prosthesis may be indicated for individuals whose erectile dysfunction is not psychogenic.

THE SEXOLOGICAL EXAMINATION

Every medical problem lies on a continuum from somatic to psychological. Sexual problems are no exception. The first important step for the physician is to establish where on this continuum the problem lies; therefore, sound medical practice is to exclude physical causes first, in order to rule out gross pathology that may be causative or contributory. A thorough history and a physical examination are essential initially. The general physical examination may provide clues concerning the etiology of the sexual dysfunction. For example, atherosclerosis may be a cause of impotence, and disturbances in peripheral sensation may indicate impairment of the autonomic nervous system.

Neurologists and urologists perform specialized tests, such as the bulbocavernosus reflex latency test and the Doppler ultrasound method, to determine the normalcy of the neural pathways or the vascularization of the penis. These specialized techniques are indicated when a precise diagnosis is required, but are not generally included in the routine physical examination. A routine, thorough physical examination, however, should always include a genital examination.

The educative sexological examination, which is a development of the genital examination, may be incorporated into the routine physical examination when sex therapy is indicated. In this examination, the physician provides sex education by suggesting that the patient look at his or her own genitals (for female patients, a mirror is required and the head of the examining table must be elevated). This increases the patient's awareness of the genitals and how they function. Many people have not seen or have avoided looking at their own sex organs because of learned injunctions, e.g., "Don't touch! Don't know what is down there!" Now, with the authority implicit in the presence of a trusted physician in the examining room, even with additional lighting to illuminate the genitals, the doctor in effect changes this message to say, "Yes, look down here. Know your sexual self." This direction and permission can be a great relief to an inhibited patient.

A good deal of sexual ignorance or misinformation may be corrected during the sexological examination. From a genital diagram in two dimensions, which a patient may have studied, to the three-dimensional perspective of "me" is a gap which even many college graduates have not bridged. Twenty per cent of women seeking help at one midwestern sex clinic had not known about their own clitoris, the function of which is sexual arousal. Some men did not even know that they were circumcised—they had not made any comparisons nor were they informed. Many persons are still sexually ignorant.

If the physician is comfortable with the sexological examination, it will be easier for the patient. If there is a sexual problem and the patient's partner has come along, then the sexological examination should be done in the presence of the partner (with written consent from both partners if they are not married). Without apology, the approach should be basic education about the body. The following are examples of what the physician can say:

For the Male. "Normally the left testis hangs lower than the right as you see." (Some men needlessly worry that asymmetry means that they are "deformed.")

"This is a circumcised (or uncircumcised) penis."

"Penises differ widely in the flaccid state, but vary little in the fully erect state."

"The buttocks, anus, upper and inner thighs, the whole groin area normally have erotic feelings."

"The muscles in the scrotal sac respond reflexively to stimuli." (Do the cremasteric reflex test of thigh stroking.)

"This is the vas where a vasectomy would be done if requested." (Let each partner feel it after the physician has located it.)

"The testes are tender to touch." (Demonstrate and let the partner feel same.)

"Here is where you would squeeze for the squeeze technique if you needed to extend the time before ejaculation." (Let the partner place her thumb on the frenulum and the second and third fingers on the coronal ridge after the doctor has done so. Some women have not touched the penis by hand throughout their married life! If it is a single male, he may be shown how to use the thumb and index finger squeeze at the root of the penis.)

"Do you have questions?"

For the Female. "The whole groin, thigh and buttock areas have erotic feelings because they have similar nerves from the lower spinal cord and this includes the rectum and bladder. This is quite normal."

"These are the outer lips and the inner lips of the vagina." (Let her look in the mirror.)

"This is the clitoris. It feels firm." (Doctor's index finger rolls the shaft laterally. Let the patient then put her index finger over the doctor's, whose finger then is removed. Let her roll it from side to side. Her partner then places his index finger over hers. She removes her finger and he rolls the shaft laterally. Mention that the tip of the clitoris is as tender as the tip of the penis, so "jabbing" should be avoided. Encourage her to guide his hand to tell him how she likes to be touched.)

"Here are the remnants of the hymen, can you see them?"

"In this lower third of the vagina, the entrance is a circular muscle. It can contract voluntarily like the circular muscles around the eyes, the mouth and the anus. Now contract tightly around my finger. Good. You can practice this as an exercise anytime. It can enhance sexual enjoyment for both of you."

"Now I shall do a gentle pelvic examination. Open your mouth and breathe slowly." (This prevents contraction of the pubococcygeus.)

"Now I want to put a speculum gently into your vagina so that you can look (adjust lamp and mirror, so that partner can see as well). This is the wall of the vagina. It lubricates automatically when you are sexually aroused. Up there is the cervix; that is the cervical canal from which a 'Pap' smear is taken. There is the vault where the sperm is deposited during your partner's ejaculation."

"Any questions?"

This sexological examination becomes a valuable "bonding" experience between physician and patient, provided the physician is comfortable in conducting it, and in doing so with both patient and partner, who can share intimate sex education. With the partner present, erotic reactions of the physician are less likely. In any case, the medical student or physician who does experience erotic sensations should recognize that this response is neither unusual nor abnormal. Precluded are a physician's sexually exploitative behaviors, not his or her feelings, which can be controlled. As the physician gains greater experience and familiarity with the procedure, troublesome erotic feelings are less likely.

For the physician, it is also a useful source of information on how each partner relates under the "stress" of this new experience, and to evaluate the concern and support each demonstrates for the other. It can be most therapeutic for persons who are sexually ignorant or misinformed. For many, this examination may be all that is required to correct sexual misconceptions. They may then proceed to work out a satisfactory sexual adjustment on their own.

The physician can end the visit with an "open door" statement: "Come back anytime if you want to ask further questions."

SEXUALLY GRAPHIC MATERIAL IN SEX THERAPY

In sex therapy, audiovisuals are the most commonly used sexually explicit materials, but occasionally photographs, models, paintings and literature are used as well. These materials can induce sexual fantasy by direct suggestion or by calculated omission. In the latter case, patients can be told that sexually explicit scenes have been deleted (or censored) from a production; that usually leads them to imagine that the scenes were more sexually explicit than they in fact were.[1]

In general, sexually graphic materials have a transient, sexually stimulating effect in normal people, and the literature suggests that viewing these materials does not in itself cause individuals to engage in sexual activities that are different from their usual sexual pattern.[2] The advantage of this finding is that these materials are probably less harmful than is believed, but the disadvantage is that they are probably somewhat less powerful than the therapist might wish them to be. This has led to the development of rather intensive workshop formats for the presentation of these materials to increase their impact. It also may be necessary to use other techniques, such as group discussions, to supplement the use of sexually graphic materials to amplify their impact.

Therapeutic Uses for Sexually Graphic Material

Sexually graphic materials are never used as the sole method of treatment for individuals with sexual difficulties. The materials can be a useful adjunct to sex therapy when there is a specific indication for them. There is even greater use of these materials in educational settings, especially for the education of professionals dealing with patients who have sexual difficulties.

There is an overlap between patients who have educational deficits causing sexual difficulties and patients who have intrapsychic conflicts leading to sexual problems. While sexually graphic materials might be quite useful in the former cases, they occasionally exacerbate psychiatric symptoms in the latter. Patients who complain of sexual difficulties should be assessed carefully. The use of sexually graphic materials in sex therapy is only one therapeutic modality among many.

Attitude Reassessment. By systematically presenting sexually explicit audiovisual materials to patients, the therapist can identify specific areas of conflict for discussion. Until patients actually see the conflict-laden behaviors, they are sometimes completely unaware that they possess negative attitudes toward or conflicts about sexuality. Group discussions after such presentations can be helpful to the patient in evaluating whether negative attitudes continue to serve a purpose in his overall adjustment.[3]

Education. Ignorance and misinformation are common causes of sexual difficulties, and viewing sexually graphic materials may help remedy these problems. Further, sexually graphic materials often teach certain therapeutic techniques much more efficiently than discussion, e.g., pleasuring techniques (sensate focus), techniques for the control of premature ejaculation and the treatment of impotence. Some films are available in cartridges that can be projected easily in the physician's office.

Fantasy Building. Some people have sexual difficulties based on their unwillingness or inability to think about sexual topics, resulting in insufficient fantasy material to permit easy sexual arousal. Many of these individuals have difficulty masturbating, which may be an important factor in perpetuating the dysfunction in an interpersonal sexual situation. Sexually graphic material, especially literature, can be very helpful in giving not only specific fantasy ideas to patients but also permission to think about sexual topics when appropriate.

Trigger Films for Group Discussions. When dealing with sexual topics in groups, people who feel inhibited will tend to avoid discussion by changing the subject. Showing a sexually explicit movie before a group discussion often serves to combat this form of avoidance; the group will tend to deal with its anxieties and inhibitions much more openly, which will generally help reduce them. This promotes interpersonal communication within the group and may transfer to intimate relationships as well.

Behavior Therapy. Sexually graphic materials have been used for aversive conditioning with moderate success.[4,5] Usually aversive conditioning is employed to change undesirable sexual object choices, such as fetish objects. Desensitization of sexual anxiety also may be aided by the use of sexually graphic materials. This can be important in the treatment of sexual dysfunctions.

Methods of Use

In general, if a therapist is attempting to alter attitudes or desensitize patients by use of these materials, he must expose his patients sufficiently. The exact amount of exposure to accomplish these purposes has not been determined yet, but most therapists agree that a minimum of six to eight hours is necessary. Interspersing group discussions with sexually graphic material tends to increase the efficacy of the materials. Occasional exposure (such as one hour at a time once weekly) generally will not accomplish the purpose of attitude reassessment or desensitization. However, that exposure schedule might be quite useful for the dissemination of information.

Exposing individuals to sexually graphic material is generally considered to be safe by most therapists who direct sexual attitude reassessment programs.[3] When individuals have negative reactions, these feelings are usually transient and relate to lowered self-esteem caused by patients observing actions they feel incapable of doing themselves or by a sense of physical inadequacy in comparison with the actors in the films. This latter difficulty has largely been corrected by producers who now choose "average-looking" subjects to use in their films.

Contraindications for Use

While these materials are generally safe for most people, there are some contraindications for their use.

Psychosis. Of greatest concern is the possibility of promoting a delusional system in a schizophrenic patient by exposing him to sexually graphic materials. If nothing else, the physician-patient relationship can be seriously disrupted if the schizophrenic believes that the physician has a hidden purpose in recommending these kinds of materials. Severe depression with feelings of inadequacy may be increased if patients see depictions of the very things they have difficulty doing themselves.

Intense Shame. On rare occasions, individuals are so embarrassed by sexually explicit material, especially films, that they have an intense physiological "riddance response," e.g., vomiting. There is danger that they will drop out of treatment.

Some individuals who have a nondefensive moral objection to the public display of sexually graphic materials may be unnecessarily traumatized by them in a sexual attitude reassessment program.

Sexually explicit materials for educational and therapeutic purposes may be obtained from many sources, a few of which are listed below.

1. Focus International, Inc.
   505 West End Avenue
   New York, N.Y. 10024
2. Multi-Media Resource Center
   1525 Franklin Street
   San Francisco, CA 94109
3. Sex Information and Education Council of the U.S.
   84 5th Avenue, Suite 407
   New York, N.Y. 10011
4. EDCOA Productions, Inc.
   12555 East 37th Avenue
   Denver, CO 80239
5. Planned Parenthood World Population
   810 Seventh Avenue
   New York, N.Y. 10019

SEXUAL ENRICHMENT PROGRAMS

A sexual enrichment program is often a helpful adjunct to marital or sex therapy. Such educational and sometimes therapeutic efforts have been given various titles in addition to "sexual enrichment," such as "sexual attitude reassessment program" and "human sexuality workshop." Programs have been conducted for newly married couples,[6] women,[7] elderly couples,[8] "normal" couples,[9,10] couples in therapy who have sexual dysfunctions or marital problems (viz., at the Marriage Council of Philadelphia) and medical students.[11] Despite the variety of titles, groups and designs, the programs have several goals in common: providing increased comfort with sexuality, making people aware of their own and others' sexual attitudes and feelings and helping them improve their sexual knowledge and skills.

Participants in many programs are exposed to—even bombarded with—explicit sexual films, slides and tapes. Some programs include fantasy experiences ("thought trips") and nonverbal experiences to increase interpersonal sensitivity and body awareness, to learn massage and pleasuring or to trigger cognitive or affective responses which are shared and discussed with one's partner or other group members. Very few programs encourage sexual activity among members other than privately between spouses.

Many programs are intensive.[7,9,10] Within 24 to 48 hours, participants may learn about coitus, masturbation, sexual fantasy, physical touch and massage and the sexual response cycle; about sex therapy techniques, such as the squeeze technique and nongenital and genital pleasuring (sensate focus); and about special topics, such as homosexuality, sexual relations during pregnancy, sexuality and aging and sex and the physically disabled. Some programs spread the experience over six to eight weeks, in periods of two or four hours,[6] and include "homework" assignments to increase body awareness and improve sexual communication and technique.

Another common element is planned, small-group participation. Groups may be self-selected, but more often the participants are randomly assigned. In programs oriented to couples, partners may be separated in different groups, where they may be less inhibited; they are encouraged to discuss their separate experiences when they reunite. Small groups may meet several times—for instance, after each film sequence and at the beginning and end of each day. The participants usually are encouraged to discuss the attitudes and feelings that the program has triggered, but to avoid intellectualizing and generalizing. Such sharing is voluntary; anyone may choose to remain silent.

Some groups share only material from the present or recent past. Others permit or even encourage excursions into the more remote past in order to relate present attitudes and behaviors to early learning and development. The therapist or group leader usually avoids probing in depth, because of the goals of the program and the brevity of the experience. With some programs, a follow-up meeting for participants is scheduled two or three weeks later.[9,10]

It is believed that the group process and saturation exposure to explicit sexual material interact to bring about change.[11] Many participants report that sharing thoughts, attitudes, feelings and concerns about previously private matters in a supportive group atmosphere is liberating and informative and contributes to a sense of being "normal." They also report increased comfort and a greater willingness and ability to risk open discussion with sexual partners. Research on the results of these programs shows that many participants attain greater sexual knowledge,[6,11] higher frequency of certain sexual activities, more sexual satisfaction and increased marital satisfaction.[6,8,10] Some participants also show greater acceptance of their own and their partners' sexual responsiveness and an increased ability to perceive accurately one another's preferences.

Although there is an increasing body of literature that suggests such positive gains for participants, several words of caution are appropriate for physicians considering the referral of patients to these programs. The psychological condition of the patients and their motivation for participation should be known. Those who are "thrill-seekers," those looking for an instant cure for a sexual dysfunction, those with a significant degree of psychoneurosis or those who respond to stress with marked emotional lability, decompensation, psychosomatic illness or counterdependent behavior should not be referred.[12]

The person or organization conducting the program should be known and trusted and have an impeccable reputation in the community.[12] Leaders should be well trained and skilled in the areas of human sexuality and group process. The goals and format of the program should be clearly specified, and participants should be prescreened in light of the guidelines mentioned previously. Since no amount of prescreening can guarantee that personal or relationship difficulties will not emerge during such programs, leaders should have appropriate clinical skills and/or a clearly defined referral network. For groups composed of couples or individuals in therapy, appropriate consultation with the referring therapist or physician before and after the program should be the norm.

A sexual enrichment program is not a cure-all, but at its best it can enhance personal and interpersonal growth, especially when combined with a therapeutic experience in which issues raised during the program can be addressed.

SYSTEMATIC DESENSITIZATION

Systematic desensitization can be highly effective in the treatment of severe sexual inhibition in some women, especially those who react to sexual approaches with such anxiety or hostility that normal sexual responsiveness is impossible.[13] Using a learning-theory model, one would say that dysphoric emotional responses have been conditioned to cues or stimuli associated with sexual behavior. The goal of systematic desensitization is to countercondition these responses by having the patient approach the sexual situation in her imagination through a series of small steps and in a psychophysiological state that inhibits or is incompatible with anxiety.

The treatment consists of three steps. First, with the aid of the therapist, the patient ranks from 10 to 15 sexual situations by how much emotional discomfort they cause. The least anxiety-provoking situation might be being touched on the hand by a potential sexual partner. The next might be the same partner kissing the patient on the cheek. For most women with severe sexual inhibition, the most discomforting scene on the anxiety hierarchy is coitus.

The second step is teaching the patient how to attain deep physical and psychological relaxation through hypnosis, progressive muscle relaxation or some other technique. Muscle relaxation is usually accompanied by psychological calm and freedom from anxiety; this mood may then be used to countercondition anxiety responses.

The third step is systematically pairing the state of relaxation with the imagined situations listed by the patient. That is, after the patient is deeply relaxed in each treatment session, the therapist describes the situations, beginning with the least discomforting one. The theory is that the small amount of anxiety elicited by the least provocative scene will be counterconditioned by the psychophysiological state of calm and tranquility that is present.

Once the patient can imagine the least anxiety-provoking scene with tranquility, the therapist moves on to the second scene on the hierarchy and so forth. Usually 15 to 20 sessions are necessary before the patient can vividly imagine the most anxiety-provoking scene calmly and comfortably.

The counterconditioning accomplished in the clinician's office typically carries over into real life. To facilitate this process, the clinician instructs the patient and her partner to practice the behaviors that have been treated in imagination. It is essential that the couple not go beyond the point where the patient begins to feel psychological discomfort; if they do so, the patient may be retraumatized and treatment will have been set back.

There are several variations to this procedure.[14] Often it is useful to have the patient's sexual partner on hand during the treatment, verbally presenting the scenes. This aids the carryover of the counterconditioning from the treatment setting to real life. The physician can prescribe small doses of antianxiety drugs during the early stages of treatment, especially if the patient has difficulty relaxing. It is desirable to discontinue medication after the first few sessions to facilitate carryover of the new learning to the "drug-free" state, i.e., to ensure that the patient will remain relaxed in her usual environment when she is not under the influence of drugs.

The physician should apply systematic desensitization only after simpler and less time consuming methods have not been sufficient to overcome severe sexual inhibition. For example, very detailed and frank sexual discussions should be carried out with the patient and her partner, because these talks often alleviate a great deal of anxiety through counterconditioning and may even be sufficient treatment in themselves. Also, the physician should be sure that the patient and her partner are adequately informed about sexual techniques and about the need of many women for fairly lengthy and gradually escalating foreplay before coitus. In fact, sexual arousal from such foreplay may itself serve as counterconditioning for anxiety responses.

Psychogenic impotence is the male analogue to sexual inhibition in women. Impotence caused by sexual anxiety often responds quickly to a program of graduated sexual experiences as described elsewhere in this book. When such a program fails to produce good results and when severe, persistent anxiety about sexual behavior is the basis of the impotence, a program of systematic desensitization similar to that described above for women should be undertaken.

HYPNOSIS FOR SEX PROBLEMS

Ever since Franz Mesmer first gave public demonstrations of hypnotism in Vienna in 1775, scientists and laymen have been fascinated by this dramatic state and have sought to use it therapeutically. Overvaluation of Mesmer's power made many women abandon their families and pursue proponents of "animal magnetism," who claimed to cure a wide variety of ills, including sexual problems. It soon became clear that exaggerated dependence on the "powerful" hypnotist can make a patient progressively more helpless unless it is emphasized from the onset of hypnotherapy that the individual enters the altered state of consciousness voluntarily. A passive, infantile "you fix me" expectation can undermine sustained change, growth and self-sufficiency.[15]

In the late 19th century, physicians applied hypnosis to syndromes involving functional elements.[16,17] The value of obtaining a history of conflictual early events under hypnosis was later noted in the United States.[15] Over the past few decades, hypnotherapy has been used for a wide variety of habits and symptoms, from smoking to sex problems.[18] The only study using long-term follow-up of sex problems treated by hypnosis (one to five years) was reported by Fuchs et al.[19] Thirty-one of 34 patients with vaginismus were treated successfully by hypnodesensitization, a combination of hypnosis and systematic desensitization. (This topic was discussed in an earlier section of this chapter). Of the 31 patients, 29 were followed up and all had maintained a normal sexual adjustment.

Orgasmic problems in 255 women were treated by Cheek,[20] a gynecologist who is also a hypnotherapist. He obtained a history of early and current sexual conflict and then directed the patient to positive responses by rehearsing negative experiences "as they should have been" (hypnosuggestion). To avoid excessive dependence on him, he described the process of autohypnosis, gave permission to use sexual fantasy and reinforced by specific suggestion the fact that the patient was in control of her sexual arousal during hypnosis and afterward. Cheek also constantly suggested during hypnotherapy that the patient redirect her fantasy toward her own partner. He reported a success rate of 60 per cent. Such therapy demands the skills of an evaluator, a sex educator, a sex therapist, a psychotherapist and a behavior therapist, as well as a hypnotherapist.

Hypnotherapy for male sexual problems uses the same or related techniques—the taking of a thorough history (excluding physical pathology), using age regression to obtain early conflictual material, densensitization to conflict situations, reassurance and positive suggestion ("ego strengthening") and specific sexual suggestions and support. Seventy-eight cases of hypnotherapy for impotence, with a 72 per cent success rate, were reported by Fabbri;[21] a 66 per cent success rate in 50 men with impotence was reported by Ward.[22] These success rates and time expenditures resemble those reported in the use of new brief sex therapy techniques without hypnosis.[23,24]

The referring physician should ensure ethical treatment for patients by screening the credentials of qualified hypnotherapists who perform sex therapy. The Society for Clinical and Experimental Hypnosis (129-A Kings Park Drive, Liverpool, New York 13088) or the American Society of Clinical Hypnosis (2400 E. Devon Avenue, Suite 218, Des Plaines, Illinois 60018) may be consulted for the names of members who practice sex therapy.

Selection of patients for sex therapy by hypnosis is usually loosely determined by request of a patient and/or by the availability of a professional who uses hypnosis and sex therapy techniques. The one symptom eliminated most successfully by hypnotherapy, with indications of long-term relief, is vaginismus. Other methods of treating vaginismus,[25] however, are equally successful (see Chapters 12 and 14).

PARTNER SURROGATES

The use of partner surrogates as an adjunct in treating sexual dysfunctions is still controversial despite the excellent results reported by Masters and Johnson.[23] The controversy revolves around legal, moral and medical issues. Nevertheless, there are reports that show that the careful use of surrogates may be indicated under very special conditions. The Conference Report on Ethical Guidelines for Research and Clinical Perspectives on Human Sexuality[26] states: "The use of sexual-partner-surrogates is justifiable if precautions are taken to avoid coercion or harm to either client or surrogate and to obtain the informed consent of both parties."

Masters and Johnson[23] described the use of 13 female partner surrogates in the treatment of 41 single men with sexual dysfunctions. Of the 41, 32 (including all 12 patients with premature ejaculation) were cured. Nineteen of the 41 had been married previously, and 24 were married after treatment. Masters and Johnson state: "In view of the statistics, there is no question that the decision to provide partner-surrogates for sexually incompetent unmarried men has been one of the more effective clinical decisions made during the past 11 years devoted to the development of treatment for sexual inadequacy." However, other therapies that do not involve surrogates can be used with reasonable degrees of success, particularly for men with premature ejaculation.[27]

Legal and moral considerations restrict the use of surrogates to unmarried persons unless there is unambiguous written consent by the patient's spouse. Even then, most therapists hesitate to refer a married patient to a surrogate. A referring therapist should know from his own experience or from the reports of his colleagues that the surrogate is reliable, sensitive and honest and will communicate frequently with the primary therapist.

Some specialists in physical medicine and rehabilitation believe that surrogates also are useful in controlled settings for isolated or disabled sexually dysfunctional people who need erotic success and practice to build the necessary confidence to find partners and maintain relationships. A different approach is to help the patient first develop a relationship and then autonomously proceed to sexual expression and emotional intimacy. This process takes time and testing over months and years.

If physical or chemical factors are the sole original causes of a sexual dysfunction, neither a surrogate nor sex therapy can help, at least not until the biogenic factors are reversed. When problems are psychogenic, there are often internal conflicts that require psychotherapy. Sexual inhibitions occasionally may be dispelled by a concerned and supportive surrogate, but additional therapy to provide sex education, support and pressure for autonomous sexual expression is usually needed. Interpersonal problems, when present, require marital therapy.

The selection and training of surrogates are still troublesome issues. Who picks them and how? Why do they volunteer? How are they trained? At the Reproductive Biology Research Foundation in St. Louis, 13 of 31 women who volunteered were chosen.[23] The 13 ranged in age from 24 to 43; all were single at the time, although 11 had once been married. Since personal detachment on the part of the surrogate was considered untherapeutic at best, even psychologically disastrous, prostitutes were never used in St. Louis. Screening apparently consisted of in-depth interviews by therapists, who obtained medical, social and sexual histories and eliminated people "with whom the co-therapist did not feel totally secure, attitudinally or socially." The training of the surrogates was not described. Because the psychological stress on the surrogates was extreme, none was used more than once a year. It may be presumed that they received individual instruction each time: "She is subjected to an exhaustive description of male sexual functioning, with explanations directed both to the physiology and the psychology of male sexual response." Surrogates also were instructed in social and conversational graces to put tense male patients at ease.[23]

Each surrogate was given detailed information about her partner's psychosexual background and the cause of his sexual dysfunction. Both patient and surrogate were cautioned to reveal only their first names and to answer no personal questions, but because of the nature of their contacts, anonymity was usually difficult to maintain. The surrogate would be contacted daily by the therapist for a progress briefing and further instructions; the therapist repeatedly emphasized that the surrogate's emotional support was as vital as her sexual cooperation. Ideally, a surrogate should approximate a concerned, cooperative partner.

Male surrogates were not used in the St. Louis program, but have since been used elsewhere. One reason they were not used in St. Louis was the greater negative reaction expected from the community if male surrogates were provided for the few single women who came to Masters and Johnson for help. Another was Masters and Johnson's view that the "social and sexual securities (that women need) cannot be established in the brief period of time available." Single women who were accepted as patients had to bring their own "replacement partners."

The surrogate program of the Reproductive Biology Research Foundation ended because of a threatened law suit that might have been contested if the patient's anonymity could have been protected by the court. When the judge refused to grant a request to keep the patient anonymous, the Foundation, in order to protect the patient, was forced to settle the case out of court.[28]

Some sex therapists, especially in New York City and California, continue to use surrogates. Data on patient and surrogate selection, resistance to treatment, stress on patient and surrogate and results of treatment are not available. Some sex therapists have commented negatively on opportunistic "therapists" with highly questionable ethics who have used prostitutes as surrogates without demonstrating the effectiveness of their methods.[24] Other therapists have stopped referring patients to surrogates because they felt like "procurers" or "madams;" there was a close association in their minds between surrogates and prostitutes. Some clinic directors say that they would not admit using surrogates even if they did so, for fear of public censure.[29]

Since the publication of *Human Sexual Inadequacy* in 1970, the financial exploitation of persons in need of sexual help has been cloaked with a semblance of respectability, in gross distortions of Masters and Johnson's therapy, by self-styled therapists who assume the dual role of surrogate and sex therapist.[30] Sometimes a prostitute is elevated to the rank of surrogate, has little or no contact with the referring therapist and knows nothing about her client before their first meeting. There is a distressing tendency for surrogates to become independent entrepreneurs, free of professional supervision.

The original reason for using surrogates was to have sex therapy occur with as close a simulation as possible of a loving, sensitive and supportive partner. Apfelbaum[31] maintains that reaching this ideal is impossible; the relationship does not permit easy and free discussion of feelings and attitudes by either patient or surrogate, and some anxiety in both is inevitable. The surrogate is supposed to be supportive, interested, confident and a good sexual partner, no matter what her feelings are. She is also supposed to give the patient the feeling that he is providing her pleasure, since her enjoyment is essential to his erotic arousal and confidence. The stress on the male patient is also rather intense; he is supposed to avoid talking about his anxieties, his concern about what the surrogate feels about him, her surrogate role, her qualifications, whether she sees him as weak and inadequate, how she compares him with other patients and what she will report to the therapist. Apfelbaum believes that this artificial situation is detrimental to overcoming sexual anxiety for most male patients, and that only men who can dehumanize the relationship can perform successfully with a surrogate.

He and Williams[32] advocate using a well-trained "therapist" who discusses with the patient not only his anxieties but her own as she verbally role-models freedom to reveal her apprehensions and concerns. The same therapist conducts so-called "body-work" with the patient; this is a euphemism for participating in sensate-focus exercises as a cooperative wife might. The massage is enhanced by her praise and sexual skills.

It should be pointed out that the "Conference Report on Ethical Guidelines for Research and Clinical Perspectives on Human Sexuality"[26] states, "It is unethical for the therapist to engage in sexual activity with a client (Section III)." In like manner, "The Principles of Medical Ethics with Annotations Especially Applicable to Psychiatry" of the American Psychiatric Association declares that " . . . sexual activity with a patient is unethical."[33]

Even under the best of circumstances, the use of surrogates remains controversial. Other therapeutic methods, such as behavioral therapy along with the learning of social skills and meeting members of the opposite sex, can be effective.[28,34] These therapies usually take longer, but the results may be more lasting. Also, transferring the success achieved with the surrogate to other partners is not always assured.[23] An experience with a surrogate—even a successful experience—may leave a patient with lower moral and sexual self-esteem. And finally, failure with a surrogate frequently does occur, because of the stress of this unnatural relationship. Failure may further decrease the low self-esteem of a sexually dysfunctional person.

The use of surrogates is not only controversial but it has special potential for sensational coverage in the media. Even if a physician is convinced that the use of a surrogate partner may be the most effective therapy for a given patient, there is a paucity of reputable programs, and he faces ethical conflicts over protecting his own reputation.

SURGICAL TREATMENT OF IMPOTENCE

References to impotence go back as far as the Old Testament and the writings of Hippocrates.[35] There has long been hope for medical techniques to correct this distressing condition, and recent advances in penile prostheses offer help for many sufferers.

First, of course, it must be determined if impotence is organic or psychogenic (see Chapter 14). Although most cases are psychogenic, a recent study indicates that hypothalamic-pituitary-gonadal disorders may be more prevalent than previously realized.[36] Other common organic causes include diabetes, arteriosclerosis, antihypertensive drug therapy, multiple sclerosis, radical pelvic surgery, pelvic fracture, spinal cord injury, alcohol abuse, antidepressant therapy, priapism and Peyronie's disease. Surgical correction obviously is meant primarily for somatogenic cases. However, patients with psychogenic impotence are also candidates for surgical correction if both the psychiatrist and urologist see no feasible alternative and if the patient desires such treatment.

Surgical treatment most commonly involves some type of penile prosthesis, which provides a mechanically assisted erection. Delayed peripheral nerve reconstruction has not proved feasible. Vascular reconstruction for "vasculogenic" impotence is in its infancy, and the results are often less than gratifying.

The surgical management of impotence is now practical and effective, but the selection of patients remains a challenge. It requires an experienced, interested and humane physician who is aware of all the possible causes of impotence and the diagnostic methods and their relative worth. He also should have access to all therapeutic modalities (medical, psychiatric and surgical) and understand their applicability to each patient.

Preprosthetic Assessment

The proper selection of candidates for penile prosthetic surgery is crucial to optimal patient satisfaction. Ultimately the decision must be based on an overall assessment of the patient and the results of any previous treatment. Even if impotence has an organic basis, psychological evaluation should always be included. The Minnesota Multiphasic Personality Index (MMPI)[37] has proved helpful in the initial screening of patients for the presence of psychosis or other severe personality disorders. Obtaining at least one psychiatric consultation to evaluate marital and psychosocial stability also is desirable. Nocturnal penile tumescence (NPT) studies should always be done if there is any question about the organicity of the impotence.

The patient must thoroughly understand and consent to the surgical procedure. His sexual partner should also be involved in the decision if at all possible. She also should participate in preoperative discussions in order to obviate misconceptions by patient and partner and facilitate postoperative sexual adjustment. A few follow-up conjoint counseling sessions to ensure adequate sexual functioning are recommended.

Other important prerequisites for optimal results are a normal libido, absence of significant depression and low surgical risk.

Patients believed to have psychogenic impotence who have not benefited from sex therapy can also be considered for a penile prosthesis, particularly if they are over 50 and impotence has lasted for more than two years. The patient must be told that the prosthesis simply provides an erect penis sufficient for penetration. If the patient could ejaculate or reach orgasm prior to surgery, these capacities will be impaired, but the prosthesis by itself cannot achieve these results. Close cooperation with a psychiatrist or sex therapist is essential to properly evaluate and advise such patients. Patients with situational impotence (impotence restricted to a particular partner) rarely are candidates for a prosthesis. All patients should be evaluated for lower and upper urinary tract disease, and any infection should be eradicated. Any necessary manipulation of the tract should be done before surgery. If a prosthesis is recommended, the patient should be thoroughly informed of the types available and their advantages and disadvantages. He should make the final decision about whether to have prosthesis surgery and which kind of prosthesis to use.

Types of Prostheses

Semirigid Rod Prosthesis. The Small-Carrion penile prosthesis consists of two semirigid medical-grade silicone rods; the penile portions have interiors of silicone sponge. The part that fits in the crura of the corpora cavernosa is tapered and of solid silicone. This prosthesis is available in various lengths and diameters; the proper size for any patient can be estimated only during surgery, so all sizes should be available then. A prosthesis that is 0.5 cm too short or too long can cause postoperative difficulties, such as pain or inadequate vaginal penetration. In some cases, each corpus cavernosum requires a prosthesis of a different size. This may occur in patients with Peyronie's disease, priapism or penile trauma.

A perineal surgical approach is used most commonly.[38] It leaves no penile scar, causes relatively little postoperative penile edema and allows earlier return to genital function. Careful operative procedure should help create a good artificial erection without buckling of the penis and prevent a beak nose-type deformity of the distal penis ("SST" deformity).

If there has been previous trauma or scarring of the cavernosa, a dorsal penile approach may be better; the midline neurovascular bundle must be carefully avoided. Complete circumferential penile skin incisions are best not made in order to prevent significant postoperative edema.

Coitus should be avoided for four weeks after either approach.

The relative advantages of a semirigid rod-type prosthesis over the inflatable type are a simpler operative procedure, shorter hospital stay, fewer complications requiring additional surgery and lower cost. The semirigid device is especially useful for the impotent patient who is also incontinent, because the permanent protrusion and semirigidity greatly help him place and maintain an external urinary collecting device. The main disadvantage is cosmetic: The penis is permanently semierect, and the prosthesis can always easily be detected by examining the penis. Loose fitting outer clothing and briefs that hold the penis against the abdomen usually make it less conspicuous. After a semirigid rod prosthesis has been inserted, ordinary transurethral procedures are difficult and contraindicated. Transurethral procedures must be done through a perineal urethrostomy in patients with this type of device.

Most partners say that they are satisfied with the results. Complications of the procedure have included infection, urethral erosion and/or intrusion, erosion through the glans penis and faulty fitting within the corpora. Removal of a prosthesis may be required for any of these reasons, but after adequate healing reinsertion is often possible.

Small[39] has reported that, in 160 patients in whom a Small-Carrion prosthesis was used, the results were excellent for 152, good for 5 and poor for 3. We have used a semirigid rod-type prosthesis in 45 patients with an 88 per cent success rate.[40] Six prostheses had to be removed because of infection and/or extrusion; so far, successful replacement has been accomplished in one of these patients.

The Finney semirigid rod prosthesis is similar to the Small-Carrion type, but the crural portion can be tailored during surgery. There is a flexible section in the subsymphyseal area that acts as a hinge to allow a more dependent resting penile position. Also, the more conical tip may allow a better fit under the glans. There are as yet few reports comparing its efficacy with that of the Small-Carrion prosthesis.

Inflatable Prosthesis. Preoperative evaluation and management of candidates for insertion of the inflatable penile prosthesis are virtually the same as for the semirigid rod-type prosthesis. Adequate intelligence to understand the device and hand control (by patient or partner) are additional requirements.

The inflatable penile prosthesis has a fluid reservoir connected to an inflate-deflate pump and two expandable penile cylinders that are available in different lengths. Insertion generally is through a suprapubic incision, usually midline and vertical. The rectus muscles are retracted laterally, and a pocket is created between the posterior rectus sheath and the posterior belly of the right rectus muscle for insertion of the reservoir. Dissection is then continued subcutaneously over the symphysis pubis to the base of the penis.

The cylinders are placed in the corporal spaces with a special tool. The reservoir is positioned beneath the rectus muscle, and the inflate-deflate pump is positioned in the dependent portion of the right hemiscrotum. Tubing from the reservoir is brought through the right inguinal canal and out the right external inguinal ring. Tubing from the cylinders is also brought into this area subcutaneously.

The system is filled with a 12.5 per cent diatrizoate (Hypaque) solution, and the cylinder and pump are connected. The cylinders are pumped fully erect, symmetry and fit are assessed, the reservoir is filled and it is connected to the pump. Patients are taught how to activate the mechanism the day after surgery and instructed to do so two or three times daily. Most patients are discharged on the eighth postoperative day. Coitus is permitted four to six weeks after surgery.

The chief advantage of this kind of prosthesis is the relatively normal appearance and feel of the penis both in the flaccid and erect state. The degree of erection can be regulated precisely. The prosthesis actually may be undetected by the occasional sexual partner. If transurethral procedures are necessary, they can be performed as usual with the prosthesis in the deflated state. The incidence of infection is about the same as for the semirigid rod; infection usually requires removal of the entire device. Erosion seems less of a problem, probably because the device is usually flaccid.

Disadvantages to the inflatable prosthesis are that both the device and the surgery cost more, the surgical procedure is more complex and time-consuming and the postoperative hospital stay is longer. Despite the fact that modifications of the reservoir, pump and cylinder continue to reduce the rate of mechanical failure, the incidence of malfunction requiring surgical correction is much higher than for the semirigid rod.

Although 27 of the first 103 patients to receive the inflatable device at Mayo Clinic have required secondary corrective surgery because of equipment malfunction, 99 had normally functioning prostheses.[41] The authors thus far have had a 93 per cent success rate with 105 patients; 29 of our patients have required 34 secondary operations for mechanical failure. Seven patients required removal of the device because of infection in three, persistent pain in two, psychological reasons in one and lack of manual dexterity sufficient to operate the pump in one. Two of these seven subsequently had a semirigid rod prosthesis placed successfully.

A third type of semirigid prosthesis was developed in 1980. The "Jonas Prosthesis" possesses the same relative advantages and disadvantages of the other semirigid types, but it does have one advantage that the others do not possess. Because it is made of a malleable silver wire core inside a silastic housing, it can be bent into a down position when not being used for intercourse and can be adjusted so that there is greater concealment of the partial erection.[42]

Whether the origin of a sexual dysfunction is psychogenic or biogenic, by the time the patient presents the problem to the physician, it usually has both physiological and psychological aspects. Thus, the physician must be prepared to deal with both in order to provide meaningful therapy.

To what extent sexual counseling is incorporated into a physician's practice is, of course, a personal decision. In the interest of providing the most comprehensive medical care one must (at the least) be aware not only of the basic principles and techniques described in other chapters, but of the specific techniques available for treatment. It is hoped that the information in this chapter will provide this awareness.

References

1. Tannenbaum H: Emotional arousal as a mediator of communication effects. *Tech Rep Comm Obscenity Porno*, vol 8. U.S. Government Printing Office, Washington, DC, 1970.
2. Bjorksten O: Sexually graphic material in the treatment of sexual disorders, in Meyer JK (ed): *Clinical Management of Sexual Disorders*. Baltimore, Williams & Wilkins Company, 1976.
3. Wollert RW: A survey of sexual attitude reassessment and restructuring seminars. *J Sex Res* 1978; 14:250-259.
4. Feldman MP, MacCullock MJ: Aversion therapy in management of 43 homosexuals. *Br Med J* 1967; 2:594-597.
5. Cautela J: Covert sensitization. *Psychol Rep* 1967; 20:459-468.
6. Mayadas NS, Duehn WD: Measuring effects in behavioral sexual counseling with newly married couples. *J Sex Educ Ther* 1977; 3:33-37.
7. Madison J, Meadow R: A one-day intensive sexuality workshop for women. *J Sex Educ Ther* 1977; 3:38-41.
8. Rowland KF, Haynes SN: A sexual enhancement program for elderly couples. *J Sex Marital Ther* 1978; 4:91-113.
9. LoPiccolo J, Miller V: Procedural outline for sexual enrichment groups. *Counsel Psychologist* 1975; 5:46-49.
10. LoPiccolo J, LoPiccolo L: A program for enhancing the sexual relationship of normal couples, in LoPiccolo J, LoPiccolo L (eds): *Handbook of Sex Therapy*. New York, Plenum Press, 1978.
11. Vines NR: Responses to sexual problems in medical counseling as a function of counselor exposure to sex education procedures incorporating erotic film. University of Pennsylvania, 1974. (unpublished doctoral dissertation)
12. AMA Council on Mental Health: Sensitivity training. *JAMA* 1971; 13: 1853-1854.
13. Brady JP: Behavior therapy in sexual disorders, in Freedman AM, et al (eds): *Comprehensive Textbook of Psychiatry*, ed 2. Baltimore, Williams & Wilkins Company, 1975.
14. Wolpe J, et al: The current status of systematic desensitization. *Am J Psychiatry* 1973; 130:961-965.
15. Wolberg L: *Hypnoanalysis*. New York, Grune & Stratton Inc, 1945.
16. Charcot JM: Clinical lectures on senile and chronic diseases. *Aging and Old Age Series*. New York, Arno Press Inc, 1979.
17. Breuer J, Freud S: *Studies on Hysteria*. New York, Basic Books Inc, 1957.
18. Crasilneck HB, Hall JA: *Clinical Hypnosis: Principles and Applications*. New York, Grune & Stratton Inc, 1975.
19. Fuchs K, et al: Hypnodesensitization therapy of vaginismus: In vitro and in vivo methods, in LoPiccolo J, LoPiccolo L (eds): *Handbook of Sex Therapy*. New York, Plenum Press, 1978.
20. Cheek DB: Short-term hypnotherapy for frigidity using exploration of early life attitudes. *Am J Clin Hypn* 1976; 19:20-27.

21. Fabbri R Jr: Hypnosis and behavior therapy: A coordinated approach to treatment of sex disorders. *Am J Clin Hypn* 1976; 19:4-8.

22. Ward LD: The hypnotherapeutic treatment of impotence. *Va Med News* 1977 (June); 104:6.

23. Masters WH, Johnson VE: *Human Sexual Inadequacy*. Boston, Little, Brown and Company, 1970.

24. Kaplan HS: *The New Sex Therapy*. New York, Brunner/Mazel Inc, 1974.

25. Renshaw DC: Are women with vaginismus frigid? *Sex Med Today* (March 23) 1977; 16-41.

26. Kolodny RC: Conference Report: Ethical guidelines for research and clinical perspectives on human sexuality. *Newsletter of Harvard University Program on Science, Technology, and Human Values*. 1978 (June); No 24:17-22.

27. Zilbergeld B: *Male Sexuality*. Boston, Little, Brown and Company, 1977.

28. Personal communication: Dr. W. Masters, St Louis, Workshop, April 1974.

29. Wolfe L: The question of surrogates in sex therapy, in LoPiccolo J, LoPiccolo L (eds): *Handbook of Sex Therapy*. New York, Plenum Press, 1978.

30. LoPiccolo J: The professionalization of sex therapy: Issues and problems, in LoPiccolo J, LoPiccolo L (eds): *Handbook of Sex Therapy*. New York, Plenum Press, 1978.

31. Apfelbaum B: The myth of the surrogate. *J Sex Res* 1977; 13(4):238-249.

32. Williams MH: Individual sex therapy, in LoPiccolo J, LoPiccolo L (eds): *Handbook of Sex Therapy*. New York, Plenum Press, 1978.

33. American Psychiatric Association: *The Principles of Medical Ethics with Annotations Especially Applicable to Psychiatry*. APA, 1978.

34. Renshaw DE: Sexual surrogates. *Sexual Med Today* 1978 (July); 2:39.

35. Gee WF: A history of the surgical treatment of impotence. *Urology* 1975; 5:401-405.

36. Spark RF, et al: Impotence is not always psychogenic. *JAMA* 1980; 243:750-755.

37. Malloy TR, Wein AJ: The etiology, diagnosis and surgical treatment of erectile impotence. *J Reprod Med* 1978; 20:183-194.

38. Small MP, et al: Small-Carrion penile prosthesis. New implant for management of impotence. *Urology* 1975; 5:479-486.

39. Small MP: Small-Carrion penile prosthesis: A report on 160 cases and review of the literature. *J Urol* 1978; 119:365-368.

40. Malloy TR, et al: Comparison of the inflatable penile prosthesis with the Small-Carrion prosthesis in the surgical treatment of erectile impotence. *J Urol* 1980; 123:678-679.

41. Furlow WL: Surgical management of impotence using the inflatable penile prosthesis. *Br J Urol* 1978; 50:114-117.

42. Jonas U, Günther HJ: Silicone-silver penile prosthesis: Description, operative approach and results. *J Urol* 1980; 123:865-867.

Part III
Management Consideration

Chapter 26

Office Procedures

Robert C. Long, M.D.

Leaders in the field of human sexuality commonly express the opinion that primary care physicians (family physicians, obstetrician-gynecologists and internists) should provide care to those couples who are experiencing sexual problems—even though these physicians, with infrequent exceptions, have had no specialized education in psychiatry, psychology, behavioral therapy or counseling beyond medical school. What is the justification for this belief which, on its face, does not seem to make much sense?

PHYSICIAN-PATIENT RELATIONSHIP

Primary care physicians establish long-term relationships with many of their patients; these relationships may extend over two to three decades or even longer. No other health care practitioners are in such a unique position to intervene to prevent a self-perpetuating cycle of sexual anxiety. These physicians see patients at every stage of life and each encounter furnishes an opportunity to provide appropriate information on the varieties of normal sexual development and behavior. The opportunities to serve as a resource person, to practice preventive medicine, to maintain health, to treat illness and to counsel patients during times of stress are numerous. They occur daily.

In times of physical and emotional illness, most patients turn first to their family physician. Although most physicians perform creditably in response to their patients' health care needs, in the field of human sexuality they have failed. No physician, for example, would ignore mitral valve insufficiency or stenosis discovered on physical examination. He or she would either carry out appropriate diagnostic studies and therapy or refer the patient to an appropriate specialist. At the same time, however, this same otherwise competent physician often ignores a specific sexual complaint. How can this behavior be explained?

There are several reasons. Many physicians separate sexual anxiety and dysfunction from the patient's general health status. This separation of sexual disease from other kinds of disease and activity is deeply rooted in our culture. Sex as a cause of illness has largely been ignored in medical education and practice. For example, most physicians, especially those in primary care, are familiar with the concept of psychosomatic medicine. Daily they encounter patients with somatic complaints whose origins lie in emotional stress. Yet all too infrequently do they recognize that how the patient feels about himself or herself as a sexual person and how he or she relates to others sexually provide a very common source of psychosomatic symptomatology. Fatigue, pelvic pain, mild depression, low back pain, headache, urinary tract symptoms, hyperacidity with or without ulcer formation and dyspareunia are commonly found in patients who lead sexual lives that they consider unsatisfactory.

Another reason for inattention to sexual problems by physicians is that many of them have never become comfortable with themselves as sexual persons. In this respect, they differ not a whit from the general population. Until recently it was believed that the study of anatomy, physiology and pathology prepared a physician to deal with the sexual problems of others. This belief and the cultural tradition that sex is a taboo subject effectively blocked the teaching of human sexuality in medical schools until a decade or so ago. Lief reported that in 1961 only 3 of 82 medical schools offered courses in human sexuality;[1] today many of the 126 medical schools offer programs in this subject. This augurs well for the future, not only because of the availability of larger numbers of trained personnel, but also because primary care physicians will have a more solid academic background for treating sexual problems.

The point of all this is that most physicians are reared to believe that sex is evil, dirty or harmful. Consequently, the changing of attitudes that results in feeling comfortable about sex, and dealing comfortably with it in relation to ourselves and others, has to be a learned experience. A physician's inability to deal comfortably with sexual questions can have a devastating effect upon patients. Physician embarrassment blocks communication and further investigation, and the patient's belief that nothing helpful can be done is often reinforced.

Another reason given by primary care physicians for eschewing investigation of their patient's sexuality is a feeling of incompetence with the subject. In addition, many are fearful of doing harm. These reasons are legitimate but, for most physicians, the lack of competence can be rather easily overcome through participation in such continuing medical education courses as sexual attitude restructuring (SAR) and office management of sexual dysfunctions.

It is essential not only that physicians be comfortable with themselves as sexual persons, but also that they learn to keep their personal, ethical and moral value system away from the counseling table. This is often difficult, but it is important to recognize that each individual has his own moral-ethical value system that must be respected by the physician. The physician's role is to serve as a resource person in a comfortable, nonjudgmental way, to establish an accurate diagnosis and to work with couples in the development of therapeutic strategies that have emerged from the work of Masters and Johnson, Kaplan and others.

MANAGEMENT

Management encompasses four dimensions: time, adjunctive aids, record keeping and insurance.

Time. Time is said to be an important barrier to the inclusion of a marital-sexual history as part of the routine investigation of a person's health care status by primary care physicians. Although this may be true, I know of no data to substantiate the conclusion. I also believe that there is a general misconception concerning the amount of time needed to investigate sexual problems with patients.

The incorporation of a marital-sexual history as a routine part of the physical examination takes only a brief period of time. The determination of whether the sexual problem is primarily marital or primarily sexual takes a bit longer but should not present a real problem to those physicians who have made a commitment to the sexual health of their patients. Much can be accomplished even in a busy practice. The physician can spend five to ten minutes to determine whether the problem is primarily marital or sexual. The differentiation is not difficult. For those patients whose problems are primarily marital, referral to a marriage counselor can be made. For those who describe a good marital relationship but for whom sex has never met the couple's expectations in terms of pleasure, intimacy and response, a choice then arises. The physician can counsel the patient himself or refer the patient to an appropriate resource within the community, i.e., health professionals, most of whom are not physicians, who are qualified sex therapists. It is essential, therefore, that physicians know the resources available within the community.

If the physician who engages in sex counseling or therapy undertakes specialized training based on the work of Masters and Johnson, Kaplan and others, special time must be allotted in his practice. There are probably as many models as there are individuals engaged in this therapy. As a solo gynecologist, I have evolved the following useful and practical model over a period of several years. The first four days of the week are engaged in the practice of general gynecology. The fifth day is devoted entirely to counseling couples whom I have carefully screened. The couples come directly from my practice or have been referred by other physicians.

Therapy in my office is confined to the diagnosis and treatment of the dysfunctions of the sexual response system: general sexual dysfunction (e.g., frigidity, lack of lubrication), anorgasmia and vaginismus in the female; premature ejaculation, retarded ejaculation and erectile incompetence in the male. Mental problems, homosexuality and deviant sexual behavior, e.g., fetishism, voyeurism, are referred. However, as a primary care physician, I often serve as a bridge in the referral of patients to other health professionals engaged in therapy in which I am not competent. This often requires two or three sessions. However, it has been my experience that after several sessions couples will accept referral more readily. Patients whom I treat are seen once a week or once every two weeks depending upon need and progress. The initial interview lasts one hour. Subsequent sessions last 25 to 40 minutes and charges are based on time.

Adjunctive Aids. Several aids are available to the primary care physician who has made a commitment to include an inquiry into the sexual health of his patient. For example, a preprinted form[2] can be given to the patient to complete prior to seeing the physician. This particular form consists of 49 questions that appear on separate cards and that the patient responds to with yes or no answers. The questions begin very generally (e.g., the existence of allergies, past serious illness or accident, immunizations, weight) and cover most of the organ systems. Those questions that concern marriage and sex appear near the bottom of the list: marital problems, husband's attitudes, pregnancy, vaginal discharges, menstrual periods, problems about sex, questions about sex or birth control and a final question indicating whether the patient wishes to talk about a problem privately. My patients and I have found this very useful. They understand that discussion of almost any subject is acceptable and encouraged, although most patients will deny that they have serious marital/sexual problems. The physician receives much general information without spending a good deal of effort and time.

Another valuable aid in obtaining information and conserving time is a detailed questionnaire that evaluates sexual performance. (See Appendix I.)

Audiovisual material also can be helpful. For example, I can describe sensate focus, the sine qua non of Masters and Johnson therapy, but illustrating this with three 10-minute audiovisual cassettes is much more effective.[3] The same applies to the "stop and go" or "stimulate/squeeze" exercises and to the employment of masturbation in cases of anorgasmia. Although I do not believe that audiovisual materials are essential to carry out sex therapy, they do serve to demonstrate and clarify, and they provide more time for dialogue in the exploration of other aspects of a problem. Such materials also increase my effectiveness and shorten therapy. The cassettes and the projector never leave my office and are used for no other purpose. I am not present in the room during the showing of the films, but there is a brief discussion about their contents immediately following.

Record Keeping. When personnel are interviewed for employment, they are apprised of the nature of the practice and the absolute necessity for confidentiality. No separate list of sex therapy patients is kept. That is, there is no cross filing. Employees are forbidden to extract charts from the files except for office visits, telephone calls, insurance purposes or other matters of absolute necessity. The objective is not to highlight the sexual aspect of my practice, but rather to regard it as an integral part no different than any other aspect. However, because of possible stigma, another precaution is taken. When a patient transfers from my practice to another physician's practice and later we receive a signed release form pertaining to her records, the patient is contacted and asked specifically whether record transfer is to include information regarding sexual, marital/sexual functioning and counseling. Those patients who instruct me to forward all material are then requested to sign a statement releasing this material.

Insurance. All patients are billed in accordance with fee-for-service based upon time. Sex therapy by physicians may be reimbursed by third-party payers if a DSM-III diagnosis, such as anxiety, generalized disorder state or depressive neurosis, can be made with respect to one of the spouses.

OFFICE THERAPY

To illustrate the types of cases that can be helped by a primary care physician, I have chosen six examples.

Case 1: A 57-year-old female, para-II, gravida-II, both deliveries by cesarean section, consulted me for dyspareunia of six months' duration. She described a good marriage, although at the time her husband was angry with her because intercourse had diminished in frequency at her insistence from two or three times a week to once every week or 10 days because of pain and vaginal dryness. Past history revealed excellent sexual functioning for many years.

Pelvic examination revealed an atrophic vagina. Wet smears confirmed this. Estrogen cream, vaginal dilators and oral cyclic estrogen therapy were prescribed. Resolution of anger through better communication was briefly discussed, and the patient was instructed to call me in four weeks.

Comment: Her report at that subsequent time was that sexual functioning had returned to normal in terms of frequency, comfort, pleasure and response. One year later at the time of annual examination she reported normal sexual functioning, and pelvic examination revealed no recurrence of atrophic vaginitis.

Case 2: A 30-year-old female in excellent health, para-II, gravida-II, reported to me during an annual examination that she had always had problems with orgasm. She had observed for years that her response was better and that the entire sexual scene was more pleasurable when she fantasized. However, because this always resulted in great feelings of guilt, fantasy was seldom employed. I simply reassured her by saying that the use of fantasy was perfectly normal and that it was the sort of behavior most couples engaged in.

When I saw her again at her annual examination and questioned her regarding sexual responsiveness and fantasy, she replied that she fantasized frequently and no longer felt guilty and that as a result her sexual life was much more satisfactory.

Comment: This case illustrates the power of authority. Physicians are authority figures in our society and, as such, they can help people greatly in such areas as masturbation and sexual fantasy simply by granting permission. The role they play in sex therapy, however, is nonauthoritarian. Obviously there is a great difference between being seen as an authority figure and behaving in an authoritarian manner.

Case 3: A 28-year-old single female first consulted me for contraceptive advice. Sexual history at that time revealed that she was orgasmic with masturbation but not with stimulation by partner or during intercourse. My records of that first visit show only that she was very goal oriented and that I had told her that worry over performance creates anxiety that in turn inhibits response, and that her responsibility was to give and receive pleasure and feel good about her body and sharing herself with someone else. I recommended some reading material and offered her some counseling.

Comment: I saw her one year later for annual examination and she volunteered the information that her sexual functioning had improved dramatically. Our talk and the book had been helpful and she was now more relaxed and not nearly so goal oriented. She stated that she is orgasmic with masturbation, stimulation by partner and occasionally during intercourse.

Case 4: A 45-year-old female, para-III, gravida-III, who has been under my care for 26 years, developed progressive stress urinary incontinence within the past year or so. I suspected that she may have been minimizing it, so after our last examination I talked to her for a few minutes and found that she was avoiding surgery because, "I feel that I would be missing something that is very important." When I asked her what that was, she referred to one of the educational booklets in my office that portrayed a diagram of the female reproductive organs. She asked me what would be missing if a hysterectomy were performed. I explained it to her and she responded "then I'll be dry, won't I, because all the secretions for intercourse come from the uterus." After I corrected that misinformation, I inquired about her sexual relationship with her husband. She said that it was excellent and that she didn't want to lose it. I pointed out that as long as their relationship and general health were good, sexual desire with vaginal lubrication and response would remain and the presence or absence of the uterus was irrelevant. She was very relieved and surgery was scheduled.

Comment: This is an example of the physician's role and responsibility as a resource person. My personal belief is that this is probably the most important role that we play. There is so much misinformation, especially in regard to female anatomy, physiology and sexual functioning.

Case 5: A 22-year-old single, never married nullipara in excellent health consulted me as a new patient. Her chief complaints were possible mass in the left breast and vaginal pruritus. Sexual history revealed that the patient was extremely naive, was virginal and had no formal sex education. During an engagement four years previously, she and her fiance attempted intercourse once but the experience was so painful that it could not be completed. Since that time she had not dated often and when she did there was almost no sexual activity. She did not know the meaning of the word masturbation. We talked about this and related matters. I strongly recommended the book, *Our Bodies, Ourselves*, and explained the importance of feeling good about oneself as a sexual person. I showed her a picture of the external genitalia and performed a sexological exam. Her hymenal ring required further dilatation which she had requested and which was carried out without difficulty.

Comment: Without a sexual history, none of the problems that really bothered her would have surfaced. Incidentally, she had no vulvovaginitis and I suspect she used this as a means to introduce related genital subjects that were of great concern to her.

Case 6: A 64-year-old widow was recently referred to me by her family physician for urgency incontinence. She was a para-X, gravida-XII, with nine children living and well. Marital/sexual history revealed that her husband of 37 years had died three years before and that since that time she had masturbated frequently, stimulating her clitoris manually and using a douche nozzle intravaginally. She was very concerned that the use of the dildo had damaged her bladder and brought about her incontinence. Examination revealed a surprisingly well supported pelvic floor, urethra and bladder. The vagina was intensely inflamed and microscopic urinalysis revealed an active lower urinary tract infection. There was no uterine prolapse. Rectovaginal examination was negative. Wet smears were negative for *Trichomonas* or yeast and positive for severe atrophic vaginitis. Estrogen cream and appropriate antibiotic medication were prescribed for the lower urinary tract infection. Upon examination four weeks later, urgency incontinence had disappeared, microscopic urine was negative and atrophic vaginitis had been eradicated.

Comment: During her first visit, I informed her that vibrators in the form of dildos were available and, when used properly, were harmless. The patient was placed on oral estrogen therapy cyclically.

Formal counseling was not employed in any of the above cases. The last case was selected to illustrate that middle-aged and elderly widows have sexual feelings and that we need to provide an environment in our office in which these feelings can be expressed and factual information can be exchanged.

The alleged shortage of time that serves to prevent a physician from engaging in sex counseling is a rationalization of anxiety about handling this part of his or her medical practice in a competent fashion. Management problems are not difficult if the physician has a reasonable amount of interest in helping patients with sexual problems. He will derive great satisfaction by enabling patients to engage in sexual behavior that is pleasurable in itself and that is an essential ingredient in happy and successful human relations. Sex counseling is generally short-term and, for a little effort, the physician will be repaid a thousandfold by the return to sexual health of his grateful patients.

References

1. Lief HI: Sex education of medical students and doctors. *Pacif Med Surg* 1965; 73:52-58.
2. Data Sheets, Series 4000, Medical Practice Systems, Inc, 1970.
3. EDCOA Productions, Inc, 310 Cedar Lane, Teaneck, New Jersey 07666.

Chapter 27

Legal Issues in Marriage Counseling and Sex Therapy

Ralph Slovenko

Physicians are aware that this is a time of proliferating laws and litigation on nearly every aspect of medical practice. Indeed, there are available today physicians' journals devoted entirely to the law-medicine interaction. Almost every recent medical decision has legal ramifications, and physicians are practicing medicine defensively. A doctor now must be able to identify and cope with potential legal problems—or else practice with a lawyer at his elbow or be covered by insurance. Suits for malpractice have become commonplace; liability insurance has become a major office expense. "Sue thy neighbor"—actually, to tap an insurance company—appears now to be the Eleventh Commandment.

Quite often, those who practice marriage counseling or sex therapy become objects of displaced hostility. Their lot is similar to that of the policeman who tries to break up or mediate a marital battle. Often the spouse most assaulted turns his or her rage on the peace officer. In Molière's *The Doctor in Spite of Himself*,[1] Sganarelle and his battered wife both turn on the interfering neighbor. Today that displaced hostility finds expression in litigation.

Hostility also may be created when a physician sees a wife or husband alone, as the other may feel left out or believe that his or her confidences are being divulged, and a sense of humiliation or anger may result.[2] In the course of consultation, a patient may reveal intimate facts that the partner did not consent to have revealed. It is often claimed that total secrecy is necessary for the conduct of psychotherapy, but the husband-wife relationship also requires confidentiality. Writing about the confessional, Fernando Diaz-Plaja[3] observes that, however Catholic the Spaniard may be, he has a great dislike of confession: "Many violent and serious bedroom quarrels are due to the disgust with which the husband sees his conjugal life regulated, or at least advised, by his wife's confessor. From this, the extreme suspicion of the psychiatrist follows logically."

Because marital counseling and sex therapy are sensitive, those who practice it must be especially mindful of public reaction. Public disfavor prompts litigation and influences jury verdicts. Yet in the practice of medicine, the primary care physician, like the specialist, has the delicate task of recognizing, diagnosing and treating his patients' sexual problems. Quite frequently, the sexual problem is disguised as a somatic complaint and calls for proper diagnosis. In other instances, the sexual concern is straightforward, such as that over impotence, sexually transmitted disease, fear of sexually transmitted disease or unwanted pregnancy. The physician may suggest a variety of techniques—counseling, contraception, oral sex, manual sex or the surgical implantation of a prosthesis. Some of the practices that he may suggest are technically illegal in the light of the old sex laws still on the books.[4]

STANDARD OF CARE

The physician is under obligation to diagnose and treat a patient with "due care." Failure to do so constitutes negligence. Due care is measured by the skill possessed or used in treating the patient. Hence, if the primary care physician is not adequately trained for dealing with his patients' sexual problems, he has the duty to refer the patient to a specialist or counselor for diagnosis or treatment and to allow the specialist to take over the case. A nonspecialist may be found liable for failure to refer when the circumstances are such that the duly careful generalist should have known that a problem existed which he was not equipped to handle. What may be accepted as the most advanced practice of medicine at one time in a physician's career may be outdated by new discoveries and advances, and it is his obligation to render treatment to his patients based on adequate understanding of these new developments.[5]

Physicians have always given advice about sexuality, and now they are asked to do so more than any other profession, especially for those problems that have a physiological basis. However, when the problem is primarily psychogenic, many physicians are less competent than counselors trained in psychotherapy or sexuality. Is a physician responsible for advice, purely and simply given, on sexual matters? Most people give advice about love and sex at some time, but the law imposes a duty of care in the giving of advice when there is a contractual or fiduciary relationship, as in the physician-patient relationship. Logically, there is no essential reason for distinguishing an injury caused by reliance on words from an injury caused by reliance on the administration of a drug. In fact, a physician is as liable for negligently advising his patient to take a drug as for negligently administering that drug. Foreseeable harm is enough to establish a duty to speak with reasonable care.

And what type of "treatment" is within the domain of a physician to prescribe? In *On the History of the Psychoanalytic Movement*,[6] Freud writes: "Although the patient had been married for eighteen years (she) was still *virgo intacta*. The husband was absolutely impotent . . . The sole prescription for such a malady . . . is familiar enough to us, but we cannot order it. It runs:

'Rx
Penis normalis
dosim
repetatur!' "

Would the doctor be responsible for the consequences of such a prescription? How would such a prescription be filled? In one case, following such advice, a woman placed an announcement in the personal column of a newspaper: "Need surrogate male partner, discreet, youngish, attractive, experienced." The men she encountered caused her endless trouble—some of these encounters are too painful to bear description. There are other consequences of such a solution. Suppose the husband should learn of it? A man, though he may not have kissed his wife in years, might sue or shoot another man who does have relations with her, or the one who arranged it. In the type of case mentioned by Freud, the physician might do well to offer nothing more than a nonprofessional opinion or refer the patient to a specialist.

The primary care physician who acts purely as a counselor has not been enmeshed in the variety of legal problems encountered by those prescribing medication or performing surgery, although physicians as a rule are not very well trained to deal with psychological problems. The reason for this is not difficult to discern. In cases involving counseling or psychotherapy, there is the difficulty of establishing standard of care, injury or a causal nexus linking the alleged fault and injury. In many cases of complaint, the only harm that can be established is that the patient wasted his time and money.

This is not to say, however, that one engaged in counseling need not be mindful of legal or economic issues. There is increasingly much to concern him. One of the most widespread recent phenomena in the health care field stemming from jurisdiction disputes among psychiatrists, psychologists and social workers is the growing attention being given to "mal-psychotherapy." The increase of public and private insurance and governmental regulation of practice have sharpened the issue on who may do what. Clinicians are being asked to specify what is being treated, what kind of treatment is being given and the outcome of treatment.

INFORMED CONSENT

Publicity has sensitized society to the issue of informed consent. The imprecision of the concept has troubled practitioners. Traditionally, to avoid a claim of battery, the physician needed only to say what he wished to do and obtain the patient's consent. However, in the early 1960's, the courts began to require that the physician also give sufficient information for the patient to decide whether he feels a procedure is desirable in light of its possible risks, benefits and alternatives (including no treatment). Uninformed consent is no consent. The law does not put the burden on the patient to ask questions, but on the physician to volunteer information; therefore, he is vulnerable to liability for not speaking.

In purely verbal therapies, there is no touching and therefore no possibility of committing a battery; recently, however, failure to disclose has been considered under negligence law. Standard for disclosure remains in controversy. Some courts[7] have said that there is no need to show what other physicians might tell patients in similar circumstances: "The jury is capable of deciding whether the doctor did not tell the patient about something that should have been revealed. The jury does not need testimony from physicians about the norm of disclosure in the community." Other courts[8] have said that the standard of disclosure is that of the "reasonable and prudent doctor."

Freud[9] advised against "lengthy preliminary discussions" before the beginning of psychoanalytic treatment, but he did recommend that the patient be told of the difficulties and sacrifices involved so that the patient would not be deprived "of any right to say later on that he has been inveigled into a treatment whose extent and implications he did not realize." Ancient wisdom teaches the healer, "Always warn the patient that the cure will take a long time, in fact make it twice as long as you really think it will be."[10]

TREATING A MINOR

Treatment of a person younger than 18 usually requires the consent of a parent or guardian. There are three exceptions. First, legally valid consent is implied on behalf of the minor when an emergency condition threatens the minor with death or serious bodily harm and the parents cannot be reached quickly. The definition of emergency in some states includes immediate danger to a minor's "health" or "well-being." Second, "emancipated minors" (those who are married or maintain their own residences and manage their own financial affairs) are legally deemed capable of consenting to treatment. Third, an increasing number of states have adopted a so-called "mature minor" rule,[11] which makes consent dependent on an individual's ability to comprehend the nature and consequences of a proposed treatment.[12]

In recent years, ad hoc exceptions have been made to parents' authority to consent, usually to help deal with health problems that have high social costs, such as sexually transmitted disease, drug abuse, contraception and pregnancy. Some states set a minimum age for consent to certain treatments; others allow treatment of any consenting minor for sexually transmitted disease.

Several court decisions recently have reduced restrictions on young people's capacity to consent, and thereby have curtailed the once exclusive authority of parents to judge and consent to the care given their children. The wide-ranging dicta in the U.S. Supreme Court's pro-abortion rulings of 1973 did not address the rights of a minor to obtain an abortion, with or without parental consent. However, in a footnote the court did say that it was specifically reserving decision on the question of whether a requirement for consent by the parents or parent of an unmarried minor may be constitutionally imposed.

In its 1973 rulings, the Supreme Court, with seven of the nine Justices concurring, determined that the "right to privacy" was "broad enough to encompass a woman's decision whether or not to terminate her pregnancy."[13,14] The Court reviewed the permissibility of state regulation in three stages. In the first trimester, the State may not interfere with the decision of the woman and her physician. In the second trimester, the State may, if it chooses, reasonably regulate the abortion procedure to preserve and protect maternal health. And in the third trimester, when the fetus might be viable, the State may proscribe abortion altogether unless the life or health of the mother is at stake.

Three years later, in 1976, in *Planned Parenthood of Missouri v. Danforth*,[15] the

Supreme Court said, "Constitutional rights do not mature and come into being magically only when one attains the state-defined age of majority. Minors, as well as adults, are protected by the Constitution and possess consitutional rights." The lower court had found "a compelling basis" for requiring parental consent in the State's interest "in safeguarding the authority of the family relationship." The Supreme Court majority disagreed: "It is difficult . . . to conclude that providing a parent with absolute power to overrule a determination, made by the physician and his minor patient, to terminate the patient's pregnancy will serve to strengthen the family unit. Neither is it likely that such veto power will enhance parental authority or control where the minor and the nonconsenting parent are so fundamentally in conflict and the very existence of the pregnancy already has fractured the family structure. Any independent interest the parent may have in the termination of the minor daughter's pregnancy is no more weighty than the right of privacy of the competent minor mature enough to have become pregnant."

There were, however, some limitations in the holding. Justice Blackmun, speaking for the majority, intimated that some limited restrictions might be imposed. He went on to say: "We emphasize that our holding . . . does not suggest *every* minor, regardless of age or maturity, may give effective consent for termination of her pregnancy" (emphasis added). Thus, from this, it might be implied that "nonmature" or "noncompetent" minors would be required to have their parents' consent to an abortion, even in the first trimester, as they would for any medical procedure.[16]

After this case, some legislatures (Massachusetts, Illinois) attempted to overcome the Court's objections to mandatory parental consent by permitting those minors whose parents refused consent to appeal to the court. Civil libertarians objected that such statutes also violate the minor's rights to privacy and equal protection of the law.

The Massachusetts statute was tested in 1979 in *Bellotti v. Baird*.[17] In an opinion by Justice Powell in which Chief Justice Burger and Justices Stewart and Rehnquist joined, the Court said that every minor must have the right to go directly to a court without consulting her parents. Justice Powell said, "A pregnant minor is entitled in such a proceeding to show either: (1) that she is mature enough and well enough informed to make her abortion decision, in consultation with her physician, independently of her parents' wishes; or (2) that even if she is not able to make this decision independently, the desired abortion would be in her best interests."

Another question that came to the Supreme Court is whether the State may require simple notification of parents, rather than their consent. Whatever the law, as a matter of practice, many clinics have made an effort to involve parents in the belief that they can be supportive, but at the same time they recognize that many young girls do not want their parents informed. In *Bellotti*, Justice Stevens remarked in a footnote: "Neither *Danforth* nor this case determines the constitutionality of a statute which does no more than require notice to the parents, without affording them or any other third party an absolute veto." In 1981 in *H. L. v. Matheson* the Supreme Court upheld a Utah parental notification law by a six to three vote. The Court said: "A statute setting out a 'mere requirement of parental notice' does not violate the constitutional rights of an immature, dependent minor. The Utah statute gives neither parents nor judges a veto power over the minor's abortion decision."[18] The Court's decision does not make parental notification mandatory nationwide but leaves it up to each state to decide whether to impose the requirement.

As a rule, pronouncements of the courts are not carried out in pure form. As a matter of practice, clinics around the country are now carrying out abortions on all women, be they adults or minors. No path is beaten to the court for its sanction. Should there be complications, however, the minor will usually find that a hospital will not admit her without parental consent. Emergency care in a lifesaving situation is available, but even then the hospital, while administering such care, will as a matter of practice attempt to contact parent or guardian.

One thing is now certain: According to *Danforth* and *Bellotti*, a parent may not veto an abortion. Under *Bellotti*, the alternative to parental consent is judicial approval depending on the circumstances. Parents, being financially responsible for the medical care given their minors though they do not consent to it, might get notice after the fact by a billing for the abortion or for emergency care.

Much less common are cases challenging the adequacy of parental consent. When a parent consents to treatment, the decision seldom comes to others' attention. Most such cases arise when a physician refuses to provide requested services, such as having a retarded child sterilized, and the parents petition the court to authorize or order the treatment. The cases seem to suggest that parental consent alone is not sufficient to authorize sterilization. The current trend is for the courts to rule on the question.[19]

The Hyde Admendment (ruled constitutional in 1980) bans Federal Medicaid payments for abortions except "where the life of the mother would be endangered if the fetus were carried to term," or in instances of promptly reported rape or incest. Abortion supporters regard the cutoff of public funds as the functional equivalent of a ban on abortion for the poor.

INTERFERENCE WITH FAMILY RELATIONSHIPS

The law protects against harm to a family relationship. In early common law, most claims were brought by husbands for loss of a wife's or child's economic services, but today there is potential for claims by any member of a family for loss of intangibles, such as companionship or affection.[20] There are three types of interference—enticement, criminal conversation and alienation of affections—but they are usually combined under the term "alienation of affections."

A change in the alienated spouse's state of mind must be evidenced by external conduct, but most courts do not require proof of an act of adultery. In fact, the defendant need not be a romantic rival; many claims are brought against relatives, especially meddling mothers-in-law or fathers-in-law. A number of states have abolished any action for alienation of affections, perhaps feeling that a home so easily broken up is not worth maintaining. One state, Louisiana, has never recognized the action; about a case in which a lover had allegedly deprived the husband of his wife's affections, Chief Justice O'Neill of the Louisiana Supreme Court quipped informally that the com - plainant had lost nothing but had learned something.[21]

There are times when a husband or wife feels that the spouse's affections have been alienated as a result of counseling or therapy, or that they have become less tolerant with one another than prior to counseling. Those who feel that counseling has hurt their relationship are sometimes right, sometimes not. In any event, the physician usually defends by saying that his patient "outgrew" the relationship. Illustrations from Molière are in this vein. In Molière's *School for Wives*,[22] Arnolphe, who carefully reared the girl to be as stupid as possible so that she would not hesitate to marry him, did not take kindly to the reshaping of his mate. Molière taught that lesson again in *The Doctor in Spite of Himself*, when Sganarelle said, "Who's the man who does not want his wife to be a fool?"[1]

There is a saying, "No man is a hero to his wife's psychiatrist." A physician may unwittingly impute blame or shortcomings to the patient's spouse. Provoked by such comments by the therapist as, "What are you getting out of the marriage?" and "Why are you so masochistic?" the patient may indeed become entirely dissatisfied with the marriage. Or the spouse may feel that the therapist is the new center of the patient's attention. Feelings of betrayal may or may not stem from earlier feelings of being left out of the "mommy-and-daddy" relationship.

A spouse may be moved to seek or threaten divorce for many reasons, sometimes with little real provocation. The following illustrations may sound fanciful, but they are true.

One husband and his wife were talking at breakfast, and she said, "Let's eat out tonight, Bob." Bob was her physician's name, not her husband's. The husband complained that her mind was on the doctor.

Another husband became angry because his wife, after a therapy session, served him squash, which he detested.

Still another husband complained that his wife, as a result of therapy, had a new language that made her so unattractive that loss of consortium resulted. She tried to sound, he complained, like Freud himself, discerning sex symbols in his pipe, his fountain pen, his hole-in-one and the bananas he ate. She said to him, "You're over-reacting," "You're having an identity crisis," "You're taking me for your mother." The psychobabble drove him up the wall.[23] He thought that the Supreme Court ought to decide whether it is cruel and inhuman punishment for him to suffer this verbal abuse. Preparatory schools promise, "Send us the boy and we will return you the man;" a patient's spouse might complain to a therapist, "I sent you my spouse and you returned me a parrot." It is no laughing matter. Legal action aside, the aggrieved husband who paid the bills for the counseling may want to get his money back.

A practitioner who suggests choices or conduct that go against an existing relationship may find himself a defendant in an action for alienation of affections or for loss of consortium. A woman says to her doctor, "I can't live with this man. He's driving me to suicide." Usually, depressed or suicidal people see no alternatives; the therapist tries to point out that there are alternatives, that the situation is not hopeless. Suggests the therapist, "You don't have to commit suicide right now; it's always an available option. Have you thought of separation?" Because many people extend great trust to a physician and consider that he is knowledgeable and is acting in the patient's best interest, physicians must be cautious in suggesting separation or divorce.

Some states, as noted, do not provide any legal remedy for alienation of affections, but when a professional is involved, there may be an action for malpractice (professional negligence). In a recent action in New York, a female physician who was counseling a couple for two years allegedly advised the husband to move out of the home. They were divorced five months after the termination of therapy and two weeks later the physician married the husband. When the former wife sued, the physician sought to have the action dismissed on the ground that it was an action for alienation of affections (an action barred in New York since 1935). This suit, though, was legally a malpractice action and thus was allowed. The case raised the question, still unanswered, of what is a "decent interval" overcoming an inference of trickery in the course of treatment.

Sexual reassignment surgery presents another possible interference with family relationships. Action for interference with a relationship was instituted (but not consummated) by a woman whose husband underwent sexual reassignment surgery.[24] The physician practicing such surgery should obtain assurance that there are no existing marital ties.

LEGAL EFFECT OF MARITAL INTERCOURSE ON DIVORCE PROCEEDINGS

A physician who explicitly or implicitly encourages reconciliation of the spouses should note the legal consequences of sexual intercourse between the parties in divorce proceedings. An act of intercourse has traditionally been viewed as condoning or forgiving the behavior that led to the divorce action. The ground for divorce thus eliminated, a court would deny the divorce. For instance, in a case in which the wife had sued the husband for separation on the ground of cruel treatment, the Louisiana Court of Appeals held that the wife's single voluntary act of coitus after leaving the marital home had wiped out the legal effects of the husband's prior acts of cruelty and effected a reconciliation.[25] The Court said, "The act of intercourse is the extreme fulfillment of the marital relationship. The voluntary performance of the action . . . could serve no purpose other than to condone the prior acts of cruelty on the part of the defendant." The Virginia Supreme Court put it this way: "It would be shocking to the moral sense of a court to grant a divorce to parties who, during the pendency of the suit, litigated by day and copulated by night."[26]

In growing number, states have in recent years adopted breakdown of marriage as the only ground or a major ground for divorce; they allow divorce without the need of establishing fault. The courts in these states do not speak with one voice on the legal effect of postseparation intercourse. It may be argued that when there is intercourse, there is no "marital breakdown." Determinations are made case by case. In Michigan it was ruled that an isolated instance of intercourse is not a sufficient basis for denying a divorce since "a marriage is based on more than just sex."[27,28]

Some states (Arizona, California, Connecticut, Florida, Illinois, Minnesota, Oregon, Washington, and Wisconsin) now provide court-connected counseling before a marriage is dissolved. The counseling is intended either to reconcile the couple or to eliminate their anger-distorted perspective so that financial, property and child-custody conflicts can be settled rationally.

PARTNER SURROGATES

The use of surrogates is controversial among sex therapists. Whatever its technical merit, it is legally questionable. Is the surrogate, who exchanges sexual services for money, a therapist or a prostitute? Prosecution is possible under criminal laws forbidding prostitution, pandering, fornication, lewd behavior and adultery.[4] The spouse of the surrogate or of the patient may have a civil claim for alienation of affections.

Some precautions have been developed, but they are not sure safeguards. Before employing a surrogate who is married, or before providing a surrogate for a client who is married, the therapist is advised to obtain consent from the surrogate's spouse or from the client's spouse. Individuals functioning as surrogates should be particularly cautioned in regard to client confidentiality and examined for any communicable disease. Therapists who provide a surrogate are responsible for the acts of the surrogate under the doctrine of vicarious liability (respondent superior).

Masters and Johnson selected and employed "partner surrogates" to engage in sexual activity with men who had not only sexual problems but personality problems that prevented them from finding partners. The sharpest attack on Masters and Johnson arose when they revealed in their book, *Human Sexual Inadequacy*, that they had treated 41 single men by partner surrogates.[29] The program had been kept secret because of this potential clash between public morals and therapeutic techniques. Masters and Johnson are no longer using surrogates—the publicity was adverse and a lawsuit was brought against them by the husband of a woman suspected of being a surrogate—but they have not abandoned their support of the technique.[30,31]

PHYSICIAN-PATIENT SEX

The medical profession, insurance companies and the law all view sex between therapist and patient as malpractice, criminal sexual assault or at best unethical conduct. The American Psychiatric Association and the American Psychological Association have both proscribed sexual contact with patients in their ethics codes. While supporting the use of surrogates, Masters and Johnson emphatically oppose therapists acting as surrogates. They view all such arrangements as exploiting "the vulnerability of men and women lost in the maze of human sexual inadequacy."[31]

In a recent case in New York, sexual contact with a physician was reported by several of his patients. The doctor was held liable for a substantial sum in compensatory and punitive damages.[32] He later sued his professional liability insurance company for its failure to assume the costs and responsibility for his defense. A malpractice insurance contract, however, does not cover acts that are not necessary for rendering professional services. The court ruled that, since the doctor's "therapy" was undertaken for his own personal satisfaction, his actions did not constitute malpractice within the meaning of the policy. The court further held that the physician could not resort to its processes to recover such expenses, since doing so would be "to indemnify immorality and to pay the expenses of prurience."[33]

In some cases, only a thin line may separate treatment and unnecessary sexual manipulation. For example, a physician must refrain from the traditional folk remedy of kissing the afflicted spot to make it better or from any unnecessary laying on of hands. A number of cases, both civil and criminal, involve the complaint that the massage was unnecessary to treatment, especially when a patient was under anesthesia.[34,35] Many such incidents occur between a male physician and a female patient, although there have been some instances of sex between female physicians and male patients. Apparently a man does not think of suing a woman physician or complaining to the authorities about her sexual relations with him.

DEFAMATION, INVASION OF PRIVACY AND BREACH OF CONFIDENTIALITY

A physician is sometimes called on when the family is in distress, confused and exposed. In his healing role, the physician may perform the most searching physical and verbal examination. Given such privileges, he is bound to almost absolute secrecy.

Certain disclosures, however, have always been accepted by the law and the medical profession. The physician is bound by ethics and law to notify authorities of any patient afflicted with certain infectious and other diseases; he is legally liable for doing so even if it is not to the patient's advantage. An improper disclosure, however, may result in liability for defamation, invasion of privacy or a breach of confidentiality. An action for defamation is subject to the defense of truth, but a breach of secrecy, even if the statement is true, may result in an action for invasion of privacy or breach of confidence. Divulgence may be regarded as a breach of an implied contract to keep information confidential; a breach-of-contract action is not covered under a malpractice policy.

The crucial question is: What is proper disclosure? May a physician, for example, divulge to a patient's wife (rather than to legally designated authorities) that the patient is committing incest with their daughter? Or that he has a sexually transmitted disease? Obviously, the husband may be reluctant to allow disclosure. Is the physician in such cases in jeopardy? Does the physician have a duty of care only to the patient or to others as well?

In an oft-cited case in Nebraska, a man who was registered at a hotel was treated by the town physician for sores.[36] This physician informed him that he believed his disease to be syphilis and advised him to leave the hotel. He refused, and the physician warned the hotel owner that he thought that the guest was afflicted with a "contagious disease." The guest brought suit against the physician, claiming a breach of confidentiality. The court, denying liability, said: "No patient can expect that if his malady is found to be of a dangerously contagious nature he can still require it to be kept secret from those to whom, if there was no disclosure, such disease would be transmitted."

In another notable case,[37] a student was sent home from school because, as a physician wrote her parents, she had a sexually transmitted disease. The dean of women added to the physician's letter that his diagnosis indicated that the student "had not been living right." The student sued the physician and the dean in an action of defamation, but they were not held liable, although the diagnosis was determined to be wrong. The statements were qualifiedly privileged because they were sent to the parents (indeed, the physician and the dean had a duty to inform them), even though a mistake was made. Every state now imposes a duty to report sexually transmitted disease and sets out the manner of reporting.

In the much publicized case of *Tarasoff v. Regents of University of California*,[38] the California Supreme Court ruled that there is a duty to report a dangerous patient to potential victims or to the authorities even if no statute imposes that duty to report. In *Tarasoff*, the Court ruled that a psychotherapist who has reason to believe that a patient may injure or kill another must notify the potential victim, his relatives or the authorities. However, when divulgence is not justified, there may be liability, as there was in the case of a physician who disclosed to the patient's husband her diagnosis and certain statements she made during therapy.[39]

Sometimes a physician warns directly or indirectly about a patient's suitability for marriage or parenthood. A girl, for example, may fail to tell her boyfriend that she has had feelings of bodily detachment or had made suicidal attempts. Her physician then might make the disclosure or otherwise attempt to disrupt the relationship, opening himself to a legal cause of action.[40]

In summary, information gained during the course of treatment may not be thrown about like custard pie. The physician has the burden of justifying a disclosure.

BREACH OF CONTRACT

To resolve a private dispute by law, only the tort solution is possible if the parties were strangers before the harm occurred. However, if the parties have entered a consensual relationship, the dispute assumes a contractual dimension even though the complaint alleges physical harm. In medical cases, however, the traditional rule has been that the parties do not contract for particular results but only for particular services, unless the physician warrants a cure for a particular ailment.

The trend toward liability has expanded the potential role of contract law as the theoretical underpinning,[41,42] and many pitfalls lie before the unwary practitioner. The line between opinion and representation of fact is often very thin; opinion can readily be taken as representation. Assurances to alleviate anxiety—"Don't worry you'll be all right"—may be taken as a promise.[43] The statement, "Premature ejaculation is the easiest sexual dysfunction to treat," may also be taken as a promise. It is a common expectation that professional consultation will "save" a marriage,[44] and many people are now viewing services as if they were commodities. If the buyer is not satisfied with the product, he or she can return it and ask for a refund. A century ago, payment for medical services—an honorarium—was made only on recovery, and that made it different from a commercial undertaking.[45] Unless the contract solution is open, dissatisfied clients or patients may find the only course open to them is to sue in tort alleging damages suffered as a result of the services.

The best protection for a practitioner is not to make exaggerated, false or misleading claims about the past or anticipated results of treatment. Such claims, like a promise of cure, could result in an action for breach of contract.[46]

TESTIMONIAL PRIVILEGE

The various states have adopted one or more testimonial privileges allowing a party in certain professional relationships to refuse to disclose confidential communications should they be demanded to do so in any legal proceeding. When information is required at a trial or in a deposition, there results no liability for disclosure. Whether testimony may be properly commanded in pretrial or trial proceedings depends on the testimonial privilege, or shield law, that a state has enacted.

The medical privilege is designed to allow the physician to keep silent about his patient if the patient so desires. Over the past 50 years, about four-fifths of the states have enacted a medical privilege. The intent was to encourage the patient to disclose to the physician all the information necessary for medical treatment—especially information about sexually transmitted disease—without the fear that public disclosure would bring embarrassment or disgrace.

So many exceptions have now been carved out of the privilege that little shield is left. Exceptions include communications not made for the purpose of diagnosis and treatment, hospital commitment proceedings, competency of a testator in contests over a legacy, actions on insurance policies, required reports (sexually transmitted diseases, gunshot wounds, child abuse), communications in furtherance of crime or fraud, malpractice action against the physician and mental or physical condition put in issue by the patient in suits claiming injury (known as the "patient-litigant" exception). Moreover, in child custody disputes, the "best interests of the child" is said to warrant exclusion from the privilege.[47] In most states, criminal prosecutions and workers' compensation proceedings also are often excluded from the scope of the privilege. A woman's statement to a doctor that she had voluntarily had coitus with a man charged with raping her is not privileged. Since criminal law in most states penalizes most sexual activity except marital coitus, almost any clinical record of sexual activity could, in these states, be used in a criminal action.

Nil Desperandum! There are legal guidelines of relevance and materiality that informally shield the physician-patient relationship. Moreover, an attorney does not put a witness on the stand unless he knows what testimony will be forthcoming. Trying to gouge testimony out of an unwilling witness may result in unfavorable distortion, so an attorney may try to subpoena records.

There is no special privilege covering research, which does not fall under the physician-patient privilege.[48] Kinsey had the sexual histories of political, social and business leaders of the first rank. Wardell Pomeroy, one of his associates, has written that divulgence "could have figuratively blown up the United States socially and politically."[49] Kinsey assured the interviewees that whatever was said would be kept in strictest confidence, no matter what happened. However, it was a promise unshielded against testimonial compulsion.[50]

The clinician's office is not a kingdom isolated from the world beyond it. Given the litigious nature of the times, the practitioner must be especially mindful of the impact of the law on himself and his patients. One could go mad trying to take into account all the possible consequences of one's work, but, more often than not, legal difficulties arise when the patient or those close to him suffer embarrassment or humiliation. The clinician dealing with sex, marriage and other relationships must be especially alert to avoid an indignity. Of course, life can bestow many indignities, and how one adjusts to them is a measure of maturity. It was the custom at one time to decide matters of honor by the point of a sword. Now it is by litigation.

References

1. Molière J: *Doctor in Spite of Himself*.
2. Kaufman S: *The Headshrinker's Test*. New York, Random House, 1970.
3. Diaz-Plaja F: *The Spaniard and the Seven Deadly Sins*. New York, Charles Scribner's Sons, 1970.
4. Leroy DH: The potential criminal liability of human sex clinics and their patients. *St Louis U L J* 1972; 16:586-603.
5. Holder AR: *Medical Malpractice Law*. New York, John Wiley & Sons, 1978.
6. Freud S: *On the History of the Psychoanalytic Movement*. New York, Macmillan Publishing Co, Inc, 1963.
7. Miller v. Kennedy: 11 Wash App 272, 522 P2d 852, affirmed 85 Wash 2d 151, 530 P2d 334, 1975.
8. Trogun v. Fruchtman: 58 Wis 2d 569, 207 NW 2d 297, 1973.
9. Freud S: *Complete Psychological Works*. New York, WW Norton & Company, 1976.
10. Burns CR (ed): *Legacies in Ethics and Medicine*. New York, Science History Publications, 1977.
11. Paul EW: Legal rights of minors to sex-related medical care. *Columbia Human Rights* 1974-75; 6:357-377.
12. Protection of human subjects: Research involving children, Report and recommendations of the protection of human subjects of biomedical and behavioral research. *Fed Reg* 1978 (Jan 13); 43:2084-2114.
13. Roe v. Wade: 410 US 113, 1973.

14. Doe v. Bolton: 410 US 179, 1973.
15. Planned Parenthood of Central Missouri v. Danforth: 428 US 52, 1976.
16. Annas GJ: Abortion and the Supreme Court: Round two. *Hastings Cent Rep* 1976 (Oct).
17. Bellotti v. Baird: 99 S Ct 3035, 1979.
18. H.L. v. Matheson: 101 S Ct 1164, 1981.
19. Dodge GA: Sterilization, retardation, and parental authority. *Brigham Young U L Rev* 1978; 380-407.
20. Prosser WL: *Handbook of the Law of Torts*, ed 4. St Paul, MN, West Publishing Co, 1971.
21. Moulin v. Monteleone: 165 La 169, 115 So 447, 1928.
22. Molière J: *School for Wives*.
23. Duffy M: Are you victimized by the verbal vigilantes? *Detroit Free Press* 1978 (Dec 15).
24. Burnell v. Catazone: Sup Ct of County of Orange, CA, Civil Action No 184985, July 21, 1971.
25. Stewart v. Stewart: 175 So 2d 692 (La App) 1965.
26. Tarr v. Tarr: 184 Va 443, 35 SE 2d 401, 1945.
27. Cowsert v. Cowsert: 78 Mich App 129, 259 NW 2d 393, 1977.
28. Peltola v. Peltola: 78 Mich App 709, 263 NW 2d 25, 1977.
29. Masters WH, Johnson VE: *Human Sexual Inadequacy*. Boston, Little, Brown and Company, 1970.
30. Repairing the conjugal bed. *Time* 1970 (May 25).
31. Wolfe L: The question of surrogates in sex therapy. *New York Magazine* 1973; 9:23-33.
32. Roy v. Hartogs: 381 NYS 2d 587, 1976.
33. Hartogs v. Employers Mutual Insurance Co: 89 Misc 2d 468, 391 NYS 2d 962, 1977.
34. Jacobi v. Texas State Board of Medical Examiners: 308 SW 2d 261, (Tex App), 1958.
35. People v. Wojahn: 337 P2d 192, 1959.
36. Simonsen v. Swenson: 104 Neb 244, 177 NW 831, 1920.
37. Kenny v. Gurley: 208 Ala 623, 95 So 34, 1923.
38. Tarasoff v. Regents of University of California: 529 P2d 342, 118 Cal Rptr 129, vacated, 17 Cal 3d 425, 551 P2d 334, 131 Cal Rptr 14, 1974.
39. Furness v. Fitchett: *New Zealand L Rep* 1958; 396.
40. Barry v. Moench: 331 P2d 814, 1959.
41. Epstein RA: Medical malpractice: The case for contract. *Am Bar Found Res J* 1976; 87-149.
42. Maynard RM: Establishing the contractual liability of physicians. *U C D L Rev* 1974; 7:84-112.
43. Miller AJ: The contractual liability of physicians and surgeons. *Wash U L Q* 1953; 413-436.

44. Brothers J: When adultery came up, her neighbor was no help. *Detroit Free Press* 1978 (Nov 30).

45. Slovenko R: Psychotherapy and informed consent: A search in judicial regulation, in Barton WE, Sanborn CF (eds): *Law and the Mental Health Professions*. New York, International Universities Press, 1978.

46. Tierney K: Contractual aspects of malpractice. *Wayne L Rev* 1973; 19:1457-1480.

47. Boulware v. Boulware: 153 So 2d 182 (La App), 1963.

48. Protection from discovery of researchers' confidential information. *Conn L Rev* 1977; 9:326.

49. Pomeroy WB: *Dr. Kinsey and the Institute for Sex Research*. New York, Harper & Row Publishers, Inc, 1972.

50. Reiss A: Selected issues in informed consent and confidentiality with special reference to behavioral/social science research/inquiry. *The Belmont Report, Ethical Principles and Guidelines for the Protection of Human Subjects of Research*. Washington, DC, US Government Printing Office, Appendix Vol 2, 1976.

Appendices

Appendix I

Self-evaluation of Sexual Behavior and Gratification

(Please check answer where indicated.)

1. **Are you satisfied with the sexual adjustment in your marriage or relationship? Do you think your partner is?**

Self		Partner	
1. Yes	( )	1. Yes	( )
2. No	( )	2. No	( )
3. Mixed feelings	( )	3. Mixed feelings	( )
4. Do not know	( )	4. Do not know	( )

If not, what is not satisfactory to you? _____
_____
_____

If not, what do you think is not satisfactory to your partner? _____
_____
_____

2. **Have you had any difficulty with any of the following?**

	Present
1. Techniques of petting and foreplay	( )
2. Positions	( )
3. Female inactivity	( )
4. Female does not achieve orgasm	( )
5. Male has difficulty with erection	( )
6. Male has orgasm too quickly	( )
7. Painful intercourse	( )
8. Fear of pregnancy	( )
9. Male wishes more frequent sexual activity than female	( )
10. Female wishes more frequent sexual activity than male	( )
11. Differences in attitudes towards sex	( )
12. Fatigue	( )
13. Lack of privacy	( )
14. Interference with sex due to working hours	( )
15. Other (specify)_____	( )
16. No difficulties	( )

3. **Have you consulted anyone for assistance with the sexual side of your marriage or relationship?**

    1. Yes   ( )
    2. No   ( )

If yes, how long ago?   Years ( )   Months ( )

If yes, indicate the type of person or agency and the extent of help you received.

	No help	Some help	Much help
Relative	( )	( )	( )
Friend	( )	( )	( )
Doctor	( )	( )	( )
Psychiatrist	( )	( )	( )
Social Agency	( )	( )	( )
Clinical Psychologist	( )	( )	( )
Clergyman (Minister, Priest or Rabbi)	( )	( )	( )
Teacher	( )	( )	( )
Other (specify) _____	( )	( )	( )

4. **How frequently on the average do you and your partner have intercourse at present?**
("Average" means typical or usual)

( )   1. No intercourse
( )   2. Less than once a month (specify) _____
( )   3. Once or twice a month
( )   4. Once a week
( )   5. Twice a week
( )   6. Three times a week
( )   7. Four times a week
( )   8. Five times a week
( )   9. Six times a week
( )   10. Seven or more times a week

5. **How do you and your partner feel about the frequency?**

Self			Partner	
1.	( )	Satisfied	1.	( )
2.	( )	Desire intercourse more frequently	2.	( )
3.	( )	Desire intercourse less frequently	3.	( )
4.	( )	Do not know	4.	( )

6A. **Are any of the following conditions affecting you and your partner so that you feel present sex activity is not representative?**
(Do not include aging or the passage of time.)

1. Pregnancy ( )
2. Unusual job situation ( )
3. Separation (not due to marital/relationship friction) ( )
4. Separation (due to marital/relationship friction) ( )
5. Marital/Relationship friction ( )
6. Housing ( )
7. Own or partner's health (mental or physical) ( )
8. Own or partner's interest in other person(s) ( )
9. Presence of children ( )
10. Personal or family crisis ( )
11. Other (specify) ( )
12. No (i.e., present sex activity is representative) ( )

B. If there are such conditions, how do you feel they affect your relationship?

1. For the better ( )
2. For the worse ( )
3. Neither better nor worse ( )

C. Approximately when did these conditions begin to affect it?
_____ Months ago _____ Years ago.

D. If you feel there is a more typical frequency of intercourse than reported in Question 4, what is it?

Use frequencies as in Question No. 4 _____
If there is no frequency, check here ( )

7. What is the duration of sex play prior to penetration?
(Be sure to answer even if there is no penetration.)

Present / Past (if different)

Present			Past (if different)	
1.	( )	No sex play	1.	( )
2.	( )	Less than 10 minutes	2.	( )
3.	( )	10 minutes to less than 20 minutes	3.	( )
4.	( )	20 minutes to less than 30 minutes	4.	( )
5.	( )	30 minutes to less than 45 minutes	5.	( )
6.	( )	45 minutes to an hour	6.	( )
7.	( )	Over one hour	7.	( )

8. **How do you and your partner feel about this duration?**

	Present				Past (if different)		
	Self	Partner			Self	Partner	
1.	( )	1. ( )	Satisfied	1.	( )	1.	( )
2.	( )	2. ( )	Desire longer sex play	2.	( )	2.	( )
3.	( )	3. ( )	Desire shorter sex play	3.	( )	3.	( )
4.	( )	4. ( )	Do not know	4.	( )	4.	( )

9. **Average duration of penetration (include time before and after orgasm).**

Present			Past (if different)	
1.	( )	No penetration	1.	( )
2.	( )	Less than 1 minute	2.	( )
3.	( )	1 minute to less than 5 minutes	3.	( )
4.	( )	5 minutes to less than 10 minutes	4.	( )
5.	( )	10 minutes to 20 minutes	5.	( )
6.	( )	Over 20 minutes (specify_____)	6.	( )

10. **How do you and your partner each feel about this duration?**

	Present				Past (if different)		
	Self	Partner			Self	Partner	
1.	( )	1. ( )	Satisfied	1.	( )	1.	( )
2.	( )	2. ( )	Desire longer time of penetration	2.	( )	2.	( )
3.	( )	3. ( )	Desire shorter time of penetration	3.	( )	3.	( )
4.	( )	4. ( )	Do not know	4.	( )	4.	( )

11. **Do you and your partner have intercourse during menstrual periods?**

Present			Past (if different)	
1.	( )	Usually	1.	( )
2.	( )	Occasionally	2.	( )
3.	( )	Rarely	3.	( )
4.	( )	Never	4.	( )
5.	( )	No menstrual periods	5.	( )

12. **How do you each feel about intercourse during menstrual periods?**
(Give your feelings whether you have intercourse at this time or not.)

	Self	Partner	
1.	( )	1. ( )	Feel the same as at other times
2.	( )	2. ( )	Dislike intercourse during menstrual periods
3.	( )	3. ( )	Prefer intercourse during menstrual periods
4.	( )	4. ( )	No objections, but believe it harmful
5.	( )	5. ( )	Do not know

13. **During your sex activity together, does partner have orgasm?**

Present
1. ( ) Always
2. ( ) Nearly always
3. ( ) About half the time
4. ( ) Seldom
5. ( ) Never
6. ( ) Do not know

Past (if different)
1. ( )
2. ( )
3. ( )
4. ( )
5. ( )
6. ( )

14. **How do you and your partner each feel about frequency of female's orgasm?**

Present				Past (if different)			
Self	Partner		Self	Partner
1. ( )	1. ( )	Satisfied with frequency	1. ( )	1. ( )
2. ( )	2. ( )	Dissatisfied, but not upset by it	2. ( )	2. ( )
3. ( )	3. ( )	Dissatisfied and upset by it	3. ( )	3. ( )
4. ( )	4. ( )	Do not know	4. ( )	4. ( )

15. **Do you have more than one orgasm during a complete sex act (the period from start of arousal to end of activity connected with that arousal)? Does your partner?**

Present				Past (if different)		
Self	Partner		Self	Partner
1. ( )	1. ( )	No orgasm	1. ( )	1. ( )
2. ( )	2. ( )	Never more than 1 per act	2. ( )	2. ( )
3. ( )	3. ( )	Occasionally more than 1 per act	3. ( )	3. ( )
4. ( )	4. ( )	Frequently more than 1 per act	4. ( )	4. ( )
5. ( )	5. ( )	Do not know	5. ( )	5. ( )

16. **When you or your partner have orgasm during sex activity together, does it always occur by penetration?**

Present				Past (if different)		
Self	Partner		Self	Partner
1. ( )	1. ( )	Always by penetration	1. ( )	1. ( )
2. ( )	2. ( )	Sometimes by penetration, sometimes by other means	2. ( )	2. ( )
3. ( )	3. ( )	Always by other means	3. ( )	3. ( )
4. ( )	4. ( )	No orgasm	4. ( )	4. ( )

17. **If your own orgasm occurs by means other than penetration, how do you and your partner each feel about it?**

	Present			Past (if different)	
	Self	Partner		Self	Partner
1.	( )	1. ( )	Not achieved by other means	1. ( )	1. ( )
2.	( )	2. ( )	Comfortable	2. ( )	2. ( )
3.	( )	3. ( )	Uncomfortable	3. ( )	3. ( )
4.	( )	4. ( )	Indifferent	4. ( )	4. ( )
5.	( )	5. ( )	Do not know	5. ( )	5. ( )

18. **If your partner's orgasm occurs by means other than penetration, how do you and your partner each feel about it?**

	Present			Past (if different)	
	Self	Partner		Self	Partner
1.	( )	1. ( )	Not achieved by other means	1. ( )	1. ( )
2.	( )	2. ( )	Comfortable	2. ( )	2. ( )
3.	( )	3. ( )	Uncomfortable	3. ( )	3. ( )
4.	( )	4. ( )	Indifferent	4. ( )	4. ( )
5.	( )	5. ( )	Do not know	5. ( )	5. ( )

19. **How frequently does your partner desire intercourse and you do not?**

Present			Past (if different)	
1.	( )	Frequently	1.	( )
2.	( )	Occasionally	2.	( )
3.	( )	Rarely	3.	( )
4.	( )	Never	4.	( )
5.	( )	Do not know when partner desires intercourse	5.	( )

20. **How frequently do you desire intercourse and your partner does not?**

Present			Past (if different)	
1.	( )	Frequently	1.	( )
2.	( )	Occasionally	2.	( )
3.	( )	Rarely	3.	( )
4.	( )	Never	4.	( )
5.	( )	Do not know when partner desires intercourse	5.	( )

21. **If you are not desirous, do you have intercourse to please your partner?**

Present   Past (if different)
1. ( ) Frequently   1. ( )
2. ( ) Occasionally   2. ( )
3. ( ) Rarely   3. ( )
4. ( ) Never   4. ( )
5. ( ) Does not apply   5. ( )

22. **If your partner is not desirous, does he/she have intercourse to please you?**

Present   Past (if different)
1. ( ) Frequently   1. ( )
2. ( ) Occasionally   2. ( )
3. ( ) Rarely   3. ( )
4. ( ) Never   4. ( )
5. ( ) Does not apply   5. ( )
6. ( ) Do not know   6. ( )

23. **In general, have you and your partner been using any method of child spacing?**

1. ( ) No method
2. ( ) Rhythm method ("safe period")
3. ( ) Withdrawal
4. ( ) Other methods _____
5. ( ) Does not apply

24. **Do you and your partner each feel secure about your method, or lack of a method, of child spacing?**

Self   Partner
1. ( ) Feel secure   1. ( )
2. ( ) Feel insecure   2. ( )
3. ( ) Do not know   3. ( )
4. ( ) Does not apply   4. ( )

25. **Apart from security, how do you and your partner each feel about your method, or lack of a method, of child spacing?**

Self   Partner
1. ( ) Satisfied   1. ( )
2. ( ) Dissatisfied   2. ( )
3. ( ) Indifferent   3. ( )
4. ( ) Do not know   4. ( )
5. ( ) Does not apply   5. ( )

26. Can you and your partner each discuss your feelings about sex frankly with one another?

Self			Partner	
1.	( )	Yes	1.	( )
2.	( )	No	2.	( )
3.	( )	About some things, not others	3.	( )
4.	( )	Do not know	4.	( )

27. Does your sex activity with your partner include the following:

	Frequency:		Satisfaction with Frequency:		Feelings about types of activity, whether or not you participate in them:	
(a) GENERAL KISSING AND CARESSING	Present 1( ) Always 2( ) Usually 3( ) Sometimes 4( ) Rarely 5( ) Never	Past 1( ) 2( ) 3( ) 4( ) 5( )	Self 1( ) Satisfied 2( ) Dissatisfied 3( ) Indifferent 4( ) Do not know	Partner 1( ) 2( ) 3( ) 4( )	Self 1( ) Like 2( ) Dislike 3( ) Mixed feelings 4( ) Indifferent 5( ) Do not know	Partner 1( ) 2( ) ( ) 4( ) 5( )
(b) DEEP KISS	Present 1( ) Always 2( ) Usually 3( ) Sometimes 4( ) Rarely 5( ) Never	Past 1( ) 2( ) 3( ) 4( ) 5( )	Self 1( ) Satisfied 2( ) Dissatisfied 3( ) Indifferent 4( ) Do not know	Partner 1( ) 2( ) 3( ) 4( )	Self 1( ) Like 2( ) Dislike 3( ) Mixed feelings 4( ) Indifferent 5( ) Do not know	Partner 1( ) 2( ) ( ) 4( ) 5( )
(c) MANIPULATION OF FEMALE'S BREASTS	Present 1( ) Always 2( ) Usually 3( ) Sometimes 4( ) Rarely 5( ) Never	Past 1( ) 2( ) 3( ) 4( ) 5( )	Self 1( ) Satisfied 2( ) Dissatisfied 3( ) Indifferent 4( ) Do not know	Partner 1( ) 2( ) 3( ) 4( )	Self 1( ) Like 2( ) Dislike 3( ) Mixed feelings 4( ) Indifferent 5( ) Do not know	Partner 1( ) 2( ) ( ) 4( ) 5( )
(d) MOUTH CONTACT WITH FEMALE'S BREASTS	Present 1( ) Always 2( ) Usually 3( ) Sometimes 4( ) Rarely 5( ) Never	Past 1( ) 2( ) 3( ) 4( ) 5( )	Self 1( ) Satisfied 2( ) Dissatisfied 3( ) Indifferent 4( ) Do not know	Partner 1( ) 2( ) 3( ) 4( )	Self 1( ) Like 2( ) Dislike 3( ) Mixed feelings 4( ) Indifferent 5( ) Do not know	Partner 1( ) 2( ) ( ) 4( ) 5( )
(e) MANIPULATION OF FEMALE'S GENITALIA	Present 1( ) Always 2( ) Usually 3( ) Sometimes 4( ) Rarely 5( ) Never	Past 1( ) 2( ) 3( ) 4( ) 5( )	Self 1( ) Satisfied 2( ) Dissatisfied 3( ) Indifferent 4( ) Do not know	Partner 1( ) 2( ) 3( ) 4( )	Self 1( ) Like 2( ) Dislike 3( ) Mixed feelings 4( ) Indifferent 5( ) Do not know	Partner 1( ) 2( ) ( ) 4( ) 5( )
(f) MANIPULATION OF MALE GENITALIA	Present 1( ) Always 2( ) Usually 3( ) Sometimes 4( ) Rarely 5( ) Never	Past 1( ) 2( ) 3( ) 4( ) 5( )	Self 1( ) Satisfied 2( ) Dissatisfied 3( ) Indifferent 4( ) Do not know	Partner 1( ) 2( ) 3( ) 4( )	Self 1( ) Like 2( ) Dislike 3( ) Mixed feelings 4( ) Indifferent 5( ) Do not know	Partner 1( ) 2( ) ( ) 4( ) 5( )

(g)	Present	Past	Self	Partner	Self	Partner
ORAL CONTACT	1( ) Always	1( )	1( ) Satisfied 1( )		1( ) Like	1( )
WITH FEMALE	2( ) Usually	2( )	2( ) Dissatisfied 2( )		2( ) Dislike	2( )
GENITALIA	3( ) Sometimes	3( )	3( ) Indifferent 3( )		3( ) Mixed feelings ( )	
	4( ) Rarely	4( )	4( ) Do not 4( )		4( ) Indifferent	4( )
	5( ) Never	5( )	know		5( ) Do not know 5( )	

(h)	Present	Past	Self	Partner	Self	Partner
ORAL CONTACT	1( ) Always	1( )	1( ) Satisfied 1( )		1( ) Like	1( )
WITH MALE	2( ) Usually	2( )	2( ) Dissatisfied 2( )		2( ) Dislike	2( )
GENITALIA	3( ) Sometimes	3( )	3( ) Indifferent 3( )		3( ) Mixed feelings ( )	
	4( ) Rarely	4( )	4( ) Do not 4( )		4( ) Indifferent	4( )
	5( ) Never	5( )	know		5( ) Do not know 5( )	

(i)	Present	Past	Self	Partner	Self	Partner
ANAL PLAY	1( ) Always	1( )	1( ) Satisfied 1( )		1( ) Like	1( )
	2( ) Usually	2( )	2( ) Dissatisfied 2( )		2( ) Dislike	2( )
	3( ) Sometimes	3( )	3( ) Indifferent 3( )		3( ) Mixed feelings ( )	
	4( ) Rarely	4( )	4( ) Do not 4( )		4( ) Indifferent	4( )
	5( ) Never	5( )	know		5( ) Do not know 5( )	

Other activity with partner? (Specify and give frequency and feelings as above)

(j)	Present	Past	Self	Partner	Self	Partner
	1( ) Always	1( )	1( ) Satisfied 1( )		1( ) Like	1( )
_____	2( ) Usually	2( )	2( ) Dissatisfied 2( )		2( ) Dislike	2( )
_____	3( ) Sometimes	3( )	3( ) Indifferent 3( )		3( ) Mixed feelings ( )	
_____	4( ) Rarely	4( )	4( ) Do not 4( )		4( ) Indifferent	4( )
	5( ) Never	5( )	know		5( ) Do not know 5( )	

(k)	Present	Past	Self	Partner	Self	Partner
	1( ) Always	1( )	1( ) Satisfied 1( )		1( ) Like	1( )
_____	2( ) Usually	2( )	2( ) Dissatisfied 2( )		2( ) Dislike	2( )
_____	3( ) Sometimes	3( )	3( ) Indifferent 3( )		3( ) Mixed feelings ( )	
_____	4( ) Rarely	4( )	4( ) Do not 4( )		4( ) Indifferent	4( )
	5( ) Never	5( )	know		5( ) Do not know 5( )	

28. What position(s) do you and your partner use in intercourse?

1. Male above usually   ( )
2. Female above usually   ( )
3. Male above and female above equally   ( )
4. Side by side   ( )
5. Usually other positions   ( )

29. To what extent have you and your partner experimented with positions?

1. Never   ( )
2. Occasionally   ( )
3. Frequently   ( )

30. **How do you and your partner each feel about the position(s) you usually use?**

Self		Partner
( )	1. Satisfied	( )
( )	2. Dissatisfied	( )
( )	3. Indifferent	( )
( )	4. Do not know	( )

31. **Who usually takes the initiative in sex activity?**

1. Self   ( )
2. Partner ( )

32. **Have you or your partner ever engaged in masturbation?**

Self		Partner
( )	1. Never	( )
( )	2. Occasionally	( )
( )	3. Frequently	( )

33. **Do you currently masturbate?**

Self		Partner
( )	1. Yes	( )
( )	2. No	( )

34. **Have you or your partner ever engaged in homosexual activity?**

Self		Partner
( )	1. Never	( )
( )	2. Occasionally	( )
( )	3. Frequently	( )
( )	4. Do not know	( )

35. **Have you or your partner ever had sexual relations with a family member?**

Self		Partner
( )	1. Never	( )
( )	2. Occasionally	( )
( )	3. Frequently	( )
( )	4. Do not know	( )

36. With which member of your family?

Self   Partner

( )   1. Parent   ( )

( )   2. Sibling   ( )

( )   3. Child   ( )

( )   4. Other   ( )

37. Have you or your partner ever been raped?

Self   Partner

( )   1. Yes   ( )

( )   2. No   ( )

Adapted from the *Sexual Performance Evaluation*
Marriage Council of Philadelphia, Inc.
Division of Family Study, Department of Psychiatry
University of Pennsylvania School of Medicine
Philadelphia, Pennsylvania

Appendix II
Physicians and Sex Therapy Clinics

Sex therapy clinics are proliferating and are being publicized widely in the popular press. Sexual dysfunction is defined as a chronic or frequent inability of an individual to fulfill his or her sexual expectations, for whatever reason. Although the etiology of sexual dysfunction is often psychological rather than organic, the effects almost always have both physiological and psychological manifestations and therefore come within the therapeutic province of the general physician. Patients are turning often to their physicians for information and advice concerning sexual dysfunction and sex therapy clinics.

Physicians should be aware of the benefits from counseling and treatment in qualified sex therapy clinics. They should be able to distinguish between sound programs and those of little value, and to determine for which of their patients referral is indicated. The well-constituted and professionally staffed sex therapy clinic has an important place in the diagnosis and treatment of sexual dysfunction.

Problems of sexual dysfunction range widely in complexity and severity, and a corresponding range of training and experience is necessary to deal with them. The physician should, however, be sensitive to indications of sexual dysfunction in his patients and make appropriate referrals when he is not able to handle the problems himself. For example:

1. If the patient's sexual dysfunction seems to be subordinate to marital difficulties or even to broaden family problems, then referral to a marriage counselor or a family therapist is appropriate.

2. If serious psychopathology is apparent or suspected, referral should be made directly to a psychiatrist.

3. When significant psychiatric problems are not present, marital or family difficulties are not the main obstacle to normal sexual functioning, and there appears to be no overriding physiological problem, referral to a competent sex therapy clinic may be indicated.

In making a referral to any sex therapy clinic, the physician should be certain that its services are appropriate, its location convenient, its course of treatment and follow-up assured and its costs acceptable.

Several parameters may be used to assess the overall merits and professionalism of a given sex therapy clinic. They include affiliation and auspices, composition and training of staff, intake and follow-up procedures and therapeutic results.

If a sex therapy clinic is part of a medical center or associated with a hospital or other medical facility, it will at least meet the criterion of medical input. Several professional organizations have issued standards relating to basic qualifications needed for sex therapists and counselors. Accreditation by, or membership in, one or more of these organizations would offer an initial measure of the training and entry competence of a therapist. Beyond the make-up and quality of the staff, the physician will want to assure himself of the soundness of the clinic's policies and procedures. In this connection, the clinic should:

— Provide for an initial evaluation of the patient/client.

— Be willing and able to refer the patient/client to other facilities and programs as necessary.

— Send periodic reports, with the consent of the patient/client, on the progress of therapy to the referring physician.

Physicians should be wary of sex therapy clinics which promise a "cure" for a designated fee or request full payment in advance.

Because sex therapy clinics do need medical supervision or backup in varying degrees, a physician may affiliate with a clinic as a consultant or as a member of the treatment staff. Before entering into such an affiliation, however, the physician should become fully cognizant of any legal or moral concomitants, and, as appropriate, discuss them with his peers and his attorney.

Report of the AMA Council on Scientific Affairs
to the House of Delegates, 1977.

INDEX

404